W9-BVO-475

AIA Guide to
CHICAGO
THIRD EDITION

7/14

AIA Guide to
CHICAGO
THIRD EDITION

American Institute of Architects Chicago

Chicago Architecture Foundation

Landmarks Illinois

with special assistance from the
Commission on Chicago Landmarks

Special support provided by
Alphawood Foundation Chicago

Introduction by **Perry R. Duis**

Preface by **Geoffrey Baer**

Alice Sinkevitch, Editor

Laurie McGovern Petersen,
Third Edition Editor

University of Illinois Press
Urbana, Chicago, and Springfield

Library of Congress
Control Number 2014936470

CONTENTS

GUIDE TO THE GUIDE

The *AIA Guide to Chicago* is the largest portable source of information on the city's built environment. The book will serve both as an introduction to Chicago's architecture for neophytes and as a sourcebook for those seeking to expand their knowledge beyond the well-documented buildings. The city's "greatest hits" are included, and many are discussed in essay form; numerous neighborhood buildings are documented in print for the first time. Much information available in other books—biographical, theoretical, statistical, and critical—is deliberately minimized, while details concerning functional requirements, client tastes, and materials are often included. The *Guide* encourages readers to discover, look at, and appreciate Chicago's built environment.

Genesis of the Book

The *Guide* was originally created for and is intended as a legacy of the 1993 American Institute of Architects/International Union of Architects World Congress, the first national convention of the AIA held in Chicago since 1969. The three sponsoring organizations—AIA Chicago, the Chicago Architecture Foundation, and the Landmarks Preservation Council of Illinois—provided the core of the Editorial Committee, which was expanded to include experts from the Chicago Park District, the Commission on Chicago Landmarks, and other groups. The Editorial Committee chose the featured tour areas and selected the bylined essayists. Each tour area had a "chapter captain" in charge of research and recommending entries. One important source of new information was the citywide Historic Resources Survey of pre-1940 buildings, conducted from 1984 to 1992 by the Commission on Chicago Landmarks. Significant additional information was uncovered by the authors and by the dedicated group of volunteer researchers.

Many photographs came from architectural firms and their clients, libraries, and other archives. Others were taken by architectural photographers, who, working as volunteers, traveled throughout the city to document neighborhood buildings.

Criteria for Inclusion

Even at its present length, the *Guide* is illustrative rather than encyclopedic, presenting a representative selection of buildings in addition to the essential landmarks. The neighborhoods chosen display a range of types, styles, and eras.

The criteria for selecting buildings, landscape and park features, bridges, public art, and cemetery monuments included not only the quality of their design but also the degree to which they either exemplified a style, trend, or functional type or stood out as unusual. Other important factors included visibility, historical significance, and the "what the heck is that" curiosity factor. Practical considerations included the geographical fit with the tour itineraries, which were laid out to connect major points of interest. Good examples of common types—the CTA station, the modernized storefront, the public school—on a route connecting featured structures were chosen over those in remote locations.

The availability of information also played a part. If dedicated research failed to produce specific data for a post-1870s building, it was likely to be omitted in favor of a better-documented example.

Building types were weighted, with criteria varying from one area to another. Houses get more attention than churches in Oak Park, for example, because of the important evolution of residential styles there.

The authors' likes and dislikes were significant factors, and we make no pretense at objectivity. Space limitations mean that many of the city's prominent but dull buildings are omitted or only briefly noted in favor of the inclusion of a greater range and number of structures. Few buildings of historic rather than architectural interest are included.

Organization

The *Guide* is organized by neighborhood chapters, beginning with the central city and radiating outward. Each chapter has a map that displays each building's name and entry number. A small inset map locates the area within Chicago. All maps have north at the top.

Because of the large areas covered in each chapter, all but the Loop have their entries ordered to facilitate driving tours. Quirks in the numerical ordering usually result from our efforts to accommodate one-way and dead-end streets, railway embankments, and other automotive impediments. Separate maps are provided for groups of entries, such as campuses and cemeteries, that lack street addresses.

A chapter introduction outlines each area's historical development and describes its neighborhoods and prominent demarcations. All neighborhoods are within the city of Chicago except for suburban Oak Park, whose concentration of Frank Lloyd Wright designs compelled its inclusion.

Information on the Entries

The heading for each nonresidential entry begins with the building's current name or address, followed by a parenthetical listing of the original name and well-known subsequent appellations, if appropriate. The use of current rather than historical names is intended to make it easier to locate buildings. In the case of a house, the name of the original owner is used.

Dashes between house numbers indicate a row of contiguous structures (such as row houses); an ampersand or the word *through* is used for a group of freestanding buildings unless they are commonly known as something else—as, for example, 860–880 N. Lake Shore Dr. Dates generally indicate the year of completion (except for prolonged construction) and are followed by the contemporaneous name of the responsible architecture firm. An ampersand joins the names of a single firm; *and* links the names of two or more separate firms.

The design architect's firm is listed first, except in the case of buildings commissioned by the City of Chicago. Subsequent work that is visually apparent is included, along with year of completion and architect. Most major buildings more than ten years old have had many alterations; only major renovations and additions are cited. *Restoration* means that the building was returned to its original appearance but *renovation* or *adaptive reuse* entries may look substantially different as a result of the work.

Interiors are generally described only if they are open to the public or are especially noteworthy. Churches are usually open only during services, when they welcome visitors.

A Final Word

The opinions expressed in the *Guide* are those of its many authors and in no way represent views or opinions of any sponsoring organization. Information is current as of April 2013; in a city as dynamic as Chicago, many changes will already have occurred before this volume's publication. Most buildings are privately owned and are not open to the public; investigation of anything not visible from the street or from a public space constitutes trespassing. Neighborhoods that are off the usual traveler's itinerary do not always treat every tourist well. Italicized commentary flags a few—but by no means all—of these areas. Readers are urged to travel in groups when exploring unfamiliar territory; visitors are encouraged to consult with Chicago residents before planning tours.

—ALICE SINKEVITCH AND LAURIE PETERSEN

ACKNOWLEDGMENTS

The cover of this book isn't big enough to acknowledge all of the people who contributed to it, so we will do it here. First, we thank the architects, contractors, craftspeople, tradespeople, and clients who created these structures. If they had been ordinary, this would be a very small book.

Third Edition Team

Our partners for the third edition, as for the previous two, were AIA Chicago, the Chicago Architecture Foundation, and Landmarks Illinois. AIA Chicago is a chapter of the American Institute of Architects, the nation's largest professional association for architects. Since its founding in 1869, the chapter has worked to advance architects' professional development and to enrich the cultural, economic, and environmental vitality of the local community.

The Chicago Architecture Foundation (CAF), founded in 1966, is a nonprofit organization dedicated to advancing public interest and education in architecture and design. CAF pursues this educational mission through a comprehensive program of tours, exhibitions, lectures, and special events designed to further the general public's awareness and appreciation of the architecture of metropolitan Chicago.

Landmarks Illinois is a private, nonprofit membership organization dedicated to promoting the vitality of Illinois's historic architecture. Landmarks is committed to community revitalization by preserving the economic and social strength of neighborhoods throughout Illinois.

For this edition we thank especially team members Joseph Frey, William Hinchliff, Kathleen Nagle, and Lisa Napoles as well as cartographer Dennis McClendon and administrative coordinator Mary Jo Graf. We are grateful to our chapter captains and our focus building essayists for reviewing and helping to update their essays. We also thank Michael Bordenaro, Benet Haller, Joan Pomaranc, Ben Schulman, and William Tyre. We appreciate Julia Bachrach's assistance with the Chicago Park District entries. We also appreciate the efforts of Eleanor Gorski, AIA, and the Commission on Chicago Landmarks. Special thanks go to our advisers Geoffrey Baer; Lisa DiChiera; T. Gunny Harboe, FAIA; Pauline Saliga; and Mark Sexton, FAIA.

AIA Chicago executive vice president Zurich Esposito guided the entire process.

At the University of Illinois Press, we thank director Willis Regier, EDP manager Jennifer Comeau, copyeditor Ellen Goldlust, designer Kaelin Chappell Broaddus, and the marketing team.

The herculean efforts of Alice Sinkevitch brought the first two editions of this book into being. This edition builds on her incomparable work.

—LAURIE PETERSEN

Third Edition Sponsors

We thank the donors whose contributions made this edition possible, especially Alphawood Foundation Chicago, the AIA Chicago Foundation, the Alexander Charitable Foundation, the Graham Foundation for Advanced Studies in the Fine Arts, and the Richard H. Driehaus Foundation.

The contributors to the previous editions deserve repeat acknowledgment.

Donors for the First Edition

The commitment of Chicago's business community, grants from many foundations, and the generosity of individuals passionately committed to the built environment made this book possible.

BENEFACTORS

Chicago Community Trust; Graham Foundation for Advanced Studies in the Fine Arts; National Endowment for the Arts; AIA Chicago; John D. and Catherine T. MacArthur Foundation

PATRONS

American Architectural Foundation; Chicago Architecture Foundation; Joyce Foundation; Landmarks Preservation Council of Illinois

SPONSORS

William B. Hinchliff; John A. Holabird Jr., FAIA; Illinois Arts Council; Henry H. Kuehn; Lohan Associates; Petersen Aluminum Corporation

CONTRIBUTORS

Baird Foundation; Chicago Dock & Canal Trust; D & K Foundation; Ernst & Young; Greater North Michigan Avenue Association; Holabird & Root; Richard J. Hoskins; Knight Architects Planners; Lucia Woods Lindley; Pamela Lohan; McClier; Hope McCormick; Murphy/Jahn; O'Donnell Wicklund Pigozzi & Peterson Architects; Pepper Companies; Perkins & Will; Seymour H. Persky; Schal Associates; Law Firm of Schiff Hardin & Waite; John I. Schlossman, FAIA; Jacqueline & Gene Summers, FAIA; U.S. Equities Realty; Harry Weese Associates; Weese Langley Weese Architects; Doreen & Steven Weiss, FAIA

FRIENDS

Anonymous; Susan M. Baldwin; Beer Gorski & Graff; Anthony Belluschi, FAIA; John Buck Company; Chicago Architecture Foundation Docents; Continental Bank Foundation; Employees of Loebl, Schlossman & Hackl; John Engman; Gerhardt Meyne Company; Gilbane Building Company; Ernest A. Grunsfeld III, FAIA; John F. Hartray Jr., FAIA; Hinshaw & Culbertson; Edward C. Hirschland; Harold S. Jensen; Joseph D. La Rue; Linpro Company; Jane Lucas; Robert G. Lyon Associates; Lynn & Eva Maddox, Assoc. AIA; Matthei & Colin; Mekus Johnson; Monadnock Building; Power Contracting & Engineering; Linda Searl, FAIA; Sears Tower; Bruce A. Simons; Stein & Company; Stein, Ray & Conway; Michael Tobin; Turner Construction Company; Carol Wyant

Volunteers

MANAGEMENT COMMITTEE

Steven F. Weiss, FAIA, chair; Susan Baldwin; John Engman; Richard Hoskins; Henry H. Kuehn; Jane Lucas; Thomas R. Samuels, FAIA; Linda Searl, FAIA; Emese Wood; Carol Wyant

EDITORIAL COMMITTEE

Wim de Wit; John F. Hartray Jr., FAIA; Robert F. Irving; Joseph D. La Rue; Vincent Michael; Joan Pomaranc; Deborah Slaton; Julia Sniderman; Cynthia Weese, FAIA

FUND-RAISING COMMITTEE

Pamela Lohan, chair; Susan Baldwin; Kathryn Godfrey Benish; Joan Goldstein; John A. Holabird Jr., FAIA; Henry H. Kuehn; John I. Schlossman, FAIA; Steven F. Weiss, FAIA

PROJECT TEAM

Alice Sinkevitch, Editor; Laurie McGovern Petersen, Associate Editor; Joan Pomaranc, Assistant Editor; Mary Alice Molloy, Special Projects Editor; Emese Wood, Photo Coordinator; Dennis McClendon, Map Designer

This book benefited from the involvement of many people. The following individuals contributed to the effort: Rolf Achilles; Deborah Allen; Margaret

Babcock; Marguerite Bailey; Margaret Balanoff; Susan Baldwin; Barry Bebart, AIA; Kathryn Godfrey Benish; Susan Benjamin; Ellen S. Berkelhamer; Alice Blum; Robert W. Blythe; Elizabeth Borden; Michael Bordenaro; Robert Bruegmann; Adam Burck; Joan Campbell; Cathy Capriglione; Constance K. Casey; Sally A. Kitt Chappell; Jane H. Clarke; Earl Clendenon; Patricia Lee Cody; Carole Cosimano; Kathleen Cummings; Barbara Cunningham; Eric Emmett Davis, AIA; Mary Dawson; Wim de Wit; Yvonne DeMuyt; Karen Dimond; Thomas Drebenstedt; David DuPre; Perry R. Duis; Joan Eggers; Janice M. Elliot; Roy Forrey; Ferne Winifred Gerulat; Ann Erickson Gifford; Blair Gifford; Paul Glassman; Patricia Goldfein; Norma Green; Mary Griffin; Florence Gurke; Louise B. Haack; T. Gunny Harboe, AIA; Elaine Harrington; Kevin Harrington; Neil Harris; John F. Hartray Jr., FAIA; Frances B. Hedlund; John Hern; Mary Beth Herr; William B. Hinchliff; Mark Hinchman; Richard Hoskins; William Jerousek; Robert F. Irving; Leo Jung; Nancy Kayman; Donald G. Kalec; Blair Kamin; Paul Kendall; Donald Kepler; Paul Kruty; Henry H. Kuehn; Joseph D. La Rue; Heather M. Lange; Bill Latoza; Beth LeGros; Margaret Lehto; Aldarcy C. Lewis; Jane Lucas; William Q. Lucas; Patricia Marks Lurie; John M. MacDonald; Laurel McCain; Harriet McShane; Suzanne Carter Meldman; Thomas Michael II; Vincent Michael; Frank P. Michalski, AIA; Mary Alice Molloy; Aurelia Moody; Harold Moody; Charlotte Myhrum; Kathleen Nagle; Kathryn Neary; Anders Nereim; Pat O'Brien; Dan O'Dair; Penny Obenshain; Lawrence Okrent; Maria Olson; Mary Lou Oswalt; Laurie McGovern Petersen; Charles Pipal; Joan Pomaranc; Helen Poot; Stephen W. Radke; Michael Ramirez; Judith Randall; John Ravitch; Diane Richard; Katherine Ross; Anne Royston; Bart H. Ryckbosch; Pauline Saliga; Thomas R. Samuels, AIA; Timothy Samuelson; John I. Schlossman, FAIA; Franz Schulze; Linda Searl, FAIA; R. Stephen Sennott; Robert A. Sideman; Joseph Siry; Deborah Slaton; Alice Sinkevitch; Julia Sniderman; C. Richard Spurgin; Joan Stinton; Patricia Talbot; Terry Tatum; Meredith Taussig; Laurence Terp; William W. Tippens; John Tomassi, AIA; Theodore Turak; David Van Zanten; John Vinci, FAIA; Gloria Wallace; Dina Wayne; Ben Weese, FAIA; Catharine Weese; Cynthia Weese, FAIA; Michael Weiland; Lauren S. Weingarden; Timothy Wittman; Carol Wyant; Ethel Zitnik; and Atie Zuurdeeg.

The "chapter captains" who led the research teams for each chapter were Adam Burck (Beverly/Morgan Park); Wim de Wit and Robert F. Irving (Lakeview/Uptown/Ravenswood); William B. Hinchliff (North Michigan Avenue/Streeterville and Edgewater/Rogers Park); Joseph D. La Rue (Near South Side and Oakland/Kenwood); Patricia Marks Lurie (Gold Coast/Old Town and Lincoln Park); Vincent Michael (Near West Side and Pilsen/Heart of Chicago/Lawndale/Little Village); Mary Alice Molloy (Loop, River North, South Loop, and Pullman/Roseland); Kathleen Nagle (Bridgeport/Canaryville/McKinley Park/Back of the Yards); Anne Royston (Chicago-O'Hare International Airport); R. Stephen Sennott (Hyde Park/South Shore); Alice Sinkevitch (Garfield Park/Austin and Oak Park); and Julia Sniderman (West Town/Wicker Park/Bucktown/Logan Square/Irving Park).

The category of special supporters and advisers is large and includes attorneys Ross Altman and Mark Feldman of Rudnick and Wolfe; the Law Firm of Jenner & Block; and the Law Firm of Sidley & Austin, all of whom helped to structure the sponsoring joint venture and our contracts. Also important were the librarians and photo specialists at the Art Institute of Chicago and the Chicago Historical Society, including Patrick Ashley, Emily Clark, Denise English, Lorraine Estreich, Eileen Flanagan, Charles McMorris, Janice McNeill, Susan Perry, Larry Viskochil, and Mary Woolever. Past AIA Chicago presidents Frank Heitzman, AIA; Sherwin Braun, AIA; and Leonard Peterson, FAIA, were instrumental in supporting the project in its infancy. Key advice and assistance were also given by Timothy Barton; Daniel Bluestone; Eric Brightfield; Janice Curtis; Jan Dubin; Charles Fiori; Mary Jo Graf; T. Gunny Harboe, AIA; Jack Hedrich; Sally Hess; Michael Houlahan; Bob Johnson; Mary Sue Kranstover; Bonita Mall; William McLenahan; Lawrence Okrent; Kevin Putz; Pat Rosenzweig; Richard Solomon, FAIA; Ann Dumas Swanson; Ben Weese, FAIA; and John Zukowsky.

The project coordinators for the first edition were Aldarcy C. Lewis, Audrey Cusack, Eva Silverman, and Joyce de Vries; for the second edition, Phil Rahill coordinated our efforts.

Second Edition Team

Our donors for the second edition were once again our partners in this project, AIA Chicago, the Chicago Architecture Foundation, and the Landmarks Preservation Council of Illinois (now Landmarks Illinois).

For this edition we thank especially team members Dennis McClendon, Mary Alice Molloy, Kathy Nagle, Joan Pomaranc, and Harold Wolff. And we thank our chapter captains and our focus building essayists for reviewing and helping to update their essays.

We also want to thank helpers and sources Catherine Bruck, Kathy Cummings, Sally Draht, Thomas Drebenstedt, Mary Jo Graf, Elaine Harrington, William Hinchliff, Joseph LaRue, Ann Royston, Tim Samuelson, Julia Sniderman, and Emese Wood.

We also thank our editor at Harcourt, Jennifer Charat, our managing editor, Gayle Feallock, and our copyeditor, Dan Janeck. And we thank the other members of the Harcourt team: Lori Asbury, Kaelin Chappell, and Elizabeth Royles.

And, again, a special thank you goes to the late Paul Gapp, the architecture critic for the *Chicago Tribune*, who gave us enthusiastic interest and support when we needed it the most.

—ALICE SINKEVITCH AND LAURIE PETERSEN

NOTE FROM THE PREFACE
TO THE FIRST EDITION

This guide should clarify our vision of Chicago. For the past two years, Alice Sinkevitch has sent into our neighborhoods a dedicated troop of scouts who have trained themselves to see the city with open minds and keen eyes. There were a few practicing architects among them, but the majority were amateurs in the most loving sense of the word. Many are docents for the Chicago Architecture Foundation and have had a critical part in creating a political and educational environment in which preservation is possible. Others are dedicated preservationists who have worked within the city government and cultural institutions.

Their greatest accomplishment, however, was not only to have cataloged the city's famous buildings but also to have captured the rich diversity of the built environment. There is a gritty integrity to Chicago's neighborhoods. Their buildings remind us that until quite recently, architecture was a craft handed down through the generations.

This guide is a monument to the breadth of our scouts' interests and to the clarity of their observations. It will help us to see Chicago as a whole and to recognize in it a much richer architectural culture than many of us might have expected.

Now that we have the book, let's go out and look at the city. It's all here— the vain efforts to scratch out a place in architectural history, the confident works of genius, and the spontaneous outpourings of decorative invention that sometimes result from the simple task of laying brick.

—JACK HARTRAY, FAIA, 1993

PREFACE TO THE THIRD EDITION

In the historically crowded working-class Chicago neighborhood of Bridgeport, on the Southwest Side, one of the city's oldest limestone quarries has been creatively converted into Palmisano Park. A sloping path leads down to a lake, where the old quarry walls tower overhead, bringing to mind the ancient limestone cliffs along the Upper Mississippi. Construction debris that had been dumped in the derelict quarry for decades has been piled up to create a soaring hill, beautifully landscaped with native plants and offering a view of the Chicago skyline.

That folks in Bridgeport can now commune with nature in their own backyard is a sea change for a neighborhood once called Hardscrabble, home to immigrant Irish ditch diggers who built the I&M Canal with picks and shovels and later the epicenter of Chicago political power. It's also a stunning example of what has changed in Chicago since the second edition of the *AIA Guide* appeared in 2004. The city best known for building big and brawny is now much more focused on building green.

To be sure, some impressive skyscrapers have gone up since the second edition, including SOM's Trump Tower and the wonderfully wiggly Aqua by Jeanne Gang. But the worst economic downturn since the Great Depression and the ominous realization that our environment is severely threatened have shifted the emphasis to sustainability in a big way.

In fact, sustainability is such a standard feature of new construction in Chicago that only pioneering or exceptional levels of sustainable design are mentioned in the entries in this book. Sustainability extends to more than just individual buildings: traditional urban density, anathema to mid-twentieth-century planners, is back, and infill development is making more neighborhoods and even suburbs walkable and transit-oriented. And adaptive reuse now gets points not only for being hip but also for being green. As the popular saying goes, "The greenest building is the one that's already built."

In addition to Palmisano Park, old industrial land is being repurposed all over the city. A multibillion-dollar mixed-use development, Lakeshore East, is rising atop the long-fallow Illinois Central rail yard at the mouth of the Chicago River. An abandoned rail line that bisects part of the city east to west is being converted to a linear park, the Bloomingdale Trail. Even the city's signature green space, Millennium Park, is built atop an old rail yard, a fact of which most Chicagoans remain completely unaware.

I experienced some of the most dramatic changes in Chicago firsthand when I hosted a 2011 public television documentary about the Loop. We spent weeks filming in the downtown area at all hours of the day and were astonished by the transformation that has taken place there. Whereas in the past it seemed like the Loop's only residents were the pastor and his wife who lived above the Chicago Temple on Washington Street, today's Loop is the 24/7 district that the city has tried to encourage for years. It's now a vibrant neighborhood with offices, shopping, restaurants, theaters, colleges, and about twenty thousand residents.

Thumbing through this book, even the most astute observer of Chicago's architecture scene will likely be amazed by all the new building that has taken place in the past ten years in every corner of the city. Much of it is in a fresh, modernist style made possible by advances in computer design and improvements in basic building materials such as concrete, metal, and glass.

Of course, a lot of other changes have occurred since the second edition. The long era of the second Mayor Daley has ended. His relentless focus on beautifying and greening the city is a hard act to follow, but his successor, Rahm Emanuel, vows to carry forward this goal, notably with a plan to realize

Daley's dream of an uninterrupted walkway along the Chicago River's main branch.

As with the previous two editions, the beauty of the *Guide* remains its scope. It features not only the famous (Willis Tower, Millennium Park, and the works of Louis Sullivan, Daniel Burnham, Frank Lloyd Wright, and Mies van der Rohe) but also hundreds of hidden gems scattered all over the city. And it fits in a backpack or a big back pocket. So lace up your walking shoes and head out on an urban adventure.

—GEOFFREY BAER, 2013

THE SHAPING OF CHICAGO

PERRY R. DUIS

Chicago holds a special place in the history of American cities.

It frequently assumes the role of the great American exaggeration, the place where common characteristics are stretched to their limits. Other cities grew during the nineteenth century, but Chicago mushroomed. Every town had its boosters, but the Windy City's were obstreperously boastful. Crime and political corruption were everywhere, but in Chicago they seemed to be elevated to an art. More positively, Chicago became a synonym for "the new" and "the first," leading the way in architecture, literature, and social reform—in part because, as a brash upstart, it possessed few encumbering traditions.

As the archetypal American industrial city, Chicago's rise and metamorphoses not only illustrate the urbanization process at its most basic but also demonstrate how the compelling forces of concentration, which allow efficiencies of space and time to outweigh all other considerations, both attract people and activities into cities and drive them outward toward the fringes.

The creative efforts of talented individuals are the substance of this book. But location, challenges, opportunities, and calamities also shaped Chicago and stimulated the city's problem solvers to reach inventive solutions. Many conditions, events, and movements have shaped the city: the following are some that have had a special impact on the built environment.

The Power of Place

Chicago's location has been both a curse and a blessing. The land at the banks of the Chicago River was swampy, and the stream itself flowed too slowly to turn a waterwheel or clear the mouth of silt. But it sat at the southwestern end of the massive Great Lakes navigation system. Via these waterways, prerailroad commerce penetrated the midsection of the continent and, interrupted only by a dry-weather portage, was linked to the Mississippi and Missouri Rivers via the Illinois and Des Plaines Rivers and the south branch of the Chicago River. Its advantages made Chicago's site a spot to control. When the first outsiders, Jacques Marquette and Louis Joliet, explored the region in 1673, the warlike Potawatomi had already displaced peaceful Indian tribes. Around 1779, Jean Baptiste Point Du Sable built a cabin roughly where the Equitable Building stands today and became Chicago's first permanent resident. A French-speaking black man, Du Sable was one of many Great Lakes traders who exchanged iron and cloth goods for furs.

In 1803, the year of the Louisiana Purchase, the United States established Fort Dearborn, the nation's westernmost military post, near what is now the south end of the Michigan Ave. Bridge. In 1812, in an incident known as the Fort Dearborn Massacre, the Potawatomi attempted to regain the valuable site. They burned the stockade, while three miles to the south, a raiding party killed most of the garrison members and their families as they fled along the lakeshore.

The fort was rebuilt in 1816, the same year that surveying began for the Illinois & Michigan Canal, which would provide a year-round link between the Chicago River and the Illinois-Mississippi River system some seventy-five miles away. A national financial panic in 1819 and fears of Indian unrest halted progress until the 1830s. On August 5, 1833, thirteen electors gathered to incorporate the Town of Chicago, and newcomers, many of them land speculators, began arriving in droves. By 1836, when work on the canal began in earnest, optimism about Chicago's future had boosted land prices to astronomical levels and attracted more than three thousand additional residents. In March 1837, Chicagoans demanded and received a city charter from the state legislature.

Illinois & Michigan Canal in Bridgeport

The Golden Funnel and the Growth of Transportation

In the mid-1840s, Chicago's merchants began to exploit the city's site by creating what might be called the golden funnel. The development of farmland throughout the West produced agricultural surpluses that could be shipped to eastern markets most efficiently via Chicago's water linkage. Wheat shipped through Chicago rose from a meager few bushels in 1840 to nearly two million bushels seven years later.

In 1848, several events improved the funnel's flow. The Illinois & Michigan Canal was finally opened, plank roads to the hinterlands made it easier for farmers to roll their grain wagons into town, and the telegraph linked national and international markets to the Chicago Board of Trade, newly formed to provide a standardized, self-policing market that farmers could trust. Most significant, on October 25, 1848, a tiny locomotive named the *Pioneer* made its inaugural run between Chicago and present-day Oak Park.

The promises of the 1840s became prosperous realities in the 1850s. Rail lines extending west to the Mississippi and east to Philadelphia and New York transformed Chicago into a national transportation hub. Grain elevators now towered over the city, while huge stacks of timber along the riverbanks proved that Chicago was the nation's leading lumber center.

The Civil War ushered in a new era for Chicago. The city's size and remoteness from military action made it an ideal site for producing war goods. The golden funnel now supplied the Union Army with horses and hay and fed its troops with carloads of bread, condensed milk, dried fruit, and cans of cooked meats from Chicago slaughterhouses. So great was the movement of livestock into the city that the need for efficiency forced packers and shippers to consolidate. On Christmas Day 1865, they opened the Union Stock Yards

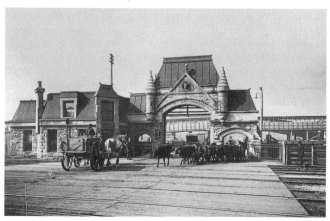

Union Stock Yards entrance gate

four miles southwest of the city. The yards soon enabled Chicago to displace Cincinnati as the nation's pork-packing capital.

Dire Necessities and Creative Technologies

The new city offered few amenities. Depending on the season, the streets were graded dust or mud that regularly disappeared under ponds left by springtime rain. Visitors were uniformly unimpressed by the buildings. Shortages of structural wood and skilled labor led to lightweight "balloon frame" construction, invented in 1833, which resulted in housing easily built by unskilled laborers.

Only gradually did more substantial masonry structures join the tiny buildings of logs or crudely cut boards. In 1837 William B. Ogden, the city's first mayor, enticed John M. Van Osdel, a carpenter and architect, from New York to begin providing something more than an architecture of expediency.

Chicago officials also turned to engineering experts to solve problems generated by exploding growth. To combat epidemics by improving drainage flow, the city's chief engineer, Ellis S. Chesbrough, designed a sewer system to be constructed on top of the existing streets, an expensive project that began in 1855 and continued for decades. The pavement grade was then raised a dozen feet, and building owners turned to youthful talents such as George Westinghouse and George M. Pullman to jack up old structures and insert new foundations. In older neighborhoods, such as Pilsen, these raised street grades are still visible.

Public health reformers began a long crusade against unsanitary burial places in 1858. Their efforts eventually closed the city cemetery (in what is now the southern part of Lincoln Park) and increased the attractiveness of landscaped plots in rural areas. Cemeteries such as Graceland, Rosehill, and Oak Woods became accessible to city dwellers because of advances in public transportation—steam railroad commuter service, a horse-drawn street railway system, and a pivoting span bridge over the river at Rush St. (1856), touted as the first iron bridge west of the Alleghenies. Architects such as W. W. Boyington, Edward Burling, and Otis L. Wheelock joined Van Osdel as designers of specialized structures for stores, public buildings, and homes.

With heavy maritime traffic keeping bridges open almost perpetually, tunnels were excavated under the river at Washington (1869) and La Salle (1871)

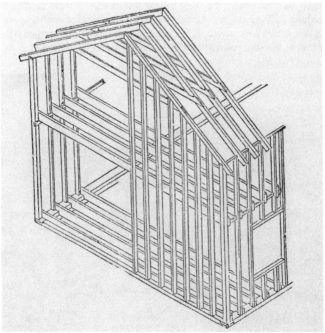

"Balloon frame" construction

Sts. When pollution from the sewage-laden river threatened the water supply, engineers designed a new water plant, the Chicago Water Tower & Pumping Station (1869), with an intake crib two miles from shore.

The Great Conflagration

To this day, no one really knows how the fire of October 8–9, 1871, started. Whether it was lightning, raucous tenants, a drunken neighbor, or even a cantankerous cow kicking over a lantern, the blaze definitely began near the barn behind Patrick and Katherine O'Leary's DeKoven St. home. Incompetent dispatchers and lookouts allowed the fire to flare out of control, and an intense firestorm consumed block after block of a city that had had no rain since July. The conflagration raged for thirty-six hours, sweeping away a third of the city before burning itself out four miles away, on the northern edge of town. More than 300 people perished, 17,450 structures were reduced to ashes, the downtown was devastated, and on the North Side, only a few scattered houses and the Water Tower were spared. At least 90,000 people were left homeless, and the livelihoods of thousands more had disappeared, along with their workplaces.

Residential Chicago would never be the same. The Common Council soon banned any new nonmasonry construction within the city limits (roughly Fullerton Ave. on the north, Pulaski Rd. on the west, and Pershing Rd. on the south). Thousands of North Siders who could not afford to rebuild in brick were forced to sell their lots and move just over the border, where developers were only too happy to put them in inexpensive new wooden houses. The contrast between the masonry city and the wooden suburbs on the old city borders can still be seen in spots along Fullerton Ave., west of Halsted St. The undamaged South and West sides were also dramatically transformed. Owners subdivided houses near the "burnt district" and rented space at premium rates. Overcrowding quickly resulted in the deterioration of thousands of these structures and hastened inner-city decay.

Downtown faced the daunting problem of reestablishing the heart of Chicago's economic and cultural life. Rebuilding began even before the rubble cooled, and Chicagoans turned to their architects and engineers. John M. Van Osdel, Edward Burling, W. W. Boyington, Otis L. Wheelock, Gurdon P. Randall, Augustus Bauer, Asher Carter, and Peter B. Wight had as many commissions as they could handle, and for two years, as crews worked around the clock and throughout the winters, they kept track of their designs in terms of miles of building fronts constructed. The new structures appeared to be much the same as those constructed before the fire, but most were slightly taller and had more elevators. Innovations were limited to improved fireproofing techniques.

Aftermath of the fire of 1871

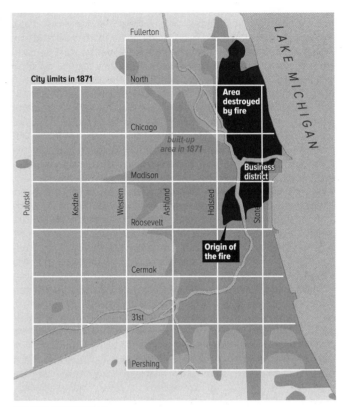

Map of the fire's destruction

The fire hastened the evolution of city-use patterns. Downtown residential use, which had been declining, was not reestablished, and most of the manufacturers whose North Side factories were destroyed soon relocated in outlying industrial districts along rail lines or the river's branches. The McCormick Reaper Co., for example, replaced its plant on the north bank of the river's mouth with what would eventually be one of the nation's largest manufacturing facilities (now demolished) at Western and Blue Island Aves. The new factories were generally much larger than their predecessors and housed heavier, more complex equipment. This reduced the mobility of the enterprises, and land-use patterns were thereby fixed for decades to come.

The Logic of Centralization

By 1870, the city's population had surged to 298,977, but wartime shortages of building materials and carpenters had hampered house building, and many areas were overcrowded. This congestion, aggravated by the noise and smoke of postbellum factories, instilled thoughts of escape. The middle and upper classes could choose to move to quiet, orderly sections of the city serviced by expanded horsecar lines and commuter railways. Those seeking permanent residential refuge found homes in subdivisions and suburban towns that sprang up along railroad routes.

Chicago's population exploded to 500,000 in 1880 and to more than 1,000,000 in 1890. The city had become big, and in this largeness was an overwhelming logic of concentration, of which factories were only one example. The savings of time and economies of scale that resulted from putting many departments under one roof—so that belts and pulleys from one huge stationary steam engine could drive the greatest number of machines—more than paid for the cost of building the structure. Downtowns were seen as also benefiting from economies of size and geographic convenience. Most of Chicago's public transit lines, which included the world's largest cable car system, were built to carry passengers into the central business district, which acquired the nickname the Loop in the early 1880s because it was encircled by transit tracks. Electric trolleys went into service in 1890, and two years later, an elevated "iron highway" was inaugurated—the first of five radial rapid transit lines that would be united in 1897 by the Union Loop above the downtown's perimeter. Steam suburban lines brought an estimated 100,000 additional daily passengers into their six depots, which also ringed the downtown.

Nineteenth-century urban residents also exercised the logic of concentration in their division of city spaces. For them, domestic dwellings were clearly private spaces, and the wealthy were better able than others to use private areas to shelter their affairs. They built their homes in exclusive districts, like Prairie Ave. on the South Side or Astor St. on the Near North, and their luxurious world of private clubs, schools, opera boxes, and carriages permitted selective contact with the rest of Chicago. Conversely, the streets, sidewalks, parks, river, and government facilities were public places—owned in common, primarily utilitarian, and usually undistinguished in design. The one great exception was Chicago's well-landscaped parks and boulevards. In 1869, Illinois Health Board member Dr. John H. Rauch, along with real estate developers and civic boosters, persuaded voters and the Illinois General Assembly to create three tax districts to fund an ambitious ring of parks several miles beyond the built-up neighborhoods.

A third category of city space might be called semipublic places—privately owned areas to which the public had access. Some were noncommercial, such as churches, which by the 1890s were often grand buildings with Sunday school or meeting facilities at least partly available to all. Most semipublic spaces, however, were designed to generate profit, and the degree to which they had become objects of civic pride reflected the progress of urbanization and centralization. Office buildings offered one example. Although they featured private offices, they also offered barbershops, restaurants, and other services, and elevator lobbies evolved into showplaces meant to make good impressions and attract tenants. In the (now demolished) Chicago Stock Exchange Building, for example, the elevator cages were enclosed in delicate metalwork; the Marquette Building presents a Chicago history lesson in mosaic tiles; and the Rookery has an airy, naturally illuminated core.

The concentration of activities downtown encouraged the creation of districts within the Loop. The railway stations girding the central business district, for example, encouraged a similarly shaped placement of hotels for the convenience of passengers. The Chicago Board of Trade at the foot of La Salle St. drew not only brokers but also law firms, banks, and insurance companies to adjacent blocks. To the east, Marshall Field had moved his retail business from Lake St. to State St. just prior to the fire. His competitors followed, so that within months a residential area had been transformed into the city's main mercantile district. Randolph St. emerged as Chicago's theater row as well as the home of

The Rookery lobby by Burnham & Root

a thriving music publishing industry. Warehousing, printing, and clothing concerns located on the edges of downtown to be near suppliers and customers.

Department stores were examples of semipublic spaces designed for public use. Before the fire, merchants had offered undifferentiated varieties of wholesale and retail goods. Eventually, merchandise and services were centralized under one roof, and the stores functioned as factories of consumption that saved consumers time and steps. The store that Marshall Field built after the fire was one of America's most lavishly furnished. By the end of the century, Field had begun what would become a complex covering more than a square block on State St.; Schlesinger & Mayer had commissioned the Louis H. Sullivan Building at State and Madison Sts. (later known as the Carson Pirie Scott store); and Siegel, Cooper & Co. had fifteen acres of floor space in the Second Leiter Building. Elsewhere on That Great Street, new buildings for Maurice Rothschild, Mandel Brothers, and the Boston Store soon created a retail district of enormous drawing power. Huge plate glass windows allowed each store to display its wares to lure passersby and provided light for counters inside.

Hotels had matured from rude inns into spectacularly appointed rivals to the palaces of European nobility. They offered such specialized amenities as billiard parlors, sunrooms, and ballrooms as well as several classes of guest rooms and dining facilities. The six major railway stations near which the hotels were concentrated had in turn evolved from homely barns into spectacular urban gateways featuring so many services that they were called "cities within cities." The Auditorium, the most remarkable structure of all, combined three types of grand semipublic places. It had an office block on its Wabash Ave. side, a luxurious four-hundred-room hotel fronting on Michigan Ave., and an acoustically perfect theater, the world's largest when it opened in 1889.

In the 1890s, the battle between centralization and dispersal continued, with new factors favoring decentralization. One of these factors was the development of small electrical motors to power individual machines, which replaced the giant steam engines that had powered entire factories. This change spawned "electrical manufacturing suburbs," such as Harvey, Maywood, and Chicago Heights that had room for both new factories and cheap workers' housing. Furthermore, those who could afford spacious homes continued to migrate to the urban fringe.

Labor Unrest in the Industrial City

Raw materials continued to flow through the golden funnel to industry, and many of the new plants required only low-skilled workers who could perform repetitive jobs. Long hours and low wages fomented worker dissatisfaction, leading to an era of labor unrest and violence. The nation's attention focused on Chicago in 1886, when demands for an eight-hour workday produced a series of strikes at the McCormick works. On the night of May 4, police charged into a labor rally at Haymarket Sq., near the corner of Randolph and Desplaines Sts. A bomb exploded, and the police opened fire. What soon became known as the Haymarket Riot led to a conspiracy trial, executions, and international protests.

The self-sufficient model factory and town thirteen miles south of Chicago, begun in 1880 by George M. Pullman, epitomized the new industrial order. Architect Solon S. Beman had designed an efficient factory, workers' housing, and amenities such as a shopping arcade, stables, a market, a park, a hotel, and a church. It was hardly utopia, however. Pullman sought a sober, dependable workforce that did not have to live in the city's slums, but workers chafed under a system that isolated them from company executives and sought to control how workers lived and where they shopped. During a serious depression that began in 1893, the company slashed wages and laid off workers, but Pullman refused to lower his rents. The 1894 Pullman strike and a nationwide boycott resulted in the firebombing of Pullman's cars and occupation of his town by federal militia. Although the company won the struggle, the courts eventually forced it to sell the houses and to hire nonresidents. The Haymarket and Pullman incidents produced front-page headlines worldwide, not only

First Infantry Armory by Burnham & Root (demolished)

because they were startling but also because Chicago's economic importance and position as the nation's fastest-growing city prompted widespread concern that battles between workers and police might eventually be repeated everywhere.

The Development of the Skyscraper

Downtown centralization required special buildings to draw together thousands of people simultaneously, and a rapid succession of technological developments made the construction of such buildings possible. Advances in foundation engineering and in metal-frame construction, reliable lighting systems (first gas, then electric), improvements in steam heating and fireproofing, and faster, safer elevators made vertical expansion possible. Soaring land values demanded the intensive use of downtown lots, just as telephone and telegraph communications were enabling business leaders to move away from their manufacturing facilities and closer to their lawyers, bankers, and other downtown services.

More than demand was required to create tall buildings, however. Chicago was blessed with a talented cadre of architects and engineers. John M. Van Osdel and Peter B. Wight were seasoned veterans among a group of varied talents. William Le Baron Jenney and William Sooy Smith concentrated on foundations and structure. Dankmar Adler, an expert in acoustics, teamed with Louis H. Sullivan, the master of detail. Daniel H. Burnham, who understood the business of architecture, formed a partnership with John Wellborn Root, who excelled in its artistry. William Holabird and Martin Roche were among the steadiest producers, with a stream of successful designs.

The architects and engineers had to find ways to secure tall buildings in Chicago's spongy soil. Initially, following suggestions from structural engineer Frederick Baumann, they designed raft foundations that spread a building's weight over as much of the subsurface soil as possible and set entrance levels high enough to compensate for expected settling. Particularly heavy or tall buildings required more substantial support. Adler & Sullivan placed the structural walls of the Auditorium on continuous reinforced concrete foundations and carried the massive weight of the seventeen-story tower on a floating raft of crisscross layers of timbers, steel rails, and I beams. In their seventeen-story Schiller Building, raft foundations were supported on wooden pilings driven to refusal; the same architects subsequently made an important breakthrough in settlement problems when they supported the west party wall of the Chicago Stock Exchange with tubular concrete caissons (the first used in Chicago) that reached fifty-five feet down to hardpan, an oxidized clay.

Framing problems also had to be resolved. The six-foot-thick walls and tiny windows of the lower floors of Burnham & Root's Monadnock Building demonstrated that extending load-bearing construction to sixteen stories limited interior space and light so severely that taller masonry projects were point-

Construction of the Marquette Building

less. But a feasible way to go higher had already been worked out gradually, so that in Jenney's Home Insurance Building (1885), metal framing had eliminated the need for exterior load-bearing walls. As the construction of tall buildings evolved into all-steel structures, curtain walls came to function only as skins and could be made of almost any material, including glass or terracotta. Interiors were flooded with light through Chicago windows (bay-filling frames holding movable sashes on either side of large fixed panes). Most important, there were now almost no theoretical limits to a building's height.

Chicago's skyline altered at a dizzying pace after 1880, and what had seemed daringly tall in one decade became the norm of the next and small twenty years later. The distinction of being the city's tallest building passed quickly from the ten-story Montauk Building (1882), the first labeled a skyscraper, to the thirteen-story Royal Insurance Building (1885). The Rookery, Austin, and Adams Express Co. buildings (all eleven stories) were exceptionally large when they were built in 1886 but of only average size once the Auditorium was under way. The Monadnock, with its load-bearing walls, and the Manhattan, with its metal frame, both reached a world's-record sixteen stories in 1890. Two years later, however, they were dwarfed by the twenty-one-story Masonic Temple.

Rampant Growth and Annexation

Only a handful of cities had fewer geographical constraints on dispersal than did Chicago. The abundance of land kept down the cost of lots or factory sites, while the transportation networks that brought passengers downtown to work or shop also made it convenient for them to live great distances away. Developers aggressively marketed life on the urban fringe. They cut building costs by mass-producing limited varieties of designs, advertised their developments heavily in multiple languages, and gave away samples—weekend excursion rides to their subdivisions. Housing for every budget was available beyond Chicago's borders, while the congestion, crime, disease,

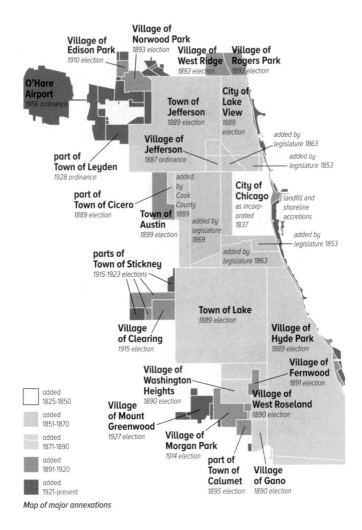

O'Hare Airport
1956 ordinance

Village of Edison Park
1910 election

Village of Norwood Park
1893 election

Village of West Ridge
1893 election

Village of Rogers Park
1893 election

Town of Jefferson
1889 election

City of Lake View
1889 election

added by legislature 1863

added by legislature 1853

Village of Jefferson
1887 ordinance

part of Town of Leyden
1928 ordinance

part of Town of Cicero
1889 election

added by Cook County 1889

City of Chicago
as incorporated 1837

landfill and shoreline accretions

Town of Austin
1899 election

added by legislature 1869

added by legislature 1853

added by legislature 1863

parts of Town of Stickney
1915-1923 elections

Town of Lake
1889 election

Village of Clearing
1915 election

Village of Hyde Park
1889 election

Village of Fernwood
1891 election

added
1825-1850

added
1851-1870

added
1871-1890

added
1891-1920

added
1921-present

Village of Washington Heights
1890 election

Village of Mount Greenwood
1927 election

Village of West Roseland
1890 election

Village of Morgan Park
1914 election

part of Town of Calumet
1895 election

Village of Gano
1890 election

Map of major annexations

and political corruption within them made daily headlines and provided the motivation to leave.

By the 1880s, Chicago risked being rivaled by its adjacent areas, which were growing far faster than the city itself. Since its founding, Chicago had grown steadily by annexation; now, the municipal government proposed a massive annexation that would take in such communities as Hyde Park, Kenwood, and Pullman to the south and Lake View and Jefferson to the north. Many of those affected realized annexation would offer the benefits of Chicago's more advanced municipal infrastructure and better services, including schools. Others, feeling safer and morally superior to their city counterparts, earnestly wanted the status quo. Nonetheless, on June 29, 1889, suburbanites spread over 125 square miles—much of it farmland—voted by a thin majority to join with Chicago. The city's territory almost quadrupled overnight, and its population was recorded at one million in the following year's census. Among American cities, only New York was larger.

"A World of Unmixed Bliss"

The success of the annexation vote aided Chicago's efforts to become host to an international exposition being proposed to celebrate the four hundredth anniversary of the discovery of America. Not only did it help the negotiations for the host city to be as large as possible, but the best sites for the fairgrounds were now inside the city limits. The self-promotion of the delegation seeking congressional approval was so aggressive that it earned Chicago its "Windy City" nickname. A struggle at home over location ended with the commissioners' choice of Jackson Park on the South Side. An illustrious group of archi-

Palace of Fine Arts by Charles B. Atwood, World's Columbian Exposition

tects from the East Coast and Chicago, led by Daniel H. Burnham, designed an immense architectural wonderland. Workers constructed a neoclassic "White City" from steel frames finished in lath and staff (a mixture of plaster, cement, and jute).

To help the city look its best for the fair, several cultural institutions opened new buildings, including the Chicago Historical Society, the Chicago Academy of Sciences, and the Newberry Library. The Art Institute rented its new home to the exposition congresses, a series of international scholarly meetings. The realization that visitors would also note what Chicago lacked motivated the founding of the Chicago Symphony Orchestra and a second University of Chicago (the first one had gone bankrupt in 1886). The World's Columbian Exposition opened amid a severe national depression, but as many as 750,000 visitors a day passed through the gates and found a plaster paradise in which the world's technical knowledge, mechanical skills, and manufacturing prowess had been collected, classified, subdivided, and displayed as never before. More than a million objects filled more than a hundred buildings. No exposition before or since ever aspired to such comprehensiveness.

The exposition left Chicago with two significant legacies. First, the fair drew hundreds of talented young people to the city, and despite a persistently depressed economy that hampered the arts in general, they created an innovative cultural milieu. Experimental theaters staged avant-garde productions. Small-scale publishers and little magazines, such as the *Chap-Book*, commissioned Art Nouveau illustrations and featured works by new authors, including Theodore Dreiser and George Ade. This creative community gathered in buildings especially designed for the arts, such as the low-rent artists' studios that Judge Lambert Tree erected in 1894 in the backyard of his N. Wabash Ave. house. The former Studebaker carriage works was remodeled by new owners in 1898 into the Fine Arts Building, housing a unique collection of studios, theaters, and music schools.

Second, Chicago's first elevated line was built to carry visitors between the downtown and the fairgrounds, and hundreds of small hotels and apartments were built along it and other South Side transit routes. Often hastily and poorly constructed by underfinanced opportunists whom the depression bankrupted, these buildings quickly fell into disrepair. From 1900 to 1930, African Americans arriving from the South could find few housing opportunities outside this broad band of exposition housing, and the so-called Black Belt emerged.

"Make Big Plans, Aim High in Hope"

By the 1890s, Chicago seemed to be choking on its own success. Each new downtown skyscraper added to traffic woes. The clatter of hoofs and metal wheels, peddlers' shouts, and streetcar bells created an unbelievable din. Some health officials worried that the darkness of the skyscraper canyons would turn the ubiquitous layers of horse manure and refuse into germ incubators. Finding one's way around was complicated by a house-numbering system that used the meandering river as its baseline and allowed countless duplicate addresses.

Proposals to relieve the city's woes took several forms. To reduce street congestion, the elevated system was extended, and a network of tunnels enabled miniature electric locomotives to haul freight, coal, and ashes to and from downtown buildings. (In 1992, a leak from the Chicago River flooded the long-abandoned system, causing an estimated one billion dollars in damage.) By the beginning of the new century, the extensive use of automobiles was being proposed as a solution to several ills. Their maneuverability would help relieve traffic jams involving fixed-route vehicles, they would eliminate the health hazards connected with manure and animal carcasses, and they would reduce the dense smoke from commuter trains because fewer trains would be needed. The city government also made several attempts to untangle Chicago's street chaos. The City Council voted in 1893 to limit building heights to 130 feet (though lobbyists soon persuaded the council to ease that restriction). The aldermen also renamed hundreds of streets and in 1909 instituted a rational house-numbering system with State and Madison Sts. as baselines.

The most significant proposal combined careful restructuring of the street system with strict planning for future development. Calling on his experience with the Columbian Exposition, Daniel H. Burnham and his assistant, Edward H. Bennett, backed by the Merchants' and Commercial Clubs, began work in 1906 on a master plan for the city. When published three years later, the *Plan of Chicago* presented a grand blueprint of transportation for the entire region and demonstrated how public spaces could be made as magnificent as semipublic ones. The plan reserved the lakefront for recreation and proposed a string of offshore islands. Monroe Harbor and Grant Park would become a formal "front door," while the seat of government would be relocated to an immense plaza at the junction of Congress and Halsted Sts. Burnham and Bennett took great pains to demonstrate how railroad facilities could be efficiently concentrated in outlying districts, how commercial and recreational use of the river's downtown banks could be compatible, and how attractive a city of uniform height might be. The most important feature, however, was the treatment of streets as the veins and arteries of a living organism. Impediment-free circulation required widening many streets, including Michigan Ave., designated as the new gateway to the North Side. Diagonal streets would improve crosstown travel. The plan was lavishly illustrated by artist Jules Guerin, who depicted the streets as low-density mixtures of automobiles, horse-drawn vehicles, and pedestrians to demonstrate the benefits of proper urban planning.

Jules Guerin rendering from Plan of Chicago

To promote Burnham's grand scheme, the Commercial Club established the Chicago Plan Commission, comprised of civic and business leaders and chaired by brewer Charles H. Wacker; Burnham served as its chief architect. The commission not only lobbied for individual projects that would conform to the plan but also campaigned intensively to sell it to the citizenry. Pamphlets on the plan blanketed the city, nickelodeon audiences found promotional movies on it sandwiched between standard features, and eighth-grade children were required to pass examinations based on *Wacker's Manual of the Plan of Chicago*, a textbook version published in 1912.

Many people objected to the plan. The Army Corps of Engineers, which was responsible for harbor development along the Lake Michigan shore, thought Chicago would be foolish to relinquish miles of potential docking facilities for recreation. The city negotiated a compromise under which Municipal (later Navy) Pier was built to combine both uses. Property owners objected to street-widening plans that destroyed their front yards or buildings. Railroads resisted consolidation. And mail-order baron A. Montgomery Ward opposed the idea of clustering public buildings in the downtown lakefront park. Ward's lawyers invoked an obscure clause in the original federal land grant that gave Michigan Ave. property owners, of which he was one, veto power over any construction there. Ward did not challenge the building of the Art Institute, but he pursued lawsuits to the Illinois Supreme Court to prevent the construction in the park of the John Crerar Library and the Field Columbian Museum.

The Burnham Plan shaped public-works construction for decades. Its success depended on a bold government that would borrow and spend on a grand scale, and William Hale "Big Bill" Thompson, who was elected mayor in 1915, was willing to do just that. Over the next eight years, Thompson began a physical transformation of the city. He enhanced the southern bank of the river with a bilevel street named in honor of Wacker and built new bridges, including the double-decker at Michigan Ave., thereby making that street a major thoroughfare on both sides of the river. Thompson also extended Ogden Ave. and Roosevelt Rd. to speed traffic across the city, and he straightened out an obtrusive bend in the Chicago River between 12th and 16th Sts.

The plan also inspired the 1923 passage of Chicago's first comprehensive zoning law, which sought to regulate both vertical and horizontal sprawl. The law replaced the rigid height limit with an elaborate formula that allowed towers above the twenty-second story provided that the structures did not occupy more than one-fourth of the area of the lot and that tower space was not more than one-sixth of the entire building. While these requirements did not help traffic problems, they slightly reduced canyon effects. The zoning law proved quite compatible with the skyscraper developments of the 1920s, a decade that witnessed an enormous building boom and the first significant appearance of tall buildings outside the Loop. The Burnham Plan made the Chicago River a focal point, and by 1929, the Merchandise Mart—the world's largest building, with more than four million square feet of floor space—was gracing the northern bank of the main branch, while the Chicago Daily News Building peered across the river at the forty-five-story Civic Opera Building, built by utilities magnate Samuel Insull. The opening of the Michigan Ave. Bridge in 1920 extended development north of the river, much as Burnham had envisioned. The dazzling white Wrigley Building was soon joined by hotels, a Northwestern University campus, and other office buildings, most notably the Tribune Tower, whose design was chosen in an international competition. A string of new apartment buildings stretched northward along Lake Shore Dr. In the Loop itself, buildings of twenty and twenty-five stories became the norm, while the 605-foot Chicago Board of Trade loomed over its neighbors.

The zoning law also not only protected property values in built-up areas from incompatible or detrimental intrusions but also provided general guidelines for developing the remaining open lands. Throughout the 1920s, developers lured workers into almost endless rows of sturdy, spacious, one-story brick bungalows. Residents of the "bungalow belt" usually found shopping nearby, because the zoning law fostered the development of outlying business districts centered on major transit intersections with heavy pedestrian traffic. These shopping districts were also likely to include the "popcorn palace" movie theaters, in which architects such as Rapp & Rapp demonstrated their mastery of sight lines and acoustics and created spectacular interiors based on escapist themes.

Poverty, Racism, and the Growth of Slums

In stark contrast to the Loop's nineteenth-century splendors were the adjacent slums. Owners had deferred maintenance on properties that they expected to raze as the downtown expanded outward. Tall-building construction had instead restricted development to the core of downtown, and decrepit transient housing soon ringed the Loop on all sides. On the South Side was the Levee, one of the nation's largest vice districts, controlled by First Ward aldermen John Coughlin and Michael "Hinky Dink" Kenna.

The residential slums began about a mile west and south of the Loop. The poor, many of them immigrants, lived in old wooden houses standing cheek by jowl with factories and bars or in once-elegant apartments and mansions converted into rooming houses and then tenements. Some lots were filled front to back with ramshackle frame houses; others became refuse pits in front of houses that had not been elevated when the street grade was raised. Many of the tiny units had no bathrooms or kitchens. While other neighborhoods were adopting electricity and steam heat, the slums had yet to see gas lighting or coal stoves in every room.

Among the few constant features of slum life were the buildings themselves, the high death rates, and political bosses who prevented reforms. By doling out city jobs, they got enough votes to remain on the City Council for decades. The "gray wolves," as the press called such grafters as Coughlin, Kenna, "Foxy Ed" Cullerton, and "Johnny De Pow" Powers, resisted efforts to end their hegemony. Political reformers could count on support only from the middle-class residents of the neighborhoods adjacent to the slums, and the political parties could not supply sufficiently strong challengers.

The multiplicity of slum problems called for a multifunctional solution. Such a "department store" approach to social reform was pioneered by Jane Addams, who arrived on the West Side in 1889 with Ellen Gates Starr to establish Hull House. The traditional approach to charity had been to dole out food and money from a downtown office or to intrude on humble homes with prying questions about worthiness. Addams, in contrast, believed that the proper way to help the poor was to live among them and create semi-public places known as settlement houses where those in need could find a variety of services. Hull House offered the arts, job training, health services, child care, physical education, domestic science instruction, a library, and a savings bank. Hull House expanded to thirteen buildings covering a square block and inspired the creation of fifty similar facilities across the city, most notably the University of Chicago and Northwestern University settlements and Chicago Commons. Ironically, by teaching job skills and thrift, settlement houses did not instill neighborhood loyalty and cohesiveness but instead contributed to the transience by showing slum residents how to move on to better lives elsewhere.

Burnham's vision of the City Beautiful made only vague comments about how deconcentration could solve slum problems and failed to recognize that racial discrimination and poverty are perversely centralizing forces. So while preservation or dispersal were options elsewhere in Chicago, the Madison St. skid row still sheltered the homeless, and the dense ring of slums surrounding the downtown continued to house those too poor to afford anything else. Moreover, racial discrimination trapped the fifty thousand African Americans who migrated to Chicago during World War I in overcrowded areas, regardless of their economic circumstances. These new arrivals subsequently competed with returning veterans for jobs and housing, leading to a bloody July 1919 race riot. Threats of violence, combined with racial covenants in sale and rental agreements, kept the Black Belt a firmly walled enclave.

After World War II, although vast neighborhood-clearance lands lay vacant, the Chicago Housing Authority began a policy of erecting high-rise buildings

Chicago Housing Authority—Stateway Gardens under construction (demolished)

on compact sites, claiming as its motives the high costs of land and federal pressure to save money on construction. Critics, however, understood that the policy ensured that the maximum number of African Americans arriving from the South would be absorbed within the existing Black Belt, thereby decreasing the possibility that middle-class black families near its edges might move into adjacent white neighborhoods. By the early 1960s, Chicago officials had accepted the widespread belief that it was easier and cheaper to demolish whole neighborhoods of substandard old flats and bungalows than to renovate individual structures. The result was massive land clearance in a swath that encircled the downtown and expanded several miles into the South Side.

The Depression and Public Works

For most Chicagoans, prosperity disappeared as the 1920s ended. Declines in construction and other economic indicators had begun around 1927, and by the time Wall Street crashed in October 1929, the number of welfare cases had exceeded the capabilities of private agencies. Ironically, the central location that underlay much of Chicago's past prosperity made the city a prime destination for homeless people traveling in boxcars. Unfinished lower Wacker Dr. provided temporary shelter for both transients and residents who found themselves evicted or foreclosed. The Winded City seemed to be moving backward. Health and education services were cut to nineteenth-century levels, streets were strewn with garbage, and at least thirty downtown buildings—among them Henry Hobson Richardson's Marshall Field Wholesale Building and Burnham & Root's Masonic Temple—were demolished as their owners sought to avoid paying taxes.

Chicago turned to dramatic solutions. Where Mayor Thompson, a Republican, had built with bonds, voters in 1931 backed a new Democratic machine under Anton Cermak and his successor, Edward J. Kelly, who funneled federal New Deal money into massive public works projects. Not only was the Outer Drive Bridge opened in 1937 and Municipal (now Midway) Airport upgraded into a major facility, but new viaducts, sidewalks, school athletic fields, and other projects put paychecks in thousands of hands. Mayor Kelly enthusiastically backed the wholesale replacement of the slum belt with public housing projects. The first three were built in 1935: the Jane Addams Homes, the Julia C. Lathrop Homes, and Trumbull Park Homes. Chicago also began work on a long-delayed subway system, the first section of which opened under State St. in 1943.

In the boldest of all moves, in 1933, at the nadir of the depression, Chicago celebrated its centennial with the Century of Progress Exposition, sprawled along the lakefront and focused on what became the site of Meigs Field. The fair offered an optimistic statement that science, industry, and business would bring a return of prosperity. Its futuristic buildings were made of such unconventional materials as rolled steel, Masonite,

Chrysler Building by Holabird & Root, 1933 World's Fair

and plywood; bright colors, accents of neon and fluorescent lights, and a whimsical midway gave the fair an escapist atmosphere.

The depression ended with the military buildup of World War II, and Chicago's central location again shaped its role. Its diverse industrial base made the metropolis second only to Detroit as a producer of war materiel; however, the need to fulfill the fourteen hundred federal contracts awarded to Chicago companies led them to seek larger quarters outside the city. The gigantic Dodge-Chicago plant at 76th St. and Cicero Ave. (in what is now Ford City Shopping Center), the Buick aircraft engine plants in Melrose Park, and the Amertorp torpedo plant in Forest Park led the industrial suburbanization, which also drew the latest influx of workers to suburban "defense housing."

The Loop Reborn versus the Logic of Decentralization

Urban patterns entrenched by the Great Depression and wartime controls crumbled with the arrival of postwar prosperity and mobility, and although few people noticed at first, among the traditions in decline was centralization itself.

Many businesses remained eager to locate downtown. Beginning with the 1952 ground breaking for the Prudential Building, the first Loop skyscraper since the Field Building of the 1930s, tower after tower appeared in rapid succession. "The tall boys are sprouting in bunches," proclaimed one journalist in 1967. The Loop seemed reborn: the Inland Steel building, the Chicago Civic Center (now Richard J. Daley Center), the Brunswick, and the First National Bank building were just a few of the additions. Most buildings of the 1960s and 1970s were at least indirectly influenced by the careful, ordered style of Ludwig Mies van der Rohe, whose strong, black-framed glass towers became the ultimate statement of the curtain wall. Innovations such as the graceful curves of Lake Point Tower and the bold bracing of the John Hancock Center gradually came into style. The greatest structural achievement of the era was the Sears Tower, at 1,454 feet the world's tallest building at the time of its construction. Although pundits questioned its site west of the Loop, Sears chair Arthur M. Wood defended it using the logic of the centralization argument. The major factor in choosing the location was "our employees—how they would get to and from work," he explained. "The site we chose offers all the advantages we were looking for . . . close to the post office, financial district, government offices, and the major attractions."

For many others, however, the trend toward dispersal greatly accelerated. The first evidence was the suburban exodus of industry made possible by a superhighway system that had begun in 1954 with the Congress (later Eisenhower) Expressway. By 1960, work was either finished or under way on the Northwest (later Kennedy), Southwest (later Stevenson), Edens, and Kingery; the Dan Ryan soon followed. Industrial developers, who had long complained that zoning in Chicago stunted expansion by preserving too much land for residential purposes, grabbed at the irresistible lure of lower taxes and cheaper

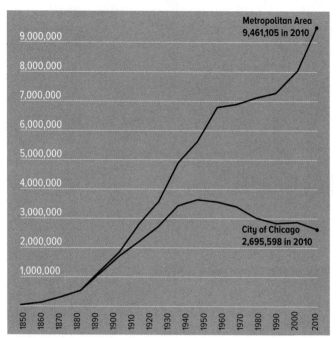

Population growth

land in suburbia. They were quick to take advantage of the independence from rail depots made possible by the increasing use of truck transportation. The opening of O'Hare International Airport in 1962, on a former Douglas Aircraft Co. plant site, provided a new form of transportation hub particularly suited for manufacturers of high-value, low-bulk goods such as electronics. Chicago reached its peak population of 3.6 million in 1950 as developers were filling in the open tracts on the Northwest and Southwest sides. But land in the suburbs was cheaper, and by the early 1960s, virtually all new single-family construction was taking place beyond the city limits. In some suburbs, failed developments from the 1920s were completed near commuter lines; in others, the dominance of the automobile was recognized and developments were oriented toward highways.

Within the city, neighborhoods became less cohesive and no longer the focus of residents' lives. Many Chicagoans had traditionally met most of their needs with local churches, stores, saloons, newspapers, movie theaters, and schools. Outings to a major park or shopping expeditions to the Loop were special events. That world evaporated after World War II, especially in the wake of 1949 federal legislation that made it easier to obtain a GI Bill or Federal Housing Administration mortgage on a house in the suburbs than on one in the city. Two new phenomena—malls anchored by large chain stores and franchise food outlets—drew clientele from wide areas, forcing many neighborhood businesses to close, while television sealed the fate of the local movie house and local newspaper. Small manufacturing plants also closed, and more breadwinners had to travel longer distances to work, often by car. As neighborhood populations aged, their schools and churches struggled to survive.

The disintegration of neighborhoods affected Chicago's Democratic machine, which had begun the postwar years in a swirl of scandals that ended Kelly's fourteen-year mayoralty. His successor, Martin H. Kennelly, a moving-and-storage company executive, presented enough of a good-government image to hold the organization together while planners were laying out the expressway and urban renewal programs, but in 1955, the aloof incumbent found himself ousted by city clerk Richard J. Daley. Promising greater emphasis on neighborhood and family concerns, the new mayor kept the machine alive for the next twenty-one years, in part because he functioned as a symbolic bulwark against change. His early years in office benefited from the infusions of federal money that built O'Hare, the expressways, and a new water-filtration plant, and he adjusted the machine to reflect Chicago's changing ethnic and racial makeup, though critics charged that his moves were too slow and too limited. He even survived charges that the police had exacerbated the riots at the 1968 Democratic National Convention.

But Daley's ability to deliver the vote began to wane in the early 1970s, and the city's Democratic political organization was slowly unraveling when he died in office in 1976. Voters now paid more attention to the media than to their precinct captains, and middle-class African Americans felt alienated. A half century of political stability was replaced by a succession of five chief executives in just over twelve years. In 1979, political maverick Jane M. Byrne upset Daley's machine successor, Michael A. Bilandic, but she, in turn, lost four years later to Chicago's first black mayor, Harold Washington, who proclaimed the machine dead. Washington's sudden death in November 1987 was followed by the interim mayoralty of Eugene Sawyer, who was defeated in a special election by Daley's son, Richard M. Daley. In 1989, Daley won a full term, but not as the head of the centralized, cohesive machine that had put his father in office.

The Birth of the Preservation Movement

The creation of the magnificent postwar skyline forced Chicagoans to deal with the constraints imposed by each generation of urbanites on its successors. Should they destroy the institutional artifacts of earlier ages, modify them to conform to present needs, or preserve them in their current forms? The earliest response was destruction. Federally funded urban renewal and land-clearance programs leveled entire neighborhoods, including churches, small businesses, and social institutions. Demolition occasionally had a specific intention, such as the clearance of the Hull House area to build the Chi-

Chicago Stock Exchange by Adler & Sullivan (demolished)

cago campus of the University of Illinois (opened in 1965), but more often, land was left vacant for decades.

In the Loop, the wrecker's ball was in the hands of private speculators who claimed many first-generation skyscrapers before Chicagoans began to realize that the demolished structures included some of the best examples of Chicago School architecture. In 1957, the City Council created a landmarks commission, but all it could do was issue plaques. Its inadequacy was underscored by the demolition of Adler & Sullivan's Schiller Building in 1960 and by its replacement with a parking structure whose facade parodied the lost classic. Nonetheless, eight years passed before Chicago had a preservation law and a commission (now the Commission on Chicago Landmarks) empowered to administer it. The subsequent loss of Adler & Sullivan's Chicago Stock Exchange in 1972 and the McCarthy Building in 1990 demonstrated that the commission could do little more than delay demolition unless the City Council designated a building for preservation and enforced that decision. At the same time, the Landmarks Preservation Council of Illinois (now Landmarks Illinois), the Chicago Architecture Foundation, the Chicago Chapter of the American Institute of Architects (AIA Chicago), neighborhood groups, and countless newspaper articles worked to foster a sense of pride in the city's physical heritage.

The Emergence of a Service Economy

A most significant postwar change was the gradual shift in employment from manufacturing to service-sector jobs. Although Chicago remained a leading industrial center, the number of blue-collar jobs in the city dropped by 77 percent between 1947 and 1982. By the early 1980s, more Chicagoans earned their money in nonmanufacturing employment than in industry. Chicago's role as the nation's transportation hub, strengthened by O'Hare's steady growth, attracted corporate headquarters and research facilities, rekindling intense competition between the city center and periphery. The continued lure of lower taxes and quick access by expressway, combined with the available acreage on which to build horizontally oriented office parks, generated a new wave of exurban construction. One hub developed in the O'Hare area, while another lay along the East-West Tollway between Oak Brook and Naperville. Even Sears, which had found the downtown so advantageous in 1974, moved in 1992 to a "campus" of low buildings in the northwestern suburbs.

The service-sector world, held together by silicon chips and fiber optics, is potentially much more mobile than the industrial world. It is no easy task to move heavy equipment; outmoded steel mills and other factories are simply closed. But service businesses can be transferred quickly and constantly seek newer, more flexible spaces that can accommodate rapidly evolving

W. Wacker Dr. in 1964

W. Wacker Dr. in 1992

office technology. This mobility has increased the competition for tenants in
the downtown towers.

The most exciting result of Chicago's transition to a service economy has
been the latest generation of downtown construction. Since the completion of
the Sears Tower, well over one hundred other new buildings have appeared in
the central area. They represent a construction boom even greater than that of
the Richard J. Daley years. On many of these buildings, the Miesian frame box
has yielded to shimmering glass and mirrors cast in curves and points. Michigan Ave.'s Magnificent Mile is the hub of a second downtown, an idea that had
been promoted since the late 1940s by real estate mogul Arthur Rubloff.

Summary

Chicagoans have discovered the depth and variety of their architectural heritage. Not only has popular interest in downtown gems expanded, but the Tax
Reform Act of 1981 sparked the interest of commercial developers, who invested heavily in renovating historic buildings. Although these incentives were
subsequently reduced, older neighborhoods have been rediscovered and rebuilt, and many old factories adjacent to downtown have been reborn as lofts
and galleries.

This trend has its negative aspects, of course, most notably in the loss
of semipublic spaces in the Loop. Except for the waiting room at Union Station, the great railway depots are only memories. The vertical malls that draw
crowds to the Magnificent Mile exemplify a new breed of semipublic space
that seems to shield customers from the city rather than immerse them in it,
as the Loop stores did. One of the most dramatic interior spaces of the type
previously associated with department stores is a public one: the atrium of the
James R. Thompson State of Illinois Center, which reinterprets the rotunda of a
capitol building.

But cities change constantly, and in Chicago that process is always cause
for optimism. If history proves any sort of guide, the city will continue to find
new ways to be a leader, both as a special place and as the quintessential
American metropolis. Chicago is both a museum and a laboratory in which
to observe how an agglomeration of peoples deploys the finite space within
the city's borders and how architects respond to the challenge of designing
for them. Chicago's story relates the triumphs and failures, the problems and
prospects, of all American cities.

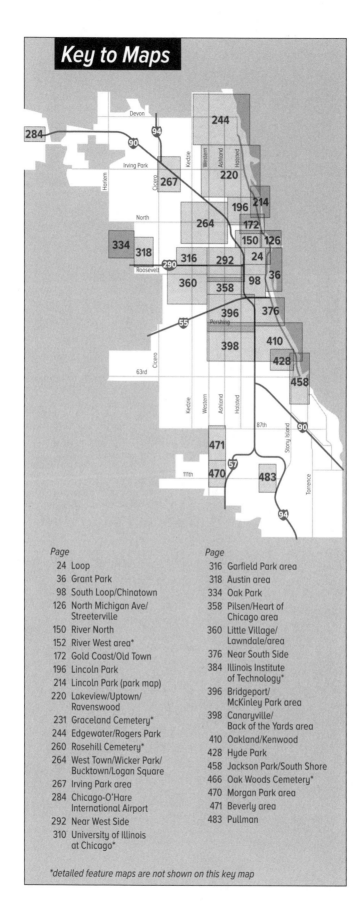

Key to Maps

244

284

90

94

Devon

Irving Park

267

220

Kedzie

Western

Ashland

Halsted

Hartem

Cicero

North

264

196 214

172

334 318

Roosevelt

290

316

292

150 126

24

98 36

360

358

396 376

398

410

428

458

55

Pershing

Cicero

63rd

Kedzie

Western

Ashland

Halsted

87th

Stony Island

90

111th

471

470

57

483

Torrence

94

detailed feature maps are not shown on this key map

LOOP AND SOUTH LOOP

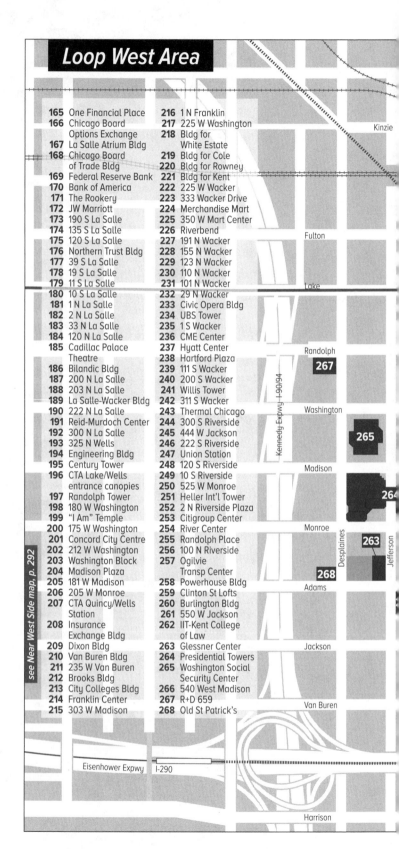

Loop West Area

165	One Financial Place	216	1 N Franklin
166	Chicago Board Options Exchange	217	225 W Washington
167	La Salle Atrium Bldg	218	Bldg for White Estate
168	Chicago Board of Trade Bldg	219	Bldg for Cole
169	Federal Reserve Bank	220	Bldg for Rowney
170	Bank of America	221	Bldg for Kent
171	The Rookery	222	225 W Wacker
172	JW Marriott	223	333 Wacker Drive
173	190 S La Salle	224	Merchandise Mart
174	135 S La Salle	225	350 W Mart Center
175	120 S La Salle	226	Riverbend
176	Northern Trust Bldg	227	191 N Wacker
177	39 S La Salle	228	155 N Wacker
178	19 S La Salle	229	123 N Wacker
179	11 S La Salle	230	110 N Wacker
180	10 S La Salle	231	101 N Wacker
181	1 N La Salle	232	29 N Wacker
182	2 N La Salle	233	Civic Opera Bldg
183	33 N La Salle	234	UBS Tower
184	120 N La Salle	235	1 S Wacker
185	Cadillac Palace Theatre	236	CME Center
186	Bilandic Bldg	237	Hyatt Center
187	200 N La Salle	238	Hartford Plaza
188	203 N La Salle	239	111 S Wacker
189	La Salle-Wacker Bldg	240	200 S Wacker
190	222 N La Salle	241	Willis Tower
191	Reid-Murdoch Center	242	311 S Wacker
192	300 N La Salle	243	Thermal Chicago
193	325 N Wells	244	300 S Riverside
194	Engineering Bldg	245	444 W Jackson
195	Century Tower	246	222 S Riverside
196	CTA Lake/Wells entrance canopies	247	Union Station
197	Randolph Tower	248	120 S Riverside
198	180 W Washington	249	10 S Riverside
199	"I Am" Temple	250	525 W Monroe
200	175 W Washington	251	Heller Int'l Tower
201	Concord City Centre	252	2 N Riverside Plaza
202	212 W Washington	253	Citigroup Center
203	Washington Block	254	River Center
204	Madison Plaza	255	Randolph Place
205	181 W Madison	256	100 N Riverside
206	205 W Monroe	257	Ogilvie Transp Center
207	CTA Quincy/Wells Station	258	Powerhouse Bldg
208	Insurance Exchange Bldg	259	Clinton St Lofts
209	Dixon Bldg	260	Burlington Bldg
210	Van Buren Bldg	261	550 W Jackson
211	235 W Van Buren	262	IIT-Kent College of Law
212	Brooks Bldg	263	Glessner Center
213	City Colleges Bldg	264	Presidential Towers
214	Franklin Center	265	Washington Social Security Center
215	303 W Madison	266	540 West Madison
		267	R+D 659
		268	Old St Patrick's

see Near West Side map, p. 292

Kinzie

Fulton

Lake

Randolph

267

Kennedy Expwy I-90/94

Washington

265

Madison

264

Monroe

Desplaines

263

Jefferson

268

Adams

Jackson

Van Buren

Eisenhower Expwy   I-290

Harrison

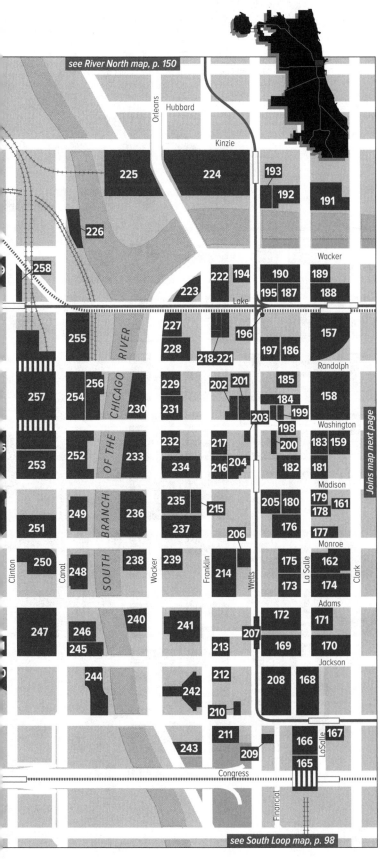

see River North map, p. 150

Orleans
Hubbard

Kinzie

225   224   193
              192   191

Wacker

226

258

222 194   190   189
223   195 187 188
        Lake

255   227   157
CHICAGO 228   196
        RIVER   197 186   Randolph

256   229   202 201   185
254   231   184   158
        230   199
                203   198   Washington
252   232   217   200   183 159
253   233   234 216 204   182   181

OF THE   Madison
249   236   235 215   205 180 179 161
BRANCH   237   176   178
251   206   177
                                Monroe
250   238   239   175   162
248 Canal   Wacker Franklin 214 Wells 173 La Salle 174 Clark
SOUTH

                            Adams
        240   172   171
247 246   241   207   169   170
245 Clinton   213   Jackson
        244   212   208 168
                242
                210
                211   166   167
        243   209   165
                LaSalle
            Congress

Financial

see South Loop map, p. 98

Joins map next page

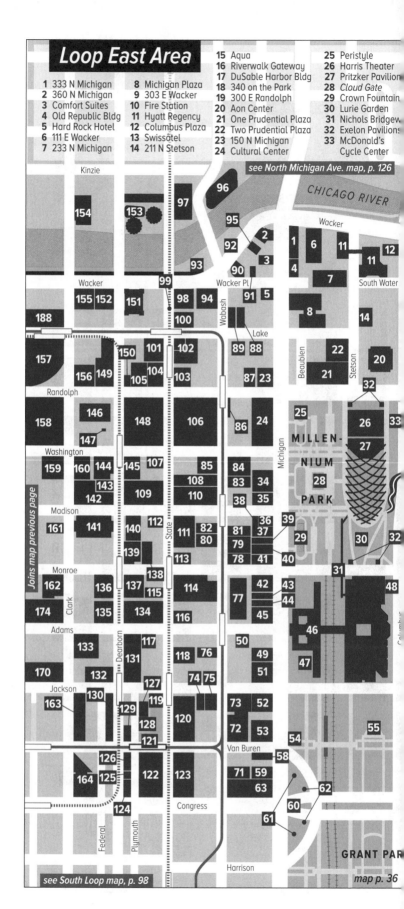

Loop East Area

1 333 N Michigan
2 360 N Michigan
3 Comfort Suites
4 Old Republic Bldg
5 Hard Rock Hotel
6 111 E Wacker
7 233 N Michigan
8 Michigan Plaza
9 303 E Wacker
10 Fire Station
11 Hyatt Regency
12 Columbus Plaza
13 Swissôtel
14 211 N Stetson
15 Aqua
16 Riverwalk Gateway
17 DuSable Harbor Bldg
18 340 on the Park
19 300 E Randolph
20 Aon Center
21 One Prudential Plaza
22 Two Prudential Plaza
23 150 N Michigan
24 Cultural Center
25 Peristyle
26 Harris Theater
27 Pritzker Pavilion
28 Cloud Gate
29 Crown Fountain
30 Lurie Garden
31 Nichols Bridgew
32 Exelon Pavilions
33 McDonald's
Cycle Center

see North Michigan Ave. map, p. 126

CHICAGO RIVER

Kinzie

Wacker

South Water

Wacker

Wacker Pl

Lake

Randolph

MILLEN-
NIUM
PARK

Washington

Madison

Joins map previous page

Monroe

Adams

Jackson

Van Buren

Congress

GRANT PAR

see South Loop map, p. 98

map p. 36

Harrison

34 20 N Michigan
35 6 N Michigan
36 Willoughby Tower
37 12 S Michigan
38 Annex Bldg
-40 Gage Group
41 University Club
42 Monroe Bldg
43 School of the
Art Institute

44 Lake View Bldg
45 122 S Michigan
46 Art Institute
47 *Fountain of the Great Lakes*
48 Chicago Stock Exchange Arch
49-50 Symphony Center
51 224 S Michigan
52 Metropolitan Tower
53 McCormick Bldg
54 Metra Canopy

55 *Abraham Lincoln*
56 Buckingham Fountain
57 Fountain Pavilions
58 Chicago Club
59 Fine Arts Bldg
60 Congress Plaza
61 Eagle Fountains
62 *The Spearman &*
The Bowman
63 Auditorium Bldg

71 Roosevelt University Wabash Bldg
72 CNA Center
73 55 E Jackson
74 DePaul O'Malley Bldg
75 DePaul Lewis Center
76 218 South Wabash Bldg
77 55 E Monroe & Park Monroe
78 Sharp Bldg
79 The Legacy at Millennium Park
80 Barker-Haskell-Atwater Bldgs
81 Jewelers Bldg
82 The Silversmith Hotel
83 Shops Bldg
84 Pittsfield Bldg
85 25 E Washington
86 Burton, Peck, Couch Facades
87 Gallery 37 Center
88 Self Park
89 Virgin Hotel
90 17th Church of Christ, Scientist
91 68 E Wacker Pl
92 Wacker Drive
93 Riverwalk & Wabash Memorial Plaza
94 35 E Wacker
95 75 E Wacker
96 Trump Int'l Hotel & Tower
97 AMA Plaza
98 One East Wacker
99 State St. Streetscape
100 The Wit Hotel
101 ABC-WLS Bldg
102 Chicago Theater
103 Joffrey Tower
104 162 N State Residences
105 Ford Center/Oriental Theatre
106 Macy's on State
107 Hotel Burnham
108 17 N State/16 N Wabash
109 2 N State/1 N Dearborn
110 1 N State
111 Sullivan Center
112 Jones Hall
113 Mentor Bldg
114 Palmer House
115 Singer Bldg
116 Thermal Chicago
117 The Berghoff
118 211-227 S State

119 John Marshall Law School
120 DePaul Center
121 CTA Harold Washington Library Station
122 Harold Washington Library
123 Robert Morris Center
124 Manhattan Bldg
125 Plymouth Bldg
126 Old Colony Bldg
127 John Marshall Law School
128 Chicago Bar Association
129 Fisher Bldg
130 Monadnock Bldg
131 Dirksen Bldg
132 Kluczynski Bldg
133 Post Office
134 131 S Dearborn
135 Marquette Bldg
136 55 W Monroe
137 33 W Monroe
138 Bank of America Theater & Majestic Hotel
139 Inland Steel Bldg
140 One S Dearborn
141 Chase Tower
142 Three First National Plaza
143 10 N Dearborn
144 Dunne Cook County Admin Bldg
145 33 N Dearborn
146 Daley Center
147 Picasso Sculpture
148 Block 37
149 Goodman Theatre Center
150 Delaware Bldg
151 Leo Burnett Building
152 55 W Wacker
153 Marina City
154 321 N Clark
155 77 W Wacker
156 161 N Clark St
157 Thompson Center
158 County Bldg/City Hall
159 Burnham Center
160 Chicago Temple
161 Loop Synagogue
162 BMO Harris Bank
163 Metcalfe Federal Bldg
164 Chicago Metropolitan Correctional Center

THE LOOP

The Loop is quintessential Chicago! Here the City of Big Shoulders flaunts its continuing vitality with an unequaled display of dazzling towers and crowded streets. Jammed with a medley of cars, trucks, buses, and darting pedestrians, the Loop is an urban canvas framed by its famous El. It is home to banks, national and international corporate headquarters, stock and commodities trading centers, and a myriad of shops, restaurants, and other support services.

The small tongue of land on which the Loop is situated, bounded by Lake Michigan on the east and the Chicago River on the north and west, determined not only the shape but also the nature of Chicago's downtown by demanding the utmost in concentration. Land for efficient corporate enterprise was at such a premium here that almost all other competing uses—factories, residences, civic institutions, and cultural facilities—were soon priced out of the area. When Chicago was developing in the second half of the nineteenth century, the dynamics of American business required that the successful businessman be on the scene, close to where the action was. Thus, the Loop witnessed an increasing concentration of fewer and fewer businesses and support functions crowded into congested streets. Even before the Great Fire of 1871, Chicago's downtown had become a business hub. Horse-drawn omnibuses, introduced on State St. in 1859, laid the groundwork for a network of transit lines to serve a commuter population.

Reconstruction in the wake of the fire reinforced these tendencies. Downtown's gridded streets were re-created as the most efficient pattern for the rapid development of business and commerce. Chicago's "new" downtown would provide little space for parks, churches, or recreational facilities and no space at all for residences. The 1880s saw the introduction of cable car lines circling part of the downtown area, the origin of the Loop's name. The term was firmly fixed when the Union Loop Elevated Railway was completed in 1897.

Technology stood ready in that same decade to generate a forest of office towers. The safety elevator, the telegraph and telephone, the flush toilet, the modern coal furnace—all already existed. Construction methods using iron and then steel developed rapidly, as did revolutionary foundation techniques that firmly anchored the new skyscraper city to the ground.

So rapid indeed were these developments that some historians have posited a whole new architecture—the Chicago School—that they claim emerged in the Loop from the early 1880s to 1910. These scholars suggest that this architecture—direct, pragmatic, and ahistorical—rests on the pioneering efforts of designers like Burnham & Root, Holabird & Roche, William Le Baron Jenney, and perhaps most notably, Louis H. Sullivan. The dictum attributed to Sullivan, "Form follows function," encapsulates the school's aesthetic and characterizes its importance as a forerunner of modernism.

More recently, some critics have challenged the concept of a Chicago School, noting that many of its designs are neither functionalist nor ahistorical. Though Sullivan had suggested the elimination of architectural ornament to the young Viennese architect Adolf Loos when the latter visited Chicago in 1893, Sullivan certainly did not follow his own advice.

Perhaps the wisest way to resolve this controversy is by reverting to a term frequently used around the turn of the twentieth century: Chicago construction. The great Chicago architects devised less a new architecture than a new means of creating it—efficient, cost-effective, and speedy. The Reliance Building, for example, whose glassy facade is often hailed as the prototype of the glass curtain-wall skyscraper, was praised in the 1890s for the rapidity with which its steel frame was erected and for the practicality of its washable terra-cotta sheathing. The speed with which Chicago's architects adopted a new and changing technology can be demonstrated in the shift from almost full bearing-wall construction in the 1891 (northern) portion of the Monadnock Building to the almost full skeletal construction of its 1893 (southern) section.

Chicago designers maintained a sense of decorum or "keeping" in their works. Martin Roche could design a simple, straightforward loft building, the Great Lakes Building, in 1910, with the verticals and horizontals of its skeletal frame neatly and modestly encased in brick and clearly expressed on its facades. That year, he also designed the lavishly ornamented Monroe Building, whose gabled roof and facades sheathed in terra-cotta reflected the structure's more prestigious location and "higher calling" as an office building.

Not long ago, some planners suggested that suburbanization and decentralization would spell the demise of the Loop as Chicago's hub. Instead, the Loop has experienced a well-nigh miraculous rebirth. New clusters of commercial activity have sprung up immediately to its north and west, making the twenty-first-century Loop more extensive and more dynamic than ever. While the 2008 recession marked a brief pause, construction has boomed, given a huge boost with the opening of Millennium Park in 2004. For the first time in years, the Loop has become a desirable residential address. Splendid new apartment towers have risen as nearby educational and cultural institutions have expanded and remodeled, notably in the east and south sections of the Loop. With a dizzying variety of stores in buildings old and new, retail activity remains strong, and a new canyon of business headquarters has been created along Wacker Dr. Despite the inevitable changes that will continue to occur in Chicago's Loop, it remains a potent urban symbol. Those who have doubts about the Loop's vitality are invited to walk from Union Station to Millennium Park and count the number of briefcases, backpacks, and shopping bags borne ceaselessly by in the hands of busy Chicagoans. They'll need no further convincing!

—ROBERT F. IRVING

1 333 N. Michigan Ave.

1928, HOLABIRD & ROOT
2014, ENTRY, LOBBY AND STOREFRONT
    RENOVATION, GOETTSCH PARTNERS

Its pronounced verticality, spare lines, and dramatic setbacks were inspired by Eliel Saarinen's second-prize entry in the 1922 Chicago Tribune Tower Competition. The polished marble base and stylized bands of ornament are the only embellishments on this elegant limestone tower. Low reliefs by Fred M. Torrey depict pioneers, traders, hunters, and Native Americans at Fort Dearborn, which occupied part of this site.

360 N. Michigan Ave.

2 360 N. Michigan Ave.

*(London Guarantee &
Accident Building)*
1923, ALFRED S. ALSCHULER
2001, RENOVATION AND LOBBY
    RESTORATION, LOHAN ASSOCS.

The river's bend dictated the building's unusual shape, which provides a graceful forecourt. The neoclassical ornament includes a triumphal-arch entry with colossal Corinthian columns, a second rank of columns

in a three-story top, and a crowning belvedere. The lobby and grand entrance were meticulously re-created in 2001.

3 Comfort Suites

320 N. Michigan Ave.
1983, BOOTH HANSEN ASSOCS.

This stylish infill building was designed for residences but was leased as offices before becoming a dormitory and then a hotel. Concrete was shaped into moldings, curves, and capitals on the main facade and expresses the building's structural grid on the sides.

4 Old Republic Building

(Bell Building)

307 N. Michigan Ave.

1925, VITZTHUM & BURNS

Classicism is stressed throughout, from the beige granite base with its triumphal-arch entrance through the cream terra-cotta shaft and colonnaded top.

5 Hard Rock Hotel

(Carbide & Carbon Building)

230 N. Michigan Ave.

1929, BURNHAM BROS.

2003, CONVERSION TO HOTEL,
    LUCIEN LAGRANGE ARCHITECTS

The most beautiful skyscraper on this stretch of N. Michigan Ave. is decidedly Art Deco in massing and detail. The polished granite base has

Carbide & Carbon Building (now Hard Rock Hotel)

a black-marble-and-bronze entrance ornamented with delicate grillwork. The dark-green-and-gold terra-cotta shaft rises without horizontal cornices or projections to a fifty-foot tower trimmed with gold leaf.

Illinois Center

Bounded by the Chicago River, N. Lake Shore Dr., N. Michigan Ave. (excluding 151, 333, and 307 N. Michigan Ave.), and E. Lake St.

MASTER PLAN BEGUN 1967, LUDWIG MIES VAN DER ROHE

6 111 E. Wacker Dr.

(One Illinois Center)

1970, OFFICE OF MIES VAN DER ROHE

7 233 N. Michigan Ave.

(Two Illinois Center)

1973, OFFICE OF MIES VAN DER ROHE

8 Michigan Plaza

205–225 N. Michigan Ave.

1981, FUJIKAWA, CONTERATO, LOHAN & ASSOCS.;
    1985, FUJIKAWA, JOHNSON & ASSOCS.

9 303 E. Wacker Dr.

1980, FUJIKAWA, CONTERATO, LOHAN & ASSOCS.

10 Fire Station

259 N. Columbus Dr.

1982, FUJIKAWA, CONTERATO, LOHAN & ASSOCS.

11 Hyatt Regency Chicago

151 E. Wacker Dr.

1974, WEST TOWER; 1980, EAST TOWER AND ATRIUM LOBBY, A. EPSTEIN & SONS

12 Columbus Plaza

233 E. Wacker Dr.

1980, FUJIKAWA, CONTERATO, LOHAN & ASSOCS.

This mixed-use development, one of the nation's largest, is a densely packed mixed bag of colors, materials, and styles, built to a colossal scale around dark, cramped plazas. Development of the eighty-three-acre site, which uses air rights over former Illinois Central Gulf Railroad tracks, has followed the original plan for a self-contained city of offices, shops, apartments, and hotels. Master planning in this case seems to have been a euphemism for a means of squeezing the highest density onto the land. There is no hierarchy of buildings or spaces, just a thicket of structures competing for land, light, and—in the postmodern era—visual dominance. A trilevel street system segregates service vehicles, arterial traffic, and local traffic; dreary and confusing pedestrian concourses link most of the buildings.

The urbanistic amenities are nil; the project lacks even a meaningful relationship to the river. Architectural discord has been the rule from the early days of construction, when the Miesian steel-and-glass towers of One and Two Illinois Center were made to share their site with the clunky, brick-faced Hyatt Regency hotel. One of Mies's successor firms, Fujikawa, Conterato, Lohan & Assocs., has stayed remarkably faithful to the original design aesthetic—for better or worse—in its office buildings while compounding the visual incoherence of Wacker Dr. with the concrete Columbus Plaza apartment building. The firm did, however, provide a small grace note of Miesian modernism in the fire station at the base of 303 E. Wacker Dr.

Lakeshore East

Bounded by N. Columbus Dr., E. Wacker Dr., and N.
Lake Shore Dr., north of Randolph St.
2002, MASTER PLAN, SKIDMORE, OWINGS & MERRILL
2005, PARK, THE OFFICE OF JAMES BURNETT, DESIGN LANDSCAPE
    ARCH.; SITE DESIGN GROUP, LANDSCAPE ARCH. OF RECORD
LOEWENBERG ARCHITECTS, ARCH. OF RECORD FOR ALL BUILDINGS AND
    DESIGN ARCH. FOR THE LANCASTER, THE SHOREHAM, THE TIDES;
    DESTEFANO & PARTNERS, DESIGN ARCH. FOR THE REGATTA, THE CHANDLER;
    THE STEINBERG GROUP, DESIGN ARCH. FOR THE PARKHOMES; BKL
    ARCHITECTURE, DESIGN ARCH. FOR COAST, GEMS WORLD ACADEMY

Beginning in 2002, the twenty-eight acres of land east of Columbus Drive became a separate development known as Lakeshore East. It is a residential enclave, totally unlike the rest of Illinois Center. Instead of decking over the site, which was cost-prohibitive given the need to include a long-promised park, the plan put the six-acre green space at grade and clustered town houses and high-rises around it. The fifty-foot gap in height from the surrounding streets was bridged with elevators and monumental stairways, two of them designed by Studio Gang. James Loewenberg was the master architect, and his firm executed some of the first buildings, but he wanted to avoid monotony by bringing in other designers. The master plan called for signature buildings on the middle of the north and east sides to mark gateways to the river and lake, but the role of iconic tower was usurped by Aqua, which seems unlikely to lose that distinction.

13 Swissôtel Chicago
(Swiss Grand Hotel)
323 E. Wacker Dr.
1989, HARRY WEESE & ASSOCS.

Wrapped in alternating bands of opaque and reflective glass, the tower reiterates the triangular massing of Weese's Metropolitan Correctional Center.

14 211 N. Stetson Ave.
(Lakeshore Athletic Club)
1990, KISHO KUROKAWA; FUJIKAWA,
    JOHNSON & ASSOCS., ASSOC. ARCHS.

This small building, the nation's first by Japanese architect Kurokawa, is the gem of the Illinois Center complex. The white-painted steel frame and window mullions are scaled to elements of traditional Japanese wooden buildings. The quartet of steel-frame rooftop towers pay homage to the towers of Louis H. Sullivan's People's Savings Bank (1911) in Cedar Rapids, Iowa. They also mark a dramatic interior space that extends an additional three stories below Stetson Ave.: a six-story skylit atrium with a curving staircase and a 100-foot rock-climbing wall.

15 Aqua
225 N. Columbus Dr.
2009, STUDIO GANG ARCHITECTS, DESIGN ARCH.,
    LOEWENBERG ARCHITECTS, ARCH. OF RECORD

It took nearly half a century, but with the completion of Jeanne Gang's Aqua, the towers of Bertrand Goldberg's Marina City finally have a true rival for the

Aqua

kind of visual audacity that makes a building a symbol of Chicago throughout the world.

Like Marina City, it is a mixed-use complex, combining condominiums, apartments, commercial space, and a hotel. Unlike Marina City, Aqua as a tower is the usual basic rectangular box. But it is set apart by the remarkable way Gang has used the idea of a "vertical topography" to give the face of the building a complex texture that ungrids the more conventional linearity that lies beneath.

The edges of the floor slabs vary continuously between floors. Where studies showed the best views (or the most need for sun shading), the slabs end in balconies, cantilevered out as much as twelve feet. In other areas, balconies are as narrow as two feet or are omitted altogether, and the curtain wall behind them deploys high-performance, more reflective glass to form "pools"—watery-looking voids resting within the vertical landforms of the rippling balconies.

Aqua not only received a large number of awards soon after its completion but also spawned a firestorm of debate over the building's claims to sustainability. The most frequent critique was that the lack of thermal blocks allows the balcony slabs to channel the cold of a Chicago winter directly into the apartments. Gang countered that the shading provided by the slabs makes the building more energy efficient in the summer and that the curtain wall was designed to reduce both solar gain and the infiltration of unwanted air, while operable doors and windows increase natural ventilation.

Despite a striking cantilever-canopied entrance at the north end, the huge three-story podium that houses ballrooms and retail engages the street in a perfunctory manner. On its roof, an 80,000-square-foot terrace incorporates extensive gardens by landscape architect Ted Wolff along with a swimming pool and other amenities.

Straight on and at a distance, especially on a gray day, Aqua's unique qualities can recede into the skyline. Add light and come closer, and the visual engagement becomes almost hypnotic. The restless variability makes the building slippery to the gaze. Stand under one of its corners and look up: with no conventional grid points to visually lock onto, the surfaces of Aqua appear to be constantly in motion.

While its quick rise to prominence has made Aqua a lightning rod for controversy, its faults are those of just about every other residential tower in Chicago, where developers calculate room layouts down to the inch to maximize return on investment. In its short life, Aqua has become indispensable. It continues to provoke discussions about fundamental architectural questions—commerce versus imagination, sustainability versus transparency, density versus sprawl, and the balance between function and form—even as it has reinvigorated the Chicago skyline by introducing the new morphologies of twenty-first-century design.

—LYNN BECKER

16 Riverwalk Gateway

**S. bank of the Chicago River
underneath N. Lake Shore Dr.**

2000, SKIDMORE, OWINGS & MERRILL

This previously menacing walkway is now a true urban amenity. The pleasant passageway under Lake Shore Dr., for use solely by pedestrians and cyclists, features a series of tile murals by artist Ellen Lanyon illustrating highlights of Chicago history. Lantern-topped towers echo the Art Deco motifs of the 1930s bridge above.

17 DuSable Harbor Building
520 E. Randolph St.

2009, DAVID WOODHOUSE ARCHITECTS

Hidden under its sloping green roof is the Chicago Park District's first LEED-certified building. On the exposed lakeside elevation, a shelf of perforated citrus-yellow louvers shades a band of windows, and sliding panels of the same hue protect the portals from Lake Michigan's worst.

18 340 on the Park
340 E. Randolph St.

2007, SOLOMON CORDWELL BUENZ

This was the first residential tower in the Midwest to achieve LEED silver certification and a pioneer in marketing sustainability to high-end condo buyers. The building is considered part of the Lakeshore East development, although it faces Grant Park, giving it a rare setting between two parks. Three of the four facades are different, and the irregular plan slants and curves to maximize views.

19 300 E. Randolph St.
1997, LOHAN ASSOCS.

2010, VERTICAL EXPANSION, GOETTSCH PARTNERS

While with Lohan Assocs., architect James Goettsch designed the thirty-two-story building to accommodate an unprecedented vertical expansion of twenty-four floors so that the client could grow without relocating. An interior atrium breaks up the large rectangular floor plates and facilitated the addition of elevator banks. The atrium also brings in north light and has open stairs and conference rooms.

20 Aon Center
(Standard Oil Building)
200 E. Randolph St.

1973, EDWARD DURELL STONE; PERKINS & WILL, ASSOC. ARCHS.

1994, PLAZA RENOVATIONS, VOY MADEYSKI ARCHITECTS

Chicago's third-tallest building was originally the world's tallest marble-clad structure but is now most famous—or notorious—as a colossal failure of building technology. To sheathe the eighty-two-story skyscraper, the architect and the client depleted the Carrara marble quarry that had served Michelangelo. Perhaps in cosmic retribution for their hubris, the slabs began to buckle at

300 E. Randolph St. and 340 on the Park

the southeast corner. Cut as thin as permitted by then-new methods, the material was unable to withstand extremes of temperature. Total recladding was the only solution; from 1990 to 1992, the marble was replaced by thicker slabs of speckled North Carolina granite.

With a new skin that is matte rather than glossy, the building's banality is even more pronounced. Structurally, it is a long hollow tube. The V-shaped perimeter columns house pipes and utility lines and allow column-free interiors.

21 One Prudential Plaza
(Prudential Building)
130 E. Randolph St.

1955, NAESS & MURPHY

Although it lacks the soaring verticality of the towers of the 1920s, this limestone and aluminum-clad skyscraper looks back to that era rather than emulating the steel-and-glass curtain walls that came into favor after World War II. Construction ended a twenty-year hiatus in major downtown building and created what was then Chicago's tallest building, complete with observation deck. The first project to use the air rights of the Illinois Central Railroad yards, it established a pattern for developers. The enormous sculpted relief of Prudential's trademark Rock of Gibraltar is by Frank Lloyd Wright collaborator Alfonso Iannelli.

22 Two Prudential Plaza
180 N. Stetson Ave.

1990, LOEBL SCHLOSSMAN & HACKL

With its soaring spire and chevroned top, Two Pru seems determined to compensate for its earlier neighbor's modesty. Although the architects cite the Chrysler Building as design inspiration, a closer parallel can be found in the work of Helmut Jahn, especially his One Liberty Place in Philadelphia (1987) and his unbuilt 1982 design for the Bank of the Southwest Tower in Houston. The best feature is the landscaped plaza to the northwest, which leads to an atrium lobby serving both Prudential buildings.

23 150 N. Michigan Ave.

1984, A. EPSTEIN & SONS

Ten more floors would be needed for the height to balance the overwhelming slice cut through the top. The light color and aggressive orientation command attention, but the proportions and detailing are a disappointment. Yaacov Agam's colorful sculpture, *Communication X9*, promises less and delivers more.

24 Chicago Cultural Center

(Chicago Public Library)
78 E. Washington St.
1897, SHEPLEY, RUTAN & COOLIDGE
1977 AND 1993, RENOVATIONS, HOLABIRD & ROOT

This latter-day Renaissance palace belongs to an illustrious family of civic and social institutions that grace Michigan Ave. and Grant Park. The spur for the founding of a free public library for the city came, ironically, from the 1871 fire. Responding to the devastation, British sympathizers sent more than 8,000 books, many of them autographed by such noted donors as Disraeli, Carlyle, Tennyson, and even Queen Victoria. To circulate the "English book donation," the Chicago Public Library was established in 1872 and temporarily housed in an old water tank while the board sought a permanent site in Dearborn Park, a remnant of the Fort Dearborn military outpost. Contending for the same parcel was a Civil War veterans' organization. A compromise reached in 1891 permitted the erection of a public library that contained a memorial hall dedicated to the Grand Army of the Republic.

The commission was awarded to the Boston-based successors to the practice of Henry Hobson Richardson, the firm of Shepley, Rutan & Coolidge, which was then completing the Art Institute. Responsibility for designing and testing the foundation went to engineer William Sooy Smith, and to this day, no appreciable settlement of the building has occurred. The library board stipulated that the new building should "convey to the beholder the idea that it is an enduring monument worthy of a great and public-spirited city." To fulfill this dictum, the final design was an amalgam of Italian Renaissance, Greek, and neo-Grec elements executed in Bedford limestone and granite.

The interior decoration is majestic, realized in rare marble, fine hardwood, stained glass, and polished bronze. Most sumptuous of all is the jewellike luster of the Cosmati work: mosaics of Favrile glass, colored stone, mother-

Chicago Cultural Center—exterior

Chicago Cultural Center—interior

of-pearl, and gold leaf inlaid in white marble. The mosaics and marble were practical as well, durable against the onslaught of Chicago's sooty air. Among the more interesting motifs are Renaissance printers' marks and quotations in ten languages. Robert C. Spencer Jr., later famed as a Prairie School architect, designed the mosaics, which were executed by Tiffany-trained J. A. Holzer.

In 1977, the building was renovated and modernized into a cultural center. It remains emblematic of Chicago in the 1890s, when, eager to no longer be identified solely for meatpacking and merchandising, the city sought to secure its status as a sophisticated and culturally conscious metropolis.

—MEREDITH TAUSSIG

Grant Park and Burnham Park

Grant Park bounded by Michigan Ave., Lake Michigan, Randolph St., and Roosevelt Rd.; Burnham Park extends south along Lake Michigan to 57th St.

1909, D. H. BURNHAM

1915–30, BENNETT, PARSONS, FROST & THOMAS AND PREDECESSORS

Though the land along the lakefront east of Michigan Ave. was among the first to be designated as public land, what is now Grant Park has been a work in progress for more than a century and a half. Chicago's formal front garden was created from sandbars, landfill, and Chicago Fire debris and was shaped by the guiding visions of the 1893 World's Columbian Exposition and the 1909 *Plan of Chicago*. The park's origins as a public space date from 1835, when federal land was given to the Illinois & Michigan Canal commissioners to be platted and sold to help fund the canal's construction. In response to residents' concerns, space was set aside for a town common on the lakeshore. The commissioners wrote on their 1836 map, on the space defined by Michigan Ave. and the lake, Randolph St., and what is now 11th St. as "Public Ground—A Common to Remain Forever Open, Clear and Free of any Buildings, or Other Obstruction whatever." The public ground was named Lake Park in 1847, but wave action caused continual erosion of the undeveloped site. In 1852, the Illinois Central Railroad offered to build a stone breakwater in the lake in exchange for an easement permitting the construction of an offshore trestle as far north as the mouth of the Chicago River. Sand, which accumulated in the lagoon created by the breakwater, was augmented by the unofficial dumping of garbage and rubble from the 1871 fire.

In 1861, the state legislature had passed a law confirming the establishment of Lake Park and requiring the consent of all adjacent property

MILLENNIUM PARK
29 Crown Fountain
30 Lurie Garden
31 Nichols Bridgeway
32 Exelon Pavilions
33 McDonald's Cycle Center

LAKE
MICHIGAN

GRANT
PARK

BURNHAM PARK

owners for any encroachments on the public ground. Nearly thirty years later, however, the park contained little more than squatters' shacks, two federal armories, and refuse awaiting removal by train. In 1890, A. Montgomery Ward, creator of the mail-order business headquartered on Michigan Ave., near Madison St., brought a lawsuit to force the city to clean up and improve the site. At this time, planning for the World's Columbian Exposition was under way; so, too, were plans for a new building for the Art Institute, which had outgrown its home on the west side of Michigan Ave. at Van Buren St. A park site was proposed for the museum and approved by adjacent property owners. After the fair, Daniel Burnham began to develop his visions for the park, which included civic and cultural institutions and had the Field Museum at its center. These plans were included in the 1909 *Plan of Chicago*. The Olmsted brothers were also involved in developing Burnham's vision, but their plans ultimately were not followed. At this point, Ward initiated a series of lawsuits to prevent further construction in the park, which had been taken over by the South Park Commission and renamed Grant Park in 1901. In 1910, the Illinois Supreme Court ruled in Ward's favor. Frequently vilified as an impediment to progress by newspaper editorials and fellow businessmen, he never wavered in his fight to protect the park "for the poor people of Chicago, not for the millionaires."

Burnham's vision of a formal Beaux-Arts plan ultimately provided the guideline for future development of the park, though without the buildings. In an agreement with the Illinois Central Railroad in 1911, the South Park Commission gained rights to an area south of the existing park. Landfill extended the park south for the new Field Museum site. In addition, this extension provided the connection to Burnham's vision of a linear park, also built on landfill, that would extend south to Jackson Park. Additional legal issues prevented work on the future Burnham Park from beginning until the early 1920s. In further cooperation with the commission and the city, the Illinois Central also agreed to electrify its trains and depress its tracks below street level to minimize its presence.

In 1915, the South Park Commission retained Edward H. Bennett, who had helped Burnham create the 1909 *Plan*, to take charge of Grant Park. In 1924, the commission adopted a comprehensive plan for the park, and the following year, philanthropist Kate Buckingham provided funds for a centerpiece that became known as Buckingham Fountain. Work on the park progressed through the 1920s, and significant improvements, including further landfill in Burnham Park, also took place in anticipation of the 1933–34 World's Fair. In 1934, Grant Park came under the auspices of the newly consolidated Chicago Park District. Over the next few years, the Park District added major plantings, including the flowering crab apples and lilacs. With Works Progress Administration funding, projects such as the Outer Dr. bridge over the river were designed in the Art Deco style.

As envisioned and developed, the park is a series of symmetrical spaces, or "rooms," defined by paths and plantings, with small enclosed spaces for passive recreation and large open areas for active pursuits. Allées of trees define promenades, and sculptures and fountains create focal points for vistas. The heart of the park is Buckingham Fountain, situated on the main east–west axis at Congress Dr.

Since the 1950s, changes to the park have, for the most part, reinforced the original plan. One glaring exception took place in 1955, when Congress Pkwy. was widened and extended through the park, destroying Congress Plaza and its grand stairway. Green space was incrementally increased with the construction of underground garages between the 1950s and 1970s and the 1986 realignment of Lake Shore Dr. at the northeast corner of the park.

Beginning in the 1990s, major improvements greatly increased park space and moved toward Burnham's vision of a continuous green lakefront. In the early part of the decade, after some thirty years of planning, the city announced its intention to relocate the northbound lanes of Lake Shore Dr.

to the west of the Field Museum, opening up a landscaped Museum Campus. Work associated with the Soldier Field addition added green space by eliminating additional surface parking. These projects strengthened the connection of Burnham Park and the Museum Campus to the southern end of Grant Park. At the park's opposite end, one of the last unimproved areas, an open pit of railroad tracks and surface parking, was covered and the park extended to Randolph St. through the creation of Millennium Park. Prompted by the new park's enormous success as well as the need to repair the parking garage under the Daley Bicentennial Plaza (1976) in the park's northeast corner, the Chicago Park District began construction in late 2012 on Maggie Daley Park. Michael van Valkenburgh's landscape plan features new types of spaces and activities connected to Millennium Park by Frank Gehry's pedestrian bridge. Maggie Daley Park reflects the city's continuous reassessment of the park's uses and is forward-looking in its emphasis on a sustainable landscape.

—JOAN POMARANC AND KATHLEEN NAGLE

Millennium Park

Between Michigan Ave. and Columbus Dr., from Randolph St. to Monroe St.

1999–2004, EDWARD K. UHLIR, FAIA, PROJECT DIRECTOR, MASTER PLANNER;
SKIDMORE, OWINGS & MERRILL, MASTER PLANNERS; TERRY GUEN
DESIGN ASSOCS. AND CAROL J. H. YETKEN, LANDSCAPE ARCHS.

The last major extension of Grant Park, Millennium Park extends the history of Grant Park development into the twenty-first century. One of the largest public projects in the city in years, the 24.5-acre park reclaims an area that was occupied by train tracks, rights-of-way, and surface parking on land leased by the city to the Illinois Central Railroad. Creation of the new park also involved removing and replacing the N. Grant Park garage and the park above it. Originally intended to be completed in time for the new millennium, this complex undertaking, requiring construction over active commuter rail lines and a new parking garage, was pushed a few years into the new century.

The park's design also attempts to straddle the centuries. Along Michigan Ave., architectural elements are consistent with the nineteenth-century Beaux-Arts vision of Grant Park. The Peristyle, McCormick Tribune Ice Rink (2001, OWP&P), railings, balustrades, and plantings are all a continuation—and in some cases a replication—of existing park features. To the east, however, the theater, outdoor pavilion, Lurie Garden, and sculptures employ forms more consistent with the new millennium yet within the framework of Beaux-Arts planning.

Millennium Park

25 Millennium Monument in Wrigley Square

(Peristyle)

Michigan Ave. and Randolph St.

2002, OWP&P (ORIGINAL PERISTYLE 1917–53, EDWARD H. BENNETT)

The semicircle of paired Doric columns is a nearly full-scale version of the original. The first Peristyle occupied the site until it was demolished to make way for the N. Grant Park parking garage. Details of the pool and base have been altered for accessibility and donor inscriptions, and the new version is in limestone rather than the original concrete. The form of the fountain's bronze spout was molded from a terra-cotta finial on the Wrigley Building.

26 Joan W. and Irving B. Harris Theater for Music and Dance

205 E. Randolph St.

2003, HAMMOND BEEBY RUPERT AINGE

In keeping with the century-old desire for Grant Park to be "forever open, clear and free," this theater is buried under landscaped terraces except for a simple two-story precast-concrete-and-glass entrance lobby on upper Randolph. The 1,500-seat theater houses twelve midsize local music and dance companies.

27 Jay Pritzker Pavilion, Trellis, and BP Bridge

Columbus Dr. and Randolph St., immediately south of the Music and Dance Theater

2004, FRANK O. GEHRY & ASSOCS.; SKIDMORE, OWINGS & MERRILL, ASSOC. ARCHS. AND ENGS.

Stainless-steel ribbons soar and twist 120 feet above the ground, framing the outdoor pavilion like a headdress. Gehry has created an urban-scale sculpture that almost lifts off from the theater buried in the earth. The pavilion backs up to the Music and Dance Theater, whose backstage facilities it shares, and faces an oval lawn south of the fixed seating area. On the Randolph St. side, the supporting structure for the proscenium was intentionally left exposed. The painted steel-pipe "trellis" over the Great Lawn distributes the sound system over a 300 × 600 foot column-free space. The sound system, designed to replicate the acoustics of an interior concert hall, is the first permanent installation of this type in the United States.

Gehry's 925-foot-long sinuous stainless-steel-clad pedestrian bridge over Columbus Dr. connects Millennium Park to Maggie Daley Park and the lakefront while providing an acoustic barrier between the traffic on Columbus and the Pritzker Pavilion.

28 *Cloud Gate*

Madison St. and Michigan Ave.

2004, ANISH KAPOOR

The structure below had to be specially engineered to carry the 110-ton load of this 33-foot-tall, 66-foot-long sculpture, locally known as the *Bean*. Its 168 stainless steel plates were assembled on site, continuously welded and polished to create the seamless effect. The lustrous elliptical form reflects Chicago's skyline and the artwork's many visitors. This sculpture is the Indian-born Kapoor's first outdoor public work in the United States.

Jay Pritzker Pavilion and Cloud Gate

29 Crown Fountain
Monroe St. and Michigan Ave.

2004, JAUME PLENSA, ARTIST;
KRUECK & SEXTON ARCHITECTS

The Crown Fountain, two fifty-foot towers at opposite ends of a shallow reflecting pool, has become one of the most popular summer attractions in Millennium Park. Like two enormous gargoyles, the towers spout intermittent streams of water, seemingly from the mouths of gigantic faces (the images of 1,000 Chicagoans) projected on the glass-block LED screens. Based in Barcelona, Plensa is one of the first artists to combine water, glass, and electronics at this scale. Images are projected throughout the year, though the water flows only seasonally.

30 Lurie Garden
Monroe St. at Columbus Dr.

2004, GUSTAFSON GUTHRIE
NICHOL AND PIET OUDOLF

Symbolic references to Chicago's past and present abound in this lush and sustainably designed garden, a collaboration between landscape architect Gustafson and perennial plantsman Oudolf. The giant Shoulder hedge references Carl Sandburg's "City of Big Shoulders" and from some angles seems to support Gehry's "headdress" proscenium. A metal armature structures the hedge and provides a guide for pruning. The Seam boardwalk follows the angle of the historic retaining walls that once defined the edge of the lake and divides the plantings of the Dark Plate (the marshy past) from the Light Plate of controlled nature in the form of perennials.

31 Nichols Bridgeway
Monroe St. between Michigan Ave. and Columbus Dr.

2009, RENZO PIANO
BUILDING WORKSHOP

From the Great Lawn, the slender 625-foot-long pedestrian bridge rises over the Lurie Garden and Monroe St. to connect Millennium Park to the third floor of the Art Institute's Modern Wing. The gentle ascent affords spectacular views of the park, skyline, and lakefront. The underside of the bridge, made of curved steel sections painted white, was inspired by the hulls of racing yachts.

32 Exelon Pavilions
North Pavilions, Randolph St. adjacent to the Harris Theater

2004, HAMMOND BEEBY RUPERT AINGE

South Pavilions, Monroe St. at the Lurie Garden

2004, RENZO PIANO
BUILDING WORKSHOP

The pavilions provide access to the parking garages below (except for the northwest pavilion, which houses a welcome center) and generate electricity through state-of-the-art photovoltaics. The North Pavilions are minimalist black cubes that complement the Beeby-designed Harris Theater. Piano's smaller South Pavilions in limestone and clear glass are sympathetic to his museum addition across Monroe St.

33 McDonald's Cycle Center
239 E. Randolph St.

2004, MULLER & MULLER

The small glass box on Randolph opens to a sunlit two-story atrium in this primarily below-grade full-service bicycle facility. Designed for commuters as well as hourly renters, the center is part of the city's larger plan to become cycling-friendly. The energy-efficient design includes solar roof panels, natural ventilation, and shading devices.

34 Illinois State Medical Society
(Ward Building)
20 N. Michigan Ave.

1885, BEERS, CLAY & DUTTON
1892, ADDITION, 1985 RENOVATION,
NAGLE, HARTRAY & ASSOCS.

A former red-brick, timber-frame warehouse for Montgomery Ward's catalog operations has been converted into a modern office building sympathetic to its past.

35 6 N. Michigan Ave.
(Montgomery Ward & Co. "Tower Building")

1899, RICHARD E. SCHMIDT
1923, FOUR-STORY ADDITION,
HOLABIRD & ROCHE
1955, REMODELING, LOEBL,
SCHLOSSMAN & BENNETT
2004, CONVERSION TO RESIDENCES,
DESTEFANO & PARTNERS

The design is attributed to Hugh M. G. Garden, a Schmidt employee who later became his partner. The firm's first major commission was much grander at the time of its construction, when it sported a ten-story tower topped by a three-story pyramidal roof, tempietto, and an eighteen-foot gilded statue of Diana. Although the addition of four floors and the demolition of the tower (1947) have drastically altered the massing, there are interesting details such as plants, birds, and fish on the terra-cotta spandrels.

36 Willoughby Tower
8 S. Michigan Ave.
1929, SAMUEL N. CROWEN & ASSOCS.
The graceful profile is complemented by the lobby with its spectacular green marble walls, rich bronze ornament, and strapwork ceilings.

37 12 S. Michigan Ave.
*(Chicago Athletic
Association Building)*
1893, HENRY IVES COBB
38 Annex Building
71 E. Madison St.
1907, RICHARD E. SCHMIDT,
   GARDEN & MARTIN
1926, SEVEN-STORY ADDITION, RICHARD
   E. SCHMIDT, GARDEN & MARTIN
Built to impress the crowds that flocked to the World's Columbian Exposition of 1893, the building is a lavish display of Venetian Gothic inside and out. The far simpler annex suggests Chicago's own Prairie School. The Athletic Association sold the property in 2007, and work began on converting it to a hotel in 2012.

Gage Group
39 Edson Keith and Theodore Ascher Buildings
24 and 30 S. Michigan Ave.
1899, HOLABIRD & ROCHE
1971, ASCHER BUILDING ADDITION,
   ALTMAN-SAICHEK ASSOCS.
2007, STOREFRONT RENOVATION OF
   24 S. MICHIGAN, KLEIN & HOFFMAN
40 Gage Building
18 S. Michigan Ave.
1899, HOLABIRD & ROCHE;
   FACADE, LOUIS H. SULLIVAN
1902, ADDITION, HOLABIRD & ROCHE
1986, RENOVATION, BOVINE GROUP,
   FOR AUBREY GREENBERG ASSOCS.

Gage Building

2010, STOREFRONT RENOVATION,
   ALTUSWORKS
These steel-frame loft buildings were built on Michigan Ave. because of the unobstructed daylight needed for the millinery businesses that they housed. Clad in the red brick common to Chicago lofts, the two southern facades clearly express their framing systems. The Gage brothers requested that Sullivan design the third facade because they felt it would benefit their business. It is finished in buff terra-cotta and displays his philosophy that a skyscraper's design should express its height. He did so by presenting the facade as a hung curtain. Because the base, originally framed in foliate cast iron, hid the first-floor columns, the piers would have appeared to exert insupportable weight on the first-floor spandrel without the pair of "clasps" on the cornice.

41 University Club of Chicago
76 E. Monroe St.
1909, HOLABIRD & ROCHE
42 Monroe Building
104 S. Michigan Ave.
1912, HOLABIRD & ROCHE
2012, RESTORATION, HOLABIRD & ROOT
The University Club's details recall the University of Chicago's Gothic inspirations. Inside are two multistory rooms, one of which features medieval hunt murals by Frederic Clay Bartlett. The height of the gabled Monroe Building

Monroe Building

The six-story limestone-and-glass addition was intended to complement the original but doesn't. Leon Harmant's frieze depicts Zeus presiding over athletic contests.

was chosen to complement its neighbor. Step inside to see the vaulted lobby with its glazed Rookwood tile. The entire building has been meticulously restored.

43 School of the Art Institute of Chicago
(Illinois Athletic Club)
112 S. Michigan Ave.
1908, BARNETT, HAYNES & BARNETT
1985, ADDITION, SWANN & WEISKOPF

44 Lake View Building
(Municipal Court Building)
116 S. Michigan Ave.
1906, 1912, JENNEY, MUNDIE & JENSEN
This white terra-cotta pencil of a building was commissioned by Jacob L. Kesner to lease as courtrooms while City Hall was being demolished and rebuilt. When the city moved out, Kesner added four stories and a vaulted ceiling in the lobby to attract other tenants.

45 122 S. Michigan Ave.
(People's Gas Co.)
1910, D. H. BURNHAM & CO.
1987, RESTORATION, ECKENHOFF
    SAUNDERS ARCHITECTS
To keep the weight of the upper stories off the ornamental granite columns, steel cantilevers at the third floor transfer the load to an interior steel frame.

46 Art Institute of Chicago
Michigan Ave. at Adams St.
1893–1916, SHEPLEY, RUTAN & COOLIDGE
Additions include:
1901, RYERSON AND BURNHAM LIBRARIES, SHEPLEY, RUTAN & COOLIDGE
1924, MCKINLOCK COURT, COOLIDGE & HODGDON
1958, FERGUSON BUILDING, HOLABIRD & ROOT & BURGEE
1962, MORTON WING, SHAW, METZ & ASSOCS.
1977, COLUMBUS DR. ADDITION AND SCHOOL OF THE ART
    INSTITUTE, SKIDMORE, OWINGS & MERRILL

Art Institute of Chicago—Stock Exchange room

1988, DANIEL F. & ADA L. RICE BUILDING, HAMMOND, BEEBY & BABKA

2001, FULLERTON HALL RESTORATION, WEESE LANGLEY
    WEESE; GILMORE, FRANZEN ARCHITECTS

2009, MODERN WING, RENZO PIANO BUILDING WORKSHOP, DESIGN
    ARCH.; INTERACTIVE DESIGN ARCHITECTS, ARCH. OF RECORD

Completion of the Modern Wing and its bridge to Millennium Park gave the Art Institute a side entrance that competes with its front door on Michigan, still guarded by the iconic bronze lions sculpted by Edward Kemeys in 1894. The original lobby (restored 1987, OFFICE OF JOHN VINCI) leads to the 1910 staircase and a collection of architectural fragments. Another highlight is the Trading Room, which was salvaged from Adler & Sullivan's demolished Chicago Stock Exchange Building, then restored and installed in the Columbus Dr. addition in 1977 by the Office of John Vinci. The room's virtuoso stenciling is one of the most lyrical examples of Sullivan's decorative talent. The Japanese Art Galleries (2010, WHY ARCHITECTURE AND PLANNING) include Tadao Ando's 1988 gallery for Japanese screens. The Modern Wing offers the de rigueur soaring lobby, prominent gift shop, and rooftop restaurant that reflect museums' twenty-first-century emphasis on consumption and socialization, executed in Piano's low-key manner. His signature gesture is the "flying carpet" sunshading system that seems to hover over the building and allows northern light into the top-floor galleries.

---

47 *Fountain of the Great Lakes*
Art Institute South Garden, S. Michigan Ave. south of main entrance

1913, LORADO TAFT; BASIN,
    SHEPLEY, RUTAN & COOLIDGE

This sculpture symbolically represents the five Great Lakes as they flow into each other. The modern garden by the Office of Dan Kiley (1962) provides a serene setting for the composition.

48 Chicago Stock Exchange Arch
Monroe St. and Columbus Dr.

1893, ADLER & SULLIVAN

This building fragment from the Chicago Stock Exchange Building (1893–1972) is the Wailing Wall of Chicago's preservation movement.

49 Symphony Center
(Orchestra Hall)
220 S. Michigan Ave.

1905, D. H. BURNHAM & CO.

1908, TOP-FLOOR ADDITION,
    HOWARD VAN DOREN SHAW

1967, REMODELING, HARRY
    WEESE & ASSOCS.

1981, REHABILITATION, SKIDMORE,
    OWINGS & MERRILL

1997, RENOVATION AND NEW
    CONSTRUCTION, SKIDMORE,
    OWINGS & MERRILL

A member of the orchestra's board, Burnham encouraged its efforts to acquire a hall of its own and as owner of this land was the logical choice for architect. The 1997 expansion created a narrow addition on Michigan Ave., the Arcade, which leads to a skylit rotunda that links all of the buildings: Orchestra Hall, the Education and Administration Wing on Adams, a single-story restaurant, and the new Artistic Support Wing, whose blank concrete facade is visible on Wabash Ave.

50 Symphony Center Education and Administration Wing
(Chapin & Gore Building)
67 E. Adams St.

1904, RICHARD E. SCHMIDT AND
    HUGH M. G. GARDEN

The facade's unusual composition reflects the special retail, storage, and office needs of the client's liquor business. Between the retail base and the office stories are two storage floors, which needed a sturdier structure and less window space. The second- and third-floor windows are joined by ornamental spandrels that show Garden's adaptation of Louis H. Sullivan's geometric forms. The windows' width matches that of the central panes in the Chicago windows of the office floors, while a decorative terra-cotta frame expands the composition to the larger overall width. The incongruously stark upper floors originally had foliate capitals crowning the piers and a projecting cornice.

224 S. Michigan Ave.

51 224 S. Michigan Ave.
*(Santa Fe Center; originally
Railway Exchange Building)*
1904, D. H. BURNHAM & CO.
1985, RENOVATION, METZ,
   TRAIN & YOUNGREN AND
   FRYE GILLAN MOLINARO

A building around a light well, a form
common to Daniel H. Burnham's
work from the mid-1880s onward,
received an undulating white-glazed
terra-cotta skin, oriel bays, and a
top floor of distinctive porthole windows. As in the Rookery, a two-story
covered court at the base of the
light well is dominated by a grand
staircase. As part of the renovation, a new skylight was placed at
the top, and the light well's inner
walls were opened up. The building
housed Daniel H. Burnham's offices,
where the 1909 *Plan of Chicago* was
worked out and a decade of buildings were planned.

52 Metropolitan Tower
*(Britannica Center; originally
Straus Building)*
310 S. Michigan Ave.
1924, GRAHAM, ANDERSON,
   PROBST & WHITE
2006, CONVERSION TO RESIDENTIAL,
   PAPPAGEORGE/HAYMES

This was the first building to take
advantage of Chicago's 1923 zoning ordinance, which permitted the
erection of occupied towers above
260 feet if setback provisions were
satisfied. In most other ways, the
main block is a variant of the firm's
La Salle St. banking buildings,
which featured second-story banking floors behind classical facades.

Behind the tall windows was the
elegant banking floor of the investment firm of S. W. Straus & Co. The
glass beehive atop the pyramidal
roof symbolized industry and thrift
and originally housed a directional
beacon signifying the company's
global reach.

53 McCormick Building
332 S. Michigan Ave.
1910, 1912 (NORTHERN EXPANSION),
   HOLABIRD & ROCHE
2000, CONVERSION OF UPPER
   FLOORS TO RESIDENTIAL,
   FITZGERALD ASSOCS. ARCHITECTS

Although dismissed by *Architectural
Record* as "not calculated to attract
remark," the McCormick Building
is one of Holabird & Roche's more
prominent and solidly designed
office buildings. Its windows are
punched out uniformly across a
neutral facade, negating the steel
frame. The Michigan Ave. site, where
legislation ensured that no building
would ever block the light, allowed
exceptionally deep offices. When the
top six floors were converted to condominiums, named the Residences
of 330 South Michigan Ave., the office entrance shifted and its address
changed to 332 S. Michigan Ave.

54 Metra Entrance Canopy
Northeast corner of Van Buren
St. and Michigan Ave.
2002

The entrance to this commuter station is a cast-iron replica of an Art
Nouveau Parisian Métro station, cast
from molds of an original designed
by Hector Guimard in the early twentieth century. It is part of a gift exchange between Paris and Chicago
organized by the Union League Club
of Chicago.

55 Abraham Lincoln: The Head
of State (Seated Lincoln)
Court of the Presidents, between
Columbus Dr. and Illinois Central
tracks at Van Buren St.
1908, AUGUSTUS SAINT-GAUDENS;
   EXEDRA MCKIM, MEAD & WHITE

Installed in 1926, Saint-Gaudens's
second Lincoln statue in Chicago
was intended as the centerpiece of a
collection of presidential statues, but
it stands—or sits—alone.

Clarence Buckingham Memorial Fountain

56 Clarence Buckingham Memorial Fountain

East end of Congress Dr.
at Columbus Dr.

1927, MARCEL FRANÇOIS LOYAU
& JACQUES LAMBERT; BENNETT,
PARSONS & FROST, ARCHS.
1995, RESTORATION, HARRY
WEESE & ASSOCS.

The fountain is the focal point of the park, terminating the Congress Pkwy. axis as envisioned in the 1909 *Plan of Chicago*. Built of pink Georgia marble, it was inspired by the Bassin de Latone at Versailles but is twice its size. Four pairs of fanciful bronze sea creatures symbolize the states bordering Lake Michigan, which the fountain is intended to represent. From 2007 to 2012, the Chicago Park District undertook significant work that included accessibility improvements.

57 Buckingham Memorial Fountain Visitor Service Pavilions

East end of Congress Dr.
at Columbus Dr.

1997, DAVID WOODHOUSE ARCHITECTS

Four low horizontal buildings sited at the corners of the plaza reinforce the park's Beaux-Arts symmetry and views. While sited and sized to minimize their presence, the pavilions' details are worth noting. The fountain's exuberant ornament has been cleverly evoked in contemporary materials. Color and structure conjure the tree canopy above, while the glazed end canopies capture the sunlight like the nearby fountain's spray.

58 Chicago Club

81 E. Van Buren St.

1929, GRANGER & BOLLENBACHER

The building was designed in the spirit of an earlier Burnham & Root

Buckingham Fountain Pavilions

structure on this site that housed the Art Institute in the late 1880s but collapsed in 1929 while being remodeled for this private club's use.

59 Fine Arts Building
(Studebaker Building)
410 S. Michigan Ave.
1885, SOLON S. BEMAN
1898, THREE-STORY ADDITION
  AND CONVERSION TO FINE ARTS
  BUILDING, SOLON S. BEMAN
1917, RENOVATION FOR STUDEBAKER
  THEATER, ANDREW N. REBORI

The Romanesque rough stone base and ranks of floors under arches established a prototypical rhythm for this stretch of S. Michigan Ave. The arches and the huge red granite columns that carry them were a means of opening the load-bearing east wall for the Studebaker carriage showrooms, which occupied the first five floors. A shift in function within was recorded in the upper stories; groupings of smaller windows mark where wagons and carriages were assembled.

When the building no longer suited Studebaker's needs, music publisher and real estate developer Charles C. Curtiss had Beman alter it into a proto-arts center with two theaters, offices, shops, and studios for musicians, artists, and writers. Among the modifications were the replacement of the top story with three new ones, including skylit studios. The building was a locus of activity for women's suffrage efforts and later for the Chicago literary movement of the 1920s. Inside are a rabbit warren of woody hallways, a light well with internal balconies (appropriately called Venetian Court), and tenth-floor muraled walls that offer reminders of former tenants.

60 Congress Plaza
Congress Dr. and Michigan Ave.
1929, EDWARD H. BENNETT
1995, RESTORATION, DLK ARCHITECTURE

Completed for the 1933 World's Fair, Congress Plaza is the formal gateway to Grant Park along the central east–west axis envisioned in the 1909 *Plan of Chicago*. The bridges and ornamental concrete elements have been restored, and lost features such as lampposts have been replaced. Two flights of stairs recall the 100-foot-wide grand stair that was lost when Congress Pkwy. was extended in the 1950s.

61 Eagle Fountains
Michigan Ave. at Congress Dr.
1931, FREDERICK C. HIBBARD

These graceful eagles grasping fish in their talons made more sense years ago, when the pools were filled with water.

62 *The Spearman* and *The Bowman*
Michigan Ave. at Congress Dr.
1928, IVAN MESTROVIC

The sculptor proposed a cowboy and an Indian, but two Native Americans were felt to be more suitable for so prominent a site, which originally featured a grand stair and plaza leading to Buckingham Fountain. Their weapons must be supplied by the viewer's imagination.

The Bowman

Auditorium Building—exterior

63 Auditorium Building

430 S. Michigan Ave.

1887–89, ADLER & SULLIVAN

1967, AUDITORIUM THEATRE RESTORATION, HARRY WEESE & ASSOCS.

2001–3, AUDITORIUM THEATRE RESTORATION, DANIEL P. COFFEY & ASSOCS.

2003, GANZ HALL RESTORATION, BOOTH HANSEN ASSOCS.

The Auditorium Building commission was the single-most-important factor in establishing the internationally recognized role of Dankmar Adler and Louis H. Sullivan in the evolution of modern architectural thought. Adler's previous successes as a theater designer secured the coveted job, while the publicity generated by the project promulgated Sullivan's innovative architectural ideals.

Created to provide a permanent home for Chicago's operatic, symphonic, and other cultural events, the building was planned with large multiuse commercial components, a 400-room hotel, and rental offices to offset possible losses from the operation of the 4,300-seat theater. The Auditorium's creation was a civic achievement of enormous stature, made even more impressive by the modernist style of its design.

The composition of the street facades, suggesting the Romanesque character of H. H. Richardson's demolished Marshall Field Wholesale Store (1887), is a highly original expression of the building's bearing-wall construction: a rugged base of supporting rusticated granite contrasts with the smooth,

Auditorium Building—interior

machined Bedford limestone skin above. Except for the entrance, the theater was almost completely enclosed from the street by the hotel, which was located along the Michigan Ave. and Congress Pkwy. frontages, and by the office section along Wabash Ave. Rising above the ten-story block on Congress Pkwy. is an eight-story tower that originally housed additional offices, tanks for the hydraulic elevators and stage equipment, and a rooftop observatory, initially the highest point in the city. Adler & Sullivan's offices were behind the stone colonnade at what is now the sixteenth floor.

In contrast to the heavy treatment of the masonry exterior, the interiors are reflections of the light, modular, post-and-beam metal frame and of the fireproof tile partitions, articulated by the creative manipulation of interior finishes in plaster, wood, cast iron, art glass, mosaic, and other materials. The primary space is the theater itself, enclosed within a fireproof brick shell. Its excellent acoustics and sight lines testify to Adler's theater expertise and received creative form through Sullivan's integral collaboration.

Other significant interior spaces can be seen by touring the facilities of Roosevelt University, which has owned the building since 1946. With the expansion of Congress Pkwy., an exterior arcade was created, destroying several first-floor spaces. The former hotel lobby is entered on Michigan Ave., and its central grand staircase leads to the second-floor parlor. The finely restored Ladies' Parlor, now the Sullivan Room and usually closed, is partially visible through a door at the south end of the loggia. The barrel-vaulted tenth-floor hotel dining room is now the university's library. The restored southern alcove reflects its original appearance, while the main room's restoration awaits funding. One of Adler & Sullivan's finest interior spaces is the hotel's banquet hall/ballroom, built of lightweight plaster and birch paneling. Now the Rudolph Ganz Memorial Recital Hall (Room 745), it was an afterthought, planned when the building was largely complete. The remarkable room spans forty feet over the theater's roof on twin bridge trusses bearing on the theater's perimeter masonry walls.

—JOHN VINCI

64 *The Spirit of Music* Sculpture and Park
S. Michigan Ave. between
Harrison St. and Balbo Dr.
1923, ALBIN POLASEK, SCULPTOR;
HOWARD VAN DOREN SHAW, ARCH.

Dedicated to the first conductor of the Chicago Symphony Orchestra, the *Spirit* has at long last been reunited with the granite relief carvings of the orchestra members. In storage since the sculpture's first relocation in 1940, the carvings were eventually found dumped along the lakefront. The entire work was restored in its present location in 1991.

65 *Agora*
Roosevelt Rd. and Michigan Ave.
2006, MAGDALENA ABAKANOWICZ

Cast in Poland and transported to Chicago, the 106 iron figures, each about nine feet tall, seem frozen in various positions suggesting movement. While they appear similar from a distance, their surface textures—described by the artist as similar to tree bark or wrinkled faces—express the individuality of the giant headless torsos.

Museum Campus
1994–98, LAWRENCE HALPRIN
AND TENG & ASSOCS.

The long-awaited relocation of the northbound lanes of Lake Shore Dr. to the west of Soldier Field and the Field Museum has created a true unified museum campus. Acres of concrete are now green space connecting the three museums, Soldier Field, and the rest of Burnham Park to the south. In addition, a vast area that had provided surface parking north of the stadium is now terraced gardens. Open pedestrian ways connect the campus to the south end of Grant Park and the rapidly developing Near South Side.

66 Field Museum of Natural History
Roosevelt Rd. and S. Lake Shore Dr.
1909–12, D. H. BURNHAM & CO.;
1912–17, GRAHAM, BURNHAM
& CO.; 1917–20, GRAHAM,
ANDERSON, PROBST & WHITE

1977, RENOVATION, HARRY
WEESE & ASSOCS.

2004, EAST ENTRANCE AND
UNDERGROUND EXPANSION,
SKIDMORE, OWINGS & MERRILL

Exhibits from the 1893 World's Columbian Exposition were the nucleus of the collections, housed for the first twenty-seven years in what was later reconstructed as the Museum of Science and Industry. The design was inspired by the Greek temple; the caryatids are especially reminiscent of the Erechtheion. The great central hall, ringed by Ionic columns, is one of Chicago's grandest neoclassical spaces, monumental yet serene.

67 Soldier Field

425 E. McFetridge Dr.

1922–26, COLONNADE,
HOLABIRD & ROCHE

2003, STADIUM, WOOD & ZAPATA;
LOHAN CAPRILE GOETTSCH
ARCHITECTS, ASSOC. ARCHS.

This enormous colonnaded stadium has been used for sports events, religious gatherings, and concerts. It was named to honor soldiers of the First World War; at the same time, Municipal Pier was renamed Navy Pier to honor sailors. But that meaning was diluted when the enormous new stadium was built in the middle of Soldier Field. The new stadium isn't so much bad as it is wrong at this location. Beautiful materials, dramatic form, a complex geometry, and all of the new amenities the players need and the fans want—this stadium has all that. In the middle of a former megamall parking lot, it would look stunning. But it is on the lakefront, blocking a substantial amount of the lake view and causing tremendous congestion on event days.

68 Northerly Island

East of Burnham Park, extending
south from Solidarity Dr.

Northerly Island (1928–30) was the only actualization of the chain of artificial islands proposed in the 1909 *Plan of Chicago*. It was intended to be a park, but its first role, and that of the parallel section of Burnham Park, was as the site for the 1933–34 World's Fair, *A Century of Progress*. After the fair, one of the temporary connections between the mainland and the island (Solidarity Dr.) was made permanent.

When Mayor Richard M. Daley ordered the middle-of-the night demolition of the Meigs Field airport in 2003, his stated goal was creating a nature sanctuary on the ninety-one-acre peninsula. To help fund the plan, a concert pavilion was constructed on the northern end in 2005 and expanded with lawn seating in 2013. The framework plan by Studio Gang and JJR landscape architects calls for gradual transition from active to passive recreational use from north to south, with six different interdependent ecosystems, including a lagoon created by a reef to the east.

69 Adler Planetarium and Astronomy Museum

1300 S. Lake Shore Dr.

1930, ERNEST A. GRUNSFELD JR.

1998, SKY PAVILION, 1999,
RENOVATION, LOHAN ASSOCS.

In a departure from the neoclassical details of the nearby museums, Grunsfeld designed a twelve-sided domed structure with simple lines and Art Deco details to house the nation's first public planetarium. Each corner of the variegated granite mass is adorned with a zodiacal sign. The central domed room is still used for viewing projected images of the sky. A panel in the lobby has emblems for each of the eight planets. The C-shaped sky pavilion addition partially wraps the historic structure with a dynamic steel-and-glass structure, a clear counterpoint to the original form. A narrow skylight separates the new from old on the inside and

Adler Planetarium & Astronomy Museum

highlights the original Alfonso Iannelli bronze plaques and richly textured walls. The new sweep of column-free exhibit space affords splendid vistas of the lake and skyline.

70 John G. Shedd Aquarium
1200 S. Lake Shore Dr.

1929, GRAHAM, ANDERSON, PROBST & WHITE

1991, OCEANARIUM ADDITION, LOHAN ASSOCS.

1999, ROTUNDA RESTORATION; 2000, AMAZON RISING EXHIBIT; 2003, WILD REEF ADDITION; PERKINS & WILL AND EHDD

Designed to harmonize with the Field Museum, the original building is covered inside and out with aquatic motifs. Additions have strived to preserve the integrity of the 1929 building while updating exhibits. The lakeside Oceanarium is a low modern extension, with the marble of its side walls obtained from the aquarium's original east wall. From the inside, the sweep of curtain wall creates the illusion of an unbroken line of water from the interior pools to Lake Michigan. The 2003 addition to the south extends the existing terrace level and creates new plaza space over underground exhibit space.

71 Roosevelt University Wabash Building
425 S. Wabash Ave.

2012, VOA ASSOCS.; JOHNSON & LEE, ASSOC. ARCH.

Brancusi's *Endless Column* sculpture inspired the building's in-and-out

Roosevelt University Wabash Building

form. Inside is a vertical campus that connects at multiple levels with the university's Auditorium Building, whose buff-colored masonry sets off the tower's shimmering two-toned blue glass. A residence hall occupies the top eighteen floors, with classrooms, lecture halls, and fitness and dining facilities below. The Wabash side incorporates the facade of Andrew Rebori's 1924 Fine Arts Building Annex.

72 CNA Center
333 S. Wabash Ave.

1972, GRAHAM, ANDERSON, PROBST & WHITE

73 55 E. Jackson Blvd.
(Continental Center)

1962, C. F. MURPHY ASSOCS.

The bays of 55 E. Jackson Blvd., originally connected to 310 S. Michigan Ave., have forty-two-foot spans; they were the largest constructed to that time but were soon surpassed by the Richard J. Daley Center's gargantuan bays. The Wabash Ave. building was an expansion for the same client.

74 DePaul University— O'Malley Building
(Finchley Building)

23 E. Jackson Blvd.

1928, ALFRED S. ALSCHULER

The Gothic style of the stone base changes incongruously to a Tudor half-timbered treatment at the top.

75 DePaul University— Lewis Center
(Kimball Building)

25 E. Jackson Blvd.

1917, GRAHAM, ANDERSON, PROBST & WHITE

Step inside to see the well-preserved L-shaped lobby of buff ceramic tile.

76 218 S. Wabash Building
(McClurg Building; originally Ayer Building)

1899, HOLABIRD & ROCHE

This steel-frame loft building is a small but resonant example of the qualities for which the Chicago School—especially the work of Holabird & Roche—is famous. The grid of the wall clearly expresses the underlying structure, with large Chicago windows set between the thinnest possible piers and spandrels. As with

Mies's I beams of a half century later, the deep fluted piers and mullions give dimensionality and rhythm to the skeletal facade. Unfortunately, the cornice that once capped the composition is missing.

77 55 E. Monroe St. and Park Monroe

(Mid-Continental Plaza)
1972, ALFRED SHAW & ASSOCS.
2007, CONVERSION OF UPPER FLOORS
   TO RESIDENTIAL, GOETTSCH PARTNERS

This International Style behemoth has closely spaced piers clad in stainless steel and ascending uninterrupted to the flat roof. Inset balconies on the upper floors show where the building changes to residential use.

78 Sharp Building

(Champlain Building)
37 S. Wabash Ave.
1903, HOLABIRD & ROCHE

This archetypal Holabird & Roche office building follows the firm's successful formula exploited between 1895 and 1910. Features include continuous piers, recessed spandrels, wide Chicago windows, and a tripartite organization of base, shaft, and cornice. The simple treatment maximizes light and air while expressing the structural steel frame.

79 The Legacy at Millennium Park

60 E. Monroe St.
2010, SOLOMON CORDWELL BUENZ

Chicago's 2002 landmark designation of the Michigan Ave. street wall put frontage from Randolph to 11th Sts. virtually off-limits to new construction. So developers went a few steps west to stake their claims. **The Heritage** (130 N. Garland Ct.), designed by Solomon Cordwell Buenz in 2005, was the first of the breed to rise on Wabash and incorporate that street's 1870s facades. Its success bred the Legacy, whose base is shoehorned behind so many buildings that it has virtually no street presence. Once again, historic Wabash Ave. buildings became a Potemkin village. Only the former Champlain Building (Sharp Building) is still partially occupied; it houses the School of the Art Institute.

80 Barker-Haskell-Atwater Buildings

18–22 S. Wabash Ave. (Barker and Haskell Buildings)
1875, WHEELOCK & THOMAS
1896, REMODELING OF 18 S.
   WABASH, LOUIS H. SULLIVAN
1903, REMODELING OF 22 S.
   WABASH, LOUIS H. SULLIVAN
28 S. Wabash Ave. (Atwater Building)
1877, JOHN M. VAN OSDEL
2009, EXTERIOR RESTORATION OF
   GROUP, HARBOE ARCHITECTS

With the loss of several Sullivan-designed buildings to fire in the early 2000s, architecture lovers were especially pleased to discover one of his previously unknown works. In the 1890s, the Schlesinger & Mayer store had begun acquiring space on Wabash Ave. near the planned Madison St. elevated station. Sullivan was commissioned to open the first two stories of the Barker Building's load-bearing facade by spanning it with ironwork finished in his decorative style and painted white. While working on this trio of buildings, Harboe discovered that Sullivan had later renovated the Haskell storefront as well. (Researchers also determined that the Barker and Haskell names had been inadvertently switched in the 1990s.) The facades and storefronts of all three buildings were reconstructed as part of the comprehensive Sullivan Center renovation.

81 Jewelers Building

19 S. Wabash Ave.
1882, ADLER & SULLIVAN

Disregard the ground-floor alterations and look up, or view this oldest surviving Adler & Sullivan design

Jewelers Building

from the El platform. The color and materials are Ruskinian Gothic; the details exhibit the emergence of Sullivan's distinctive ornament. The chunky, rather stiff plant forms are akin to the work of Philadelphia architect Frank Furness or the designs of Owen Jones as found in such publications as *The Grammar of Ornament* (1854).

82 The Silversmith Hotel and Suites
(Silversmith Building)
10 S. Wabash Ave.
1897, D. H. BURNHAM & CO.
1998, CONVERSION TO HOTEL,
FITZGERALD ASSOCS. ARCHITECTS

On a richly colored facade composed of expressed structural elements, brick mullions placed on the spandrels and the column faces emphasize verticality.

83 Shops Building
21 N. Wabash Ave.
1875, ARCHITECT UNKNOWN
1912, REMODELING, ALFRED
S. ALSCHULER

An old loft building became a retail center with the addition of a metal-frame facade covered with polychrome terra-cotta.

84 Pittsfield Building
55 E. Washington St.
1927, GRAHAM, ANDERSON,
PROBST & WHITE

This tower was briefly Chicago's tallest building. Its emphasis on verticality and use of setbacks recall the era's Art Deco high-rises, but it uses the Gothic vocabulary of earlier skyscrapers. The building accommodated the special electrical and plumbing needs of medical and dental offices and the security requirements of jewelers. Beyond the Washington St. lobby is a well-preserved five-story shopping arcade surrounded by balconies and shop windows.

85 25 E. Washington St.
(Marshall Field & Co. Annex)
1914, GRAHAM, BURNHAM & CO.

Field's established what soon became a popular practice of offering a separate men's store. The six retail levels of this mixed-use building are surmounted by fourteen office floors.

86 Facades of the Burton Estate, Peck, and Couch Estate Buildings
129, 137, and 139 N. Wabash Ave.
1872, 1877 (BURTON ESTATE),
JOHN M. VAN OSDEL

This fragment of commercial streetscape built after the Fire shows the variations possible in Italianate facades.

87 Gallery 37 Center for the Arts
66 E. Randolph St.
1872, WILLIAM W. BOYINGTON
2000, ADAPTIVE REUSE, DANIEL
P. COFFEY & ASSOCS.

The city's Dept. of Cultural Affairs purchased two decrepit buildings—a nondescript 1920s structure and a rare remnant of early post-Fire construction—and commissioned their reuse as an art center with studios, theater, art gallery, and café. A unified storefront and canopy joins the disparate structures at street level.

88 Self Park
60 E. Lake St.
1986, STANLEY TIGERMAN & ASSOCS.

A classic touring car inspired the facade. The turquoise of the baked enamel panels was selected from the 1957 Chevrolet color schedule.

89 Virgin Hotel
(Old Dearborn Bank Building)
203 N. Wabash Ave.
1928, C. W. AND GEORGE L. RAPP
2014, CONVERSION TO HOTEL,
BOOTH HANSEN

Movie palace confectioners Rapp & Rapp also designed relatively sober business buildings. Ornament here is concentrated at the spandrels and at the top.

90 Seventeenth Church of Christ, Scientist
55 E. Wacker Dr.
1968, HARRY WEESE & ASSOCS.

A 200-foot travertine curve marks the auditorium and creates a commanding presence for this low building set among skyscrapers. Structural elements, including the lower columns and roof ribs, are clearly visible. A school is located under the auditorium level; offices are slipped in behind.

91 68 E. Wacker Pl.

(Chicago Motor Club)

1928, HOLABIRD & ROOT

This modestly scaled tower equals the firm's more celebrated Art Deco skyscrapers in refinement and soaring verticality. The theme of travel is beautifully elaborated in a large lobby mural by John W. Norton.

92 Wacker Dr. East–West segment

1926, EDWARD H. BENNETT

2001–4, REBUILDING, CHICAGO DEPT. OF TRANS., JOHNSON LASKY ARCHITECTS

Along the south bank of the main branch of the Chicago River is a double-level street and embankment built of reinforced concrete with Bedford limestone details. Called Wacker Dr., it honors the first president of the Chicago Plan Commission. The initial conception was part of Daniel H. Burnham's 1909 *Plan of Chicago*; the design was elaborated with business's needs in mind. The world's first two-level street replaced the congested, dilapidated South Water St. Market in little more than two years. Demolition and construction had to safeguard existing buildings and tunnels, contain the river, and mesh with streets, bridges, and ramps.

The upper level is a flat slab system, supported by octagonal columns that carry a 110- to 115-foot-wide roadway plus sidewalks and a riverfront promenade. Images of the banks of the Seine are deliberately encouraged by such garniture as balustrades similar to those on the Pont de la Concorde, grand staircases from street to dock level, and obelisk lampposts modeled on a Parisian example. The lower level provides truck access to the area and carries four lanes of through traffic.

Wacker Dr. was extended southward to W. Congress Pkwy. along the former Market St. from 1949 to 1958, but this time without water contact. East of Michigan Ave. it was extended to Lake Michigan as Illinois Center developed.

93 Chicago Riverwalk and Wabash Memorial Plaza

South bank of the Chicago River from State St. to Michigan Ave.

2005–9, ROSS BARNEY ARCHITECTS; JACOBS/RYAN, LANDSCAPE ARCH.

This is the first phase of a master plan that calls for a pleasant walking and cycling path to extend along the south bank of the river from the lake all the way to Lake St. The rebuilding of Wacker Dr. freed up space near Wabash Ave. to incorporate a plaza, which features a memorial to fallen soldiers of the Vietnam War. Under the Michigan and Wabash bridges, stainless steel panels—matte at ground level, polished above—protect pedestrians from falling debris and create lively reflections of people and water. Phase 2 plans by Ross Barney Architects and Sasaki Assocs. were unveiled in 2012. They call for a variety of amenities, including a kayak pier, floating gardens, and many types of seating and gathering places.

94 35 E. Wacker Dr.

(Pure Oil Building; originally Jewelers Building)

1926, GIAVER & DINKELBERG; THIELBAR & FUGARD, ASSOC. ARCHS.

2005, LOBBY RESTORATION, GOETTSCH PARTNERS

The initials *JB* in the terra-cotta commemorate the original name of the building, which was planned to attract tenants in the jewelry trade. When new, the building was noted for its internal garage. Tenants could drive in from lower Wacker Dr. and have their cars taken by elevator to assigned stalls on the lower twenty-two floors. In 1940, the system was abandoned because of mechanical failures and increases in car size, and the garage space was converted to office use. The setbacks at floors 24 and 26 created terraces punctuated by corner tempietti that artfully hid water towers. On top, the belvedere, whose dome hides mechanical equipment, originally provided an expansive view above a restaurant and lounge. Since the

35 E. Wacker Dr.

1980s, it has served as a dramatic presentation room for Murphy/Jahn, which occupies space below.

95 75 E. Wacker Dr.

(Lincoln Tower; originally Mather Tower)

1928, HERBERT HUGH RIDDLE
1983, RENOVATION, HARRY
    WEESE & ASSOCS.

The city's slenderest skyscraper, a twenty-four-story rectangle topped by a telescoping eighteen-story octagon, is like a terra-cotta Gothic rocket poised for takeoff. Its crumbling crown was rebuilt in 2002–3.

96 Trump International Hotel & Tower

401 N. Wabash Ave.

2009, SKIDMORE, OWINGS & MERRILL

The concrete core-and-outrigger structural system hidden behind the reflective curtain wall represents the next generation in high-rise structural design after the trussed-tube of the Hancock and bundled-tubes of the Sears (now Willis) Tower. In the tradition of the Fazlur Khan–Bruce Graham partnership that produced those two buildings, SOM structural engineer Bill Baker worked with architect Adrian Smith; they also collaborated on the record-breaking Burj Khalifa in Dubai. The concrete core is connected to perimeter columns by deep outrigger beams at three of the double-height mechanical floors, just below the setbacks. Perimeter "belt walls" at these floors provide additional stiffness. The building becomes more slender as it rises, reflecting changes in use from parking to hotel to condominium. In a contextual gesture that is almost impossible to discern, the setbacks occur at the heights of the Wrigley, Marina City, and IBM Buildings. Trump is the tallest building constructed in North America since the Sears (Willis) and is the tallest residential tower on the continent. It is also notable for its complex phas-

75 E. Wacker Dr.

Trump International Hotel & Tower

ing; the hotel was occupied while the last thirty-two floors were still under construction. The Trump glitz factor is toned down for the Midwest, although from a distance and in certain lights, the mirror-finish mullions make it shimmer like a disco ball.

97 AMA Plaza
(One IBM Plaza)
330 N. Wabash Ave.
1971, OFFICE OF MIES VAN DER ROHE; C.
F. MURPHY ASSOCS., ASSOC. ARCH.

Mies's last American building and his largest, this structure follows his familiar model. It is sited to avoid obstructing Marina City and to capture the lake views made possible by a bend in the river.

98 One East Wacker
1962, SHAW, METZ & ASSOCS.
1989, RENOVATION, LUCIEN
LAGRANGE & ASSOCS.

The luxe marble finish does little to disguise the absence of the pristine detailing and proportions of stronger modernist designs. The 1989 renovation interrupted the rhythm of the facades—which had never been better than dull—with new, elegantly detailed entries.

99 State St. Streetscape
State St. from Congress Pkwy. to Wacker Dr.
1996, SKIDMORE, OWINGS & MERRILL

The redesign and reconstruction removed all vestiges of the disastrous 1979 "malling" that had widened sidewalks, narrowed the street, and restricted traffic to buses. The historic elements that look as though they have been there for decades in fact date from the 1996 renovation. Streetlights are reproductions of those that lined the sidewalks between 1926 and 1958, and the subway entrances feature festive new designs with abundant clear glass. Planters, tree grates, and signage all recall the era of "that great street."

100 The Wit Hotel
201 N. State St.
2009, KOO AND ASSOCS.

This theater-district hotel has a split personality: conservative straight man on the north, jazzy drama queen on the south. A chartreuse "lightning bolt" zips down the glassy facade and terminates in a marquee-like canopy, bringing kinetic energy to the narrow site. The glazed two-story lobby brings in the El as a surprising costar.

101 ABC-WLS Building
(State-Lake Theater)
190 N. State St.
1917, C. W. AND GEORGE L. RAPP
1984, RENOVATION, SKIDMORE,
OWINGS & MERRILL
2006, RENOVATION AND VIDEO
SCULPTURE, LEGAT ARCHITECTS

This former movie palace and office building now serves the television industry.

102 Chicago Theater Center
(Chicago Theater; Page Bros. Building)
175 N. State St. and 177–191 N. State St.
175 N. State St.
1921, C. W. AND GEORGE L. RAPP
177–191 N. State St.
1872, JOHN M. VAN OSDEL
1902, STATE ST. FACADE, HILL & WOLTERSDORF
1986, RENOVATION, DANIEL P. COFFEY & ASSOCS.

Though the architects went on to design larger movie palaces, the Chicago, along with the Tivoli Theater (1921, demolished) at Cottage Grove Ave. and 63rd St., set the standards for the type. Their success was so great that Rapp & Rapp became architects in residence for their client, Balaban & Katz, and later for the entire Paramount/Publix theater chain.

The theater has been restored to its condition in 1933, when it was refurbished in preparation for the World's Fair. The triumphal-arch facade of off-white terra-cotta opens into a series of lavish, Versailles-inspired spaces. The 3,800-seat auditorium's excellent sight lines derive from the unusually shaped site.

Page Bros. Building

The Page Bros. Building was built immediately after the Great Fire and in the same style and materials as the destroyed buildings. It has one of the Loop's two remaining cast-iron facades, which became unpopular after the fire because they melted in the heat, bringing down masonry walls with them. The Page Bros. Building originally fronted on Lake St.; its brick side wall was given a fancy facade after State St. had become the city's premier mercantile address. In 1986, the building was rehabilitated to provide speculative office space that would support the Chicago Theater, which wraps around it in an L-shaped plan. The linkage could be accomplished only after upgrading the Page Bros. Building's wood-frame structure, which did not conform to building codes. To preserve the delicate Lake St. cast-iron facades, the original structure was used as formwork for the new concrete system and was then replaced in stages.

103 Joffrey Tower

8–10 E. Randolph St./151 N. State St.
2008, BOOTH HANSEN

The podium of this condominium building offers views of dancers rather than parked cars, because the Joffrey Ballet purchased the third and fourth floors for rehearsal studios, offices, and a small theater. Unfortunately, the massing of the two-legged tower does not quite match the grace of the occupants below. From 1892 to 1939, this site featured Burnham & Root's Masonic Temple, whose gabled top inspired that of 191 S. La Salle.

104 162 N. State St. Residences

2000, BOOTH HANSEN ASSOCS.

This dormitory commissioned by the School of the Art Institute of Chicago features a pale facade of undulating bays that emulates the Hotel Burnham one block to the south. Precast, glass-fiber-reinforced concrete mimics terra-cotta. Circular windows at cornice level illuminate a common room. The complex includes the renovated former Butler Building (1924, CHRISTIAN A. ECKSTORM) to the north and steps back to the west on Randolph behind the remnants of the Old Heidelberg restaurant (1934, GRAHAM, ANDERSON, PROBST & WHITE).

When plans were announced for the renovation of the Oriental and Palace Theaters and the building of a new Goodman Theatre (entries 105, 149, and 185), the long-deferred dream of a theater district along Randolph St. finally became a reality. The 1998 streetscape, designed by Skidmore, Owings & Merrill, celebrates the area's vitality with historic streetlights hung with banners, sidewalk elements such as medallions and "doormats" beneath theater marquees, and kiosks. Although concentrated on Randolph St. from Michigan Ave. to Wacker Dr., the streetscape improvements were extended to the surroundings of nearby landmarks such as the County Building/City Hall and Daley Plaza.

105 Ford Center for the Performing Arts
(Oriental Theatre)
24 W. Randolph St.
1925, C. W. AND GEORGE L. RAPP
1998, RESTORATION AND EXPANSION,
   DANIEL P. COFFEY & ASSOCS.

To be commercially viable in the modern theater world, this fanciful cinema palace needed a much deeper stage, but there was no room for expansion—except in the adjacent Oliver Building, which was gutted to accommodate a pair of twenty-ton trusses that transfer the load of a stage-obstructing column. The Oliver's preserved facade (1908, 1920, HOLABIRD & ROCHE), with its cast-iron spandrels decorated with typewriters, is visible on Dearborn St.

106 Macy's on State Street
(Marshall Field & Co.)
111 N. State St.
ON N. WABASH AVE.: SOUTH
   SECTION, 1892, D. H. BURNHAM;
   MIDDLE SECTION, 1906,
D. H. BURNHAM & CO.; NORTH
   SECTION, 1914, GRAHAM, BURNHAM
   & CO.; ON N. STATE ST.: NORTH
   SECTION 1902 AND SOUTH SECTION
   1907, D. H. BURNHAM & CO.
1992, RENOVATION, HTI/SPACE
   DESIGN INTERNATIONAL

The grande dame of State St. has an appropriately massive, stolid design that contrasts with the more skeletal facades of its competitors. The southeastern structure is the earliest, designed with load-bearing walls and heavy arched windows by Charles B. Atwood in complete contrast to his contemporaneous Reliance Building. The high ceilings are supported by forests of decorated columns; the two arcades are topped by a skylight and by shimmering Tiffany mosaics.

107 Hotel Burnham
(Reliance Building)
32 N. State St.
1891, FOUNDATIONS AND BASE,
   BURNHAM & ROOT
1895, ADDITIONAL STORIES,
   D. H. BURNHAM & CO.
1996, EXTERIOR RESTORATION (ABOVE
   STOREFRONT LEVEL), MCCLIER
1999, RECONSTRUCTION OF
   STOREFRONTS AND LOBBY; ADAPTIVE
   REUSE, ANTUNOVICH ASSOCS.;
   MCCLIER, RESTORATION ARCH.

The building's chief virtue is as clear support for the Chicago School's claim to be a precursor of modern architecture: it is very glassy. Designer Charles B. Atwood used glass at every opportunity. He folded the bay windows out from the frame to completely hide the columns, and he balanced huge picture windows with narrow ones of double-hung sashes in the fullest early example of the Chicago window. His achievement is all the more remarkable because his work had to use the foundations and base executed four years earlier according to John Wellborn Root's plans. Root, Daniel H. Burnham's original design partner, died in 1891, and his plans for the elevations are lost.

Hotel Burnham

On the terra-cotta facades, Atwood stressed the overriding continuity of the horizontal spandrels. This was a clear break with the prevailing tradition of letting vertical load-bearing piers carry down to the ground. At the corner, where the structural columns could not be suppressed behind the glass, two bundled sets of colonnettes slide up the covering pier to dematerialize it, a technique used by Gothic stonemasons for exactly the same purpose. This corner treatment makes an interesting comparison with those on tall buildings designed by Mies van der Rohe.

The Reliance Building is almost as weightless as it looks. The vertical loads are borne down to preexisting foundations by lightweight, open trusswork columns. Constructing the frame out of factory-assembled two-story columns with staggered joints reduced the number of field connections and allowed the steel for the top ten stories to be erected in fifteen days. Structural engineer Edward C. Shankland relied for wind bracing on these tall, stiff columns rigidly coupled to extra-deep girders. This method of construction constituted a significant departure from the heavier portal bracing derived from railroad viaducts and used frequently for such tall buildings as Holabird & Roche's Old Colony Building (1894) and Cass Gilbert's Woolworth Building (1913) in New York. The Reliance's construction methods have much in common with more recent construction and wind-bracing techniques, such as those used in the Aon Center (1973).

Predominantly glassy facades could be found before 1895 on, for example, the Crystal Palace in London (1851, JOSEPH PAXTON) and on Oriel Chambers in Liverpool (1864, PETER ELLIS JR.), but the promise of these early aesthetic speculations had to wait a generation for delivery. The perfection of the high-speed elevator made the Reliance Building's height possible; the explosive demand for modern office space in Chicago after the 1871 fire made it essential.

After decades of decay, the building was brought back to life in two phases. In 1994, the City of Chicago purchased it and commissioned a thorough restoration of the terra-cotta exterior, including reconstruction of the original cornice. A private developer then converted the building into a hotel, faithfully reconstructing the storefront level and historic elevator lobby.

—ANDERS NEREIM

108 17 N. State St./16 N. Wabash Ave.
(Charles A. Stevens Store Building)
1912, D. H. BURNHAM & CO.

Recognizing the need to accommodate small retailers on a street that had become filled with grand emporiums, the Stevens brothers topped the seven floors of their own department store with eleven levels of shops for others.

109 2 N. State St./1 N. Dearborn St.
(Boston Store)
1905, 1917, HOLABIRD & ROCHE
2001, RENOVATION, OWP&P (1 N. DEARBORN), DANIEL P. COFFEY & ASSOCS. (SEARS ON STATE)

Sears's return to State St. capped the resurgence of retail here that was spurred by the street's 1996 "de-malling."

110 1 N. State St.
(Wieboldt's Department Store; originally Mandel Bros. Store)
1912, HOLABIRD & ROCHE
8–14 N. Wabash Ave.
(Mandel Bros. Annex)
1900, HOLABIRD & ROCHE
1905, TOP TWO FLOORS ADDITION, HOLABIRD & ROCHE

The restored State St. building has been subdivided to accommodate smaller retailers. The more distinguished Wabash Ave. structure has unusually wide bays, very narrow spandrels, and slim projecting courses, all of which stress horizontality.

Carson Pirie Scott (now Sullivan Center)

111 Sullivan Center

(Carson Pirie Scott & Co.; originally Schlesinger & Mayer Department Store)
1 S. State St.
1899; 1903, LOUIS H. SULLIVAN
State St. Addition (five bays)
1906, D. H. BURNHAM & CO.
State St. Addition (three bays)
1961, HOLABIRD & ROOT
1980, RESTORATION, OFFICE OF JOHN VINCI
2006–11, EXTERIOR RESTORATION, HARBOE ARCHITECTS; REHABILITATION
   AND CONVERSION TO OFFICES, DEPALMA GROUP

One of the first large department stores erected entirely with fireproof steel-frame construction, Carson Pirie Scott served American and European architects as a model for this modern building type. Designers perceived it as a representation of its architect's axiom, "Form follows function," for in it Louis H. Sullivan had ingeniously extended the technology of skyscraper construction to the department store. However, as he had in his office buildings, Sullivan took artistic license with the expression of practical forms and their functions.

On his skyscrapers, Sullivan modified the expression of the grid of steel construction by emphasizing the vertical dimension with unbroken lines of piers and recessed spandrels. The main portion of the Carson Pirie Scott Store comprises a corner entrance pavilion and tower, flanked by twelve-story elevations. In the tower, Sullivan reproduced the skyscraper effect, but on the elevations, he emphasized the horizontal dimension by using unbroken stringcourses to unite expanses of Chicago windows.

Sullivan's emphasis on horizontality was initially determined by the lighting and spatial requirements of modern merchandising practices. Steel framing required minimal internal support, allowed the maximum amount of daylight for merchandise display, and increased open space for easy movement around display cases and between floors. This post-and-lintel construction is exhibited on the exterior as a thin white-tiled grid that frames recessed windows and defines layered floors. Its clearest expression is in the plate-glass show windows, which are as wide as the vertical supports allow.

The ornamented display windows at the base sought to attract customers. Equally important, they served Sullivan's artistic purpose: to show the originality

Carson Pirie Scott (now Sullivan Center) detail

of his style of ornament close up. Sullivan used ornament as an artistic finish or, in his words, as "a garment of poetic imagery." He wrote extensively about architecture as a kind of poetic representation of nature capable of offsetting the materialist culture of an industrialized modern city. The intertwining geometric forms and botanical motifs (and his initials, *LHS*, above the corner entrance) are cast in iron and painted green over a red undercoat, emulating both oxidized bronze and dappled sunlit foliage. Sullivan's metaphor of the natural landscape is made manifest by strolling along the base and walking through the entrance. Together with the mahogany-paneled vestibule and foliate column capitals, the experience recalls a tree-lined forest walk.

Sullivan's store was built in two sections for the retail firm of Schlesinger & Mayer. The first section (1899), three bays wide on Madison St., has nine stories. The twelve-story corner section (1903) extended the frontage through the seven northernmost State St. bays. The building lease and business were sold to Carson Pirie Scott & Co. virtually upon completion. As a department store, the building was twice extended southward and was subjected to numerous external and internal alterations, including the unfortunate removal of original ornamentation in metal, wood, and mosaics and the twelfth-story open colonnade-and-cornice ensemble. Major restoration work was done on the facades and the main entrance in 1978–80. In 2007, Carson Pirie Scott closed the store. Property owner Joseph Freed & Assocs. then renamed the building the Sullivan Center and began its refurbishment as a mixed-use office, retail, and entertainment facility. Twenty-first-century restorations have returned the building to its original glory, restoring the gleaming white terra-cotta facing and the dark green metal work and reconstructing the twelfth-story ensemble, with its lush botanical ornament.

—LAUREN S. WEINGARDEN

112 Jones Hall
(Chicago Building; originally Chicago Savings Bank Building)
7 W. Madison St.
1904, HOLABIRD & ROCHE
1997, ADAPTIVE REUSE, BOOTH HANSEN ASSOCS.

Highly visible on State St. from the north because of an eastern shift in the roadway is this Holabird & Roche archetype. Large Chicago windows—flat on State St., alternately projecting and flat on Madison St.—dominate the facades. The emphasized corners and the rare intact cornice are also noteworthy. Everything above the first floor is now dormitory space for the School of the Art Institute of Chicago.

Chicago Building (now Jones Hall)

into Gothic tracery and the polygonal top floor are arresting, and the exceptionally tall lower floors provide maximum street exposure and daylight.

116 Thermal Chicago State St.
137 S. State St.
1995, ECKENHOFF SAUNDERS ARCHITECTS
Above the ground-floor retail space, this is an industrial facility that supplies chilled water from ice melt to cool nearby buildings via a below-ground distribution network. Behind the structurally expressive grid of glass block and concrete panels are huge ice tanks and chillers, while fiberglass walls on the upper stories conceal cooling towers. When ice making occurs at night, the glass block glows and small blue rooftop lights are illuminated.

113 Mentor Building
39 S. State St.
1906, HOWARD VAN DOREN SHAW
Shaw's only skyscraper presents an unusual amalgam of styles, with windows grouped in horizontal bands between a four-level base of large showroom windows and a classically inspired top. The details are typically robust and idiosyncratic, retaining the character of their classical sources but used as large-scale, conspicuous motifs.

114 Palmer House
17 E. Monroe St.
1927, HOLABIRD & ROCHE
2009, RESTORATION, LOEBL SCHLOSSMAN & HACKL
Built by the same architects and at the same time as the Stevens (Hilton) Hotel and only slightly smaller, the Palmer House shares its massing of narrow towers grouped around light courts. Below the palatial second-floor lobby is an elegant commercial arcade.

115 Singer on State Building
120 S. State St.
1926, MUNDIE & JENSEN
1997, ADAPTIVE REUSE, HASBROUCK PETERSON ZIMOCH SIRIRATTUMRONG
The Singer Sewing Machine Co. wanted a distinctive building but had only twenty-five feet of frontage. The white glazed terra-cotta molded

117 The Berghoff
17 W. Adams St.
1872, ARCHITECT UNKNOWN
27 W. Adams St.
1872, CHARLES M. PALMER
The Berghoff is housed in the Loop's only surviving public-hall building; the top-floor meeting room is indicated by the larger-scaled windows. One of two remaining cast-iron facades in the Loop is at 27 (the other is the Page Bros. Building).

118 211–227 S. State St.
1949, SHAW, METZ & DOLIO
The holdover Moderne facade has strong vertical strips of windows and dark spandrels to counteract the boxy horizontally.

119 John Marshall Law School
(Maurice L. Rothschild Building)
300 S. State St.
1906, HOLABIRD & ROCHE
1910, THREE-BAY SOUTH ADDITION, HOLABIRD & ROCHE
1928, FOUR-STORY ADDITION, ALFRED S. ALSCHULER
The original eight-story building had foundations and walls that would accommodate an additional four floors; but when they were added, the building lost its cornice to a simple parapet. The chamfered corner was designed to admit extra daylight to the selling floors.

120 DePaul Center
(Goldblatt's; originally Rothschild & Co. Store)
333 S. State St.
1912, HOLABIRD & ROCHE
1993, RENOVATION, DANIEL
P. COFFEY & ASSOCS.

On the remarkably intact facade, the deep, bracketed cornice is especially noteworthy. Converted to a multiuse structure, the building has shopping and food courts on the lower levels, rental offices in the middle, and academic floors on top.

121 CTA—Harold Washington Library Station
2001, DLK ARCHITECTURE

With the ticket functions placed under the track level, platform and street-level spaces are open and light. The new station, which replaced an aging facility at the same location, uses color, material, and traditional forms to relate to the adjacent library and the historic buildings nearby.

122 Harold Washington Library Center
400 S. State St.
1991, HAMMOND, BEEBY & BABKA; A. EPSTEIN & SONS INTERNATIONAL, ASSOC. ARCHS.

The winner of a highly publicized 1988 design competition, the library was the most overtly traditional of the diverse proposals designed to house the main library collection, which had been in temporary quarters for a decade. The building recalls neoclassical institutions but is not literal in all its details. Classical details such as the garlands and flamboyant acroteria adorn a massive red-brick-and-granite block that anchors the south end of the Loop at State St. The building's sense of solidity and permanence is reinforced by small, deeply recessed openings in its rusticated base and deep-set arches above. A completely different impression is created, however, when one views the facade along Plymouth Ct. Here, the building appears to have been sliced away to reveal a taut glass skin. The intention was to create a neutral mirror for the Manhattan and Old Colony Buildings to the west. Its neutrality is a counterpoint to the way glass is a vehicle for reinterpreting classicism elsewhere in the building, particularly in the pediments. The grand interior space that one would expect to enter in a building this scale is found not on the ground floor but at the top. The skylit Winter Garden is a restful space that recalls an exterior courtyard.

123 Robert Morris Center
(Second Leiter Building; originally Siegel, Cooper & Co. Store)
403 S. State St.
1891, WILLIAM LE BARON JENNEY

In the Second Leiter Building, what seems to support *does* support. Cornices and colonnettes articulate the underlying skeleton, with piers and spandrels resolving themselves into magnificent ranks of glass-filled grids. The exterior reflects an interior extraordinarily spacious, especially for its time. Each of the eight stories is an open composition of broad avenues and slender iron columns sixteen feet high. Contemporaries saw the building as a manifestation of a new age.

The building constitutes the response of William Le Baron Jenney, who must be considered one of the century's most significant architects, to the demands of its developer, Levi Z. Leiter, Marshall Field's partner from 1867 to 1881. Leiter wanted a "complete and perfect" building to house a single major retail establishment, but he also wanted the ability to subdivide if required. In the diminutive First Leiter Building (1879), which stood at Monroe and Wells Sts. until 1972, Jenney had given Leiter a predominantly glass envelope by supporting timber joists and girders on cast-iron columns. For Leiter's second commission, all of the beams and girders were steel; supports remained cast iron. The steel's high tensile strength enabled Jenney to open the exterior walls to glass to an unprecedented extent. The system, introduced by Jenney with wrought-iron horizontals on the demolished Home Insurance Building (1884), obviated the need for supporting partitions, permitting Leiter to arrange the interior as he saw fit. The extensive exterior glazing made space-consuming light courts unnecessary.

Second Leiter Building (now Robert Morris Center)

For most of its history, the building functioned as a store for a single retailer, originally Siegel, Cooper & Co. and later Sears, Roebuck & Co. Until the building was subdivided in 1981, the open qualities of its steel framing were instantly obvious.

Striking in its formal excellence, the Second Leiter Building recalls Jenney's training in the early 1850s at the École Centrale des Arts et Manufactures in Paris: the school's architectural curriculum taught that purpose and structure determine form. Leiter was the rare client who made the fullest use of Jenney's training, permitting the most modern materials and their expression in the building's design. The forward-looking qualities of the building's functionalism have fascinated historians such as Sigfried Giedion, who described it as "the first high building to exhibit the trend toward pure forms." And so it does. With a little imagination, one can see the Second Leiter Building as a modern composition of the mid-twentieth century.

—THEODORE TURAK

124 Manhattan Building
431 S. Dearborn St.
1891, WILLIAM LE BARON JENNEY
1982, RENOVATION, HASBROUCK
   HUNDERMAN
2005, EXTERIOR RESTORATION,
   BAUER LATOZA STUDIO

Viewed with awe by visitors to the 1893 World's Columbian Exposition, who called it Hercules, the Manhattan was the first tall building to use skeleton construction throughout; the first sixteen-story building in the United States and briefly the world's tallest building; and the first building with a structurally sophisticated wind-bracing system. The north and south bays are cantilevered to avoid overloading the footings of adjacent buildings.

Manhattan Building

125 Plymouth Building

417 S. Dearborn St.

1899, SIMEON B. EISENDRATH

1945, WEST FACADE REMODELING,
W. SCOTT ARMSTRONG

The Gothic face-lift was intended to give a collegiate image to a correspondence school. Eisendrath's design remains visible on Plymouth Ct. with Sullivanesque ironwork executed by Winslow Bros. Inside is a newel post identical to those executed by Winslow for the Schlesinger & Mayer (Carson Pirie Scott & Co.) store—not surprising, since Eisendrath had worked for Adler & Sullivan.

Old Colony Building

126 Old Colony Building

407 S. Dearborn St.

1894, HOLABIRD & ROCHE

Here is the Loop's sole survivor of a group of Chicago School skyscrapers with gracefully rounded corner bays. To offset its narrowness, continuous piers and recessed spandrels visually contract the long sides, while enhanced spandrels on the narrow elevations attempt to emphasize the horizontal. This was the first American structure to use portal arches (fillets joining column and girder) for wind bracing. The Phoenix columns are wrought iron, and the girders and floor beams are steel.

127 John Marshall Law School

(City Club)

315 S. Plymouth Ct.

1910, POND & POND

The gently curving limestone arch that ties together windows on the second floor is repeated at the top of the building.

128 Chicago Bar Association Building

321 S. Plymouth Ct.

1990, TIGERMAN MCCURRY

Gothicism à la Eliel Saarinen imbues this small building with a vivid presence. Emphasis is on the decorative facade at street level and at the pinnacled top. The cast-aluminum figure above the entry is *Themis*, by Mary Block.

129 Fisher Building

343 S. Dearborn St.

1896, D. H. BURNHAM & CO.

1907, NORTHERN ADDITION,
PETER J. WEBER

2001, RESTORATION AND ADAPTIVE
REUSE, PAPPAGEORGE/HAYMES,
COORDINATING ARCH.; EIFLER &
ASSOCS., LOBBY ARCH.; DESMAN
ASSOCS., FACADE RESTORATION ARCH.

The building's lavish facade—full of marine creatures in homage to the developer's name, Lucius G. Fisher—was painstakingly restored in a process that required replacement of more than 6,000 pieces of terra-cotta. The destroyed main entrances on Dearborn St. and Plymouth Ct. were re-created, and 1,200 wood-frame windows were repaired or replaced. Mosaic flooring and Carrara marble walls on the interior were also restored. The main lobby is a mixture of restoration and new design.

Fisher Building

53 W. Jackson Blvd.

1889–91, BURNHAM & ROOT

Addition, 54 W. Van Buren St.

1893, HOLABIRD & ROCHE

The Monadnock Building was erected in two parts along Dearborn St. for Peter C. and Shepherd Brooks, Boston developers who commissioned many prominent Chicago buildings. The northern section was designed with exterior masonry walls; the southern addition has a steel frame clad in terra-cotta. At sixteen stories, it was briefly the world's tallest office building.

The northern half has always been the subject of attention and wonder. It was constructed as a thick-walled brick tower, 66 feet wide, 200 feet long, and 200 feet high. In 1892, the *American Architect* described the building as a chimney.

Monadnock Building

Two cross walls divide the interior space into three flue-like cavities, the centers of which are open from street to roof. A freestanding staircase spirals down from the brilliance of the skylit sixteenth floor to the dark lobby cut lengthwise through the ground floor. Around this open stairwell a light structural grid sustains stacks of rental floors. From these extend the modular alcoves pushing through the facade to become bay windows.

The thick, perforated exterior wall is an expansion of the series of thick wall slabs that Burnham & Root originally proposed to divide the building vertically, like bookends, into a series of steel-framed cells. This modification of the steel system was first decisively demonstrated in Holabird & Roche's demolished Tacoma Building (1889), where two such thick walls were set at right angles to discipline the grid and achieve stability. In the Rookery (1888), Burnham & Root used two perforated masonry facade walls and four elevator and stair stacks to stabilize the iron skeleton. Each of these designs features a nice play of hard and soft, enclosure and exposure. Steel and masonry are in balance. The old material has not yet been abandoned; the new material has not yet supervened.

Contemporaries did not particularly comment on the Monadnock's remarkable constructive organization but instead noted its lack of exterior ornament. Burnham & Root shaped it as a single massive unit: a plinth-like base below a curved brick plane moving inward and upward transformed into a subtle batter for fourteen floors before returning outward to overhang in a cavetto cornice, giving the whole a shape suggestive of an Egyptian pylon. As the walls retreat, the window alcoves emerge as bays. Bevels at each corner expand and pace the rise of the facade.

The windows are not outlined with decoration but remain mere holes cut in this huge shape. Contemporary critics saw this as rational, honest, and exemplary of the starkness that a commercial building should accept; the Monadnock came to be cited as a model for steel-framed buildings of entirely different structure. But, as Sigfried Giedion observed in *Space, Time, and Architecture* (1941), the nature of steel construction is a grid of panels, as in the Reliance Building (1895). The Monadnock was exceptional. Its sense of upward thrust and the contrast of thick masonry and fragile steel look back to the traditional craft of building brick by brick and are appropriate to its fiercely archaic Egyptoid form.

—DAVID VAN ZANTEN

Chicago Federal Center

Chicago Federal Center

Dearborn St. between Adams St. & Jackson Blvd.

1959–74, LUDWIG MIES VAN DER ROHE; SCHMIDT, GARDEN & ERIKSON;
C. F. MURPHY ASSOCS.; A. EPSTEIN & SONS, ASSOC. ARCHS.

131 Everett McKinley Dirksen Building

219 S. Dearborn St.

(1959–64)

132 John C. Kluczynski Building

230 S. Dearborn St.

(1966–74)

133 U.S. Post Office—Loop Station

219 S. Clark St.

(1966–74)

By accident rather than design, the axial siting of three great plazas forms a rhythmic pattern that adds a discernibly urbanistic unity to the Loop. The outermost spaces, at the Richard J. Daley Center to the north and the Federal Center to the south, are oriented inward, as if addressing the intervening First National Bank (now Chase Tower) plaza. The symbolism of government bowing to finance, while fortuitous in this instance, is not without poetic appropriateness to Chicago's history. Such a metaphor, however, would have meant little to the chief architect of the Federal Center, Ludwig Mies van der Rohe, whose design is notable as much for its indifference to a traditional iconography of government as for the evidence it offers of his lifelong search for a universal order and grammar of the building art.

Outwardly, the Chicago Federal Center reads as many of Mies's residential and commercial works do: as abstract and nonallusive rather than representational architecture. It has been criticized for doing so. Nevertheless, Mies's uncompromising devotion to principle, together with his vaunted sensitivity to proportion and structural detail and in this case the organizational scale, combine to give the complex a monumental urban presence.

Three buildings occupy a space divided by Dearborn St. The thirty-story Dirksen courtroom building takes up a half square block to the east. The forty-two-story Kluczynski office building and a one-story postal facility are sited on the full block to the west. This ensemble encloses a large space at the southwest corner of Adams and Dearborn Sts., where in 1974 Alexander Calder's vermilion-painted steel construction, *Flamingo*, was installed. Its color and organic contours serve as a counterfoil to the matte-black geometries of Mies's buildings.

Both towers are curtain-wall structures characteristic of the high-rise designs of Mies's American period. Their steel frames, suppressed behind uniform walls of glass and steel, are marked off by projecting steel I-beam mullions. The Post Office, a unitary space with a central core, is similarly typical of Mies's reductivist concept of the single-story pavilion. Externally thin yet powerful structural steel columns brace enormous panes of tinted glass.

Commissioned by the U.S. General Services Administration, the Federal Center was part of a 1950s plan to modernize the federal government's administrative and judiciary buildings. Begun in 1959, the center had been fully designed by 1964 and was the first of Mies's urban, mixed-land-use projects. Budgetary problems delayed completion until 1974.

—FRANZ SCHULZE

134 131 S. Dearborn St.
2003, RICARDO BOFILL ARQUITECTURA,
DESIGN CONSULTANTS; DESTEFANO
& PARTNERS, ARCH. OF RECORD

The classically inspired limestone detailing that is so prominent on the skin of the architects' earlier 77 W. Wacker Dr. is here reduced to a thin wall just inside the lobby's glass exterior. The effect of the reflective glass skin is fearsome.

135 Marquette Building

140 S. Dearborn St.
1893–95, HOLABIRD & ROCHE
1906, WESTERNMOST ADAMS ST. BAY, HOLABIRD & ROCHE
1980, RENOVATION AND RESTORATION, HOLABIRD & ROOT
2003, CORNICE RE-CREATION, MCCLIER

The Marquette Building is an exemplar of the Chicago style: the rectangular grid of its structural steel skeleton is clearly articulated by its brick–and–terra-cotta cladding. The decorative treatment establishes the organization of the elevation, with its hierarchy of base, shaft, and capital, and gives it a sense of verticality that is expressed through the greater sculptural depth of the piers in comparison to the spandrels. The arms of the E-shaped building embrace a large light well with the elevator and service shafts in the central projection.

Marquette Building

All of the offices, which line the arms of the plan, have a window either to the street or to the light well. This design, combined with the structural and aesthetic treatment of the wall, guaranteed the maximum amount of natural light for the interior spaces.

The architects, William Holabird and Martin Roche, would become recognized as among the most prolific working in the Chicago commercial style. They had met as draftsmen in the office of pioneer skyscraper designer William Le Baron Jenney and founded their own firm in the early 1880s. A prominent structural engineer, Corydon T. Purdy, collaborated on this design.

The building was named in honor of Jacques Marquette, a Jesuit priest and explorer. His journal, in which he recorded his expedition through the Illinois Country in 1674–75, included the first description by a European of the site of Chicago. Owen F. Aldis, a real estate developer, an amateur historian, and one of the building's original owners, had translated Marquette's journal in 1891, providing the inspiration for the structure's name and decorative program. Hermon A. MacNeil's relief sculptures over the main portal depict events associated with Marquette's expedition. The two-story lobby is sumptuously decorated with marble trim and mosaic scenes of Marquette's trek designed by J. A. Holzer and executed by the Tiffany Glass and Decorating Co. Edward Kemeys's bronze reliefs above the elevator doors depict French explorers and Native Americans.

Alterations include the removal of the original Ionic columns from the main portal and the replacement of the cornice by the top floor (1950).

—TIMOTHY WITTMAN

136 55 W. Monroe St.
1980, C. F. MURPHY ASSOCS.

Taut and streamlined, the curtain wall slides around the corner, while diagonals in the sidewalk and on the roof slice across it. To cut energy costs, the proportion of glass to aluminum paneling changes from 75 percent on the north elevation, which receives little direct sun, to 50 percent elsewhere.

137 33 W. Monroe St.
1980, SKIDMORE, OWINGS & MERRILL

The three stacked atria were a first in office design, but the colors, materials, and lighting are unusually dreary.

138 Bank of America Theater & Majestic Hotel
16–22 W. Monroe St.
1905, EDMUND R. KRAUSE
2006, RENOVATION, BOOTH HANSEN

Here is a celebration of the terra-cotta modeler's skills at imitating heavy stonework.

139 Inland Steel Building
30 W. Monroe St.
1954–58, SKIDMORE, OWINGS & MERRILL

In Chicago, such measurable superlatives as *largest*, *tallest*, and *busiest* have always been the cornerstones of civic pride. It is indeed ironic that the Inland Steel Building, an office tower of modest scale and limited visual prominence, has achieved celebrity status, while its taller, larger, and significantly more conspicuous contemporary, the Prudential Building, is now virtually ignored.

Inland Steel's pioneering attributes are well known. Its unobstructed floor plate (177 × 58 feet) was unprecedented. It was created by placing core services in the adjacent tower to the east. For the first time, steel pilings, driven 85 feet through mud and clay into bedrock, were used to support a high-rise structure. Inland Steel was Chicago's first fully air-conditioned building, the first with dual glazing, and the first to provide indoor below-grade parking. It pioneered the use of stainless steel as a cladding material. Critics and scholars have consistently praised its graceful proportions, the elegance of its detailing, and the sophistication of its public art.

But the Inland Steel Building has not been adequately cited for one of its most praiseworthy attributes, the civic benefit of its presence on the streetscape. Avant-garde for its time, the building has become increasingly engaging, compatible, and understated as the character of the surrounding area has evolved, in large part as a consequence of the excellence of its site plan and the civility of its scale. The placement of its principal mass respects and reinforces the established building lines of the fronting streets. The longer dimension, along the line of Dearborn St., is interestingly maintained by seven projecting columns encased in stainless steel. The alignment of the shorter Monroe St. dimension not only enhances the sculptural quality of the services tower but also imparts a personal scale and orientation to the entrance, which is recessed at grade, glazed on three sides, and flooded by natural light. A

Inland Steel Building

substantial single-story annex houses loading docks, mail rooms, and the garage entrance. Its skillful placement on the site's northeastern corner makes it all but invisible to the public.

The economics of modern urban development and current code standards have secured the uniqueness of the Inland Steel Building and have qualified it as a protected architectural landmark. It survives as an enduring reminder of an optimistic period when the future was a beacon and long-restrained architectural skill and creativity blossomed once again. While its designers could not possibly have anticipated the adjacent construction, especially of the plaza on the west side of Dearborn St., they could not have prepared for it more effectively.

—LAWRENCE OKRENT

140 One South Dearborn

2005, DESTEFANO KEATING PARTNERS

Set back on a plaza, the only project completed by this short-lived partnership defers street-level attention to the adjacent Inland Steel Building. The design makes multiple references to its neighbor: a shared palette and materials, voids between bands of windows, and a Dearborn St. elevation that changes subtly at the height of that landmark's glass box.

141 Chase Tower

(First National Bank of Chicago)
Block bounded by S. Dearborn, W. Madison, S. Clark, and W. Monroe Sts.
1969, PERKINS & WILL; C. F. MURPHY ASSOCS., ASSOC. ARCHS.

Because Illinois laws at the time prohibited branch banking, the building had to accommodate tens of thousands of daily transactions on a single site. Departments with public access required large spaces at or

Chase Tower

near street level; tenants needed traditional office-building floors and access outside of banking hours. The graceful solution was this tapering shape and a pair of end cores that hold all services. The spread base and the cores combine to achieve stability and efficient load carrying; they also create the landmark profile. The multilevel, sunken plaza combines services with spaces around a fountain and Marc Chagall's mosaic mural, *The Four Seasons* (roof structure, 1996, SKIDMORE, OWINGS & MERRILL). The ancillary building at 20 S. Clark St. was known as the **Two First National Building** (1973, C. F. MURPHY ASSOCS.).

142 Three First National Plaza
W. Madison St. at N. Dearborn St.
1981, SKIDMORE, OWINGS & MERRILL

SOM broke its own mold with this carnelian granite-clad companion to Chase Tower (formerly First National Bank). Two towers are connected by a nine-story atrium with exposed steel truss supports. The sawtooth, setback configuration provides many corner offices and greenhouses at the top, which is lower than Chase Tower so that the views from the bank's boardroom remain unobscured.

143 10 N. Dearborn St.
(Covenant Club)
1923, WALTER W. AHLSCHLAGER
1987, FACADE RESTORATION AND
INTERIOR REMODELING, ECKENHOFF
SAUNDERS ARCHITECTS

Designed for a Jewish men's social and service club, this Renaissance Revival structure was completely gutted and rebuilt for office and retail uses.

144 George Dunne Cook County Administration Building
(Brunswick Building)
69 W. Washington St.
1965, SKIDMORE, OWINGS & MERRILL
2001, CHILD DEVELOPMENT CENTER,
ROSS BARNEY & JANKOWSKI

The weight is carried by the innovative tube-in-a-tube system—a concrete elevator core at the center and concrete exterior walls—that allows flexible, column-free floors. To provide a visually open base, a massive ring girder (behind the thick windowless line at the second floor) transfers and distributes the weight of more than five dozen vertical members to the perimeter first-floor columns. Above the girder, the walls curve gracefully inward, recalling the profile of the nearby Monadnock Building. In the plaza to the west is Joan Miró's *Miss Chicago* (1981). The outdoor play area for the building's day care center is located directly behind the Miró sculpture and is enclosed by a fence whose bollards mimic the artwork.

145 33 N. Dearborn St.
(Connecticut Mutual Life Building)
1967, SKIDMORE, OWINGS & MERRILL

On this masonry-clad Miesian steel frame, visual enhancement is limited to subtle emphasis around the window openings. The first floor was originally arcaded, a configuration favored by Chicago's zoning ordinance, but was later filled in to provide better retail spaces.

146 Richard J. Daley Center
(Chicago Civic Center)
Block bounded by W. Washington, W. Randolph, N. Dearborn, and N. Clark Sts.
1965, C. F. MURPHY ASSOCS.; LOEBL, SCHLOSSMAN & BENNETT
AND SKIDMORE, OWINGS & MERRILL, ASSOC. ARCHS.

Sternly elegant in its skin of rusting steel, the Daley Center is an outstanding example of Chicago's love for Miesian architecture. The scale is remarkable: at 648 feet it is immensely tall for only thirty-one stories, and its structural bays are an unprecedented 87 feet wide and 47 feet, 8 inches deep. Warren trusses frame each floor, stiffening the overall structure and allowing ample room between floors for service ducts and conduits. In its logic and execution, the resulting structure resembles a beautifully detailed bridge.

A framework of such scale and precision was deemed necessary to allow varied interior spaces. The structure was built to house more than 120 court and hearing rooms, a law library, and office space. Offices were accommodated by normal floor-to-ceiling heights of twelve feet, while twenty-six-foot-high courtrooms extended through two floors. Future space needs were taken into consideration; courtrooms can be converted into office space—and vice versa—with minimal structural rearrangement.

In its interior flexibility, the Daley Center is truly Miesian in spirit. The ruggedly handsome exterior reflects the underlying structure in its refined detailing. Cruciform columns stand outside the exterior wall plane, which is composed of six-foot-high spandrel panels and twelve-foot-high bronze-tinted windows. Both the spandrels and columns are clad in Cor-Ten, a self-weathering steel developed in the 1930s for use in railway hopper cars and not previously used in building construction. The building's bronzed coloring and hefty proportions give it a Promethean character, conjuring images of the foundry infernos of WPA murals.

Richard J. Daley Center

The Daley Center brought a building of immense visual power to the Loop but at a heavy price—the destruction of an entire block of shops and restaurants that encouraged downtown pedestrian traffic day and night. Yet something wonderful was gained: the Daley Center plaza has become Chicago's Forum. With its large-scale sculpture by Pablo Picasso, the plaza is the location of events as diverse as concerts, farmers' markets, peace rallies, and memorial services. Through these and other activities, the Daley Center fulfills a civic purpose consistent with its architectural dignity.

—TERRY TATUM

147 Untitled Sculpture (*The Picasso*)

Daley Center Plaza, W. Washington St. between N. Dearborn and N. Clark Sts.

1967, PABLO PICASSO, ARTIST

Though many people initially hated it, locals and visitors alike have come to love this enigmatic Cor-Ten head, which resembles the artist's drawings both of his wife and of his Afghan hound, Kaboul. The frontal view looks more like the dog; the profile is more like that of a woman.

148 Block 37

108 N. State St.

2010, GENSLER

22 W. Washington St.

2008, PERKINS & WILL

Decades of false starts—a process so Byzantine it was chronicled in Ross Miller's book, *Here's the Deal*—culminated in nothing more than a four-story mall and short office tower. Financial setbacks and changes in ownership led to cutbacks throughout. A CTA superstation with express service to the airports was scotched, and

the north tower is unbuilt. The CBS broadcast center TV screen overlooking Daley Plaza was designed to be more than twice as long and to wrap around the corner. The tiny Art Deco electrical substation on Dearborn St. (1931, HOLABIRD & ROOT, relief sculpture by Sylvia Shaw Judson) soldiers on as the complex's lone indispensable element.

149 The Goodman Theatre Center

170 N. Dearborn St.

2000, KUWABARA PAYNE MCKENNA
BLUMBERG ARCHITECTS AND
DLK ARCHITECTURE; SOUTH
FACADE, LIGHTSWITCH

A round pavilion marks the corner and a kinetic display of colored lights enlivens the Randolph St. elevation, but the real action is on Dearborn St., where glass walls reveal the two-story lobby. Anchoring the north end are the preserved facades of the Harris and Selwyn Theaters (1923, CRANE & FRANZHEIM), which, like the Oliver Building across the street, sacrificed their interiors to a larger new facility.

150 Delaware Building

(Bryant Building)
36 W. Randolph St.
1874, WHEELOCK & THOMAS
1888, TWO-STORY ADDITION,
  JULIUS H. HUBER
1982, RENOVATION, WILBERT
  R. HASBROUCK

A rare survivor from the first years after the Fire demonstrates High Victorian variety: bays of differing widths, rectangular and segmental arches, dissimilar stringcourses, and competing horizontal and vertical emphases. Added to the mix are a variety of materials: glass and cast iron on the first two floors, cast stone (an early form of precast concrete) on the next four levels, and pressed metal on the top two floors. Step into the lobby from Randolph St. to see the interior court. The beveled glass blocks, which allow light to filter down from the skylight, are also a product of Huber's addition.

151 Leo Burnett Building

35 W. Wacker Dr.
1989, KEVIN ROCHE—JOHN
  DINKELOO & ASSOCS.; SHAW &
  ASSOCS., ASSOC. ARCHS.

Roche's Chicago debut is an overly detailed and dreary interpretation of the columnar skyscraper: rows of columns and pilasters constitute the base and capital as well as a midpoint break for a mechanical floor. Stainless-steel bullnose mullions, which have been compared to pencils, add sparkle but do not make a brilliant design.

152 55 W. Wacker

(Blue Cross–Blue Shield Building)
1968, C. F. MURPHY ASSOCS.

Concrete is both the major structural material and the primary design element. Eight huge pylons act as structural members; duct enclosures are counterbalanced by concrete spandrels and cornices. Vertical surfaces have bush-hammered corrugations; horizontal ones are smooth, with exposed tie holes.

153 Marina City

300 N. State St.
1959–67, BERTRAND GOLDBERG ASSOCS.

Few Chicago buildings were as innovative in design or have had as great an impact on their environments as Marina City. Marina City stood out immediately among Chicago's many architectural highlights and was for a long time one of the most photographed buildings in the city. The two round apartment towers, with their semicircular balconies—thought by many people to resemble corncobs—were especially intriguing, as were the spiraling garages that occupy the lower half of each tower.

Marina City was designed for the yuppie avant la lettre. Goldberg and his client, the Building Service Employees International Union, decided that despite the exodus to

Marina City—under construction

the suburbs, many of those employed in the Loop were single or childless and wanted apartments close to their work. Goldberg and his client were right. The complex was a success from the start and a prototype for many others on the edge of the Loop.

In the absence of facilities that would glamorize living in an area previously devoted to railroading, Goldberg incorporated stores, a restaurant, a health center, a swimming pool, a skating rink, an exhibition space, a theater, a marina, a bowling alley, and an office tower. The complex was advertised as a "city within a city," a place for "24-hour urban living," both clearly commentaries on the suburbs, in which commuters spent only their nights.

Marina City

Goldberg's masterful design imparts an open feeling to the small, packed complex, every part of which seems to defy gravity and move upward; the plaza, for example, is lifted above the water and dematerialized by the windows of the restaurant. Despite recent additions, it is experienced as a thin slab, very different from the heavy box beneath its neighbor, Mies van der Rohe's One IBM Plaza. Because of the spiraling garage floors, the apartment towers seem to grow out of the plaza. Indeed, the towers appear virtually transparent, with the garage floors and balconies cantilevering from the perimeter columns. The office tower, now a hotel, is also lifted off the plaza, standing on columns above a windowless slab containing the bowling alley. This structure in turn is separated from the plaza by a glass-enclosed floor housing the hotel lobby and retail space. The irregularly shaped theater is the only structure that seems to rest on the plaza instead of taking off from it.

The apartments are also designed to create feelings of openness. Not only are they placed above the garages and the warehouses formerly in the vicinity, but their pie shapes allow for ever-expanding views of the city. More than in any other high-rise apartments, in Marina City, one has the feeling of having the whole city at one's feet.

Although modernistic in design, Marina City's round, cast-concrete forms were a clear reaction against the glass-and-steel towers of Mies van der Rohe, whose style prevailed in Chicago at the time.

—WIM DE WIT

154 **321 N. Clark St.**
(Quaker Tower)
1987, SKIDMORE, OWINGS & MERRILL
This late example of flat-topped, rectangular modernism includes a transparent ground floor, designed to the departed client's taste. Semi-circular stainless-steel mullions stress verticality.

Construction began on a ninety-story hotel and condominium building at **111 W. Wacker Dr.** *in 2006 and was stalled two years later by the* *economic crisis. The twenty-six-story shell was purchased by developers and redesigned in 2012 by Handel Architects as a fifty-nine-story luxury rental tower.*

155 77 W. Wacker Dr.

1992, RICARDO BOFILL ARQUITECTURA, DESIGN ARCH.; DESTEFANO & PARTNERS, SUPERVISING ARCHS.

For his first American skyscraper, this Spanish proponent of modern classicism supplied a square, silver-tinted glass column under four pedimented roofs. At night, theatrical lighting downplays the inglorious mismatch between the glazing and the white granite exoskeleton.

156 161 N. Clark St.

1992, KOHN PEDERSEN FOX

Lacking the prominent unobstructed sites of their 225 and 333 W. Wacker Dr. buildings, the designers created an intriguing top to make the building leap out of the skyline. An identical tower is intended for the site's northern half.

157 James R. Thompson Center
(State of Illinois Building)
100 W. Randolph St.

1979–85, MURPHY/JAHN; LESTER B. KNIGHT & ASSOCS., ASSOC. ARCHS.

It's either breathtaking or exhausting, depending on your threshold for retinal fatigue, but it draws crowds of tourists and ennobles such humble tasks as renewing driver's licenses and picking up tax forms. A series of dazzling concepts traveled

James R. Thompson Center

a rocky road in translation to actual buildable materials. Helmut Jahn's original design called for silicone glazing, which would have produced a mullionless skin but scared off contractors fearful of liability problems. Salmon, silver, and blue were already in Jahn's palette and fit the standard governmental red, white, and blue but as executed look tawdry and ill chosen. But the central "people place," the massive atrium that rises a full seventeen floors and is expressed by a sliced-off cylindrical crown, is a resounding success. Champions of Illinois artists resented the plaza placement of Jean Dubuffet's fiberglass sculpture, *Monument with Standing Beast.*

158 County Building and Chicago City Hall
118 N. Clark St. (County Building) and 121 N. La Salle St. (City Hall)

1911, HOLABIRD & ROCHE

This is in essence an office building—or, rather, two office buildings built around light wells—one of which has its offices interrupted for two stories to accommodate the City Council. The goal was to erect a building of eleven very high stories that would not look like a skyscraper. This was accomplished by doubling the scale of the exterior mask, minimizing fenestration, and introducing what were at construction Chicago's biggest columns, seventy-five feet high, hollow, and comprising fifteen arc-shaped granite segments. The Corinthian capitals are the height of an entire floor. Supporting these purely decorative elements required caissons ten feet in diameter. In 2006, a green roof was installed on the City Hall half of the building, allowing energy consumption comparisons with the traditionally covered County Building.

159 Burnham Center
(Conway Building)
111 W. Washington St.

1913, D. H. BURNHAM & CO. AND GRAHAM, BURNHAM & CO.
1986, RENOVATION, JACK TRAIN ASSOCS.

Burnham's version of the Chicago skyscraper (this was the firm's last before his death in 1912) continued to use the open light well introduced in the Rookery. Designed by Frederick P. Dinkelberg, the Conway Building eschewed the expression of its skeleton frame in favor of the image (but not the low scale) of the Beaux-Arts city that permeated the pages of the 1909 *Plan of Chicago*.

160 Chicago Temple
(First Methodist Episcopal Church)
77 W. Washington St.
1923, HOLABIRD & ROCHE

A twenty-one-story office tower is crowned by an eight-story spire, the Loop's only church spire, which tops the world's tallest church (568 feet), according to Guinness World Records. The shaft uses the vertical styling, small windows, and Gothic detailing that characterize the Tribune Tower; the spire, however, is more accurately executed. Officially, this is the home of the First United Methodist Church of Chicago, which has a ground-floor sanctuary and a chapel in the spire.

161 Chicago Loop Synagogue
16 N. Clark St.
1957, LOEBL, SCHLOSSMAN & BENNETT

This congregation began in a hotel room where travelers and businessmen could assemble a daily minyan. The building now serves that function in a ground-level chapel and an upper sanctuary. Reached by a ramp, the sanctuary is dominated by an eastern wall of Abraham Rattner's stained glass, *Let There Be Light*.

162 BMO Harris Bank
111 W. Monroe St.
1911, SHEPLEY, RUTAN & COOLIDGE
1960, EAST TOWER, SKIDMORE, OWINGS & MERRILL; 1974, WEST TOWER, 115 S. LA SALLE ST., SKIDMORE, OWINGS & MERRILL

Stainless-steel Miesian towers are fitted around a neoclassical red-granite-and-brick "traditional" bank in a way that affords each its own identity. The centerpiece features a five-story base in which three stories are deeply recessed behind Ionic columns. The East Tower uses thin window mullions to obtain a lively vitality and to avoid the surface distortion characteristic of large flat surfaces. It also makes a virtue of a midheight mechanical floor, recessing it to fully expose the columns. The West Tower's wide bays and huge spandrels add horizontality to the mix.

163 Ralph H. Metcalfe Federal Building
77 W. Jackson Blvd.
1991, FUJIKAWA, JOHNSON & ASSOCS.

Tall, rectangular, flat-topped (rare in 1991), and designed to blend with Mies's Federal Center buildings, this concrete structure is finished in granite rather than painted steel.

164 Chicago Metropolitan Correctional Center
(William J. Campbell U.S. Courthouse Annex)
71 W. Van Buren St.
1975, HARRY WEESE & ASSOCS.

More people ask "What the hell is that?" about the Chicago Metropolitan Correctional Center than about any other building in the Loop. And well they should, for there are few buildings like this twenty-seven-story triangular federal detention center. However, a simple analysis of the concrete, slit-windowed exterior reveals much about the prison's interior, which houses only those awaiting trial in nearby federal courts.

The shape is a response to the U.S. Bureau of Prisons' mid-1970s' approach to incarceration. In an attempt to reform prisons, the bureau had Weese's office experiment with placing cells around a lounge-like

Chicago Metropolitan Correctional Center

common area supervised by an unarmed officer. Weese found that a triangular floor plan allowed the maximum number of cells to be most efficiently centered around the lounge. The triangular plan was not intended to symbolize the three branches of government, although some members of those branches have been guests at the facility.

The first nine floors contain administrative facilities. The windows in this section are ten inches wide, to provide ample light and views for the staff. Above the tenth-floor mechanical room, identifiable by its angled air intakes, are five-inch-wide windows for the inmates' rooms. The long, thin windows were meant to symbolize an opening through which people could not pass. Not caring much about symbolism, some architecturally disrespectful inmates discovered a way around this design feature and escaped. Lights now wash the exterior, and bars have been added to the interiors of the cells.

The eight two-level housing units have recreation and private meeting rooms. These secured areas are represented by the long strips of horizontal windows at the upper floors. A rooftop basketball and volleyball court, covered by wire mesh, tops the building. Attempted helicopter escapes necessitated the installation of struts to support cables that deter unauthorized aerial exits.

Although the Metropolitan Correctional Center can be seen as a straightforward solution to a building program, it is not without its architectural precedents. It owes a great deal to Le Corbusier, whose mixed-use Unité d'Habitation in Marseilles (1952) includes two-level housing units, a rooftop garden, and smooth concrete finishes. Although Le Corbusier hoped to create designs that would inspire worldwide imitation, it is Weese's building that has been widely copied.

The direct-supervision method of running correctional facilities has been successful, and Weese's triangular plan has been the basis for many of the housing units. His provocative but graceful building form, however, has not been matched.

—MICHAEL BORDENARO

165 One Financial Place
440 S. La Salle St.
1985, SKIDMORE, OWINGS & MERRILL

Built on the site of the La Salle St. Station's shed and tracks are an unadorned, flat-roofed office tower with forty bay windows per floor—a recollection of a Chicago School characteristic—and the five-story Midwest Stock Exchange straddling the Eisenhower Expressway approach. The Stock Exchange's two arched windows (lighting a fitness center, not the trading area) are meant to honor Adler & Sullivan's demolished Chicago Stock Exchange Building. Access to the present La Salle St. commuters' station is through these buildings. The plaza, a gentle element in an otherwise hard environment, contains a bronze horse created by Ludovico de Luigi in homage to the horses of St. Mark's, Venice.

166 Chicago Board Options Exchange
141 W. Van Buren St.
1985, SKIDMORE, OWINGS & MERRILL

This virtually windowless box occupies the site of the La Salle St. Station's head house and turns its back on Van Buren St. It features a 44,000-square-foot trading floor.

167 La Salle Atrium Building
(Fort Dearborn Hotel)
401 S. La Salle St.
1914, HOLABIRD & ROCHE
1985, RENOVATION, BOOTH HANSEN ASSOCS.

Strategically positioned next to the La Salle St. Station, this relatively modest former hotel has a symmetrical Georgian facade, a luxurious lobby sheathed in Circassian walnut and Rookwood tile, and a mezzanine adorned with murals depicting early Chicago. These elements were refurbished, retained, or replicated when the hotel was converted into offices. This was accomplished by closing the south end of the original U shape with an elevator bank and adding skylights at the second floor and roof.

141 W. Jackson Blvd.

1930, HOLABIRD & ROOT
1980, ADDITION, MURPHY/JAHN;
    SHAW & ASSOCS. AND SWANKE,
    HAYDEN, CONNELL, ASSOC. ARCHS.
1997, SECOND ADDITION, FUJIKAWA,
    JOHNSON ARCHITECTS
1998, FOUNTAIN IN EAST PLAZA,
    DESTEFANO & PARTNERS
2007, LOBBY RESTORATION AND
    EXTERIOR REHABILITATION, AUSTIN
    AECOM; HARBOE ARCHITECTS,
    PRESERVATION ARCH.

The Chicago Board of Trade is that rare hybrid in American architecture that successfully combines designs from two periods. The main portion, which faces north from the foot of La Salle St., Chicago's main financial artery, is a striking forty-five-story tower whose facade features setbacks often associated with Art Deco skyscrapers. The twenty-four-story steel-and-glass postmodern addition to the south is entered on Van Buren St. Although its black-and-silver exterior contrasts sharply with the gray limestone cladding of the original, the new is visually linked to the old through a skillful updating of the Art

Chicago Board of Trade Building

Deco building's vocabulary of setbacks and symmetry and a recapitulation of its pyramidal roof.

Likewise, the lobbies throughout the building complement each other, with the abstracted sculptural forms of the 1930 entry inspiring equally intriguing spaces in the 1980 structure. The original building's three-story lobby features streamlined cascades of buff-colored marble that alternate with massive black marble piers. Its sculptural volumes are further articulated by dramatic lighting, particularly through a panel that cuts a wide swath across the ceiling and down the wall.

In the 1980 addition, the first-floor lobby is a compact, two-story variation of its antecedent executed in shades of jade and turquoise. On the twelfth floor is a second lobby (closed to the public) whose north wall is the limestone exterior of the original building, a skillful combination of contemporary and historic structures.

Sculpture and painting were important in both building campaigns. The carved figures holding wheat and corn on the La Salle St. facade were designed by Illinois artist Alvin Meyer; the pyramidal roof is topped by an aluminum statue of Ceres, the Roman goddess of agriculture, by renowned American sculptor John Storrs. The similarly shaped skylight

Chicago Board of Trade Addition

on the addition features an ornamental abstraction of a trading pit. Finally, re-installed in the addition's atrium is a monumental mural of Ceres by Chicago artist John Warner Norton, removed years earlier from the original trading room.

—PAULINE A. SALIGA

169 Federal Reserve Bank Building

230 S. La Salle St.

1922, GRAHAM, ANDERSON,
PROBST & WHITE

1957, SOUTHWEST ADDITION,
NAESS & MURPHY

1989, RENOVATION AND NORTHWEST
ADDITION, HOLABIRD & ROOT

170 Bank of America
(Illinois Merchants Bank Building)

231 S. La Salle St./230 S. Clark St.

1924, GRAHAM, ANDERSON,
PROBST & WHITE

1990, RENOVATION, SKIDMORE,
OWINGS & MERRILL

Bank of America

The southern end of La Salle St. is flanked by a pair of virtually identical buildings with classical columns and cornices neatly lined up. The Federal Reserve Building has Corinthian columns; the Bank of America's columns are Ionic. On the interiors, similarity ends. The B of A's second-level banking floor is a richly appointed re-creation writ large of a Roman temple, lacking only the god's statue, prompting Louis H. Sullivan to suggest that bankers here wear togas and speak Latin. Jules Guerin's murals adorning the frieze are allegorical references to international commerce. The Federal Reserve's dictate to avoid extravagance left the corresponding space dressed in white limestone under a restrained coffered ceiling. B of A is largely unchanged except for the introduction of escalators; most of the Federal Reserve has been reworked.

171 The Rookery

The Rookery—exterior

209 S. La Salle St.

1885–88, BURNHAM & ROOT

1907, LOBBIES AND LIGHT COURT
RENOVATION, FRANK LLOYD WRIGHT

1931, LOBBIES RENOVATION,
WILLIAM DRUMMOND

1992, RESTORATION AND
REHABILITATION, MCCLIER

After the Great Fire of 1871, a temporary city hall stood at the southeast corner of La Salle and Adams Sts. The site and nearby stables attracted pigeons and these—together with roosting politicians—gave the building the name the Rookery. When a new city hall was completed in 1885 and a group of investors acquired the lot, the name stayed with the new structure, to be designed by Daniel H. Burnham and John W. Root.

The Rookery—interior

More than two dozen Burnham & Root designs for commercial buildings were under construction in downtown Chicago in the 1880s and 1890s. Of these, only the Rookery remains. To support the building on Chicago's notorious clay soils, Root utilized a rail-grillage foundation. The street facades are entirely load-bearing masonry construction, while the lower floors on the alleys are supported by cast-iron columns and wrought-iron beams. The floor system and the walls of the light well are supported by iron framing, allowing large expanses of glazing. The design took advantage of other innovations: fireproof clay tile, plate glass, improved mechanical systems, and that remarkable invention, the hydraulic passenger elevator.

The nearly square Rookery is organized around a central court surmounted by a skylight above the second story. A cast-iron oriel stair extends the height of the light well above. A walkway encircles the court at the mezzanine level, with grand stairways leading to that preeminent rental floor from two light-filled lobbies.

The bold facades feature a red granite base, pressed brick facades, terra-cotta ornament, and turrets. The light court is faced with light-colored glazed brick and terra-cotta. All public spaces are clad in incised and gilded marble and copper-plated and Bower-Barff ironwork. Contemporaries extolled the Rookery as "the most modern of office buildings" and "a thing of light."

In 1905, Frank Lloyd Wright was commissioned to redesign the lobbies and light court, and he replaced Root's iron railings and terra-cotta cladding with those of his own, more geometric, design. Wright's former student, William Drummond, later altered the lobbies into one-story spaces and replaced the open-grille elevator cages with solid doors ornamented with rook motifs designed by Annette Byrne. During the following decades, the skylight was covered over, the mosaic floor was removed, and the interior surfaces grew dim.

A comprehensive program completed in 1992 revitalized the offices and public spaces and restored the Rookery's historic features. The exterior was returned to its original ruddy hues, the public lobbies were re-created to approximate the 1907 renovation, and Drummond's elevator lobbies were retained. The skylight over the light court was reopened, and a second skylight was added at the top of the light well. The court's 1905 marble and ironwork were restored. Because of this remarkable commitment to preservation, the Rookery offers a rare glimpse of downtown Chicago at the turn of the twentieth century.

—DEBORAH SLATON

172 JW Marriott Chicago

*(City National Bank; originally
Continental & Commercial
Bank Building)*
151 W. Adams St. and
208 S. La Salle St.
1914, GRAHAM, BURNHAM & CO.
2010, CONVERSION TO HOTEL,
   LUCIEN LAGRANGE ARCHITECTS

The street-level colonnade establishes the "financial" look of La Salle
St. in many minds. The granite Doric
columns have steel cores to support
the block-filling structure. The colonnade reappears atop the building,
where loss of the cornice destroys
the "temple" effect. The lower
twelve floors have been converted
to a hotel.

173 190 S. La Salle St.

1987, JOHN BURGEE ARCHITECTS
   WITH PHILIP JOHNSON; SHAW
   ASSOCS., ASSOC. ARCHS.

Philip Johnson's only Chicago building is postmodernism at its most
serious and successful, responding
strongly to its context and proclaim-
ing its deep roots in Chicago's architectural history. The granite base is
topped by a many-gabled summit
that echoes similar elements on
neighboring buildings. Its arched windows and doors parallel those on the
Rookery; its overall design is drawn
from John W. Root's demolished Masonic Temple (1892); the upper elevations alternate the punched-window
limestone facades of the 1920s with
contemporary curtain walls. The overscaled, barrel-vaulted lobby features
rich marble and a gold-leaf ceiling.

174 135 S. La Salle St.

*(La Salle Bank Building;
originally Field Building)*
1934, GRAHAM, ANDERSON,
   PROBST & WHITE

Conceived as the Loop's largest
office building, the Field Building
was one of the city's last sizable
buildings under construction as the
Great Depression deepened. It is an
H-plan building with a central rectangular tower rising from a base with
four lower corner towers. The limestone exterior creates strong verticals alternating with window tiers of
similar size. Embellishment consists

135 S. La Salle St.

only of a dark granite base and incised lines at the summits of the five
shafts. The marble lobby is lush by
contrast, offsetting beige walls with
white pilasters and metalwork of
nickel silver bronze. Mirrored Art
Deco bridges connect the north and
south balconies.

175 120 S. La Salle St.

(State Bank of Chicago Building)
1928, GRAHAM, ANDERSON,
   PROBST & WHITE
1994, BANKING HALL
   RESTORATION, VOA ASSOCS.
1998, RENOVATION, LOHAN ASSOCS.

The overall lines are slimmer and
the colonnade is reduced to a four-
column entrance, but the outline
is similar to the firm's bank at 208.
Furthermore, the second-floor banking space is intact.

176 Northern Trust Building

50 S. La Salle St.
1905, FROST & GRANGER
1928, TWO-STORY PENTHOUSE
   ADDITION, FROST & HENDERSON

This banking house *without* an office
tower above it is singular on a street
that is a virtual canyon.

177 39 S. La Salle St.

*(La Salle–Monroe Building;
originally New York Life Building)*
1894, JENNEY & MUNDIE
1898, EASTERN HALF, JENNEY & MUNDIE
1903, ONE-STORY ADDITION,
   ARCHITECT UNKNOWN

This early steel-frame building is one
of the first whose walls were built
simultaneously at several stories
instead of from the ground up.

178 **19 S. La Salle St.**
(Association Building; known
as Central YMCA building)
1893, JENNEY & MUNDIE

The heavy banding and the shifting
design characterized much of Jenney's work at this time.

179 **11 S. La Salle St.**
(Roanoke Building; originally
Lumber Exchange Building)
1915, HOLABIRD & ROCHE
1922, FIVE-STORY ADDITION,
   HOLABIRD & ROCHE
1926, TOWER, HOLABIRD & ROCHE;
   REBORI, WENTWORTH, DEWEY &
   MCCORMICK, ASSOC. ARCHS.
1984, RENOVATION, HAMMOND,
   BEEBY & BABKA

This building with an unusual number
of changes and additions began as
the Lumber Exchange, a sixteen-story
late–Chicago School commercial
building with windows under arches
at the fourth and top floors. The top
rank of arches disappeared in 1922,
when five floors were added under
a re-creation of the original cornice.
The vertical ranks of paired windows
were later adapted to a tower addition at the eastern end of the
Madison St. frontage. The tower, one
of the first to incorporate setbacks,
was primarily the design of Andrew
N. Rebori. The 1984 renovation replaced a 1950s modernization with a
postmodern evocation of the original
profusely ornamented features.

180 **10 South La Salle**
1989, MORIYAMA & TESHIMA;
   HOLABIRD & ROOT, ASSOC. ARCHS.

The exterior walls of the base of the
Otis Building (1912, HOLABIRD & ROCHE)
were reused to retain the scale of
La Salle St. in this sleek tower. No
attempt was made to disguise either
the old or the new: the stone base
is contrasted by the facade, whose
grid it sets. The new elevations are of
matching blue-painted aluminum and
glass with details picked out in bright
green. The surface is interrupted for a
seven-story semicircular entry and for
a single strip of bay windows from the
nineteenth floor to the roof.

181 **1 N. La Salle St.**
1930, VITZTHUM & BURNS

Slim strips of windows and lime-

stone alternate to assert the tower's
verticality. Virtually the only break is
at the fifth floor, where sculptured
panels commemorate the explorations of Robert Cavalier, Sieur de La
Salle, who allegedly camped on this
site in 1679.

182 **2 N. La Salle St.**
1979, PERKINS & WILL

Ribbons of windows, set flush in
alternating bands with structural
aluminum wall panels, stress the
smoothness of this building's skin;
rounded corners emphasize its continuity. The unglazed corners at the
second level identify the mezzanine
of transfer beams that allowed the
building to reuse the foundations of
the demolished La Salle Hotel.

183 **33 N. La Salle St.**
(Foreman State National
Bank Building)
1930, GRAHAM, ANDERSON,
   PROBST & WHITE

The upward thrust is enhanced by
facing the recessed spandrels on the
central portion of each facade in a
darker terra-cotta than the piers. The
gradual tapering of the peak and the
sculpted relief on the rose granite
base, which includes suggestions
of pediments at the fourth floor, are
forms of stripped eclecticism.

184 **120 N. La Salle St.**
1991, MURPHY/JAHN

Through carefully executed, elegant
detail, the building enriches the La
Salle St. corridor with a vigorous

120 N. La Salle St.

three-dimensionality. East and west facades feature a gently curving, gray-tinted, butt-glazed window wall, bordered by a contrasting, deeply suppressed vertical bank of windows. Both facades are crowned by a glazed three-story half vault. A cantilevered trellis on the north wall extends the length of Court Pl. Curving over the entrance is artist Roger Brown's *Flight of Daedalus and Icarus*, a colorful mosaic. Above the entrance loggia, all masonry is coursed in alternating bands of light and dark gray flame-cut granite. Dividing the facade into two unequal parts, a vertical granite-clad plane pulls the window wall out over the sidewalk and separates the office spaces from the service and mechanical areas. Polished granite clads the horizontally banded, deeply rusticated lobby walls; at the height of the door lintels, a brass strip lines the horizontal joint in the granite.

185 Cadillac Palace Theatre and Hotel Allegro Chicago
151 and 171 W. Randolph St.
1925, C. W. AND GEORGE L. RAPP
1999, RENOVATION, DANIEL
    P. COFFEY & ASSOCS.

This is the western anchor to the Randolph St. Theatre District. The theater's historic elements were restored or re-created and its stage and support spaces greatly expanded. The Allegro's cultural image contrasts with the smoke-filled, backroom-political identity of the predecessor Bismarck Hotel.

186 Michael A. Bilandic Building
(Burnham Building)
160 N. La Salle St.
1924, BURNHAM BROS.
1992, RENOVATION AND ADDITION,
    HOLABIRD & ROOT

A U-shaped office building with a traditional tripartite facade was retrofitted to create courtrooms and offices for the State of Illinois. A mechanicals floor was added, sheathed in limestone and fitted with a cornice and belt courses that resemble the original summit. The walls of the light well were opened up behind

a reflective glass curtain wall. The single arched entry was expanded into a new lobby resembling a walled Italian courtyard.

187 200 N. La Salle St.
1984, PERKINS & WILL

This "extruded ice cube" is clad in a curtain wall of green-tinted glass, half of which has been sprayed from behind to make it opaque. The perimeter is serrated to create ten corner offices per floor. The taller windows at these corners help to emphasize verticality.

188 203 N. La Salle St.
1985, SKIDMORE, OWINGS & MERRILL

The horizontal slits ventilate the parking levels and are repeated for unity above. The massive glass column on Clark St. houses the elevator, and slanting skylights cover two interior atria.

189 La Salle–Wacker Building
221 N. La Salle St.
1930, HOLABIRD & ROOT;
    REBORI, WENTWORTH, DEWEY &
    MCCORMICK, ASSOC. ARCHS.

Dramatically sited at the "gateway to finance" on La Salle St., this building allows a clear reading of the H-shaped plan devised in response to the 1917 ordinance restricting buildings to floor areas one-quarter of their site above a certain height. Stripped-down classicism and setbacks mark the changes. The three-story base shifts to an H configuration, with north and south light courts. At the twenty-third-story cross of the H, the tower ascends uninterrupted for another eighteen floors.

190 222 N. La Salle St.
(Builders Building)
1927, GRAHAM, ANDERSON,
    PROBST & WHITE
1986, RENOVATION AND ADDITIONS,
    SKIDMORE, OWINGS & MERRILL

This is a late appearance of Daniel H. Burnham's tripartite, limestone-clad, flat-roofed office block around a light court. Don't miss the central atrium: the building trades that developed the structure used it as an indoor fair.

Reid-Murdoch Center

191 Reid-Murdoch Center
(Reid, Murdoch & Co. Building)
325 N. La Salle St.
1914, GEORGE C. NIMMONS
2002, RENOVATION, DANIEL
P. COFFEY & ASSOCS.

The most visible of Nimmons's warehouse designs, this is regarded as perhaps his best work. The building lost its rigid symmetry with the removal of the westernmost bay in 1930, when La Salle St. was widened.

192 300 North La Salle
2009, PICKARD CHILTON; KENDALL/
HEATON ASSOCS., ASSOC. ARCHS.

The tower's water-level plaza, green-gray glass cladding, fourth-story balcony, and projecting overhang reflect the revised perception of the river as an amenity. Delicate vertical detailing terminating in finials and too-subtle setbacks help to mitigate the blocky massing required to maximize revenue-generating office space.

193 325 N. Wells St.
(Helene Curtis Building)
1912, L. GUSTAV HALLBERG
1984, RENOVATION, BOOTH
HANSEN ASSOCS.

An old riverfront warehouse was transformed into a distinctive office building by inserting green glass topped by a terraced crystalline addition housing the company boardroom.

194 Engineering Building
205 W. Wacker Dr.
1928, BURNHAM BROS.
1982, RENOVATION, HIMMEL BONNER

This U-shaped building had its original entrance below an open court on Wells St. The windows are uniform except at the corners; ornament is restricted to the base and top, where it projects slightly in the manner of Art Deco skyscrapers. Traces of the original lobby were retained in a renovation that moved the entrance to the Wacker Dr. side.

195 Century Tower
(Trustees System Service Building)
182 W. Lake St.
1930, THIELBAR & FUGARD
2003, CONVERSION TO RESIDENTIAL,
FITZGERALD ASSOCS. ARCHS.

This was Chicago's last skyscraper begun before the October 1929 stock market crash. It introduced to the city an Art Deco device used elsewhere: above the fourth floor, the brick is purple, shading lighter

Century Tower

to the top, which is buff to match the sunburst terra-cotta ornament. It is topped by a ziggurat and lantern. Around the original banking entrance on Lake St. are panels depicting finance through the ages. They were designed by Eugene van Breeman Lux, who also designed the allegorical figures at the second-floor level. The lead panels of workingmen are by Edgar Miller.

196 CTA—Lake/Wells Entrance Canopies
Northeast and southeast corners of W. Lake and N. Wells Sts.
1997, TENG & ASSOCS.
Each sleekly modern entrance canopy is a beautiful piece of street furniture and brightens the way out of this station.

CTA—Lake/Wells entrance canopy

197 Randolph Tower City Apartments
(Steuben Club Building)
188 W. Randolph St.
1929, VITZTHUM & BURNS
1993, RENOVATION, STENBRO LTD.
2011, CONVERSION TO
    RESIDENTIAL, HARTSHORNE
    PLUNKARD ARCHITECTURE
This is possibly the last of the historicist limestone tower buildings whose shapes were conditioned by the 1923 zoning ordinance. The silhouette of telescoping "towers" also characterizes the firm's later design for 1 N. La Salle St.

198 180 W. Washington St.
(Equitable Building)
1929, HYLAND & CORSE

199 "I Am" Temple
(Elks Club Building)
176 W. Washington St.
1916, OTTENHEIMER, STERN & REICHERT
Two narrow eccentric structures: 180 is a veritable terra-cotta catalog, while the Temple's unusual character is ascribed to the fact that the Viennese-born Rudolph Schindler was working for this firm. It was his first American job, after his studies with Otto Wagner and before joining the office of Frank Lloyd Wright.

200 175 W. Washington St.
(Chicago Federation of Musicians)
1933, N. MAX DUNNING
1949, ADDITION, ARCHITECT UNKNOWN
The added third story of this tiny Bedford limestone gem carefully respects the original facade.

201 Concord City Centre
208 W. Washington St.
1926, GRAHAM, ANDERSON,
    PROBST & WHITE
2002, CONVERSION TO CONDOMINIUMS,
    HARTSHORNE & PLUNKARD
202 212 W. Washington St.
1912, HOLABIRD & ROCHE
2002, CONVERSION TO CONDOMINIUMS,
    FITZGERALD ASSOCS. ARCHS.
The unusual sight of flower-bedecked balconies on this block heralds a pioneering residential conversion in this previously business-only district.

203 Washington Block
40 N. Wells St.
1874, FREDERICK & EDWARD BAUMANN
This rare survivor from immediately after the Great Fire has remained virtually intact. It is singularly well conceived, with a facade of alternating wide and narrow stone courses and windows clearly outlined and topped with a variety of Italianate crowns. Frederick Baumann advocated isolated-pier foundations as more suitable than continuous perimeter ones to Chicago's compressible soil. This building is assumed to have them, since it was designed just after he published a pamphlet on the subject.

The exposed truss of **215 W. Washington St.** (2010, SOLOMON CORDWELL BUENZ) hangs like the Sword of Damocles over the Washington Block.

204 Madison Plaza
200 W. Madison St.
1982, SKIDMORE, OWINGS & MERRILL
2006, WINTER GARDEN,
  POWELL KLEINSCHMIDT

The serrated front creates a distinctive plaza (now enclosed) and a setting for Louise Nevelson's steel sculpture *Dawn Shadows*; the stepped-back top allows views to the east from the top floors. A partially prefabricated steel framing system limited on-site welding, resulting in high-speed erection of the exterior tube.

205 181 W. Madison St.
1990, CESAR PELLI & ASSOCS.

Frankly echoing Eliel Saarinen's second-prize design in the 1922 Chicago Tribune Tower Competition, this symmetrical tower has truncated setbacks to enhance the strongly expressed—even exaggerated—verticality. The cladding is white granite, reflective metal mullions are set forward from the windows, and the finials are nickel-plated. A five-story lobby with a vaulted, coffered ceiling is meant to echo an entrance to the Uffizi Gallery in Florence, Italy. Each of the lobby's end walls displays a large sculpture by Frank Stella.

206 205 W. Monroe St.
1898, HOLABIRD & ROCHE

This wholesale building clearly reveals its metal framing on its upper floors and its low cost in the sparse ornament around the doorways.

207 CTA—Quincy/Wells Station
W. Quincy and S. Wells Sts.
1897, ALFRED M. HEDLEY
1988, RESTORATION, CITY OF
  CHICAGO, DEPT. OF PUBLIC WORKS,
  BUREAU OF ARCHITECTURE

Lightweight and inexpensive materials were used in elevated stations. This one had its wood framing and

CTA—Quincy/Wells station

decorative, pressed sheet-metal cladding restored to the original design and what paint analysis indicated was the original color.

208 Insurance Exchange Building
175 W. Jackson Blvd.
1912, D. H. BURNHAM & CO.
1928, SOUTH ADDITION, GRAHAM,
  ANDERSON, PROBST & WHITE
2001, RENOVATION, LUCIEN
  LAGRANGE ARCHITECTS

Finished in enameled brick and terra-cotta trim, it has the styling of the first-quality buildings by the Burnham firm and its successors. Architect Ernest R. Graham was part owner of this project; its success enabled him to endow the Graham Foundation for Advanced Studies in the Fine Arts.

209 Dixon Building
411 S. Wells St.
1908, NIMMONS & FELLOWS

This loft design is easily identified by the firm's characteristic ahistorical capitals, the banding of the piers near the summit, and the portions blocked out in light limestone against the dark brick.

210 Van Buren Building
212 W. Van Buren St.
1893, FLANDERS & ZIMMERMAN

A second-floor Romanesque oriel adds a graceful touch to this mid-block building.

211 235 West Van Buren
2010, PERKINS & WILL

The semaphore-like patterns of projecting balconies that inspired the moniker Dot-Dot-Dash Building are

235 W. Van Buren

S. Frost and Alfred H. Granger received many commissions, including the demolished Chicago & North Western Railway Terminal; they were not known for their office buildings. This one, like their railway stations, stresses structural sufficiency: strong corners, larger-than-necessary piers, a heavy base tapering into the wall above, and an entrance marked by sturdy columns.

214 Franklin Center
(AT&T Corporate Center and USG Building)
227 W. Monroe St. and 222 W. Adams St.
1988, 1992, SKIDMORE, OWINGS & MERRILL

There is a lot to be said for quality materials and craftsmanship, and this building says it all. The block-long complex of two high-rises with a connecting base represents a re-interpretation of the conventions of the late 1920s setback office tower. Pronounced vertical lines, granite cladding, spiky pinnacles at the roof and setbacks, and lavish lobbies characterize this Adrian Smith design. The materials and general approach are the same for both buildings, but the details vary. The centers of the main facades are set-in vertical curtain walls; elsewhere, windows are punched into the granite sheathing. On the Monroe building, the granite shades from deep red at the base to a light rose-beige at the top. Sporting a hipped roof, the Adams building has a lower profile. The lobby is a sequence of spaces of varying ceiling heights and a symphony in stone.

215 303 W. Madison St.
1988, SKIDMORE, OWINGS & MERRILL

Designer Joseph Gonzalez integrated references to the work of Frank Lloyd Wright, Otto Wagner, and the Chicago School in a design that emerges as distinctly his own. The debt to Wright is in the interlocking right-angle geometries; Wagner is quoted in the glass-block storefronts; and the facade's tripartite composition and Chicago windows evoke the Chicago School. The relatively small building is clad in granite and tinted glass in white-painted

on the highly visible south and west facades. The other two elevations respond to their no-nonsense Loop context with terraces recessed into regular grids. A thin ribbon wends through the austere parking podium to admit narrow bands of light and air. The apartment floors typically pack in twenty-two mostly shoebox-shaped units. The phenomenon of a windowless bedroom with walls that stop short of the ceiling was written into the building code to accommodate loft conversions but is now often found in new construction as well.

212 Brooks Building
223 W. Jackson Blvd.
1910, HOLABIRD & ROCHE

Gothic shafts and moldings in beige terra-cotta articulate the columns, presaging the Gothic office towers of the coming decades. But the walls are as clear and precise an articulation of their skeleton frame as the Chicago School could produce. The clasp-like ornament atop the piers recalls its use a decade earlier by Louis H. Sullivan on the Gage Building.

213 City Colleges Building
(Chicago & North Western Railway Office)
226 W. Jackson Blvd.
1904, FROST & GRANGER
1978, RENOVATION, ALTMAN-SAICHEK ASSOCS.

As sons-in-law of Marvin Hughitt, the railroad's president, Charles

aluminum frames. The horizontal banding of contrasting-colored granite broadens the narrow facades. The general scale, treatment of the Washington St. entrance, and arcading at the top are reminiscent of Wright's unbuilt 1912 Press Building project in San Francisco.

216 1 N. Franklin St.

1991, SKIDMORE, OWINGS & MERRILL

Sheathed in cast stone, the primary facade has various window types arranged in vertical rows; in sharp contrast, the south facade has uniform ranks of Chicago windows. Two cylindrical glass towers set within square railings suggest the Art Moderne of the 1930s. The notched corners at the base are filled with glassy bays cantilevered over the sidewalk.

1 N. Franklin St.

217 225 W. Washington St.

1986, SKIDMORE, OWINGS & MERRILL

This slablike building makes several references to the Chicago School. Within its tripartite facade, the shaft is articulated with full-bay variations of the Chicago window, drawing attention to the underlying frame. The glassy corner bays are another reference to the first Chicago School. The top floors on Franklin St. have a three-bay-wide recessed arcade. Prominent arches signal the entrances on both streets, but the arch on Wash-

ington St. leads to a blank stone wall.

218 Building for the Alexander White Estate
227–229 W. Lake St./177 N. Franklin St.

1872, BURLING & ADLER

219 Building for Samuel Cole
233 W. Lake St./185 N. Franklin St.

1873, BURLING & ADLER

220 Building for William Rowney
235 W. Lake St.

1873, ARCHITECT UNKNOWN

221 Building for Albert E. Kent
175 N. Franklin St.

1875, GEORGE H. EDBROOKE
1983, RENOVATION, STUART COHEN & ANDERS NEREIM

Building for Albert E. Kent

Known informally as the Lake-Franklin Group, this quartet constitutes the Loop's largest concentration of 1870s commercial buildings. They are typical of construction before the general use of passenger elevators and steel framing. All have load-bearing walls and relatively narrow Italianate windows.

222 225 W. Wacker Dr.

1989, KOHN PEDERSEN FOX; PERKINS & WILL, ASSOC. ARCHS.

The skillfully combined glass-and-granite cladding lightens considerably near the top, crowned by corner lanterns that pierce the skyline without dominating it.

333 W. Wacker Dr.

223 333 W. Wacker Dr.

1979–83, KOHN PEDERSEN FOX; PERKINS & WILL, ASSOC. ARCHS.

Sited at the bend of the Chicago River, this green glass tower has been called Chicago's first postmodern skyscraper. But William E. Pedersen, the design partner of Kohn Pedersen Fox, never uses that term to describe his buildings. He does, however, use such phrases as "a strategy of assemblage or collage—pieces, each of which has references to its context."

Indeed a "collage" of contextual "references," 333 is a quintessentially Chicago building in its tripartite structure of base, shaft, and clearly defined top. But base and shaft are strikingly different: a modern tower rests on a classically inspired base. These disparate forms are united by their color, utilized uniformly for the curtain wall and as a strong accent in the base, where bands of dark green polished marble alternate with gray granite. The same verde antique marble, combined with black granite, sheathes octagonal entrance columns that take their shape from the towers on the Merchandise Mart, which dominates the opposite bank of the river.

Above all, 333 is site-specific, its form adapted to its triangular lot. The Wacker Dr. facade is a graceful arc that follows the river's curve. The taut skin of mirrored glass reflects water, sky, and buildings in a constantly changing montage and, in an unmodern fashion, conceals the cross-braced steel supporting skeleton. The entrance is flush with the street, elegantly detailed and exactly centered.

The opposite facade, facing the edge of the Loop at the junction of Franklin and Lake Sts., is sliced and notched. To defy the neighborhood's generally dilapidated state in the late 1970s, Pedersen gave this side a splendid center entrance that invites passersby to ascend its curving steps, symbolic of his belief that the tall urban office building should be brought into a "more social state of existence." Three decades later, this entrance faces an area that has undergone rapid redevelopment, and the riverside entrance looks out on one of the city's grandest boulevards, the totally reconstructed and beautifully landscaped Wacker Dr.

This thirty-six-story tower established the seven-year-old firm as award-winning skyscraper designers. Worldwide commissions followed, including

333's immediate neighbors at 225 W. Wacker Dr. and 191 N. Wacker Dr. An element of contextualism with 225 is porthole medallions that recall the ventilation covers for 333's third-story mechanicals. This circular motif has become almost a signature of Pedersen's designs. It appears, for example, on the firm's Procter & Gamble complex in Cincinnati and as blind medallions on 900 N. Michigan Ave.

—JANE H. CLARKE

224 Merchandise Mart
222 Merchandise Mart Plaza
1930, GRAHAM, ANDERSON,
PROBST & WHITE
1992, RENOVATION, BEYER
BLINDER BELLE; JACK TRAIN
ASSOCS., ASSOC. ARCHS.

Impressive for its size, beautiful in its detail, the Merchandise Mart remains a major Chicago icon. Built as a wholesale store by Marshall Field & Co., it now serves primarily as a display center for furniture and furnishings dealers, apparel and gift wholesalers, and major art and art furniture shows. With some 4.2 million square feet of rentable space, it was the world's largest building at the time of its construction.

The design is typical of the late 1920s: prominent piers, recessed spandrels of darker color, and geometric ornament. Jules Guerin murals glow in the lobby and depict worldwide trade and commerce. Juniper berries and foliage combine to enrich the metalwork around the windows and on the elevators. The pedestrian bridge (1991, MURPHY/JAHN) that spans Orleans St. echoes the Deco geometry.

225 350 West Mart Center
(Apparel Center)
350 N. Orleans St.
1977, SKIDMORE, OWINGS & MERRILL

The building was designed so that its concrete infill panels could be replaced by windows if the tenant mix changed from showrooms to offices, which happened during the early to mid- 2000s—not long before an announcement that the spectacular southern views would soon be blocked by new high-rises.

*In late 2012, Pelli Clarke Pelli Architects revealed a master plan for a trio of skyscrapers on **Wolf Point**, the land that juts into the river where the north and east branches converge. The first structure will be a residential tower on the western end of the site, designed by bKL Architecture. The plan calls for south and east towers by Pelli Clarke Pelli to contain offices and hotel rooms, with a park overlooking the river.*

226 The Residences at Riverbend
333 N. Canal St.
2002, DESTEFANO & PARTNERS

The building's massing was determined by the curve in the river and

Merchandise Mart

a rail line to the west. Sleek upper floors top a concrete midsection for parking and town houses at ground level. A single corridor on the west side of the apartment floors gives all the units an eastern orientation, with western light coming through high transom windows.

Ground was broken in 2013 for the forty-five-story River Point office tower at **444 W. Lake St.**, *designed by Pickard Chilton.*

227 191 N. Wacker Dr.
2002, KOHN PEDERSEN FOX; KENDALL/
    HEATON ASSOCS., ASSOC. ARCH.

Given a once-in-a-lifetime opportunity to design a riverfront triptych with their two earlier buildings, the architects created a simple glass box that complements but does not compete with their 333 W. Wacker Dr. The transparent facade at lobby level reveals how the structure cantilevers to the west above the second floor, an accommodation to the 2002 widening of Wacker Dr.

The reconstruction of the north–south leg of Wacker Dr. (DLK CIVIC DESIGN) was completed in 2012.

228 155 N. Wacker Dr.
2010, GOETTSCH PARTNERS

As with Goettsch's earlier Wacker Dr. buildings, clear glass walls visually open a dramatic lobby to the street, while colossal columns support the office floors above. Here an almost dizzying array of diagonals on the lobby's floor, walls, and ceiling play connect-the-dots with the structural elements. Suppressing the corner columns on the south side creates dramatic cantilevers.

229 123 N. Wacker Dr.
1988, PERKINS & WILL

An arcade repeats the one on the Civic Opera Building; both the opera house and the Merchandise Mart are echoed in the pyramidal roof, the granite skin with punched windows, and the tripartite organization.

230 110 N. Wacker Dr.
1961, GRAHAM, ANDERSON,
    PROBST & WHITE

The Wacker Dr. elevation of this International Style building is balanced with a central limestone wall, flanked by matched, three-story curtain-wall segments with fluted stainless-steel panels above and below paired windows.

231 101 N. Wacker Dr.
1980, PERKINS & WILL
1990, ARCADE ALTERATION,
    KOBER/BELLUSCHI

Energy efficiency was a major aim in this design. Monitors behind the white aluminum curtain wall adjust to shifting sunlight, and vision and spandrel glass reflect or absorb light and heat as needed.

232 29 N. Wacker Dr.
2000, SKIDMORE, OWINGS & MERRILL

An undistinguished 1950s remodeling received a dramatic face-lift with new glass and a suspended metal grid, making for a richly textured facade.

233 Civic Opera Building
20 N. Wacker Dr.
1929, GRAHAM, ANDERSON,
    PROBST & WHITE
1996, RENOVATION, SKIDMORE,
    OWINGS & MERRILL
2012, RESTORATION OF ARCADE
    LIGHTING, STOREFRONT AND OFFICE
    LOBBY, GOETTSCH PARTNERS

The last big real estate venture of Chicago's traction and utilities mogul Samuel Insull is an office building wrapped around a 3,500-seat opera house. Art Deco and French Renaissance styling pervade the building, along with musical motifs. An arcade runs the entire length of the east facade, with pediments marking the entrances to the theaters (the smaller one was converted to support space). The opera theater's Grand Foyer is forty feet high, with colors chosen by Jules Guerin, the designer of the theater's fire curtain.

234 UBS Tower
1 N. Wacker Dr.
2001, LOHAN CAPRILE
    GOETTSCH ARCHITECTS

This office tower makes its most dramatic moves at street level, where clear glass walls encase the lobby on three sides. Using technology pioneered in Europe, the cable net wall allows huge sheets of very

UBS Tower

transparent glass to be supported with minimal structure, advancing the integration of plaza and lobby first seen in Mies van der Rohe's buildings.

235 1 S. Wacker Dr.

1982, C. F. MURPHY ASSOCS.

Designer Helmut Jahn speaks of such buildings as a synthesis of Sullivanian and Miesian Chicago architecture with 1980s technology. Here he faces a concrete stepped-back structure with a curtain wall of black, silver, and coral tones in which the dark glass defines grouped vertical bands of "windows." The "draped curtain" entrance leads to a streamlined, well-ordered lobby.

236 CME Center

(Chicago Mercantile Exchange Center)
10 and 30 S. Wacker Dr.

1983 (30 S. WACKER DR.), 1988 (10 S. WACKER DR.), FUJIKAWA, JOHNSON & ASSOCS.

To get a pair of office buildings and two large trading floors onto the site required cantilevering substantial portions of the towers over the trading rooms in the intervening base pavilion. Doing so while keeping trading floors column-free required diverting loads to the ground via a system of thickened walls, wide columns, and huge trusses. The serrations boost the number of corner offices to sixteen per floor.

237 Hyatt Center

71 S. Wacker Dr.

2005, PEI COBB FREED & PARTNERS, DESIGN ARCH.; A. EPSTEIN AND SONS INTERNATIONAL, ARCH. OF RECORD

The family that established architecture's Pritzker Prize played it safe by rejecting the initial choice, Lord Norman Foster, and instead commissioning Harry Cobb for the headquarters of their flagship corporation. The gently curving walls offer a fine counterpoint to the angular geometry that pervades the Loop.

238 Hartford Plaza

(Hartford Fire Insurance Building)
100 S. Wacker Dr.

1961, SKIDMORE, OWINGS & MERRILL

"Simple technique uncelebrated" marks this column-and-slab concrete frame, later covered in polished gray granite.

239 111 S. Wacker Dr.

2005, LOHAN CAPRILE GOETTSCH ARCHITECTS

The internal parking ramp is celebrated rather than concealed,

111 S. Wacker Dr.

rising like a celestial stairway through the middle of the glass-walled lobby. The ramp is hung from the third floor framing, and columns spaced at eighty-foot intervals lift the office tower up to allow maximum visibility for this tour de force. The radial pattern of the lighting, particularly stunning at night, is echoed by the floor pattern that extends out to the plaza. The beauty is not just skin-deep: the building was the first to be certified gold in the LEED CS (core-and-shell) category.

240 200 S. Wacker Dr.

1981, HARRY WEESE & ASSOCS.

Responding to an irregularly shaped riverfront site, Weese experimented with triangular geometries, as he had in the Metropolitan Correctional Center, designing a building composed of two triangles joined at the hypotenuse. One segment is seven stories taller than the other, making the scheme most apparent at the top of the building. The perimeter columns of the concrete frame are rotated 45 degrees to present a slim edge on a taut curtain wall of white-painted aluminum and tinted glass.

241 Willis Tower

(Sears Tower)

233 S. Wacker Dr.

1968–74, SKIDMORE, OWINGS & MERRILL

1985, GROUND-FLOOR RENOVATION AND WACKER DR. ATRIUM
   ADDITION, SKIDMORE, OWINGS & MERRILL

1994, RENOVATION AND LOWER-LEVEL REMODELING, DESTEFANO & PARTNERS

2010, THE LEDGE AT SKYDECK CHICAGO, SKIDMORE, OWINGS & MERRILL

Stand back . . . waaaaaay back . . . and look at the 110-story tower. Its modernist rendition of base, middle, and top clearly illustrates the goals of client Sears, Roebuck & Co. and architect Bruce Graham: housing 5,000 Sears

Sears (now Willis) Tower

employees in the base, leasing the middle to tenants, and using the top to establish the world's tallest building for the world's largest retailer.

By creating the massive, 50,000-square-foot floor plates in the first fifty floors, Sears was able to consolidate its merchandising group employees from seven Chicago locations. The large floors allowed the greatest amount of employee interaction without moving up and down elevators. By stepping the building back above the fiftieth floor, Graham created prestige leasable space that helped Sears pay for—and profit from—the $186 million project.

One-third of that amount went toward the superstructure. Structural engineer Fazlur R. Khan skillfully carried out his duties by designing a "bundled tube" consisting of nine squares, sixty-five feet each. These squares, formed by I beams spaced fifteen feet apart, are anchored in a deep concrete slab below the three subbasements. The slab rests on 114 steel-and-concrete caissons embedded in bedrock sixty-five feet below.

Two of the nine tubes stop at the fiftieth floor, two more end at the sixty-sixth floor, and the last three terminate at the ninetieth, leaving two tubes to rise the full 1,454 feet. The termination of the tubes was determined as much by the lateral stiffness required to resist wind loads as by spatial conditions or aesthetic needs.

The daily movement of 25,000 tenants and visitors in and around the building has been problematic. The windswept plaza was difficult to access and rarely used. A redesign of the entry and lower levels in 1985 improved the original circulation design, which was confusing. Following Sears's move to Hoffman Estates in 1992, another lower-level renovation sorted out circulation for the building's new post-Sears life.

The tower has always been more of a structural engineering triumph than an architectural accomplishment. While Graham and Khan were like a well-oiled, twin-cam engine firing on all cylinders when they designed the elegant John Hancock Center, the architectural manifold was slightly backfiring when they were running the Sears 500.

—MICHAEL BORDENARO

242 311 S. Wacker Dr.

1990, KOHN PEDERSEN FOX; HARWOOD
K. SMITH & PARTNERS, ASSOC. ARCHS.

The world's tallest concrete-framed building (a title it took away from Water Tower Place) was to have had two companions, presumably with their own back walls and tower projections; the Winter Garden, which serves as an open space, would have been blocked off from sunlight. The summit, a seventy-foot drum surrounded by four smaller ones, now looks overdone at any hour. At night, lit by nearly 2,000 fluorescent tubes, it is a visual poke in the eye. Three of them are unthinkable.

Thermal Chicago Franklin St.

243 Thermal Chicago Franklin St.

400 S. Franklin St.

1996, ECKENHOFF SAUNDERS
ARCHITECTS

A giant ice factory, like its predecessor at State and Adams, this chilled water plant houses the world's largest reinforced cast-in-place concrete ice tank, measuring 110 × 100 × 40 feet high. The "prow" oriented toward the river features the main supply-and-return chilled water piping as a signature element. The curving green glass wall is a reference to 333 W. Wacker at the north end of the drive. The rooftop metal screen, reminiscent of nearby freeway signage, masks evaporative condensers.

244 300 S. Riverside Plaza

1983, SKIDMORE, OWINGS & MERRILL

This ungainly addition to the riverfront has an odd curve meant to echo the bend in the river.

245 444 W. Jackson Blvd.
(MidAmerica Commodity Exchange)
246 222 S. Riverside Plaza
1971, SKIDMORE, OWINGS & MERRILL
2001, REMODELING, PRISCO
SERENA STURM ARCHITECTS

The complex that replaced Union Station's vaulted concourse comprises a bland tower and a low building designed to accommodate a trading-exchange floor. Enormous black aluminum trusses make the latter look like a supine version of the John Hancock Center.

Union Station

247 Union Station
210 S. Canal St.
1913–25, GRAHAM, ANDERSON,
PROBST & WHITE
1992, RENOVATION, LUCIEN
LAGRANGE & ASSOCS.

One of the last of the grand American railroad stations, Union Station was intended as the major element in West Loop development under Burnham's 1909 *Plan of Chicago*. The austere facade encloses a huge travertine-clad waiting room. The eight-story office tower above, set well back from the base and virtually invisible from the sidewalk, was meant to be twenty stories high. The double "stub end" tracks are the only ones in the United States where northbound and southbound tracks for different railroads end at the same point.

248 120 S. Riverside Plaza
1968, SKIDMORE, OWINGS & MERRILL
1986, ESPLANADE RENOVATION,
SKIDMORE, OWINGS & MERRILL

249 10 S. Riverside Plaza
1965, SKIDMORE, OWINGS & MERRILL

This pair of Miesian office buildings is carried over active rail yards by columns. "Riverside Plaza" is listed as the address of virtually all of the waterfront buildings east of Canal St., although no such street actually exists.

250 525 W. Monroe St.
1983, SKIDMORE, OWINGS & MERRILL

This pedestrian office building was overshadowed soon after construction when developers expanded the West Loop glitz zone from Franklin St. and Wacker Dr., bringing taller, more dramatic "signature" buildings.

251 Heller International Tower
500 W. Monroe St.
1992, SKIDMORE, OWINGS & MERRILL

This granite-clad skyscraper stands in contrast to the firm's glassy modernism as seen at its S. Riverside Plaza buildings. A tower marks the southeastern corner, where the structure is built to the street edge; the building steps down to the west.

252 2 N. Riverside Plaza
(Daily News Building)
1929, HOLABIRD & ROOT

For evidence of the continuing cheapening of the urban vista, just compare the grand civic enhancement of this former newspaper building with Freedom Center, the *Chicago Tribune*'s modern printing plant. The interlocking vertical masses of the office block rise from the public plaza, Chicago's first to be planned as part of an office building.

2 N. Riverside Plaza

253 Citigroup Center
500 W. Madison St.
1987, MURPHY/JAHN

Designer Helmut Jahn's sinuous curtain wall reads like a waterfall that cascades in precise sheets down the southern facade. Enter through the receding arch at the base or via the walkway from 2 N. Riverside Plaza to a dazzling multilevel space where the steel structure is articulated, exposed, and celebrated.

254 River Center
111 N. Canal St.
1913, D. H. BURNHAM & CO.
1982–2002 RENOVATION,
  BALSAMO/OLSON GROUP

255 Randolph Place
(Butler Bros. Warehouses)
165 N. Canal St.
1922, GRAHAM, ANDERSON,
  PROBST & WHITE
1992, RENOVATION, GRAHAM-
  THOMAS ARCHITECTS
1999, CONVERSION TO RESIDENTIAL,
  HARTSHORNE & PLUNKARD

Detailed like a nineteenth-century armory, complete with machicolations, the design of these warehouses was *retardataire* by 1913 but greatly admired by Andrew Rebori, who found remarkable the "very noble largeness and simplicity." The building at 111 stands in its original spot; its twin originally stood on its eastern side but was demolished and reincarnated at 165.

256 100 N. Riverside Plaza
1990, PERKINS & WILL

Located atop active train tracks, the building accommodates lower floors

100 N. Riverside Plaza

with large uninterrupted spaces for computer operations. With much smaller floor plates for offices, the tower rises from a long base, an entire corner of which is suspended over the tracks from an exposed truss on the roof.

257 Ogilvie Transportation Center
(Chicago & North Western Station Yards)
Bounded by N. Canal, W. Lake, and N. Clinton Sts. and Citigroup Center
1911, FROST & GRANGER
1996, RENOVATION AND REBUILDING,
  HARRY WEESE & ASSOCS.

The new lightweight canopy structure has only half as many columns as the original and has perforated beams that harmonize with the modern industrial vocabulary of the Citigroup Center.

258 The Powerhouse Building
(North Western Terminal Powerhouse)
211 N. Clinton St.
1911, FROST & GRANGER
2006, RENOVATION AND
  ADAPTIVE REUSE, HARTSHORNE
  PLUNKARD ARCHITECTURE

A 226-foot chimney is the exclamation point of the complex, which began four blocks to the south. The powerhouse's nine arches along Clinton St. recall the Beaux-Arts styling of the demolished station. A new interior structure within the historic shell provides three floors of office space above a ground-level restaurant.

259 Clinton St. Lofts
**226 N. Clinton St. and
541–547 W. Fulton St.**
1888–89, FREDERICK WAESCHER;
  ADLER & SULLIVAN
1997, CONVERSION TO RESIDENTIAL,
  HARTSHORNE & PLUNKARD

E. W. Blatchford, trustee of the Newberry estate, used its architect, Waescher, to design the southern building for his own business, which manufactured lead pipe and linseed oil. After a fire, Adler & Sullivan rebuilt the interiors and designed the structure to the north to replace an existing Blatchford building. Sullivan's characteristic ornament is absent from these utilitarian edifices.

260 Burlington Building
547 W. Jackson Blvd.

1911, MARSHALL & FOX

Gleaming terra-cotta celebrates steel construction in the former headquarters of the Chicago, Burlington & Quincy Railroad. The arched arcades of the base are repeated at the top.

261 550 W. Jackson Blvd.

2001, BELLUSCHI/OWP/P

One of many high-rises to spring up west of the commuter train stations, this one is unusual in that it was built atop an existing four-story building whose telephone switching station could not be disrupted. Exterior columns and inverted V-shaped trusses transfer the weight of the new floors around the old structure. The curving roof hides the mechanical system and adds interest to the profile.

262 Illinois Institute of Technology—Chicago-Kent College of Law
565 W. Adams St.

1992, HOLABIRD & ROOT

With security a paramount planning issue, public spaces such as classrooms and auditoriums were located on lower floors; more private areas such as faculty offices and the library are on higher ones. The reading room, atop the building, features a ceiling with an exposed lamella truss.

263 Glessner Center
(Warder, Bushnell & Glessner Co. Office and Warehouse)
130 S. Jefferson St.

1883, JAFFRAY & SCOTT;
WILLIAM W. BOYINGTON
1985, CONVERSION TO OFFICES,
BOOTH HANSEN ASSOCS.

Comprising a southern office and a northern warehouse, the building was completed by Boyington after a series of construction disasters. The firm made farm machinery; partner John J. Glessner commissioned Glessner House, H. H. Richardson's masterpiece.

264 Presidential Towers
555, 575, 605, and 625
W. Madison St.

1986, SOLOMON CORDWELL
BUENZ & ASSOCS.

These four enormous and mundane apartment towers are noteworthy for the neighborhood change they hastened—the eradication of several blocks of seamy, colorful, and "underdeveloped" Skid Row.

265 Harold Washington Social Security Center
600 W. Madison St.

1976, LESTER B. KNIGHT & ASSOCS.

The design of this dull office building has one saving grace—the reflective curtain wall that is a beautiful backdrop to Claes Oldenburg's strong and structural yet totally whimsical *Batcolumn*.

Batcolumn

266 540 W. Madison St.
(ABN AMRO Plaza)

2003, DESTEFANO & PARTNERS

Placement of the tower on its podium is designed to maximize views for its occupants as well as those of the planned second tower. Raised floors and multiple risers accommodate the extensive and changing technological needs of the client, a bank consolidating several Loop offices in this location.

267 R+D 659
659 W. Randolph St.

2009, BRININSTOOL & LYNCH

The concrete condo formula is elevated to a higher plane in this crisply organized and well-detailed building. Street-side balconies are inset, and those overlooking the south terrace project from the wall.

268 Old St. Patrick's Church

140 S. Desplaines St.

1852, 1856, CARTER & BAUER
1990–2000, RENOVATION,
    BOOTH HANSEN ASSOCS.

Chicago's oldest church has a simple facade of Milwaukee common brick above a Joliet limestone base. The onion dome symbolizes the church in the East, while the spire symbolizes the church in the West. The renovation created a Celtic wonderland of decoration in the building's interior. It is a masterpiece of the harnessing of computer technology to fulfill a historic decorative program. The adjacent campus for Frances Xavier Warde Schools was master-planned and designed by Eckenhoff Saunders Architects; it opened in 2004.

Old St. Patrick's Church

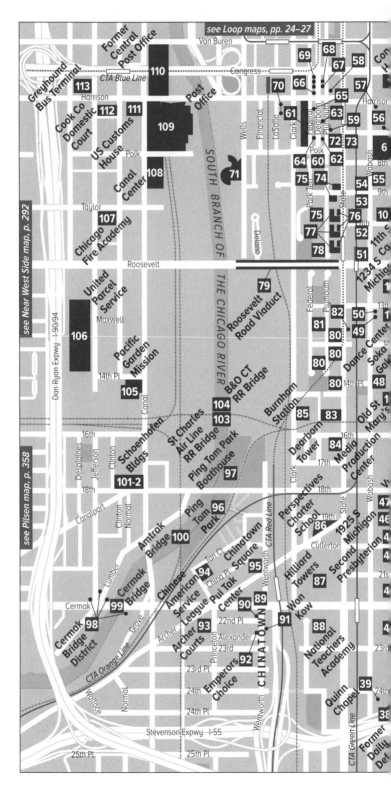

see Loop maps, pp. 24–27

Van Buren

Congress

CTA Blue Line

Former Central Post Office

110

Greyhound Bus Terminal

113

Harrison

Cook Co Domestic Court

112

111

US Customs House

109

Post Office

Polk

108

Canal Center

Taylor

107

Chicago Fire Academy

Roosevelt

United Parcel Service

Maxwell

106

Pacific Garden Mission

14th Pl

105

16th

Schoenhofen Bldgs

St Charles Air Line RR Bridge

103

104

B&O CT RR Bridge

Ping Tom Park Boathouse

97

101-2

18th

Amtrak Bridge

100

Ping Tom Park

96

Chinese American Service League Pui Tak Center

94

Chinatown Square

95

Cermak Bridge

Cermak

99

98

Cermak Bridge District

93

Archer Courts

22nd Pl

90

89

91

Princeton

Alexander

23rd

92

Emperors Choice

23rd Pl

24th

24th Pl

Stevenson Expwy I-55

25th Pl

25th Pl

SOUTH BRANCH OF

THE CHICAGO RIVER

Roosevelt Road Viaduct

79

71

Burnham Station

85

83

Dearborn Tower

84

16th

17th

Perspectives Charter School

86

Cullerton

Hilliard Towers

87

Won Kow

88

National Teachers Academy

Quinn Chapel

39

Dan Ryan Expwy I-90/94

see Near West Side map, p. 292

see Pilsen map, p. 358

Delano

Harrison

Van Buren

69

68

67

58

66

70

65

57

61

63

59

56

72

73

6

64

60

62

75

74

54

55

53

76

10

77

52

78

51

1234 S Michigan

82

50

81

80

49

80

80

80

48

Wells

Financial

LaSalle

Clark

Federal

Dearborn

Plymouth

State

Wabash

Polk

Park Terr

Federal

Plymouth

Dance Center

Soka Gak

Old St Mary's

Media Production Center

18th

19th

1925 S

Second Presbyterian

Michigan

47

46

4

4

21s

23rd

24th

CTA Red Line

CTA Orange Line

CTA Green Line

Former Daily Def

Con H

57

Harrison

8th

9th

11th

Michigan

18th

14th Pl

CHINATOWN

Wentworth

Tan Ct

China Pl

Archer

Clark

State

Wabash

V

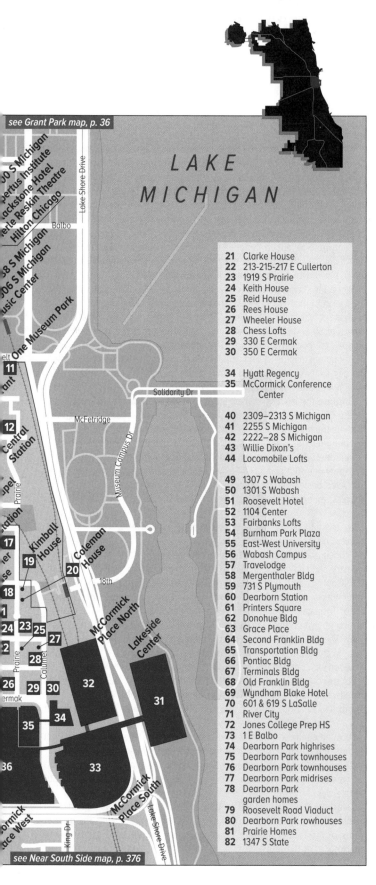

see Grant Park map, p. 36

LAKE
MICHIGAN

Lake Shore Drive

Balbo

One Museum Park

Solidarity Dr

McFetridge

Museum Campus Dr

Kimball House

Coleman House

18th

McCormick Place North

Lakeside Center

Prairie

Calumet

ermak

32

31

33

McCormick Place South

McCormick Place West

King Dr

Lake Shore Drive

21	Clarke House
22	213-215-217 E Cullerton
23	1919 S Prairie
24	Keith House
25	Reid House
26	Rees House
27	Wheeler House
28	Chess Lofts
29	330 E Cermak
30	350 E Cermak
34	Hyatt Regency
35	McCormick Conference Center
40	2309–2313 S Michigan
41	2255 S Michigan
42	2222–28 S Michigan
43	Willie Dixon's
44	Locomobile Lofts
49	1307 S Wabash
50	1301 S Wabash
51	Roosevelt Hotel
52	1104 Center
53	Fairbanks Lofts
54	Burnham Park Plaza
55	East-West University
56	Wabash Campus
57	Travelodge
58	Mergenthaler Bldg
59	731 S Plymouth
60	Dearborn Station
61	Printers Square
62	Donohue Bldg
63	Grace Place
64	Second Franklin Bldg
65	Transportation Bldg
66	Pontiac Bldg
67	Terminals Bldg
68	Old Franklin Bldg
69	Wyndham Blake Hotel
70	601 & 619 S LaSalle
71	River City
72	Jones College Prep HS
73	1 E Balbo
74	Dearborn Park highrises
75	Dearborn Park townhouses
76	Dearborn Park townhouses
77	Dearborn Park midrises
78	Dearborn Park garden homes
79	Roosevelt Road Viaduct
80	Dearborn Park rowhouses
81	Prairie Homes
82	1347 S State

see Near South Side map, p. 376

SOUTH LOOP/CHINATOWN

As one of Chicago's earliest settlements, the South Loop was among the first areas to experience the typical urban cycles of prosperity, decay, and renewal, and it now contains the city's most intensely polyglot collection of buildings and neighborhoods. Its shifting boundaries testify to the area's increasing vitality. Originally thought of as bounded by Congress and Roosevelt, east of Interstate 90/94, it is now considered to stretch all the way south to the Stevenson Expressway. It is home to the conventioneers' mecca of McCormick Place, cultural and educational institutions, and a variety of housing from rehabbed factories to new town houses to skyscrapers. And on its southwestern edge is the thriving ethnic community of Chinatown, which has grown as the rail yards have been removed.

When the City of Chicago was incorporated in 1837, its southern boundary was at Cermak Rd. (22nd St.), but the area south of the original riverfront settlement was still a wilderness. Henry B. Clarke's house stood at what is now 16th St. and Michigan Ave., in a rural setting that would remain undeveloped for more than a decade. The railroads arrived in the 1850s, spurring development of industry and working-class housing near the tracks. In 1853, the city limits were extended a mile south to 31st St., and a decade later they moved another eight blocks farther south.

Because the North and West Sides were separated from the central city by the Chicago River, the South Side was the most accessible and quickly became the neighborhood of choice for wealthy homeowners. After the 1871 fire burned virtually everything to the north and west, businesses rebuilt in or near their original locations, but displaced residents moved south. Prairie Ave. between 16th and 22nd Sts. was soon lined with mansions, and Michigan Ave., designated a boulevard in 1880, also became a very fashionable address; meanwhile, the area west of State St. filled up with workers' cottages.

By the late 1890s, the area had already peaked as a residential community and was beginning a long process of decay. The city's growth and the concentration of railroad terminals on the Loop's southern flank pushed industry and commerce (including the thriving vice business) farther south. The Illinois Central Gulf Railroad tracks stretched along the lakefront, and other tracks converged at the four depots clustered at the Loop's south edge. They carried freight as well as passengers, and printing industries sprang up just north of the Dearborn Station to take advantage of this proximity. The residential exodus accelerated after the turn of the century; by 1910, Michigan Ave. was known as Automobile Row, and the lakefront was crowded with railroad tracks, breweries, and industrial complexes.

As trucks and planes superseded trains after World War II, vast tracts of railway land became available for development, but the question of by whom and for what purpose was subject to continuing debate. Municipal government skirted the issue by drawing up master plans for every area except the central city. Concerned about the Loop's economic and cultural decline, a group of business leaders formed the Chicago Central Area Committee; in 1973, the committee proposed that the abandoned South Loop rail yards be used for mixed-use development that would include abundant middle-class housing.

Dearborn Park, developed on that land, found success as a residential neighborhood. To the north, restaurants and shops were filling the ground floors of the former printers' buildings, which began to be converted to apartments in the late 1970s. In the early 1990s, another self-contained housing development began to take shape on abandoned railway land. Central Station extended the residential popularity of Dearborn Park farther east, linking the built-up city to the newly created Museum Campus. Like Dearborn Park, Central Station was envisioned as a mixture of office, commercial, and residential uses, but only the housing proved easily marketable.

In the late 1990s, Columbia College expanded its campus southward, purchasing several historic buildings that now anchor the area around Michigan and Wabash Aves. Just a decade earlier, these streets were the missing links in the South Loop's development, but with the conversion of old business buildings to residential lofts and construction of new infill town houses and apartments, the area has been transformed into a desirable, mixed-use neighborhood. Big-box retail along Roosevelt Rd. serves the burgeoning population; Motor Row is slated for development as an entertainment district; and the once-derelict Prairie Ave. neighborhood has both important house museums and fashionable new residences.

—LAURIE MCGOVERN PETERSEN

1 Congress Plaza Hotel
(Auditorium Annex)
520 S. Michigan Ave.
1893, CLINTON J. WARREN
1902, 1907, HOLABIRD & ROCHE

Built as an extension of the Auditorium Hotel, the "Annex" was designed to harmonize with it, even though its steel frame made the arcaded windows anachronisms more appropriate to the Auditorium's load-bearing walls. The additions respected the original section, including the generous bay windows overlooking the lake, but without the arcades.

2 Columbia College
(Harvester Building)
600 S. Michigan Ave.
1907, CHRISTIAN A. ECKSTORM
2011, EXTERIOR RESTORATION, KLEIN & HOFFMAN AND GENSLER

One of the most colossal cornices remaining on a Chicago high-rise was replaced with a replica made of glass-fiber-reinforced concrete.

3 Spertus Institute for Jewish Learning and Leadership
610 S. Michigan Ave.
2007, KRUECK & SEXTON ARCHITECTS

A ten-story wall of glass, with sections folding in and out from the vertical plane like origami, stands dramatically apart from its predominantly masonry neighbors on Michigan Ave. The faceted facade is composed of 726 pieces of unusually thick and flat glass cut into 556 shapes. The facade required specially designed mullions

Spertus Institute

and had to be mocked up in Texas prior to installation. Behind the glass wall lie a variety of spaces for this distinguished institution founded by Herman and Maurice Spertus in 1924. At the client's request, the facade extends upward rather than ending with a cornice, symbolizing the unending nature of the study of Judaism.

The glass screen installed immediately to the south at **620 S. Michigan Ave.** (2012, GENSLER) robs Spertus of some of its visual punch.

4 Blackstone Hotel
636 S. Michigan Ave.
1908, MARSHALL & FOX
2008, RENOVATION, LUCIEN LAGRANGE ARCHITECTS; WISS, JANNEY, ELSTNER ASSOCS.

5 Merle Reskin Theatre
(Blackstone Theatre)
60 E. Balbo Dr.

1910, MARSHALL & FOX

The elegance of this opulently roofed palace is shared by the adjacent theater.

6 Hilton Chicago
(Stevens Hotel)
720 S. Michigan Ave.

1922–27, HOLABIRD & ROCHE

1986, RENOVATION, SOLOMON
    CORDWELL BUENZ & ASSOCS.

Built to be the world's "largest and most sumptuous" hotel and designed in a "modification of the style of Louis 16th," this twenty-five-story behemoth contained 3,000 rooms—all of them outside rooms with private baths—plus a convention hall seating 4,000, an exhibition hall "equal in dimensions to the Coliseum," and a rooftop golf course. Because the number and size of the public rooms on the lower floors required the frequent displacement of loads throughout the steel framing system, fewer than half of the 300 columns on a typical floor extended from the basement to the attic. In some cases, trusses ran through several stories and required that corridors be threaded through them.

Purchased by the U.S. War Dept. for use as a barracks in 1942, the Stevens changed hands several times until it was acquired in 1945 by Conrad Hilton, who renamed it in 1951. The renovated building has 1,600 rooms as well as parking and fitness facilities.

7 888 S. Michigan Ave.
(Crane Co. Building)
1912, HOLABIRD & ROCHE

This virtually intact classical revival version of the tripartite high-rise formula lacks the Chicago School's vertically emphasized central shaft.

8 Columbia College
(Lightner Building)
1006 S. Michigan Ave.

1904, EDMUND R. KRAUSE

This highly refined office building features large amounts of glass set in Chicago windows as well as columns and beams that have been reduced to the minimum.

9 Columbia College Music Center
1014 S. Michigan Ave.

1912, CHRISTIAN A. ECKSTORM

1998, REMODELING, SAS ARCHITECTS

The mansard roof with pedimented pairs of windows is an unusual touch on what was constructed as a speculative commercial building.

10 Columbia College— 11th St. Campus
(Chicago Women's Club Building)
72 E. 11th St.

1929, HOLABIRD & ROCHE

1985, REMODELING, MICHAEL ARENSON

The building for the city's premier women's service club included a recital room, various clubrooms, and three floors of hotel rooms. The Art Deco style was chosen to affirm the fifty-year-old club's youthful outlook.

Columbia College—11th St. Campus

11 One Museum Park and The Grant
1211 and 1201 S. Prairie Ave.

2009, 2010, PAPPAGEORGE/HAYMES

Even as the Michigan Ave. street wall was landmarked and East Randolph St. began to fill in, the invisible "south wall" of Grant Park escaped attention. But as Central Station's northward creep resulted in ever-taller structures near the Museum Campus, it became clear that the site called for better design than the bland concrete boxes proliferating throughout the central city. These curving, glassy towers are the response, and if they fall short as icons, they are a substantial step above most of their peers. Another two are planned, again proceeding east to west.

12 Central Station

S. Michigan Ave./S. Indiana Ave.
east to Lake Shore Dr., between
E. Roosevelt Rd. and E. 21st St.
BEGUN 1992

Conceived as a mixed-use project with a significant office component, the development proved most popular for residential buildings. Everything is built on land and air rights over existing railroad tracks. The former Illinois Central station stood on Roosevelt Rd. at the north end of what is now this project.

Film Row

Wabash and Michigan Aves. from
Roosevelt Rd. to W. 16th St.

For almost fifty years, exhibitors who ran Chicago's 1,100 movie theaters came here for everything they needed: feature films, cartoons, short subjects, and coming-attractions trailers; movie projectors and sound heads; lobby posters, billboards, and still photographs; numbered tickets, popcorn, and candy; seats, canopies, carpeting, lightbulbs for marquees; and even dishes to be given away as premiums. By the 1930s, more than two dozen studios and independents were operating film exchanges here, mostly near 13th St. In the 1960s, television changed the movie world, and neighborhood squalor began driving the exchanges elsewhere.

13 1234 S. Michigan Ave.

(Universal Pictures Film Exchange)
1947, ARCHITECT UNKNOWN

This former film exchange replicates the Art Deco style of the earlier exchanges on Wabash Ave.

14 Columbia College Dance Center

(Paramount Pictures Film Exchange)
1306 S. Michigan Ave.

Columbia College Dance Center

1930, ANKER S. GRAVEN
2000, ADAPTIVE REUSE,
   SAS ARCHITECTS

A calm, sedate limestone skin serves as a backdrop to Art Deco ornament highlighting flowers, with no suggestion of things cinematic.

15 Grace Episcopal Church Chapel

1448 S. Indiana Ave.
1928–31, TALLMADGE & WATSON

The chapel for the old St. Luke's Hospital (whose buildings include **1439 S. Michigan Ave.**, 1908, FROST & GRANGER; and **1440 S. Indiana Ave.**, 1925, CHARLES S. FROST) is a diminutive version of the Gothic churches that became a mainstay of this firm after the demise of the Prairie School.

16 Old St. Mary's Catholic Church

1500 S. Michigan Ave.
2002, PRISCO SERENA
   STURM ARCHITECTS

The light colors of the metallic roof and precast concrete walls were chosen for their ability to reflect light and heat. High-performance glass used throughout also reduces the amount of solar gain.

17 Metra (Metropolitan Rail) Substation

*(Commonwealth Edison
E. 16th St. Substation)*
1620 S. Prairie Ave.
1925, HERMANN V. VON HOLST

Many substations are found near the Chicago Transit Authority's elevated tracks or Metra electrified rail lines. They were built by Commonwealth Edison between about 1900 and 1930 to supply power to the traction conglomerate of Samuel Insull, who also controlled Commonwealth Edison. They are usually of brick, with details that run the gamut of styles; many exhibit Prairie School massing and were designed by von Holst. This delightful polychromatic substation has whimsical limestone trim with reliefs of a 1920s electric locomotive and other traction devices.

John J. Glessner House

18 John J. Glessner House

1800 S. Prairie Ave.

1885–87, HENRY HOBSON RICHARDSON

Glessner House is the finest urban residence designed by Henry Hobson Richardson. Richardson used a corner site to create a dwelling of extraordinary distinction, one eloquently expressing his desire for a modern American architecture. The house has two powerful facades: the primary one on Prairie Ave. calls on American colonial design, while the subsidiary one on 18th St. has an English prototype. Two striking arched doorways were derived from the Romanesque sources that Richardson favored. The seemingly symmetrical main facade includes a porte cochere leading to a walled courtyard. Norcross Bros. constructed the building with facade walls of pink-gray granite and courtyard elevations of rosy brick with limestone trim. The roof is terra-cotta.

John Jacob Glessner, the vice president of a company that manufactured farm implements, and his wife, Frances Macbeth Glessner, commissioned the house in 1885 for use primarily as a winter residence. Richardson finished the design before his death in 1886, and his successors, Charles A. Coolidge and George F. Shepley, carefully carried it to completion in 1887. The functional plan is one of Richardson's best: principal living spaces face the southern courtyard and have large windows to capture the winter sun, while a service passage to the north mitigates Chicago's chilliest winds. The house served the Glessners perfectly for the next half century. Daniel H. Burnham, one of their earliest dinner guests, observed that it was in Chicago that the great Boston architect took new departures and did his most successful work.

John J. Glessner House—interior

The settings, furniture, and decorative objects assembled within Glessner House are a cohesive grouping of items designed by architects or designers with architectural training. These include masterpieces of Modern Gothic case goods by Isaac E. Scott; a library double desk, dining room chairs, and a grand piano by Charles A. Coolidge and Francis Bacon, both designing for the A. H. Davenport firm; and wallpapers, upholstery and hanging fabrics, chairs, lamps, carpets, and ceramic tiles and vases from the British workshops of William Morris and William De Morgan, both known and admired by Richardson. Woodwork for paneling, doors, and mantels is primarily quartersawn oak. Wall colors were terra-cotta red, gold, and green, while gold leaf highlighted the dining room ceiling.

Understanding of the Glessners' uniquely close relationship with their architect, their home, and their lives is enhanced by extensive documentation, much of it used by restoration architects who have worked on the house, among them John Thorpe, Wilbert R. Hasbrouck, John Vinci, Walker Johnson, and Anne Sullivan.

Glessner House Museum is a private not-for-profit foundation, open to the public for tours.

—ELAINE HARRINGTON

19 William W. Kimball House
1801 S. Prairie Ave.
1890–92, SOLON S. BEMAN

As the Second Empire's influence faded in the 1880s, wealthy clients increasingly abandoned the eccentricities of the Queen Anne style in favor of more historically correct designs, such as those imitating the great French châteaus of the reign of Francis I (1515–47). The "châteauesque" was an ideal choice for an era of pastiche. Its prototype was a polyglot style that had applied classical motifs newly introduced from Renaissance Italy onto the irregularly massed forms of the medieval castle. Following the lead of New York architect Richard Morris Hunt on the Vanderbilt châteaus, Beman here recalled picturesque, fragmented sixteenth-century French facades with pavilions and windows of varied shapes and sizes. His immediate inspiration was the design of the sixteenth-century dormers of the Château de Josselin in Brittany, the model for the massing for the three-story bay on the main facade.

William W. Kimball House

20 Joseph G. Coleman House
(Miner T. Ames House)
1811 S. Prairie Ave.
1885, COBB & FROST

The entrance is a superb example of contrasting surfaces. Huge sandstone blocks form roundheaded arches atop squat, clustered, smooth columns with Romanesque capitals, while in the second story a window-filled bay of smooth stone stands out against the rusticated walls. Buildings in the rear courtyard now connect it to the Kimball House.

21 Henry B. Clarke House
1827 S. Indiana Ave.
1836, ARCHITECT UNKNOWN
1981, RESTORATION, JOSEPH W. CASSERLY, CHICAGO CITY ARCH.;
  WILBERT R. HASBROUCK, RESTORATION ARCH.
2004, RESTORATION, MCCLIER CORP.

Chicago's only visibly Greek Revival building is the oldest surviving structure within the original city limits. Built at 1631 S. Michigan Ave., it was moved

Henry B. Clarke House

twice, returning in 1977 to this, its original neighborhood. Its colonnaded grandeur still projects an aura of the civilizing influence that pioneers attempted to bring to frontier Chicago. The ancient forms of pedimented porticoes, Doric columns, and pilasters (although Roman, not Greek), and the "entablature" were considered most appropriate for a growing democracy. Greek Revival buildings were invariably white, regular, and symmetrical, with a central-hall plan. The Greek Revival style reigned from 1820 to 1860, and rebellion against its ordered predictability stimulated the development of picturesque and irregular revival styles. The Italianate belvedere added ca. 1855 is a reflection of this push-back. Clarke House Museum is owned by the City of Chicago and is open to the public for tours. It is furnished to the 1853–60 period by the National Society of the Colonial Dames of America in the State of Illinois.

To the north of the house is ***Helping Hands***, sculpted by Louise Bourgeois in 1993 to commemorate the work of Jane Addams. In 2011, it was relocated to the **Chicago Women's Park**, which was designed in 2000 by landscape architect Mimi McKay and architect Tannys Langdon.

---

22 213, 215, and 217 E. Cullerton St.

213
1891, THOMAS & RAPP
215
LATE 1860S, ARCHITECTS UNKNOWN
217
1892, THOMAS & RAPP

The houses at 213 and 217, built for Dr. Charles W. Purdy and John M. Clark, respectively, replaced houses that would have matched the surviving Italianate at 215. No. 217 was occupied by George Pullman's daughter, Florence, following her 1896 marriage to future Illinois governor Frank Lowden.

23 1919 S. Prairie Ave.
(Marshall Field Jr. House; originally William H. Murray House)
1884, SOLON S. BEMAN
1902, D. H. BURNHAM & CO.
2007, CONVERSION TO CONDOMINIUMS,
   SCHOCH ASSOCS.

Beman's original Queen Anne house was significantly enlarged and remodeled by Burnham's firm for Marshall Field Jr., who died under mysterious circumstances just three years later. Carved faces in the stone capitals over the squat columns of the recessed porch may represent members of the Field family.

24 Elbridge G. Keith House
1900 S. Prairie Ave.
1870, JONATHAN W. ROBERTS
CA. 1880, MANSARD ADDITIONS,
   ARCHITECT UNKNOWN

This is the quintessential "marble front" of the 1870s, a brick house whose main facade is faced with Joliet limestone, then known as Athens marble. This type almost universally has a single projecting bay running the full three-story height. The stable at the rear of the property may hint at the house's original roofline.

25 William H. Reid III House

2013 S. Prairie Ave.

1894, BEERS, CLAY & DUTTON

This house has a central, first-floor skylit room in an open plan made possible by the building's steel frame, the first documented use of this building technology in a Chicago residence. The third-floor Palladian window marks the location of the ballroom.

26 Harriet F. Rees House

2110 S. Prairie Ave.

1888, COBB & FROST

The twenty-five-foot Richardsonian facade formula is polished and emboldened by the team that introduced it to Chicago. The smooth facade features an elegantly controlled use of ornamentation.

27 Calvin T. Wheeler House

(Joseph A. Kohn House)

2020 S. Calumet Ave.

1870, O. L. WHEELOCK

Style sleuths will delight in Second Empire details and the mansard roof. The incised hood moldings around the windows are typical of the Italianate style; the matching incised pilasters are unusual. The two-story copper oriel window was added later, probably in the 1880s.

28 Chess Lofts

(Columbian Colortype Co.)

320 E. 21st St.

1920, ALFRED S. ALSCHULER
2007, CONVERSION TO
    RESIDENTIAL, K2N CREST

A pivotal building in the career of a prolific factory designer features innovations that became standard.

Entrance, docks, stairwells, and all services were pushed to the west wall to minimize interference with clear floor spaces and natural lighting. Economical flat-slab concrete construction reduced vibration. The concrete columns were exposed on the main elevations so that—when used in combination with terra-cotta detailing at the base, entry, and cornice—the effect of a totally brick–and–terra-cotta facade was achieved without its expense.

29 330 E. Cermak Rd.

(American Book Co.)

1912, N. MAX DUNNING

This company shared with the other South Side presses the notion that books deserved to be made and stored more artistically than other goods. This red-brick–and–terra-cotta warehouse features excellent surface-shadow effects accomplished by slight vertical and strong horizontal projections. Rooftop tanks and sprinkler equipment assume the usual tower disguise.

30 350 E. Cermak Rd.

(R. R. Donnelley & Sons
Co. Calumet Plant)

1912–24, HOWARD VAN DOREN SHAW
1929, WEST-CENTRAL AND SOUTH
    SECTIONS (INCLUDING TOWER),
    CHARLES Z. KLAUDER
2000, ADAPTIVE REUSE, PDA ASSOCS.

The Donnelleys had commissioned Shaw to design their Lakeside Press Building on S. Plymouth Ct., and they returned to him for a master plan and design for a new printing facility, to be built in stages over two decades. Shaw

350 E. Cermak Rd.

took the opportunity to create one of the city's—perhaps the nation's—finest essays in Industrial Gothic. Buttress-like piers separate large vertical bands of windows capped by limestone arches. Stone medallions and terra-cotta plaques depict stylized marks and devices of early printers such as Johannes Gutenberg, William Caxton, and John Baskerville. At the main entry are six seals, three with the initials of the architect and owners, and carved relief panels of a Prairie Indian and a frontiersman. The taller tower, designed after Shaw's death by collegiate Gothicist Klauder, contained a two-story Gothic library.

31 Lakeside Center at McCormick Place
2301 S. Lake Shore Dr.
1971, C. F. MURPHY ASSOCS.

This structural tour de force, which brutally interrupts the sweep of the lakefront, is one of Chicago's biggest planning gaffes. As early as 1954, the South Side Planning Board had proposed an exposition hall, to be designed by Mies van der Rohe, for a site on the south side of Cermak Rd. between King Dr. and Michigan Ave. The Metropolitan Fair and Exposition Authority, established in 1955 by the state, instead accepted the city's offer of a Burnham Park site east of the 23rd St. viaduct. Howls of protest, ignored by City Hall, greeted this proposal, which violated the dreams of city visionaries from A. Montgomery Ward to Daniel H. Burnham to keep the lakefront "forever open, clear and free." When the first McCormick Place (1960) burned in 1967, civic

groups mounted a campaign to relocate it, but the economic pressures of getting the lucrative convention hall back in operation as quickly as possible dictated that the foundations on this site be reused.

Designer Gene R. Summers, who had worked for Mies from 1950 to 1966, brought to life an airy, powerful hall. The statistics are staggering. The 1,360-foot roof, which cantilevers so gracefully 75 feet beyond supporting columns, covers nineteen acres and weighs 10,000 tons. Yet the 300,000-square-foot main exhibit space contains only eight columns. The cross-shaped columns of reinforced concrete poured into steel shells form a superstructure of 150 150-foot bays of unencumbered space and carry the roof 50 feet above the floor level. It's an impressive engineering feat and a keystone of the city's convention business— but neither built to nor intended for human scale.

32 McCormick Place North
450 E. 23rd St.
1986, SKIDMORE, OWINGS & MERRILL

The diamond patterning symbolizes the hidden truss system and is a faint echo of Mies's convention hall project of the 1950s. As in the Lakeside Building, the roof is the dramatic focal point, using a fifteen-foot-deep truss system, supported by seventy-two four-inch, 450-strand cables hung from twelve concrete pylons. The system is designed to withstand abrupt changes in temperature, high winds, and broken cables. The pylons contain conduits for air-conditioning and heating, making ceiling vents unnecessary. The fixed

McCormick Place North

vertical pipes on the long sides are designed to help stabilize the roof when it moves (normally up or down an inch or so) in certain kinds of weather.

33 McCormick Place South

2301 S. King Dr.

1996, THOMPSON, VENTULETT,
STAINBACK & ASSOCS., DESIGN
ARCH.; A. EPSTEIN & SONS
INTERNATIONAL, ARCH. OF RECORD

The most graceful of all the buildings in this complex, it engages well with the outdoors both at the entrance and on the east side. Because it is not meant solely for trade shows but for meetings as well, windows are plentiful.

34 Hyatt Regency McCormick Place

2233 S. King Dr.

1998, MC3D

2013, RENOVATION AND ADDITION,
CBG HOTEL DESIGN-BUILDERS

The Hyatt is better composed than its predecessor hotel, and its extended roof strengthens its identity from the Loop.

The western elevation of the MPEA energy building at **2201 King Dr.** incorporates the facade of Howard Van Doren Shaw's 1907 Platt Building.

35 McCormick Place Parking, Office, and Conference Center

301 E. Cermak Rd.

1996, MC3D

The parking and office structure now blends in with the West Building.

36 McCormick Place West

2300 S. King Dr.

2007, MC4WEST (A. EPSTEIN & SONS
INTERNATIONAL, ARCH. OF RECORD;
TVS, CONCEPTUAL DESIGN)

The superlatives continue with this latest addition to the world's largest convention center, but now it is not just about size but also sustainability: at time of completion, it was the country's largest LEED–New Construction building and had the city's largest green roof. A massive tunnel, 12 feet in diameter and 3,500 feet long, collects the roof's rainwater and sends it directly into the lake, keeping it out of the sewer system.

37 Motor Row

S. Michigan Ave.; originally
Roosevelt Rd. to 29th St.

In the 1880s, the fashionable residential area of S. Michigan Ave. acquired a "magnificent stretch" of asphalt pavement "as level as a billiard table." After 1900, car dealers were eyeing the wide, deep (180 feet) lots for showrooms, and by 1910, they had created what *Architectural Record* called "the longest and best automobile course in any city of this country," with at least forty new buildings selling or servicing cars.

The earliest showroom buildings were only slightly more elaborate than factories, typically three stories high and on corner lots and almost invariably three bays wide. Spans of up to thirty feet permitted windows low and wide enough to show an entire car. Construction methods varied from semi-mill to steel and reinforced-concrete framing. Interior finishes were kept close to utilitarian even in the salesrooms, which had easily maintained red terrazzo floors and inexpensive wood wainscotings. Exteriors were initially brick with terra-cotta trim and logos.

In the 1920s, designers began addressing the problem of how to effectively display indoors an item meant to be seen outdoors. Interiors, often with offices tucked away on mezzanines, were made to look like exteriors, with walls of stucco or stone. Mediterranean and California Spanish styling were deemed highly suitable.

Since the 1960s, most Motor Row buildings have been converted to other uses, many of them associated with activities at McCormick Place. The pace of restoration and adaptive reuse accelerated in the early twenty-first century, as the local population began to grow and the city began encouraging development of an entertainment district here.

38 Former *Chicago Daily Defender* Building

(Illinois Automobile Club)

2400 S. Michigan Ave.

1936, PHILIP B. MAHER

Built on the site of Adler & Sullivan's Standard Club (1887) and

Former Chicago Daily Defender *Building*

using the abandoned foundations of a predecessor organization's planned clubhouse, this two-story brick building with its lantern-topped clock tower employs a simplified Spanish Mission styling. Many of the social aspects of automobile clubs vanished after World War II, when cars became more readily available to the average person. This building housed one of the nation's leading African American newspapers from 1960 to 2005.

39 Quinn Chapel
(African Methodist Episcopal)
2401 S. Wabash Ave.
1891–94, EXTERIOR, HENRY F. STARBUCK; INTERIOR, CHARLES H. MCAFEE

Named for William P. Quinn, bishop of the Midwest diocese of the African Methodist Episcopal Church in the 1840s, the chapel houses the city's oldest black congregation. Brick walls are faced with gray stone; the Victorian Gothic facade is distinguished by the north tower, with its belfry and tourelle. The church proper is a second-floor amphitheater with seating arranged in a fan pattern and a balcony wrapping around three sides. The William H. Delle pipe organ was purchased from the German Pavilion at the Columbian Exposition.

40 2309–2313 S. Michigan Ave.
(Automobile Buildings for Alfred Cowles)
1915, HOLABIRD & ROCHE

Two small automotive buildings reveal lively uses of terra-cotta in the jagged blind arcade of the northern

building and in the three-dimensional geometric patterning entirely covering the southern one. Holabird & Roche also designed the building at **2347 S. Michigan Ave.** for the Fiat Co. in 1910, when the Italian firm established its American division.

41 2255 S. Michigan Ave.
(Thomas Flyer Garage & Service Building)
1910, HOLABIRD & ROCHE
1916, ADDITION, ALFRED S. ALSCHULER

Although two stories have been added, the base still reveals its origins as a classic auto-sales facility; varieties of brickwork and multicolored terra-cotta panels articulate the structural system.

2222–2228 S. Michigan Ave.

42 2222–2228 S. Michigan Ave.
(Hudson Motor Co. of Illinois)
1922, ALFRED S. ALSCHULER

H (for Hudson) medallions sit above the Palladian window in the central bay. Exuberant terra-cotta imitates stone in twisted columns and rope moldings.

43 Willie Dixon's Blues Heaven
(Chess Records; originally McNaull Tire Co.)
2120 S. Michigan Ave.
1911, HORATIO R. WILSON
1957, REMODELING, JOHN S. TOWNSEND JR. AND JACK S. WEINER

This is Chicago's only building to inspire a Rolling Stones song, an instrumental that was named for the building's address as a tribute to Chess Records and that was recorded here in 1964. From 1957 to 1967, the company's headquarters were in this building, which—like its neighbors—began life "in the motor trade."

44 Locomobile Lofts
(Locomobile Showroom)
2000 S. Michigan Ave.
1909, JENNEY, MUNDIE & JENSEN

Here is a quintessential early auto facility: a three-story corner building made of reinforced concrete and trimmed in brick and terra-cotta.

45 Second Presbyterian Church
1936 S. Michigan Ave.
1874, JAMES RENWICK
1884, BELL TOWER, JOHN ADDISON
1900, REBUILDING, HOWARD VAN DOREN SHAW

Renwick, architect of the Smithsonian Institution in Washington, D.C., and St. Patrick's Cathedral in New York City, designed Chicago's first Gothic Revival church for this congregation in 1849. It was destroyed in the 1871 fire. This replacement was built of a local limestone featuring bituminous mottling; it is trimmed with sandstone. The interior is imbued with the Arts and Crafts influences introduced by Shaw after a devastating fire in 1900. A

Second Presbyterian Church

series of thirteen Pre-Raphaelite murals by Frederic Clay Bartlett, elaborate plaster decoration, dark oak furniture and paneling, original brass lighting fixtures, and a palette of muted red, blue, green, and gold form a backdrop for an unrivaled collection of stained-glass windows, including nine examples embracing every phase of Louis C. Tiffany's career. Two windows in the narthex were designed by the British Pre-Raphaelite painter Edward Burne-Jones and executed by the William Morris studio.

46 1925 S. Michigan Ave.
(B. F. Goodrich Co. Building)
1911, CHRISTIAN A. ECKSTORM

The elaborate facade of this structure, sheathed in white terra-cotta beneath a copper-clad mansard roof, would have made this showroom for automobile-related rubber products a worthy neighbor to the exclusive Calumet Club, which abutted the building on the south.

47 Vue 20
1845 S. Michigan Ave.
2003, BRININSTOOL & LYNCH

The five-story base, containing the requisite multilevel parking garage above retail, is enlivened with a palette of clear, perforated, translucent, and opaque materials. Floor-to-ceiling glass on the east and west elevations exposes the building's structure, which is of post-tension concrete that allows for column-free residences and a minimal number of caissons. Balconies are concentrated on the north and south shear walls, maintaining the clean lines of the principal facade on Michigan Ave. Slightly later condominium buildings designed by the firm are at **1620 and 1720 S. Michigan Ave.**

48 Soka Gakkai International USA Chicago Culture Center
1455 S. Wabash Ave.
1995, HARDING PARTNERS

The Midwest headquarters for Soka Gakkai, Japan's largest religious organization, includes a Buddhist temple. A 150-seat chapel is located in the base of the masonry cylinder, with an office and conference room above. A Japanese garden atop the second floor is visible from the lobby, which is centered on the axis of 14th Pl.

49 1307 S. Wabash Ave.
(Warner Bros. Film Exchange)
1929, ZIMMERMAN, SAXE & ZIMMERMAN
Integral zigzag brickwork rather than applied ornament lends interest to this Art Deco exchange.

50 1301 S. Wabash Ave.
(Universal Studios Film Exchange)
1937, OLSEN & URBAIN
This yellow-brick structure features an intact, curving glass-block corner.

51 Roosevelt Hotel
1152 S. Wabash Ave.
1892, JULES DE HORVATH
2003, REHABILITATION FOR APARTMENTS, PAPPAGEORGE/HAYMES
The abandoned and severely deteriorated hotel gained new life as moderate-income apartments. The gently undulating bays of the facade are reminiscent of some of Holabird & Roche's work of the 1880s.

52 Columbia College 1104 Center
(Ludington Building)
1104 S. Wabash Ave.
1891, JENNEY & MUNDIE
2002, RESTORATION AND ADAPTIVE REUSE, SAS ARCHITECTS
This unusually well preserved high-rise is one of the first all-steel structures, built at the same time as the Second Leiter Building (now Robert Morris Center), which has a steel-

and-wrought-iron frame. In both, the exterior exactly reflects the form of the skeleton frame, and the demand for light is well satisfied.

53 Fairbanks Lofts
(Fairbanks, Morse & Co. Building)
900 S. Wabash Ave.
1907, CHRISTIAN A. ECKSTORM
This completely intact loft building has showrooms that are outlined in ornamental cast-iron trim and separated from the rest of the facade by a molded limestone sill.

54 Burnham Park Plaza
(YMCA Hotel)
828 S. Wabash Ave.
1916, ROBERT C. BERLIN; JAMES GAMBLE ROGERS, CONSULTING ARCH.
1988, CONVERSION, SCHROEDER MURCHIE LAYA
The hotel provided simple and wholesome quarters at moderate cost. The small rooms, placed around light wells, were completely gutted in the conversion to apartments. A penthouse and roof deck and a new building containing

Burnham Park Plaza

Columbia College 1104 Center

theaters, commercial space, and a garage were constructed.

55 East-West University
The Loftrium
(Munn Building)
819 S. Wabash Ave.
1909, CHRISTIAN A. ECKSTORM
Student Life Center
825 S. Wabash Ave.
2013, HOLABIRD & ROOT

The Loftrium's cast-iron storefront is framed by handsome Sullivanesque ornament. Above, the brick-sheathed frame is fully expressed, and wide windows light the interior. The Student Life Center has a large atrium on the lower floors and living accommodations above.

56 Columbia College— Wabash Campus
(Second Studebaker Building)
623 S. Wabash Ave.
1896, SOLON S. BEMAN

Look past the added story (1941) and lower-floor alterations to the strikingly modern structural expression and Gothic detailing.

57 Travelodge
65 E. Harrison St.
1930, ALFRED S. ALSCHULER

High-style Art Deco embellishments include voluptuous figures and stylized foliage.

Printing House District
The Dearborn St. Station was a source for paper and supplies and an easy route for outgoing publications, making Dearborn St. south from Jackson Blvd. a convenient center for the printing trades from the 1880s through the 1950s. Plymouth Ct. and Federal St. provided back doors for Dearborn St. buildings and were direct routes to the depot's loading docks. The widening of Congress St., called for in the 1909 *Plan of Chicago*, was finally accomplished (1945–55) to create an expressway link. Construction destroyed twelve buildings on Dearborn St. and many others on adjacent streets, effectively separating everything south of Congress St. from the Loop. Rejuvenation began in the late 1970s, spurred by the development of the former rail yards as Dearborn Park.

58 Mergenthaler Lofts
(Mergenthaler Linotype Building)
531 S. Plymouth Ct.
1886, ARCHITECT UNKNOWN
1917, RENOVATION, RICHARD E.
  SCHMIDT, GARDEN & MARTIN
1980, REHABILITATION, KENNETH
  A. SCHROEDER & ASSOCS.

This early example of a loft building converted to stylish apartments is also one of the best. The new work included the introduction of windows in colorful framing on the south wall and the incorporation of the shell of Tom's Grill, a former adjacent eatery, as a sculptural objet trouvé (now demolished).

Mergenthaler Lofts

59 731 S. Plymouth Ct.

(Lakeside Press Building)
1897, 1902 (FOUR NORTH BAYS),
  HOWARD VAN DOREN SHAW;
  SAMUEL A. TREAT, ASSOC. ARCH.
1986, RENOVATION, LISEC & BIEDERMAN

This exceptionally creative amalgam
of traditional and nontraditional
architectural detailing was Shaw's
first nonresidential commission. It
established his and owner R. R. Donnelley & Sons Co.'s reputations as
creators of printing plants that are a
joy to behold.

60 Dearborn Station

*(Polk St. Station; also known
as Dearborn St. Station)*
47 W. Polk St.
1885, CYRUS L. W. EIDLITZ
1923, RECONSTRUCTION AFTER
  FIRE, ARCHITECT UNKNOWN
1985, CONVERSION, KAPLAN/
  MCLAUGHLIN/DIAZ AND
  HASBROUCK HUNDERMAN

Chicago's oldest train station is a
U-shaped Romanesque building
whose Italian brick tower closes
the Dearborn St. vista. The tower
is a replacement of a Flemish one,
destroyed in a 1922 fire that also
took the building's hipped roofs.
The reworked station, comprising a
cleaned-up but historic north facade
and a modern galleria to the south,
acts as a transition between the
renovated printing district and the
Dearborn Park development.

61 Printers Square

(Borland Manufacturing Buildings)
700, 740, and 780 S. Federal St.
1909, 1912, AND 1928, FROST &
  GRANGER AND SUCCESSOR FIRMS
1983, CONVERSION TO
  APARTMENTS, LOUIS WEISS

This series of simply detailed loft
buildings was constructed in sections from the designs of one architect. It now has 356 apartments and
underground parking.

62 Donohue Building & Annex

711 and 727 S. Dearborn St.
1883, JULIUS SPEYER
1913, ALFRED S. ALSCHULER

This was the first major printers'
structure in the district. The main
portion exhibits the basic masonry
construction system with punched
window openings, one window per
opening. It utilizes both Romanesque
rustication and incised designs, and
its slightly enhanced round-arched
sandstone and granite entrance bay
was originally topped with a tower.
The simple and functional annex
harmonizes with the original.

63 Grace Place

637 S. Dearborn St.
1915, ARCHITECT UNKNOWN
1985, RENOVATION, BOOTH
  HANSEN ASSOCS.

The second floor of this renovated
printers' building contains a worship
space encircled by an internal wall
with pointed-arch windows. A skylight
floods the altar with natural light.

Dearborn Station

Second Franklin Building

Pontiac Building

64 Second Franklin Building
720 S. Dearborn St.

1912, GEORGE C. NIMMONS
1987, CONVERSION TO APARTMENTS,
    LISEC & BIEDERMAN

Using the modified Prairie School style that characterized his factory and warehouse work, Nimmons incorporated colorful tile work designed by Oskar Gross depicting the history of printing. The sloped roofline, a frequent feature on factories of this era, permitted a very high top floor under an enormous skylight—helpful for hand binding.

65 Transportation Building
600 S. Dearborn St.

1911, WILLIAM STRIPPELMAN
1980, REHABILITATION, BOOTH
    HANSEN ASSOCS.

Twenty bays wide but only four bays deep, this structure was designed to be built in sections and to have its great breadth broken regularly by vertical bands of roughened brickwork. The contrast is not enough to do the job. The rehabilitation of this building was crucial to the area's rejuvenation.

66 Pontiac Building
542 S. Dearborn St.

1891, HOLABIRD & ROCHE
1985, RENOVATION, BOOTH
    HANSEN ASSOCS.

An air of substance and repose emerges from this earliest extant Holabird & Roche skyscraper. The heavy corner piers rise from base to cornice, interrupted only by the shelf angles supporting each floor of brick sheathing; the windows are small and double-hung. The gently projecting oriels that span two bays are unique in the firm's work.

67 Terminals Building
(Ellsworth Building)
537 S. Dearborn St.

1892, JOHN M. VAN OSDEL & CO.
1986, RENOVATION, COMMUNITY
    RESOURCES CORP.

A heavily rusticated rock-faced limestone base is balanced by the crisp modeling of the brick into vertical elements above.

68 Old Franklin Building
525 S. Dearborn St.

1887, BAUMANN & LOTZ

This printers' building demonstrates how, in an effort to provide light for detail work, architects began to group windows by using iron spandrels between brick piers and supporting them with cast-iron mullions. The lobby shows the beamed ceilings found in the loft apartments.

69 Wyndham Blake Chicago
(Hyatt on Printers Row;
originally Morton Hotel)
500 S. Dearborn St.

1987, RENOVATION AND ADDITION,
    BOOTH HANSEN ASSOCS.

Duplicator Building
530 S. Dearborn St.

1886, EDWARD P. BAUMANN

Morton Building
538 S. Dearborn St.

1896, JENNEY & MUNDIE

This hotel combined new construction with two old buildings. The Duplicator

River City

is a traditional loft structure; the Morton shows how classical elements, in the form of atlantes supporting the projecting bay, were supplanting the vigorous expression of skeleton construction that had characterized Jenney & Mundie's earlier commercial work.

70 601 and 619 S. La Salle St.
(Brock & Rankin Building)
1901–2, NORTH PORTION; 1903, TWO-
    STORY ADDITION; 1909, SOUTH
    ADDITION; HOLABIRD & ROCHE

What looks like two attached buildings is one loft built during two phases of Holabird & Roche's work. The northern part has colored tiles set on angle; the southern part relies on brickwork, especially the "zippered" window surrounds.

71 River City
800 S. Wells St.
1986, BERTRAND GOLDBERG ASSOCS.
2003, CONVERSION TO CONDOMINIUMS,
    ROULA ASSOCS. ARCHITECTS

The curves for which Goldberg's buildings are famous result here in a complex form, a four-story base for a pair of S-shaped apartment buildings supported on concrete piers with penthouse towers above the rooflines. River Rd., the combination corridor and atrium, has an array of monumental and undulating shapes softly lit from above.

72 William Jones College Preparatory High School
700 S. State St.
1965–68, PERKINS & WILL
2013, PERKINS & WILL

A skyscraper to house a secretarial and office training school was first suggested for this site in 1909 by Dwight H. Perkins. The successor building to the 1960s reinforced-concrete tower continues Perkins & Will's tradition of innovative educational design.

73 1 E. Balbo Ave.
(East 7th St. Hotel)
1930, MICHAELSEN & ROGNSTAD

Behind the fire escapes is an Art Deco building with an intact entry floor and window surrounds of terra-cotta.

Dearborn Park I
State to Clark Sts., Polk St. to Roosevelt Rd.
1974–77, MASTER PLAN, SKIDMORE, OWINGS & MERRILL
1979–87, VARIOUS ARCHITECTS

Enter the Dearborn Park I community at 9th and State Sts. (the only vehicular access point) to tour the self-contained streets of Plymouth Ct. and S. Park Terr./Federal St.

Dearborn Park grew out of SOM's comprehensive blueprint for the central city, drafted in 1973 for the Chicago Central Area Committee and exploiting the abandoned rail yards immediately south of downtown.

The site was split into two parcels, with the twenty acres north of Roosevelt Rd. to be developed first. The original scheme of high-density superblocks was scaled down to a mixture of town houses, mid-rises, and high-rises—a "suburb in the city"—with parks and heavily landscaped open space but no offices or entertainment complexes. Internal roads end in cul-de-sacs. In 1977, the design was parceled out to several architecture firms, with the first occupancies in 1979. Phase I was substantially complete by 1985, with just over 1,200 units, about half of them in mid-rise buildings.

Design guidelines specified white brick for the two-story town houses and red brick for all other buildings. Such cohesiveness as there may be relies on the abundant landscaping rather than a shared aesthetic. The tallest buildings, sited on the street perimeter, are centered on the landscaped spaces surrounding the town house clusters. The two **74 | High-Rises** (EZRA GORDON–JACK M. LEVIN & ASSOCS.) flank the 9th St. access road but fail to provide a significant gateway, serving only to create an inward-focused enclave. The **75 | Two-Story Town Houses** (HAMMOND, BEEBY & BABKA) cluster around parking areas and are oriented toward private gardens that overlook shared green spaces. Recessed corner entrances and exterior corner columns are the main design elements. The **76 | Three-Story Town Houses** in turn enclose the courtyards formed by the **77 | Mid-Rise Buildings** (BOOTH HANSEN ASSOCS.). The **78 | Garden Homes of Dearborn Park** (MICHAEL J. REALMUTO), developed last, were intended as luxury housing, presaging the low-density, upmarket development of Phase II.

---

79 Roosevelt Rd. Viaduct
Roosevelt Rd. from the
Chicago River to State St.
1995, DLK ARCHITECTURE

The sculptural program included in the rebuilding of this elevated roadway recalls nearby bridges built in the twentieth century. The iconography of the sculptures emphasizes the link between the University of Illinois at Chicago to the west and the Museum Campus to the east. The repetitive use of three sizes of obelisks along the 1,500-foot bridge weakens the potential power of that form, but the positive civic message is clear.

Dearborn Park II
State to Clark Sts., Roosevelt
Rd. to W. 15th St.
1988–97

Phase II proceeded very differently from its predecessor. There is more parking, and buildings are no more than four stories high, with an abundance of luxury housing. The parcel lacks even minimal cohesiveness, with the variety of building types and architects making for something of a hodgepodge.

80 Row Houses, Metropolitan Mews, and Park Homes
1300 and 1400 blocks of S. State St.
1989–92, BOOTH HANSEN ASSOCS.

The properties east of Plymouth Ct. are organized formally in long rows around central green spaces, while the freestanding Park Homes are far more suburban and seem out of place.

81 Prairie Homes
1300 to 1356 S. Plymouth Ct.,
1301 to 1357 S. Federal St.
1992, FITZGERALD ASSOCS. ARCHITECTS

Prairie School elements such as brackets under hipped roofs and horizontal divisions of the facades make these the liveliest buildings, but the crowded siting and essentially vertical massing detract.

82 1347 S. State St.
*(Arthur Dixon Transfer
Co. Truck Garage)*
1921, HOLABIRD & ROCHE

Making an admirable virtue of spareness, this handsome, flat brick facade adorned only with stepped detailing conceals a single wood-framed space lit from rooftop monitor windows.

83 Dearborn Tower
1530 S. State St.
2001, ADDITION AND CONVERSION TO
RESIDENTIAL, PAPPAGEORGE/HAYMES

This cold-storage warehouse was converted to residential use by placing a recessed window wall behind the exposed concrete frame on the north side. The south facade has long balconies that provide shade from the summer sun. The seven-story addition is articulated with a smaller, lighter grid. A clock tower marks the building entry and unifies old and new construction.

84 Columbia College Media Production Center
1600 S. State St.

2010, STUDIO GANG ARCHITECTS

Cinematic history is referenced both literally, with a terra-cotta arch salvaged from a film warehouse, and figuratively, with spatial layering inspired by moviemaking techniques. A multiple frame-within-frame shot is created by looking through the glass walls of a classroom to a transparent corridor and out to the street. The exterior and the lobby, where a wide stairway provides a popular perch, feature the vibrant colors of television test patterns. The rest of the interior is blank-canvas monochromatic but is filled with light from skylights and clerestories. The concrete structure

Columbia College Media Production Center

absorbs noise from the nearby El trains and the studios themselves.

85 Burnham Station
61 W. 15th St.

1997, TIGERMAN MCCURRY ARCHITECTS

Architect Stanley Tigerman describes the concrete and glass mid-rise as his "Mies-building-as-a-wedding-cake."

86 Perspectives Charter School Rodney D. Joslin Campus
1930 S. Archer Ave.

2004, PERKINS & WILL

This streamlined school addresses its difficult triangular site with a point as crisp as a newly sharpened pencil. In the core of the triangle is shared two-story space that functions as a town square for the school community. It receives light from a clerestory formed by the roof's upward slope to the west. Long bands of windows illuminate classrooms at two different heights. The library at the eastern end can be opened outside school hours for student and community use. The school's corrugated metal skin is a budget-conscious salute to the area's industrial heritage and the nearby El trains.

87 Chicago Housing Authority— Hilliard Towers Apartments
2030 S. State St.

1966, BERTRAND GOLDBERG & ASSOCS.
2003–6, REHABILITATION,
LISEC & BIEDERMAN

The revolutionary design theories that Goldberg developed for Marina City were applied here to the problem of public housing, creating what is still regarded as one of the city's best examples of humane high-rise living

Perspectives Charter School Rodney D. Joslin Campus

Hilliard Towers Apartments

for low-income families. In a parklike setting, a pair of twenty-two-story curving slabs accommodates families, and two sixteen-story cylindrical towers are devoted to seniors. The curved walls and windows express the character of poured concrete while providing structural stability; curved windows also distribute stress in the building's skin. The floor plan of the round towers, with wedge-shaped apartments ringing the elevator core, minimizes corridor distances for the elderly occupants. The complex's national landmark status and continued appeal to tenants inspired an exterior restoration paired with a gut rehab of the interiors to give it another half century of life.

In 2012, Ross Barney Architects designed the new **CTA—Cermak–McCormick Place Station** *for the Green Line at Cermak Rd.*

88 National Teachers Academy—Professional Development School
55 W. Cermak Rd.
2002, DESTEFANO & PARTNERS

This unusual four-story building houses a functioning elementary school (preschool through grade 8) that also serves as a showcase center for professional teacher training. An adjacent community center connected by a pedestrian bridge contains a natatorium, gymnasium, and day care center.

89 Chinatown
In 1912, a large group of Chinese residents and business owners were displaced from the South Loop by new construction. The On Leong

tong (benevolent association) was responsible for the establishment of this Chinatown, arranging for group members fifty leases in the 22nd St. and Wentworth Ave. area, a neighborhood of modest stores and flats. Wentworth Ave. south of 22nd St. is lined with typical nineteenth-century buildings remodeled to look more Chinese. Many of the buildings constructed after 1912 are inspired by traditional Chinese architecture, in which the wall is not load-bearing. Instead, columns ascend toward the roof to support elaborately cantilevered brackets below wide eaves that extend far beyond the building's envelope. The wall is treated as a screen, and attention is focused on the brackets, which are often highly painted. The wall of the top floor is often recessed behind the columns to create a loggia.

90 Pui Tak Center
(On Leong Chinese Merchants' Association Building)
2216 S. Wentworth Ave.
1928, MICHAELSEN & ROGNSTAD

After relocating from downtown, the On Leong tong carried on its activities—a hostel for immigrants, a Chinese-language school, and business, job-placement, and dating services—in various nearby locations. For its new building, the tong turned to Michaelsen & Rognstad, who had done restaurant remodelings for a prominent member. Although unfamiliar with Chinese architecture, they were willing students. Rognstad was responsible for the sculptural program, executed in terra-cotta, a very good substitute for the *liu li*

Pui Tak Center

glazed ceramic of traditional Chinese architecture. Polychrome terra-cotta flowers, vases, and moths cover the walls. Lions guard the doorway, their heads twisted so they face us but do not turn their backs on each other, which would be bad luck.

91 Won Kow Restaurant
2233 S. Wentworth Ave.
1928, MICHAELSEN & ROGNSTAD
The top two stories have recessed balconies supported by brick piers. Decorative roundels display herons and parrots; again, stylized lions guard the doorway. The building's central portion is flanked by square towers that symbolize the pagoda form but are flat-topped, with enameled urns at the corners.

92 Emperor's Choice Restaurant
2238 S. Wentworth Ave.
1928, MICHAELSEN & ROGNSTAD
1932, TWO-STORY ADDITION,
MICHAELSEN & ROGNSTAD
Graceful terra-cotta herons fold sinuously around the door frame, while dragons encircle a pair of columns. More Chinese details appear at the top, which has a traditional Chinese profile.

93 Archer Courts
2220 S. Princeton Ave.
2000, RENOVATION AND COMMUNITY
CENTER, LANDON BONE ARCHITECTS
This is the city's most dramatic renovation of a dismal public housing project into an attractive complex. The simple gesture of placing a curtain wall over the long, exposed corridors was enhanced by dividing the glass into panels, some clear and some frosted, and by painting the entry doors in bright hues that

make the wall a tapestry of color, especially at night. A new community building provides a simple but light-filled gathering space for residents, all of whom are former Chicago Housing Authority tenants who now use Section 8 vouchers to pay rent to the private owner. Asian design motifs are integrated into features such as the fence and gateway. To complete the transformation of the property into a mixed-income community, the western portion of the site has town houses (2003, LANDON BONE BAKER ARCHITECTS), of which the majority are market rate.

94 Chinese American Service League Kam L. Liu Building
2141 S. Tan Court
2004, STUDIO GANG/O'DONNELL
Evoking the scales of a dragon, a mythological beast revered in Chinese culture, Kam Liu's glittering titanium skin snaps this shoebox-shaped building to life. A lattice sunscreen on the west helps shade the double-height community room. Amid the mostly brick and less-than-inspired buildings in Chinatown Square, Kam Lui is a silvery fire-breather.

95 Chinatown Square
Archer Ave., Cermak Rd., Chicago River, 18th St., and Wentworth Ave.
1992–94, HARRY WEESE & ASSOCS.
Hemmed in for years by highways and railroad tracks, Chinatown was finally unleashed when the Santa Fe Railroad abandoned its yards north of Archer Ave. The first buildings to rise on the thirty-acre site were brick retail strips, followed by a variety of housing.

96 Ping Tom Memorial Park
S. Branch of the Chicago River, East Side, at 18th St.
1999, SITE DESIGN GROUP
(ALSO MCCLIER, LAND
DESIGN COLLABORATIVE, E.
C. PURDY & ASSOCS.)
Old rail yards along the river's edge have been transformed into a park that celebrates the neighborhood's Chinese heritage. Gingko trees and a bamboo grove on a terraced site evoke a Chinese landscape. A courtyard entry and columns with dragon details are other traditional Chinese elements.

97 Ping Tom Memorial Park Boathouse

2013, JOHNSON & LEE

In 2002, additional land was purchased to expand the park north of 18th St. A field house, adapted from a Booth Hansen prototype, was added in 2013. The boathouse is one of four announced in 2011 to provide increased recreational opportunities on the river. It offers a canopied shelter adjacent to restrooms and vending facilities, storage for kayaks and canoes behind red metal ornamental screens, and a boat launch off a floating dock that is ADA accessible.

98 Cermak Rd. Bridge Historic District

465 W. Cermak Rd., W. M. Hoyt Co. Building

1909, NIMMONS & FELLOWS

500 W. Cermak Rd., Thomson & Taylor Spice Co. Building

1911, CHATTEN & HAMMOND

2141 S. Jefferson St., Western Shade Cloth Co. Building

1924, LOCKWOOD GREENE & CO.

600 W. Cermak Rd. and 2130–2146 S. Jefferson St., Wendnagel & Co. Warehouse

1901, 1906, ARCHITECT UNKNOWN

99 Cermak Rd. Bridge

Cermak Rd. and the Chicago River

1906, SCHERZER ROLLING LIFT BRIDGE CO.

The ensemble of industrial buildings and bridge, listed on the National Register of Historic Places in 2012, offers a rare reminder of the time when the city's businesses relied on the river and rails to ship raw materials and finished goods. Three of the four buildings have chamfered corners to accommodate their irregular sites. The Hoyt building features one of Nimmons & Fellows's liveliest facades, with pronounced vertical piers that rise to Prairie Style "capitals." With the facilities no longer suitable for manufacturing, the city hopes to encourage development of a Cermak Creative Industries District here.

Designed by William Scherzer, the rolling lift bridge was the first of the two bascule types to replace the cumbersome nineteenth-century center-pier swing bridges. The bridge was patented in 1893; the Chicago-based Scherzer Co. designed bridges constructed around the world. The Scherzer bridge works like a rocking chair, utilizing overhead counterweights to balance its truss double leaves, which roll into place on large steel girder rockers at their bases. The counterweights slide into the slots between roadway and sidewalk, as the teeth on the rounded tracks engage holes in the rockers. Despite its global success, the Scherzer type was soon surpassed locally by the trunnion bascule bridge. The Cermak Rd. Bridge is the last Scherzer-type owned and operated by the city.

100 Amtrak Bridge

(Pennsylvania Lines—South Branch Chicago River Bridge)
S. Branch of the Chicago River, East of Canal St. at 2000 South

1915, WADDELL & HARRINGTON; FABRICATED BY THE PENNSYLVANIA STEEL CO.

With a pair of 195-foot towers, it's the kinetic cathedral of this rail yard area, carrying southbound freight and passenger traffic out of the city. Engineers J. A. L. Waddell and J. L. Harrington of Kansas City were the masters of the vertical lift bridge, designing two dozen between 1907 and 1914. Because of its dominating profile, this type was never popular downtown; remaining examples are in industrial areas. The entire center span lifts straight up and is balanced by heavy counterweights, visible

Amtrak Bridge

here on the sides of the towers. A vertical-lift configuration was chosen for this site because it was more economical than a bascule for this long span. Because the tracks cross the river at an angle, the towers are trapezoidal to hug the shoreline and make the movable span no longer or heavier than necessary. The span is a 1,500-ton riveted steel Pratt through truss, which is 272 feet long and lifts to a height of 130 feet over the river. The original tenders' cabin on the upper chord of the lift span now houses only the electric drive motors that operate the span. Attendants in a control tower five blocks away at 14th and Lumber Sts. operate the span via television monitors.

101 Peter Schoenhofen Brewing Co. Administration Building
Northwest Corner W. 18th
St. at S. Normal Ave.
1886, ADOLPH A. CUDELL

102 Powerhouse-Warehouse
1770 S. Canalport Ave.
1902, RICHARD E. SCHMIDT
1992, RENOVATION, NORMAN
   KOGLIN & ASSOCS.

Beer making was a thriving industry in Chicago, with more than fifty breweries in operation by 1890; the proximity of rail lines and the river made this a logical spot for industry. These surviving buildings sum up the startling leap made by Chicago architects between the mid-1880s and 1900. The fussy Administration Building has Renaissance and Baroque detailing,

with an elaborate cornice, terra-cotta keystones, and medallions sporting sheaves of grain. In contrast, the Powerhouse is a spare, strong statement in brick that fully exploits the expressive potential of masonry. On the west facade, the building's dual functions are clearly visible in the organization of the wall. The north half of this rectilinear trapezoid housed the boiler rooms; the Canalport Ave. side was the hops warehouse. Shooting through the roof is the tower, which hid the water tanks and surmounted the stairs and elevator. Although longer than it is tall, the Canalport Ave. facade appears proudly vertical, with full-height brick panels on the ends and recessed windows divided by thin brick piers. The powerful Bedford limestone arch, with voussoirs up to seven feet long, is gracefully beribboned with the company name, sheltering what was surely the city's most graphically blessed loading dock.

103 St. Charles Air Line Railroad Bridge
S. Branch of the Chicago
River at 1500 South
1919, ILLINOIS CENTRAL RAILROAD,
   A. S. BALDWIN, CHIEF ENG.;
   1931, RELOCATION

104 Baltimore & Ohio Chicago Terminal Railroad Bridge
S. Branch of the Chicago
River at 1500 South
1930, B & O RAILROAD AND
   STRAUSS BASCULE BRIDGE CO.

After 1900, the obstructive center-

Schoenhofen Brewing Co.—Powerhouse-Warehouse

pier swing bridge was replaced by the trunnion bascule type, whose leaves swing up like one end of a seesaw. The "seam" in the middle of a double-leaf bridge is a potential pivot point as a heavy train begins to cross; movable railway bridges are usually single spans, which also require only one set of machinery.

On these single-leaf Strauss trunnion bascules, the trunnions are very high and balanced by concrete counterweights that slip in underneath. The St. Charles Air Line Bridge was originally 260 feet, the longest of its type in the world, and weighed 3,500 tons. When it was built, the straightening of the south branch of the river was already anticipated. The bridge was designed to pivot to its new position but instead was dismantled, shortened (to 200 feet), and rebuilt in 1931. The Baltimore & Ohio Bridge led to a large train yard on the east side of the river and to Grand Central Station at Wells and Harrison Sts., demolished in 1971.

105 Pacific Garden Mission
1458 S. Canal St.
2007, TIGERMAN MCCURRY ARCHITECTS
The unassuming concrete-and-brick structure reflects its industrial context, low budget, and challenging program. The shelter provides beds, meals, and services for 1,000 men, women, and children and transmits a weekly radio show from the auditorium. The lone touch of whimsy is indoors, where a colorful corridor is dubbed the Yellow Brick Road. Residents grow food in greenhouses and on the roof.

106 United Parcel Service—Distribution Center
1400 S. Jefferson St.
1965, EDWARD D. DART
By the mid-1960s, highly automated package handling had helped the trucking industry supersede the archaic operations of the Chicago tunnel system. This center uses two conveyor assemblies to sort parcels and has a midfloor control center that employs a carousel with giant pigeonholes. Separate loading docks and marshaling areas, each with its own traffic control station, are sheltered under second-floor office space and steel sheds.

107 Chicago Fire Academy
558 W. DeKoven St.
1960, LOEBL, SCHLOSSMAN & BENNETT
Firefighters are trained on the site of the Patrick O'Leary barn, where a cow allegedly kicked over a lantern, setting off the 1871 holocaust. The tall building is the drill hall, where trainees learn to operate snorkels, maneuver on fire escapes, and open windows. The red-glazed brick is a backdrop for the flame-shaped sculpture by Egon Weiner.

108 Canal Center
(Northern Trust Co. Operations Center)
801 S. Canal St.
1990, ECKENHOFF SAUNDERS ARCHITECTS
The length of the precast concrete facade is mitigated by a recessed glass-walled entrance on Canal St. and by the terraces of a cafeteria and a day care center on the eastern side.

109 U.S. Post Office—Cardiss Collins Center
433 W. Harrison St.
1996, KNIGHT ARCHITECTS ENGINEERS PLANNERS
Constructed just south of the outdated Central Post Office, the building spans thirteen commuter rail lines with 10-foot-deep, 100-foot-long steel I beams and encloses an elevated roadway that is nearly a mile long.

110 Former Central Post Office
433 W. Van Buren St.
1921, 1932, GRAHAM, ANDERSON, PROBST & WHITE
This building was designed to straddle the broad Congress St. projected in the 1909 *Plan* but not realized until decades after the building's completion. When it opened, this was the world's largest post office. With four large corner towers, the rectangular mass is further subdivided into base, shaft, and top; the verticality of uninterrupted piers and narrow windows somewhat mitigates the length. The Van Buren St. lobby is clad in cream marble with French glass and tile reliefs. Multistory postal operations require the heavy use of elevators and are regarded as inefficient, so a new post office to the south was

Former Central Post Office

completed in 1996. The building's mammoth size has stymied a series of redevelopment schemes.

111 U.S. Customs House
610 S. Canal St.
1932, JAMES A. WETMORE, ACTING SUPERVISING ARCH.; BURNHAM BROS. AND NIMMONS, CARR & WRIGHT, ASSOC. ARCHS.

Eagles hover in the parapets of this sleekly massed, pristine government facility.

112 Cook County Domestic Court
555 W. Harrison St.
2005, BOOTH HANSEN

The key move in creating a welcoming courthouse from a nondescript commercial structure was placing a new entry facade on the north side, sixteen feet in front of what had been the back of the building. The terra-cotta–and–aluminum rain screen wall has large windows and a south-facing clerestory that fill the new atrium with light.

113 Greyhound Bus Terminal
630 W. Harrison St.
1991, NAGLE, HARTRAY & ASSOCS.

Drivers zooming past on the Eisenhower Expressway get an elevated view of this elegant essay in architectural engineering (structural design by COHEN-BARRETO-MARCHERTAS). The striking roof is suspended by steel supporting stays connected to ten slim vertical masts whose upward sweep creates a taut, graceful contrast.

Greyhound Bus Terminal

NORTH AND NORTHWEST

NORTH MICHIGAN AVENUE/ STREETERVILLE

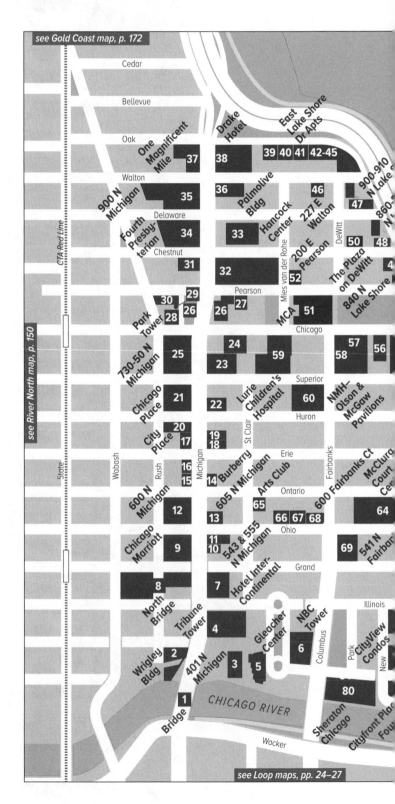

see Gold Coast map, p. 172

Cedar

Bellevue

Oak

Drake Hotel

East Lake Shore Dr Apts

One Magnificent Mile

37

38

39 40 41 42-45

900-910 N Lake S

Walton

900 N Michigan

35

36

Palmolive Bldg

46

47

860- N

Fourth Presby-terian

Delaware

34

Hancock Center

227 E Walton

DeWitt

50

48

Chestnut

31

33

200 E Pearson

The Plaza on DeWitt

4

32

52

840 N Lake Shore

Park Tower

30 29
28 26

27

26

Mies van der Rohe

MCA

51

Pearson

Chicago

730-50 N Michigan

25

24

23

59

57 56

58

Chicago Place

21

22

Lurie Children's Hospital

Superior

60

NMH–Olson & McGaw Pavilions

City Place

20
17

19
18

Huron

St Clair

Michigan

16
15

14

Burberry

605 N Michigan

Arts Club

Erie

Fairbanks

600 Fairbanks Ct

McClurg Court Cen

Wabash

Rush

600 N Michigan

12

13

Ontario

65

64

Chicago Marriott

9

11
10

543 & 555 N Michigan

66 67 68

Ohio

69

541 N Fairba

8

7

Hotel Inter-Continental

Grand

Illinois

North Bridge

Tribune Tower

4

Gleacher Center

NBC Tower

6

Columbus

Park

CityView Condos

New

Wrigley Bldg

2

401 N Michigan

3

5

1

80

Bridge

CHICAGO RIVER

Sheraton Chicago

Cityfront Pla
Fou

Wacker

see Loop maps, pp. 24–27

CTA Red Line

see River North map, p. 150

State

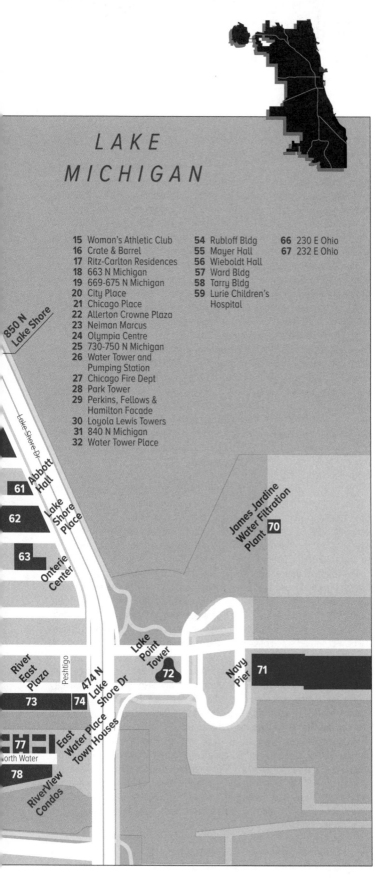

LAKE
MICHIGAN

15 Woman's Athletic Club
16 Crate & Barrel
17 Ritz-Carlton Residences
18 663 N Michigan
19 669-675 N Michigan
20 City Place
21 Chicago Place
22 Allerton Crowne Plaza
23 Neiman Marcus
24 Olympia Centre
25 730-750 N Michigan
26 Water Tower and
   Pumping Station
27 Chicago Fire Dept
28 Park Tower
29 Perkins, Fellows &
   Hamilton Facade
30 Loyola Lewis Towers
31 840 N Michigan
32 Water Tower Place

54 Rubloff Bldg
55 Mayer Hall
56 Wieboldt Hall
57 Ward Bldg
58 Tarry Bldg
59 Lurie Children's
   Hospital

66 230 E Ohio
67 232 E Ohio

850 N
Lake Shore

Lake-Shore-Dr

Abbott
Hall

61

Lake
Shore
Place

62

63

Onterie
Center

James Jardine
Water Filtration
Plant 70

River
East
Plaza

Peshtigo

Lake
Point
Tower

474 N
Lake
Shore Dr

72

Navy
Pier

71

73

74

East
Water Place
Town Houses

77

orth Water

78

RiverView
Condos

NORTH MICHIGAN AVENUE/ STREETERVILLE

In a city notable for dramatic transformations, the story of North Michigan Avenue/Streeterville deserves a special place. It is amazing to contrast a picture of today's densely built-up neighborhood with an aerial photograph taken in 1926. Then, apart from a handful of scattered buildings, the roughly square-mile area was a gigantic vacant lot awaiting development. More remarkably, forty years earlier, there had been little land there at all. Lake Michigan then covered virtually all of Streeterville, from the east side of N. Michigan Ave. (then Pine St.) reaching from Chicago Ave. north to Oak St. The scruffy land south of Chicago Ave. was mostly uninhabited sand dunes.

Now one of Chicago's most valuable real estate parcels, the area was created almost by accident. A breakwater, constructed to the north of the mouth of the Chicago River in the early 1830s, was extended eastward during the following decades, creating sand dunes along the shoreline to the north. By the 1880s, there was a considerable accumulation up to about Chicago Ave.

In July 1886, George Wellington "Cap" Streeter arrived on the scene. A show and circus promoter and surely one of Chicago's most memorable mavericks, Streeter ran aground with his rickety ship on a sandbar near today's John Hancock Center. As the weeks went by and the water failed to rise and free his ship, the wily captain built a crude causeway to the land and encouraged the builders developing the nearby Gold Coast residential area to dump their excavated materials around his ship. Since the land thus created stood outside the official boundaries of the State of Illinois as depicted in the 1821 shoreline survey, he declared it a free "federal district" answerable only to the national government—and set himself up as its governor. He was soon selling off the land to gullible investors.

The rapid development of the Near North Side increased the size of the "District of Lake Michigan," and Chicago's initial indifference to Streeter's claim turned to indignation. Repeated attempts to evict him met with no success until 1918, when the enormous clout arrayed against him proved overwhelming, and his claim was rejected by the courts. He was finally evicted for selling whiskey on Sundays.

The southern part of Streeterville, along with Ogden Slip and the Chicago River, burgeoned in the 1890s with warehouses and dock facilities. After 1900, additional factories, lofts, and offices appeared to the north and west; the Pugh warehouses (now River East Plaza) date from this period. The other area of early development lay to the north, when the elegant Gold Coast residential district spread south of Oak St., beginning with the construction of 999 N. Lake Shore Dr. in 1911–12.

Between these industrial and residential areas lay an extensive tract of land that remained largely undeveloped until 1920, when Northwestern University purchased a large parcel along E. Chicago Ave. as a campus for its professional schools. The university soon expanded to the west and south, primarily to accommodate a large hospital complex.

Michigan Ave. experienced as rapid and dramatic a transformation as Streeterville itself. A new and Europeanized "grand" boulevard for Pine St., proposed in the 1909 *Plan of Chicago*, became a reality with the opening of the monumental Michigan Ave. Bridge in 1920. The great building boom of the Soaring Twenties left its distinctive mark on the new avenue in the modestly scaled, limestone-clad neoclassical and Art Deco buildings that made this street unique in Chicago.

Although comparative "skyscrapers" anchored its northern and southern ends, Michigan Ave. retained its human scale until the 1969 erection of the 100-story John Hancock Center. This behemoth amply demonstrated the truth of the real estate adage that giants attract giants, for five more towers only slightly less titanic now cluster around it. What astute real estate developer Arthur Rubloff dubbed the Magnificent Mile in 1947 has become, alas, the Manhattanized Mile.

The Gold Coast has gradually expanded southward east of Michigan Ave. to Pearson St. Postwar development has generally followed the pattern set by Mies van der Rohe's pathbreaking steel-and-glass towers at 860–880 N. Lake Shore Dr.

That old visionary scoundrel Cap Streeter must be saying, "I told you so." Only a stone's throw from where he ran aground a century ago, twenty million people come every year to shop, dine, see, and be seen at this shopping mall mecca of the Middle West.

—WILLIAM B. HINCHLIFF

1 Michigan Ave. Bridge, McCormick Bridgehouse, and Chicago River Museum
Chicago River at N. Michigan Ave.
1920, EDWARD H. BENNETT; THOMAS G. PIHLFELDT, CITY BRIDGE ENG.; HUGH YOUNG, ENG. OF BRIDGE DESIGN
2006, RENOVATION FOR MUSEUM, MCBRIDE KELLEY BAURER

Chicago has more movable bridges than any other city in the world, and most, like this one, are trunnion bascules. Ideal for this visible and busy location, it spans the river gracefully and economically, with no protruding superstructure, while leaving a wide, navigable channel. Construction of this bridge was a top priority in the

Michigan Ave. Bridge

1909 *Plan of Chicago*, and it led the way to the rapid redevelopment of real estate on N. Michigan Ave. The exemplar for its design was Paris's Alexander III Bridge (1900), with four corner pylons, ornamental abutments, a graceful flat arch profile, and integrated embankments. The forty-foot pylons are functional operator houses. Each is embellished with sculptural reliefs depicting events in Chicago's history: *Defense* and *Regeneration* by Henry Hering grace the south pylons, while the north pylons feature *The Discoverers* and *The Pioneers* by James Earle Fraser. The southwest structure now houses a museum run by Friends of the Chicago River. Open seasonally, it offers the opportunity to see the gears that turn to open and close the bridge.

2 William Wrigley Jr. Building

400 and 410 N. Michigan Ave.
1919–24, GRAHAM, ANDERSON,
PROBST & WHITE
2013, RENOVATION, GOETTSCH PARTNERS

William Wrigley Jr. Building

London has Big Ben, Paris has the Eiffel Tower, and Chicago has the Wrigley Building. With its towering form, its lively white cladding, and its incomparable setting on the Chicago River, the Wrigley symbolizes the city in the hearts of its citizens. Because of the bend in Michigan Ave. at the river, the building is also the glittering climax of the Magnificent Mile's southern end. From the east and west its impact is doubled by its watery reflection.

But the Wrigley is not just a popular emblem: it embodies the essentials of the history of Chicago architecture up to the 1920s as transformed into a new synthesis by gifted young architect Charles G. Beersman of Graham, Anderson, Probst & White, one of the city's most prolific firms. Beersman gave the building a tripartite division, borrowing from the European tradition, as Chicago commercial architects had done since the rebuilding after the 1871 fire. The dazzling effects of the 1893 White City inspired the sparkling terra-cotta cladding, and Beersman further specified six shades of tiles, ranging from creamy white at the bottom to blue-white at the top, so that the brightness increases as the building rises. At night, banks of floodlights mounted on adjacent buildings illuminate the building in ever-increasing intensity upward. At noon or at midnight, it stands out in a brilliant blaze against the sky.

The Wrigley Building is actually two structures conceived consecutively, but the parts stand side by side almost like fraternal twins. The taller, southern building with its tower seems stately; the shorter, northern building, constructed later, seems monumental. The seeming subservience of the "annex" is all the more noteworthy given the area of its site: 21,000 square feet, compared to 11,000 of the "original." The pleasantly proportioned offices have large windows and handsome moldings, but there are no great public rooms. The tower soars to 398 feet, where an observation room in the round, templed Lysicrates cupola once allowed visitors to view the city from its highest peak.

Ernest R. Graham and Beersman, the architects, and William Wrigley Jr., their client, were keenly aware of the soaring verticality in the Manhattan skyline. They must have admired Cass Gilbert's Woolworth Building (1913), but it was more likely McKim, Mead & White's Municipal Building (1913), with its combination of classicism and a tower, that inspired the Chicagoans. They hoped their new building would have the dignity of the traditional architecture of Daniel H. Burnham's day and the great heights of the modern age, the best of both worlds, a synthesis of aspiring monumentality.

—SALLY A. KITT CHAPPELL

3 401 N. Michigan Ave.
(Equitable Building)
1965, SKIDMORE, OWINGS & MERRILL

401 N. Michigan Ave.

The height and setback were dictated by the Tribune Co. when it sold the land, to ensure the prominence of its own building. The Tribune also mandated the development of an intervening plaza, christened Pioneer Court. In 1992, it received a welcome face-lift designed by Cooper, Robertson & Partners to harmonize with the pedestrian spaces of Cityfront Center to the east. In a gracious urbanistic gesture that was twenty years ahead of its time (although it had been recommended in Burnham's 1909 *Plan*), the plaza continues down to the riverfront via a curving staircase. The building itself is a strong Miesian statement, with an articulated facade that emphasizes the underlying steel frame.

4 Tribune Tower
435 N. Michigan Ave.
1923–25, HOWELLS & HOOD
Addition, 441–445 N. Michigan Ave.
1934, JOHN MEAD HOWELLS;
   HOOD & FOUILHOUX AND LEO J.
   WEISSENBORN, ASSOC. ARCHS.
1997, GROUND FLOOR RENOVATION,
   VINCI/HAMP ARCHITECTS

Tribune Tower

In 1922, in honor of the paper's seventy-fifth anniversary, the *Chicago Tribune* announced an international competition for the design of "the most beautiful office building in the world." Hyperbole notwithstanding, the competition was a major event: the 264 entries constituted a compendium of skyscraper design and sparked considerable debate about the proper form of the modern office building.

Approximately 90 percent of the entries relied on the historical precedents that had dominated American architecture at the beginning of the decade: Beaux-Arts ideals inspired nearly 40 percent of them, and another 20 percent employed the neo-Gothic style popularized by Cass Gilbert's Woolworth Building (1913) in New York, then the tallest and one of the best-known American office buildings. Other entries reflected an emerging modernism: Walter Gropius submitted an exercise in the International Style, and Eliel Saarinen's second-prize entry, with its abstract and insistent verticality and graduated setbacks, pointed toward the skyscrapers of the late 1920s.

First prize went to the studied Gothic design of New York architects John Mead Howells & Raymond M. Hood. Rising thirty-six stories (460 feet), its structural steel frame is sheathed in Indiana limestone elaborately carved

Tribune Tower—Eliel Saarinen's design

at the base and top in Gothic forms. At its base, the structure covers a rectangle that extends 100 feet along Michigan Ave. and 326 feet eastward to adjoin the newspaper's former printing plant (1920, JARVIS HUNT). At the twenty-first floor the easternmost portion ends, and the tower becomes square in plan. Above the twenty-fourth floor, the building steps back and rises as an octagonal tower. Two prominent piers from each of the four sides continue in the form of flying buttresses above the setback, creating a spidery crowning silhouette that recalls the thirteenth-century Butter Tower of the Rouen Cathedral.

The three-story arched entryway contains a richly detailed stone screen depicting characters from Aesop's fables. The howling dog and Robin Hood figures at the midpoint of the arch's curve are visual allusions to the architects' names. Embedded in the exterior walls are stones from well-known structures throughout the world. Some were gifts to Colonel Robert R. McCormick, the *Tribune*'s publisher; others were secured at his request by the paper's foreign correspondents.

The Tribune Tower, together with the Wrigley Building to the west and the 333 and 360 N. Michigan Ave. buildings across the Chicago River, frames the monumental Michigan Ave. Bridge (1920), a major gateway to the North Side. Each of these office towers represents a facet of 1920s architecture documented by the contest entries; as a group, they define one of Chicago's most dramatic spaces.

—ROY FORREY

5 University of Chicago Graduate School of Business, Gleacher Center

450 N. Cityfront Plaza Dr.

1994, LOHAN ASSOCS.

The windowless west side, where the classrooms are, has been criticized for its empty look at a vivid neighborhood. But it is a deliberate device to help the students focus. The public spaces make the most of the location, with windows facing east and south to the Chicago River.

6 NBC Tower at Cityfront Center

454 N. Columbus Dr.

1989, SKIDMORE, OWINGS & MERRILL

This popular skyscraper borrows from New York's Rockefeller Center in its streamlined verticality and from the Tribune Tower in its upper-floor buttresses. Good proportions and the high level of finish in the lobby and entries show what extra care and a little extra money can do. The west lobby has a special treat: a 1989 painting by Roger Brown, *City of the Big Shoulders*.

NBC Tower at Cityfront Center

Hotel Inter-Continental Chicago

7 Hotel Inter-Continental Chicago
(Medinah Athletic Club)
505 N. Michigan Ave.
1929, WALTER W. AHLSCHLAGER
1989, RESTORATION, HARRY
  WEESE & ASSOCS.

The decorative program and the idiosyncratic gold-leafed dome hint at the feast of illusion and artifice within. Neo-Egyptian low reliefs designed by George Unger are carved into three sides of the facade, depicting masons on the south, builders on the north, and architects presenting a model of the building to the pharaoh on the west. The interior spaces are modest in scale but grandiose in spirit, infused throughout with a romantic historicism. The indoor swimming pool rivals that at Hearst Castle in San Simeon, California.

8 The Shops at North Bridge
(McGraw-Hill Building)
520 N. Michigan Ave.
1929, THIELBAR & FUGARD
2000, ANTHONY BELLUSCHI
  ARCHITECTS; FARR ASSOCS.,
  PRESERVATION CONSULTANTS

Chicago's largest "facadectomy" was performed here in response to public outrage at the proposed destruction of the McGraw-Hill Building. More than 6,000 pieces of the limestone skin were removed, cleaned, and re-hung on a new steel frame structure. The Art Deco panels were designed by Eugene and Gwen Lux. Four panels that were not reattached are on display in the atrium. The glassy four-story shopping arcade that spans both Grand and Rush Sts. and slices through the lower floors of the building is designed to provide Michigan Ave. frontage for a new Nordstrom

McGraw-Hill Building (now The Shops at North Bridge)

store one block west—the market driver of the whole development. The new building clad with the old limestone skin houses a hotel on its upper floors.

9 Chicago Marriott Downtown
540 N. Michigan Ave.
1978, HARRY WEESE & ASSOCS.
1998, FACADE REPLACEMENT,
DESTEFANO AND PARTNERS

The original "faceless, graceless clunk" is now a shiny, dressy box on a still-clunky hotel.

10 543–545 N. Michigan Ave.
(Jacques Building)
1929, PHILIP B. MAHER

Maher had studied in France in 1925–26, and his supremely elegant buildings lent credibility to the appellation *Boul Mich*. Easily overlooked among its larger, more strident neighbors, this narrow retail building combines classical proportions and a mansard roof with the flattened ornamentation of Art Deco. The female figures in panels above the doors recall the building's origins as a luxury dress shop.

543–545 N. Michigan Ave.

11 555 N. Michigan Ave.
1999, TIGERMAN MCCURRY ARCHITECTS

Compatible in scale to its older neighbors, this limestone-clad retail building combines the open modern grid with subtle references to classical and Gothic details.

12 600 N. Michigan Ave.
1996, BEYER, BLINDER, BELLE

To preservationists' dismay, the entire block, including a building housing

Mies van der Rohe's Arts Club interior, was razed to make room for yet another retail box on Michigan Ave. Adding insult to injury, materials such as terra-cotta and dark granite were employed to supposedly recall traditional storefronts, a poor replacement for the two 1920s facades that gave the boulevard its original character.

13 605 N. Michigan Ave.
(Lake Shore Trust Building)
1922, MARSHALL & FOX
1982, RENOVATION AND
ADDITION, PERKINS & WILL
1996, RENOVATION, LUCIEN
LAGRANGE & ASSOCS.

The original windows were replaced with large, undivided panes of glass, drastically altering the bank's character and making the wall vanish between the colossal engaged Corinthian columns. The monumental, freestanding bank modeled on a temple, though common in many cities, is relatively rare in Chicago.

14 Burberry
633 N. Michigan Ave.
2012, CALLISON BARTELUCE

Burberry's previous store on the site was quietly discreet. This shiny black-glass box amps up the volume to attract attention amid the growing cacophony of signature retail buildings on North Michigan Ave.

15 Woman's Athletic Club
626 N. Michigan Ave.
1928, PHILIP B. MAHER

This unusually well preserved reminder of the avenue's gentility has a sober elegance typical of

Woman's Athletic Club

Crate & Barrel

Maher's French-influenced work. Tall windows at the second and seventh floors indicate the location of the important public spaces.

16 Crate & Barrel
646 N. Michigan Ave.
1990, SOLOMON CORDWELL
    BUENZ & ASSOCS.

Wearing summer whites to a black-tie affair, Crate & Barrel's flagship store issues a brazen challenge to the architectural conventions of Michigan Ave. Unlike its masonry-clad neighbors, the building is bright, shiny, and shamelessly transparent; a glass-enclosed, crisp corner cylinder nestles slightly inward from the outer walls. The smooth, white skin and continuous bands of windows pay homage to Le Corbusier, while the continuation of the specially finished sidewalk through to the building's interior flooring is a favorite Miesian device. Nothing constructed on the avenue since the Hancock Center has made such a strong modernist statement.

17 Ritz-Carlton Residences
118 E. Erie St.
2012, LUCIEN LAGRANGE ARCHITECTS

Rather than providing a modern counterpoint, the concrete tower overwhelms and competes unsuccessfully with the preserved facade of the elegant Farwell Building (1927, PHILIP B. MAHER).

18 663 N. Michigan Ave.
1966, HOLABIRD & ROOT
19 669–675 N. Michigan Ave.
(Blackstone Shops, later expanded for Saks Fifth Avenue)
1925, PHILIP B. MAHER

1966, RENOVATION, HOLABIRD & ROOT

The verticality of the earliest two buildings was re-created surprisingly well in all of the subsequent work.

20 City Place
676 N. Michigan Ave.
1990, LOEBL, SCHLOSSMAN & HACKL

One of the trio of mixed-use behemoths that invaded Michigan Ave. in the late 1980s, this building presents its slimmest profile to the avenue but commands attention from the side, with its garish pink-red palette and potpourri of window patterns. In an inversion of the typical formula, the hotel is located on the middle floors, giving offices the best views.

City Place

21 Chicago Place
700 N. Michigan Ave.
1990, RETAIL BASE, SKIDMORE,
    OWINGS & MERRILL; CONDOMINIUM
    TOWER, SOLOMON CORDWELL
    BUENZ & ASSOCS.

The exterior of the base is meant to recall the great emporiums of State St.—Marshall Field & Co. (classical columns) and Carson Pirie Scott (curved corners)—but the result is ersatz. In a formula firmly established by Water Tower Place, the skyscraper tower is set well back from the mid-rise base. The mall never succeeded in creating a viable retail environment.

22 Allerton-Crowne Plaza
(Allerton House)
140 E. Huron St.
1924, MURGATROYD & OGDEN;
  FUGARD & KNAPP, ASSOC. ARCHS.
1999, RENOVATION, ECKENHOFF
  SAUNDERS ARCHITECTS

Built as part of a New York City–based chain of residential "club hotels" for single men and women, the Allerton has a northern Italian Renaissance style that proved popular as a model for other hotels and

Allerton-Crowne Plaza

apartments. The throne-like massing reflects Chicago's 1923 zoning ordinance, which required setbacks on large buildings that covered their entire lot. The 1999 rehabilitation revealed a good look at another age. The renovation architects convinced the new owners of the hotel to emphasize its historic character. The limestone base and the arched windows on the twenty-third-floor towers were restored. And although the former bar is now a ballroom, the Tip Top Tap sign shines again.

23 Neiman Marcus
737 N. Michigan Ave.
1983, SKIDMORE, OWINGS & MERRILL

24 Olympia Centre
161 E. Chicago Ave.
1986, SKIDMORE, OWINGS & MERRILL

Postmodernism was slow to penetrate the citadels of Chicago orthodoxy; Neiman Marcus, in design beginning in 1978, was one of the first examples. The large glass arch evokes the work of H. H. Richardson and Louis H. Sullivan but with an obligatory wink: the glass slit in place of a keystone underscores the arch's structural irrelevance. The high-rise Olympia Centre tapers on two sides as it rises. The changes in fenestration reflect reduced structural loads, with larger windows where the function shifts from office to residential.

25 730–750 N. Michigan Ave.
1997–98, ELKUS/MANFREDI ARCHITECTS

The block-long Michigan Ave. frontage is divided into four storefronts, each with a distinct style. The Peninsula Hotel entrance is on Superior St.

26 Chicago Water Tower and Pumping Station
806 and 811 N. Michigan Ave.
1866, PUMPING STATION, WILLIAM W. BOYINGTON
1869, TOWER, WILLIAM W. BOYINGTON
1997, TOWER EXTERIOR RESTORATION AND 2002, PUMPING STATION
  EXTERIOR RESTORATION, BAUER LATOZA STUDIO
2003, PUMPING STATION ADAPTIVE REUSE FOR LOOKINGGLASS
  THEATRE, MORRIS ARCHITECTS/PLANNERS

One of only a few buildings to survive the Great Fire, the Water Tower is a potent symbol of Chicago's "I Will" spirit. In three days in October 1871, the city's commercial center and a third of its residences were leveled by fire. But the tower stood, holding out the promise of a rise from the ruins and ashes. Within months, Chicago was rebuilding, resuming its role as the nineteenth century's fastest-growing city.

The famous 154-foot tower was actually a secondary structure. It was built to house a 138-foot standpipe that stabilized the pressure of the water distributed from the adjacent pumping station. Both buildings were built in the

Chicago Water Tower and Pumping Station

"castellated Gothic" style of locally quarried Joliet-Lemont limestone, widely used in Chicago before it was replaced by Indiana graystone in the 1890s. The stone is recognized by its distinctive yellow patina.

The Pumping Station and Tower are two of only a few surviving buildings by William W. Boyington, one of the city's most prominent early architects, who gave shape to the Chicago that burned as well as to the phoenix that replaced it. Working in the popular revival styles, Boyington designed major hotels, commercial structures, churches, and other institutions from the 1850s to the 1890s.

The four facades of the Water Tower are identical and feature a massive arched door flanked by pointed-arch windows surmounted by drop moldings. Small towers with lancet windows, castellated crowns, and tourelles frame each level as the base rises to the tower itself, which is surmounted by a crown of eight tourelles and a copper cupola. The overall effect led Oscar Wilde to call it "a castellated monstrosity with salt and pepper boxes stuck over it." Boyington used the same styling not only on the pumping station but also on the first University of Chicago (demolished); the prison at Joliet, Illinois (1858); and the entrance to Rosehill Cemetery (1864).

A Chicago landmark of great visceral magnitude, the Water Tower has nonetheless battled three times for its life. In 1906, the standpipe became obsolete, and only a public outcry saved the tower from demolition. In 1918, the tower obstructed the northward progress of the new Michigan Ave., but preservationists prevailed over planners. A 1948 plan for an art center on the site was also defeated, and the first restoration of the tower began in 1962. Today, the Water Tower is a focus of Michigan Ave., whose buildings have come to dwarf the structure that once stood tall amid smoldering ruins.

—VINCENT MICHAEL

27 Chicago Fire Dept.
202 E. Chicago Ave.
1902, CHARLES F. HERMANN,
CHICAGO CITY ARCH.

This tiny fire station repeats in miniature the castellated Gothic of the Water Tower and Pumping Station.

28 Park Tower
800 N. Michigan Ave.
2000, LUCIEN LAGRANGE & ASSOCS.

The sixty-eight-story mixed-use building has forty-eight floors of luxury condominiums above a Park Hyatt hotel and a retail base. The reinforced concrete structure is clad in precast concrete except for the first two stories, which are of limestone. The east and west sides look quite different than the narrower north and south sides. Balconies are sculpturally woven into the facade.

29 Facade of former Perkins, Fellows & Hamilton Studio and Office

814 N. Michigan Ave.

1917, PERKINS, FELLOWS & HAMILTON

This is a rare example of an originally freestanding building designed by architects for their own offices. The brick facade, with Gothic details and extensive sculpture by Emil R. Zettler, is all that remains; behind it is the Park Hyatt that is part of the Park Tower.

30 Loyola University—Lewis Towers

(Illinois Women's Athletic Club)
820 N. Michigan Ave./111 E. Pearson St.

1927, RICHARD E. SCHMIDT, GARDEN & MARTIN

This Gothic skyscraper had shops on the first two floors, offices to the ninth floor, and club facilities above. A relief of Diana with her dog guards the east entrance, which now leads to the Loyola University Museum of Art (2005, SOLOMON CORDWELL BUENZ).

31 840 N. Michigan Ave.

1992, LUCIEN LAGRANGE & ASSOCS.

This dignified low-key addition to the avenue extends the human scale that reigns on its western side between Superior St. and Delaware Pl. The corner tower and mansard roof evoke earlier retail establishments, and the six shades of limestone harmonize with the masonry of the streetscape.

32 Water Tower Place

845 N. Michigan Ave.

1976, LOEBL, SCHLOSSMAN & HACKL
2001, RENOVATION, WIMBERLY ALLISON TONG & GOO

This marble-clad monument to mammon forever changed the avenue's character—for better or worse. It moved the retail center of gravity north from State St. in the Loop and heralded the arrival of a more international and luxurious marketplace. Despite the setback of the building's tallest part, great violence was done to the streetscape by Water Tower Place's blank walls and recessed storefronts, a mistake avoided by its imitators. The bland marble walls cover a reinforced-concrete frame that was the world's tallest until the construction of 311 S. Wacker Dr.

33 John Hancock Center

875 N. Michigan Ave.

1969, SKIDMORE, OWINGS & MERRILL
1994, LOWER-LEVEL REMODELING, INCLUDING PLAZA, HILTSCHER SHAPIRO

Of the four giants that dominate the early twenty-first-century Chicago skyline, the Willis Tower, Trump Tower, and Aon Center are taller, but the John Hancock Center best exemplifies the Chicago tradition of combining bold structural advances with brawny architectural form.

Despite its gigantism, the 1,127-foot-tall, 100-story, 2.8-million-square-foot Hancock is a beloved urban icon. Nicknamed "Big John" soon after its completion, it features a distinctive tapering profile and exterior cross-bracing that have inspired countless schoolchildren to portray it as a cartoonlike series of stacked Xs. So deeply is the building ingrained in the Chicago psyche that in 1989, Mayor Richard M. Daley attacked the owner's plan to fill in the tower's sunken plaza and add a three-story retail atrium to its base. The scheme was replaced by one that reconfigured the rectangular plaza into an elliptical space that was more welcoming and less moatlike. The happy result is that the Hancock's striking silhouette remains intact, a high-water mark for Skidmore, Owings & Merrill and a triumph of modern architecture.

Designed by SOM architect Bruce Graham and engineer Fazlur R. Khan, the Hancock exemplifies another Chicago tradition, the multipurpose building. Floors 1–2 are devoted to retail space; 3 to mechanical equipment; 4–12 to parking; 13–41 to offices; 42–43 to mechanical equipment; 44–92 to residences; and 93 to broadcast equipment. The 94th floor houses a public observatory. A bar and restaurant occupy floors 95 and 96, with television and communications equipment housed on 97, a mix of televi-

John Hancock Center

sion, communications, and mechanical equipment on 98, and mechanical equipment alone on 99–100. Supporting it all, as well as the television and radio antennas that bring the building's total height to about 1,500 feet, are 46,000 tons of steel. Exterior columns, horizontal beams, and cross-braces form a highly efficient structural system comparable to a rigid box; the tower was erected for the cost of a conventional forty-five-story office building.

The tapering form provides large floor areas for retail and office use and smaller spaces for the condominiums. The form also evokes the permanence and monumentality associated with the obelisks of ancient Egypt or the Washington Monument.

Monumental presence is both a blessing and a curse. For all its swaggering presence on the skyline, the Hancock has a history of stumbling as it meets the street. The base of the black aluminum tower originally was covered in travertine marble, leading tour guides to compare the Hancock to a man in a tuxedo wearing white socks. The 1994 remodeling of the tower's base replaced the travertine with a gray granite cladding that is far more sympathetic to the dark colossus.

Still, the Hancock maintains an uneasy relationship with its ever-shifting environs. Before the tower was built, N. Michigan Ave. largely resembled a Parisian boulevard of elegant low- and mid-rise classical buildings. After the Hancock shattered that fragile scale, the avenue became an urban canyon of hulking blockbusters. That trend, which has since spread to the streets flanking N. Michigan, makes the open space of the Hancock's sunken plaza all the more valuable, even if it dims somewhat the tower's brilliant synthesis of engineering and architecture, pragmatism and poetry.

—BLAIR KAMIN

Fourth Presbyterian Church

34 Fourth Presbyterian Church
866 N. Michigan Ave.

1914, RALPH ADAMS CRAM; HOWARD
VAN DOREN SHAW, ASSOC. ARCH.

1914, CLOISTER, HOWARD
VAN DOREN SHAW

1925, MANSE, PARISH HOUSE, BLAIR
CHAPEL, HOWARD VAN DOREN SHAW

2012, GRATZ CENTER, GENSLER

One of Chicago's wealthiest congregations turned to a nationally renowned practitioner of the Gothic Revival for their church. Parishioner Shaw collaborated with Cram on the interior and designed the less formal buildings that create a peaceful courtyard, or garth. The stained glass is by Charles J. Connick of Boston; local artist Frederic Clay Bartlett designed the illuminated ceiling and the wooden statuary. After decades of failing to gain approval for a revenue-producing high-rise on the rear portion of the property, the church instead built a parish center there. The weathered copper cladding enhances the side street, but from Michigan Ave., the glassy office facade forms an incongruous backdrop to the lovely cloister.

35 900 N. Michigan Ave.

1989, KOHN PEDERSEN FOX; PERKINS
& WILL, ASSOC. ARCHS.

Known as the Bloomingdale's Building, this mixed-use structure by the developers of Water Tower Place builds on that project's commercial success and corrects some of its errors. The eight-story shopping block extends to the lot line with a welcoming entrance and plenty of large display windows. The spacious, understated neo-Deco atrium has the anchor store at the back, so that shoppers pass the boutiques first. The hotel, office, and condominium floors have entrances on the side streets. Like Water Tower Place, the exterior is a stack of embellished boxes but with a more ambitious decorative program. Though it does not all hang together, the four huge lanterns atop the building are a visual delight.

36 The Palmolive Building
159 E. Walton St.

1929, HOLABIRD & ROOT

1982, STOREFRONT RENOVATION,
SKIDMORE, OWINGS & MERRILL

2006, CONVERSION TO CONDOMINIUMS,
BOOTH HANSEN ASSOCS.

The Palmolive Building

Like New York, Chicago enacted a zoning law for skyscrapers (in 1923) that set the stage for the Art Deco buildings soon in vogue. This building, like the Chicago Board of Trade by the same architects, is a shining example of the style, with setbacks making it a powerful sculptural object. The crowning Lindberg beacon was restored when the office building was converted to condominiums.

999 N. Lake Shore Dr.

37 One Magnificent Mile
940–980 N. Michigan Ave.

1983, SKIDMORE, OWINGS & MERRILL

Although it uses the bundled tube structure of the Sears Tower, this pink granite triad is clad in 1980s garb. The window patterns express the familiar divisions of retail, office, and residential use.

38 Drake Hotel
140 E. Walton St.

1920, MARSHALL & FOX

This luxurious hotel anchors both the north end of Michigan Ave. and the west end of the E. Lake Shore Dr. Historic District, combining the public splendor of the avenue with the residential elegance of the drive. The H-shaped plan maximizes lake views. The Italian Renaissance–inspired facades effectively incorporate a *piano nobile* treatment for the public spaces on the lower floors.

E. Lake Shore Dr. Historic District
From Michigan Ave. east through 999 N. Lake Shore Dr.

39 Drake Tower Apartments
179 E. Lake Shore Dr.

1929, BENJAMIN H. MARSHALL

40 The Mayfair
(Lake Shore Dr. Hotel)
189 E. Lake Shore Dr.

1924, FUGARD & KNAPP

41 199 E. Lake Shore Dr.
(The Breakers)

1915, MARSHALL & FOX

42 209 E. Lake Shore Dr.

1924, MARSHALL & FOX

43 219 E. Lake Shore Dr.

1922, FUGARD & KNAPP

44 229 E. Lake Shore Dr.

1919, FUGARD & KNAPP

45 999 N. Lake Shore Dr.

1912, MARSHALL & FOX

This remarkable group creates a harmonious street wall that is one of the few lakefront stretches with no recent structures interrupting its cohesiveness. It also provides an intriguing glimpse of Benjamin H. Marshall's design evolution, from the Second Empire exuberance adorning the corner at 999 to the sober ahistoricism of the Drake Tower Apartments.

46 227 E. Walton St.

1956, HARRY WEESE & ASSOCS.

While Mies was refining and simplifying the glass-and-steel curtain wall that would become de rigueur for high-rise facades, Weese was moving toward greater variety and plasticity. Inspired by the multibayed facades of the early Chicago School, he used a warm palette of red brick with concrete trim here.

47 900–910 N. Lake Shore Dr.
(Esplanade Apartments)

1953–56, LUDWIG MIES VAN
DER ROHE; PACE ASSOCS. AND
HOLSMAN, HOLSMAN, KLEKAMP
& TAYLOR, ASSOC. ARCHS.

The success of 860–880 N. Lake Shore Dr. led developer Herbert Greenwald to commission another pair. They have a sleeker version of the expressive curtain wall, with dark-tinted glass and without the contrasting aluminum window frames. The structural system is not a steel skeleton but a flat-slab concrete frame, resulting in complete independence of skin and structure.

1949–51, LUDWIG MIES VAN
DER ROHE; PACE ASSOCS. AND
HOLSMAN, HOLSMAN, KLEKAMP
& TAYLOR, ASSOC. ARCHS.

2009, RESTORATION, KRUECK &
SEXTON ARCHITECTS; HARBOE
ARCHITECTS, PRESERVATION ARCH.

860–880 N. Lake Shore Dr.

These towers constitute the first
and most forceful demonstration of
Ludwig Mies van der Rohe's ideas
for tall buildings. No other building
by Mies had as immediate or strong
an impact on his American contemporaries, and the influence of these
structures went on to pervade much
of modern architecture.

Mies had come to Chicago from
Germany in 1938 to become director
of the school of architecture at what would later become the Illinois Institute
of Technology. He also established an architecture practice and in 1948 designed the concrete-framed Promontory Apartments in Hyde Park, the first
of many projects for developer Herbert Greenwald. Mies had prepared two
versions of the Promontory. One was the form actually used; the other had a
steel-and-glass exterior on the long elevations, his first use of the curtain wall
that came to be his hallmark.

While the Promontory was under construction, Greenwald commissioned
these apartments. The plan was developed from the alternative version for the
Promontory and from sketches that Mies had drawn between 1919 and 1921 for
two radically innovative glass towers, which had brought him to the forefront of
the modern movement. The unexecuted designs reemerged here and in 1968,
through the hands of Mies's former students, in Lake Point Tower.

The buildings acquire their strong verticality from the narrow I beams
welded to the columns and mullions, a feature necessitated in part by the
building code's requirement that steel-framed buildings be fireproofed with
concrete. Mies satisfied the code and achieved the appearance he desired by
finishing the framing elements with steel plate, which served as formwork for
poured concrete, and by welding I beams onto the plate.

Questioned on his use of a structural material as applied ornament, Mies
gave a good reason and then the real reason. He noted that the I beams
would function well as mullions. "But why weld them onto the column
plates?" he was asked. "It strengthens the plates," Mies replied. "Do the
plates need strengthening?" "Well, no," he confessed, "but if you leave out
the I beams there, it breaks the rhythm!"

The "Glass Houses" were startling not only in terms of form but also as habitation; critics wondered about the psychological impact of transparent homes.
The apartments were a financial success, however. The buildings became the
international prototype for steel-and-glass structures and engendered an architecture now so commonplace that it is almost impossible to appreciate their
initial impact, when it was "as if steel and glass [were] seen for the first time."

—JOAN POMARANC

49 850 N. Lake Shore Dr.

(Lake Shore Athletic Club)

1924, JARVIS HUNT

Built as a combination clubhouse
and apartment building, the hulking
mass consists of a large neoclassical
base topped by rather plain upper
floors.

50 The Plaza on DeWitt

(DeWitt-Chestnut Apartments)

260 E. Chestnut St.

1963, SKIDMORE, OWINGS & MERRILL

This was Chicago's first building
with a tubular structural system, in
which closely spaced exterior columns create a load-bearing screen

wall. The reinforced-concrete frame is sheathed in marble. It was the first collaboration of SOM architect Bruce Graham and engineer Fazlur R. Khan, the team that created the Hancock Center and Sears Tower.

51 Museum of Contemporary Art
220 E. Chicago Ave.
1996, JOSEF PAUL KLEIHUES;
A. EPSTEIN & SONS INTERNATIONAL,
ARCH. OF RECORD

This boxy bunker landed on the streetscape with a dull thud rather than the anticipated splash. The steep front stairway is intimidating rather than inviting, and the cast-aluminum facade panels lend the dreariness of concrete but at a much higher cost. Glittering stainless-steel screws fasten the panels to the building frame at precise intervals but offer little visual relief. Fortunately, the interior has more to recommend it. The four-story atrium has glass walls that offer spectacular views. Barrel-vaulted top-floor galleries are lit with indirect natural light. And tucked against the northern wall, a curving stairway wraps around an almond-shaped reflecting pool.

52 200 E. Pearson St.
1916, ROBERT S. DEGOLYER

This vintage palazzo was home to Ludwig Mies van der Rohe, who chose not to live at his free apartment at 860–880 N. Lake Shore Dr., the story goes, because he didn't want the tenants to treat him like the maintenance man.

53 840 N. Lake Shore Dr.
2003, LUCIEN LAGRANGE ARCHITECTS

Of the group of three buildings that comprise the Residences on Lake Shore Park, 840 N. Lake Shore Dr. is the most interesting. Chicago had not attempted Gallic grandeur on this scale since the Belden Hotel was completed in 1922.

Northwestern University— Chicago Campus
This campus houses law, business, and medical schools and is concentrated between Chicago Ave. and Huron St., from the lake west to St. Clair St. James Gamble

Rogers created a campus plan in 1924 and designed a row of buildings in his signature Collegiate Gothic style. The original group marched west from the lake along Chicago Ave., with the buildings increasing in height. This pattern has been broken by subsequent construction, but Rogers's Gothic precedent has proved amazingly durable. Fallen from grace and superseded by modernist buildings, the style was strongly evoked in two major additions of the 1980s: the Law School's Rubloff Building and the Medical School's Tarry Building. The 1990s and early 2000s saw explosive growth of the medical campus, but its architecture was generally uninspired. The announcement in 2012 of the impending demolition of the original Prentice Women's Hospital (1975, BERTRAND GOLDBERG & ASSOCS.) set off a firestorm of protest that received national attention but failed to save the building, whose curving concrete bed tower stood out amid its rectilinear neighbors.

54 Northwestern University School of Law—Arthur Rubloff Building
375 E. Chicago Ave.
1984, HOLABIRD & ROOT

This handsome addition to the campus has a finely detailed curtain wall, the base of which gestures to its Gothic neighbors with abstracted buttresses. A glazed atrium links it with the Gary Law Library building.

Northwestern University School of Law— Arthur Rubloff Building

55 Northwestern University School of Law—Levy Mayer Hall
357 E. Chicago Ave.
1927, JAMES GAMBLE ROGERS;
CHILDS & SMITH, ASSOC. ARCHS.

The Law School quadrangle surrounds a leafy courtyard and

includes Rogers's Albert H. Gary Law Library (1927; note the owls perched atop the buttresses) on Chicago Ave. and Robert R. McCormick Hall (1960, HOLABIRD & ROOT) at 350 E. Superior St., executed in a self-effacing and harmonious nonstyle.

56 Wieboldt Hall
339 E. Chicago Ave.
57 Montgomery Ward Building
303–311 E. Chicago Ave.
1926, JAMES GAMBLE ROGERS;
   CHILDS & SMITH, ASSOC. ARCHS.

An attractive arcade links these two buildings (a twin links Wieboldt to the Law School complex) and creates a peaceful courtyard, a hallmark of Rogers's campus designs. The Ward Building was the nation's first Collegiate Gothic skyscraper. Although stylistically dull in comparison with the architect's better-known buildings at Yale University, the planning makes the most of the cramped urban site.

58 Tarry Research and Education Building
300 E. Superior St.
1990, PERKINS & WILL

Collegiate Gothic returned in 1990s materials in this addition, which completes the block begun by the Montgomery Ward Building and continued in the Morton (1955) and Searle (1956) Medical Research Buildings (310 and 320 E. Superior St.). Method Atrium (part of Tarry), an elegant glassy lobby, links all four buildings.

59 Ann and Robert H. Lurie Children's Hospital of Chicago
225 E. Chicago Ave.
2012, ZGF ARCHITECTS; SOLOMON
   CORDWELL BUENZ; ANDERSON
   MIKOS ARCHITECTS

Children's Memorial Hospital got a new name along with its new building when it left the Lincoln Park neighborhood for the Northwestern medical campus. The twenty-three-story tower has whimsical and welcoming interior spaces. The standout (literally as well as figuratively) is the glassy sky garden on the eleventh floor that cantilevers seven feet from the wall below.

60 Northwestern Memorial Hospital—Northwestern University Health Sciences Building/Olson and McGaw Pavilions
710 N. Fairbanks Ct.
1979, HOLABIRD & ROOT

This unabashedly high-tech building lost some of its edge when its gleaming white metal panels were painted buff to blend in with the surrounding limestone and concrete. Pedestrian bridges with exposed trusses make connections to buildings across both streets.

61 Abbott Hall
710 N. Lake Shore Dr.
1939, HOLABIRD & ROOT

Built as a student residence, this unadorned limestone structure has more bulk than style. The ornamental wrought-iron gate, designed for the original 1920s campus, sits uselessly on the site's southeast corner.

62 Lake Shore Place
(American Furniture Mart)
680 N. Lake Shore Dr.
1924, EAST END, HENRY RAEDER
   ASSOCS.; GEORGE C. NIMMONS & CO.
   AND N. MAX DUNNING, ASSOC. ARCHS.
1926, WEST END, GEORGE C.
   NIMMONS AND N. MAX DUNNING
1984, CONVERSION, LOHAN ASSOCS.

This lavishly ornamented monument to the wholesale furniture trade was built when Chicago was at the indus-

Lake Shore Place

try's center. Although the exterior seems all of a piece, a closer look reveals a difference between the sixteen-story east end, which has a reinforced-concrete structure, and the twenty-story western section, which is a steel-framed skyscraper. The Gothicism of the exterior reaches its apogee in the thirty-story tower, which was inspired by the British Houses of Parliament. The interior carries out the theme in the lavish Whiting Hall lobby, which runs the length of the building. The Furniture Mart declined with the industry's decentralization and the move of many showrooms to the Merchandise Mart. It is now a mixed-use building of apartments, offices, parking, and stores.

63 Onterie Center
446–448 E. Ontario St./441 E. Erie St.
1979–86, SKIDMORE, OWINGS & MERRILL
This building was the final collaboration between architect Bruce Graham and engineer Fazlur R. Khan, who died in 1982 after completing the structural design. A pair of reinforced-concrete tubes, their cross-bracing expressed by concrete infill panels, embrace a central core. This system combines the cross-bracing of the Hancock Center with the tubular structure of the Sears Tower, though it lacks their elegance. Retail and office space occupy the lower floors, with apartments in the tower.

64 McClurg Court Center
333 E. Ontario St.
1971, SOLOMON CORDWELL BUENZ & ASSOCS.
This apartment complex offers the kind of self-contained, multiuse environment popular since the 1970s. Although some shops face the street, it presents a forbidding presence. The curved corner towers are placed at right angles to each other to maximize views.

65 The Arts Club
201 E. Ontario St.
1997, VINCI/HAMP ARCHITECTS
This understated two-story building is a comfortable permanent home for the club, which lost its Mies van der Rohe–designed interior to the wrecking ball. The focal point for the new building is the Mies stair (1951), which was salvaged from the old location two blocks west. Galleries on the first floor and salon and dining on the second are simple and restrained in their materials and detailing, as is the exterior, with its Norman brick and large steel-framed windows.

66 230 E. Ohio St.
(Pelouze Building)
1916, ALFRED S. ALSCHULER
67 232 E. Ohio St.
(Pelouze Scale & Manufacturing Co. Factory)
1916, HILL & WOLTERSDORF
These are among the few remaining loft buildings in this former industrial area.

68 600 Fairbanks Ct.
2008, MURPHY/JAHN
The high quality of the curtain wall, with its ultrasmooth glass, makes this high-rise look more like an expensive office building than a condominium tower. And the usual bugaboos of the building type—balconies and a massive parking base—are handled with uncommon elegance. The inset terraces are protected by clear glass panels rather than metal railings. The parking podium is sheathed in glass set in front of aluminum mesh, making this one of the rare instances where accommodating cars enhances rather than deadens the design. To the north, the structure cantilevers gracefully over an existing building.

600 Fairbanks Ct.

541 N. Fairbanks Ct. Building

unusual at the time, conserves energy. Double-deck elevators are programmed to stop at two floors at the same time during rush hours and to provide regular service at other times.

When condominium construction screeched to a halt during the Great Recession, developers began building luxury rental properties instead. Two of the most prominent examples completed in 2013 are **500 Lake Shore Dr.** *(*SOLOMON CORDWELL BUENZ*) and* **Optima Chicago Center** *(*OPTIMA*) at 200 E. Illinois St.*

69 541 N. Fairbanks Ct. Building
(Time and Life Building)
1968, HARRY WEESE & ASSOCS.
1989, RENOVATION, PERKINS & WILL
This brawny building of Cor-Ten steel with bronze-tinted mirror glass is a foray by Weese into the Miesian realm. The reflective glass,

70 James Jardine Water Filtration Plant
(Central District Filtration Plant)
1000 E. Ohio St.
1952–64, C. F. MURPHY ASSOCS.
On this long finger of landfill is a campus of buildings that filter and purify water for the metropolitan area. The low buildings are of steel-frame construction with metal-and-glass curtain walls.

71 Navy Pier
(Municipal Pier No. 2)
600 E. Grand Ave. at Lake Michigan
1916, CHARLES S. FROST
1976, RENOVATION, JEROME R. BUTLER JR., CHICAGO CITY ARCH.
1995, RECONSTRUCTION, BENJAMIN THOMPSON & ASSOCS.; VOA ASSOCS., ASSOC. ARCHS.
Shakespeare Theater
1999, VOA ASSOCS.
A 1910 plan called for the construction of five municipal piers, of which only Navy Pier was built. Its 3,000-foot length, set on 20,000 wooden piles, made it the world's largest pier at the time. During its golden age (1918–30), it was an important terminal for freight and passenger traffic as well as a site of public entertainment. The rise of trucking combined with the Great Depression to curtail both uses; it became a naval training facility during World War II and served as the Chicago branch of the University of Illinois from 1946 until 1965. When the east buildings were restored in 1976, the pier again began to host civic and cultural events.

The 1995 rebuilding of deteriorating infrastructure and the new construction of museums, shops, and entertainment and recreational facilities made the pier one of Chicago's most popular attractions. The Crystal Garden and the 230,000-square-foot Festival Hall convention facility join the Grand Ballroom in making the pier a prime site for small conventions and large parties. A food court, stores, and museums offer something for everyone. The Shakespeare Theater has multilevel glass corridors that wrap around the main performance space, insulating it from noise and providing patrons with spectacular views. In an effort to refresh the pier's appeal, a design competition was held in 2012. Plans by the winning team of James Corner Field Operations and nArchitects include a grand staircase and extensive landscape improvements.

72 Lake Point Tower

505 N. Lake Shore Dr.

1968, SCHIPPOREIT-HEINRICH;
GRAHAM, ANDERSON, PROBST
& WHITE, ASSOC. ARCHS.

Inspired by a 1919–21 visionary
project of Mies van der Rohe,
two of his former students and
employees designed this undulating glass tower as their firm's first
commission. The first skyscraper
with curving glass walls, it still out-
shines its imitators. The Y-shaped
plan (which differs from Mies's
asymmetrical model) provides the
optimal combination of density,
views, and privacy. The tower sits
on a large podium that contains

Lake Point Tower

parking and commercial space
and is topped with a private park
designed by Alfred Caldwell.

Cityfront Center

Bounded by the Chicago River,
N. Lake Shore Dr., E. Grand
Ave., and N. Michigan Ave.

MASTER PLAN: 1985, COOPER,
ECKSTUT ASSOCS.; SKIDMORE,
OWINGS & MERRILL

PLANNING: LOHAN ASSOCS. (EAST OF
COLUMBUS DR.); SKIDMORE, OWINGS
& MERRILL (WEST OF COLUMBUS DR.)

Scaled to the pedestrian but convenient for traffic, Cityfront Center
consciously repudiates the kind
of urban planning that resulted
in bleak landscapes of isolated
towers. Its pleasant river orientation could be possible only in this
postindustrial era, when waterways
are more important as pleasure
grounds than as transportation
arteries. Development has been
carried out separately, with land-
ownership divided between the
Chicago Dock & Canal Trust (east
of Columbus Dr.) and the Equitable
Life Assurance Society (between
Columbus Dr. and Michigan Ave.).

73 River East Plaza

(North Pier Chicago;
originally Pugh Terminal)
435 E. Illinois St.

1905–20, CHRISTIAN A. ECKSTORM
1990, RENOVATION, BOOTH HANSEN
ASSOCS.; AUSTIN CO., ASSOC. ARCHS.

Constructed as an exhibition center
for wholesale products, this sprawling building capitalized on Chicago's
emerging role in American merchandising to locate numerous manufacturers and product lines under one

roof. It was originally more than twice
as long and stretched east across the
path of Lake Shore Dr. The conversion
to a three-story retail mall with four
office floors was the first completed
project at Cityfront Center.

Fan-shaped steel canopies punctuate the ground floor on Illinois St. between windows that were originally
loading docks. This facade is of face
brick and, although simple, presents
a more finished appearance than the
common-brick river and side walls,
which are now more prominent. Inside, a three-story rotunda introduces
the inventive combination of materials that evoke the area's nautical and
industrial past in a 1990s vocabulary.
The Ogden Slip facade has been
extended with two neo-Miesian glass-
and-steel gallerias.

74 474 N. Lake Shore Dr.

1991, DUBIN, DUBIN & MOUTOUSSAMY;
FLORIAN-WIERZBOWSKI,
DESIGN CONSULTANTS

75 CityView Condominiums

440 and 480 N. McClurg Ct.

76 Cityfront Place

400 N. McClurg Ct.

1991, GELICK FORAN ASSOCS.

The grim sixty-one-story tower faced
with precast concrete panels was
Cityfront's first major residential project. The thirty-story mid-rise tower
and pair of linked twelve-story structures were a welcome improvement.
A grand staircase leads to a terrace
whose west section features a long,
low fountain and glorious views of the
skyline. To the east, a curving section

like the prow of a boat provides a good perch for people watching

77 East Water Place Town Houses
430 E. North Water St.
1997, BOOTH HANSEN ASSOCS.
Town house living close to Lake Michigan is an unusual kind of luxury. Fifty-six units are clustered in eight buildings laid out around private roads that create a mews effect.

78 RiverView Condominiums
445 E. North Water St.
2001, DESTEFANO & PARTNERS
The steel cornice and restrained yet lively palette of materials elevate this twenty-seven-story tower above its more mundane neighbors.

79 Nicholas J. Melas Centennial Fountain
McClurg Ct. at the Chicago River
1989, LOHAN ASSOCS.
This monument honors the centennial of the Metropolitan Water Reclamation District, the agency charged with ensuring the area's constant supply of healthy drinking water. The summit of the stepped granite pavilion represents the eastern continental divide (located just southwest of Chicago), with water flowing east to the Atlantic Ocean and west to the Gulf of Mexico. During the day (in season), a cannon shoots an eighty-foot arc of water across the river every hour.

80 Sheraton Chicago Hotel & Towers
301 E. North Water St.
1992, SOLOMON CORDWELL BUENZ & ASSOCS.
This enormous but well-articulated convention hotel anchors the southwest corner of the Chicago Dock & Canal property. Automobile access is from the north; to the south, the hotel opens onto a river esplanade linking it with the rest of Cityfront Center.

RIVER NORTH

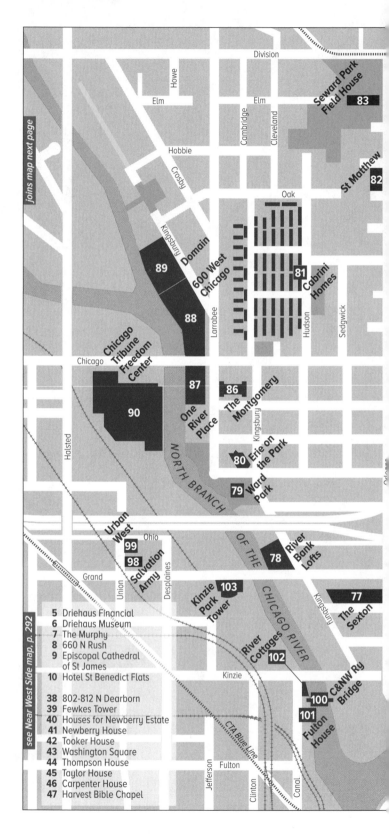

Division

Seward Park Field House

83

Howe

Elm

Elm

Cambridge

Cleveland

St Matthew

82

Hobbie

Crosby

Oak

joins map next page

Kingsbury

Domain

89

600 West Chicago

81

Cabrini Homes

88

Larrabee

Hudson

Sedgwick

Chicago Tribune Freedom Center

Chicago

87

86

The Montgomery

Kingsbury

90

One River Place

80 Erie on the Park

Halsted

NORTH BRANCH

79 Ward Park

Urban West

Ohio

99

98

Salvation Army

Grand

Union

Desplaines

OF THE

78 River Bank Lofts

Kinzie Park Tower

103

CHICAGO RIVER

Kingsbury

77 The Sexton

5   Driehaus Financial
6   Driehaus Museum
7   The Murphy
8   660 N Rush
9   Episcopal Cathedral
    of St James
10 Hotel St Benedict Flats

38 802-812 N Dearborn
39 Fewkes Tower
40 Houses for Newberry Estate
41 Newberry House
42 Tooker House
43 Washington Square
44 Thompson House
45 Taylor House
46 Carpenter House
47 Harvest Bible Chapel

River Cottages

102

Kinzie

100 C&NW Ry Bridge

101

Fulton House

Jefferson

Fulton

Clinton

Canal

CTA Blue Line

see Near West Side map, p. 292

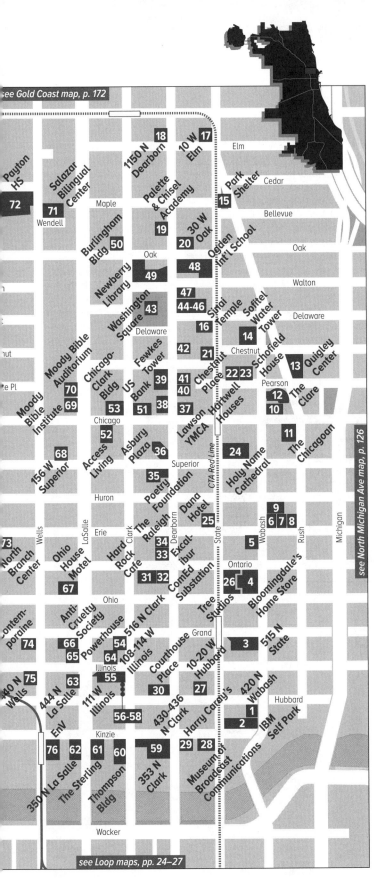

see Gold Coast map, p. 172

Payton HS

72

Salazar Bilingual Center

71
Wendell

Maple

18 1150 N Dearborn

10 W Elm **17**

Elm

Cedar

Park Shelter

15

Bellevue

Palette & Chisel Academy

Burlingham Bldg **50**

19

30 W Oak

20

Ogden Int'l School

Oak

Walton

Newberry Library

Oak

49

48

47
44-46

Sinai Temple

Sofitel Water Tower

Delaware

Washington Square **43**

Delaware

16

14

Schofield House

Quigley Center **13**

Moody Bible Auditorium

Chestnut

42

21

Chestnut

Chicago-Clark Bldg

US Bank

Fewkes Tower

39

41
40

Chestnut Place

22 23

Pearson

12

The Clare

70
69

53

51 **38**

37

Lawson YMCA

Hartwell Houses

10

Moody Bible Institute

Chicago

52

Access Living

Asbury Plaza

36

24

Holy Name Cathedral

11

The Chicagoan

156 W Superior

68

Superior

35

Poetry Foundation

9

Huron

Dana Hotel

6 7 8

Erie

Ohio House Motel

The Raleigh

Hard Rock Cafe

34
33

Excalibur

25

5

North Branch Center

73

67

Ohio

31 32

ComEd Substation

Ontario

26 **4**

Bloomingdale's Home Store

Anti-Cruelty Society

Powerhouse

54

516 N Clark

Tree Studios

74

Contemporaine

66
65

64

108-114 W Illinois

Courthouse Place

Grand

3

515 N State

Illinois

63

55

30

10-20 W Hubbard

27

420 N Wabash

75

440 N Wells

444 N La Salle

111 W Illinois

56-58

430-436 N Clark

Harry Caray's

Hubbard

1
2

IBM Self Park

EnV

Kinzie

76 **62**

61 **60**

59

29 28

Museum of Broadcast Communications

350 N La Salle

The Sterling

Thompson Bldg

353 N Clark

Wacker

see Loop maps, pp. 24–27

see North Michigan Ave map, p. 126

RIVER NORTH

RIVER NORTH

River North is the newest name for one of Chicago's oldest neighborhoods. In the 1970s, the long-forgotten area north and west of the towers that border the Chicago River and N. Michigan Ave. featured open blocks of surface parking in its southeastern sector, with ranks of mill-construction factory and warehouse buildings, many dating from the 1880s, in other parts of the neighborhood. Loft conversions to commercial and residential use brought new life and a new name, and by 2000, new construction had filled the parking lots with high-rise apartments, multistory garages, and retail complexes.

The poorest part of the city when it was incorporated in 1837, River North was the site of Chicago's first industries, first railroad line (down Kinzie St.), and first slum (an Irish ghetto near the fork of the north branch). In the late 1850s, three bridges—at Rush St., Erie St., and Grand Ave.—established the first stable links between the North Side and the rest of the city. From then on, the area's role as the city's industrial district expanded, with the river and the rail lines attracting more factories, warehouses, and lumber- and brickyards. Miles of frame cottages soon housed the neighborhood's laborers.

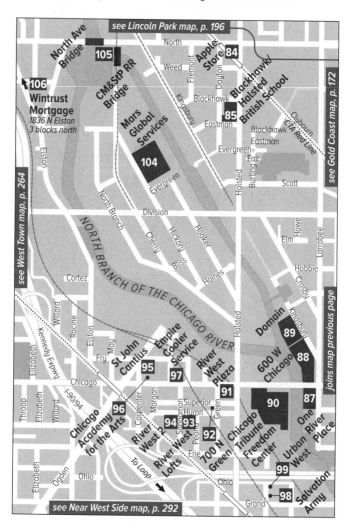

In an exception to this pattern of land use, an exclusive residential enclave emerged north of Grand Ave. along Rush and adjacent streets. Leading citizens established estates on quarter-block parcels. The city's oldest park, Washington Square, was a developer's creation to stimulate upscale residential expansion north of Chicago Ave.; a legacy of this venture is the deviation of the city's grid in the surrounding blocks.

The 1871 fire devastated the residential portions but left the lumberyards and industries untouched. Rebuilding followed the old patterns, with luxury neighborhoods east of La Salle St. and ethnic enclaves—first Irish and Swedish, later Italian—to the west. After 1900, however, factory construction spread northward and eastward from the river edges and gradually turned poor neighborhoods into slums.

The opening of the Michigan Ave. Bridge in 1920 was the coup de grâce that sent everything west of the Magnificent Mile into a decline. As grand mansions were subdivided into rooming houses, the residential area near the Water Tower briefly became a Left Bank bohemia known as Tower Town. Washington Square, dubbed Bughouse Square, became a lively forum for free speech. The slums to the west were razed beginning in the 1940s for the enormous public housing complex that became known as Cabrini-Green. Industries in the southwest corner gradually closed or moved their operations elsewhere.

The transformation in the 1970s was begun by artists, gallery owners, and photographers who converted warehouses into inexpensive, light-filled living and working spaces. As in other cities, the artists' alterations raised real estate values, and they ultimately found themselves edged out by boutiques, trendy restaurants, and luxury apartments. Offices, hotels, and major retail development followed, especially in the southeast corner, in essence expanding the Loop northward and the Magnificent Mile westward. The area west of the north branch of the Chicago River, dubbed River West in the late 1980s, was touted as a less-expensive location for loft residences and small businesses.

The 1990s saw the rapid rise and swift demise of garish theme restaurants and entertainment venues, a few of which remain in toned-down incarnations. The twentieth century ended with the death of one of its great failed experiments, the high-rise public housing of Cabrini-Green, as the increasingly valuable land filled with retail and market-value housing. The building boom to the south and east resulted in luxury skyscrapers so brutally banal that in 2003 Mayor Richard M. Daley delivered a headline-grabbing decree, "No More Ugly Buildings." A subsequent wave of construction included several notable contemporary designs.

—MARY ALICE MOLLOY

Buildings on the north bank of the river are included in the Loop chapter.

1 420 N. Wabash Ave.
1983, CONVERSION,
  PAPPAGEORGE/HAYMES
One of the city's best-designed loft conversions creatively uses negative space by inserting a second skin of glass and metal behind the partially hollowed-out brick facade.

2 IBM Self Park
401 N. State St.
1974, GEORGE SCHIPPOREIT
A delicate screen of vertical, self-weathering Cor-Ten fins conceals intricate scissor ramps and space for 800 cars. The gentle curve of the

Wabash Ave. elevation has a sculptural quality.

3 515 N. State St.
1990, KENZO TANGE; SHAW &
  ASSOCS., COORDINATING ARCHS.
Modernism is alive and well in this strong opening statement in the redevelopment of almost twelve acres controlled by the American Medical Association. The sculptural glass-and-aluminum curtain-wall building creates a distinctive top with a four-story cutout near its summit. The leftover wedge of space houses mechanical equipment. The southern half of the property was not developed with offices as originally planned but

RIVER NORTH

Medinah Temple (now Bloomingdale's Home Store)

instead has the **Palomar Hotel** (2010, GREC ARCHITECTS).

4 Bloomingdale's Home Store
(Medinah Temple)
600 N. Wabash Ave.
1913, HUEHL & SCHMID
2002–3, RENOVATIONS, DANIEL
P. COFFEY & ASSOCS.

Built for the Shriners to host conventions, circuses, and concerts, it displays the Arabic motifs that lent exoticism to the organization's rituals. The textured brickwork is laid in an unusual variety of Flemish bond. Huehl & Schmid created scores of fanciful Shriners' auditoriums; this is one of the largest and best preserved. It now has new life as a retail store that incorporates many of the original decorative elements. Exterior changes were kept to a minimum.

5 Driehaus Financial Services
(Ransom R. Cable House)
25 E. Erie St.

Driehaus Financial Services

1886, COBB & FROST
1992, RENOVATION, JOHN
VICTOR FREGA ASSOCS.
2008, RESTORATION,
ANTUNOVICH ASSOCS.

This house introduced to Chicago such Richardsonian design elements as rock-faced ashlar (here of Kasota stone), the slightly battered foundation, the low-sprung triple arches of the corner entry, and encrustations of neo-Byzantine carving. The medieval coach house is a superb complement.

6 The Richard H. Driehaus Museum
(Samuel M. Nickerson House)
40 E. Erie St.
1883, BURLING & WHITEHOUSE
2008, RESTORATION,
ANTUNOVICH ASSOCS.

A painstaking restoration returned the Gilded Age glory to what was known as the Marble Palace, named for its opulent interior that featured seventeen types of that stone along with alabaster and onyx. The porous Berea sandstone facade, long blackened with grime, was cleaned using laser technology—the first time the process was

Driehaus Museum

used for an entire building in this country. It is a sedate foil for the lavish interior, whose restored rooms now showcase Driehaus's collection of decorative arts.

7 The Murphy

(American College of Surgeons—John B. Murphy Memorial Auditorium)
50 E. Erie St.
1922–26, MARSHALL & FOX
2006, RESTORATION,
    ANTUNOVICH ASSOCS.

This auditorium-library was intended as the center of a complex devoted to postgraduate medical education. It is modeled remarkably closely on the Chapelle de Notre-Dame de Consolation in Paris (1900, ALBERT GUILBERT), including the central street-level door and the curving stairs to the pillared and porticoed upper entrance, with its bronze doors by Tiffany Studios.

8 660 N. Rush St.

(Double House for Leander McCormick and son, Robert Hall McCormick)
1875, FREDERICK AND EDWARD BAUMANN
1997, CONVERSION TO OFFICES,
    SEARL & ASSOCS.
2010, EXTERIOR RESTORATION,
    ANTUNOVICH ASSOCS.

Built as a double house for the brother and nephew of the reaper's inventor, Cyrus H. McCormick, it was converted into a single building after Leander's death in 1900.

9 Episcopal Cathedral of St. James

65 E. Huron St.
1857, EDWARD J. BURLING
1875, REBUILDING, BURLING & ADLER
1913, CHAPEL OF ST. ANDREW,
    BERTRAM GROSVENOR GOODHUE
1928, MEMORIAL NARTHEX,
    GOODHUE ASSOCS.
1985, RESTORATION, HOLABIRD & ROOT

The stenciled nave, a chorus of color, is one of the nation's finest Victorian interiors. It was designed in 1888 by Edward Neville Stent, a student of William Morris. The church tower still bears the scars of the Great Fire.

10 Hotel St. Benedict Flats

42–50 E. Chicago Ave./801 N. Wabash Ave.
1882, JAMES J. EGAN

This is a rare and prominent example of the early years of the "flat craze" (1881–93), when apartments were marketed to the upper middle class as "French flats." It uses Second Empire elements to create the effect of attached houses.

Hotel St. Benedict Flats

Episcopal Cathedral of St. James

11 The Chicagoan
750 N. Rush St.

1990, SOLOMON CORDWELL
 BUENZ & ASSOCS.

This "lipstick building" is oval with octagonal bays at opposite corners, allowing six "corner" apartments per floor and living rooms with 180-degree views.

12 The Clare at Water Tower
55 E. Pearson St.

2008, PERKINS & WILL

The unusual program of creating a full-service retirement community in a high-rise was made even more complex with the addition of a three-story classroom structure leased to Loyola University. The tower contains six levels of parking, surmounted by floors for increasingly independent levels of living. Balconies are so skillfully tucked into the building's curves and notches as to be almost invisible.

13 Archbishop Quigley Center
(Archbishop Quigley Preparatory Seminary and Chapel of St. James)
831 N. Rush St.

1919, ZACHARY T. DAVIS
2008, ADAPTIVE REUSE AND
 CHAPEL RESTORATION, JAEGER
 NICKOLA & ASSOCS.

The former seminary is Flamboyant Gothic, with energetic stonework throughout; the chapel on the southwest corner is modeled after the mid-thirteenth-century Sainte-Chapelle in Paris. Like that building, the chapel was conceived as an armature for a dazzling display of stained glass, executed in thousands of pieces of antique English glass by Robert T. Giles.

14 Sofitel Chicago Water Tower
20 E. Chestnut St.

2002, JEAN-PAUL VIGUIER; TENG
 & ASSOCS., ASSOC. ARCHS.

There is welcome drama and grace in this thirty-three-story hotel. The wedge and curve and thin vertical band of windows on the western

Sofitel Chicago Water Tower

Chapel of St. James, Archbishop Quigley Center

facade make one stop, look, and go inside. The hotel lobby is atypical, with the bar to the side of the lobby and not even visible from the front door. This location allows the bar to have sidewalk tables when the weather is right. The glass staircase carves the lobby into a relatively small space but provides maximum effect.

15 Green Bay Triangle Shelter/Mariano Park
Rush St., State St., and Bellevue Pl.
1900, BIRCH BURDETTE LONG

Though almost smothered by commercial signage, the hardy, humble terra-cotta morning glory climbs the columns and blooms on the capitals of this simple Prairie School park shelter. The fountain was installed in 1998.

16 Chicago Sinai Temple
15 W. Delaware Pl.
1997, LOHAN ASSOCS.

The sanctuary is elevated above street level. A monumental exterior stair is placed sideways against the long elevation, providing a ceremonial approach on a tight urban site. An octagonal stained-glass window, designed by architect Dirk Lohan, marks the location of a small chapel.

Chicago Sinai Temple

17 10 W. Elm St.
1928, B. LEO STEIF

With chevrons, zigzags, and fancifully imagined plant and animal forms, a group of French terra-cotta modelers brought a vivid new decorative vocabulary to Chicago. This high-rise apartment is clothed at top and bottom in the pastel decorative essays of Edouard Chassaing and his colleagues at the Northwestern Terra Cotta Co. He was one of six sculptors imported by the company in 1927 after the Exposition Internationale des Arts Décoratifs et Industriels Modernes (1925) in Paris. In contrast to the magisterial streamlining of Holabird & Root and Graham, Anderson, Probst & White, here is the brash side of the late 1920s.

18 1150 N. Dearborn St.
(John DeKoven House)
1874, EDWARD J. BURLING

This imposing Second Empire house has elaborate window surrounds and the original wrought-iron roof cresting and stoop railing.

19 Palette and Chisel Academy of Fine Art
(William Waller House)
1012 N. Dearborn St.
1874, ARCHITECT UNKNOWN

A relic of post-Fire residential grandeur, this Italianate mansion retains its principal features under the care of the academy, founded in 1895 under the sponsorship of sculptor Lorado Taft.

20 30 West Oak
2007, BOOTH HANSEN

The generous balconies are true outdoor rooms, not the usual bicycle-and-barbecue perches. An underground garage removes another source of visual blight, the dreaded

10 W. Elm St.

parking podium. Most floors are split east–west into just two units, with open-plan living in the glassy south tower and bedroom suites in the more private north portion. Closer inspection of the southern structure reveals horizontal white-painted steel beams that were used as the concrete formwork and left in place to frame the floor-to-ceiling glass. Booth Hansen also designed the town houses to the north.

21 Chestnut Place Apartments
850 N. State St.
1982, WEESE, SEEGERS, HICKEY, WEESE

A vicarious trip to Florence awaits tenants in their private lobby, whose painted walls (by Richard Haas) evoke San Miniato al Monte. Bands of brick, dark at street level and lighter above, delineate each floor.

22 Edwin S. Hartwell Houses
14–16 E. Pearson St.
1885, JULIUS H. HUBER
1980, RENOVATION, BAUHS & DRING

This pair of town houses features terra-cotta portrait roundels of Hartwell's son and daughter, for whom these houses were built.

23 Frank Schofield House
18–20 E. Pearson St.
1934, FLORA SCHOFIELD; EUGENE
  B. REINER, SUPERVISING ARCH.

Designed by an artist, this simple but lively building has garages and an exhibition room on the ground floor, her studio and family's living quarters on the second floor, and a top-floor studio for her son. The facade has the handcrafted charm of Sol Kogen's work on W. Burton Pl., with mottled bricks, multicolored tiles, and a copper parapet.

24 Holy Name Cathedral
735 N. State St.
1875, PATRICK C. KEELEY
1890–93, RENOVATION,
  WILLETT & PASHLEY

1914, ADDITION, HENRY J. SCHLACKS
1969, REMODELING, C. F.
  MURPHY ASSOCS.

Although not the archdiocese's most beautiful building, it is one of the hardiest and most embellished. Brooklyn architect Keeley was a very successful if unimaginative church specialist who usually relied on formula, which is Gothic here. Schlacks's ambitious changes moved the apse and inserted an additional fifteen feet of nave.

25 Dana Hotel and Spa
660 N. State St.
2008, ECKENHOFF SAUNDERS ARCHITECTS

The slender tower flaunts its exposed concrete aesthetic with wedge-shaped balconies. The glass curtain wall visually opens the public spaces to the street.

26 Tree Studios
601–623 N. State St.
1894, PARFITT BROS., BAUER & HILL,
  AND HILL & WOLTERSDORF
Addition, 4–10 E. Ohio St.
1912, HILL & WOLTERSDORF
Addition, 3–9 E. Ontario St.
1913, HILL & WOLTERSDORF
2005, RESTORATION, DANIEL
  P. COFFEY & ASSOCS.

Built to entice out-of-town artists working at the Columbian Exposition to remain in Chicago, the studios comprise ground-floor shops with large windowed studios above. Once slated for demolition along with Medinah Temple, the block was saved after a huge public outcry. The restoration created an office entrance in the charming courtyard that had previously been closed to the public.

27 10–20 W. Hubbard St.
1883, STEPHEN V. SHIPMAN
1965, CONVERSION, 1976 REMODELING,
  HARRY WEESE & ASSOCS.

These quintessential examples of investor-built industrial lofts have interior brick walls twenty feet apart

Tree Studios

Excalibur

spanned by wood floors and plain, non-load-bearing facades. Weese, an early and strong Chicago preservationist, adapted the building for his own and other architects' offices.

28 Museum of Broadcast Communications
360 N. State St.
2012, ECKENHOFF SAUNDERS
ARCHITECTS

The tradition of creating small museums out of improbable buildings is carried forward in this conversion of a derelict 1920s parking garage. Stainless steel mesh covers the Kinzie St. facade, while aluminum panels and large expanses of glass open the museum to State St.

29 Harry Caray's
(Chicago Varnish Co.)
33 W. Kinzie St.
1900, HENRY IVES COBB

This "quoin bank" is filled with Dutch Renaissance exuberance.

30 Courthouse Place
(Cook County Criminal Courts Building)
54 W. Hubbard St.
1892, OTTO H. MATZ
1986, RENOVATION, SOLOMON
CORDWELL BUENZ & ASSOCS.

This Romanesque Revival mass, with more history than artistry, has a lavish if less than authentic lobby.

31 Hard Rock Café
63 W. Ontario St.
1985, TIGERMAN, FUGMAN, MCCURRY

32 Commonwealth Edison Substation
Southwest corner, Dearborn and Ontario Sts.
1989, TIGERMAN, FUGMAN, MCCURRY

It's the T-shirts and the decor that draw the tourists, not the Tuscan proportions and neo-Palladian windows. These elements were meant to identify the building with an adjacent Commonwealth Edison substation that was subsequently demolished. The replacement substation was then designed to respond to the Hard Rock Café, reusing the original's medallions, tympanum, and wrought-iron fence.

33 Excalibur
(Chicago Historical Society)
632 N. Dearborn St.
1892, HENRY IVES COBB

Vigorous and picturesque, this fine Richardsonian Romanesque edifice housed the city's oldest cultural institution for more than thirty-five years before sheltering a Moose lodge, a school of design, a recording studio, and several nightclubs. Admiringly called a "pyramidal pile of brownstone" by an 1890s critic, this behemoth conveys a stability that belies its checkered past.

34 The Raleigh
650 N. Dearborn St.
1891, ARCHITECT UNKNOWN
1912, TOP-FLOOR REMODELING,
ARCHITECT UNKNOWN
1990, RENOVATION, BERGER & ASSOCS.

With its serpentine stone skin, this was one of the more colorful hotels to open in anticipation of the World's Columbian Exposition.

35 Poetry Foundation
61 W. Superior St.
2011, JOHN RONAN ARCHITECTS

A visitor experiences this subtle modernist building one layer at a

Poetry Foundation

time, starting with the delicately perforated screen of gray zinc at the sidewalk. Behind the screen, almost as a surprise, one enters a quiet courtyard framed by a two-story glass wall. The journey ends in a light-filled interior with walls of blond birch. The first-floor public spaces include a library on the west side, a lobby/exhibit area in the middle (overseen by a large image of Harriet Monroe, founder of *Poetry Magazine*) and an acoustically fine poetry-reading room to the east. Everything in the building is understated, beautifully crafted, and elegant.

36 Asbury Plaza
750 N. Dearborn St.
1981, GEORGE SCHIPPOREIT

The intriguing geometry, which gives this concrete high-rise a different massing from every angle, also serves to reduce its bulk and maximize the lake views.

37 Lawson House YMCA
30 W. Chicago Ave.
1930–34, PERKINS, CHATTEN & HAMMOND

Intact if timeworn, this limestone-and-brick skyscraper emulates more lavish office buildings of the period. The Art Deco ornament includes spandrels with low-relief athletes above the main entrance. A second-floor drawing room preserves its Deco fireplace, paneling, and etched-glass doors.

38 802–812 N. Dearborn St.
EARLY 1870S, ARCHITECTS UNKNOWN

These well-preserved Italianate row houses have neo-Grec ornament on the low buildings to the south and lavish Second Empire trim on the four-story north buildings. At 810 is the fine Alliance Française de Chicago, remodeled by DeStefano & Partners in 1998 to include a building around the corner on Chicago Ave. At the rear of the property is a courtyard with a steel-and-glass addition that links the two buildings.

39 John Fewkes Tower
55 W. Chestnut St.
1967, HARRY WEESE & ASSOCS.

Fenestration is everything in this Ben Weese–designed tower. Eight-inch masonry walls alternate with thirty-story strips of trapezoidal bay windows and corners chamfered with slim windows. The windows even prompted a trapezoidal silhouette for interior partitions.

40 Houses for the Newberry Estate
827–833 N. Dearborn St.

41 Newberry House
(Grant's Seminary for Young Ladies)
839 N. Dearborn St.
1878, FREDERICK H. WAESCHER

Although constructed as a set, the row houses have incised ornament that only hints at the Frank Furness–style detailing evident on the corner building's compressed columns and angled bay. The wall in front of

Newberry House

827–831 includes portrait roundels from Adler & Sullivan's demolished Schiller Building. Waescher was the Newberry estate's architect for more than a decade, specializing in heavy structures such as warehouses and factories.

42 Robert N. Tooker House
863 N. Dearborn St.
1886, JENNEY & OTIS

One of the few remnants of the two-year Jenney-Otis partnership has a two-tone rosy granite facade. Tooker Place, the adjacent alley, was the site of the Dill Pickle Club, a 1920s hangout for local bohemians and denizens of Bughouse Square.

43 Washington Square
The land for this park was donated to the city in 1842 by the American Land Co. when it purchased Bushnell's addition bounded by State, Chicago, Division, and La Salle Sts. By the 1890s, it was a genteel place of crossing walks, benches, and a central fountain. In 1906, it needed improvements, so Jens Jensen redesigned the park with a new fountain (removed in the 1970s). As the buildings to the east were acquired by the Masonic Oriental Consistory in the early 1900s, and as other homes in the area were divided into rooming houses, the square became "the outdoor forum of garrulous hobohemia" known as Bughouse Square. The Chicago Park District acquired the park in 1959 and re-created the Jensen-era fountain in 1999.

44 John Howland Thompson House
915 N. Dearborn St.
1888, COBB & FROST

Superb masonry design, second only to that on H. H. Richardson's Glessner House, patterns the reddish brown Lake Superior sandstone, which provides rich texture but never overwhelms with massiveness. The balanced but asymmetrical bays on the Delaware Pl. elevation, the steeply pitched slate roof of gables and turrets exuberantly outlined in copper, and the tripartite entrance separated by bundled columns with rock-faced lintels below a handsome panel of foliate diaperwork combine to demonstrate what can happen in an inspired partnership.

45 George H. Taylor House
919 N. Dearborn St.
1895, TREAT & FOLTZ

46 George B. Carpenter House
925 N. Dearborn St.
1891, TREAT & FOLTZ

These neighboring houses are a lesson in shifting tastes. The rough stonework on portions of the Carpenter House seems to be peeled away to reveal Georgian Revival forms like those of the Taylor House.

47 Harvest Bible Chapel
(Scottish Rite Cathedral; originally Unity Church)
929 N. Dearborn St.
1867, THEODORE VIGO WADSKIER
1873, REBUILDING, BURLING & ADLER
1882, SOUTH TOWER, FREDERICK B. TOWNSEND

RIVER NORTH

2010, RESTORATION, WISS,
JANNEY, ELSTNER ASSOCS.
The original structure with a matched set of towers, touted as one of the grandest of the city's Joliet limestone churches, lost all of its wooden portions in the 1871 fire. Rebuilding within the original walls gave Dankmar Adler his first experience with acoustical design by installing raked seating. The 2010 restoration included a new west window to replace one that had been filled in by the Scottish Rite owners.

48 Ogden International School of Chicago
24 W. Walton St.
2011, SMNG-A, DESIGN ARCH.; NAGLE
HARTRAY DANKER KAGAN MCKAY
PENNY, ARCH. OF RECORD
The exceptionally dense urban site required going both up and down: parking is underground, and the main playground is atop the roof. In a deviation from the L-shaped elementary school prototype, the library and gymnasium are at opposite ends of the building rather than stacked in a single tower. The raised plaza is both protective and welcoming.

49 Newberry Library
60 W. Walton St.
1890–93, HENRY IVES COBB
1981, ADDITION, HARRY WEESE & ASSOCS.
The "uncommon collection of uncommon collections" provided for in the will of Walter Loomis Newberry (1804–68) has an impressive housing whose original building is only half as deep as what Cobb intended. The jagged lines where the addition was

to have picked up are visible on the side elevations. Cobb was asked to abandon his partnership with Charles S. Frost to devote full attention to this commission. The facade, which centers on a triple-arched entrance inspired by the twelfth-century church of Saint-Gilles-du-Gard in southern France, is attributed to Cobb employee Louis C. Mullgardt. The interior plan was conceived by the Newberry's first librarian, William F. Poole.

In the addition, whose brickwork hints at the arches of the original, even the walls and their plenum spaces are part of the mechanical system, which provides climate-controlled storage for twenty-one miles of books, maps, and manuscripts. The replicated chandelier in the restored lobby has bulbs that point downward to prove that this was one of Chicago's first electrified buildings.

50 Burlingham Building
1000 N. Clark St.
1883, 1897, TWO-STORY
ADDITION, ALFRED SMITH
A cast-iron corner turret, bays that feature cast-iron piers, slate spandrels, and colored window glass constitute an elaborate array of Queen Anne details. The bays have unusual proportions, with the central window narrower than those to the side.

51 U.S. Bank
(Cosmopolitan State Bank)
801 N. Clark St.
1920, RICHARD E. SCHMIDT,
GARDEN & MARTIN
1997, ADDITION, TILTON & LEWIS ASSOCS.
In 1921, *American Architect* called

Newberry Library

it "a fine example of unfashionable bank designing," in notable contrast to the classical temples being erected everywhere else. Especially praiseworthy were the large, unbroken wall surfaces, simple and severe lines, and rich and neutral colors.

52 Access Living
115 W. Chicago Ave.
2007, LCM ARCHITECTS

Executed by a firm specializing in accessible architecture, the Chicago Ave. elevation—comprised of a five-story brick block and a four-story glass box—offers no hint of the universal design required by the client, a disability advocacy organization.

53 Chicago-Clark Building
(Bush Temple of Music)
100 W. Chicago Ave.
1901, J. E. O. PRIDMORE

Unashamedly overblown and *retardataire*, it originally contained studios, practice rooms, rehearsal halls, and a large theater used by German performers.

54 516 N. Clark St./101 W. Grand Ave.
1872, 1873, ARCHITECT UNKNOWN
1883, 1884, CYRUS P. THOMAS
1985, RENOVATION, SWANKE HAYDEN CONNELL

Beginning as a four-story grocery with lofts, it grew additions and extra stories until it became the Albany, an 1880s first-class apartment building with hardly a seam visible.

55 111 W. Illinois St./451 N. La Salle Blvd.
2008, SOLOMON CORDWELL BUENZ

The triangular prow of Martin Wolf's design takes advantage of an awkward site to create a separate identity for the Erickson Institute, which owns and occupies the western portion of what is otherwise a speculative office building.

56 430 N. Clark St.
1872, ARCHITECT UNKNOWN
57 432 N. Clark St.
1988, FACADE, FLORIAN-WIERZBOWSKI
58 436 N. Clark St.
1872, WILLIAM W. BOYINGTON

A clever copy filled in a gap between two of the city's oldest business buildings.

59 353 N. Clark St.
2009, LOHAN ANDERSON, DESIGN ARCH.; A. EPSTEIN & SONS INTERNATIONAL, ARCH. OF RECORD

To provide a Clark St. address for a building that is set well back from that street and has most of its frontage along Kinzie St., the plan features a lobby on the south side that is accessed via entry plazas from the flanking north–south streets as well as a Carroll Ave. auto court. Columns are pulled in from the corners to maximize views.

60 John R. Thompson Building
350 N. Clark St.
1912, ALFRED S. ALSCHULER
1983, RENOVATION, METZ, TRAIN & YOUNGREN

Known for years as the Commissary Building, it housed the general offices of the Thompson restaurant chain. Its creamy terra-cotta facade bespeaks good hygiene as well as Chicago School proportions.

61 The Sterling
345 N. La Salle Blvd.
2002, SOLOMON CORDWELL BUENZ & ASSOCS.

This actually is a sterling design, much better than most of the rows of high-rise apartments and condos filling River North. The painted concrete skin looks as good as many fancier materials because it is kept simple, as it curves around the building and peaks at the top, on the northwest corner.

N. La Salle Blvd. Renovations

From the river north to its terminus at Lincoln Park, La Salle was an avenue in the post-Fire years, when it was lined with elms and some of the city's finest residences. In 1930—already a little seedy and with commercial structures encroaching on its southern end—it became a street, as trees, lawns, porches, and often entire facades were sliced off to widen the roadway by fourteen feet on each side. The project had been proposed as part of the 1909 *Plan of Chicago* to provide fast motor access to the Loop. Evidence of the widening can be seen along the length of the street, with the best examples of Art Deco facades on the east side between Chestnut and

Widening of La Salle Blvd.

Delaware Sts. An estimated thirteen million dollars in private funds was spent in 1978–79 to revitalize the street after decades of unbenign neglect. The move led to another name change to indicate its upscale image: La Salle Blvd.

62 350 N. La Salle Blvd.
1990, LOEBL, SCHLOSSMAN & HACKL IN CONSULTATION WITH WOJCIECH LESNIKOWSKI

A conscious reuse of Chicago School elements articulates the skeleton frame with red brick and fills the bays with green glass. The curved and towered corners create internal variety in a very slim building.

63 444 N. La Salle Blvd.
1930, REMODELING, GEORGE F. LOVDALL

The street widening cost this old warehouse its front, but in the remodeling it gained a dazzling polychrome Art Deco terra-cotta facade.

64 108–114 W. Illinois St.
(Grommes & Ullrich Warehouse)
1901, RICHARD E. SCHMIDT

This former liquor distribution center, designed by Hugh M. G. Garden,

108–114 W. Illinois St.

expresses its structure boldly. Horizontality is emphasized by discontinuous recessed piers and unusually broad Chicago windows.

65 Former Cable Car Powerhouse
500 N. La Salle Blvd.
1888, NORTH CHICAGO STREET RAILROAD

The El is Chicago's iconic form of transportation, but the city once boasted the world's largest cable car system, in use from 1882 to 1906. This unadorned building is the most tangible remnant of that era. It housed power-generating equipment and winding machinery for the cables that pulled cars through the North Chicago Street Railroad's downtown loop and the La Salle St. tunnel.

66 Anti-Cruelty Society
157 W. Grand Ave.
1935, LEON STANHOPE
1982, ADDITION ON LA SALLE BLVD., STANLEY TIGERMAN & ASSOCS.
2011, REMODELING, INTERACTIVE DESIGN ARCHITECTS

The original sleek Art Moderne building displays its purpose with low-relief carvings of animals and owners on either side of the door. The PoMo mojo of Tigerman's cheeky "doggy in the window" storefront was muzzled by a too-tame remodeling.

67 Ohio House Motel
600 N. La Salle Blvd.
1960, SHAYMAN & SALK

This may be the city's best-preserved expression of the colorful, angular, space-age design of the Sputnik era.

Anti-Cruelty Society ca. 1982

Valerio Dewalt Train Assocs. designed a hotel at the southeast corner of La Salle Blvd. and Huron St. that was put on hold during the Great Recession, then resurrected as **The Godfrey Hotel** in 2013.

156 W. Superior

68 156 W. Superior
2006, MILLER/HULL PARTNERSHIP,
  DESIGN ARCH.; STUDIO DWELL
  ARCHITECTS, ARCH. OF RECORD

The way this small condo building flaunts its structure and modern materials gives it an outsize presence on the physical and architectural landscape. Its success reinforced the appeal of modernism for small-scale residential development.

69 Moody Bible Institute
820 N. La Salle Blvd.
1937–39, THIELBAR & FUGARD

70 Moody Bible Auditorium
840 N. La Salle Blvd.
1954, FUGARD, BURT,
  WILKINSON & ORTH

English Gothic styling gives a quasi-religious look to this high-rise school. The auditorium was completed after a fifteen-year hiatus.

71 Ruben Salazar Bilingual Center
(James A. Sexton Public School)
160 W. Wendell St.
1882, ARCHITECT UNKNOWN

This typical Italianate school is remarkable for its age and unusual cornice.

72 Walter Payton College Preparatory High School
1034 N. Wells St.
2000, DESTEFANO & PARTNERS,
  MANAGING ARCH.; MANN, GIN, DUBIN
  & FRAZIER, ARCH. OF RECORD

A glass circulation spine creates an internal "street" that links the academic and public wings of the building. The latter includes after-hours activity centers such as the gymnasium and lecture/performance hall. The steel-framed building is clad in brick to harmonize with neighboring housing stock.

73 North Branch Center
223 W. Erie St.
CA. 1896, ARCHITECT UNKNOWN
1899, ADDITION, JOHN H. WAGNER
1980, RENOVATION, JEROME BROWN

This large industrial building uses exposed metal mullions to open up the facade, a technique unpopular after miles of cast-iron facades melted in the 1871 fire.

Contemporaine

74 Contemporaine

516 N. Wells St.

2004, PERKINS & WILL

Designed at the same time as Sky-bridge, this much smaller building also makes visual poetry by shaping raw concrete into tall, thin columns and dramatic cantilevers. The floor-to-ceiling clear glass of the garage podium remains a rarity in Chicago, but the unpainted concrete and folded roof plane have been repeated often—usually to less felicitous effect.

75 440 N. Wells St.

(Liquid Carbonic Acid Manufacturing Co.)

1903, HOLABIRD & ROCHE

1982, RENOVATION, HAMMOND, BEEBY & BABKA

This loft building has the large windows, high ceilings, and open-beam construction that made this type of structure so popular for office conversions in the 1980s. The facade is unusually well detailed, with terra-cotta ornament and recessed courses of brick.

76 EnV Chicago

161 W. Kinzie St.

2011, VALERIO DEWALT TRAIN ASSOCS.

Cantilevered balconies hover above the El tracks, their crisply engineered glass planes a lofty rebuke to the clatter and grit of a nineteenth-century transportation system. The glazing is a quarter-inch thicker on the west walls and on half of the north and south facades to mitigate the noise.

77 The Sexton

(John Sexton & Co.)

500 N. Orleans St.

1916, 1919, ALFRED S. ALSCHULER

2001, CONVERSION TO RESIDENCES, FITZGERALD ASSOCS. ARCHITECTS

Built by a grocery and food-processing company for use as its office, manufacturing plant, and warehouse, this building represents the final stage in Chicago loft construction. Unlike the previous generation of lofts, the elevations not only reflect the various uses of the interior space but also identify stairwells, light shafts, and elevators. Appearance and image were so important that the addition, which added the easternmost 150 feet, matched the original building's load-bearing walls, even though the structural system was now reinforced concrete.

During the 2000–2001 conversion to condominiums, balconies and additional stories were added.

78 River Bank Lofts

(Railway Terminal and Warehouse Co.)

550 N. Kingsbury St.

1909, NIMMONS & FELLOWS

1995, CONVERSION TO RESIDENCES, FITZGERALD ASSOCS. ARCHITECTS

John Sexton & Co. (now The Sexton)

The self-banding at the base and top, also reflected in the stone capitals, is tantamount to the original firm's signature. The metal balconies bolted onto brick facades became ubiquitous in River North residential conversions.

79 A. Montgomery Ward Park
630 N. Kingsbury St.

This small park was created in 2005 to accommodate the influx of residents to a formerly industrial area. Sheila Klein calls her aluminum sculpture, *Commemorative Ground Ring* (1989, relocated here in 2005), "a tangible symbol of my love for Chicago architecture." It takes the form of a colossally scaled engagement ring: the band is a circle of Chicago windows, and the "stone" represents the Sullivan-designed Getty tomb, set atop abstract skyscraper facades and crowned by a Prairie School roof.

80 Erie on the Park
510 W. Erie St.

2002, LUCIEN LAGRANGE ARCHITECTS

The narrow condominium tower, a parallelogram in plan, rises

Erie on the Park

from a context of low brick warehouse and office buildings. The expressed steel structure with its distinctive cross-bracing and terrace setbacks is visible from all directions and is a welcome architectural expression in comparison to the more typical condominium construction. It was followed in 2003 by Lagrange's **Kingsbury on the Park** at 653 N. Kingsbury, which conceals its structure and aims for drama with balconies on projecting steel trusses.

81 Chicago Housing Authority— Frances Cabrini Homes
Chicago Ave., Larrabee St., Oak St., and Hudson Ave.

1942, HENRY HOLSMAN, GEORGE BURMEISTER, MAURICE B. RISSMAN, ERNEST A. GRUNSFELD JR., LOUIS R. SOLOMON, GEORGE M. JONES, KARL M. VITZTHUM, I. S. LOEWENBERG, AND FRANK A. MCNALLY

One of the nation's most notorious housing projects became one of its most closely watched models for the redevelopment of public housing. The 1990s brought demolition of most of Cabrini's red-brick high-rises and the construction of numerous private developments that have 20 percent of their units set aside for Chicago Housing Authority (CHA) tenants. Public works projects include two new schools, a branch library, and a police station. The redevelopment pioneered here was continued and extended throughout the city under the auspices of the CHA's ten-year, $1.5 billion Plan for Transformation. Inaugurated in 2000, the plan calls for the demolition of all of the agency's high-rises that house families (not seniors) and their replacement with units that are interspersed with market-rate and affordable housing. Cabrini's prime location between River North and Old Town virtually assured the success of the mixed-income model here. The subsequent economic downturn and foreclosure crisis stalled the even more ambitious plans for the south and west sides, which have lost their high-rises and await much of their replacement housing.

82 St. Matthew United Methodist Church
1000 N. Orleans St.
1969, SKIDMORE, OWINGS & MERRILL

A pastor seeking to expand community programs in a very depressed area admired the University of Illinois at Chicago and consequently engaged Walter Netsch Jr. to apply his field theory to this church. A series of rotated squares constitutes the church, fellowship hall, classrooms, and two suites for day care. Sculptor Richard Hunt's Cor-Ten cross marks the church end of the site.

83 Seward Park Field House
375 W. Elm St.
1908, DWIGHT H. PERKINS
1999, CLOCK TOWER, JOHNSON JOHNSON & ROY

The Prairie School tradition is manifest in the clear, logical expression and use of materials. Sloping brick piers with metal capitals support the wood knee brackets, which in turn support the overhanging eaves with their exposed wooden rafters.

84 Apple Store
801 W. North Ave.
2010, BOHLIN CYWINSKI JACKSON

Stainless steel slabs create an elegant jewel box that contrasts with nearby big box stores. The luminous interior draws people in through transparent entrance walls at either end of the narrow building. Trees and a long, thin display window enliven the otherwise blank Halsted St. elevation.

85 Blackhawk-Halsted and the British School of Chicago
**1460 N. Halsted St. and
814 W. Eastman St.**
2007, 2008, VALERIO DEWALT TRAIN ASSOCS.

A building housing the British School is set at a right angle to the retail and office structure along Halsted, the complex visually unified by the corrugated metal skin. A large parking garage is on the northwest part of the two-acre site, which was previously occupied by a factory.

Former Montgomery Ward & Co. Complex
86 The Montgomery
*(Montgomery Ward & Co.—
Corporate Offices)*
500 W. Superior St.
1974, MINORU YAMASAKI & ASSOCS.
2004–6, CURTAIN WALL RENOVATION, SKIDMORE, OWINGS & MERRILL; CONVERSION TO RESIDENCES, PAPPAGEORGE/HAYMES

87 One River Place
(Administration Building)
619 W. Chicago Ave.
1930, WILLIS J. MCCAULEY
2002, CONVERSION TO RESIDENCES, FITZGERALD ASSOCS. ARCHITECTS

88 600 W. Chicago
(Catalog Building)
**600 W. Chicago Ave./800
N. Larrabee St.**
1906–8, RICHARD E. SCHMIDT, GARDEN & MARTIN
2002, CONVERSION, GENSLER

89 Domain
(Catalog Building North)
900 N. Kingsbury Ave.

Montgomery Ward Catalog Building (now 600 W. Chicago)

1917; 1940, 1970, NORTH ADDITIONS,
MONTGOMERY WARD & CO.

2002, CONVERSION TO RESIDENCES,
PAPPAGEORGE/HAYMES

Despite its massive size, the former
Montgomery Ward complex was
redeveloped for residential and
commercial uses in a relatively
short time. Offices on the south
side of Chicago Ave. became
condominiums, with the *Spirit of
Progress* sculpture still perched
gracefully atop the tower of the
former administration building. The
architectural highlight is Richard E.
Schmidt's 1908 Catalog Building,
whose original facades of exposed
concrete with red-brick infill are now
visible after decades of being hidden
beneath a uniform white coating.
Schmidt was a master of concrete
construction, and this unmistakably
horizontal building is his most impressive achievement.

90 Chicago Tribune
Freedom Center
777 W. Chicago Ave. at N.
Branch of the Chicago River
1982, SKIDMORE, OWINGS & MERRILL
Built on a site that includes railroad
air rights, this sprawling structure
houses the nation's largest newspaper printing and distribution facility.

91 River West Plaza
(Devoe & Raynolds Co.)
770 N. Halsted St.
1902, HILL & WOLTERSDORF
1989, CONVERSION TO OFFICES,
BERGER & ASSOCS.
Buildings formerly used by a paint-
making business were converted
into a four-building office complex.
The frontispiece, the two buildings
at the Halsted-Chicago corner,
acquired a glass link and an atrium
inserted around the old elevator
tower.

92 700 N. Green St.
(Koenig, Henning & Gaber Co.)
1877, ARCHITECT UNKNOWN
Common brick walls set off with
small windows, tie rods, and occasional touches of red brick characterize this furniture factory. After
being burned out in the 1871 fire,
John Koenig moved his mechanized
operations here to be near the riverfront lumberyards and railroads.

700 N. Green St.

93 River West Lofts
(J. P. Smith Shoe Co.)
915–925 W. Huron St.
1912, HORATIO R. WILSON & CO.
1919, HURON ST. ADDITION,
SHANKLAND & PINGREY
1987, CONVERSION, BERGER & ASSOCS.
This factory was built within three
years of Albert Kahn's demonstration
of the advantages of metal sash
windows at Ford's Highland Park,
Michigan, plant. The introduction of
metal sash windows—in this case,
covering fourteen-foot-wide areas—
changed the configuration of mullions and fenestration and the overall
composition of factory facades. Vertical wall surfaces are merely thin piers
rising from sidewalk to cornice; walls
are embellished with very simple
patterns of projecting and recessed
brickwork. The building was dilapidated and underutilized when its
conversion to apartment units
sparked the revitalization of an area
designated a slum.

94 River West 2
939 W. Huron St.
1991, BERGER & ASSOCS.
This poured-in-place concrete building is a modern application of the
old loft concept: concrete ceilings
and columns, heating and air-conditioning ducts, and other industrial
finishes are exposed. Stylistically,
the elevations call on contemporary
German and Japanese sources.

95 St. John Cantius
Roman Catholic Church
813–817 N. Carpenter St.
1893–98, ADOLPHUS DRUIDING
1901, RECTORY, ARCHITECT UNKNOWN
96 Chicago Academy for the Arts
(St. John Cantius Parish School)
1010 W. Chicago Ave.
1903, THEODORE OSTROWSKI, MASON
These three buildings exhibit very
different styles. Parish publications

RIVER NORTH

St. John Cantius Roman Catholic Church

describe the church as "Roman-esque Baroque"—perhaps meaning that the main elevation spans the history of round-arch styles. The Rectory's high mansard roof with gabled dormers shows the influence of S. S. Beman's Kimball House. The parish school is a heavy-handed rendition of Northern European Baroque.

97 Empire Cooler Service
(Paepcke-Leicht Lumber Co.)
940 W. Chicago Ave.
1906, LOUIS GUENZEL

This small industrial building makes a bold statement with nontraditional stone ornament on a textured brick facade. Above the roofline, the tower of the Italianate house that it enveloped is visible.

98 Salvation Army Thrift Store
(Braun & Fitts Butterine Factory)
509 N. Union Ave.
1891, FURST & RUDOLPH
1917, ADDITION AND ALTERATIONS,
    POSTLE & FISCHER
1947, ALTERATIONS AND REMODELING,
    ALBERT C. FEHLOW

99 Urban West Assocs. Building
685 W. Ohio St.
1992, REMODELING, KEITH TALBERT &
    JAY KELLER, URBAN WEST ASSOCS.

These side-by-side examples of adaptive reuse were done forty-five years apart. The Salvation Army, as the client converting a margarine factory to institutional use, employed an Art Moderne seam of an elevator core and light well to wed the seven- and five-story pieces of the Braun & Fitts structure. Talbert & Keller, as owner-architects of a two-story

heavy timber structure, slathered multicolored Dryvit on masonry bearing walls that had been wrecked by permanent imitation brick.

100 Chicago & North Western Railway Bridge
N. Branch of the Chicago River South of W. Kinzie St.
1908, STRAUSS BASCULE BRIDGE
    CO. AND WILLIAM H. FINLEY

This single-leaf bascule has an atypical counterweight: it is visible above ground and hangs free of the bridge. No longer in use and therefore in a perpetually upright position, the bridge is a photogenic foreground for many a Chicago photograph.

101 Fulton House
(North American Cold Storage Co.)
345 N. Canal St.
1898, FRANK B. ABBOTT
1981, CONVERSION, HARRY
    WEESE & ASSOCS.

102 River Cottages
357–365 N. Canal St.
1988, HARRY WEESE & ASSOCS.

Sailor Weese's enthusiasm for riverfront living manifested itself in these very different projects. Fulton House's windows are carved out of the thick walls of an insulated warehouse. At the opposite end of the scale—and style—spectrum are River Cottages' futuristic facades adorned with porthole windows.

103 Kinzie Park Tower
501 N. Clinton St.
2001, NAGLE HARTRAY
    DANKER KAGAN MCKAY

This condominium tower achieves what many River North apartment and condo buildings miss. Instead of having balconies sticking out of the facade, on this building they are tucked neatly between sculptural curves and angles. Those curves also provide unusually expansive views for a great number of the units.

104 Mars Global Services
(Republic Windows and Doors)
930 W. Evergreen St.
1998, BOOTH HANSEN ASSOCS.

This sleek complex is the star of a new generation of industrial buildings on Goose Island, a protected manu-

Republic Windows and Doors (now Mars Global Services)

facturing district. A three-story corporate headquarters fronts a large, single-floor factory whose twenty-seven-foot ceilings offer abundant light from huge roof monitors.

105 North Ave. Bridge

2008, MULLER & MULLER; HNTB, ENG.

Chicago, Milwaukee & St. Paul Bridge

1902; 2009, RESTORATION AND ADAPTIVE REUSE, CHICAGO DEPT. OF TRANSPORTATION

W. North Ave. at N. Branch of the Chicago River

The North Ave. bridge is a hybrid of structural types: suspension (the middle span) and cable-stayed (at either end). The railway bobtail swing bridge was rehabilitated to provide Goose Island access for pedestrians and cyclists as well as the rare freight train.

106 Wintrust Mortgage

(Hyde Park Bank Investment Real Estate Loan Processing Center)
1836 N. Elston Ave.
2009, FLORIAN ARCHITECTS

Like the mouse that roared, this tiny outpost has a mighty presence that allows it to hold its own on a gritty industrial corridor. A black steel frame extends above the two-story box to convey monumentality.

Wintrust Mortgage

GOLD COAST/OLD TOWN

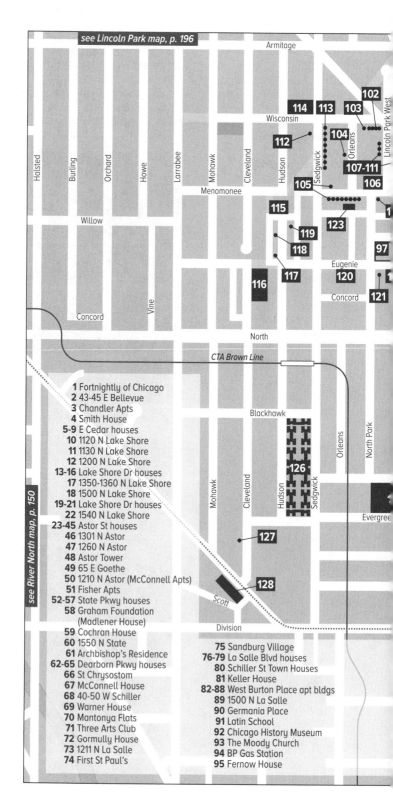

see Lincoln Park map, p. 196

Armitage

Wisconsin

Menomonee

Willow

Concord

North

CTA Brown Line

Halsted
Burling
Orchard
Howe
Larrabee
Mohawk
Cleveland
Hudson
Sedgwick
Orleans
Lincoln Park West
Vine

114 **113** **103** **102**
112 **104**
107-111
105 **106**
115 **123** **1**
119 **97**
118
117 **120** **121**
116

Eugenie
Concord
Blackhawk
Scott
Division

Mohawk
Cleveland
Hudson
Sedgwick
Orleans
North Park
Evergree

126
127
128

see River North map, p. 150

1 Fortnightly of Chicago
2 43-45 E Bellevue
3 Chandler Apts
4 Smith House
5-9 E Cedar houses
10 1120 N Lake Shore
11 1130 N Lake Shore
12 1200 N Lake Shore
13-16 Lake Shore Dr houses
17 1350-1360 N Lake Shore
18 1500 N Lake Shore
19-21 Lake Shore Dr houses
22 1540 N Lake Shore
23-45 Astor St houses
46 1301 N Astor
47 1260 N Astor
48 Astor Tower
49 65 E Goethe
50 1210 N Astor (McConnell Apts)
51 Fisher Apts
52-57 State Pkwy houses
58 Graham Foundation
   (Madlener House)
59 Cochran House
60 1550 N State
61 Archbishop's Residence
62-65 Dearborn Pkwy houses
66 St Chrysostom
67 McConnell House
68 40-50 W Schiller
69 Warner House
70 Mantonya Flats
71 Three Arts Club
72 Gormully House
73 1211 N La Salle
74 First St Paul's

75 Sandburg Village
76-79 La Salle Blvd houses
80 Schiller St Town Houses
81 Keller House
82-88 West Burton Place apt bldgs
89 1500 N La Salle
90 Germania Place
91 Latin School
92 Chicago History Museum
93 The Moody Church
94 BP Gas Station
95 Fernow House

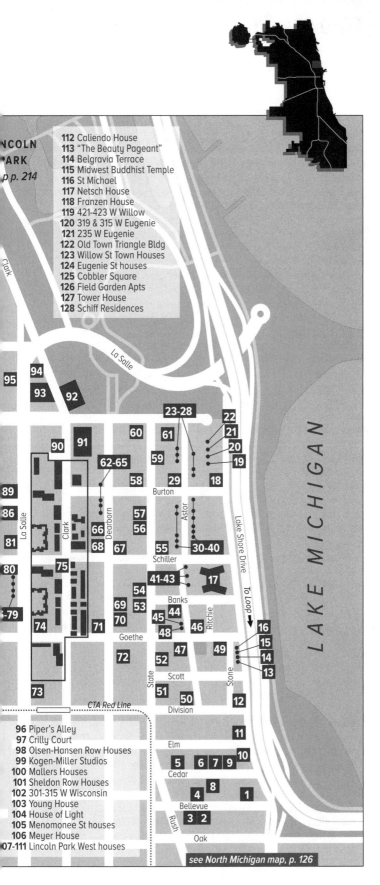

NCOLN
ARK
p p. 214

112 Caliendo House
113 "The Beauty Pageant"
114 Belgravia Terrace
115 Midwest Buddhist Temple
116 St Michael
117 Netsch House
118 Franzen House
119 421-423 W Willow
120 319 & 315 W Eugenie
121 235 W Eugenie
122 Old Town Triangle Bldg
123 Willow St Town Houses
124 Eugenie St houses
125 Cobbler Square
126 Field Garden Apts
127 Tower House
128 Schiff Residences

La Salle

Clark

95 94
    93 92

89
86

81

80

-79

LA SALLE

Clark

La Salle

Dearborn

90 91

62-65

58

66
68 67

75

74 71

73

23-28   22
          21
61   20
59   19
       29   18
      Burton

57
56

       55   30-40
      Schiller

41-43   17

54
69 53   Banks
70   45 44
     48 46   Ritchie

     47   49
72 52

51
50   12
Division

Astor

Lake Shore Drive

To Loop

16
15
14
13

11
Elm
                10
5   6 7 9
Cedar
        8
    4   1
Bellevue
    3 2

Rush

Oak

LAKE MICHIGAN

Scott

Goethe

State

Stone

CTA Red Line

96 Piper's Alley
97 Crilly Court
98 Olsen-Hansen Row Houses
99 Kogen-Miller Studios
100 Mallers Houses
101 Sheldon Row Houses
102 301-315 W Wisconsin
103 Young House
104 House of Light
105 Menomonee St houses
106 Meyer House
07-111 Lincoln Park West houses

see North Michigan map, p. 126

GOLD COAST/OLD TOWN

Throughout most of their history, the neighborhoods of the Gold Coast and Old Town presented a sharp contrast between rich and poor, elegance and squalor. Today, however, their demographics are surprisingly similar. While many Gold Coast mansions have been replaced by high-rises or subdivided into smaller but still desirable apartments, a tidal wave of money has swept over the workers' cottages and flats of Old Town, many of which have been converted into expensive single-family residences or sold as tear-downs.

The streetscapes of the two communities are still worlds apart. Old Town is filled with charmingly restored cottages, row houses, and small flats as well as coach houses, many of which were built for Gold Coast residents. The Gold Coast, apart from its many modern high-rises, has an abundance of mansions and large row houses. Along the Clark St./La Salle Blvd. boundary between the two neighborhoods is that exemplar of 1960s redevelopment, Carl Sandburg Village, constructed as the Gold Coast's Maginot Line against the creeping disintegration of Old Town and points west.

Old Town, as one might guess, is the earlier community, although the entire area was not included in the city's 1837 charter. It was settled by German produce farmers, who were numerous enough to form St. Michael's Parish in 1852. After the devastation of the Great Fire of 1871, wooden cottages sprang up to house the homeless. Most of the tiny, crudely built "relief shanties" are long gone, but many wooden cottages remain from the short period between the fire and the northward extension of the city's strict building code in the 1874 fire ordinance. The area remained heavily Germanic throughout the following decades, and by 1900, North Ave. as far west as Halsted St. was known as German Broadway.

Industry, which located in the heart of the area as well as along the river, provided employment for many. Housing west of La Salle Blvd., built for the working class and new immigrants, deteriorated in the twentieth century. By the 1940s, most of the Germans had moved away, replaced by Italians, African Americans, Asians, and later Hispanics.

Artists took advantage of depressed real estate values. In the 1920s, Sol Kogen and Edgar Miller turned decrepit housing on Burton Pl. into masterpieces of folk art, and in the 1960s, artists began buying and rehabilitating many of Old Town's small houses. Wells St. became the center of Chicago's counterculture, with head shops selling drug paraphernalia and psychedelic posters and record stores catering to flower children and the inevitable gawking tourists.

The massive urban renewal that resulted in the 1960s construction of Sandburg Village, together with the pioneering efforts of artists and architects, bolstered the area's reputation and effectively extended the Gold Coast west of its traditional boundaries. Apart from the Sandburg complex and a few tall buildings near the lake, Old Town has retained its low scale. Scattered urban renewal and private projects in the 1960s and 1970s were confined mostly to three- to four-story apartment buildings and town houses that met the sidewalk with high brick walls.

Beginning in the 1980s and accelerating into the twenty-first century, many early cottages were replaced by neotraditional multibathroom extravaganzas whose overblown character and/or scale are frequently jarring. But the area also has much exemplary new construction: town houses that extend welcoming stairways to the sidewalk, freestanding houses that echo the materials and styles of their more modest neighbors, and renovations that return buildings to their original character after decades of concealment beneath ugly siding materials. Old Town's projects span the careers of such well-known residential architects as Stanley Tigerman, Ben and Harry Weese, Larry Booth, and Jim Nagle from early town houses and renovations to large new houses.

The Gold Coast was created almost single-handedly by State St. retail mogul Potter Palmer and his wife, Bertha, Chicago's reigning socialite. When they built their Henry Ives Cobb–designed castle (demolished) at 1350 N. Lake Shore Dr. in 1882, the locus of social power began an inexorable shift north from S. Prairie Ave. to this area. Palmer also bought land for speculative development to profit from his self-created gold rush, in which land values soared 400 percent within a decade.

Early development concentrated on the drive itself and on adjacent streets from Bellevue Pl. north to Burton Pl. The north half was developed after the turn of the century, when the Catholic archbishop subdivided property on Dearborn, State, and Astor Sts. just south of his North Ave. mansion. Modest 1870s Italianate row houses farther west were joined in the 1880s by flashier Queen Anne and Romanesque residences. Commissions for houses from New York architects McKim, Mead & White in the 1890s started a trend toward neoclassical and Georgian Revival styles; the latter was particularly well suited to the town house format and proliferated after 1900.

Apartment buildings had appeared in the Gold Coast as early as the 1890s, but their construction was concentrated in two great eras. The boom of the 1920s brought large revival-style towers, mostly on Lake Shore Dr. In the 1950s and 1960s, many mansions were replaced by behemoths that forever changed the area's character. Even the narrow streets farther west have had their scale disrupted by high-rise apartment buildings. Yet the Gold Coast remains a desirable address.

—PATRICIA MARKS LURIE WITH LAURIE MCGOVERN PETERSEN

1 Fortnightly of Chicago
(Bryan Lathrop House)
120 E. Bellevue Pl.
1891–93, MCKIM, MEAD & WHITE
1972, RESTORATION, PERKINS & WILL

New Yorker Charles F. McKim, a leading architect of the 1893 World's Columbian Exposition, designed this elegant Georgian Revival trendsetter when Romanesque was still the dominant residential style. By 1900, Georgian was the favorite Gold Coast style. This exceptionally graceful example has gently curving bays at each end of the unusually wide house. The symmetry is broken only by the off-center placement of the door. Occupied by a women's club since 1922, the building is in excellent condition, with a fiberglass cornice that replicates the original.

2 43–45 E. Bellevue Pl.
1892, CHARLES M. PALMER

This Romanesque double house, built by Potter Palmer as an investment, is on a much larger scale than many he built in the area. The rustication diminishes with each floor. Unfortunately, the cornice is gone.

Fortnightly of Chicago

3 Chandler Apartments
33 E. Bellevue Pl.
1911, RICHARD E. SCHMIDT,
GARDEN & MARTIN

This Georgian Revival apartment building has lavish classical detail. Some of it is treated rather originally, such as the keystone-and-lintel arrangement on the fifth-floor projecting bays.

4 Lot P. Smith House
32 E. Bellevue Pl.
1887, BURNHAM & ROOT

One of John Wellborn Root's few extant residential designs displays his flair for decorative detail in the unusual dormer with its knobby finials and in the pattern of circles in the pediment and above the entry door.

5 20 E. Cedar St.
1924, FUGARD & KNAPP

Splendid Gothic terra-cotta frames huge windows that illuminate two-story living spaces. The deep fourteenth-floor setback creates a large terrace and a "castle in the air" crown.

6 42–48 E. Cedar St.
1896, CHARLES M. PALMER
7 50–54 E. Cedar St.
1892, L. GUSTAV HALLBERG

Rusticated stone, roundheaded windows, and foliate capitals mark Hallberg's Romanesque town houses. Each of the two groups was designed as a unit, with gabled ends flanking a flat-topped central section. The symmetry breaks down for the group at 42–48 (built by Potter Palmer), because 42 has a fourth floor with a ballroom.

8 49 E. Cedar St.
1908, MARSHALL & FOX

This was an early "joint ownership apartment building" in which Marshall had one of the full-floor units. The elegant semicircular bay recalls Marshall & Fox's larger buildings nearby, such as 1200 N. Lake Shore Dr. and 1550 N. State Pkwy. By contrast, this structure is Georgian, with its Flemish bond brickwork alternating red stretchers with dark brownish-black headers.

9 60 E. Cedar St.
1890, CURD H. GOTTIG

Flamboyant even in this ritzy neighborhood, a gable and three turrets squeeze onto the roofline, while six squat columns support ground-floor arches. The facade is of rusticated Georgia marble, with abundant copper trim above the cornice line.

10 1120 N. Lake Shore Dr.
1926, ROBERT S. DEGOLYER

The prosperous 1920s produced a variety of residential high-rises in this neighborhood. This one offered smaller, customized apartments rather than the floor-throughs of nearby luxury buildings.

11 1130 N. Lake Shore Dr.
(90 E. Elm St.)
1911, HOWARD VAN DOREN SHAW

One of the first tall apartment buildings to invade the line of mansions along the drive was also a pioneer cooperative apartment, where occupants were shareholders in a corporation. Each apartment occupied an entire floor; Shaw was among the first owners. Tudor Revival, his favorite domestic style, gives the building the appeal and character of his country houses. The facade is dotted with medieval motifs and carved panels of fruit. Like many apartments with corner sites on the drive, its entrance is on the side street, but the address has been changed to emphasize the lakefront location.

12 1200 N. Lake Shore Dr.
(Stewart Apartments)
1913, MARSHALL & FOX

The architects' trademarks include the graceful Adamesque detailing, the rounded bays, and the spacious plan, which places living room and dining room on either side of a sun parlor with a generous bay.

13 Carl C. Heisen House
1250 N. Lake Shore Dr.
1890, FRANK B. ABBOTT
14 Mason Brayman Starring House
1254 N. Lake Shore Dr.
1889, L. GUSTAV HALLBERG
1990, RENOVATION, MARVIN
HERMAN & ASSOCS.

This pair of single-family houses offers a fragmentary glimpse of the drive's early appearance. The arched entries, squat towers,

Carl C. Heisen House

1350 and 1360 N. Lake Shore Dr.

and deeply recessed porches are hallmarks of the Richardsonian Romanesque. The house at 1250 is rough and rugged, even down to the small columns and piers, while 1254 has smoothly polished columns with elaborately carved capitals, one of which includes a grinning face. In 1990, the buildings were joined and the interiors were gutted to create four new residences.

15 Arthur T. Aldis House
1258 N. Lake Shore Dr.
1896, HOLABIRD & ROCHE

Even no-nonsense architects had occasional flights of fancy. While designing this Venetian Gothic palazzo, they were also working for Aldis's brother, Owen (agent for Boston developers Peter and Shepherd Brooks), on the Marquette Building.

16 Lawrence D. Rockwell House
1260 N. Lake Shore Dr.
1911, HOLABIRD & ROCHE

This is far more characteristic of the firm than the Aldis House. With its simple rectangular massing, minimal classical details, restrained surfaces, and overall symmetry, it is typical of houses built just after the turn of the century.

17 1350 and 1360 N. Lake Shore Dr.
1949–51, LOEBL, SCHLOSSMAN & BENNETT

Just as the construction of Potter Palmer's crenellated castle on this site in 1882 spurred a local boom in mansion building, its replacement by this pair of twenty-two-story towers led a new generation of high-rise

development on the drive. Richard M. Bennett's overriding concern was to give every unit a view of the lake. The brick walls, with their windows set flush, bend like paper around the irregular plan. The angled bay windows and the mid-building bends create a multitude of planes on the long facades.

18 1500 N. Lake Shore Dr.
1931, ROSARIO CANDELA, DESIGN ARCH.; MCNALLY & QUINN, ARCH. OF RECORD

This is the only Chicago work by Candela, who was the premier designer of luxury apartment buildings in New York City during the 1920s boom years. It has a characteristically sedate old-money street presence and a lavish three-story penthouse complete with gardens and reflecting pool.

19 International College of Surgeons
(Edward T. Blair House)
1516 N. Lake Shore Dr.
1914, MCKIM, MEAD & WHITE

20 International Museum of Surgical Science
(Eleanor Robinson Countiss House)
1524 N. Lake Shore Dr.
1917, HOWARD VAN DOREN SHAW

21 Polish Consulate
(Bernard A. Eckhart House)
1530 N. Lake Shore Dr.
1916, BENJAMIN H. MARSHALL

This trio's austere neoclassicism belies their separate authorship. The Blair House's setback and restrained use of classical ornament on a smoothly polished facade set the standard for the others. The Countiss House is a rare Shaw essay in French architecture. His

1500 Astor

strong-minded clients insisted on a copy of the Petit Trianon at Versailles but with four stories instead of three. Go inside to see the many intact interior features, including the stone staircase with partially gilded iron balustrade and a lovely paneled library on the second floor.

22 1540 N. Lake Shore Dr.
1925, HUSZAGH & HILL

Mundane at ground level, it has a top inspired by medieval French châteaus. The elaborate upper floors are best seen from the drive.

23 1524 N. Astor St.
1968, I. W. COLBURN & ASSOCS.

This 1960s essay in contextualism almost pulls a vanishing act by continuing the brick wall of its neighbors to the south. Look at the north wall to see the U-shaped plan that brings light to the interior.

24 1520 N. Astor St.
1911, JEREMIAH K. CADY
25 1518 N. Astor St.
1911, JENNEY, MUNDIE & JENSEN
26 1525 N. Astor St.
1916, ARCHITECT UNKNOWN
27 1511 N. Astor St.
1911, ARTHUR HEUN
28 1505 N. Astor St.
1911, JENNEY, MUNDIE & JENSEN

These are variations on the popular Georgian row house theme. Each floor has three window openings stacked above those of the floor below, usually decreasing in height, and some have especially tall windows on a second-floor *piano*

nobile. The parapet is frequently crowned by a balustrade whose openings align with those of the windows below. The few details present are usually classically inspired (pediments above windows or doors, etc.), as is the rigid system of proportions.

29 1500 Astor
(Elinor Patterson–Cyrus H. McCormick Mansion)
20 E. Burton Pl.
1893, MCKIM, MEAD & WHITE
1927, ADDITION, DAVID ADLER
1978, CONVERSION TO CONDOMINIUMS, NAGLE, HARTRAY & ASSOCS.; WILBERT R. HASBROUCK, CONSULTANT

Together with the Lathrop House of a year earlier, this Stanford White design is, for Chicago, an early and influential example of a neoclassical residence. Closer to an Italian palazzo than its predecessor, the materials here are orange Roman brick with terra-cotta trim. McCormick bought the house in 1914, and in 1927, David Adler doubled its size to the north.

30 Peter Fortune Houses
1451 N. Astor St. and 43 E. Burton St.
1910, HOWARD VAN DOREN SHAW

By 1910, Jacobethan was a close competitor of Georgian Revival, although better suited to expansive country properties than narrow city lots. The corner site makes this an only slightly scaled-down version of the country houses that Shaw was designing so prolifically at the time. His favored motif of carved fruit baskets tops the strapwork panels flanking the Astor St. entrance.

31 C. D. Peacock Jr. House
1449 N. Astor St.
1898, E. R. KRAUSE

The massive château, made fashionable by Solon S. Beman's Kimball House, was even more difficult to adapt to narrow city lots than the Tudor Revival. The large bay and massive entry porch dominate the facade, which has an unusual frieze pattern of shells under the cornice and rather odd, twisted half columns at each end.

32 Edward P. Russell House
1444 N. Astor St.
1929, HOLABIRD & ROOT

Sleek, urbane, sophisticated, and very French, this elegant Art Deco town house is timeless and unique. The poised and polished facade is of stone from Lens, France, with gleaming granite trim, a barely suggested three-story bay, and incised ornament.

33 C. Vallette Kasson House
1442 N. Astor St.
1891, POND & POND

The doorway's pointed stone arch is echoed in tracings of arches in brick above the windows.

34 Horatio N. May House
1443 N. Astor St.
1891, JOSEPH LYMAN SILSBEE

The quarry-faced granite blocks of the rigidly symmetrical facade are on a colossal scale.

Horatio N. May House

35 George W. Meeker House
1431 N. Astor St.
1894, HOLABIRD & ROCHE

The gently curving bay is reminiscent of those on Boston's Federal-style houses, but the pedimented porch is a later addition. The best original feature is the metal cornice with its unusual ball motif.

36 Eugene R. Hutchins House
1429 N. Astor St.
1891, POND & POND

This quirky design combines rough Romanesque masonry with such Gothic details as the pointed arch above the door and the crocketed dormers with small-paned windows.

37 Rensselaer W. Cox House
1427 N. Astor St.
1889, WILLIAM LE BARON JENNEY

The rock-faced brick is an unusual feature of this otherwise mundane design.

38 Thomas W. Hinde House
1412 N. Astor St.
1892, DOUGLAS S. PENTECOST

This unusually decorated facade combines classical elements with diamond-paned windows and medieval motifs.

39 Joseph T. Ryerson Jr. House
1406 N. Astor St.
1922, DAVID ADLER
1931, ADDITION, DAVID ADLER

Adler fluidly adapted French style to the Chicago town house formula. His mansarded fourth-floor addition accommodated a large collection of Chicago memorabilia later donated to the Chicago Historical Society. The owner's initials appear in the decorative ironwork over the entrance.

40 Perry H. Smith House
1400 N. Astor St.
1887, COBB & FROST
1991, ADDITION, HAMMOND,
    BEEBY & BABKA

Despite the Astor St. address, the entrance is on Schiller St., punctuated by a magnificent Romanesque arch. So beautifully matched that it is almost indistinguishable from the original is the 3,000-square-foot west addition, which contains the kitchen and a master bedroom suite.

Charnley-Persky House

41 Charnley-Persky House
1365 N. Astor St.
1892, ADLER & SULLIVAN
1982, RESTORATION, THE
   OFFICE OF JOHN VINCI
1988, RESTORATION, SKIDMORE,
   OWINGS & MERRILL
2003, RESTORATION, JOHN
   EIFLER & ASSOCS.

The house was designed when Frank Lloyd Wright was Sullivan's chief draftsman, so it presents a rare opportunity to see the genius of both architects under one broad roof. It is owned by the Society of Architectural Historians, whose weekly tours allow visitors to experience the breathtaking atrium that occupies the large central portion of the house.

42 Astor Court
(William O. Goodman House)
1355 N. Astor St.
1914, HOWARD VAN DOREN SHAW

In this very formal exercise in neoclassical/Georgian Revival com-position, the details are alternately robust (the second-floor window surrounds) and delicate (the design of stacked urns around the central window, the feathery pilaster capitals, and animal heads and skulls topped with fruit baskets forming keystones). The entrance on the south, originally a drive, leads to a landscaped court and entries to several units.

43 Edwin J. Gardiner House
1345 N. Astor St.
1887, TREAT & FOLTZ

The sandstone from Dunreath quarry, Ohio, in a mélange of fruit sherbet colors, is one of the street's most vivid materials—and the only notable element of this otherwise ordinary Romanesque town house.

44 Houses for Potter Palmer
**1316–1322 N. Astor St.
and 25 E. Banks St.**
1889, CHARLES M. PALMER

Four of this group are textbook examples of rustication, especially the striated or banded variety on 1316 and 1320.

45 James L. Houghteling Houses
1308–1312 N. Astor St.
1887–88, BURNHAM & ROOT

Root designed four town houses (1306 was demolished) for Houghteling and moved into 1310. The large second-floor bay is not part of his original design, which had a series of three arched windows. The group of houses shows a remarkably coherent combination of stylistic influences.

Astor Court

James L. Houghteling Houses

46 **1301 N. Astor St.**
1932, PHILIP B. MAHER
47 **1260 N. Astor St.**
1931, PHILIP B. MAHER
These severe, decorous Art Moderne apartment buildings were among the first Gold Coast high-rises west of Lake Shore Dr.

1301 N. Astor St.

48 **Astor Tower**
(Astor Tower Hotel)
1300 N. Astor St.
1963, BERTRAND GOLDBERG
1996, FACADE, DESTEFANO & PARTNERS
Concrete columns raise the lowest floors above the rooflines of surrounding houses. The metal jalousies, which originally screened the windows in this design experiment, were replaced with plain glass in the massive 1996 facade renovation.

49 **65 E. Goethe**
2002, LUCIEN LAGRANGE ARCHS.
Lagrange continues his reign as the master of Gallic luxury with this condominium development. The roofline and massing fit well into the neighborhood. The lower two floors feature maisonettes, which are townhouses incorporated into an apartment building.

50 **1210 N. Astor St.**
(McConnell Apartments)
1897, HOLABIRD & ROCHE
Perhaps the ultimate Chicago School apartment building, this is a forthright composition in red brick with strong bays that echo the firm's Old Colony Building and many demolished hotels.

51 **Frank F. Fisher Apartments**
1209 N. State Pkwy.
1937, ANDREW N. REBORI; EDGAR MILLER, DESIGN ASSOC.

Frank F. Fisher Apartments

Ignoring the street's parade of Revival styles, Rebori wrote a new chapter with this coolly masterful Art Moderne block. Onto a long, narrow, unpromising lot, he shoehorned thirteen duplex apartments oriented around a sliver of private space. The terra-cotta plaques (some are missing) are by Edgar Miller, and his carved animals originally posed atop the wooden beams that project above the entrance.

52 Charles Henry Hulburd and Charles C. Yoe Double House
1243–1245 N. State Pkwy.
1880, ARCHITECT UNKNOWN

This Second Empire design uses a contrasting stone to join window heads and sills. The abstract foliate ornament in the keystones has a neo-Grec crispness.

53 1328 N. State Pkwy.
1938, ANDREW N. REBORI
1956, REMODELING,
   BERTRAND GOLDBERG

A simple brick zigzag unites the facade and leads the eye to the small entry sculpted from the severe front. Two houses were built on opposite ends of this narrow lot, each with the main second-floor living space designated a studio. Goldberg made the houses into a home and studio for his mother-in-law, sculptor Lillian Florsheim. Look for Rebori's tiny initials in the wooden spandrel.

54 George S. Isham House
1340 N. State Pkwy.
1899, JAMES GAMBLE ROGERS

The leaden sobriety of this stiff, French-inspired mansion became an odd backdrop for later owner Hugh Hefner's 1960s *Playboy* excesses.

55 1411 N. State Pkwy./10 E. Schiller St.
1914, ANDREW SANDEGREN

This unique Tudor-Craftsman hybrid smoothly incorporates generous balconies, not only enhancing the floor plans but also strengthening the facades.

56 George A. Weiss House
1428 N. State Pkwy.
1886, HARALD M. HANSEN

Gold Coast clients' deep pockets enabled the use of highly worked, unusual materials such as this pink Georgia marble and the copper crockets, crests, and parapets.

57 Charles K. Miller House
1432 N. State Pkwy.
1884, A. M. F. COLTON

Remarkable individual elements give the facade that vigorous incoherence so typical of the early Queen Anne style. Most peculiar is the plaque with florid Sullivanesque ornament appearing to spew from a flaming brazier.

Charles K. Miller House

58 Graham Foundation for Advanced Studies in the Fine Arts
(Albert F. Madlener House)
4 W. Burton Pl.
1902, RICHARD E. SCHMIDT
1963, RESTORATION, BRENNER,
   DANFORTH & ROCKWELL

Heaven's gate can be no more finely crafted than this doorway. The building's cubical massing and Teutonic severity owe a debt to the early nineteenth-century villas of Karl Friedrich Schinkel, but the precise ornament is pure Chicago. Schmidt employee Hugh M. G. Garden is credited with the design. A collection of architectural fragments is on display in the court on the west. The building hosts exhibitions and is open to the public.

59 J. Lewis Cochran House
1521 N. State Pkwy.
MID-1890S, GEORGE W. MAHER

Developer Cochran selected Maher from among the many architects who designed for his Edgewater subdivision and elsewhere.

Graham Foundation for Advanced Studies in the Fine Arts

60 1550 N. State Pkwy.

1912, MARSHALL & FOX

This was the ultimate in luxury when it was built, by architects who set the standards for early twentieth-century hotels and apartments. Each apartment originally had fifteen rooms and occupied an entire floor—more than 9,000 square feet. From the bowed windows and metal balconies to the *orangerie*, it is the *dernier cri* in French elegance. There is an ordered rhythm to the lively facade, with more dimension to the wall plane.

1550 N. State Pkwy.

61 Residence of the Roman Catholic Archbishop of Chicago

1555 N. State Pkwy.

1880, ALFRED F. PASHLEY

This early Queen Anne residence still has Italianate windows but is dominated by the busy, picturesque roofline typical of the style, punctuated by nineteen chimneys.

*The **wood block alley** (connecting N. Astor and N. State) behind the archbishop's house was constructed in 1909 and restored in 2011.*

62 George E. Rickcords House

1500 N. Dearborn Pkwy.

1889, WILLIAM W. CLAY

The Richardsonian Romanesque style frequently gives substance and street presence to a house squeezed onto a narrow lot. The entry is carved from the body of the house and is framed by low-springing arches.

63 Joseph C. Bullock House

1454 N. Dearborn Pkwy.

1877, EDBROOKE & BURNHAM

64 John P. Wilson House

1450 N. Dearborn Pkwy.

1877, ARCHITECT UNKNOWN

65 Philo R. King House

1434 N. Dearborn Pkwy.

1876, ARCHITECT UNKNOWN

The Bullock House is a fine rare example of a full-blown Second Empire town house. In addition to the characteristic mansard roof (still shingled in slate), there is abundant classical detail. A pavilion effect was created by setting back the entrance bay and emphasizing the north corner with pilasters and incised quoins. The Wilson and King houses share many of these details, with crisp incised ornament giving them even more of a French flavor.

66 St. Chrysostom's Episcopal Church

1424 N. Dearborn Pkwy.

1913, BROWN & WALCOTT
1922, ADDITION TO CHURCH & PARISH
HOUSE, CLARK & WALCOTT
1925, ONE-STORY ADDITION &
BELFRY, CHESTER H. WALCOTT
1925, REMODELING, CHESTER
H. WALCOTT AND BENNETT,
PARSONS & FROST

The intimate church has the feeling of a campus chapel. The complex swallowed a house by William Le Baron Jenney to the south to create the parish house.

67 Luther McConnell House

1401 N. Dearborn Pkwy.

1877, ASA LYON

One of Chicago's oldest Queen Anne houses exhibits the style's characteristic variety. A rotated corner bay enlivens the irregular but not excessively polygonal facade. The severe planar surfaces are enriched with carved terra-cotta plaques—like the griffin crouched in a niche under the chimney.

68 40–50 W. Schiller St.

1922, REBORI, WENTWORTH,
DEWEY & MCCORMICK

To envision the original aspect of this elegant small apartment building, picture the garden opening onto the street where a low wall now partially fills the arches. The primary entrances used to face this garden, and the doors that now serve as street entries were for servants and tradesmen.

69 Augustus Warner House

1337 N. Dearborn Pkwy.

1884, L. GUSTAV HALLBERG

The deep overhanging bay is the major design element, making the house look as if it had been plucked from a narrow European street.

70 Lucius B. Mantonya Flats

1325 N. Dearborn Pkwy.

1887, CURD H. GOTTIG

The facade is bedecked with seventeen Moorish arches, many infilled with rich leaded glass.

71 Three Arts Club

1300 N. Dearborn Pkwy.

1914, HOLABIRD & ROCHE

This former residence for female art students was John A. Holabird's first design for his father's firm, which he joined after returning from Paris. The ornament is highly eclectic, drawn from a variety of European sources. The sculptural panels on the east facade were inspired by Jean Goujon's Fontaine des Innocents (1549) in Paris. The building was vacated in 2003.

72 R. Philip Gormully House

1245 N. Dearborn Pkwy.

1884, ARCHITECT UNKNOWN

The pink slate is a foil to the magnificent copper work of the second-floor windows and third-floor dormer. It must have served as a billboard-size advertisement for Gormully's business, galvanized iron cornices and metalwork.

73 1211 N. La Salle Blvd.

1929, OLDEFEST & WILLIAMS
1981, RENOVATION, WEESE
SEEGERS HICKEY WEESE

An old apartment hotel with one decorated facade was converted to an apartment building whose walls became a canvas for artist Richard Haas. His *Homage to the Chicago School of Architecture* arranges the windows into trompe l'oeil bays on the eastern facade. On the south wall, Louis H. Sullivan's round, terra-cotta–encrusted window from the Merchants' National Bank

1211 N. La Salle Blvd.

Carl Sandburg Village

in Grinnell, Iowa, rises above the Golden Doorway of his Transportation Building at the 1893 World's Columbian Exposition. Between them, the Board of Trade Building two miles south is "reflected" in painted windows.

74 First St. Paul's Evangelical Lutheran Church

1301 N. La Salle Blvd.

1970, EDWARD D. DART

Severe on the outside but serene and comfortable inside, the church has an inward focus; north windows bring gentle, clear light to the extremely simple chancel.

75 Carl Sandburg Village

Clark St. and La Salle Blvd. between Division St. and North Ave.

1960–75, LOUIS R. SOLOMON AND JOHN D. CORDWELL & ASSOCS.

A blighted area of run-down housing was demolished for this new urban neighborhood, part of the Clark–La Salle Redevelopment Project. Most prominent are the high-rises, which do not match the charm of the low-rise apartments or town houses.

Following is a fragment of fashionable La Salle Blvd. (entries 76–79 and 81), once the western fringe of the Gold Coast, walled off from old neighbors to the east by Carl

Sandburg Village. Most of the houses were demolished or converted to apartments or commercial spaces. Many survivors were badly remuddled, but several have been restored.

76 Anna A. Wolf House

1338 N. La Salle Blvd.

1888, FREDERICK W. WOLF

The tiny copper turret has gusto, from its engaged column "leg" to its fish-scale panels to its bell-shaped roof. In the gable is a wolf's head, a pictorial reference to the owners' name.

77 Double House for John McEwen

1340–1342 N. La Salle Blvd.

1888, BURLING & WHITEHOUSE

Mirror images up to their mismatched gables, these chocolate brown sandstone houses are distinguished by fine craftsmanship on the bays and in the stonework.

78 John McEwen House

1346 N. La Salle Blvd.

1872, ARCHITECT UNKNOWN

Although altered, this grand mansard-roofed villa with its projecting central pavilion still reveals a French influence. In the late nineteenth and early twentieth centuries, the neighborhood was heavily Swedish; the house was both a Swedish Lutheran hospice and a home for the elderly before its 1986 rehabilitation as luxury housing.

79 John F. Jelke House
1352 N. La Salle Blvd.
1895, BEERS, CLAY & DUTTON
1981, RENOVATION, MARVIN ULLMAN

This facade playfully exaggerates its classically derived elements. The Palladian window stretches to five panes across, while a low row of rolling swan's-neck pediments forms the parapet. The appendage to the north is a 1980s elevator.

80 Schiller St. Town Houses
141–149 W. Schiller St.
1988, NAGLE, HARTRAY & ASSOCS.

Bulging exaggerated bays grab for the maximum north light.

81 Frederick Keller House
1406 N. La Salle Blvd.
1882, ARCHITECT UNKNOWN

Far from the spartan "octagon front" formula of the 1870s is this finely crafted fussbudget. It has a distinctly French flavor with its mansard roof, stringcourses, and colonnettes.

82 W. Burton Pl.
(Carl St.)

Across the street from the ordered universe of Carl Sandburg Village is a small, happily slapdash dreamworld, credited as the birthplace of Old Town as an artists' community. In 1927, a lively group of artists and craftspeople began to reinvent W. Burton Pl., then called Carl St. This neighborhood of "tumble-down old flats and cheap rooming houses," as the *Chicago Daily News* described it in 1940, became their urban canvas.

Entrepreneur and artist Sol Kogen and artist Edgar Miller had met at the School of the Art Institute in 1917. Chicagoan Kogen then worked several years in his family's yard goods business before moving to Paris. Miller grew up in Idaho, where he was influenced by Native American artists and developed a love for animals—including the antelopes, horses, and weasels that populate his work. After returning to Chicago, Kogen began his conversions by inviting Miller to join him in the work at 155 W. Burton Pl.

Kogen and the others began with Victorian houses like those still visible at 147 or 164–166 W. Burton Pl. (both built in 1881) and remade them in a richly decorative, freehand Art Deco style. Some were merely embellished; others were entirely slipcovered with brick and sported additions and new profiles.

Much was done without building permits, and when architects were retained, they apparently had only a minor influence on the designs, which were directed by the artist-owners and their artist-craftsmen friends. Andrew N. Rebori, for example, who worked with Kogen on 155 W. Burton Pl., recalled, "Yes, I was the consulting architect, but only when I was consulted—which was damned little."

Low on capital but high on vision, the owners went scavenging in Maxwell St. flea markets for tiles, copper tubs, wooden doors, and hardware. Construction was often limited to one apartment at a time, using rents to capitalize slow unit-by-unit conversions. Some were never really finished, as their owners continued to add new art objects. Appreciative tenants and owners care for and continue to carefully embellish their buildings. In 2006, architect Ann Temple renovated one around the corner at **154 W. Schiller St.**

83 Theophil Studios
143 W. Burton Pl.
1940, RENOVATION, FRANK J. LAPASSO

With Kogen's advice, artist Theophil Reuther rebuilt an 1892 house to a Moderne look with stucco facades sporting red-brick trim, porthole windows, and Milleresque decorative plaques. Note the leaded-glass windows.

84 151 W. Burton Pl.
1932–35, REMODELING, ARCHITECT UNKNOWN

Self-confident pizzazz transformed an 1887 house into this stylish apartment building. Kogen served as an adviser to owner and rehabber William Giuliani, a former opera singer. A front addition brought the house out to the street, while at the

151 W. Burton Pl.

and spaces open up in unanticipated directions, with a surprise around every corner. Miller's beloved animals, especially weasels, enliven the stained-glass windows and wooden carvings, while Kogen's vigorous hand can be seen in the mosaic sidewalk.

86 161 W. Burton Pl.

1940, REMODELING, WILLIAM WENDLAND

An 1879 Italianate house with a Joliet limestone front (the brick side wall is still visible on the alley) was rebuilt into a snazzy four-unit apartment building. The enclosed stair is lit by four slit windows that climb the facade. The two-story windows on the front and side lend the stylistic cachet of artists' studios, though the owner, Norman E. Johnson, intended the dwellings "for the average person in commercial life."

87 160 W. Burton Pl.

1887, ARCHITECT UNKNOWN
1938, REMODELING,
LAWRENCE MONBERG

The original window locations on this 1887 house still show through the paint and the patching on the severe facade. Miller maintained that Kogen duplicated some existing sculptured plaques by Miller without his permission and installed them on several Burton Pl. buildings, including this one.

rear it grew to engulf the old coach house. The deliberately rough brick walls, set with flagstones and tiles, serve as artful foils to three sets of rounded corner windows. Glass and tile scavenged from the 1933 World's Fair form the curving windows and line the stairway and halls.

85 155 W. Burton Pl.

(Carl St. Studios)

1927, REMODELING, SOL KOGEN,
ARTIST/CONTRACTOR; EDGAR
MILLER, ARTIST; ANDREW N.
REBORI, CONSULTING ARCH.

Lovingly detailed and devotedly maintained, this apartment complex is intriguing, beguiling, unpredictable, and visually bounteous. A mansarded Victorian was converted to seventeen (now sixteen) idiosyncratic studio apartments. Corridors

88 152–156 W. Burton Pl.

1933–39, REMODELING, ARCHITECTS
UNKNOWN; SOL KOGEN, CLIVE
RICKABAUGH, AND CARL PETER
KOCH, ARTISTS/CONTRACTORS

The resident artists created a courtyard complex by combining two rooming houses and three coach houses. They bricked up old windows and added new ones, leaving a roundheaded third-floor dormer on 156 as a clue to the original nineteenth-century look.

89 1500 N. La Salle Blvd.

1892, EDMUND R. KRAUSE

Bays serve this apartment building as well as they did the skyscrapers downtown, providing light, ventilation, and a pleasingly rhythmic facade.

155 W. Burton Pl.

Germania Place

90 Germania Place
1536 N. Clark St.
1888, AUGUST FIEDLER

This ethnic meeting hall is a symbolic gateway to the Old Town Triangle, settled by German immigrants in the late 1840s. The club was built by the Germania Maennerchor, organized in 1865 to sing a requiem for President Lincoln when his bier rested in Chicago. The elaborate terra-cotta ornament includes lyres centered on the Ionic capitals.

91 Latin School of Chicago
59 W. North Blvd.
1969, HARRY WEESE & ASSOCS.
1993–94, FIRST-FLOOR INFILL
AND LOBBY RENOVATION,
NAGLE, HARTRAY & ASSOC.
1995–96, TOP-FLOOR CLASSROOM
ADDITION AND ALLEY EXPANSION,
NAGLE, HARTRAY & ASSOC.
2007, MIDDLE SCHOOL ADDITION,
NAGLE HARTRAY DANKER KAGAN
MCKAY PENNEY ARCHITECTS

This concrete-and-brick structure houses the upper grades of the private Latin School, founded in 1888.

Completely filling its limited site, the school also uses the playing fields of Lincoln Park for recreation.

92 Chicago History Museum
Clark St. at North Ave.
1932, GRAHAM, ANDERSON,
PROBST & WHITE
1988, ADDITION, HOLABIRD & ROOT
2006, RENOVATION, HAMMOND
BEEBY RUPERT AINGE

It has grown in all directions—but, happily, it has done so in the hands of skillful designers respectful of precious park space. The major remaining Graham, Anderson, Probst & White facade faces Lincoln Park in a sober Federal Revival style. The plaza surmounts underground storage areas that accommodate growing collections without infringing on open space. The Clark St. addition, which consumed a previous addition, blends with the original's massing, colors, and materials but has a more open and welcoming appearance at the entry under its precisely gridded pediment and curtain wall.

93 The Moody Church
**1630 N. Clark St./1635
N. La Salle Blvd.**
1925, FUGARD & KNAPP
2007, NORTH ADDITION,
MCBRIDE KELLEY BAURER

Evangelist Dwight L. Moody came to Chicago in 1856 as a businessman but soon devoted his life to uplifting working people and the poor. According to the dedication-day program, the church design was inspired in part

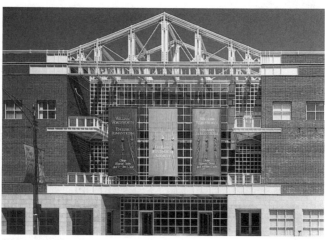
Chicago History Museum

by the Byzantine Hagia Sophia in Istanbul; the offices and meeting rooms on the La Salle Blvd. side were based on various Romanesque churches from Lombardy. A brick structure with sparing use of terra-cotta ornament, the building provided a large gathering place at limited cost.

94 BP Gas Station
Clark St. and La Salle Blvd.
1971, STANDARD OIL OF INDIANA
(NOW BP); GEORGE W. TERP
JR., SUPERVISING ARCH.

Standard Oil used the prominent location to make a bold corporate statement with a space-age gas station, while placating developer Arthur Rubloff, who did not want unattractive views from his planned high-rise across the street. A shipyard welded steel beams into the desired curves, and an innovative white material originally covered the roof.

95 Emma Fernow House
1620 N. La Salle Blvd.
1883, FROMMANN & JEBSEN

While delighting modern eyes, this type of early Queen Anne eclecticism drove critics to exasperation: French Second Empire roof; an almost Gothic third-floor window; slate-, brick-, stone-, and metalwork; and a carved stone head commonly found on homes of this period designed or owned by Germans.

96 Piper's Alley Commercial Mall
Wells St. North of North Ave.
1974–77, STANLEY TIGERMAN & ASSOCS.

The renovation of a bakery on the west side of Wells St. and new construction on the east created a retail complex around this busy intersection. While Tigerman's building for the Walgreens drugstore chain has functioned successfully, the building to the west has been through many changes, and any sense of an ensemble is long gone. One part that has remained constant is Second City, the popular theater company, which occupies space behind a terra-cotta frieze salvaged from Adler & Sullivan's demolished Schiller Theatre. Designed for the third-floor balcony, the frieze features the heads of great German writers and philosophers and is the largest of several Schiller fragments scattered around the near North Side. At Walgreens, the exterior light fixtures of crouching frogs supporting light globes are from Navy Pier.

The streets of Old Town are inviting but narrow and difficult to navigate by car. The area between Wells St. and Cleveland Ave. (entries 97–124) is best seen on foot or by bicycle.

97 Crilly Ct. Development
North Park Ave. and Wells St.,
St. Paul Ave. and Eugenie St.

This late nineteenth-century mixed-use Queen Anne development offered many housing options and convenient retail space. Real estate developer Daniel F. Crilly purchased this block in 1885,

Crilly Ct. Development

cut a street (Crilly Ct.) through it, and built the row houses on the west side. Three years later, **1717–1719 N. North Park** was moved to its present site from Germania Pl., just south of North Ave. The combination commercial and apartment building at **1700–1718 N. Wells St.**, designed by Flanders & Zimmerman (1888), was followed in 1893 by the three apartment buildings designed by that firm at **1701 to 1713 N. North Park Ave.** Crilly's undertaking culminated in 1895 with four apartment buildings on the **east side of Crilly Ct.**, named after his children, Isabelle, Oliver, Edgar, and Erminnie.

98 Olsen-Hansen Row Houses
164–172 W. Eugenie St.
1886, HARALD M. HANSEN

Of the twelve houses that the Norwegian-born Hansen designed for Adolph Olsen at this corner, only five survive; 164 was the architect's own residence. The fanciful facades of these Queen Anne structures, together with their irregular rooflines and combinations of materials and colors, typify the most exuberant Victorian design.

99 Kogen-Miller Studios
1734 N. Wells St.
1928–32, REMODELING, SOL
  KOGEN, CONTRACTOR/ARTIST;
  EDGAR MILLER, ARTIST

As with their W. Burton Pl. collaborations, Kogen and Miller designed and built with great enthusiasm and imagination but little documentation. They built onto the front in 1928, raised the building in 1931, and put on a top addition in 1932. Their handiwork includes carved doors and windows, Miller's stained glass, small decorative plaques, and ceramic tiles from Kogen's scavenged collection.

100 Houses for John B. Mallers
1834–1836 N. Lincoln Ave.
1876, JOHN J. FLANDERS
1838 N. Lincoln Ave.
1879, JOHN J. FLANDERS

An Italianate variation popular in Chicago after the Fire is this triangular bayed type, usually executed—as it was here—in Joliet limestone.

101 Row Houses for Edwin B. Sheldon
1841–1849 N. Lincoln Ave.
1881–82, ARCHITECT UNKNOWN

These well-preserved Second Empire houses feature sunburst pedimented dormers and corbeled brick cornices.

102 301–315 W. Wisconsin St.
1878, ARCHITECT UNKNOWN
103 John N. Young House
317 W. Wisconsin St.
1879, ARCHITECT UNKNOWN

Here is a long row of the classic "octagon front" Italianates that sprang up all over Chicago after the Fire. The bays not only increase light and ventilation but also set up a lively rhythm. The remodelings show the many approaches to altering the facade that result from changing the entrance from the very high first floor to the English-basement level.

104 House of Light
1828 N. Orleans St.
1983, BOOTH HANSEN ASSOCS.

The widely imitated plan overcomes the disadvantages of the narrow city lot with a central stairwell that floods the interior with daylight. The limestone facade has prominent joint lines, echoed by the window mullions, that describe its proportional elements and call attention to its classical derivation.

105 325 through 345 W. Menomonee St.
These cottages, all in various states of remodeling, give a good idea of what the community looked like before the 1871 fire. The tiny cottage on the edge of the alley, now part of the house at **1801 N. Sedgwick St.**, is a rare surviving example of a "fire relief cottage." Immediately after the Fire, the Relief & Aid Society supported the construction of these one-room dwellings, which could be moved by wagon to burned-out lots.

106 Henry Meyer House
1802 N. Lincoln Park West
1874, ARCHITECT UNKNOWN

The narrow end, on Lincoln Park West, has window hoods with carved wooden keystones that imitate those on more expensive masonry buildings.

107 1829 N. Lincoln Park West
1875, 1882, ARCHITECT UNKNOWN
108 1835 N. Lincoln Park West
1874, ARCHITECT UNKNOWN

These Italianate wood houses have very well preserved trim. The structure at 1829 has a pilaster-and-pediment surround on all the window and door openings as well as incised scrolling designs. The trim on 1835 is mostly of the bull's-eye type found in many interiors, but it also has pierced work above the door and rope molding around the attic window.

109 Houses for Ann Halsted
1826–1828 N. Lincoln Park West
1884, ADLER & SULLIVAN
1830–1834 N. Lincoln Park West
1885, ADLER & SULLIVAN

Built as rental property, these houses are rare examples of the early Picturesque phase of the firm's work. The bold ornament shows the influence of Sullivan's early employer, Frank Furness of Philadelphia. The three houses were designed as a symmetrical group.

110 Charles H. Wacker House
1836 N. Lincoln Park West
EARLY 1870S; 1884, REMODELING,
  ARCHITECT UNKNOWN

The Wackers' coach house, in which the family lived while 1838 was under construction, was relocated from the rear of the property to this position and remodeled by Frederick's son, Charles. The namesake of Wacker Dr., Charles was the youngest director of the World's Columbian Exposition of 1893 and a vigorous promoter of Daniel H. Burnham's 1909 *Plan of Chicago*.

111 Frederick Wacker House
1838 N. Lincoln Park West
1874, ARCHITECT UNKNOWN

A Swiss-born brewer, Wacker built his frame house just before new regulations prohibited wood construction in that part of the city destroyed by the Great Fire of 1871. The form is typical of a Chicago cottage, but the ornament is unusually elaborate, with incised pilasters around the doors and windows and a large overhanging porch that recalls a Swiss chalet.

112 Caliendo Residence
1852 N. Sedgwick St.
2004, WILKINSON BLENDER ARCHITECTS

This house inverts the usual residential formula (formal rooms at the front, daily living spaces at the back), with a street-side kitchen opening to a balcony. The overhang also diminishes the visual intrusiveness of the garage, which is lowered below sidewalk level.

113 "The Beauty Pageant"
1811 through 1847 N. Sedgwick St.

In the early 1970s, the Dept. of Urban Renewal closed Ogden Ave., a major southwest thoroughfare, from North Ave. at Larrabee St. to Armitage Ave. at Clark St. The former roadbed and some adjacent property was offered for development, including ten lots on the east side of Sedgwick St. that were sold in 1977. The various buyers considered unified design guidelines for their new houses but ultimately preferred to go their own ways. Of the resulting diversity, Stanley Tigerman, who designed 1847, said,

Houses for Ann Halsted

"This is an American street. . . . It's quiet, dumb, Wild West, egocentric, and typically American. Americans have always seen themselves as individuals, and that individual imperative governs everything." Several buildings have already been replaced by larger, more luxurious houses. In one of several small parks aligned with the former street is a sculpture of two horses by Chicago artist John Kearney, who uses old car bumpers to create creatures with great character.

114 Belgravia Terrace
W. Wisconsin St. between Sedgwick St. and Hudson Ave.
1989, GELICK FORAN ASSOCS.

In a gracious urbanistic gesture, these row houses come out to the lot line with split staircases designed to invite entry rather than repel intruders. This approach offers a welcome change from the usual formula at that time: high brick walls separating front yard from sidewalk.

115 Midwest Buddhist Temple
435 W. Menomonee St.
1971, HIDEAKI ARAO

The base contains classrooms and meeting rooms and serves as a terrace for ceremonial processions. The temple's combination gable and hip roof is traditionally Japanese. A rectory stands to the west.

116 St. Michael's Roman Catholic Church
447 W. Eugenie St.
1869; 1872, REBUILDING, AUGUST WALLBAUM
1888, ALTERATIONS AND STEEPLE, ADAM F. BOOS
1889, CLOCK, SCHWALBACH CO.
1913, REMODELING AND BRICK FACADE, HERMANN J. GAUL

Generations of German architects, craftspeople, designers, and parishioners made St. Michael's a Romanesque monument with a Bavarian Baroque interior. The church was largely destroyed in the Fire, but the exterior walls survived, and the church was rebuilt within them. The grandest single element is the high altar, designed and installed along with four subsidiary altars by E. Hackner & Sons of La Crosse, Wisconsin. Within an arched niche, flanked by the archangels Gabriel and Raphael, St. Michael stands high above a defeated Lucifer. The altar was installed in celebration of the parish's golden jubilee in 1902, as were the stained-glass windows by the Mayer Window Institute of Munich.

117 Walter A. Netsch Jr. House
1700 N. Hudson St.
1974, WALTER A. NETSCH JR.

This is a rare example of the domestic work of the former general partner at Skidmore, Owings & Merrill best known for his design of the Air Force Academy Chapel in Colorado Springs and the University of Illinois at Chicago. While ensuring privacy from the street, the interior offers a lofty, open central space, thirty-three feet high, under skylights covered with a passive solar collector.

118 Anton Franzen House
1726 N. Hudson Ave.
1880, ARCHITECT UNKNOWN

The form of the Chicago cottage lent itself to brick construction, although it was more typically built of economical wood.

Anton Franzen House

119 421–423 W. Willow St.
1982, FREDERICK PHILLIPS & ASSOCS.

Two divided by three equals these twin town houses, joined behind a painted steel frame that suggests the shape of a third.

235 W. Eugenie St.

120 319 and 315 W. Eugenie St.
1874, ARCHITECT UNKNOWN

These well-preserved frame cottages have lively woodwork, including dentils and paired brackets below the gabled cornices.

121 235 W. Eugenie St.
1962, HARRY WEESE & ASSOCS.,
   BEN WEESE, DESIGNER

The varied layouts of the apartments were intended to lure renters to this pioneering example of modern design in Old Town. Constructed of Chicago common brick, the building maintains a nineteenth-century scale all the way up to its mansard roof.

122 Old Town Triangle Association Building
1763 N. North Park Ave.
1922, GRAHAM, ANDERSON,
   PROBST & WHITE

Throughout the Triangle are brick buildings designed as garages with apartments above. They were chauffeurs' quarters for employees of Gold Coast residents whose narrow lots could not accommodate cars. The garage space of this building was remodeled to house meeting rooms and classrooms.

123 Willow St. Town Houses
312–318 W. Willow St.
1974, HARRY WEESE & ASSOCS.

The architect and three friends built these row houses for themselves. Their inspiration was London's row house "terrace" altered to accommodate the automobile. Their plan has become standard: garage, entrance foyer, family room, and garden at street level; living room,

215 W. Eugenie St.

dining room, and kitchen on the second floor; and bedrooms on the third and fourth floors.

124 225, 219, 217, and 215 W. Eugenie St.
1874, ARCHITECTS UNKNOWN

This unusual concentration of one- and two-story frame cottages was built just before the 1874 ordinance banning wooden construction. They all have high basements (in some cases a full story), gabled roofs with bracketed cornices, and simple trim that reflects the prevailing Italianate style. To the west, **229 W. Eugenie St.** was connected to its neighbor by a glass link to form a single house (2004, EIFLER & ASSOCS.)

125 Cobbler Square
(Western Wheel Works)
1350 N. Wells St.
1889, BLOCK ON W. SCHILLER ST. AT
   NORTH PARK AVE.: HENRY SIERKS
1891, BLOCK ON W. EVERGREEN ST. AT
   NORTH PARK AVE.: HENRY SIERKS
1895, BLOCK ON W. EVERGREEN ST.
   AT WELLS ST.: JULIUS H. HUBER
1985, RENOVATION, KENNETH
   A. SCHROEDER & ASSOCS.

This residential and retail complex was created from some twenty buildings put up from 1880 to 1959. The oldest structures, of heavy wooden-beam mill construction, belonged to the Western Wheel Works, which made bicycles, and reflect the vertical organization of the manufacturing process. In 1911, the company founded

Cobbler Square

by Dr. William M. Scholl acquired the property for the manufacture of his foot-care products, adding structures in the 1940s and 1950s. After the company vacated the site in 1981, some of the interior buildings were demolished, and a slice was cut out of a building on Wells St. to create an entry to the 295 residential units. An engaging series of courtyards, hollowed out of the center of the site, is ringed by steel walkways and entered through a three-story atrium.

126 Marshall Field Garden Apartments
N. Sedgwick St., W. Evergreen Ave.,
N. Hudson Ave., and W. Blackhawk St.
1928–29, ANDREW J. THOMAS;
GRAHAM, ANDERSON, PROBST
& WHITE, ASSOC. ARCH.
1993, RENOVATION, DUBIN,
DUBIN & MOUTOUSSAMY

Under the direction of Marshall Field III, the Marshall Field Estate built this low-income housing complex of ten buildings on two city blocks with a large central courtyard, communal interior spaces, and retail space on Sedgwick St. One of the nation's largest such efforts, it was an attempt to see if private initiatives could eliminate slum housing and become economic successes. A New York architect, Thomas was a preeminent designer of housing projects; his spartan, almost Art Deco complex was a success on aesthetic grounds. But it failed to provide housing to low-income tenants because costs proved greater than anticipated and required moderate rather than low rents.

127 Tower House
1306 N. Cleveland St.
2001, FREDERICK PHILLIPS & ASSOCS.

This modern urban "tree house" has two floors of interior space sandwiched between a roof terrace and an open carport. Much is achieved with a small building footprint. An exterior circular stair provides code-required redundancy to the concrete block stair tower. The living spaces are on the third floor to take advantage of the best views.

Marshall Field Garden Apartments

Schiff Residences

128 Margot and Harold Schiff Residences—Mercy Housing
1244 N. Clybourn Ave.
2007, MURPHY/JAHN; SMITH & SMITH ARCHITECTS, ASSOC. ARCHS.

The industrial materials and loaf-shaped massing recall Jahn's slightly earlier State St. Village at the Illinois Institute of Technology—not surprisingly, since dormitories and single-room-occupancy buildings share many requirements, particularly the need to provide small rooms with privacy and security while fostering a sense of community. Sustainable features include a rooftop wind turbine, solar panels, and reuse of gray water for landscaping.

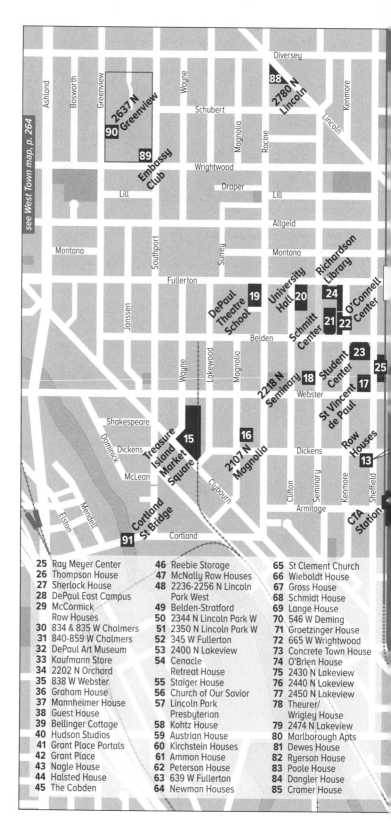

see West Town map, p. 264

Diversey

88 2780 N Lincoln

Lincoln

Kenmore

Ashland
Bosworth
Greenview

90 2637 N Greenview

Wayne

Schubert

Magnolia

Racine

89 Embassy Club

Wrightwood

Draper

Lill

Lill

Altgeld

Montana

Southport

Surrey

Montana

Richardson Library

Fullerton

Janssen

DePaul Theatre School **19**

University Hall **20**

24

O'Connell Center

Schmitt Center

21 **22**

Belden

Wayne
Lakewood
Magnolia

2218 N Seminary

18

Student Center

23

25

Webster

17

St Vincent de Paul

Shakespeare

Dominick

Dickens

Treasure Island Market Square **15**

16

2107 N Magnolia

Dickens

Row Houses

13

McLean

Clybourn

Clifton
Seminary
Kenmore
Sheffield

Armitage

Mendell
Elston

Cortland St Bridge

91

Cortland

CTA Station

25 Ray Meyer Center
26 Thompson House
27 Sherlock House
28 DePaul East Campus
29 McCormick
   Row Houses
30 834 & 835 W Chalmers
31 840-859 W Chalmers
32 DePaul Art Museum
33 Kaufmann Store
34 2202 N Orchard
35 838 W Webster
36 Graham House
37 Mannheimer House
38 Guest House
39 Bellinger Cottage
40 Hudson Studios
41 Grant Place Portals
42 Grant Place
43 Nagle House
44 Halsted House
45 The Cobden

46 Reebie Storage
47 McNally Row Houses
48 2236-2256 N Lincoln
   Park West
49 Belden-Stratford
50 2344 N Lincoln Park W
51 2350 N Lincoln Park W
52 345 W Fullerton
53 2400 N Lakeview
54 Cenacle
   Retreat House
55 Staiger House
56 Church of Our Savior
57 Lincoln Park
   Presbyterian
58 Kohtz House
59 Austrian House
60 Kirchstein Houses
61 Ammon House
62 Peterson House
63 639 W Fullerton
64 Newman Houses

65 St Clement Church
66 Wieboldt House
67 Gross House
68 Schmidt House
69 Lange House
70 546 W Deming
71 Groetzinger House
72 665 W Wrightwood
73 Concrete Town House
74 O'Brien House
75 2430 N Lakeview
76 2440 N Lakeview
77 2450 N Lakeview
78 Theurer/
   Wrigley House
79 2474 N Lakeview
80 Marlborough Apts
81 Dewes House
82 Ryerson House
83 Poole House
84 Dangler House
85 Cramer House

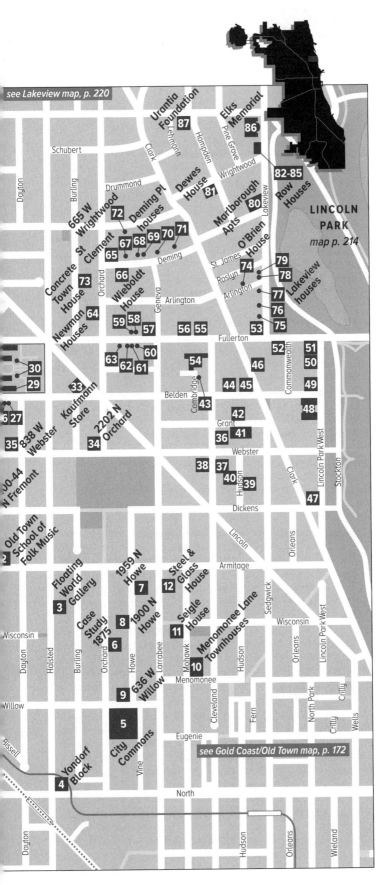

see Lakeview map, p. 220

Schubert

Dayton

Burling

665 W Wrightwood

Drummond

Clark

Lehmann

Hampden

Urantia Foundation **87**

Pine Grove

Elks Memorial **86**

Dewes House **87**

Wrightwood

82-85

Row Houses

Deming Pl houses **72**

Marlborough Apts **80**

Lakeview

LINCOLN PARK

map p. 214

Clement St

67 68 69 70 71

65

Deming

O'Brien House

St. James

74

Roslyn

79
78

Lakeview houses

Concrete Town House **73**

Orchard

66

Wieboldt House

Geneva

Arlington

Arlington

77
76

Newman Houses **64**

59 58

57

56 55

53
75

Fullerton

63

62 61

60

54

Commonwealth

52

51
50

49

30
29

33

Kaufmann Store

46

44 45

48

6 27

35

838 W Webster

Webster

2202 N Orchard

Belden

Cambridge

43

42

Grant

36
41

34

00-44 N Fremont

Old Town School of Folk Music

38

37
40 39

Webster

Hudson

Lincoln Park West

Stockton

47

Dickens

Lincoln

Orleans

Clark

Floating World Gallery **3**

1959 N Howe

7

Steel & Glass House **12**

Armitage

Sedgwick

Wisconsin

Lincoln Park West

Orleans

Wisconsin

Case Study 1875 **8**

1900 N Howe

Seigle House **11**

Menomonee Lane Townhouses

Hudson

Dayton

Halsted

Burling

Orchard

Howe

6

636 W Willow

9

Larrabee

Mohawk

10

Menomonee

Cleveland

Fern

North Park

Crilly

Crilly

Wells

Willow

5

City Commons

Eugenie

Vine

see Gold Coast/Old Town map, p. 172

Russell

Yondorf Block **4**

North

Dayton

Hudson

Orleans

Wieland

LINCOLN PARK

No other Chicago neighborhood has witnessed as dramatic a resurgence as Lincoln Park. The 1950 *Local Community Fact Book*, the city's decennial oracle of sociological trends, predicted "the end of much of Lincoln Park as a residential community." Today, however, many people see it as the city's most desirable neighborhood—with real estate prices to match. The density and congestion that constitute its chief drawbacks are the inevitable side effects of its popularity. Yet unlike the Gold Coast, the only neighborhood with higher median home values, high-rise construction has invaded only a small area of Lincoln Park, and the vast majority of streets retain their late-nineteenth-century character.

Lincoln Park had distinctly inauspicious origins. Like the rest of the North Side, it was less accessible to the central city because of the intervening river. The lakefront just beyond North Ave. was considered remote enough for use as the city's cemetery, until the growth of the North Side population (still primarily farmers) led Dr. John H. Rauch and other public health crusaders to demand the removal of the bodies to cemeteries farther north. In 1864, the city replaced the cemetery with Lake Park; it was renamed for the assassinated president the following year.

The Great Fire of 1871 destroyed the North Side as far as the city limits at Fullerton Ave., and an 1874 ordinance extended the fireproof building codes to the entire city. The growth of industry along the north branch of the river in the 1880s provided an impetus for the construction of workers' housing to the west. Cable cars arrived on Clark St. and Lincoln Ave. later in the decade, increasing middle-class settlement near those streets. The 1889 annexation of Lake View bumped the city boundary well north of Fullerton Ave., ending the construction of wooden houses, which had flourished just north of the former city limits. Construction of the Northwestern Elevated Railroad Co.'s tracks along Sheffield Ave. in the late 1890s spurred further commercial development.

By 1900, ethnic patterns were well established, with wealthy Germans living in large houses near the lake and middle- and working-class Irish and Poles in modest flats farther west. The 1920s and 1930s brought an extensive turnover, with poorer immigrants moving in and buildings subdivided to accommodate them. New construction was limited to the ever-desirable lakefront, while west of Halsted St., rooming houses were carved out of already modest dwellings.

After World War II, most of Lincoln Park was considered a slum. The housing stock resembled that of most other close-in neighborhoods: fifty-year-old buildings that were aging badly as a consequence of neglect and subdivision into tenement-size units. But because the situation was less desperate than on the Near South Side and in other neighborhoods, urban renewal arrived at a slower, more measured pace. Funds were not allocated until 1964, eight years after most of the community had been included in a 226-acre urban renewal area. By then, there was less enthusiasm—and money—for the wholesale replacement of the housing stock with clusters of high-rises. Private owners had already begun to renovate their properties, sometimes in ways that horrify today's preservationists. An influx of Baby Boomers in the 1970s filled the rehabbed graystones, vintage apartments, and new high-rises, bolstering the demand for shopping and entertainment. Restaurants, bars, theaters, and boutiques quickly made Lincoln Park one of the city's liveliest neighborhoods.

Gentrification proceeded slowly westward, crossing Halsted St. in the early 1980s. Deconversion became the rage: not only were rooming houses returned to their original configuration of large apartments, but structures built as two- and three-flats were remodeled into luxurious single-family residences. The passion for preservation also led to the increasingly authentic restoration of facades, even where the interiors (whose original features were sometimes unsalvageable) had been redone in white-on-white modern.

Retail and entertainment establishments followed the westward expansion, creating a new frontier along the formerly industrial Clybourn Ave. The availability of large parcels of land hard by the Chicago River's north branch led to the creation of suburban-style strip malls that offer the abundant free parking that is in woefully short supply closer to the lake.

Twenty-first-century developments include the inexorable expansion of DePaul University and the creation of a Millionaires' Row in a formerly modest neighborhood southwest of Armitage Ave. and Mohawk St. More than sixty years after its predicted demise, Lincoln Park remains one of the city's most vital residential communities.

—PATRICIA MARKS LURIE WITH LAURIE MCGOVERN PETERSEN

1 CTA—Armitage Ave. Station
944 W. Armitage Ave.
1900, WILLIAM R. GIBB; J. A. L.
  WADDELL, CONSULTING ENG.
2009, REHABILITATION,
  GONZALEZ HASBROUCK

This station of the Northwestern Elevated line from the Loop to Wilson Ave. resembles five others by Gibb at Belmont, Fullerton, Diversey, Sedgwick, and Chicago. The brick walls are trimmed with cast stone tinted to look like terra-cotta.

2 Old Town School of Folk Music
(The Aldine)
909 W. Armitage Ave.
1896, JOSEPH BETTINGHOFER
1987, RENOVATION AND STOREFRONT
  RESTORATION, LISEC & BIEDERMAN

In anticipation of the Northwestern Elevated Railroad Co.'s Center St. (Armitage Ave.) station, business blocks sprang up here during the mid-1890s; **917**, **919**, **921**, and **925** all date from 1895 to 1897. Their Baroque embellishments—cherubs, figures, and banded pilasters—and elaborate corner bays compete for shoppers' attention.

3 Floating World Gallery
1925 N. Halsted St.
2009, S. CONGER ARCHITECTS

A new facade of purple-gray slate creates an elegant street presence for a tired commercial building. The original commission was to create a very private second-floor gallery, accessed from a path along the south side of the building, but it expanded to include a ground-floor exhibit space as well.

4 Yondorf Block and Hall
758 W. North Ave.
1887, FREDERICK AHLSCHLAGER
1989, RENOVATION, FITZGERALD
  ASSOCS. ARCHITECTS; OFFICE OF
  JOHN VINCI, ASSOC. ARCH.

This combination retail and hall building was constructed by the owners of a clothing business that occupied a nearby storefront on North Ave. In 1910, the storefronts were remodeled with a white terra-cotta facade for a bank, and roof cresting at the corner was removed. The largest of the six halls is complete with a stage and gallery. They were rented for social gatherings and meetings by unions and fraternal organizations. The building has stylistic elements of both the Victorian Gothic and the Romanesque Revival.

Old Town School of Folk Music

Yondorf Block and Hall

5 City Commons

W. Willow St. between N.
Orchard and N. Vine Sts.

1986, PAPPAGEORGE/HAYMES

Trendsetting developers Horwitz-
Matthews worked with the architects to devise a project that orga-
nizes town houses around a private,
secured courtyard. Walled gardens
act as a buffer between the street
and the unbroken perimeter wall
and increase the fortresslike quality. But through the Tinseltown
entrance with its backlit glass block
is a ring of row houses that honor
their Italianate grandparents, complete with long flights of stairs up to
the stoops.

As the massive public housing towers of Cabrini-Green were being
demolished south of Division St.,
several blocks between North and
Armitage Aves. were quietly under-
going their own demographic shift to
become a new Gold Coast. Modest
cottages and flats were bulldozed
and replaced by lavish multistoried,
lot-filling houses or mansions that
sprawl across multiple lots. Many
dramatic examples can be found on
the blocks between Cleveland and
Halsted.

6 Case Study 1875

1875 N. Orchard St.

2007, WHEELER KEARNS ARCHITECTS

The most discreetly lavish of all
the new houses is also one of the
few to be modern rather than Old
World. One of the biggest luxuries
is land: to create a property large
enough for a generous side garden,
four houses were demolished,
including Nagle Hartray's 1986
House with a Bay. Even more impressive is the structural tour de
force: forty-foot cantilevers extend
from the concrete core, allowing
the first floor to open to the garden
via enormous glass walls that hang
from the ceiling and slide open at
the corners.

7 1959 N. Howe St.

2010, THOMAS HICKEY & ASSOCS.

Part of the brick shell of an 1890s
cottage forms an entry courtyard for
the new house behind it.

8 1900 N. Howe St.

1991, MAX GORDON; OFFICE OF
JOHN VINCI, ASSOC. ARCH.

This 10,000-square-foot house
meets the neighborhood standard
of lavishness but is a quiet island of
understatement and good taste. Executed in rosy brick, with long, taupe
window frames divided into small
panes, it was designed to accommodate the owners' art collection.

9 636 W. Willow St.

1995, PETER DE BRETTEVILLE, ARCHITECT

Designed around a glassy courtyard,
this corner-lot house presents a
private face to the street. Roman
brick and horizontal mullions reinforce the overall horizontal massing.
Vertical piers on the entrance facade
suggest the double-height space
concealed within, lit with clerestory
windows.

636 W. Willow St.

10 Menomonee Lane Town Houses

1801–1813 N. Mohawk St.

1986, MICHAEL LUSTIG & ASSOCS.

English row houses were the inspiration for this fourteen-unit project.
Lines of contrasting brick are laid
over Flemish bond, uniting the windows and doors and enlivening the
surfaces with a crisply articulated
grid.

11 Seigle Residence

1856 N. Mohawk St.

2008, LOHAN ANDERSON

A limestone fence enclosing a front
courtyard becomes a solid wall as it
turns the corners, defining the pedestal for a box of terra-cotta, striated
in long tiles of vibrant earth tones
and accentuated by ribbons of stainless steel. On the north elevation, a
glass curtain wall bisects the house
vertically, revealing a dramatic staircase that is the focus of its interior.

12 Steel and Glass House
1949 N. Larrabee St.

1981, KRUECK & OLSEN ARCHITECTS

It's aloof and mechanically pristine—but at night, when the light shines alluringly through the windows and steel grating, who'd turn down an invitation to step inside this beautiful cage? This 5,000-square-foot house is made of shop-fabricated steel angle frames joined to form structural bays. The U-shaped plan has two levels, with a two-story living space. A central court and an informal garden provide private outdoor space.

Steel and Glass House

13 2100–2144 and 2101–2145 N. Bissell St.

1883, IVER C. ZARBELL

John Davis developed these rental row houses, which are clustered in pairs and triplets to resemble grand homes. Second Empire mansard roofs and central pavilions blend with the Queen Anne's quirky variety of shapes, colors, and materials.

14 2100–2144 N. Fremont St.

1875, EDWARD J. BURLING

Rebuilding after the fire filled entire blocks with Italianate houses and flats. The ritzier dwellings were termed *marble fronts* because they were built of Joliet limestone. For this more modest project, common brick walls and cast stone (concrete) sills and hood molds were used all around. An elaborate cornice unites this monolithic block with end houses set slightly forward. The porches closest to original are probably those with a simple bracketed canopy over the door. An almost identical set of houses is at **2225–2245 N. Burling St.**

15 Treasure Island Market Square
Clybourn, Wayne, Lakewood, and Webster Aves.

1987, BOOTH HANSEN ASSOCS.

This complex is notable less for its design, a serviceable postmodern composition of industrial materials, than for its site plan, which places shops on the periphery and parking in the middle. Regrettably, the other shopping centers lining Clybourn Ave. did not follow this pattern, offering instead the standard sea of surface parking between sidewalk and storefronts.

16 2107 N. Magnolia St.
(Joel T. Headley Public School)

1875, ARCHITECT UNKNOWN

1985, CONVERSION TO
  APARTMENTS, BAUHS & DRING

The city's oldest public school building now houses condominium lofts, but the Italianate exterior and spartan lobby are little changed.

2107 N. Magnolia St.

17 St. Vincent de Paul Roman Catholic Church
1004 W. Webster Ave.

1897, JAMES J. EGAN

Egan's smooth and graceful interpretation of the Romanesque does not evoke the sense of shelter associated with the style's fortresslike Richardsonian version. The high altar (1903–9), of Carrara marble, is inlaid with mother-of-pearl and mosaics.

18 2218 N. Seminary Ave.

1996, SCHROEDER MURCHIE LAYA

What at first may appear to be a renovation/addition is all-new construction, built on a double lot. The limestone portion of the house was designed to relate to its late nineteenth-century neighbors, while the steel-and-glass box that intersects it at a twelve-degree angle provides a multistory interior space.

DePaul University— Lincoln Park Campus
Webster Ave., Fullerton Ave., Halsted St., and Clifton Ave.

Founded as St. Vincent's College in 1898 and chartered under its current name in 1907, DePaul increased its presence in Lincoln Park in the 1960s and 1970s with the purchase of the McCormick Theological Seminary and the construction of a pair of brutalist megabuildings on Seminary Ave. In 1988, Lohan Assocs. produced a master plan that guided the creation of a more campus-like environment, looking outward to its gentrified surroundings. The subsequent building boom resulted in dormitories and academic and recreational buildings that are contextual and low-profile neighbors rather than attention-getters. A landscaped quadrangle, created by closing the 2300 block of Seminary Ave. to traffic in 1992, provides a central focus. The 2009–19 master plan was drafted by Antunovich Assocs., which has designed the vast majority of post-1990 buildings, including dormitories, the student apartment building at **1237 W. Fullerton Ave.**, both McGowan science buildings, and Arts and Letters Hall.

19 The Theatre School at DePaul University
2350 N. Racine Ave.

2013, PELLI CLARKE PELLI ARCHITECTS, DESIGN ARCH.; CANNON DESIGN, ARCH. OF RECORD

The modern limestone-and-glass home for DePaul's top-ranked theater school is a departure from the traditional brick additions to the campus. The luminous flex theater cantilevers over the street corner as a beacon for the campus, while the building steps back from the street to break down its scale. Normally behind-the-scenes construction shops are visible from the street, and the glass-fronted lobby displays the activity inside.

20 University Hall
2345 N. Clifton Ave.

1986, LOHAN ASSOCS.

Architect and client worked to create

housing with massing and materials sympathetic to surrounding nineteenth-century houses and flats. The window hoods are inspired by the Italianate, although the openings that they top are almost square rather than tall and narrow.

21 Arthur J. Schmitt Academic Center
2323 N. Seminary Ave.

1968, C. F. MURPHY ASSOCS.

Since its companion building has been demolished, this massive concrete bunker is the lone relic of the "university as fortress" image that DePaul has successfully shed.

22 Michael J. O'Connell Center
(Hall of Science)
1036 W. Belden Ave.

1938, SHAW, NAESS & MURPHY

This modest Art Moderne building denotes chemistry, biology, and physics in spandrel panels that depict laboratory beakers, splayed frogs (presumably awaiting dissection), and engines and gears.

23 DePaul Student Center
2250 N. Sheffield Ave.

2002, WTW ARCHITECTS WITH VMC ARCHITECTS

This three-story block is big but respectful to the street and neighbors. Two main entrances at opposite corners are linked by a curved interior street of student services.

24 Richardson Library
2350 N. Kenmore Ave.

1992, LOHAN ASSOCS.

This is the first major building designed in accordance with the 1988 master plan. The red brick trimmed in pale masonry establishes a strong presence yet blends well with the neighborhood. Piers suggestive of buttresses lend a collegiate air, while the towers anchor the building. The eclectic vocabulary—classical keystones, Gothic buttresses, and Chicago School towers—fails to speak with a clear voice, although it is too subdued to be cacophonous.

25 Ray Meyer Fitness and Recreation Center
2235 N. Sheffield Ave.

1999, ANTUNOVICH ASSOCS.

One of four buildings on the east

DePaul University Richardson Library

side of Sheffield that Antunovich designed for DePaul, it has the requisite brick-and-limestone detailing and sensitivity to neighborhood scale but a higher degree of transparency to maximize daylight and views.

26 Hiram J. Thompson House
851 W. Belden Ave.

1885, BURLING & WHITEHOUSE

This Queen Anne house retains the flat-fronted sobriety of the Italianate style on the first two floors but explodes in scale at the top, where the huge dormer pierces an oversized cornice ornamented with giant shells between brackets. These bulky elements and the wide variety of materials (red brick trimmed in brownstone, hung with a metal bay) are typical of the uninhibited if awkward early Queen Anne style.

27 James P. Sherlock House
845 W. Belden Ave.

1895, LOUIS BRODHAG

Sedate and cohesive compared to its next-door neighbor, it shows the relative quietness and monochromatic palette of the later Queen Anne style, here executed in the Romanesque mode. The once-popular variety of brown sandstone known as Lake Superior raindrop stone shows characteristic "spattering."

28 DePaul University—Lincoln Park Campus (East Portion)
(McCormick Theological Seminary)
Halsted St., Belden Ave., Fullerton Ave., and the El tracks

The Presbyterian Theological Seminary was founded in Indiana in 1829, moved to Chicago in 1859, and relocated here in 1864. All of the original academic buildings, which faced Halsted St. and Belden Ave., were demolished, most of them during a 1960s building campaign. The most notable remnant is the collection of Queen Anne row houses, now a designated landmark district. Dissatisfied with the return produced by investing the endowment in bonds and mortgages, the seminary began constructing row houses in 1882 to produce rental income and create a comfortable island of Protestants in a sea of German Catholics.

The next building phase began in 1929, when architect Dwight G. Wallace created a grand plan to redesign the entire campus in the Collegiate Gothic style. What is now DePaul's **Commons Building** (1932) is the sole remnant of Wallace's efforts. (The 1929 gymnasium was demolished in 2005.) After moving to Hyde Park in 1973, the seminary sold its institutional buildings to DePaul University and the houses to private owners.

29 McCormick Row Houses
832–840, 844–858 W. Belden Ave., 833–841, 845–859, 901–913, 917–927 W. Fullerton Ave.

1884–89, A. M. F. COLTON

These modest Queen Anne dwellings have lively rooflines, street walls that step in and out, and

McCormick Row Houses

Ferdinand Kaufmann Store and Flat Building

ornamental brick patterns. Construction proceeded from east to west, and the later buildings in the 900 block of Fullerton Ave. differ slightly.

30 834 and 835 W. Chalmers Pl.

834: 1889, A. M. F. COLTON & SON
835: 1882, WILLIAM LE BARON JENNEY

These two freestanding houses were built for the seminary's faculty members; 835 was for high-rankers and was moved from its original location on Belden Ave. when a library (now demolished) was constructed there in 1894.

31 840–858 and 841–859 W. Chalmers Pl.

1889–91, A. M. F. COLTON & SON

The row houses surrounding the greensward on Chalmers Pl. are more subdued than their predecessors on the avenues. Each group shares a long gabled roof broken by a symmetrical pattern of round and triangular cross gables. They have smooth brick facades with recessed windows and deep arches sheltering the doorways. The dark color, arched entries, and corner tourelles convey a Victorian—or is it Presbyterian?—sobriety.

32 DePaul Art Museum

935 W. Fullerton Ave.

2011, ANTUNOVICH ASSOCS.

A glass box pops out of the brick facade at the level of the Fullerton El platform to trumpet the museum's presence to commuters, whether they are waiting on the platform or zipping by on a train.

33 Ferdinand Kaufmann Store and Flat Building

2310–2312 N. Lincoln Ave.

1883, 1887, ADLER & SULLIVAN

The south portion is earlier, although the entire building was probably designed at the same time. The only element distinguishing it as the firm's work is the robust ornament in the stone moldings and terra-cotta lunettes and the small lotus flowers topping the first-floor pilasters.

34 2202 N. Orchard St.

2010, DIRK DENISON ARCHITECTS

The house is a study in asymmetrical solids and voids that blur transitions from exterior to interior. The long elevation is on Webster St. across from Oz Park. The lot-filling design incorporates a green roof, a water-retention tank for irrigation, sustainable wood siding, and other environmentally friendly features.

2202 N. Orchard St.

838 W. Webster Ave.

35 838 W. Webster Ave.

2005, DESTEFANO & PARTNERS

Striking yet deceptively simple, the house is unapologetically of its time while contextual in scale and materials. The three-story volume extends along the west side of the lot to create a courtyard with the two-story elements at the front and back.

36 Bruce Graham House

2215 N. Cleveland Ave.

1969, BRUCE GRAHAM

Unabashedly different and fiercely private is this home designed by and built for a former Skidmore, Owings & Merrill partner. It tries no harder to fit in here than does his Sears Tower in the Loop. It is oriented around a walled garden, with a steel gate guarding the entrance.

37 Leon Mannheimer House

2147 N. Cleveland Ave.

1884, ADLER & SULLIVAN
1995, RESTORATION, LUCIEN LAGRANGE

The outsized chunks of lotus-like metal ornament are close to the scale of decoration on the firm's business buildings downtown. Along with the idiosyncratic semi-circle topping the window and the triangular bay, they are the only clues to Sullivan's involvement.

38 Walter Guest House

2150 N. Cleveland Ave.

1932, REMODELING, EDGAR
    MILLER, ARTIST

The Art Deco street-side and topside additions of buff brick gave this old house a face-lift. The facade is dominated by large expanses of Miller's characteristic chevron-patterned leaded-glass windows. The screen on the front door displays another

Walter Guest House

Miller favorite: animals from antelopes to sea horses.

39 Richard Bellinger Cottage

2121 N. Hudson Ave.

1869, WILLIAM W. BOYINGTON

Like Boyington's Water Tower, this house survived the Fire and became a legendary landmark. Located near the northernmost edge of the Fire's reach, it was saved when Bellinger allegedly soaked the roof with cider (his wife claimed it was water). This superb example of an 1860s Chicago cottage is clapboarded and shingled and was ultimately raised for a new foundation.

40 Hudson Studios

2134–2138 N. Hudson Ave.

1948–52, REMODELING AND
    ADDITIONS, FRANK LAPASSO

Attorney Lawrence S. Adler and commercial artist Clive Rickabaugh developed this courtyard complex with the bohemian, do-it-ourselves charm of W. Burton Pl., where Rickabaugh lived near his friend, Sol Kogen. A long-vacant burned-out shell at 2138 was replaced by four apartments in 1948, with duplexes on the second and third levels. The building at 2134 was converted next and still has the bricked-in windows of its earlier incarnation as a Victorian house. In 1952, additions were built on the back of each structure, with diamond-shaped bays and "Miami windows." The maple railings, doors, carvings, and fireplaces were scavenged from the La Salle St. Methodist Church, which had burned.

The Cobden

41 Grant Place Portals
415–443 W. Grant Pl.
1972, BOOTH & NAGLE

These stacked town houses meet the street with the walled yards typical of others nearby, but within is a village atmosphere. Despite the density (fifty houses on less than an acre), the slice of landscaped space knits them together.

42 Grant Place
432 W. Grant Pl.
2005, PAPPAGEORGE/HAYMES

Although Lincoln Park's side streets were primarily residential, a scattering of commercial buildings on this block have been replaced with infill housing. The concrete and tinted glass of this condominium building are foreign materials, but the scale and restrained design help it fit in.

43 James Nagle House
2321 N. Cambridge St.
1978, BOOTH, NAGLE AND HARTRAY

Taking advantage of an unusually shaped lot, this modernist house has a square rather than rectangular plan that features a two-story atrium at the center and allows for a generous garden at the back. The modest scale and materials make it a good neighbor.

44 Ann Halsted House
440 W. Belden Ave.
1883, ADLER & SULLIVAN

The lotus motif that decorates many Sullivan houses and business buildings of this era adorns the gable of this severely simple early Queen Anne house.

45 The Cobden
418–424 W. Belden Ave.
1892, CHARLES S. FROST

On busy Clark St., it is a typical flats-above-storefronts building, while the facade on residential Belden Ave. derives its picturesque variety from its bays and the shaped gable that breaks the roofline.

46 Reebie Storage & Moving Co.
2325 N. Clark St.
1923, GEORGE S. KINGSLEY

"If Old King Tut were alive today, he'd store his goods the Reebie way!" Thus did the enterprising

Reebie Storage & Moving Company

Reebie brothers capitalize on the Egyptomania occasioned by the opening of King Tut's tomb in 1922. The well-preserved polychrome terra-cotta facade (missing only its cavetto cornice, similar in shape to those above the second-floor windows) is guarded by two statues of Ramses II, representing William C. and John C. Reebie. The hieroglyphics at the base say, "Forever I work for all of your regions in daylight and darkness" (left statue) and "I give protection to your furniture." Much of the elaborate sculptural program, which extends to the interior foyer and office lobby, was devised by Northwestern Terra Cotta Co. sculptor Fritz Albert.

47 Row Houses for Andrew McNally

2103–2115 N. Clark St./310–312 W. Dickens Ave.

1885, JOSEPH LYMAN SILSBEE

Queen Anne variety enlivens this corner block, designed by one of Frank Lloyd Wright's first employers.

48 2236–2256 N. Lincoln Park West

1910, SIMEON B. EISENDRATH

The influence of Eisendrath's former employer, Louis H. Sullivan, shows in the hearty foliate terra-cotta surrounding each entrance.

49 Belden Stratford

(Belden Hotel)

2300 N. Lincoln Park West

1922, FRIDSTEIN & CO.

This elegant apartment building seems almost to have been plucked from a Parisian boulevard and enlarged to Chicago scale. The mansard roof dominates the skyline, and the smooth limestone facade is embellished with quoins and classical carving.

50 2344 N. Lincoln Park West

1917, KARL M. VITZTHUM

1991, PENTHOUSE ADDITION, FREDERICK PHILLIPS & ASSOCS.

A small sixth-floor apartment was remodeled and a 2,000-square-foot seventh floor added to create a dazzling penthouse that is still low enough to be seen from the street. With its twin limestone belvederes, it fits securely atop this Beaux-Arts facade.

51 2350 N. Lincoln Park West/305 W. Fullerton Ave.

1916, ANDREW SANDEGREN

A master of quiet elegance, Sandegren created signature sunrooms with million-dollar views of Lincoln Park.

52 345 W. Fullerton Ave.

1973, HARRY WEESE & ASSOCS.

The concrete frame surrounding the dark glass windows is made less severe by the gradual stepping back of each facade.

53 2400 N. Lakeview Ave.

1963, LUDWIG MIES VAN DER ROHE

This is the last residential high-rise that Mies designed for Chicago.

54 Cenacle Retreat House

513 W. Fullerton Ave.

1967, CHARLES POPE

Siting the parking lot on Fullerton Ave. was unfortunate, but it lessens the impact of the tall buildings behind, which house sleeping rooms. The complex is a terrific example of the warm side of clean, quiet modernism in brick, with narrow piers forming strong verticals. Inside the chapel is the same sensibility, augmented by boldly abstract windows.

55 Carl M. Staiger House

520 W. Fullerton Pkwy.

1891, LAMSON & NEWMAN

All the bang is in the bay. With a swan's-neck pediment and large acroterion, it projects from the facade like a corsage.

56 Church of Our Savior (Episcopal)

530 W. Fullerton Pkwy.

1888, CLINTON J. WARREN

The tourelled Romanesque facade blends seamlessly with the rector's house on the west. The nave has walls of unglazed terra-cotta tiles and a beautifully trussed ceiling. Some of the original, geometrically patterned leaded-glass windows were replaced with figural stained glass, several by Tiffany Studios.

57 Lincoln Park Presbyterian Church

(Fullerton Ave. Presbyterian Church)

600 W. Fullerton Pkwy.

1888, JOHN S. WOOLLACOTT

1898, ADDITION, WILLIAM G. BARFIELD
Every corner on this massive Richardsonian Romanesque church is soft and rounded. Fat disks of greenish sandstone are stacked to form giant tourelles, and blocks of many sizes are knit into a tall tower (minus its steeple since 1970). This variety of green stone, called Michigan buff sandstone, was popular from the mid-1880s to the mid-1890s. From the pulpit on the west wall, the aisles radiate in a semicircle on an ascending grade as in "all the first-water Presbyterian churches of the city," as the *Daily Inter Ocean* noted. Barfield's addition pushed the west wall back twenty-five feet but maintained this orientation.

58 Louis O. Kohtz House
620 W. Fullerton Ave.
1886, ARCHITECT UNKNOWN
59 Leo Austrian House
624 W. Fullerton Ave.
1886, THEODORE KARLS
The Austrian House sets itself apart from its neighbor with a flattened Romanesque castle front that includes a corner tower, parapet, and shallow machicolations.

Leo Austrian House

60| Herman Kirchstein Houses
621 and 627 W. Fullerton Ave.
1888, JULIUS H. HUBER
623–625 W. Fullerton Ave.
1887, JULIUS H. HUBER
Awkwardly massed but beautifully detailed, the two slightly later houses stiffly bookend the double house. All are enlivened by robust wooden porches whose cornices feature disks that look like flying saucers impaled on spikes.

61 Ernest Ammon House
629 W. Fullerton Ave.
1889, FROMMANN & JEBSEN
62 Peter Peterson House
631 W. Fullerton Ave.
1889, JULIUS H. HUBER
At 629, the two colors of sandstone are an unexpected combination, while 631 features a more subdued palette of red brick and matching terra-cotta.

63 639 W. Fullerton Ave.
EARLY 1890S, ARCHITECT UNKNOWN
This house is saved from formula by the fabulous acanthus-leaf symphony at the entry. The fingered leaves swirl and twist, framing jesters' faces at the bottom. At the top they become spiky collars that frame facing dog faces—or are they caricatures of humans?

639 W. Fullerton Ave.

64 Newman Bros. Houses
2424, 2430, and 2434 N. Orchard St.
1895, JOHN M. VAN OSDEL II
S. S. Beman popularized the châteauesque locally with his Kimball House (1891); many elements of his design are squeezed here into a narrower, high-shouldered version. This trio was to have been done in shades of red stone, but the middle house was executed in limestone. John M. Van Osdel II was the nephew of John Mills Van Osdel, Chicago's first architect.

65 St. Clement Roman Catholic Church
646 W. Deming Pl.
1918, BARNETT, HAYNES & BARNETT
1989, RESTORATION, HOLABIRD & ROOT

Newman Bros. Houses

St. Clement Roman Catholic Church

The architects of the St. Louis Cathedral produced a scaled-down version here, complete with a Byzantine dome inspired by Istanbul's Hagia Sophia. Trompe l'oeil mosaic, plasterwork, and marble make the interior a riot of colors and faux textures.

66 William A. Wieboldt House
639 W. Deming Pl.

1896, ROBERT C. BERLIN

The plain but vaguely Italian facade is topped by a determinedly German Baroque third-floor gable.

67 Jacob Gross House
632 W. Deming Pl.

1892, EDMUND R. KRAUSE

Krause prized the massiveness and geometries of the Queen Anne style while eschewing its fussiness. This facade is a balance of squares and rectangles topped by triangles and cones. The monochromatic palette quiets the clamor.

68 William Schmidt House
618 W. Deming Pl.

1889, FREDERICK FOEHRINGER

Tourelles on the third-floor dormer, a classical cornice with modillions and brackets, a mansard roof, a rusticated stone facade, and Ionic porch columns create a house with an identity crisis.

69 Frederick J. Lange House
612 W. Deming Pl.

MID-1890S, THOMAS W. WING

The handsomest stone detailing on the street is on the porch parapet.

70 546 W. Deming Pl.
(Chateau VI)

1968, JEROME SOLTAN

Ranging from banal to bruising, the curse of city neighborhoods in the

1960s and 1970s was the infamous four-plus-one, invented by Soltan in 1960. Here, twenty-four apartments on four floors are squeezed onto a space that originally accommodated a single-family home. The ground-level parking is partially screened by decorative concrete blocks. All but filling the lot, the four-plus-one not only provides little light to the units on the sides and back but also cuts off light to neighboring buildings. The four-plus-one was never built with sufficient parking, and streets were clogged with the overflow cars. The lack of parking was its ultimate downfall.

71 William C. Groetzinger House
526 W. Deming Pl.

1895, FREDERICK B. TOWNSEND

Ponderous but comfortably cave-like and beautifully detailed, the Romanesque facade is Gothicized with pointed arches.

William C. Groetzinger House

72 665 W. Wrightwood Ave.

1998, TADAO ANDO ARCHITECT
AND ASSOCS.

The high quality of Ando's exacting concrete work is apparent in this, his first building in the United States. Typical of Ando's houses in Japan, this minimalist residence focuses inward and reveals nothing of its interior life to the street. The intensely private house occupies three lots, though close to half of that area is devoted to a walled garden with reflecting pool.

73 Concrete Town House
2465 N. Burling St.

2005, JOHN RONAN ARCHITECTS

By emphasizing rather than dis-

guising the impressions of the planks used to form them, the exposed concrete walls almost take on the characteristic of sun-baked clapboard. The walnut cladding around the tunnel-like entrance seems to serve as a vestigial reminder of that construction process.

74 William V. O'Brien House
426 W. Arlington Pl.

1894, FLANDERS & ZIMMERMAN

Built for an art dealer, this house is one of the city's most unusual for its era. The band of windows tucked under the eave was a favorite device of Frank Lloyd Wright, although it predates his use of the motif. The enormous dormer that continues the wall plane in an upward surge is also an anomaly, perhaps inspired by Adler & Sullivan's towered Victoria Hotel (1892) in Chicago Heights. The house is well preserved, although at some point (possibly in 1921) the front entrance was moved to the side, and the eastern arch was transformed from a door to a window.

William V. O'Brien House

75 2430 N. Lakeview Ave.

1927, REBORI, WENTWORTH,
DEWEY & MCCORMICK

Although Rebori's most distinctive work is his interpretation of the Deco and Moderne styles, he was also a fluent translator of the Georgian idiom so beloved of his wealthy clients. The horizontal separation of living spaces and bedrooms is evident in the window arrangement.

76 2440 N. Lakeview Ave.
(Lake View Ave. Apartments)
1927, RISSMAN & HIRSCHFELD
Despite its frilly facade, six units per floor make for less luxury than its more sober neighbors possess.

2440 N. Lakeview Ave.

77 2450 N. Lakeview Ave.
1924, HOWARD VAN DOREN SHAW
Servants lived on the second floor of this simplified Georgian building, which was designed with only one unit per floor. Shaw was one of the original owners, but he died at the age of fifty-six only two years after its completion, having just received the gold medal of the American Institute of Architects.

78 Joseph Theurer/ Philip K. Wrigley House
2466 N. Lakeview Ave.
1897, RICHARD E. SCHMIDT
The monochromatic scheme of orange brick and terra-cotta and the palazzo form have a kinship with Stanford White's Patterson-McCormick Mansion, but the asymmetrical bays and exaggerated quoins add a German neoclassical flavor. This was Schmidt's first major commission.

79 2474 N. Lakeview Ave.
1993, LOHAN ASSOCS.
The architects describe the elevation as "an abstract collage on which the spatial and constructive elements are realized." The most prominent element is a sinuous skylighted galleria that runs the length of the interior.

80 Marlborough Apartments
400 W. Deming Pl./2600–2608 N. Lakeview Ave.
1923, ROBERT S. DEGOLYER
The clever massing and delicate Adamesque ornament diminish the bulk. Apartments on the Lakeview Ave. side were for the building's investors; the much smaller units on Deming Pl. were rented to others.

81 Francis J. Dewes House
503 W. Wrightwood Ave.
1896, CUDELL & HERCZ
1998, RENOVATION, HAMMOND BEEBY RUPERT AINGE
This Prussian confection can't decide whether to be neoclassical, Baroque, or Rococo, but it does succeed in being impressive. The rich carving includes statues supporting a balcony above the entrance. The house next door at **509 W. Wrightwood** was built at the same time (architect unknown) for Dewes's brother, August.

Francis J. Dewes House

82 Mrs. Arthur Ryerson House
2700 N. Lakeview Ave.
1917, DAVID ADLER
83 Abram Poole House
2704 N. Lakeview Ave.
1917, DAVID ADLER
84 Henry C. Dangler House
2708 N. Lakeview Ave.
1917, HENRY C. DANGLER
85 Ambrose C. Cramer House
2710 N. Lakeview Ave.
1917, AMBROSE C. CRAMER
Although designed by different architects, this cohesive block seems straight out of Georgian London—up to the cornice line, at least. The houses share an

Elks National Memorial Building and Headquarters

Adamesque sensibility in the details as well. Dangler was Adler's partner, and he stamped all of the construction drawings because Adler had never passed the engineering test needed to obtain an architect's license.

86 Elks National Memorial Building and Headquarters
2750 N. Lakeview Ave.
1923–26, EGERTON SWARTWOUT
1967, MAGAZINE BUILDING,
   HOLABIRD & ROOT
2013, RESTORATION,
   HARBOE ARCHITECTS

This memorial to fallen Elks of World War I (rededicated after subsequent conflicts to include latter-day heroes) contains one of the city's grandest public spaces. The Memorial Rotunda is a riot of colored marble and mural painting, dazzling in opulence if not taste. Eugene Savage painted the enormous and rather cryptic murals here and in the reception room (on axis with the main entrance); Edwin H. Blashfield was responsible for the more subdued wall paintings in the small lobby between the two rooms. Adolph A. Weinman sculpted the gesticulating figures in the niches; James Earle Fraser was responsible for the sculpture in the entry vestibule; and Laura Gardin Fraser designed the life-size elks that flank the steps where they meet the sidewalk on Lakeview Ave. Weinman also designed the monumental bronzes in the pair of exterior niches.

Urantia Foundation

87 Urantia Foundation
(Sylvan Kunz Flats)
533 W. Diversey Pkwy.
1908, FROMMANN & JEBSEN

Light-years from the firm's turgid, tourelled stone-front houses on Fullerton Ave. is this grand flat, the star of this graceless southside stretch of Diversey Pkwy. Lavish ornament grows out of the wall organically, recalling Art Nouveau and Jugendstil masters. The integration of the metal railing with the stone balcony is the jewel in the crown of this sculptured facade.

88 2780 N. Lincoln Ave.
(John E. Hufmeyer Building)
1888, CHARLES F. HERMANN

The diagonal path of Lincoln Ave. creates dozens of six-point intersections that are a motorist's nightmare but provide high-visibility sites for storefronts. This mansard-roofed block is one of the city's most elaborate flatiron flats-above-shops buildings.

89 Embassy Club

Southport Ave., Greenview Ave., and Wrightwood Ave. just south of Diversey Pkwy.

1989–92, PAPPAGEORGE/HAYMES

One of Chicago's grandest yupscale developments has narrow row houses grouped around cobbled streets. The elaborate facades feature the bay windows and lively street-wall rhythms of their Queen Anne ancestors but with a Georgian formality. The resulting Queen George amalgam conveys a Disneyland ambience of virtual reality, with none of the quirks or messiness—or vitality—of a true cityscape.

90 2637 N. Greenview Ave.

1996, KRUECK & SEXTON ARCHITECTS

The modernist planes of brick and glass are a rebuke to the traditionalism of the surrounding Embassy Club. On the west elevation, a slot window extends as a continuous skylight across the roof.

91 Cortland St. Bridge

(Clybourn Pl. Drawbridge)
Cortland St. (1400 W.) at the Chicago River

1902, JOHN E. ERICSON, CITY ENG.;
    THOMAS G. PIHLFELDT, CITY BRIDGE ENG.

This was the nation's first trunnion bascule bridge. The leaves are hinged at the shore end on a trunnion, or shaft. Chicago's conception and execution of this type of bridge became a textbook example around the world.

LINCOLN PARK

Lincoln Park

Oak St. to Ardmore Ave.; Lake Michigan to N. Lake Shore Dr., N. Clark St., Lincoln Park West, Lakeview Ave., Lake Shore Dr., Marine Dr.

1865–80S, SWAIN NELSON & OLAF BENSON
1903–21, OSSIAN C. SIMONDS
1920S–60, ERNST G. SCHROEDER
1936–38, ALFRED CALDWELL

Chicago's largest and busiest park has more noteworthy features than any other and offers a variety of landscapes, buildings, and activities. It reflects more than a century of design and the work of many talents, but each succeeding designer knit his contributions into the existing fabric, resulting in an overall unity of appearance. The landscape also reflects a century of competing interests and ideas about how parkland should best be used.

Lincoln Park's history is unusually complex. Much of its 1,212 acres, which stretch along almost six miles of Lake Michigan shoreline, were created from landfill. The southern section, from North to Webster Aves., comprised the municipal cemetery, established in 1837. The first area used as parkland was 60 vacant acres of the cemetery between Wisconsin St. and Webster Ave. As the population of surrounding neighborhoods increased, pressure grew to relocate the bodies for health reasons. In 1864, the Common Council prohibited the sale of burial plots and designated the land for Lake Park, although reinterment in private cemeteries outside the city limits did not begin in earnest until 1871 and continued for several years. In 1865, the park was renamed for the recently assassinated president, and three years later a zoo was established when New York City's Central Park donated two pairs of swans. In 1869, state legislation created the Lincoln Park Commission to manage the park and permitted its northward expansion.

Landscape gardener Swain Nelson drew up the first plan for the park in 1865. His plan enhanced the existing topography of low glacial ridges by creating three interconnected ponds encircled by hills, including a thirty-five-foot-tall "lookout mountain." Lawn areas and winding pathways and drives completed the scheme. Nelson formed a partnership with his cousin, Olof Benson, and they continued to work on the park, expanding it north to Diversey Ave. The ponds and waterfowl lagoon as well as the hill known as Mount Prospect are legacies of their work. The first landfills were created in the 1880s, beginning a process that continued for the next seven decades.

In 1903, Ossian C. Simonds began to promote a midwestern style of naturalistic landscaping inspired by the landforms, rock outcroppings, waterways, and native plants of the prairies. Simonds proposed extending the park all the

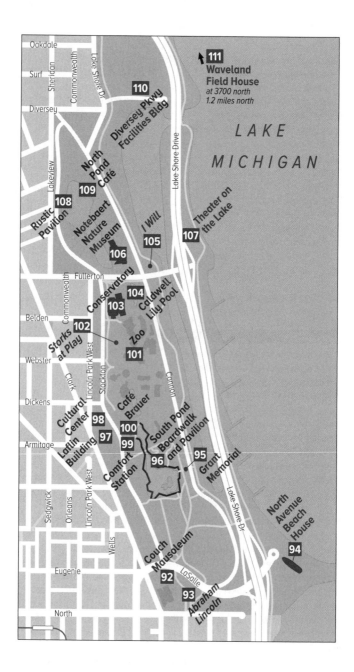

way to Devon Ave., a mile past its present terminus, and during his tenure it grew north to Cornelia St.

Beginning in the 1930s, engineer Ernst G. Schroeder directed the park's growth to the north, and it finally terminated at Ardmore Ave./Hollywood Beach in 1957. The newly created sections were laid out in a naturalistic style that incorporated interesting rockwork elements. The most important designer during this period was Alfred Caldwell, a disciple of landscape architect Jens Jensen. Caldwell brought the Prairie School spirit into the park, most dramatically in the Lily Pool. His work can also be seen in the broad open spaces defined by groves of hawthorn trees in the Montrose Point area.

The biggest changes since the 1950s have been made to accommodate the ever-increasing demands of the automobile. Wheeled traffic has been an issue since 1873, when a speed limit was established for the park's roadways; two years later, a separate speeding track was built. Encroachment on parkland began in earnest in 1938, when La Salle Dr. was extended through the park's south end. Lake Shore Dr. now cuts a wide swath through the entire length of the park, separating the lakefront from the rest of the city. The many issues concerned with the use of Lincoln Park—cars versus pedestrians, passive versus active recreation, buildings versus open space—continue to generate lively dialogue and inspire strong passions.

—JOAN POMARANC

92 Couch Mausoleum
Northwest of *Abraham Lincoln*
1857–58, JOHN VAN OSDEL

The only tomb left from the park's early days as the municipal cemetery is here because the family refused to move it. Construction excavations have uncovered adjacent remains unknowingly left behind.

93 *Abraham Lincoln (Standing Lincoln)*
East of the Chicago History Museum
1887, AUGUSTUS SAINT-GAUDENS; BASE AND EXEDRA MCKIM, MEAD & WHITE

One of America's greatest nineteenth-century sculptures and widely considered Saint-Gaudens's most significant work, this imposing statue commands its handsome setting. The face and hands are based on life casts by sculptor Leonard W. Volk, but Saint-Gaudens had also seen Lincoln, once in life as well as when his body lay in state. The great orator is portrayed in the penultimate moment before a speech, as he gathers his thoughts to step forward and address the crowd.

Abraham Lincoln (Standing Lincoln)

94 North Ave. Beach House
Lakefront at North Ave.
1999, G.E.C. DESIGN GROUP WITH WHEELER KEARNS ARCHITECTS

When the popular 1939 beach house just north of this location had deteriorated to the point of necessitating its replacement, public sentiment strongly favored a new facility that would capture the playful nautical spirit of the original. The new, more durable cast-in-place concrete "steamship" updates and reinterprets many original elements and adapts them to a larger scale. Elliptical "smokestacks," functional counterparts of the decorative originals, contain open-air stairs to the rooftop restaurant. Nautical imagery pops up in playful details throughout the building. The new siting relieves congestion and opens up vistas of the lake from North Ave.

95 Ulysses S. Grant Memorial
1891, LOUIS T. REBISSO; FRANCIS M. WHITEHOUSE, ARCH.

The aesthetic quality of this ponderous monument has been the subject of debate since its unveiling. One early newspaper account called it suitable only for impressing country cousins.

96 South Pond Nature Boardwalk and Peoples Gas Education Pavilion
2010, BOARDWALK AND PAVILION, STUDIO GANG ARCHITECTS, DESIGN ARCH.; SHAW SUSTAINABLE SOLUTIONS OF ILLINOIS, ARCH. OF RECORD MASTER PLAN, SHAW ENVIRONMENTAL & INFRASTRUCTURE

Created as one of the park's original ornamental water features, South Pond was brought out of its

Peoples Gas Education Pavilion

ecological death throes through dredging and shoreline restoration and is now a wetland habitat. It is ringed by a new boardwalk of recycled plastic, the planks changing in hue from concrete-colored to brown. The bridge features a plaque identifying buildings visible on the skyline, but a small-scale icon—the education pavilion—is right here. What could have been a simple shelter for outdoor classes is instead one of the park district's most exquisitely sculptural structures. Once again, Gang's materials investigations lead to a unique solution. Using techniques drawn from boatbuilders and furniture makers, a shape inspired by a tortoise shell is fabricated from Douglas fir laminated and bent to just short of its breaking point. Fiberglass domes provide shelter from rain and strong sun. The siting deviates slightly from true north/south to frame the skyline, increasing the pavilion's irresistible quality to everyone from yoga enthusiasts to photo-snapping tourists and locals.

97 Matthew Laflin Memorial Building
(Chicago Academy of Sciences)
2001 N. Clark St.
1893, PATTON & FISHER
1996, RENOVATION FOR OFFICES, SOLOMON CORDWELL BUENZ & ASSOCS.

The building is named after the pioneer businessman who provided this Renaissance Revival home for Chicago's oldest museum, founded in 1857 to promote knowledge of the region's natural history. That museum became the Notebaert Nature Museum.

98 Lincoln Park Cultural Center
2045 N. Lincoln Park West
1927, EDWIN H. CLARK

This Georgian Revival building recalls the architect's contemporaneous work for the Lincoln Park Zoo.

99 Comfort Station
(Carlson Cottage)
Stockton Dr. southwest of Café Brauer
1888, JOSEPH LYMAN SILSBEE
2008, RESTORATION, INTERACTIVE DESIGN ARCHITECTS

One of the earliest park structures, it was first identified as Men's and Ladies' Cottage. Although it no longer nestles into a berm on the north side, its picturesque charm has been restored.

100 Café Brauer
(South Pond Refectory)
2021 N. Stockton Dr.
1908, PERKINS & HAMILTON
1989, RENOVATION, LAWRENCE B. BERKLEY & ASSOCS.; MEISEL & ASSOCS.; WISS, JANNEY, ELSTNER ASSOCS.

On the banks of the South Pond, the Lincoln Park Commission constructed a new refectory financed by restaurateurs Paul and Caspar Brauer. The building is a masterpiece of designer Dwight H. Perkins, a leader of the Prairie School.

The massing includes a large closed central pavilion flanked by two graciously curving loggias. A broad expanse of green tile roof with deep

Café Brauer

overhangs, combined with earthy red brick, subtle terra-cotta details, and polychromatic mortar, settles the building into the landscape. Viewed from Stockton Dr. to the west, the large block of the central pavilion dominates, while the curving loggias recede. But on the lagoon side, the main pavilion is opened up with large expanses of glass, and the two loggias are seen to wrap around the end of the pond. Simultaneously, the loggias contain the water, and the lagoon's form controls their curves.

The centerpiece of the building is the Great Hall, located on the second floor of the pavilion. It is accessed from a lobby that has low ceilings and rich, earth-toned colors. At the top of the stair, the Great Hall rises thirty-four feet to the peak of the skylight that bathes the room in sunlight. The large glass doors on the lagoon side also provide soothing natural light to the room. Two art-glass chandeliers hang from the trusses. The walls are buff speckled brick, and Rookwood mosaics enhance recessed corner alcoves and a musicians' gallery. From the loggias, which open off the Great Hall, the skyline unfolds to the south.

The café was a favored establishment during its early years and throughout Prohibition. The dining room fell into decline after repeal, however, because state law forbade the sale of liquor in the parks. The Great Hall closed in 1941, and throughout the late 1950s and 1960s, the space was used as a winter theater.

Not until legislation in 1989 permitted the sale of liquor at Café Brauer could a viable restoration plan be undertaken. At that time, the clay tile roof and skylight, which had been removed in the 1940s, were reinstalled; the original wall sconces, which were also missing, were reproduced; and all the original paint colors were re-created. Remarkably, the two chandeliers, which had hung in place throughout the hall's incarnations, required only cleaning and minor repairs. They are the centerpieces of that room as restored to its original elegance.

Café Brauer is an outstanding example of the Prairie School style in a public building.

—WILLIAM W. TIPPENS

101 Lincoln Park Zoo
Armitage to Fullerton Aves., Stockton to Cannon Drs.
Early zoo buildings, little more than decorative cages for the separation of species, evolved into settings designed to appropriately frame the animal for human eyes. Modern design stresses the re-creation of natural habitats, with human intrusion kept to a minimum. The beasts in the beautifully detailed **Lion House** (1912, PERKINS, FELLOWS & HAMILTON; 1986, RENOVATION, HAMMOND, BEEBY & BABKA) had indoor and outdoor quarters, not just for their own comfort but to increase their visibility. The Georgian Revival architecture popular in the 1920s is represented by the **Park Pavilion** (AQUARIUM & FISH HATCHERY, 1923; RENOVATION 1998, VALERIO DEWALT TRAIN ASSOCS.) and **Primate House** (SMALL ANIMAL HOUSE, 1927), both by Edwin H. Clark and renovated by John Macsai & Assocs. in 1984 and 1992, respectively. The **McCormick Bird House** (1900, JARVIS HUNT)

has been completely renovated to house naturalistic habitats. The **Waterfowl Lagoon** (1865, SWAIN NELSON; 1978, RENOVATION, CHICAGO PARK DISTRICT) re-creates the naturalistic landscape planned by the park's original designer.

In the 1990s, the zoo undertook a major building campaign to provide more visitor services. Entrance from the Cannon Dr. parking lot is through the whimsical **Entrance Gate** (2002, DAVID WOODHOUSE ARCHITECTS). On the north side of the landscaped plaza are the **Gateway Pavilion** (1995, KATHRYN QUINN) and the **Mahon-Theobald Pavilion** (1999, VALERIO DE-WALT TRAIN ASSOCS.), which houses the

Wild Things! Gift Shop in the Mahon-Theobald Pavilion

Wild Things! Gift Shop and Big Cats Café. A replacement bridge (1996, TENG & ASSOCS.) spans the Swan Pond, and the firm created a new **Flamingo Habitat** in 2003. Other major buildings include the **Regenstein Center for African Apes** (2004, LOHAN CAPRILE GOETTSCH ARCHITECTS) and the **Pritzker Family Children's Zoo** (2005, EHDD/ARCHITECTURE, DESIGN ARCH.; ARCHITECTUREISFUN, INTERIOR ARCHITECT). The **Farm-in-the-Zoo** was renovated in 2002 by Interactive Design Architects. West of the antelope area is the bas-relief *Rites of Spring* that Milton Horn sculpted in 1952 for the Seneca-Walton apartment building (demolished).

---

102 *Storks at Play*
(The Bates Fountain)
1887, AUGUSTUS SAINT-GAUDENS AND FREDERICK WILLIAM MACMONNIES

Saint-Gaudens received this commission together with that for the *Standing Lincoln*, which so absorbed him that he called on a former student to work on the fountain. He later gave MacMonnies primary credit for this popular work.

103 Lincoln Park Conservatory
Stockton Dr. between Belden Ave. and Fullerton Pkwy.
1894, JOSEPH LYMAN SILSBEE, ASSISTED BY MIFFLIN E. BELL

The Crystal Palace–inspired conservatory (its entrance was enlarged in the 1950s) overlooks a formal French garden to the south and an English-style perennial garden on the west, across Stockton Dr. Both gardens have been in place at least since 1887.

104 Alfred Caldwell Lily Pool
Fullerton Pkwy. between Stockton and Cannon Drs.
1937, ALFRED CALDWELL
2001–2; RESTORATION, CHICAGO PARK DISTRICT AND THE FRIENDS OF

LINCOLN PARK; WOLFF CLEMENTS AND ASSOCS., LANDSCAPE ARCH.; EIFLER & ASSOCS., ARCH.

Caldwell redesigned a Victorian lily pool to evoke the midwestern landscape by way of Japan and the Prairie School, with stratified stonework, a wooden pavilion, and native plants. After years of overuse and insensitive maintenance, a $2.5 million rehabilitation brought Caldwell's vision back to life. Nonnative invasive trees and plants were replaced with native prairie and woodland plants. Trees, shrubs, and grasses now protect the shoreline from erosion, enabling the removal of slabs of concrete and stone. A council ring, a favorite element of both Caldwell and Jens Jensen, adds seating for conversation and contemplation. The Lily Pool once again takes its place as one of the loveliest pockets of nature in the city.

105 *I Will*
Cannon Dr. at Fullerton Pkwy.
1981, ELLSWORTH KELLY

The park's first contemporary sculpture honors Chicago's unofficial motto of the 1890s, recalling the rebuilding after the Great Fire of 1871.

Alfred Caldwell Lily Pool

106 Peggy Notebaert Nature Museum

2430 N. Cannon Dr.

1999, PERKINS & WILL

The color and angular massing are meant to recall the shifting sand dunes that earlier occupied the site. The building is composed of a series of paths, some breaking through the wall to be exterior walkways, layered atop one another. Large expanses of glass emphasize the close relationship of building to landscape.

107 Theater on the Lake

(Chicago Daily News Fresh Air Sanitarium)
Lakefront northeast of Lake Shore Dr. and Fullerton Pkwy.

1920, PERKINS, FELLOWS & HAMILTON

Major changes to Lake Shore Dr. and Fullerton Pkwy. in 1937 necessitated significant alterations to this Prairie School structure, later remodeled into a theater.

108 Rustic Pavilion

Lakeview Ave. at St. James Pl.

1883, MIFFLIN E. BELL
2012, RESTORATION, CHICAGO
    PARK DISTRICT

An artesian well once briefly bubbled up nearby. The site's naturalness has been obscured, but the structure has been restored to its original color. The Adirondack twig detailing recalls a bygone era of pleasure grounds and picturesque vistas.

109 North Pond Café

(Warming House)
2610 N. Cannon Dr.

1914, PERKINS, FELLOWS & HAMILTON
1998, 2002, CONVERSION TO
    RESTAURANT, NANCY WARREN

This warming shelter for skaters was set into the slope of the landscape and given a flat roof and very simple facade. It now has a new life as an Arts and Crafts–style restaurant.

110 Diversey Pkwy. Facilities Building and Driving Range

(Golf Course Shelter)
Diversey Pkwy. east of Lake Shore Dr. West

1916, 1919, ANDREW N. REBORI
1998, DRIVING RANGE,
    DESTEFANO & PARTNERS

Originally open to the golf course, the north side of the shelter was filled in by Rebori's expansion.

111 Waveland Field House

(Refectory)
East of Lake Shore Dr. opposite Waveland Ave.

1932, EDWIN H. CLARK

At the north end of Lincoln Park is one of Clark's finest park buildings. The Collegiate Gothic field house includes a clock tower with the Wolford Memorial Chimes. In 1992, a dedicated group of volunteers finished restoring the long-silent chimes and the clock's previously immobile hands.

LAKEVIEW/RAVENSWOOD/UPTOWN

see Edgewater map, p. 244

Foster
Winona
Carmen
Winnemac
Argyle

Argyle
Ainslie
Gunnison
Lawrence

Claremont
Lincoln
Western
Oakley
Bell
Leavitt
Hamilton
Hoyne
Seeley
Damen

Winchester
Wolcott

Wolcott Gardens

77

75 Doblin House

76 Yannell House

Ashland
Ainslie

Sandburg House

Ravenswood

Farr
Foste
Wino
Carm
Winn
Argy

Studio V Design

85

Giddings
Leland

Hamilton

78 Abbott House

79 Ravenswood Methodist

Clark

CTA Brown Line

Eastwood

Eastwood

Windsor

Seeley

Lawrence

All Saints Episcopal

Ravenswood

Wilson
80
81 Sunnyside

Black En

82

Old Town School of Folk Music

86 **87**

Agatite

Sulzer Library

Montrose

Claremont
Lincoln

Rockwell
Maplewood
Campbell
Artesian

Pensacola

Hutchinson

Warner

Cuyler

Pensacola
Cuttom
Hutchinson

Winchester
Wolcott
Honare

Berteau
Warner
Bette Plaine
Cuyler
Irving Park

83 Ravenswood School

Hermitage
Paulina

Greenview

Pensa
Cutlor
Hutchi
Warne

Lakeview HS **45** Cuyler

St Benedict

88

Dakin

89

Claremont House

Berenice

Bradley

Talman
Campbell
Artesian
Western
Claremont
Oakley
Bell
Leavitt
Hamilton
Hoyne
Seeley
Damen

Larchmont
Byron
Berenice
Grace
Bradley
Waveland
Patterson

Ravenswood
Ravenswood

Hermitage
Paulina
Marshfield
Ashland

Byron

Wave

90 Lane Tech HS

91

Clark Park Boathouse

Metrose

Eddy
Cornelia
Newport
Roscoe
Henderson
School
Metrose

Ravenswood

84 Ravenswood Corridor

Bosworth
Greenview

Her

NORTH BRANCH

Fletcher
Barry
Nelson

Oakley
Leavitt
Hamilton
Hoyne

Belmont
Fletcher
Nelson

Jahn School **92**

93 Brundage Bldg

Schub

OF THE CHICAGO

Oakdale
George
Wolfram

Washtenaw
Elston
Talman
Rockwell
Maplewood
Campbell

Damen
Wolcott

Oakdale
George
Wolfram

Picardy Pl
Hermitage

Ge
Wol

St Alpho

RIVER

Logan

Clybourn

see West Town map, p. 264

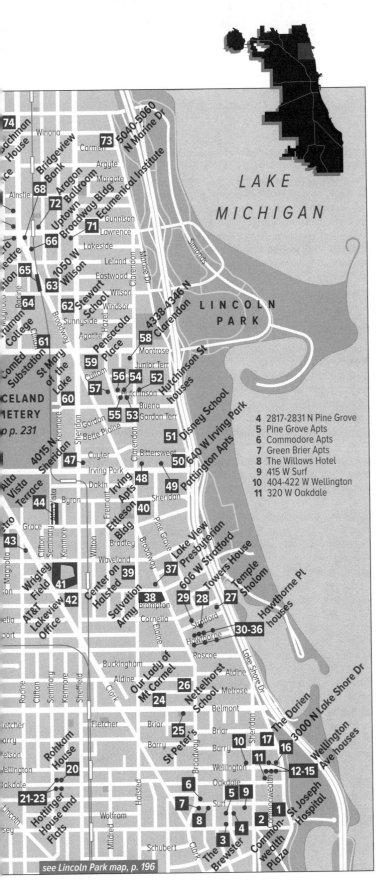

74

Winona

Bridgeview
Bank

73

5040-5060
N Marine Dr

Carmen

Argyle

Margate

Ainslie

68

72
Uptown

Aragon
Ballroom

Broadway Bldg

Ecumenical Institute

71

Lawrence

66

1050 W
Wilson

Lakeside

Leland

Clarendon

Marine Dr

Simonds

LAKE
MICHIGAN

65

Eastwood

63

Stewart
School

62

Wilson

Windsor

LINCOLN
PARK

Truman
College

64

Sunnyside

Agatie

Hazel

Pensacola
Place

4338-4346 N
Clarendon

ComEd
Substation

61

St Mary
of the
Lake

58

Montrose

59

Cuttom

Junior Terr

GRACELAND
CEMETERY

60

56 54

52

Hutchinson

Hutchinson St
houses

see pp. 231

57

Buena

Sheridan

55 53

Gordon Terr

Gordon

Disney School

4015 N
Sheridan

Belle Plaine

51

540 W Irving Park

47

Cuyler

Clarendon

Bittersweet

Pattington Apts

Alta
Vista
Terrace

Irving Park

Dakin

50

44

Byron

48

Sheridan

4 2817-2831 N Pine Grove
5 Pine Grove Apts
6 Commodore Apts
7 Green Brier Apts
8 The Willows Hotel
9 415 W Surf
10 404-422 W Wellington
11 320 W Oakdale

LAKEVIEW/RAVENSWOOD/UPTOWN

43

Grace

Fremont

Irving
Apts

40

49

Ettleson
Bldg

Bradley

Pine Grove

Broadway

Lake View
Presbyterian

Wrigley
Field

41

Waveland

39

37

606 W Stratford

Towers House

Temple
Sholom

42

AT&T
Lakeview
Office

Center on
Halsted

38

Salvation
Army

Brompton

29

28

27

Stratford

Hawthorne Pl
houses

Cornelia

Elaine

Hawthorne

130-36

Roscoe

Buckingham

Aldine

Our Lady of
Mt Carmel

26

Nettelhorst
School

Aldine

Metrose

24

Belmont

Fletcher

Fletcher

Briar

25

Briar

10

17

The Darien

3000 N Lake Shore Dr

Rohkam
House

Barry

St Peter's

Barry

16

Wellington
Ave houses

20

Wellington

11

12-15

Oakdale

Oakdale

6

5 9

St Joseph
Hospital

21-23

Hottinger
House and
Flats

7

Surf

2

1

8

4

Common-
wealth
Plaza

3

The
Brewster

see Lincoln Park map, p. 196

LAKEVIEW/RAVENSWOOD/UPTOWN

Over time, the North Side communities of Lakeview, Uptown, and Ravenswood carved themselves out of a much larger government entity, the township of Lake View. When organized in 1857, Lake View Township extended north from Fullerton Ave. to Devon Ave. and from the lake to Western Ave. Today, the name survives in that of just one of the many neighborhoods developed in the township. Lakeview extends from (roughly) Diversey Pkwy. to Addison St. Communities to its north include Wrigleyville (Addison to Irving Park Rd.), Buena Park (east and west of Graceland Cemetery), Uptown (north of Montrose Ave.), and Ravenswood (west of Ashland Ave. from Addison to Lawrence Ave.). The history of the area can be divided easily into the nineteenth-century saga of Lake View Township and the twentieth-century stories of these individual communities.

Throughout the nineteenth century, Lake View Township resembled the garden in Chicago's motto, *Urbs in Horto* (City in a Garden). Farms dominated the landscape to the west, and country estates lined the lakefront. In 1836, Conrad Sulzer established a farm near the present intersection of Clark St. and Montrose Ave., and the truck farmers who followed his lead made Lake View Township the center of the Midwest's greenhouse industry and the nation's largest shipper of celery.

Along the lakeshore, developers James B. Rees and Elisha E. Hundley acquired 225 acres between Belmont Ave. and Irving Park Rd. in 1852. Two years later, they opened a first-class lakefront hotel, the Lake View House. When the State of Illinois conferred township status on the area three years later, Lake View became the first North Side community named for a resort hotel. Rees and Hundley subdivided their acreage into spacious residential lots, and wealthy Chicagoans, among them real estate investor Samuel H. Kerfoot, laid out beautifully landscaped lakefront estates that attracted visitors from miles around. To the west, in Ravenswood, other developers built frame houses near the Chicago & North Western right-of-way to attract families displaced by the Great Fire of 1871. Beer gardens in the vicinities of Clark and Diversey and Broadway and Lawrence and a baseball park at Sheffield and Addison emphasized outdoor entertainment.

Lake View Township went out of existence in 1889, when annexation by Chicago brought improved municipal services and increasing urbanization. Lakeview developed a split personality as early frame houses remained concentrated west of Halsted St. while graystone and brick houses, flats, and apartments predominated to the east. Pockets of spacious homes, such as those found at Buena and Sheridan Parks, continued to bear witness to the area's suburban origins even after elegant 1920s apartments filled Sheridan Rd. Outdoor enjoyments now centered on Riverview Amusement Park at Belmont and Western and National League baseball at Wrigley Field. In Ravenswood, the residential neighborhoods were pierced by an industrial corridor along the railroad line.

The pace of urbanization accelerated northward to Wilson Ave. after 1900, along with new elevated train service. By the 1920s, the area around Wilson and Broadway had been christened Uptown, a name that reflected the glamour and urbanity of a vibrant commercial and entertainment district. However, Uptown never really recovered from the Great Depression. Its famous movie palaces and dance halls went dark, and poverty overtook its once-fashionable neighborhoods. Although it continued to attract weekend crowds of the young and the restless, Uptown lagged ever further behind adjacent neighborhoods over the next few decades. Private renewal began slowly in the 1980s, just as the area began to benefit from the vitality that immigrants invest into port-of-entry neighborhoods.

Postwar construction initially concentrated on the ever-desirable lakefront, creating canyons of concrete high-rises and infill pockets of "four-plus-one" apartments. Around the turn of the twenty-first century, teardown mania raged through all of these communities. Density soared as new multiple-unit buildings replaced razed frame houses. Many masonry two-flats were converted into single-family residences, some with added setback third floors. The least successful examples of this new construction are overscaled with cartoonish period ornament, while the best designs are contemporary yet contextual.

—MARY ALICE MOLLOY

1 St. Joseph Hospital
2900 N. Lake Shore Dr.
1963, BELLI & BELLI

Forgive the blue walls with their diamond-shaped windows and the dark glass cylinder that hangs like a uvula from the front. The eleventh-floor Dan Ryan Memorial Chapel, open every day, is a great treat. It may be the city's most perfectly preserved 1960s interior, from the mosaic-lined, concrete baldachin to the pointy-legged altar furniture. Architects would like to think the 1960s looked like Mies's Federal Center, but this is what that era *really* looked like.

Commonwealth Plaza

Walk this densely built lakefront neighborhood from Diversey Ave. to Wellington Ave. to see a variety of Chicago housing types popular from the 1890s until the present.

2 Commonwealth Plaza
(Commonwealth Promenade Apartments)
330–340 W. Diversey Pkwy.
1953–56, LUDWIG MIES VAN DER ROHE; FRIEDMAN, ALSCHULER & SINCERE, ASSOC. ARCHS.

This is curtain-wall modernism in full stride. The project was commissioned by developer Herbert S. Greenwald, Mies's early and influential client, whose death in 1959 halted development of two additional towers planned for the site. The glass-and-aluminum skin is suspended in front of the columns, which comprise two different structural systems (reinforced concrete on the lower floors and steel above). The space between the columns and the skin contains vertical ventilation shafts, allowing for more efficient heating and cooling than in Mies's previous buildings.

St. Joseph Hospital

The Brewster

3 The Brewster
(Lincoln Park Palace)
2800 N. Pine Grove Ave.

1893, ENOCH HILL TURNOCK
1972, RENOVATION, MIEKI HAYANO

It looks like a brooding high-rise armory from the outside, but beg your way indoors to see the "sky lobby," a fantasy in steel and glass block. Every apartment opens onto a gabled, skylighted court. Turnock's early years in the office of William Le Baron Jenney may account for the steel frame and the atrium design, which resembles bridge construction. The rugged "Jasper stone" (quartzite) walls set off an outstanding Sullivanesque terra-cotta frieze on the top floor. The polished granite entry on Pine Grove Ave. was originally the ladies' entrance.

4 2817–2831 N. Pine Grove Ave.

1891, OSTLING BROS.

The use of a uniform building material increases the apparent size of the units, while varied bay shapes, rooflines, and stone cuts provide individuality.

5 Pine Grove Apartments
(Pine Grove Apartment Hotel)
2828 N. Pine Grove Ave.

1924, LOEWENBERG & LOEWENBERG

Upper-class vintage apartment buildings frequently have remarkably understated entrances to downplay the communal nature of the accommodations. But apartment hotels, which offered dining, recreation, and other services, flaunted their congregate nature. Playing up the grand public spaces, an octagonal entry pavilion leads to an enormous lobby, and

an ornate belt course separates the monumental and heavily detailed first floor (which contained the public spaces) from the private residential floors above.

6 Commodore Apartments
550–568 W. Surf St.

1897, EDMUND R. KRAUSE
1985, RENOVATION, NAKAWATASE, RUTKOWSKI, WYNS & YI

This exemplary Chicago School apartment building owes as much to the skyscrapers of Holabird & Roche as to the flats of the era. A massive building, it is broken into smaller blocks to increase ventilation and light. The Roman brick facade is crisply edged and sparingly ornamented, with oculi at the top story and an Ionic temple front entrance.

Commodore Apartments

7 Green Brier Apartments
559–561 W. Surf St.

1904, EDMUND R. KRAUSE
1985, RENOVATION, ARCHITECTS INTERNATIONAL—CHICAGO

Familiar from the Commodore are the temple front entrance and the use of Roman brick, but the flat facades—with their pox of brackets—are repetitious by comparison.

8 The Willows Hotel
555 W. Surf St.

1925, RISSMAN & HIRSCHFELD

Behind the ornate terra-cotta facade is an apartment hotel shaped like a bowling alley: the footprint is 36 × 216 feet!

9 415 W. Surf St.

1910, SAMUEL N. CROWEN

Crowen was more successful than most in marrying Prairie School detailing to apartment-house formulas. This brick three-flat has Wrightian

geometric decoration and an unusual stepped elevation ending in a
large square bay.

10 404–422 W. Wellington Ave.

1939, LOEBL & SCHLOSSMAN

The enduring desirability of this lakefront community called for the successful reintroduction of a decades-
old housing type, the row house.
These ten streamlined Lannon stone
examples are densely packed on the
site. The courtyard is an important
amenity, made private by its half-
story elevation from the street.

Arthur H. Apfel House

11 320 W. Oakdale Ave.

1953, MILTON M. SCHWARTZ

Milton Schwartz was a highly original postwar Chicago architect who
rejected minimal Miesian modernism
in favor of more exuberant and typically American design vocabulary.
In this building, he extended the
concrete floor slabs beyond the
aluminum-and-glass curtain wall
to screen the sun, deflect rain and
snow, reduce vertigo, and provide
a dramatic horizontal view. Through
the use of a complex series of transfer girders on the third floor, the
bulk of the building appears to float
above the glass lobby.

On this short block of Wellington
Ave. are elegant single-family
houses dating from the 1920s (entries 12–15). This area developed
later than the Gold Coast because
much of the land east of Sheridan
Rd. between Diversey and Belmont
Aves. had been created by an
ongoing process of filling in the
shoreline. In the early twentieth
century, Lincoln Park expanded
north of Diversey, and the streets
immediately to the west filled up
with stately homes in fashionable
revival styles.

12 Arthur H. Apfel House

341 W. Wellington Ave.

1925, E. H. FROMMANN

13 Oscar Mayer Houses

333 and 335 W. Wellington Ave.

1926, RISSMAN & HIRSCHFELD

14 Philip T. Starck House

330 W. Wellington Ave.

1925, MAYO & MAYO

15 Lester Armour House

325 W. Wellington Ave.

1915, HOWARD VAN DOREN SHAW

1925, REMODELING, HOWARD
   VAN DOREN SHAW

These houses are as substantial and
bourgeois as their owners, bastions
of the business community. Individual but not eccentric, they exude
fine craftsmanship while blending
nicely in the streetscape. Starck's
French neoclassical house is the
most elegant; Apfel's Tudor Revival
is the most charming.

16 3000 N. Lake Shore Dr.

2011, WHEELER KEARNS ARCHITECTS

The firm's residential work is characterized by a deft interplay of solids
and voids that provides a combination of privacy and openness in
dense urban areas. The roof slopes
down to the west to accommodate
solar panels and a sunscreen for the
second-floor terrace. Most unusually,
the client kept about two-thirds of
the lot as open space.

Philip T. Starck House

17 The Darien
(Darien Apartment House)
3100 N. Lake Shore Dr.
1948–51, LOEBL, SCHLOSSMAN & BENNETT

Bennett folded the masonry curtain wall like paper, arranging the floor plans to maximize lake views. The metal-framed windows are laid almost flush with the brick, emphasizing the wall's thinness.

Farther west in Lake View were more ethnic neighborhoods. Two reminders of the large German community still stand on Southport Ave. (entries 18–19).

18 Schuba's
3159 N. Southport Ave.
1903, FROMMANN & JEBSEN

At the turn of the century, the Joseph Schlitz Brewing Co. bought many corner lots and built its own saloons to increase its market share and ensure maximum distribution. A busy street in a German neighborhood was a prize location. Vice president Edward G. Uihlein purchased the properties and hired the architects. Although no emphasis was placed on unique design, the Schlitz trademark, the terra-cotta globe, was always prominent on the facade.

19 St. Alphonsus Roman Catholic Church
2950 N. Southport Ave.
1889–97, ADAM BOOS AND JOSEPH
    BETTINGHOFER, SCHRADER & CONRADI

The unusual central placement of the large tower follows a German Gothic precedent that was later translated to a smaller scale in nineteenth-century English parish churches. The small lantern windows high atop the roof were a popular feature in nineteenth-century German neo-Gothic churches. In the nave, a steel support system with exposed rivets tops the ornate decor.

From 1048 to 1059 W. Oakdale Ave. is Terra-Cotta Row, a group of houses and flats built for executives of the Northwestern Terra Cotta Co. (entries 20–23). Established in 1877, the company opened a large plant at Clybourn and Wrightwood Aves. in 1883 and became a leader in the booming industry of architectural ornament.

20 Henry Rohkam House
1048 W. Oakdale Ave.
1887, THEODORE KARLS

Built for one of the founders of Northwestern Terra Cotta, this exuberant brick house and ornate fence display the company's products with great flair. A full range of wares is on display, from small geometric stock pieces to elaborately sculpted plaques, tympana, and chimney pots. The wild eclecticism of the ornament is held in check by a monochromatic color scheme. Don't miss the relief of a woman at a spinning wheel on the west side.

Henry Rohkam House

21 Gustav Hottinger House
1054 W. Oakdale Ave.
1886, JULIUS H. HUBER

This more modest house, built for Northwestern's founder and presi-

St. Alphonsus Roman Catholic Church

dent, has been substantially altered but retains a terra-cotta panel at the peak of the gable and volutes bracketing the east window.

22 Adolph Hottinger Flat
1057 W. Oakdale Ave.
1916, MORITZ F. STRAUCH

23 Gustav Hottinger Flat
1059 W. Oakdale Ave.
1901, THEODORE ANDRESEN

Terra-cotta's ability to ape any material in any style made it equally appropriate for the banded Ionic columns at 1059 and the geometric ornament on 1057.

24 Our Lady of Mt. Carmel Roman Catholic Church
700 W. Belmont Ave.
1914, EGAN & PRINDEVILLE

An imposing English Gothic edifice of Indiana limestone, this rib-vaulted Catholic church has two organs and frequently hosts concerts of sacred and modern music. The reredos behind the altar continues the Gothic vocabulary in a backdrop for statues of the four evangelists.

25 St. Peter's Episcopal Church
615 W. Belmont Ave.
1895, WILLIAM A. OTIS

This small and beautifully detailed structure looks like the top stories of a regulation-sized church, but it is whole and complete according to the architect's plans.

26 Louis Nettelhorst Public School
3252 N. Broadway
1892, JOHN J. FLANDERS
1911, ARTHUR F. HUSSANDER

The public schools' Queen Anne period was shaped by Flanders, who between 1884 and 1893 designed more than fifty projects for the Board of Education. His earliest formula was gloomy and Flemish-gabled, but after William Carbys Zimmerman joined Flanders in practice in 1886, his designs brightened, with lively ornament and larger, more varied windows. Flanders's portion faces Broadway; its polygonal forms and bands of ornament typify Chicago's public schools of the early 1890s. Hussander's addition defers to the original.

27 Temple Sholom
3480 N. Lake Shore Dr.
1930, LOEBL, SCHLOSSMAN & DEMUTH AND COOLIDGE & HODGDON

Loebl, Schlossman & Demuth conceived this project while in graduate school at the Armour Institute. Byzantine in inspiration, the octagonal limestone synagogue is elaborately ornamented with friezes, ornate column capitals, and a portal with stained-glass windows over a trio of paneled doors. The sanctuary is illuminated by indirect light, and a movable wall doubles the seating capacity.

28 Albert B. Towers House
551 W. Stratford Pl.
1894, GEORGE W. MAHER

A great gambrel roof and enormous boulders at ground level hint at the rustic grandeur of this much-altered house.

29 606 W. Stratford Pl.
1912, HUEHL & SCHMID

This is a two-flat masquerading as an urbane single-family house. The monochromatic color scheme suits the severity of the pared-down facade, which seems to anticipate the angular crispness of Art Deco architecture.

Hawthorne Pl. between Broadway and Lake Shore Dr.
Subdivided in 1883 by John and Benjamin F. McConnell, this tree-lined street is a rare and cohesive remnant of the single-family-house district that once stretched for miles along the lakefront.

30 Nicholas J. Sheridan House
587 W. Hawthorne Pl.
1906, BORST & HETHERINGTON

The battered sides, art glass, and projecting roof with exposed supports are Craftsman touches.

31 Alfons Bacon House
580 W. Hawthorne Pl.
1937, MAYO & MAYO

This house presents an elegant Art Deco interpretation of the Georgian style.

32 George E. Marshall House
574 W. Hawthorne Pl.
1886, BURNHAM & ROOT
1896, ADDITION, ARCHITECT UNKNOWN
1938, ALTERATIONS,
ARCHITECT UNKNOWN

The original Queen Anne design is visible only in the half-timbered third-floor gables. Subsequent alterations, such as the pedimented front door and Palladian window, were mostly classical revival.

33 Benjamin F. McConnell House
568 W. Hawthorne Pl.
1884; 1887, REMODELING,
GEORGE BEAUMONT
1987, ADDITION, SCHROEDER
MURCHIE LAYA

The oldest house on the block has been spectacularly transformed by the rear addition of a funhouse for people and plants. Inside this luxuriously modern version of a Victorian conservatory are a swimming pool and a hot tub.

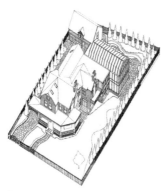

Benjamin F. McConnell House

34 Herman H. Hettler House
567 W. Hawthorne Pl.
1892, JOSEPH LYMAN SILSBEE
1899, ADDITION AND REMODELING,
JULIUS H. HUBER

This lavish Queen Anne, built by a wealthy lumber merchant, is pierced and anchored by a great round bay.

35 John McConnell House
546 W. Hawthorne Pl.
1885, ARCHITECT UNKNOWN

This brick-and-limestone villa with rotated corner bay seems like the city cousin of the rambling clapboard house at 568.

36 Chicago City Day School Additions
541 W. Hawthorne Pl.
1990, 1997, WEESE LANGLEY WEESE

The clock tower and low canopy create a modest civic presence and an inviting entrance. An addition to a classroom facility built in 1969 and 1973, the building was sited on the rear of the property to lessen the impact on the residential streetscape. The architects expanded the school westward again in 1997, this time matching the brick of the earliest buildings to bracket and emphasize the central stone facade.

37 Lake View Presbyterian Church
716 W. Addison St.
1888, BURNHAM & ROOT
2005, RESTORATION, HOLABIRD & ROOT

This simple Shingle Style structure, now gloriously restored, has a high

Chicago City Day School

Lake View Presbyterian Church

40 Isaac G. Ettleson Building
3837–3845 N. Broadway

1911, HARRY HALE WATERMAN

Wingtip to wingtip, terra-cotta eagles flap in formation across the top of this otherwise typical retail and office building.

Isaac G. Ettleson Building

pitched roof and octagonal tower with conical steeple. Built shortly before the annexation of Lake View, it features the wood frame construction that had been prohibited in Chicago after the Fire. In the 1890s, the church was enlarged, shifting the axis to north–south.

38 Salvation Army College for Officers' Training
(Joseph E. Tilt House)
700 W. Brompton Ave.

1914, HOLABIRD & ROCHE

The grand Tudor Revival mansion, built for the owner of a shoe company, has been almost obscured by later buildings. The Salvation Army's Mumford Hall was renovated in 2009 by Harding Partners.

39 Center on Halsted
3656 N. Halsted St.

2007, GENSLER; FACADE RESTORATION, MCGUIRE IGLESKI & ASSOCS.

This mixed-use building for Chicago's lesbian, gay, bisexual, and transgender (LGBT) community incorporates the facade of the former Sexauer Garage (1924, DAVID SAUL KLAFTER) for ground-floor retail and offices above. The entry pavilion presents a modern contrast, its expanses of clear glass signaling pride and openness to the community. Facilities include a gymnasium, theater, office, café, and other gathering spaces. In 2011, the Center announced plans for affordable senior housing (also designed by GENSLER) that would extend to the south and incorporate the former police station (1907, ARCHITECT UNKNOWN).

41 Wrigley Field
(Weeghman Park)
1060 W. Addison St.

1914, ZACHARY TAYLOR DAVIS
2006, BLEACHER EXPANSION, HOK SPORT AND VINCI HAMP ARCHITECTS

Chicago's beloved Cubs Park is the oldest surviving National League ballpark and one of only two survivors (with Boston's Fenway Park) of baseball's golden age (1910–25). Key features from that era include the use of permanent materials (steel and concrete instead of wood); large seating capacity (usually more than 10,000); post-and-beam construction, which allowed spectators to be close to the action; and an urban context that frequently determined the dimensions of the playing field (as was the case here). Davis had designed several other ballparks (including Chicago's original Comiskey Park, demolished in 1991), and his knowledge and foresight facilitated the park's constant enlargements and remodelings. Little of the original structure remains visible, but Wrigley still has the ambience of an old-time ballpark, offering views of surrounding three-flats instead of parking lots.

Alta Vista Terrace

42 AT&T—Lakeview Office
*(Chicago Telephone Co.—
Lakeview Office)*
3532 N. Sheffield Ave.
1914, HOLABIRD & ROCHE

In the early twentieth century, Holabird & Roche developed a generic Georgian brick box to house telephone switching equipment throughout Chicago and its suburbs. This example is less altered than most, with a pedimented entrance and simple limestone lintels, cornice, and base.

43 The Metro
(Northside Auditorium Building)
3730 N. Clark St.
1928, MICHAELSEN & ROGNSTAD

Spanish Baroque Revival, with its exotic connotations and exuberant ornament, was the style of choice for many Roaring Twenties entertainment halls.

44 Alta Vista Terrace
3800 block of N. Alta Vista Terr.
1904, JOSEPH C. BROMPTON

This tiny street is well worth the circuitous route needed to reach it. Alta Vista Terrace was one of the last real estate ventures of Samuel Eberly Gross, a prominent developer of working-class housing during the 1880s and 1890s. Inspired by a European sojourn, Gross re-created the character of London row houses on newly purchased land. As with Georgian terraces, the street wall is designed as a unit, but with a wealth of contrasts in color, rooflines, and stylistic detail. Twenty small row houses on each side of the narrow street create an intimate streetscape; the designs are mirrored diagonally across the block. All are two-story buildings of Roman brick except for a quartet of three-story graystones in the center. In 1971, Alta Vista Terrace was designated Chicago's first historic district.

45 Lakeview High School
4015 N. Ashland Ave.
1898, NORMAND S. PATTON
1916, ARTHUR F. HUSSANDER
1939, JOHN C. CHRISTENSEN

Lakeview High School

The influence of Oxford and Cambridge is evident in American college and university designs of the 1890s, including those of the University of Chicago. This magnificent complex, intended to emulate the style and quality of a university building, was the city's first public high school in the Tudor style. Patton's design comprises the section running from the gatehouse tower (with 1898 carved above the entry) north to the center of the block; it was an addition to a building (now demolished) on Irving Park Rd. Patton's work was echoed by Hussander's quarter blocks to the north and south: note especially the fine doorway on Irving Park Rd. The extreme northern quarter came last. Gables, crenellated towers, ornamentation, and fenestration create a unified whole.

46 Graceland Cemetery

4001 N. Clark St.

These 121 acres were a rural area when the cemetery was founded in 1860 by Thomas B. Bryan, a lawyer and real estate investor who received a state charter in 1861 exempting the property from condemnation for public purposes. The first designer was William Saunders, who also worked at Rosehill, assisted by Swain Nelson and followed by Horace W. S. Cleveland, who may also have worked on the design for Oak Woods Cemetery. Bryan's nephew, Bryan Lathrop, served for many years as Graceland's president and was a self-taught naturalist. Under his influence, architects William Le Baron Jenney and Ossian Cole Simonds were brought in to improve the site in 1878. Simonds decided to devote his practice to landscape design and held the post of the cemetery's superintendent from 1881 until his death in 1931. His harmonious settings using native flora presaged the Prairie School movement.

Holabird & Roche designed the **A | Entrance Gates and Fence** as well as the adjacent **B | Administration Building and Waiting Room** in 1896. The firm received many commissions at Graceland from Simonds, who had been a founding partner of the architecture firm in 1880. Eifler & Assocs. designed the renovation of the Waiting Room in 2002 and the Administration Building in 2003.

C | Howard Van Doren Shaw designed his family plot with a tall central column and separate stones for the families of two of his daughters. A traditionalist in his architectural work, Shaw created a flat-sided column topped by a bronze ball, cast with the words of the Twenty-Third Psalm.

LAKEVIEW/RAVENSWOOD/UPTOWN

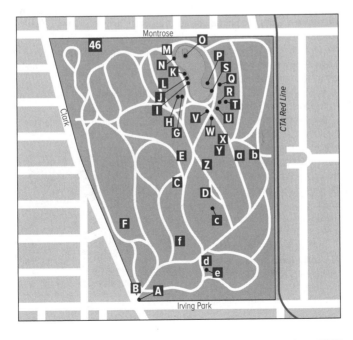

The rusticated red granite **D | Chapel and Mortuary Crypt** was designed by Holabird & Roche and constructed in 1888. Expansions and alterations in 1934 and 1958 caused the chapel to lose its original interior design, and changes in funeral practices limited its usefulness. A reconsideration of functions for the chapel resulted in a renovation (2009, NORTHWORKS ARCHITECTS AND PLANNERS) that entailed removing the additions and creating a new interior. Adjacent to the chapel is a columbarium and fountain completed in 1996, the work of architect Eifler & Assocs. and landscape architect Wolff Clements and Assocs., who have collaborated on many improvements at the cemetery since the early 1990s. Look for the plaque marking the interment of **Marion Mahony Griffin,** designed by Eifler and incorporating a flower copied from one of Griffin's renderings for Frank Lloyd Wright. Along with her husband, Walter Burley Griffin, and her cousin, Dwight H. Perkins, Marion Griffin was an architect of the Prairie School movement, known for her beautiful Japanese-influenced drawings.

E | William A. Hulbert founded the National League of Professional Baseball Clubs in 1876. The names of the league's eight teams are carved into the giant baseball that marks his grave.

The columnar monument with an urn-like top, designed by Richard E. Schmidt for his parents, **F | Ernst and Therese Schmidt,** is a handsome and personal example of his Prairie School style.

The grave of structural engineer **G | Fazlur Rahman Khan,** whose work at Skidmore, Owings & Merrill included the John Hancock Center and the Sears Tower, is marked by a square stone of red granite and is snugly surrounded by low, tight greenery.

Photographer **H | Richard Nickel** was an early crusader for architectural preservation, renowned for his efforts to document and save the great works of Chicago architecture. He was killed by falling masonry while salvaging ornament from Adler & Sullivan's Stock Exchange Building during its demolition in 1972. His black granite stone was designed by architects John Vinci and Lawrence Kenny.

Architect **I | Bruce Goff** was influenced by Louis Sullivan and the Prairie School architects. Although he lived in Chicago for only a few years, Graceland Cemetery was an appropriate place in which to place his ashes in 2000. The marker, designed by Seattle architect Grant Gustafson, incorporates a chunk of cullet glass from the house Goff designed for Joe Price in Oklahoma (1956), which was destroyed by arson in 1996.

The flat slab of black granite that marks the grave of **J | Ludwig Mies van der Rohe** was designed by his grandson, architect Dirk Lohan. Mies came to Chicago from Germany in 1938 to direct the architecture department of the Armour Institute, which became the Illinois Institute of Technology. His designs for steel-and-glass buildings revolutionized modern architecture and established the International Style.

Architect Peter Weber designed the **K | Lucius Fisher** columbarium in 1916, and sculptor Richard W. Bock designed the hooded figure.

Architect Henry Bacon and sculptor Daniel Chester French designed the monument for **L | Marshall Field,** which French titled *Memory*. On the base of the statue is the emblem of the caduceus, the staff of Mercury, Roman god of commerce. Bacon and French later collaborated on the design of the Lincoln Memorial in Washington, D.C.

Getty Tomb

Louis H. Sullivan designed the **M | Getty Tomb** for lumber merchant Henry Harrison Getty after the death of his wife, Carrie Eliza, in 1890. Getty was a partner of Martin

Ryerson, whose nearby tomb was also Sullivan's work. Freed from addressing the normal practical requirements of a working building, Sullivan gave free rein to his decorative talents in designing this monument, planning the ornament in full-scale drawings. The frilly acanthus leaf, a favorite plant form of Sullivan and his contemporaries, is lushly but delicately rendered in Bedford limestone and bronze. Look through the gates to the explosion of ornament on the massive door. Frank Lloyd Wright said of this work, "Outside the realm of music, what finer requiem?"

N I Ernest Robert Graham was one of Daniel Burnham's partners and established the firm of Graham, Anderson, Probst & White in 1917, after Burnham's death.

O I Daniel Burnham and his family are buried on an island in the lake that is reached by a plain concrete footbridge; boulders mark the burial sites. As an architect, chief of construction for the 1893 World's Columbian Exposition, and coauthor of the 1909 *Plan of Chicago*, Burnham was a central figure of the Chicago School.

New York architects McKim, Mead & White designed the **P I Potter and Bertha Palmer** tomb, tall twin sarcophagi set within an open-air temple of Ionic columns.

Across the road from the Palmers, McKim, Mead & White designed a French Gothic tomb for Bertha's parents, **Q I Henry H. and Eliza Honoré.** Southeast of the Palmer tomb is an equally grandiose McKim, Mead & White monument to piano manufacturer **R I William Kimball.**

The **S I Goodman Family** tomb, designed by Howard Van Doren Shaw in 1918, nestles into the lakeshore, its top appearing as an overlook and its entrance reached by a flight of stairs leading to the water's edge.

The grave of **T I Louis H. Sullivan** was designed by Thomas Tallmadge in 1929, five years after Sullivan's death. Upon a wide boulder Sullivan's profile is set in one of his own ornamental designs; Tallmadge wrote the tribute on the back of the stone. On the narrow sides, a setback skyscraper seems to be emerging, reflecting Sullivan's role in the development of the high-rise. Tallmadge wrote a history of nineteenth-century Chicago architecture and coined the term Chicago School.

Martin Ryerson Tomb

Lumber merchant and real estate speculator **U I Martin Ryerson** died in 1887; his son, Martin A. Ryerson, commissioned this mausoleum from Louis H. Sullivan, who had designed four downtown office buildings for the senior Ryerson. The polished black granite tomb is inspired by Egyptian funerary forms, the mastaba for the lower portion and the pyramid for the top. Unlike most Egyptian-style tombs, the design calls on Egyptian precedents not for detailing but for the dark and massive form, which seems as timeless as the concept of eternity itself.

Solon S. Beman, who was responsible for the design of the company town of Pullman, also designed the **V I George M. Pullman** monument, a very tall Corinthian column placed in a terraced setting with an exedra on either side. Pullman died after a bitter and violent strike had disrupted his town. Fearing that his remains might be vandalized, the family had him interred below the monument inside a concrete block topped with railroad ties set in concrete.

Brewer **W I Peter Schoenhofen** rests in a steep-sided pyramid entered through an Egyptian portal with a sun disk. A sphinx and a rather out-of-place Victorian angel stand guard, the latter holding a key and gazing heavenward.

Burnham's partner, **X I John Wellborn Root,** died of pneumonia while their firm was planning the World's Columbian Exposition. Included among the abstract ornament on the Celtic cross that marks his grave is his last

John Wellborn Root Monument

drawing, a design for the entrance to a building proposed for the fair. The cross was designed by Jules Wegman, a member of the firm.

Y | William Holabird, another central figure of the Chicago School, is buried in a family plot tucked into a low ridge.

The work of **Z | George Grant Elmslie** is a highly personal interpretation of the Chicago and the Prairie Schools. His name is engraved on a flat slab of black granite along with the names of members of his wife's family.

"Above All Things Truth Beareth away the Victory" are the only words on this monument to **a | Victor F. Lawson.** Lorado Taft sculpted the larger-than-life polished black granite figure of a medieval crusader. The statue was erected in 1931, six years after the death of the philanthropic publisher of the *Chicago Daily News*.

b | Peirce Anderson was one of Daniel Burnham's partners and later a founding member of Graham, Anderson, Probst & White. Anderson's profile is featured on a large pink granite monument that bears his name and birth and death dates in very small letters near the lower edge.

Designer **c | László Moholy-Nagy** came to Chicago in 1937, after the Nazis had closed the Bauhaus. He then opened the New Bauhaus, which was later renamed the Institute of Design and subsequently merged with the Illinois Institute of Technology. His cremated remains are buried under a small, standardized granite square behind the chapel.

The family plot of pioneer Chicagoan and hotel owner **d | Dexter Graves** features a mysterious and haunting bronze sculpture, *Eternal Silence,* by Lorado Taft.

e | When **William Le Baron Jenney** died in 1907, his ashes were scattered over the marked grave of his wife, Elizabeth, but the name of the man popularly known as the Father of the Skyscraper was absent. In 2007, the cemetery trustees commissioned Northworks Architects and Planners to design a monument to honor the architect.

f | Dwight H. Perkins played an important role in the Prairie School movement, designing innovative schools and park buildings. He also helped to establish the Cook County Forest Preserves.

Other architects buried at Graceland include David Adler, Augustus Bauer, Edward Burling, James J. Egan, L. Gustav Hallberg, Richard G. Schmid, and Alfred Shaw.

—JOAN POMARANC

47 4015 N. Sheridan Rd.
(Marmon Hupmobile Showroom)
1920, PAUL GERHARDT

Things Egyptian were very popular in this era of archaeological marvels, which culminated in the opening of King Tut's tomb in 1922. Gerhardt was so enamored of Egyptian motifs that he incorporated them into two entries for the Chicago Tribune Competition.

48 Irving Apartments
(Kellshore Apartment Hotel)
718–756 W. Irving Park Rd.
1915, E. NORMAN BRYDGES

Describing this project, *The Book of the North Shore* said, "Much as one may regret the necessity of people living in apartments instead of in attractive vine-covered houses, the problem is with us and so has to be

Pattington Apartments

met in a manner which will insure the maximum of comfort, light, air, and pleasing composition." Although basking in the reflected glory of the grand Pattington Apartments, the units here are small studios and one-bedrooms designed to appeal to young marrieds and single office workers. Shallow urns that flank the courtyard entryways and top the corner piers provide a Prairie School touch.

Immaculata High School (now 640 W. Irving Park Rd.)

49 Pattington Apartments
660–700 W. Irving Park Rd.

1902–3, DAVID E. POSTLE

Chicago's best courtyard building was the largest built to that time. All seventy-two units were capacious apartments with servants' quarters, and they were marketed to upper-middle-class families as an alternative to single-family residences. Each of the two courtyards has five elaborate neoclassical entrances. The design provides complete cross-ventilation for each apartment, enhanced by bay windows that flood the rooms with light and air.

50 640 W. Irving Park Rd
(Immaculata High School)
Former Mary Hall
600–634 W. Irving Park Rd.
1922, BARRY BYRNE
Former Convent
4030 N. Marine Dr.
1955, BARRY BYRNE
Former St. Joseph's Hall
636 W. Irving Park Rd.
1956, BARRY BYRNE

This important early modern school displays Byrne's characteristic combination of Prairie School massing and forms with a very personal interpretation of Gothic detailing. Shared facilities such as the assembly hall and the gymnasium dominate the pavilion, which breaks out slightly from the southeast corner; the window treatment here reflects the scale of the interior spaces. Classroom windows are arranged in groups of three, enframed by slender pointed arches rising the building's full height. The spare ornament (which originally included sculpture by Alfonso Iannelli) is concentrated at the entrances.

51 Walt Disney Magnet School
4140 N. Marine Dr.

1973, PERKINS & WILL

Chicago's first magnet school draws students from large areas rather than just the surrounding neighborhood. Innovations include flexible classroom space organized into nine "pods."

Hutchinson St. Landmark District
Hutchinson St. between
Marine Dr. and Hazel St.

This two-block area, a showcase for residential architecture of the late nineteenth and early twentieth centuries, is particularly rich in designs by George W. Maher, spanning two decades of his career.

Claude Seymour House

52 Edwin J. Mosser House
750 W. Hutchinson St.
1902, GEORGE W. MAHER

The cream-colored Roman brick walls flower with luxuriant Sullivan-esque ornament, especially around the main entrance facing west. The south facade is dominated by a one-story sunporch, with a projecting roof that forms a porte cochere.

53 Claude Seymour House
817 W. Hutchinson St.
1913, GEORGE W. MAHER

Maher's last house on Hutchinson St. is broad, monumental, and digni-fied. It includes a favorite motif, the flanged segmental arch over the door, and features such Prairie Style characteristics as a hipped roof, pronounced horizontality, and bands of windows under deep eaves.

54 William H. Lake House
826 W. Hutchinson St.
1904, GEORGE W. MAHER

Asymmetrical but formal and subtly balanced, the monumental facades are topped by great overhanging low hipped roofs.

55 Grace Brackebush House
839 W. Hutchinson St.
1909, GEORGE W. MAHER

This mature design combines the straightforwardness and severity that Maher admired in such English contemporaries as C. F. A. Voysey with the long horizontals of the Prai-rie School.

56 John C. Scales House
840 W. Hutchinson St.
1894, GEORGE W. MAHER

This is the earliest house in the dis-trict, designed for the street's de-veloper in the Queen Anne style of Maher's early career. Complex roof forms, beautifully reshingled, and high chimneys top heavily textured walls of boulders and half-timbering.

---

57 Louis Wolff House
4234 N. Hazel St.
1904, RICHARD E. SCHMIDT

Long attributed to Schmidt's chief designer, Hugh M. G. Garden, this house is now credited to another employee, William Drummond. The very closed facade, with small windows and large brick walls, has beautifully carved stone around the front door.

58 4338–4346 N. Clarendon Ave.
1905, SAMUEL N. CROWEN

Crowen frequently blended Prairie Style elements with a dash of the Egyptian in his blocky apartment buildings. The delicate Sullivanesque frieze contrasts with robust entrance canopies.

59 Pensacola Place Apartments
4334 N. Hazel St.
1981, STANLEY TIGERMAN & ASSOCS.
WITH ROBERT FUGMAN, ASSOC. ARCH.

The eastern facade of this two-faced structure mirrors the **Boardwalk Apartments** at 4343 N. Clarendon Ave. (1974, STANLEY TIGERMAN & AS-SOCS.). The western facade is an essay in pop architecture. Semi-circular balconies are intended to suggest the shafts of gigantic columns that culminate in huge Ionic volutes—a visual joke more clearly read in drawings than on the build-ing. Above the altered ground floor

Pensacola Place Apartments

with retail space is a mezzanine of aluminum-sided town houses.

60 St. Mary of the Lake Roman Catholic Church
4200 N. Sheridan Rd.
1913–17, HENRY J. SCHLACKS
1915, SCHOOL, JOSEPH W. MCCARTHY
1939, CONVENT, MCCARTHY,
    SMITH & EPPIG

Unlike an earlier generation of church designers who knew historic architecture more through drawings and photos than direct experience, Schlacks traveled extensively in Europe in search of inspiration. This Renaissance design freely combines several major fourth- and fifth-century Roman churches: the freestanding campanile was patterned after that of St. Pudentiana, while the facade borrows from the Basilica of St. Paul Outside the Walls. The richly painted interior, decorated by Arthur Hercz, features fine stained-glass windows by F. X. Zettler.

St. Mary of the Lake Roman Catholic Church

61 Commonwealth Edison Electric Power Substation
4401 N. Clifton Ave.
1916, HERMANN V. VON HOLST

Like many of von Holst's power stations, this strong, block-like design is enriched with brickwork in geometric patterns.

62 Stewart Elementary School
4525 N. Kenmore Ave.
1907, DWIGHT H. PERKINS

Pairs of enormous copper brackets support the massive hipped roof of this imposing brick and limestone structure. Features in common with Perkins's other schools include the robust consoles serving as keystones atop the large arched windows of the central block and vertical pairs of windows on the end pavilions with only the lower of the two pairs pedimented.

63 1050 W. Wilson Ave.
(Standard Vaudeville Theater)
1909, WILLIAM F. BEHAN
1989, RENOVATION, MAYES-
    VOSTAL ARCHITECTS

A building with many lives, the original theater closed in 1922 and was replaced by a series of banks. The Bank of Chicago arrived in 1947 and added a trompe l'oeil mural that hides a wall left bare by the demolition of an adjacent building in the 1980s. Through the "arch" is a southern Italian formal garden.

64 Truman College
1145 W. Wilson Ave.
1977, DUBIN, DUBIN, BLACK
    & MOUTOUSSAMY

This city college in a gritty neighborhood has an appropriately sturdy, hard-edged Miesian campus. Subsequent buildings have followed the formula.

Because Northwestern University's original charter specified a "four-mile limit" banning liquor sales, for many years no alcohol could be served north of Devon Ave. Uptown thus became the city's northernmost outpost for taverns and the first spot south of suburban Highwood where alcoholic drinks were available. With the advent of Prohibition, the booze just went underground, making this neighborhood a bootlegging and roadhouse center filled with young people and entertainment complexes (entries 65–72).

65 CTA—Wilson Ave. Station
(Uptown Union Station)
4604–4634 N. Broadway
1923, ARTHUR U. GERBER
This small building served as a transfer point between suburban railroads and elevated trains that ran downtown. HNTB designed a complete rebuilding of the station, and facade restoration began in 2013.

66 Uptown Broadway Building
4707 N. Broadway
1927, WALTER W. AHLSCHLAGER
2006, REHABILITATION, SPACE
  ARCHITECTS AND PLANNERS
Uptown boomed when terra-cotta was at its peak of popularity, and this commercial building is a visual encyclopedia, with human faces, animal heads, foliage, columns, and ribbons rendering the Spanish Baroque style in yellow and gray. A popular claim that the building was built by Al Capone is unsubstantiated.

67 Riviera Theatre
4746 N. Broadway
1918, C. W. AND GEORGE L. RAPP
This was the second theater built by Balaban & Katz and the first for which they used Rapp & Rapp. Its success led B & K to use Rapp & Rapp almost exclusively. Originally started by another owner, the project went broke during construction. The facade and adjacent commercial building were by another architect (unknown) and were probably left intact by the

Rapps; the facade is tame by comparison with the firm's subsequent work.

68 Bridgeview Bank
(Uptown Bank Building)
4753 N. Broadway
1924, MARSHALL & FOX
1928, ADDITION, HUSZAGH & HILL
Originally constructed with only eight floors and later expanded, the building has two cornices. The base reflects the importance of the second and third floors, which contain the main banking spaces. Step inside to see original fixtures and ornamental work. The plaster ceiling was originally cast in Italy and shipped in pieces for installation.

Bridgeview Bank

69 Uptown Theatre
4814 N. Broadway
1925, C. W. AND GEORGE L. RAPP
Eight stories tall and with 4,381 seats, it was the largest theater

Uptown Theatre

ever for both the architects and the developers, Balaban & Katz. The Uptown was an important addition to the entertainment district, which included the Aragon Ballroom and the Green Mill Lounge. The Spanish Baroque Revival style, with its emphasis on the grandly ornamented portal, was perfect for a movie palace. Through those doors lay a world much grander and more exotic than the neighborhood's cramped apartments and smoky bars.

70 U.S. Post Office—Uptown Station
4850 N. Broadway
1939, HOWARD L. CHENEY
Polished granite eagles guard this small Moderne post office. Inside, murals (1943) by Henry Varnum Poor depict Carl Sandburg and Louis H. Sullivan, who holds a model of the Carson Pirie Scott store.

71 Ecumenical Institute
(Mutual Insurance Building)
4750 N. Sheridan Rd.
1921, FUGARD & KNAPP
1926, ADDITION AND
   ALTERATIONS, B. LEO STEIF
Handsomely clad in gleaming terra-cotta, this office building was originally a four-story retail building with an arcaded corridor; its facade was "stretched" to insert three more floors.

72 Aragon Ballroom
1106 W. Lawrence Ave.
1926, HUSZAGH & HILL
The golden age of ballroom dancing came to life in this Moorish dreamland. A grand entrance lobby running the length of the building culminated in a wide staircase flanked with plaster dragons. Double-tiered, ornate terra-cotta arches, mosaics, tiles, palm trees, and a promenade surrounded the dance floor. Lights from Spanish-style fixtures glowed under the twinkling stars in the cobalt blue dome. Ceilings that imitated the night sky were key features of 1920s "atmospheric" theaters and dance halls, transporting snowbound midwesterners to warm Mediterranean landscapes. The Spanish or Moorish—or sometimes Oriental—decor enhanced the appealing exoticism.

When ballroom dancing faded after World War II, the Aragon was used for a series of unsuccessful ventures before becoming a concert hall in the 1970s.

73 5040–5060 N. Marine Dr.
(Marine Dr. Apartments)
1939, OMAN & LILIENTHAL
This development followed close on the heels of the Granville Gardens and Wolcott Gardens and shows the same simple Art Moderne detailing: corner windows (originally metal casements), multicolored stripes of brick, and a very thin wall plane with windows set close to the surface. Six staggered blocks are arranged to take advantage of lake views and maximize ventilation.

74 Myron Bachman House
1244 W. Carmen Ave.
1948, REMODELING, BRUCE GOFF
If the Jetsons had remodeled a house after World War II, it might have looked like this. Goff had designed Quonset huts during the war and applied his interest in corrugated metal to this renovation of an old house, incorporating a recording-studio control room in front. Though hardly contextual, it is fascinating—especially the combination of corrugated metal and weeping mortar.

Myron Bachman House

75 Doblin House
5017 N. Ravenswood
2002, VALERIO DEWALT TRAIN ASSOCS.
Looking more like an industrial building than a dwelling place, the windowless facade is clad entirely with galvanized steel. One of the two twenty-three-foot-wide bifold garage doors opens (rarely) to reveal a landscaped entry court before a glass curtain wall residence hidden from view.

Yannell Net Zero Energy Residence

76 Yannell Net Zero Energy Residence
4895 N. Ravenswood St.
2009, FARR ASSOCS.

Green goes glam in Chicago's first net-zero residence, designed to produce more energy than it consumes and look good doing it. V-shaped roofs provide optimal angles for photovoltaic and solar thermal panels while channeling rainwater and blocking the summer sun. Living and sleeping functions are split into two wings of unequal heights to increase southern exposure for passive solar heating and to maximize cross-ventilation. The garage is tucked into the basement, which houses technology that includes the first graywater system approved for a Chicago single-family house. Beneath the native-plant landscape are geothermal wells. The building garnered enough LEED points to easily exceed a platinum rating and was at the time of construction the "Greenest House in America."

77 Wolcott Gardens
4901–4959 N. Wolcott Ave.
1939, MICHAELSEN & ROGNSTAD

A full block of twenty-one modest Art Moderne apartment buildings is arranged around open space, creating courtyards that are more private than those in traditional U-shaped flats of the 1920s. The detailing varies subtly, usually around the doorways. This project was made possible by Federal Housing Administration mortgage insurance, and construction was not started until all of the flats in Granville Gardens on N. Hoyne Ave. had been leased.

78 Carl Sandburg House
4646 N. Hermitage Ave.
EARLY 1890S, ARCHITECT UNKNOWN

Sandburg moved into the second-floor flat in 1912 with his wife and

Wolcott Gardens

infant daughter and wrote "Chicago" while living here.

79 Wallace C. Abbott House
4605 N. Hermitage Ave.

1891, DAHLGREN & LIEVENDAHL

One of the finest Victorian homes lining Hermitage and Paulina Aves. is this one built for the founder of Abbott Laboratories. Beautifully restored and maintained, it also retains a nineteenth-century stable.

80 All Saints Episcopal Church
4550 N. Hermitage Ave.

1883, JOHN C. COCHRANE

This distinctive Stick Style structure may be the city's oldest frame church. The bell in the corner tower summoned the volunteer fire department and announced services, which Carl Sandburg attended here.

All Saints Episcopal Church

81 Ravenswood United Methodist Church
(Ravenswood Methodist Episcopal Church)
4501 N. Hermitage Ave.

1890, JOHN S. WOOLLACOTT

Behind the prim rusticated facade is a sculpted space inspired by H. H. Richardson and Louis H. Sullivan. A great roundheaded arch filled with organ pipes dominates the almost square worship space. A hammer-beam ceiling rises above gently curving amphitheatrical seating and a balcony. The church was designed to accommodate these leaded-glass windows, which were brought from an earlier church nearby.

82 Black Ensemble Theater
4450 N. Clark St.

2011, MORRIS ARCHITECTS PLANNERS

Morris has designed theaters for some of Chicago's best-known companies, including Steppenwolf and Lookingglass. BET's first permanent home has a 300-seat theater and glassy, double-height lobby in a new building of concrete, ipe wood, and cement panels. Parking and support services are in a remodeled garage to the south.

83 Ravenswood Public School
4332 N. Paulina Ave.

1892, JOHN J. FLANDERS

1912, ARTHUR F. HUSSANDER

The broad-eaved Flanders design was echoed by copycat Hussander; cut-stone ornament is reproduced in terra-cotta on later sections.

84 Ravenswood Corridor
N. Ravenswood St. east of the Metra tracks between Irving Park Rd. and Addison St.

Around the turn of the twenty-first century, the character of this light-industrial corridor became increasingly residential. Brick factories and warehouses were rehabbed into lofts and single-family homes, sometimes almost invisibly (views from the Metra train are often the best). Notable examples are the Loft House at **3813 N. Ravenswood St.** (2008, JOHN RONAN ARCHITECTS), whose addition is best seen from the alley; Byron Station Studios at **1754 W. Byron St.** (2003, ANN TEMPLE ARCHITECT); and a residence at **1757 W. Nelson St.** (2002, LANDON BONE BAKER ARCHITECTS).

85 Studio V Design
(Krause Music Store)
4611 N. Lincoln Ave.

1922, WILLIAM C. PRESTO WITH LOUIS H. SULLIVAN, ASSOC. ARCH.

2007, FACADE RESTORATION, MCGUIRE IGLESKI & ASSOCS.; ADAPTIVE REUSE AND REAR ADDITION, WHEELER KEARNS ARCHITECTS

Unlike his professional fortunes, Sullivan's talent never waned, as this, his final design, testifies. William Krause asked his neighbor, Presto, to design a building to house his music store showroom below and his family

Studio V Design

above. Presto in turn asked his former employer, Sullivan, to design the facade, which he did while working out of an office of the American Terra Cotta Co. With the help of the company's modeler, Kristian Schneider, Sullivan's characteristic foliate ornament bloomed as beautifully on this modest project as it had on the magnificent Auditorium Theater built more than thirty years earlier. The elaborate system of ornament culminates in a large cartouche rising three feet above the parapet.

86 Old Town School of Folk Music

(Chicago Public Library—Frederick H. Hild Regional Branch)

West Building: 4544 N. Lincoln Ave.
1931, PIERRE BLOUKE
1998, ADAPTIVE REUSE, WHEELER/
KEARNS ARCHITECTS WITH MORRIS
ARCHITECTS PLANNERS
East Building: 4545 N. Lincoln Ave.
2012, VOA ASSOCS.

The restrained Art Deco facade on the 1931 building is smooth and blocky, a discreet owl the only playful element. The centerpiece of the transformation from library to music center is the semicircular concert hall that once housed four floors of book stacks. Large sliding doors in the backstage wall open the space to the lobby, creating an informal gathering space at the hub of the complex. Highlights of the interior are two reused Works Progress Administration murals by Francis F. Coan. The East Building is the school's first-ever new construction. Though it lacks the

homey, improvised quality of the other locations, it is a handsome, welcoming presence—especially up close, where one doesn't notice the corrugated steel sides and back.

87 Chicago Public Library— Conrad Sulzer Regional Branch

4455 N. Lincoln Ave.
1985, HAMMOND BEEBY & BABKA WITH
JOSEPH W. CASSERLY, CITY ARCH.

This friendly, whimsical, and inviting public building is worth exploring for its decorative delights. The long facade continues the street wall of Lincoln Ave. and ends in a graceful curve. The entrance is subtly indicated by a large gabled window that opens into the second-floor reading room. Inspired by neoclassical architecture, the building is nonetheless modern in its revelation of metal structure with infills of glass or brick. The division of functions is logical, with noisy activities (circulation desk, audio and video materials, children's library) concentrated on the first floor. Whimsically painted furniture, originally intended for the children's area, now delights patrons throughout the building.

Chicago Public Library—Conrad Sulzer Regional Branch

88 St. Benedict's Roman Catholic Church

2201 W. Irving Park Rd.
1918, HERMANN J. GAUL

The large German congregation built

its church in the Rundbogenstil, a nineteenth-century revival of Romanesque forms that predates the more robust Richardsonian Romanesque. It is exuberantly studded with short columns outside as well as inside. The interior is also Germanic and features art-glass windows by F. X. Zettler.

89 Claremont House
3909 N. Claremont St.
2007, BRININSTOOL & LYNCH
Nothing as prosaic as a front door mars the glass expanse of the first floor—the entrance is off a walkway on the south side. The interior organization is visible through the windows: an open-tread stairwell on the far right is separated from the living spaces by a core of cabinetry. The second floor is as concealed as the first floor is open; bedroom windows are on the north.

90 Albert G. Lane Technical High School
2501 W. Addison Rd.
1934, PAUL GERHARDT
1940, STADIUM, JOHN C. CHRISTENSEN
The Board of Education took technical education seriously, creating special facilities for these schools and endowing them with the dignity and focused purpose of a college campus. Lane Tech looks like an Industrial Gothic factory, with its large glazed areas, clock tower, and smokestack. A light court gives outside exposure to all classrooms and shops. The interior is worth a visit to see sculptures in the library by Peterpaul Ott and frescoes in the audito-

Albert G. Lane Technical High School

rium lobby glorifying *The Teaching of Art* (late 1930s, Mitchell Siporin). The concrete football stadium, a 1930s version of Gothic, was built by the Works Progress Administration.

91 Chicago River Boathouse at Clark Park
3400 N. Rockwell St.
2013, STUDIO GANG ARCHITECTS
The motion of rowing a boat inspired the rhythm of the roofs, constructed with trusses in alternating inverted V and M shapes. The result creates generous south-facing clerestories for winter warmth and summer ventilation.

92 Friedrich Ludwig Jahn Public School
3149 N. Wolcott Ave.
1907, DWIGHT H. PERKINS
This is a Prairie form with simplified Gothic details. The depth of the facade and the Secession-style entrance link it with Perkins's other powerfully modeled schools of this period.

Friedrich Ludwig Jahn Public School

93 Brundage Building
3325 N. Lincoln Ave.
1923, WILLIAM G. UFFENDELL
The robust neoclassical facade of this elegant flatiron building (note the four-foot-wide pilasters) looks like limestone but is entirely of terra-cotta. Avery Brundage, famous as the long-time head of the International Olympic Committee, acquired properties that he had built as a contractor and that went under in the 1930s.

LAKEVIEW/RAVENSWOOD/UPTOWN

EDGEWATER/ROGERS PARK

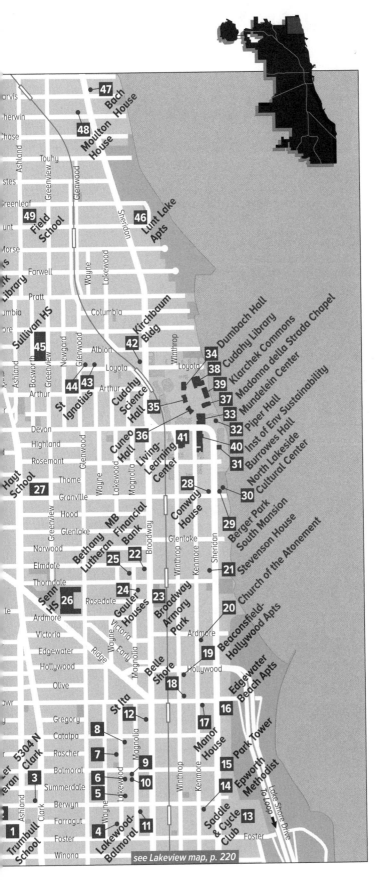

see Lakeview map, p. 220

EDGEWATER/ROGERS PARK

EDGEWATER/ROGERS PARK

The story of Edgewater and Rogers Park is a tale of metamorphosis from gen-teel suburb to urban neighborhood. As usual, the catalyst was the extension of a transit line that made the community more accessible to legions of Loop office workers. Highway construction brought further changes, turning quiet streets into congested thoroughfares. But behind the row of Sheridan Rd.'s high-rises are pockets of elegance that hint at the area's enduring appeal.

Edgewater and Rogers Park began as farming communities but originally belonged to different townships, separated at Devon Ave. Edgewater joined the city as part of the Lake View annexation in 1889; four years later, Rogers Park voted to secede from Evanston and become part of Chicago.

Edgewater's landscape of celery farms began its suburban transforma-tion in 1885, when J. Lewis Cochran purchased lakefront property—the first of his many subdivisions—bounded by Foster Ave., Broadway, and Bryn Mawr Ave. Known as the Father of Edgewater, Cochran installed roads, sidewalks, drainage, and electricity; gave the area its name; and built about fifty "stylish mansions" on streets named for towns along the Main Line of his native Philadelphia. By 1910, Sheridan Rd. had become an exclusive stretch lined with mansions, while developments west of Broadway (such as Cochran's Lakewood-Balmoral) retained the suburban ambience on a more modest scale. Farther west, working-class Swedes and Germans built single-family homes and two-flats near industries clustered along the Chi-cago & North Western tracks. The extension of the Northwestern Elevated Railroad (now the CTA Red Line) through Edgewater in 1908 spurred further residential growth, and by the 1920s, some of the original houses had given way to high-rise hotels and apartments.

In addition to Lakewood-Balmoral, Edgewater's other historic district in-cludes a mix of retail and residential buildings along a much-revitalized stretch of Bryn Mawr Ave. between Sheridan Rd. and Broadway. Other notable group-ings of houses are in Edgewater Glen and the Highlands of Edgewater, which lie on either side of Clark St., south of Devon Ave.

Edgewater can claim one of Chicago's most vibrant retail corridors along Clark St. north and south of Foster Ave. For decades, this area has been known as the heart of Andersonville, an old neighborhood name evocative of its Scandinavian history. Although significant numbers of Swedes have not lived here for a long time, the Swedish connection persists in a variety of shops and restaurants as well as in the terrific Swedish American Museum.

Rogers Park was incorporated as a village in 1878. It was named by its chief promoter, Patrick L. Touhy, for his father-in-law, Phillip Rogers, an early settler. Development took place first along the Ridge, a shelf of land left by the reced-ing lakeshore and the site of an Indian trail that was the area's only north–south road for decades. Farmers, especially Luxembourgers and Germans, built cottages here, and the Touhys and other wealthier families built sub-stantial homes in picturesque styles. Even after the coming of two railroads, development remained slow until the 1908 extension of the elevated line to Evanston. With stops every three blocks, the El set off a boom in apartment and hotel building adjacent to the lakefront.

In the southeastern corner of Rogers Park, Loyola University opened in 1922 on sand dunes acquired by the Jesuits in 1906, and Mundelein College (now part of Loyola) opened its skyscraper campus in 1930. With less pub-lic transportation, West Ridge (west of Ridge Blvd.) was sparsely settled until after World War I, when brick bungalows and flats sprouted along its streets.

After decades as the site of nurseries, truck farms, and greenhouses, it was extensively developed after World War II.

—WILLIAM B. HINCHLIFF

1 Lyman Trumbull Public School

5200 N. Ashland Blvd.

1910, DWIGHT H. PERKINS

Shorn of traditional ornament and showing the influence of the progressive Prairie School movement, this massive block has the power and purity of form that distinguishes Perkins's work as Chicago Board of Education architect. Towering and percussive, the walls roll from pier to pier, punctuated with deep vertical window reveals. The strong entrance pavilion rises above the busy intersection, marking the site as a community anchor. Innovations of this era include a ground-floor (rather than top-story) auditorium to facilitate community use of the space, generous corridors to improve circulation, washrooms on every floor instead of solely in the basement, and skylights. The facade cleaning in 2003 has revealed the brick's subtle original two-tone color scheme. The renovation was part of a ten-year campaign to upgrade school buildings throughout Chicago. In 2013, officials announced that Trumbull and forty-eight of the city's other elementary schools would be closed.

2 Ebenezer Lutheran Church

1650 W. Foster Ave.

1912, ANDREW E. NORMAN

A tall steeple, the highest point in the area, identifies Andersonville's dominant church, visited twice by the king and queen of Sweden. In addition to this limestone-clad, neo-Gothic church, which features Norman's own woodcarvings on the interior, the architect designed about a dozen religious buildings and more than a hundred houses, many of them in Edgewater.

3 5304 N. Clark St.

(Erickson Jewelers)

EARLY 1940S, REMODELING,
ARCHITECT UNKNOWN

In 1935, America's aging and dowdy retail areas were suffering from the effects of the Great Depression; for years, merchants had put little money into remodeling. That year the Federal Housing Administration began insuring loans for store improvements up to $50,000, and in June, *Architectural Record* announced a competition sponsored by the Libbey-Owens-Ford Glass Co. to "Modernize Main Street," with a jury that included Albert Kahn, William Lescaze, and John W. Root. Architects were directed to rethink the typical cluttered storefront as a merchandising device: "The store front with its plate glass show windows establishes the character of the store. . . . It must serve to make the passer *buy*, inviting him or her to stop and shop." The glassmakers sponsored the competition to promote Vitrolite, an opaque, pigmented structural glass (marketed

Lyman Trumbull Public School

Erickson Jewelers (now 5304 N. Clark St.)

under different names by other companies). Attached by adhesive to masonry, Vitrolite was a perfect modernizing material for storefronts: low maintenance, extremely durable, sleek, and shiny. According to the *Record*, the properly "modernized" storefront should feature a prominent sign or logo against an unadulterated surface. Although the black-glass background no longer sets off the brushed metal Erickson name and the diamond ring logo, this is still one of the best preserved examples of its type.

Lakewood-Balmoral Neighborhood

Lakewood, Magnolia, and Wayne Aves. from Foster to Bryn Mawr Aves.
Developer J. Lewis Cochran began energetically promoting his Edgewater subdivisions in the mid-1880s. Almost all of the grandest houses, built on lots east of the railroad (now CTA) tracks, have been replaced by apartments. These more modest dwellings, substantial yet often half the price of those closer to the lake, form a still-desirable neighborhood of single-family residences. Cochran sold unimproved lots and built houses on spec, frequently five or ten at a time. Between 1885 and 1896, he commissioned designs from Joseph Lyman Silsbee, L. Gustav Hallberg, Henry H. Sprague, George W. Maher, J. N. Tilton, Joseph C. Brompton, Julius H. Huber, Church & Jobson, and Handy & Cady. Attributions are difficult because of the number of architects Cochran commissioned and the extensive remodeling that many houses have undergone. But even the unattributable Victorians are of interest, as they reemerge under the care of owners who remove artificial siding, repair the porches, and strip the woodwork.

4 Herman C. Lammers House

5222 N. Lakewood Ave.
1898, JULIUS H. HUBER
1901, ADDITION; 1911, REMODELING
The Hansel-and-Gretel remodeling was intended to make the house look more "European."

5 5313 N. Lakewood Ave.

1903, ARCHITECT UNKNOWN
The pinched verticality of the dormers gives a piquant silhouette to Cochran's spec house.

6 Angelica Holzaffel House

5347 N. Lakewood Ave.
1910, LEON E. STANHOPE
Features typical of the Craftsman style include diamond-paned windows and a pergola-like porch.

7 5426 N. Lakewood Ave.

1893, ARCHITECT UNKNOWN
Cochran built this Queen Anne with an unusual lidded third-floor window surround.

8 Patrick H. McNulty House

5453 N. Lakewood Ave.
1898, HOLABIRD & ROCHE
The centrally placed door and second-floor bay of this classically inspired house are a play on Palladian window composition.

Patrick H. McNulty House

9 Arthur Deppman House

5356 N. Magnolia Ave.
1904, GEORGE W. MAHER
Maher's simple, rectilinear design is firmly rooted in the twentieth century.

10 H. Mark Flat
5344 N. Magnolia Ave.
1913, HENRY L. NEWHOUSE
The huge two-story bay makes both floors equally grand, revealing this house's true nature as a two-flat. Corinthian columns as attenuated as toothpicks rise the full height of the bay.

11 5247 N. Magnolia Ave.
1899, HARVEY L. PAGE & CO.
The classical language is bold and self-confident; Ionic columns support a double-height porch.

12 St. Ita's Church
1220 W. Catalpa Ave.
1927, HENRY J. SCHLACKS
The *M* carved in the stone parapet honors the powerful Cardinal Mundelein, whose preference for French Gothic was not lost on Schlacks: he made this church solidly thirteenth-century inside and out. The graceful, cohesive interior is warmed by wood wainscoting with Gothic detailing.

Lincoln Park and Lake Shore Dr. ended at Foster Ave. until the early 1950s, when a huge landfill project extended them to Hollywood Ave. On the lake north of Foster Ave. were the private beach areas of the Saddle and Cycle Club and the Edgewater Beach Apartments and hotel complex (entries 13 and 16).

13 Saddle and Cycle Club
900 W. Foster Ave.
1898, JARVIS HUNT
1904, 1909, ADDITIONS, JARVIS HUNT
1968, ADDITION, C. F. MURPHY ASSOCS.
You can catch a fleeting glimpse of this private club from Sheridan Rd. or Lake Shore Dr. In the mid-1890s, the main club facilities were downtown; the Edgewater location was originally for cyclists and equestrians riding on the lakefront. The Shingle Style clubhouse and its first additions, designed by club member Hunt, are now barely visible; the tower with its bell-shaped cap is their most prominent remaining feature. The private beach was originally only 100 feet from the veranda and at the end of the nineteenth century had a boathouse and pier.

14 Epworth United Methodist Church
(Epworth Methodist Episcopal Church)
5253 N. Kenmore Ave.
1890, FREDERICK B. TOWNSEND
1930, ADDITION AND RENOVATION, THIELBAR & FUGARD
The massive boulders that form the craggy, random-coursed stone walls were floated down Lake Michigan from Wisconsin to a shoreline slip. The composition is beautifully balanced by three towers: square, round, and octagonal. An early drawing shows entrances in the square and octagonal towers; the current entrance dates from the 1930 addition and sanctuary renovation.

15 Park Tower Condominiums
5415 N. Sheridan Rd.
1974, SOLOMON CORDWELL BUENZ & ASSOCS.
The beautifully detailed and proportioned curtain wall stands out among Edgewater's lakeside cliff of largely dreary high-rises.

16 Edgewater Beach Apartments
5555 N. Sheridan Rd.
1928, BENJAMIN H. MARSHALL
This is the sole survivor of the Edgewater Beach Hotel complex, a sophisticated luxury resort and center of Roaring Twenties nightlife. A central octagonal tower and four Y-shaped wings rise from a rectangular base. When it was first built, three out of every four apartments had a view of the lake.

Edgewater Beach Apartments

17 Manor House
1021–1029 W. Bryn Mawr Ave.
1908, J. E. O. PRIDMORE
The British-born Pridmore designed this elegant Tudor Revival apartment

building with only six units (later sub-divided) of twelve to sixteen rooms—and two of the apartments had ball-rooms. Once the home of the British consul and known as the Prince of Wales House, it bears the royal coat of arms in terra-cotta at the rear of the courtyard. Other upscale features were the rounded sunporch on the corner (the orangerie) and the private "family room" at the rear.

18 Belle Shore Apartment Hotel
1062 W. Bryn Mawr Ave.

1929, KOENIGSBERG & WEISFELD

Behind the Art Deco terra-cotta facade are 138 one-room/kitchenette apartments. Sculptural embellishments include an Egyptian frieze above the storefronts and Art Nouveau–influenced figures.

19 Beaconsfield-Hollywood Apartments
1055–1065 W. Hollywood Ave.

1913, J. E. O. PRIDMORE

This complex of connecting three-flats has fanciful terra-cotta ornament that culminates in an elaborate portal with diamond-patterned columns and a crest modeled on that of Castile, Spain.

20 Episcopal Church of the Atonement
5751 N. Kenmore Ave.

1890, HENRY IVES COBB
1910, 1920, J. E. O. PRIDMORE

Pridmore's additions enveloped Cobb's original church but were executed in the same rock-faced red sandstone, running counter to the tidal wave of smooth Bedford limestone that clad most Gothic churches built between 1910 and 1930.

Episcopal Church of the Atonement

21 Harry M. Stevenson House
5940 N. Sheridan Rd.

1909, GEORGE W. MAHER

Signature details include the dormer window (a complex play on a Palladian theme) and the second-floor window recessed behind colonnettes. At the rear, the broad cornice unites the garage, porte cochere, and house.

22 MB Financial Bank
(Riviera-Burnstine Motor Sales)
5960 N. Broadway

1925, R. BERNARD KURZON

Terra-cotta is spun like sugar across a brick facade to form French Gothic lancets, finials, and drop-pendant window hoods. The interior is a fine example of a 1920s automobile showroom. The Mediterranean decor, with its stuccoed walls, columns, and grand staircase, was meant to suggest an outdoor setting such as a plaza or courtyard, which were considered the most appropriate backdrops for displaying cars.

MB Financial Bank

23 Broadway Armory Park
(Winter Garden Ice Skating Rink)
5917 N. Broadway
1916, CARPENTER & WELDON
2005–12, REHABILITATION, VOA ASSOCS.

Built as an ice rink, the structure became an armory during World War I, with the drill hall continuing to host recreational activities, including the national roller-skating derby in 1922. The Chicago Park District made the building into a recreation center in 1985, and it is their largest indoor facility, with five gymnasiums and thirteen rooms.

24 John Gauler Houses
5917–5921 N. Magnolia Ave.
1908, WALTER BURLEY GRIFFIN

Griffin achieved maximum impact by carefully placing these twin Prairie School houses on their narrow lots. Framed by embracing porches, the intervening space—a gangway in less skillful hands—offers an additional architectural experience. The visitor is deep into this space before even seeing the very private front doors. Griffin's characteristic touches are the wood-mullioned windows and unbroken vertical piers.

25 Bethany Evangelical Lutheran Church
1244 W. Thorndale Ave.
1914, GRANT C. MILLER
1908, BIBLE CHAPEL, PATTON & MILLER

Patton & Miller was among the few firms that designed churches in the informal, domestically scaled, simply but beautifully detailed Craftsman style. The Tudor Revival–Craftsman Bible Chapel, which served as the first church, blends well with the larger Craftsman church on the corner. Religious motifs are limited to the stone crosses on the bell tower and small medallions in the grapevine-patterned leaded-glass windows.

26 Nicholas Senn High School
5900 N. Glenwood Ave.
1912, ARTHUR F. HUSSANDER
1931, ADDITIONS, PAUL GERHARDT

Grand but bland, it is greatly enhanced by the broad lawn, a rarity on Board of Education properties. Hussander's block, the north–south rectangle, contains a 2,000-seat auditorium. Gerhardt's perpendicular additions form a broad U-shaped court.

27 Stephen K. Hayt Public School
1518 W. Granville Ave.
1906, DWIGHT H. PERKINS

Bold arches top vertical rows of windows in this school, which is closely related to the Francis Scott Key School in the Austin neighborhood.

28 Richard F. Conway House
6200 N. Sheridan Rd.
1906, WILLIAM CARBYS ZIMMERMAN

29 Berger Park South Mansion
(Joseph Downey House)
6205 N. Sheridan Rd.
1906, WILLIAM CARBYS ZIMMERMAN
1988, RENOVATION, CHICAGO
PARK DISTRICT

30 North Lakeside Cultural Center
(Samuel H. Gunder House)
6219 N. Sheridan Rd.
1910, MYRON H. CHURCH
1988, RENOVATION, ROULA ASSOCS.
ARCHITECTS AND SIMON & CO.

This prestigious residential area resembled neighboring North Shore suburbs until high-rises replaced

John Gauler Houses

most of the mansions during the 1950s and 1960s. A hint of grandeur survives in the lavish, historically inspired detail of the Conway House, which contrasts with the sobriety of the other two houses.

On Sheridan Rd. are several Loyola University buildings that belonged to Mundelein College, a women's school that merged with the university in 1991 (entries 31–33).

31 Burrowes Hall
(Adolf Schmidt House)
6331 N. Sheridan Rd.
1917, GEORGE W. MAHER
The decorative motif on this late work of Maher is the water lily, used on the capitals of the octagonal columns.

32 Piper Hall
(Albert G. Wheeler House)
956 W. Sheridan Rd.
1909, WILLIAM CARBYS ZIMMERMAN
Wheeler, chief engineer of the Chicago Tunnel Co., provided the architect with a lavish budget, enabling him to create classical, Romanesque, Tudor, and Prairie details from rough-textured white Vermont marble. Mundelein retained the interior detail and first-floor grandeur. A breathtaking art-glass window fills the wall behind the stair landing.

33 Mundelein Center
(Mundelein College)
6363 N. Sheridan Rd.
1930, NAIRNE W. FISHER AND
JOSEPH W. MCCARTHY

Mundelein Center

The first "skyscraper college," Mundelein's thoroughly modern school for women was headquartered in the impressive fifteen-story tower. With its Art Deco massing and zigzags, curves, and stylized floral patterns, it could house the *Daily Planet*—except for the colossal archangels flanking the entrance. Uriel (Light of God) holds a book inscribed with a cross and points skyward; Jophiel (Beauty of God) holds aloft the torch of knowledge and grasps a celestial globe.

Loyola University Chicago, Lake Shore Campus
6525 N. Sheridan Rd.
In 1906, the Jesuits of St. Ignatius College on Roosevelt Rd. purchased a twenty-acre site between Devon and Loyola Aves. and Sheridan Rd. They established Loyola Academy, a high school, in 1909. The first col-

Loyola University Chicago, Lake Shore Campus

lege building followed in 1912; the university moved from Roosevelt Rd. in 1922. Andrew Rebori's 1920s campus plan envisioned Lake Shore Dr. extending northward along the lake, which explains the eastern orientation of his two buildings as well as the name Madonna della Strada (the drive being the *strada*, or way). The 1960s saw a boom of quick and cheap modern buildings that are gradually being replaced. In 1990, a plan for expanding east on landfill was stopped by environmental concerns, so the campus grew southward by absorbing Mundelein College and moving into the neighborhood south of Devon. Solomon Cordwell Buenz has designed most of the recent buildings and has created a master plan that goes through 2020 as well as a sustainable action plan that targets energy-reduction strategies throughout the campus.

The Loyola campus occupies the lakefront north and east of Sheridan's right-angle turn at Broadway and Devon. Major entrances are on the north side of W. Sheridan Rd. at Kenmore Ave.; and on Loyola Ave. at Winthrop Ave. Street addresses are of little help in locating buildings, which are best found by checking the prominently posted campus maps.

Loyola's earliest years are best represented by entries 34–35:

34 Dumbach Hall
(Loyola Academy)
1909, WORTHMANN & STEINBACH
35 Michael Cudahy Science Hall
1912, WORTHMANN & STEINBACH
These near twins blend Spanish Mission Style with Renaissance details such as elaborately decorated arched windows. Dumbach was originally the high school, Cudahy the first college building.

36 Cuneo Hall
2012, SOLOMON CORDWELL BUENZ
This uncanny simulacrum forms the trio with Dumbach and Cudahy Halls that had been envisioned in Rebori's original plan, although it is much larger than those two. Cuneo Hall replaced a 1960s build-

ing that was so reviled that campus officials refused to consider anything remotely modern despite the success of the nearby Information Commons.

37 Madonna della Strada Chapel
6525 N. Sheridan Rd.
1939, ANDREW N. REBORI
38 Elizabeth M. Cudahy Memorial Library
1930, REBORI & WENTWORTH
1968, ADDITION, BARRY & KAY
In vivid contrast to the historical styles of the early buildings, Loyola's library and chapel are fresh and bold. Facing each other across a broad lakefront lawn, they offer a striking display of Rebori's distinctive interpretation of modernism. Although designed as an ensemble in the late 1920s, the buildings were constructed nearly ten years apart as a consequence of the Great Depression.

The artless library addition obscures most of Rebori's work. But walk around to the lake side to view the carved frieze with Latin names of subjects, the tower with its ziggurat, and the sundial. Go inside to see the main reading room with its large mural by John Warner Norton, who also painted the murals in the Board of Trade and Chicago Daily News Buildings. It celebrates the seventeenth-century French explorers of the region and re-creates Father Marquette's map of Illinois.

Rebori reworked his earlier design for the chapel in the late 1930s. The curving Art Moderne form is reminiscent of a small dirigible or airplane hangar. The walls of the apse are "accordioned"—the folds were originally filled with glass blocks to admit slim slices of light. Names of famous Jesuits are crisply incised along the roofline; the tall tower is flat-topped and windowless.

39 Richard J. Klarchek Information Commons
2008, SOLOMON CORDWELL BUENZ
The masonry bookends pay homage to Rebori's buildings and frame a dazzlingly transparent box that opens the campus to the lake. The west facade is Chicago's first double-skin glass wall, trapping and utilizing or venting solar heat, and

is also one of the country's first tensioned-cable-net walls. The highly efficient LEED silver building can be ventilated mechanically, naturally, or both simultaneously.

40 Institute of Environmental Sustainability
6349 N. Kenmore Ave.
2013, SOLOMON CORDWELL BUENZ
An enormous greenhouse is the centerpiece of this complex that incorporates a residence hall, offices, classrooms, and research laboratories.

41 Simpson Living-Learning Center
6333 N. Winthrop Ave.
1991, SOLOMON CORDWELL BUENZ & ASSOCS.
This residence hall is a model of architectural collegiality, fitting well into its dense residential neighborhood. The varied roof heights of the interconnected buildings signal different functions, which include student housing as well as a conference and study center.

42 Kirchbaum Building
6560 N. Sheridan Rd.
1922, RONNEBERG, PIERCE & HAUBER
Look above the cluttered storefronts to see the Northwestern Terra Cotta Co.'s panorama of Chicago's growth. The long panel between Fort Dearborn, on the left, and the newly completed Wrigley Building, on the right, shows the contemporary skyline and features many of Northwestern's greatest hits, including the Railway Exchange Building and the Blackstone Hotel.

43 St. Ignatius Auditorium
1320 W. Loyola Ave.
1931, REBORI & WENTWORTH
Art Deco lettering over the entrance hints at Rebori's authorship.

44 St. Ignatius Roman Catholic Church
6559 N. Glenwood Ave.
1917, HENRY J. SCHLACKS
Here is a monument to God and to Bedford limestone. Each giant column of the Roman Renaissance portico is carved from a single block of stone. A six-story campanile anchors the eastern end.

45 Roger C. Sullivan High School
6631 N. Bosworth Ave.
1927, JOHN C. CHRISTENSEN
Low and laid out close to the sidewalk, Sullivan was designed to a residential scale. Take in the delightful Tudor details—finials, quoins, medallions, and gargoyles—in a trip around the block. Gothic-lettered panels identify various sections from boiler room to assembly hall.

46 Lunt Lake Apartments
1122–1140 W. Lunt Ave.
1949, HOLSMAN, HOLSMAN, KLEKAMP & TAYLOR
The same January 1950 issue of *Architectural Forum* that featured Mies van der Rohe's Promontory Apartments and his 860–880 N. Lake Shore Dr. (for which the Holsman firm was consulting architect) gave equal space to this project and the firm's Winchester-Hood Garden Homes. What most impressed the magazine were the innovative con-

Simpson Living-Learning Center

Roger C. Sullivan High School

struction techniques, especially the use of "rowlock bond" brickwork, developed by structural engineer Frank Kornacker. Steel rods reinforce concrete poured in the cavity between outer and inner courses of brick, creating a very strong yet very thin bearing wall.

47 Emil Bach House
7415 N. Sheridan Rd.
1915, FRANK LLOYD WRIGHT
2013, RESTORATION,
HARBOE ARCHITECTS

One of the few Wright houses in Chicago proper, this is also one of the last small urban commissions of his Prairie Style period. It is a compact version of Wright's suburban residences, with a cantilevered second story. The floor plan is a condensed version of the open layouts he pioneered.

48 J. Benjamin Moulton House
1328 W. Sherwin Ave.
1908, WALTER BURLEY GRIFFIN

The massing follows a scheme developed by Frank Lloyd Wright, Griffin's employer from 1901 to 1905: the first-floor living room wing projects from the main two-story block, creating a tiered effect. Griffin preferred windows with thick wood mullions to the more delicate, leaded art glass favored by most Prairie School architects.

49 Eugene Field Public School
7019 N. Ashland Blvd.
1898, NORMAND S. PATTON
1916, ADDITION, ARTHUR F. HUSSANDER
1940, ADDITION, JOHN C. CHRISTENSEN

Many elementary schools in older neighborhoods were built over several decades, and until the 1960s, the Board of Education's architects

J. Benjamin Moulton House

Eugene Field Public School

designed additions to match. The oldest part is the central section facing Ashland Ave.; it was built as an addition to Rogers Park's prean-nexation East Side School, which faced Greenleaf Ave. The propor-tions, the hipped roof, and the rusticated base were all respected when the complex was expanded to a harmonious block-long campus.

50 Chicago Public Library—Rogers Park Branch
6907 N. Clark St.

1999, ANTUNOVICH ASSOCS.

Prairie School influences are evident in this building's massing, horizontal band of limestone, and the slablike clock tower. This is the first of four "prototype" buildings developed by four architectural firms in collabora-tion with the CPL.

51 Indian Boundary Park
2500 W. Lunt Ave.

1922, RICHARD F. GLOEDE

1929, FIELD HOUSE, CLARENCE HATZFELD

Through this thirteen-acre park runs the northern boundary of an 1816 Indian treaty ceding the Chicago area to the federal government. In 1922, when the park opened, the surrounding area was almost com-pletely undeveloped. A 1989 addi-tion to the park is an elaborate playground designed by Robert Leathers and constructed by local residents. The field house combines Tudor and American Indian motifs. In the assembly hall, the beamed ceiling features chandeliers sport-ing peace pipes, drums, and arrow-heads. Eifler & Assocs. was hired to restore the building following a devastating 2012 fire.

Chicago Public Library—Rogers Park Branch

Park Gables

52 Park Gables
2438–2484 W. Estes Ave.
1927, JAMES F. DENSON

53 Park Castle
2416–2458 W. Greenleaf Ave.
1925, JENS J. JENSEN

54 Park Manor
2415–2437 W. Greenleaf Ave.
1926, MELVILLE GROSSMAN

55 Park Crest
2420–2434 W. Lunt Ave.
1925, JAMES F. DENSON

This magnificent ensemble is crowned by Park Gables, a Tudor Revival double-courtyard complex with enormous projecting gables, slate roofs, tall casement windows, and ornamented chimney pots. Cathedral ceilings grace the upper-floor apartments. Park Castle reaches back to the medieval castle for its machicolations, crenellations, and gargoyles. The two smaller buildings to the south are less flamboyant but reiterate the English theme.

56 Fred B. Marshall House
2238 W. Greenleaf Ave.
1915, FRED B. PRATHER

57 Fred Winter House
2246 W. Greenleaf Ave.
1928, FRED WINTER

Marshall's house is monastically simple, honest, and unadorned, while down at the corner, Winter pulled out all the stops when he designed his own massive bungalow. The red-tiled roof, Tudor half-timbering, battered walls, and Georgian windows are a raucous blend of colors, textures, and materials.

58 Casa Bonita Apartments
7340–7350 N. Ridge Ave.
1928, ALEXANDER CAPRARO
& MORRIS KOMAR
1974, RENOVATION, WARNER,
BREJCHA, EVANS & ASSOCS.

Glistening white terra-cotta facades define the deep courtyard.

Casa Bonita Apartments

Jackson-Thomas House

59 **7221 N. Ridge Ave.**

EARLY 1870S, ARCHITECT UNKNOWN

1914, REMODELING, NIELS BUCK

Ridge Ave. follows the still-discernible contour of an ancient beach. Because the lower land to the east was frequently swampy, many of the first houses in Rogers Park were built on this street. A few cottages, some from the 1870s, remain. This one was remodeled in the Craftsman style popular before World War I. Characteristics include the exposed rafters under overhanging gables, bands of casement windows, and wood strips decorating stucco walls. Another Craftsman house is next door at **7215**.

60 **7114 N. Ridge Ave.**

1913, ROBERT E. SEYFARTH

61 **7106 N. Ridge Ave.**

1913, ROBERT M. HYDE

62 **7100 N. Ridge Ave.**

1916, A. J. SMITH

Built during Ridge Ave.'s heyday as a fine residential street, 7100 has elaborate Craftsman style brackets under a gabled roof. The house at 7106, similar to Hyde's Charles A. Carlson House in the Austin area, has an asymmetrical gabled roof that extends over the recessed entrance with battered piers. Other Craftsman features include decorative brickwork, exposed rafters, and floral-design leaded windows on the south wall. The Dutch Colonial house at 7114 presents an unusual treatment of a common style, with its gambrel roof exaggeratedly broad-

ened to hold down the entire house, which is built at grade.

63 **Jackson-Thomas House**
7053 N. Ridge Ave.

EARLY 1870S, ARCHITECT UNKNOWN

Commissioned by Andrew B. Jackson, a founding trustee of Rogers Park, this was one of the first generation of grand houses on Ridge Ave. that rose above the modest cottages in bracketed splendor. The symmetrical facade with its central pavilion, the tall windows, and the bracketed hood molding and eaves make this a fine example of the Italianate style at its zenith.

64 **6901 N. Ridge Ave.**

1959, DONALD E. ERICKSON

While many neighborhood apartment buildings were being built to a watered-down Georgian Revival formula, former Frank Lloyd Wright Foundation fellow Erickson curved this flagstone and curtain-wall building to give every apartment a view of open space. The steel-rod stairway gave the building its nickname, the Birdcage, and originally rose above a fish pond whose reflections doubled the structure's pizzazz.

65 **Angel Guardian**
Croatian Catholic Church
(St. Henry's Roman Catholic Church)
6346 N. Ridge Ave.

1906, HENRY J. SCHLACKS

This towered and gabled church is Schlacks's most folkloric design. St. Henry's Parish was founded in the early 1850s by German-speaking Catholics, many from Luxembourg, who decided in 1904 to replace their church buildings with this brick-and-limestone Gothic edifice. Clocks fill in the tops of the tower's louvered arches, and in a niche above the round window on Ridge Ave. is a statue of St. Henry standing next to a model of Bamberg Cathedral, which he built.

Winchester-Hood Garden Homes

66 Unity Church in Chicago
(Chicago Town and Country Tennis and Swim Club)
1925 W. Thome Ave.
1925, GEORGE W. MAHER & SON

The chimney of this grand Tudor manor house bears a limestone shield sporting the club's emblem: tennis racquets flanking intertwined initials. Though best known for his modern Prairie School–influenced work, Maher also did revivalist buildings between World War I and his death in 1926. Given the late date of this building, his son, Philip, may have been responsible for the design.

67 Winchester-Hood Garden Homes
1823–1825 W. Granville Ave., 1908–1922 and 1940–1960 W. Hood Ave., 6149–6175 N. Wolcott Ave., 6113–6129 N. Winchester Ave., and 1920–1922 W. Norwood Ave.
1949–51, HOLSMAN, HOLSMAN, KLEKAMP & TAYLOR

This ambitious project encompasses twenty-two four- and five-story apartment buildings and contains some 800 units. Like the similar Lunt Lake Apartments by the same architect-developer-engineer team, Winchester-Hood combines innovative construction techniques—including concrete-reinforced brick walls and radiant-heated ceiling beams—with a "Scandinavian modern" look that recalls the work of Eliel Saarinen and Alvar Aalto. Ornament is used sparingly but effectively. The stair halls rise behind walls punctuated by a series of three concrete panels depicting stylized signs of the zodiac that were designed by architect Coder Taylor.

68 Granville Gardens
6200–6242 N. Hoyne Ave.
1938, RISSMAN & HIRSCHFELD

Federal Housing Administration mortgage insurance stimulated a slow resumption of residential construction in the few years before America's entry into World War II halted nonessential building. Several stripped-down Art Deco housing projects were built on the Far North Side, where undeveloped land was still available. Granville Gardens was Chicago's first large, privately financed housing complex since the onset of the Great Depression and the first built under direct government supervision. The carefully tailored design kept construction costs low enough to charge a monthly rent of no more than fifteen dollars per room. Fourteen buildings, each containing fourteen units, face two garden courts. To increase the sense of spaciousness, steel-framed casement windows were placed at the corners of each unit. The wall planes are very flat, with windows recessed only slightly. Decoration is limited to horizontal brickwork, which defines the ground floor and enhances the corners. Amazingly, the entire complex is in close to original condition.

69 Rosehill Cemetery
5800 N. Ravenswood Ave.

The Chicago area's largest nonsectarian cemetery was established in 1859 on a rural 350-acre site more than four miles north of the existing city limits. The name came from an error in the charter documents, which referred to

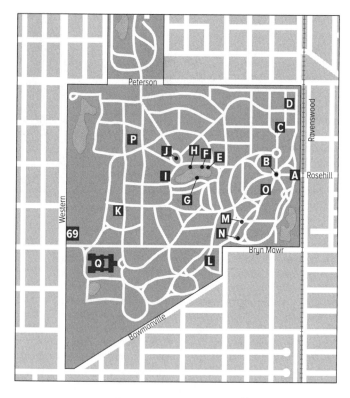

Hiram Roe's tavern on a nearby hill as Roe's Hill. The cemetery's founders ensured the success of their investment by placing the entrance adjacent to the Chicago & North Western Railroad line. They also sought advice from John Jay Smith, founder of Philadelphia's Laurel Hill Cemetery. He recommended his associate, William Saunders, who provided the initial landscaping in a parklike setting of drives and walkways amid artificial lakes and well-tended grounds.

Rosehill Cemetery Entrance Gate and Office Building

Built of Joliet limestone, the

A | Entrance Gate and Office Building (1864, WILLIAM W. BOYINGTON) were designed in the castellated Gothic style, which employed the forms of medieval English architecture for picturesque effect.

Mid-nineteenth-century rural cemeteries were located on the outskirts of the city near rail lines. Railroads owned special funeral cars that could be rented to transport funeral parties to and from the city center. When the train tracks were elevated after 1900, a new Rosehill station and an elevator (for caskets) were designed to match the nearby entrance. The station has been demolished, although part of the platform remains. The elevator tower remains but is no longer in use.

Atop the hill is the **B | Civil War Soldiers Memorial**, in the grassy center of a circular driveway ringed with other memorials to the Civil War. The columnar monument, *Our Heroes*, designed by sculptor Leonard Volk, is topped by a figure of a Union soldier. Four bronze plaques near the base represent the four service branches: army, navy, artillery, and cavalry.

George S. Bangs tomb

C | George S. Bangs invented the railway mail car, which made it possible to collect and sort mail on a moving train. His monument depicts a dead tree that represents the deceased; despite death, the trunk continues to support life in the form of plants and animals. A "fast mail" rail car emerges from a tunnel at the base of the trunk.

D | "Long John" Wentworth, one of twelve mayors buried at Rosehill, has a seventy-two-foot obelisk, the cemetery's tallest monument.

Around the lake, near the center of the cemetery, is an impressive row of mausoleums representing the popular styles of the late nineteenth century. The Egyptian temple for railroad president **E | Darius Miller** reflects the popularity of a cultural style whose greatest monuments focused on death and eternity.

A Greek temple with Doric columns marks the resting place of **F | Charles Gates Dawes,** the U.S. vice president under Calvin Coolidge.

Darius Miller tomb

Look across the lake for the best view of banker **G | Norman W. Harris's** mausoleum, with its Corinthian columns and copper-clad dome. The tomb is a perfect classical tempietto in the eighteenth-century manner. The burial chambers lie below the floor of the structure.

H | Charles M. Hewitt, a manufacturer and financier, has a rusticated Romanesque mausoleum.

Another very impressive temple form, for **I | Adam Schaaf**, has two lions resting at the front steps.

The picturesque design of the **J | Horatio N. May Chapel** (1899, JOSEPH LYMAN SILSBEE) combines Gothic and Romanesque elements. The chapel is generally kept locked, but walk through the porte cochere and note the handsome mosaic ceiling.

K | William B. Mundie was William Le Baron Jenney's partner from 1891 to 1907 and worked on the design of the Manhattan Building.

Horatio N. May Chapel

The mausoleum of banker **L | Oscar G. Foreman** is noteworthy for its unusual Art Nouveau architecture (designer unknown) and because it is empty: the Foremans are buried in Graceland Cemetery.

Sculptor **M | Leonard W. Volk** carved the life-size statue of himself that marks his family plot. His wife's cousin, Senator Stephen A. Douglas, and his political opponent, Abraham Lincoln, were frequent and popular subjects for Volk's work.

N | John M. Van Osdel, Chicago's first professional architect, was responsible for more than seventy commercial and public buildings in the Loop alone.

O | William W. Boyington, an early Chicago architect, was a leading designer of Chicago railroad stations and other public buildings.

The grave of architect **P | George W. Maher** is marked with a small unadorned block of granite. Maher's work is generally classified with that of the Prairie School, but his was a highly personal interpretation of ideas from various contemporary sources.

Within the marble-lined hallways of the **Q | Rosehill Mausoleum** (1914, SIDNEY LOVELL), family crypts open off long corridors embellished with stained-glass windows. The most impressive is the Tiffany window in the John G. Shedd Memorial Room.

—JOAN POMARANC

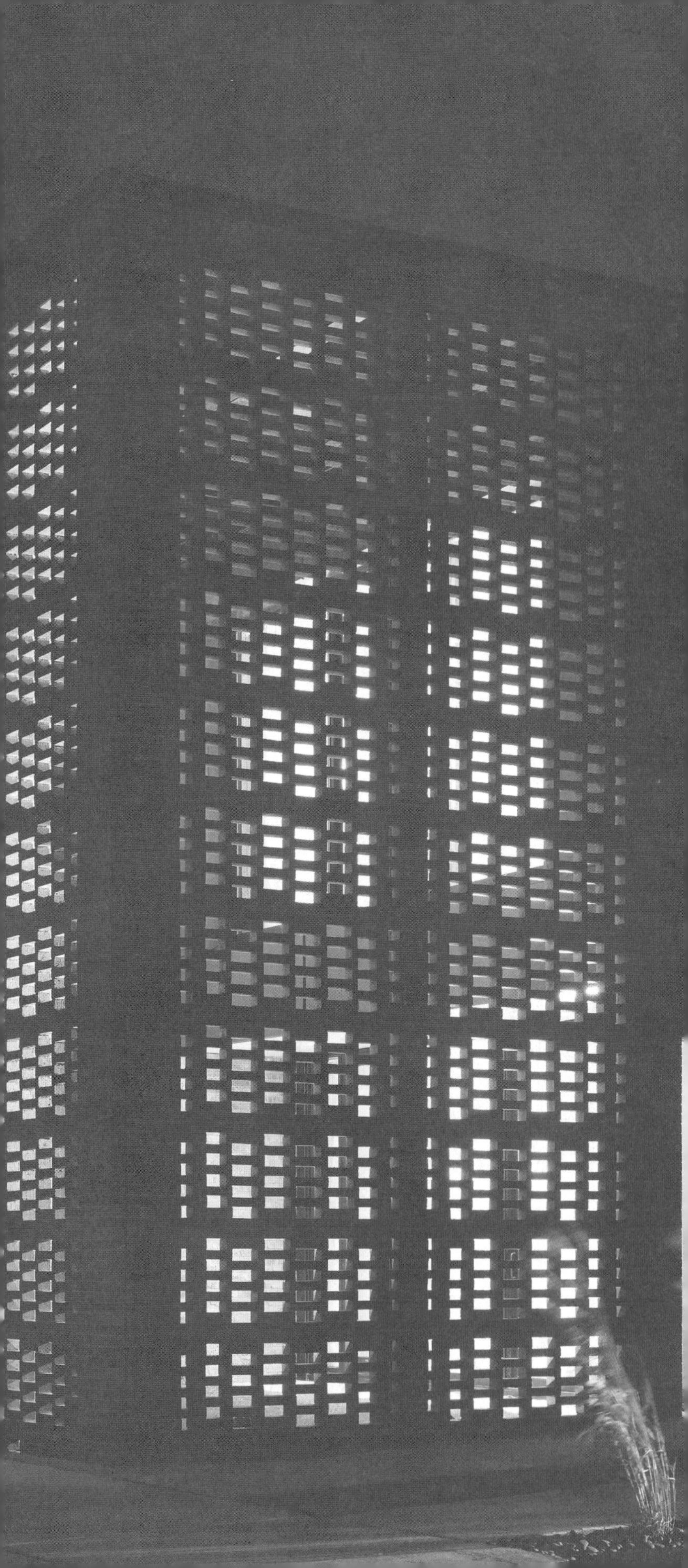

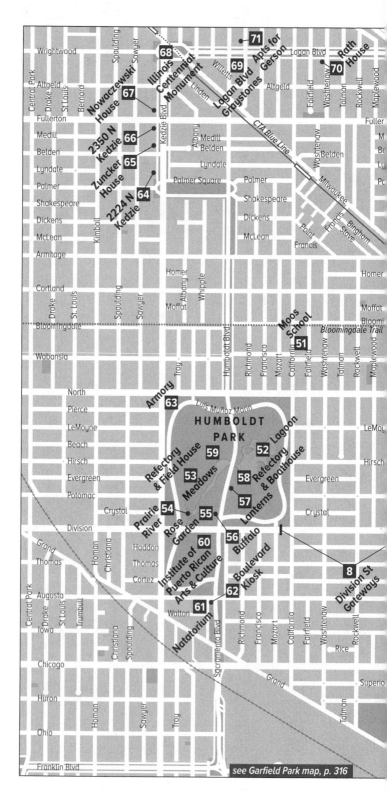

see Lakeview map, p. 220

72 Green Exchange
2545 W Diversey
2 blocks northwest

Wrightwood

Ashland

Altgeld

Fullerton

Janssen

see Lincoln Park map, p. 196

I-90/94 Fwy

Oakley

Holstein Park

Seeley

Winchester

Lister

Honore

Wood

Elston

Ashland Avenue Bridge

50

Wayne

Lakewood

47 Palmer

Hamilton

Avondale

St Hedwig

Bell

Webster

44
45 Shakespeare **46**

Kamka Bldg

Charleston

Dickens

43 McLean

Leavitt

Ranquist House

Homer

Cortland

Moffat

41 Flats

Wilmot

Milwaukee

Winnebago

31-32 Caton

Concord

29 Essex Two

25-28

Wicker Park houses

24

Pierce

23

22 LeMoyne

21

Schiller

20

19 **18**

Evergreen

Potomac

6 St Mary of Nazareth Hospital

Crystal

5 Holy Trinity

Division

Haddon

Thomas

Cortez

Augusta

Walton

4 St Nicholas

Iowa

Rice

3 Sts Volodymyr & Olha

Chicago

Lee

Huron

Erie

Ohio

Race

1 Brick Weave House

Grand

Ferdinand

Damen

Winchester

Wolcott

Avondale

Armitage

Churchill

Willow

St Paul

40 Willow Court

33 Caton St houses

35

34 North Ave Baths

North

Pierce

LeMoyne

Schiller

17

Wicker Park

Wolcott

Bloomingdale

39

St Mary of the Angels

Cortland

1713 N Wood

38

Wabansia

36

37

1600 block Wolcott

Marshfield

Wis

Marshfield

Honore

Paulina

Hermitage

Wood

Pierce

LeMoyne

Julian

Beach

Blackhawk

Etten

Marion

Honore

Wolcott

Moorman

CTA Blue Line, Milwaukee

Dean

Paulina

Division

Haddon

Thomas

Cortez

Augusta

Walton

Walton

Iowa

Rice

9 Division St Baths

Winchester

Wolcott

Wood

Damen

Rice

Pearson

Chicago

Lee

Superior

Huron

Erie

Ohio

Hartland

Hermitage

Ontario

see Near West Side map, p. 292

Shakespeare

Dominic

Dickens

McLean

Cortland

Willow

Wabansia

Ada

Concord

Throop

Bestly

Kennedy Expwy I-90/94

Noble

Elston

To Loop

see River North map, p. 150

Pulaski Park

16

14

15

St Stanislaus Kostka

Ashland

Bosworth

Greenview

Cleaver

Noble

Ada

Bishop

Elizabeth

Throop

13 Holy Trinity

12 Northwestern Settlement House

Thomas

Cortez

Augusta

Walton

Chestnut

Fry

11 1537 W Chestnut

Greenview

Armour

Bishop

Noble

Ancona

Ada

Elizabeth

10

C3 Prefab

Grand

Ogden

WEST TOWN/WICKER PARK/BUCKTOWN/ LOGAN SQUARE/IRVING PARK

The Northwest Side comprises disparate neighborhoods united by the important artery of Milwaukee Ave. Like many of Chicago's diagonal streets, it began as an Indian trail, was developed as a plank road and streetcar route, and remains a heavily traveled commercial thoroughfare. The many changes in neighborhood names and boundaries along the Milwaukee Ave. corridor reflect the area's shifting populations and their various motives of ethnic pride, historical interest, and real estate promotion.

The major community areas, which extend west from the north branch of the Chicago River for about two miles, are West Town, from Kinzie St. to about Bloomingdale Ave.; Logan Square, from Bloomingdale to Diversey Aves.; Avondale, from Diversey Ave. to Addison St.; and Irving Park, from Addison St. to Montrose Ave. West Town includes the neighborhood of Wicker Park; the section of Logan Square east of Western Ave. is known as Bucktown.

In 1851, Chicago's boundaries were extended to Western and North Aves. The earliest housing in West Town was built by German Catholics who came after the 1848 revolutions in Europe and settled around Milwaukee Ave. and Division St. By the mid-1860s, they were joined by large numbers of Polish immigrants, and animosities between nationalities caused conflicts. Both Germans and Poles emphasized the establishment of "national" parishes and built large churches that served as community and religious centers.

The boulevard system radiating from Humboldt Park is a major feature of the area. An 1869 act of the state legislature established the West Park Commission, one of three municipal bodies responsible for creating a system of peripheral boulevards and pleasure grounds intended to ring the city. William Le Baron Jenney, better known as the Father of the Skyscraper, was hired in 1870 to design the West Side parks and boulevards. Conceived as an ensemble and originally named Upper, Central, and Lower Parks, these landscapes are now known as Humboldt, Garfield, and Douglas Parks and are linked by broad boulevards lined with stately houses and apartments.

The creation of Humboldt Park attracted real estate speculators, and the 1871 fire was another impetus to population growth, driving many workers from damaged areas to this expanding industrial and residential corridor. Much of what is now the Northwest Side lay beyond the city limits, with the housing stock consisting of inexpensive wooden buildings free from the ban on frame construction enacted within Chicago itself.

In 1868, a public park, Wicker Park, was established on a small triangle of land and named for two brothers, Charles G. and Joel H. Wicker, who were major local real estate developers. By the late 1880s and early 1890s, the surrounding area had developed as fashionably middle and upper class. The construction of streetcar lines and the extension of the elevated line to Logan Square in 1895 fostered growth north along the boulevards. Many of the successful immigrants who ran businesses on Milwaukee Ave. and had lived there in "flats above the store" built elegant graystones, brick town houses, and two- and three-flats emulating single-family homes on Kedzie and Logan Blvds.

In the great annexation of 1889, Chicago added 125 square miles, and the extension of the city's north and west boundaries placed the boulevard system in the center of the city rather than on its periphery. North along Milwaukee Ave. the annexation of part of Jefferson Township added the suburb of Irving Park. Evidence of this nineteenth-century community is still visible in the cluster of fine Victorian homes in the area of Irving Park Rd. and the Kennedy

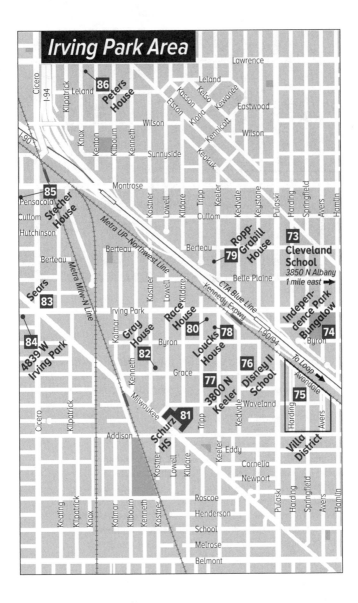

Irving Park Area

Expressway. Many of them have shed their siding to emerge as clapboard Cinderellas. Electric streetcar lines were established along Irving Park Rd. and Milwaukee and Elston Aves. in the 1890s, and the neighborhood began to develop as part of the city. But even greater development occurred between 1910 and 1920, when Irving Park's population more than doubled.

Early settlers of West Town included not only Germans and Poles but also Scandinavians and Italians. After World War I, a tremendous influx of Russian Jews replaced some of the Poles and Germans. A more recent wave of newcomers includes Hispanics as well as Polish immigrants. St. Stanislaus Kostka offers masses in English, Polish, and Spanish, testifying to the area's continuing diversity.

A significant number of artists began moving to the area in the 1980s, and young professionals soon followed. Condominiums began to line the main arteries and to replace cottages and modest flat buildings on the side streets. Elegant mansions in Wicker Park and Logan Square have regained their original splendor even as clean-lined modern architecture has appeared throughout the area.

—JULIA S. BACHRACH

Brick Weave House

1 Brick Weave House
1922 W. Race St.
2009, STUDIO GANG ARCHITECTS

A dilapidated horse stable was the starting point for another of Gang's virtuoso exercises in materials exploration. Upending the traditional perception of a solid brick wall by creating an elaborate twenty-six-foot-high screen presented an engineering challenge. The single-brick-deep wall is attached to a steel frame with customized hardware. Behind the small enclosed front garden is a predominantly glass wall that admits an ever-changing pattern of light during the day and glows through the brick screen at night.

2 Ohio House
2301 W. Ohio St.
1989, 1999, JOSEPH VALERIO
AND LINDA SEARL

Ohio House

The square masonry base was part of the first project and houses all of the public spaces. The forty-two-foot-diameter aluminum-clad cylinder was added to the second floor a decade later. It shimmers in the right light. The two front doors, at right angles to each other, lead to the same space.

3 Sts. Volodymyr and Olha Church
739 N. Oakley Blvd.
1975, JAROSLAW A. KORSUNSKY

4 St. Nicholas Ukrainian Catholic Cathedral
2238 W. Rice St.
1915, WORTHMANN,
STEINBACH & PIONTEK

Liturgical differences split St. Nicholas's congregation, leading the traditionalists to build their own church, Sts. Volodymyr and Olha. The cathedral's thirteen domes represent Christ and the Apostles; the application of intricate mosaics derives from the Cathedral of St. Sophia in Kiev. The church has a simpler profile but still includes five domes and an enormous mosaic commemorating the conversion of Grand Duke Vladimir of Kiev to Christianity in 988, an occasion also celebrated in the sculpture of the two saints northwest of the church. The mosaics and paintings are dazzling.

Holy Trinity Russian Orthodox Cathedral

**5 Holy Trinity Russian
Orthodox Cathedral**
  1121 N. Leavitt St.
  1899–1903, LOUIS H. SULLIVAN

Sullivan synthesized Orthodox iconography and Byzantine tradition
with his own design ideals and the
theories of the nineteenth-century
Gothic Revival architect Eugène-
Emmanuel Viollet-le-Duc. The portal's ogee-arched canopy derives
from Russo-Byzantine precedent,
while the decorative sheet metal
under the canopy, though subsidiary,
is as fine and fluid as Sullivan's contemporaneous work on the Carson
Pirie Scott & Co. Building. The Eastern Orthodox central plan creates an
intimate interior; the congregation
stands in a square space surmounted by a painted octagonal
dome. The sacred apse is screened
from view by an elaborate iconosta-
sis. Although most of the decoration
is stenciled, it is not by Sullivan.

6 St. Mary of Nazareth Hospital
  2233 W. Division St.
  1975, PERKINS & WILL

The fluted exterior resembles the
AT&T Long Lines Building in New
York and could have inspired the
sets of the futuristic movie *Brazil*.

7 Roberto Clemente High School
  1147 N. Western Ave.
  1974, FUJIKAWA, CONTERATO,
    LOHAN & ASSOCS.

To squeeze a large high school onto
a limited site split by a major street,
Clemente's instruction building rises
nine stories and is connected to the
athletic building by a steel bridge
over Division St.

8 Division St. Gateways
  **Division St. at Artesian
  Ave. and Mozart Dr.**
  1995, DESTEFANO & PARTNERS

The Puerto Rican flag, abstracted
and rendered in forty-five tons of
steel, spans the street in two places
to celebrate the neighborhood's
ethnic identity. Related street
ornamentation includes seating
with game tables as well as metal
light-pole banners with laser-cut
silhouettes of Puerto Rican cultural
themes.

**9 Division St. Russian
and Turkish Baths**
  (Kaplan Baths)
  1916 W. Division St.
  1907, MAURICE SPITZER

Unlike the municipal baths, these
provided more than just hygiene;

behind the classically derived limestone facade, they offered a luxurious retreat.

Wheeler Kearns Architects designed a 99-unit apartment building at **1611 W. Division St.** *that was scheduled for completion in late 2013.*

10 C3 Prefab
1404 W. Ohio St.
2011, SQUARE ROOT
   ARCHITECTURE & DESIGN
C3 (Cube, Copy, Cut) is a prototype infill house that is prefabricated and certified LEED platinum. It consists of five modules built in an Indiana factory and assembled in a single day. The U-shaped plan brings extra light into the interior. A slightly wider version is at **1650 W. Huron St.**

11 1537 W. Chestnut St.
1994, FREDERICK PHILLIPS & ASSOCS.
To stay in scale with other houses on the block, this residence on a double lot is articulated as two volumes, allowing room for a side garden. The eastern wing is a steel structure that houses a top-floor bedroom from which a screen porch is suspended. To increase security, the building features indoor parking and a minimum of ground-floor openings.

12 Northwestern University Settlement House
1400 W. Augusta Blvd.
1910, POND & POND
The solid massing and finely detailed brickwork are typical of the settlement houses designed by these architects. Geometric trim on piers and diaper brickwork are their trademarks.

13 Holy Trinity Roman Catholic Church
1120 N. Noble St.
1906, HERMAN OLSZEWSKI
   AND WILLIAM G. KRIEG
The exuberant pilastered facade with its balustrades, urns, and obelisks is based on Roman Baroque models, with additional homage to the Pantheon's pedimented portico. Under the iron-vaulted ceiling, the column-free space is adorned with unusual ceiling paintings and windows by F. X. Zettler and Mayer & Co.

St. Stanislaus Kostka Roman Catholic Church

14 St. Stanislaus Kostka Roman Catholic Church
1327 N. Noble St.
1876–81, PATRICK C. KEELEY
1892, TOWERS, ADOLPHUS DRUIDING
The dazzling interior focuses on the apse, with Thaddeus Zukotynski's richly embellished paintings of the life of St. Stanislaus. The southern tower was destroyed by lightning in 1964.

15 St. Stanislaus Kostka School
1255 N. Noble St.
1959, BELLI & BELLI
The John F. Kennedy Expressway was routed around the church but displaced many parishioners and destroyed the old school. The replacement is a slightly kitschy take on Corbusian modernism with a classroom block atop pilotis.

16 Pulaski Park
Blackhawk St., Potomac Ave., Noble St., and Cleaver St.
1912, JENS JENSEN
1913, LOCKER BUILDING, 1914, FIELD
   HOUSE, WILLIAM CARBYS ZIMMERMAN
The West Park Commission carved this Progressive Reform movement park out of a densely populated neighborhood and designed it to meet a wide range of needs. The bathing facilities of the Locker Building, intended for men and boys, served 500 patrons per hour. Dominated by a multiplaned, clipped gable roof, the Tudor Revival/Craftsman-style field house is as grand as a manor house, its generous scale and high style contrasting

sharply with the modest flats nearby. It housed men's and women's gyms (with separate entrances), an auditorium, and a branch of the Chicago Public Library, hinted at by the sculptured owl and open book in the western gable.

17 Wicker Park
Damen, Schiller, and
Wicker Park Aves.
The 1892 Gurgoyle Fountain was rebuilt in 2002 (DESTEFANO & PARTNERS) from castings made from the original molds. Other historic elements such as benches and urns have also been reproduced. The field house (1985, CHICAGO PARK DISTRICT) is reminiscent of John S. Van Bergen's Oak Park playground shelters of the 1920s (now remodeled or demolished), built to a domestic scale with Prairie School lines.

Often called Chicago's ethnic Gold Coast, the Wicker Park neighborhood housed many prosperous Scandinavian and German immigrants who could have afforded to live farther east and south but chose to build here, alongside their successful compatriots (entries 18–28 and 31–33).

18 Harris Cohn House
1941 W. Schiller St.
1891, THEODORE LEWANDOWSKI
A standout among its more sedate Italianate neighbors, this costly Queen Anne has a rusticated and towered stone facade with granite columns—a fine display of the style's forms, materials, and window shapes.

19 Nels T. Quales House
1951 W. Schiller St.
CA. 1873, ARCHITECT UNKNOWN
1890, ADDITION AND REMODELING,
THIEL & LANG
The original, Italianate house was set far back from the street; its stone window hoods are still visible on the sides. The Queen Anne front addition, complete with Moorish arch, is a stylish update. It distinguished the house from adjacent properties such as **1955–1957 W.**

Schiller St. (1883, CHARLES O. HANSEN), which Quales, a Norwegian immigrant who became a Chicago city physician, developed.

1407 N. Hoyne Ave.

20 1407 N. Hoyne Ave.
1879, ARCHITECT UNKNOWN
This high-shouldered Second Empire house is tall and exuberantly French, with its curbed mansard roof, incised foliate detailing, sawtooth window hoods, and cast-iron porch details.

21 Louis Hanson House
1417 N. Hoyne Ave.
1879, ARCHITECT UNKNOWN
2009, RESTORATION, VINCI/
HAMP ARCHITECTS
The side porch on this Italianate house has nothing to do with entry but was intended as a frame for viewing the garden.

22 Henry Grusendorf House
1520 N. Hoyne Ave.
1886, GUSTAV BLOEDNER
23 Adolph Borgmeier House
1521 N. Hoyne Ave.
1895, HENRY T. KLEY
Bloedner's Second Empire design is embellished with a carved portrait of a woman, a decorative element frequently seen on houses designed by or built for Germans. Kley's turreted Queen Anne has an intricately detailed stoop framed with wooden "lace."

24 Albin Greiner House
1559 N. Hoyne Ave.
1876, ARCHITECT UNKNOWN
This elaborate gabled brick cottage with Italianate window hood

moldings is one of the area's oldest houses, featuring the side garden porch common in this neighborhood.

25 Hermann Weinhardt House
2135 W. Pierce Ave.
1889, WILLIAM OHLHABER

Fancy houses in neighborhoods of successful immigrants often looked to Europe for inspiration and in-genuously used elements that had gone out of style elsewhere. The side porch with the garden view is a holdover; the rich and heavy metal bargeboards recall Northern Europe.

Hermann Weinhardt House

26 John D. Runge House
2138 W. Pierce Ave.
1884, FROMMANN & JEBSEN

The elaborate two-story porch beautifully frames the views through robust posts and finely worked motifs, such as the Masonic insignias under the eaves of the gabled dormer.

John D. Runge House

27 Theodore Juergens House
2141 W. Pierce Ave.
1895, HENRY T. KLEY

28 2146, 2150, and 2156 W. Pierce Ave.
1890, LUTKEN & THISSLEW

These fine examples of rusticated Romanesque show how the style was better adapted in the long run to the more durable limestone (2141 and 2150) than to the softer sandstone (2146 and 2156).

29 Essex Two Live/ Work Structure
2210 W. North Ave.
1995, WHEELER KEARNS ARCHITECTS

The clean, simple elevation could be the business card of the two graphic designers who live and work here. To construct a solid, high-quality house on a restricted budget, a prefabricated structure of insulated concrete beams, walls, floors, and a roof was erected in four days atop six site-cast concrete caissons. Concrete is left exposed, although it is visually softened on the interior floors with integral pigment.

30 Clock Tower Lofts
2300 W. Wabansia Ave.
1919, ALFRED ALSCHULER
1995, CONVERSION TO LOFTS, HARTSHORNE & PLUNKARD

This unusually fine loft conversion leaves the best of the old building and beautifully complements it with new material. It fits well into its side street.

31 Flats for Iver Christianson
1658 N. Leavitt St.
1893, CHARLES F. SORENSEN

32 Flats for Gustaf Murbach
1644 N. Leavitt St.
1896, CHARLES THISSLEW

Using high-quality materials such as stone, cast iron, and art glass, the owners built many handsome flats, such as these rusticated Roman-esque graystones, in this presti-gious area of single-family houses.

33 2138, 2142, 2146, 2152, and 2156 W. Caton St.
1891, FABER & PAGELS

"No two alike!" the architects boasted. When built, 2152 was de-

2156 W. Caton St.

scribed as Renaissance; 2146 was called Swiss.

34 North Ave. Baths Building
2039 W. North Ave.
1921, LLOYD & KLEIN
1997, RESTORATION, JAY R. KAISER
Bathhouses often served as social centers in ethnic neighborhoods, and this building has found new life as a restaurant and residential structure.

35 Northwest Tower
1608 N. Milwaukee Ave.
1929, PERKINS, CHATTEN & HAMMOND
The peaked tower of this neighborhood skyscraper was intended to house a revolving red, green, and white beacon. The first two floors were designed for retail, with medical offices on the middle floors.

Northwest Tower

36 Urban Sandbox
1615 N. Wolcott St.
2009, MILLER/HULL PARTNERSHIP,
    DESIGN ARCH.; OSTERHAUS MCCARTHY
    ARCHITECTS, ARCH. OF RECORD
1617 N. Wolcott
2009, STUDIO DWELL ARCHITECTS
1625 and 1627 N. Wolcott St.
2007, 2009, OSTERHAUS
    MCCARTHY ARCHITECTS
This block illustrates the rapid change in Bucktown's character as well as a more general shift to modernism in that most conservative of housing types, the speculative single-family home. In 1994, Brininstool & Lynch designed a custom house at **1614 N. Wolcott St.**, its modern style and tough materials a pioneering gesture in what was still a somewhat rough-edged area. Just a decade later, Ranquist Development razed an old warehouse and planned five houses and a condominium building whose size and amenities evoke the city's most expensive zip codes. Looming over the street and filling the lot lines, the houses are behemoths. The multifamily building offers a relatively open street presence, with floor-to-ceiling windows screened by the steel frame that supports generous balconies.

37 Wis Tavern
1825 W. Wabansia Ave.
2007, WILKINSON BLENDER
    ARCHITECTURE
The owners of a record label wanted to use green technology to reinvigorate the tradition of living above the store. Remodeling of the classic corner tavern reused structural elements and many of its materials. On the roof deck, wind turbines double as kinetic sculpture, and a solar panel trellis provides shade. This design prompted a change in the Chicago Building Code to exempt wind turbines from building height

Wis Tavern

restrictions, underscoring the city's interest in promoting green construction.

38 1713 N. Wood St.

2010, MILLER/HULL PARTNERSHIP, DESIGN ARCH.; OSTERHAUS MCCARTHY ARCHITECTS, ARCH. OF RECORD

As ever-larger homes squeeze onto urban lots, the challenge of providing green space means that no horizontal surface goes unused. Here, a series of level changes elevates the main floor to the height of the garage roof and provides easy access to it via a short bridge. An even larger deck sits atop the house itself.

39 St. Mary of the Angels Roman Catholic Church

1850 N. Hermitage Ave.

1914–20, WORTHMANN & STEINBACH
1992, REHABILITATION, HOLABIRD & ROOT

An ambitious pastor's architectural aspirations, combined with a devout and generous congregation's funds, created this neo-Renaissance "Polish cathedral," where angels tread on the parapets and hover in the massive nave. The tile–and–terra-cotta dome recalls the silhouette of St. Peter's in Rome.

40 Willow Court

2008–2050 W. Willow St. and 1757–1767 N. Hoyne Ave.

1999, PAPPAGEORGE/HAYMES

A difficult site—an abandoned railroad switching yard that sloped twenty feet from one end to the other—led to a creative solution for this fifty-six-unit complex. Staggered town houses around a series of landscaped entry courts at varying levels along Willow St. create gateways to the housing behind, which is also accessed by car from Hoyne Ave. The entry courts as well as two colors of brick and boxcar-like steel bays create a neighborly scale. The rear units back up to the Bloomingdale Trail.

41 Ranquist House

1804 N. Leavitt St.

2007, MILLER/HULL PARTNERSHIP, DESIGN ARCH.; STUDIO DWELL ARCHITECTS, ARCH. OF RECORD

This is a masterful essay in making a home out of a nondescript, awkwardly shaped commercial building. The entrance was moved to the north end of the roughly triangular plan, while the south part was converted into a courtyard that brings light deep into the house. A new glass wall at the back of the property extends the house out and up to increase transparency and create a master suite on the top level.

Across Leavitt St. is **Churchill Row** *(*2002, HIRSCH ASSOCS.*), one of the area's first large-scale redevelopments. Immediately to the south is the* **Bloomingdale Trail***, a 2.7-mile-long disused elevated rail spur that the city and the Trust for Public Land plan to turn into a linear park like New York City's High Line. Ross Barney Architects and Michael Van Valkenburgh Assocs. unveiled plans in January 2013 that include walking and bike trails on the former tracks as well as a variety of street-level parks to provide access points. Later that year, the project was named The 606, for the three digits common to all Chicago zip codes.*

42 2227–2245 W. Homer Ave.

1888, THEODORE N. BELL

Still remarkably well preserved, these tiny Queen Anne cottages miniaturized the style for the budget-conscious.

43 Bucktown Three

2215 W. McLean Ave.

2010, STUDIO DWELL ARCHITECTS

Instead of filling the oversized lot, the design creates a variety of

Bucktown Three

garden spaces with a staggered, irregular floor plan. Windows are judiciously placed to maximize light and privacy. One of the firm's slightly earlier houses (**Bucktown One**) is at 2041 W. Cortland Place.

44 St. Hedwig Roman Catholic Church
2100 W. Webster Ave.
1899–1902, ADOLPHUS DRUIDING

In this high-octane Renaissance Revival design for a Polish congregation, the geometric facade is anchored by square corner piers topped by robust cupolas. The aedicula above the entry is echoed by a pedimented reredos behind the altar.

45 St. Hedwig Rectory
2226 N. Hoyne Ave.
1892, ADOLPHUS DRUIDING

This kind of Second Empire grandeur was already out of style in more fashionable neighborhoods. Essentially a boardinghouse, the rectory is masquerading as a mansion, its breadth visually diminished by setbacks.

46 Joseph Kamka Building
2121 W. Webster Ave.
1910, WORTHMANN & STEINBACH
1940, REMODELING,
 ARCHITECT UNKNOWN

The first-floor funeral parlor was modernized with a pigmented, structural glass facade that is sleek and elegant—and completely at odds with the prim slice of dull flats above it.

47 Holstein Park
Shakespeare Ave., Oakley Ave., and Lyndale St.
1912, FIELD HOUSE, WILLIAM
 CARBYS ZIMMERMAN

In 1854, three developers donated just under two acres of their Holstein District property in the hope that a city park would increase the value of their surrounding land. But development did not pick up until after the city's 1901 donation of the land to the West Park Commission, which began improvements five years later. This block-

wide recreation center contained many of the same elements as the Pulaski Park field house: gymnasiums, a library, assembly rooms, showers, and lockers.

48 2100 Block of N. Oakley Ave.
Tall, narrow, and stiff, the gabled brick cottages and two- and three-flats ringing Holstein Park are curious anachronisms created between 1901 and 1908 by neighborhood architect Joseph A. Wilkowski and contractor John Konczik. Their monotonous uniformity is relieved only by slightly varying colors and setbacks. German names were originally given to the park and surrounding streets, but by 1901, many Germans had moved out and been replaced by Poles.

49 Finfrock House
2318 N. Oakley Ave.
2009, CURT FINFROCK

The architect-homeowner built most of the house himself, with help from friends and day laborers. The inexpensive and reclaimed materials include the unusual cladding, which consists of cement hand-troweled onto fiber-cement panels. Also unusual is the interior plan: principal living spaces are on the second floor, and the ground level could be divided so that part of it would become a duplex with the clerestory-lit basement.

50 Ashland Ave. Bridge
Ashland Ave. north of Webster St.
1937, SCIPIONE DEL CAMPO

The Art Deco bridge houses feature bas-reliefs of classical figures proudly showing off bridge elements, including gears, trusses and a sleek tower.

51 Bernard Moos Public School
1711 N. California Ave.
1910, DWIGHT H. PERKINS

Best described as castellated Chicago School, with crenellated parapets above the projecting stair towers, this is a close cousin of the architect's contemporaneous George M. Pullman School.

Humboldt Park

W. North Ave., N. Kedzie Ave., W. Augusta Blvd., N.
Sacramento Blvd., W. Division St., N. California Ave.
1912, ADDITION: W. AUGUSTA BLVD., N. WHIPPLE ST., W.
   WALTON ST., WEST OF N. SACRAMENTO BLVD.
1871–77, WILLIAM LE BARON JENNEY
1877–90S, OSCAR F. DUBUIS
1906–9, JENS JENSEN

The most impressive of the three great nineteenth-century West Side parks, Humboldt Park gives no hint of its originally flat and boggy site. Jenney, like his colleagues in the naturalistic landscape movement such as Frederick Law Olmsted, strove to create human-designed vistas that aspired to the beauty of the natural. His work is best seen in the section east of Humboldt Dr., where the irregularly shaped **52 | Lagoon and Islands** typify the picturesque ideal. The concrete bases of lamp standards marking Jenney's northeast entrance to the park still stand at the corner of California and North Aves.

Jensen was the superintendent of Humboldt Park in the mid-1890s (with an office in the turret of the stables building). After he took over as general superintendent and chief landscape architect of the entire West Park System in 1905, Humboldt Park became an important place for his experimentation with design ideas. The area west of Humboldt Dr. shows his hand in the three large **53 | Meadows,** sheltered from Kedzie Ave. by berms and heavy landscaping. He narrowed the western section of the **Lagoon** (called the "New Lake") to form a signature **54 | Prairie River** (RESTORED IN 2004) that imitates one of his beloved native Illinois landscapes. Nearby, he surrounded with berms and set below grade the formally designed **55 | Rose Garden,** which in 1911 gained bronze castings of Edward Kemeys's **56 | Buffalo** sculptures, originally created for the 1893 World's Columbian Exposition.

Jensen also introduced Prairie School architecture into Humboldt Park, hiring Schmidt, Garden & Martin and William Carbys Zimmerman. The former firm's **57 | Lanterns** (1907) are identical to those in Columbus Park.

58 Refectory and Boathouse
East side of Humboldt Dr.
north of W. Division St.
1907, RICHARD E. SCHMIDT,
   GARDEN & MARTIN
2002, RESTORATION, BAUER
   LATOZA STUDIO

The hovering hipped roof and the three great arches are bounteously reflected in the lagoon to the north. This great Prairie School amenity encouraged visitors to stay outdoors, sheltering summer guests on the terraced open-air room and their rental boats below and serving as a warming house for ice-skaters in the winter. The parking lot to the south was once the Music Court.

59 Refectory and Field House
1400 N. Sacramento Blvd.
1928, MICHAELSEN & ROGNSTAD

Georgian and Tudor details combine in this eclectic facility, grandly historic in derivation.

Humboldt Park Refectory and Boathouse

Institute of Puerto Rican Arts & Culture/Humboldt Park Receptory and Stables

60 Institute of Puerto Rican Arts & Culture

(Receptory and Stables)
South side of W. Division St.
west of Humboldt Dr.
1896, FROMMANN & JEBSEN
1998, RESTORATION, MCCLIER

Domestically detailed but lavishly scaled, this structure was intended to resemble "the old German Style of country house architecture," according to the West Park Commission. The nearby Lily Pond (1897) is thought to be an early Jensen project.

61 Natatorium

W. Augusta Blvd. west of
N. Sacramento Blvd.
1914, WILLIAM CARBYS ZIMMERMAN

This simple Prairie School pool house provided other recreational opportunities as well.

62 Boulevard Kiosk

1995, DLK ARCHITECTURE

Map station kiosks and additional new signage were designed as part of an improvement project for the city's twenty-eight-mile boulevard system. The kiosks reinterpret nineteenth-century forms in contemporary materials.

63 Illinois National Guard, Thirty-Third Division—Northwest Armory

1551 N. Kedzie Ave.
1940, CHATTEN & HAMMOND

Late-nineteenth-century armories were fortified like castles to preserve public order against possible workers' demonstrations and other civil unrest. By the 1930s, the typical armory was more civil, with more entrances and windows, because its drill hall could also serve as a convention hall or sports arena. This strong Art Deco limestone block gives the reassurance of a fort but has the modern styling of an office building or movie palace. The panels of men in uniform are by John J. Szaton.

Illinois National Guard, Thirty-Third Division—Northwest Armory

Humboldt and Kedzie Blvds. and Logan Square

No part of the twenty-eight-mile boulevard system offers more pleasure than the drive from Humboldt Park to Logan Square, a trip that would have been even more pleasant at a nineteenth-century pace. The 250-foot-wide roadways were designed with central "carriage drives" and service roads framed by formal lines of elm and catalpa trees. The roadway widens to 400 feet at Palmer Square, a popular raceway for nineteenth-century carriage drivers and cyclists.

64 2224 N. Kedzie Blvd.

1915, JEAN B. ROHM & SON

A stolid square facade is enlivened by inventive Art Nouveau stone trim, especially the cartoonish human face.

65 Peter M. Zuncker House

2312 N. Kedzie Blvd.

1911, HUEHL & SCHMID

The quirkiness of the unusual dormer, with its ski slope profile, ornaments a conservative Prairie School design.

66 2350 N. Kedzie Blvd.

(Chicago Norske Club)

1916, GIAVER & DINKELBERG

The stylized dragons and hefty brackets of this heavily altered building are borrowed from Norwegian vernacular architecture.

Chicago Norske Club (now 2350 N. Kedzie Blvd.)

67 William Nowaczewski House

2410 N. Kedzie Blvd.

1897, ARCHITECT UNKNOWN

One can only wonder at the appetite for display that funded this virtuoso panorama of carved limestone. Flemish stepped gables, a medieval crenellated tower, Gothic crockets and window hood molds, and classical capitals and modillions compete for attention on the ashlar front.

68 Illinois Centennial Monument

Logan Square

1918, HENRY BACON, ARCH.; EVELYN BEATRICE LONGMAN, SCULPTOR

Around the base range Native Americans, explorers, workers, and farmers, an honor roll of citizens from Illinois's first century of statehood. Longman frequently collaborated with Bacon, the designer of the Lincoln Memorial in Washington, D.C.

69 Logan Blvd. Graystones

After the Fire and through the early 1890s, architects experimented with a variety of decorative sedimentary stones, from yellow Joliet-Lemont limestone to Minnesota's pink Kasota stone to the dark red sandstones of the northern Wisconsin shores of Lake Superior. But by the mid-1890s, Chicago's proximity by rail to Indiana's limestone quarries and a shift to simpler styles had created a demand for Bedford limestone not only among developers of skyscrapers and mansions but also among first-generation citizens building homes and flats.

The ace of sedimentary stones, limestone is hard and durable, takes carving beautifully, and holds its crisp lines even through Chicago's vicious freeze-thaw cycles. Smooth or rusticated, it weathers well, discoloring little and adapting to any style of masonry.

Logan Blvd. has the city's finest and most easily viewed collection of graystones. Classical detailing abounds, as at **2955** (1908, DOUGLAS S. PENTECOST) and **2947, 2949,** and **2951** (1907, ALBERT J. FISCHER). Groups are frequently built to a uniform height, usually with roofline emphasis above the bay. Checkerboard patterning, alternating solids and open spaces, is popular for balcony walls. Curious amalgams abound: at **2959** (1909, HERMANN J. GAUL) the porch piers are embellished with stripes that are apparently Prairie School at

2959 W. Logan Blvd. (Logan Blvd. Gray-stones)

3024 W. Logan Blvd. (Logan Blvd. Gray-stones)

the corners but become meander patterns on the central piers. Classical and Gothic details combine at **2715** and **2741** (1905, BURTAR & GASSMANN), which bracket **2735** and its pronounced Richardsonian Romanesque porch arch. Even the grandest buildings are flats masquerading as houses, like the immense gabled and balconied examples at **2820** (1904, FRED & JOHN AHLSCHLAGER) and **3024** (1908, JOHN AHLSCHLAGER).

Because of limestone's durability, few elements have been replaced on these homes, which retain unusual integrity. The front porches and steps alone deserve landmark designation—perhaps as a historic Stoop District, to celebrate the six- to eight-inch-wide railings and eight-foot-wide treads.

70 John Rath House

2701 W. Logan Blvd.

1907, GEORGE W. MAHER

The low, Prairie School profile and characteristic Maher detailing, such as the flanged segmental arch shapes of the entrance bay and doorway, are resolutely individual. The floral-patterned art glass is remarkable, as is the carved wood and stone. Under the exaggeratedly deep eaves of the low, hipped roof, the curious boulevard facade features impressive second-floor art-glass windows across the immense porch opening.

Apartments for John Gerson

71 Apartments for John Gerson

2934–2936 W. Logan Blvd.

1909, FREDERICK R. SCHOCK

The Art Nouveau doorway leads through a mosaic-lined hall to Craftsman-style apartments lavishly decorated with art glass and decorative tiles. The stacked porches make the facade rhythmic while capturing the boulevard's beauty for outdoor living rooms.

In 2010, the Chicago Park District created a skate park under the Kennedy Expressway at Logan Blvd. and Western Ave. and commissioned the **Silver-surf Gate** *by artist Lucy Slivinski.*

72 Green Exchange (Vassar Swiss Underwear Co. Building)

2545 W. Diversey Ave.

1914, 1924, WESTERN ADDITION,
L. G. HALLBERG & CO.

2012, REHABILITATION, HARTSHORNE PLUNKARD ARCHITECTURE

Two centuries of innovation are represented in this building. Architect Hallberg specialized in factories of reinforced concrete frame construction (which overtook the heavy-timber frame around 1900) and held more than a thousand patents related to concrete flooring and foundations. Client Vassar Swiss was known for improving the fit and comfort of "union suits for gentlemen" and boasted that the factory would have "the finest knitting mill in the world." The latest incarnation is a LEED platinum home for a variety of green businesses that claims to be the largest such facility in the country. The four-story tower that once housed a water tank and sported a clock on each side now overlooks a rooftop organic garden and future restaurant.

Villa District

this historic Villa District, stipulating that purchasers build single-family homes "of bungalow appearance." Two popular types appear here. The Chicago bungalow is narrow, long, and built of brick with a side entrance; it is represented at **3700 N. Avers Ave.** and on the west side of the **3600 block of N. Hamlin Ave.** The California bungalow is usually wider and has a front entrance, an open front porch, wide eaves, and more varied materials; **3700 N. Springfield Ave.** (1920, JOHN C. CHRISTENSEN) is a good example. Prairie School touches enliven **3640 N. Avers Ave.** (1912, HATZFELD & KNOX), while generic Sullivanesque ornament, such as that on many Irving Park Rd. storefronts, graces the facade at **3608 N. Avers Ave.** (1917, HARLEV & AGA).

73 Grover Cleveland Public School

3850 N. Albany Ave.
1910, DWIGHT H. PERKINS

The bold, almost intimidating massing is warmed by bands of subtly colored brick that run like a tapestry along the edges of the elevations.

74 Independence Park Bungalow

(John L. Coppersmith House)
3900 N. Hamlin Ave.
1920, BENEDICT BRUNS
2012, RESTORATION, BAILEY EDWARD ARCHITECTURE

This sizeable bungalow received a top-to-bottom green restoration and remains open to the public as a showcase of sustainability and preservation strategies. Many of the replacement clay roof tiles came from the Chicago Park District's stock. The house had been purchased by the Irving Park District in 1929 as part of its park enlargement plan and used as the Woman's Club House. Architect Bruns designed an almost identical bungalow at **2839 W. Wilson St.**

75 Villa District

Bounded by Addison St., Hamlin Ave., Avondale Ave., and the alley east of Pulaski Rd.

In 1907, Albert Haentze and Charles M. Wheeler subdivided the land of

76 Disney II Magnet School

(Irving Park Public School)
3815 N. Kedvale Ave.
1912, DWIGHT H. PERKINS

Best viewed from the corner of Grace St., the assembly hall is treated like a separate block, with massing similar to a Louis H. Sullivan bank.

77 3800 N. Keeler Ave.

BEFORE 1870, ARCHITECT UNKNOWN

The earliest houses on these blocks can be identified by their brick foundations. This delicate villa combines Gothic Revival (steeply pitched gabled roofs), Italianate (high corner tower), and Second Empire (mansard roof) elements.

78 Charles N. Loucks House

3926 N. Keeler Ave.
1889, CLARENCE H. TABOR

Despite alterations, this house remains one of the area's finest Queen Annes, especially because of its rich art glass and idiosyncratically capped turret.

79 Ropp-Grabill House

4132 N. Keeler Ave.

BEFORE 1871, ARCHITECT UNKNOWN

This lovely Italianate house still has its cupola, an ornamental feature useful as a chimney for drawing fresh air up through the house.

80 Stephen A. Race House

3945 N. Tripp Ave.

CA. 1870, ARCHITECT UNKNOWN

This Italianate house originally faced Irving Park Rd. but was turned on the lot in 1905.

81 Carl Schurz High School

3601 N. Milwaukee Ave.

1908–10, DWIGHT H. PERKINS
1915, ADDITION, ARTHUR F. HUSSANDER
1924, ADDITION, JOHN C. CHRISTENSEN
1993–2000, RENOVATIONS, ROSS BARNEY & JANKOWSKI

Schurz High School is an ideal model for urban development and for its expression in architectural form.

Commissioned by a reform-minded school board headed by Jane Addams, the project was one highlight of a broad program for rescuing the immigrant poor from the ignorance and isolation engendered by the industrial city. One revolutionary aspect of this program was linking the development of schools with the development of neighborhood parks. In 1904, Perkins, in partnership with landscape designer Jens Jensen, had written Chicago's first citywide park plan, promoting a network of "breathing holes" that would bring the social and health benefits of natural landscapes to the common citizen. Perkins was thus the ideal choice to serve as the Board of Education's architect, a position that enabled him to bring these qualities to the expanding school system.

Before 1905, Chicago's typical Dickensian public school was a poorly lighted and ventilated box, set into the city grid with no significant playgrounds. Toilet facilities were archaic and located in the basement. The forty-odd schools that Perkins designed between 1905 and 1910 brought grass and trees, sunlight and fresh air, safety from fire, and good sanitation.

At the same time that these functional transformations were taking place, a similar revolution was developing in the art of architecture. A circle of young architects—among them, Perkins, Frank Lloyd Wright, Hugh M. G. Garden, Purcell & Elmslie, Walter Burley Griffin, Pond & Pond, and Robert Spencer— transformed the concepts of the Arts and Crafts movement into the indigenous Prairie School.

Schurz High School represents the translation of what was mainly a domestic vocabulary into an institutional one. A centralized composition that telescopes out from a dominant center, it sits astride its site. Its syncopation of horizontal sills and eaves with vertical piers, together with its hovering

Carl Schurz High School

roofs and earth-toned brick–and–terra-cotta trim, place it squarely among the contemporaneous Prairie School explorations undertaken by Perkins's colleagues. The interiors and decoration are somewhat generic Prairie designs. Lighting fixtures, trim, and other details are highly geometric, often reflecting stylized natural forms; the auditorium, which has benefited from more recent alterations, was a cubic volume with spatial, planar, and linear transparencies similar to—if not as bold as—Wright's spectacular Unity Temple.

Carl Schurz High School asserted that the urban public school belonged much higher on the architectural hierarchy than had been allowed. Beyond its task of providing a safe, healthy, and beautiful place to learn, it towers over the trees, sheltering the entire community, an immense Prairie house for the new citizens of its immigrant, working-class neighborhood.

—ERIC EMMETT DAVIS

82 John Gray House
4362 W. Grace Ave.

BEFORE 1870, ARCHITECT UNKNOWN

The nearby Chicago, Milwaukee & St. Paul Railroad station was named Grayland after this early settler, as was the neighborhood created when his farm was subdivided in 1873 and this country villa became a suburban home.

83 Sears, Roebuck & Co.
4730 W. Irving Park Rd.

1938, NIMMONS, CARR & WRIGHT

In the early 1930s, Sears established a department to design stores built around the presentation of merchandise; this was one of the first five constructed to the company's specifications. Intended as a kind of transparent billboard, windows were for display, not illumination; products inside were better lit artificially. The plain, vaguely Art Moderne concrete facades provide a backdrop for these windows and for a giant logo.

84 4839 W. Irving Park Rd.
(Peoples Gas Co.—Irving Park Store)

1926, GEORGE GRANT ELMSLIE
AND HERMANN V. VON HOLST

Elmslie was Louis H. Sullivan's chief draftsman, and this finely carved facade shows his mastery of the Sullivanesque ornamental style. Bedford limestone blooms in delicately embellished carvings atop the side piers and across the cornice.

Within a mile of this area are two unusual houses by Walter Burley Griffin, a leading Prairie School architect (entries 85–86).

85 Karl Stecher House
4840 W. Pensacola Ave.

1910, WALTER BURLEY GRIFFIN

The soaring roof seems poised for takeoff from its ground-hugging base. Horizontal board-and-batten siding, stucco, and corner windows with geometric mullions are prominent Prairie School motifs.

86 Harry V. Peters House
4731 N. Knox Ave.

1906, WALTER BURLEY GRIFFIN

A broad side-gabled roof dominates this small house, with eaves extending far beyond the wall plane. The front door is tucked into a tunnellike entry passage.

4839 W. Irving Park Rd. (Peoples Gas Co.— Irving Park Store)

CHICAGO-O'HARE
INTERNATIONAL AIRPORT

In June 1942, the federal government bought 1,000 acres surrounding the small Orchard Place Airport to establish the Douglas Aircraft Co. factory, which built C-54 transport planes there during World War II. In 1945, an urgent search to replace Midway Airport, then the world's busiest, led to this wartime factory site. Although it was located fifteen miles northwest of the Loop and would require changes to the existing infrastructure of streets and railroads, it offered the best chance for rapid development. The federal government gave the site to the city, retaining 280 acres for the Army Air Force, and the first commercial flight took off the following year. In 1948, city engineer Ralph H. Burke published his phased master plan for a commercial airport, which was renamed in 1949 to commemorate Edward H. "Butch" O'Hare, a flying ace lost over the Pacific in 1942. *Orchard* lives on, however, in *ORD*, the call letters appearing on all inbound luggage tags.

The introduction of commercial jet service in Europe in 1952 and the anticipated debut of American jets demanded a facility with different terminal and concourse configurations as well as longer runways. By 1955, city money had funded the rerouting of railroads and highways as well as construction of a terminal building, new runways, and a control tower, enabling several airlines to operate regularly scheduled flights. In 1956, recently elected Mayor Richard J. Daley invited the architectural and engineering firm Naess & Murphy (which became C. F. Murphy Assocs. in 1957 and Murphy/Jahn in 1981) to examine the existing master plan for O'Hare development. More important, Daley established an airport funding mechanism whereby landing fees would be used to pay revenue bonds, allowing a series of connecting but separate terminals to be constructed.

Naess & Murphy, consulting with others—most notably airport specialists Landrum & Brown—focused on the design concepts of "concentration, consolidation, and connections." The airport's original terminal was the International Terminal, now the site of the United Airlines Terminal. The location of the new terminals (now Terminals 2 and 3) was determined by the airlines' requirements for five two-story concourses, radiating like fingers, with covered accordion ramps to planes. The boarding functions would be on the terminals' upper levels, arrival functions on the lower levels, and the administrative ser-

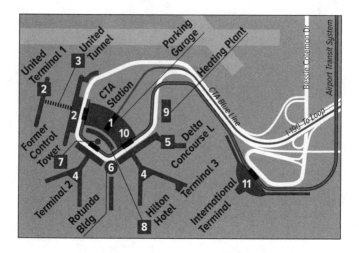

vices on a mezzanine level. The three terminals would form a half hexagon, with parking in the center.

In 1958, as the Air Force Academy was completed in Colorado, many members of the Skidmore, Owings & Merrill design team left that firm to join this project. Among them was Stanislav A. Gladych, who became O'Hare's chief designer. The new terminals were Miesian in concept, exploiting concrete, steel, and specially fabricated glass as the principal exterior materials.

Construction of the $120 million airport, the largest public works project ever undertaken in Chicago, began in 1959. Most of the work was completed within thirty-three months and much of it under adverse weather conditions. In 1946, Ralph Burke had predicted an almost unbelievably high 12 million passengers at O'Hare by 1960, but his estimate proved low: although the airport was still under construction, traffic that year topped 13 million.

As the airlines added jets, operations shifted from Midway to O'Hare, serving passengers from temporary facilities that were quickly demolished as the project progressed. Construction included two terminals, a restaurant pavilion, an underground utilities tunnel, a fire station, a fuel farm, two new runways, a post office, a telephone exchange, a heating plant, and hangars. Existing runways, portions of which are still in use, were reinforced and lengthened in their east–west configuration, and the parking lot was enlarged. The design was unusually consistent throughout, from baggage handling to furnishings and signage, with high-quality materials and craftsmanship.

At the airport's March 1963 dedication, Mayor Daley hailed the terminals as an "engineering and administrative wonder," and they have proved durable and surprisingly flexible, even under post-9/11 security conditions. The adjacent terminals are now connected only for ticketed passengers, and the amenities are located beyond security checkpoints.

Increasing traffic and bigger planes have constantly challenged the terminal facilities. Initiated by the city's Dept. of Aviation, O'Hare's current configuration was forged in the $2 billion O'Hare Development Plan for 1982–95. Improvements made in accordance with that plan include the United Airlines Terminal and the separate International Terminal. These expanded terminal areas are linked to parking facilities by the Airport Transit System (ATS), an automated, high-speed people mover, 3.2 miles long with five stations at each of the terminals and the parking lot. American Airlines acquired the G Concourse and rebuilt it as designed by Teng & Assocs.; it now has six clerestory vaults and more capacity for American's aircraft. A new $28 million Federal Aviation Administration prototype control tower, embedded in front of the former restaurant rotunda building, was designed by Holmes & Carver of California and customized with a glass skin by Murphy/Jahn; it opened in 1996. The old control tower remains in place, now used for managing airfield operations.

Concern about O'Hare's congestion again became a national issue in the 1990s, leading to the announcement of the $10 billion World Gateway program in 1998. In addition to reconfigured runways, plans featured two new terminals, gate modifications at Terminals 2 and 3, a new maintenance facility, hangars and cargo depots, parking for the International Terminal, and extension of the ATS. T6-Partners, a consortium led by Bechtel Infrastructure Corporation, had completed 30 percent of the design of the first terminal when the project was put on hold by the financially strapped airlines in October 2002.

Chicago-O'Hare International Airport remains a design gateway to the city with the implementation of numerous improvements and a major modernization program. Murphy/Jahn upgraded Terminals 2 and 3 with a new curtain wall and metal canopy to improve the drop-off process. exp (formerly Teng) has improved interiors in those terminals and provided elegant service buildings. A $6.6 billion modernization plan to reconfigure runways requires additional control towers, so in 2009, Parsons designed a north tower, and exp has designed a south tower and offices scheduled to open in 2015.

—ANNE ROYSTON

CTA—O'Hare Station

O'Hare is exciting on many levels and is well integrated, with connecting terminals, underground moving sidewalks, and the ATS. It is easier on Chicagoans, who never change flights here, than on out-of-towners, who are frequently seen sprinting across the great plains of terrazzo to make a connecting flight. But the airport is logical, well signed, and suitable for an indoor walking tour.

1 CTA—O'Hare Station

1984, CITY OF CHICAGO, DEPT. OF PUBLIC WORKS, BUREAU OF ARCHITECTURE; MURPHY/JAHN, ASSOC. ARCH.

If only air travel could live up to the glamour of this subway terminal! The backlit glass-block walls undulate slowly to deaden sound and please the eye. The abrupt transition into the basement of the parking garage is eased by the Jahn-designed wall treatments.

2 United Airlines Terminal 1 Complex

1982–88, MURPHY/JAHN; A. EPSTEIN & SONS, ASSOC. ARCH.

United's terminal is that rarest of species, an instant landmark: conspicuously, singularly, and clearly an expression of its time, place, and function.

Any terminal initially designed to serve 35 million passengers a year would have to be conspicuous, but designer Helmut Jahn and his colleagues confounded expectations by refusing to match the two handsome structures already in place around O'Hare's tight U-shaped core—a move that would have completed the three-part configuration as originally conceived. Far from being capricious, the new architectural expression derived from changes in air travel. In the early jet age, terminal designers had used the logic of railroad and bus stations, with their large waiting rooms in which passengers arrived, bought tickets, and waited to depart. Such configurations proved unsatisfactory as air traffic grew and as greater distances between ticket counters and planes encouraged passengers to cluster at woefully underscaled gates.

One way out of the impasse, used by Eero Saarinen at Dulles International Airport outside Washington, D.C., was to reinforce the terminal's centrality and to provide access to aircraft with shuttle buses. Although this approach created a magnificent architectural space, it raised new functional problems and ducked the issue of using architectural form to express the linkage between automobile and airplane. The more common solution was to decentralize, pulling apart terminals so that cars could deliver passengers close to airplanes. At its extreme, this technique produced Dallas–Fort Worth, one of the nation's newer and more impressive airports. But the enormous distances between terminals created functional problems, and the possibility of significant interior spaces was almost ruled out.

United Airlines Terminal 1 Complex

United's terminal represents a cross between the two approaches. It is necessarily compact because of its position within the tight O'Hare horseshoe, but it is split into two main concourses connected by an underground tunnel to increase the interface with airplanes. Its longer, lower profile along the curb gives maximum access to automobiles.

The straightforward, steel-framed simplicity of the earlier terminals is brilliantly fused with a more elaborate development of the building's section and a richer palette of materials. The resulting monumentality is as grand as Dulles's but much lighter and more luminous. It also expresses more directly the reality of the contemporary airport as the place where the automobile meets the plane.

—ROBERT BRUEGMANN

3 United Airlines Terminal Pedestrian Tunnel

Connecting Concourses B and C is an 860-foot-long pedway submerged thirty-five feet below the apron with its parked and taxiing jets. An integral part of the United complex, it is a gigantic version of the undulating glass-walled tube of the CTA's O'Hare Station. The colored walls ripple over white vertical bands symbolizing trees whose canopies cover the walkways. The passage compels forward motion with a four-lane moving sidewalk and a neon-on-Dexedrine ceiling sculpture, Michael Hayden's *Thinking Lightly.*

4 Terminals 2 and 3; Concourses E, F, G, H, and K

1961, C. F. MURPHY ASSOCS.
1990, AMERICAN AIRLINES CONCOURSES H AND K REMODELING, KOBER/BELLUSCHI AND WELTON BECKET ASSOCS.
1995, AMERICAN AIRLINES CONCOURSE G REMODELING, TENG & ASSOCS.

5 Delta Airlines Concourse L

1982, PERKINS & WILL; MILTON PATE & ASSOCS., ASSOC. ARCH.

Originally identical, the concrete-framed, column-free, 770-foot-long terminals spin off the Rotunda. Specially formulated tinted glass, terrazzo floors, and Charles Eames–designed waiting-area chairs have

O'Hare Heating Plant

worn exceptionally well, visually and practically. Because of changes in baggage handling, ticketing, and seat-assignment procedures, passengers now spend less time in the terminals and more time in the concourses. E and F are no fun; they are still spartan 1960s in style. By comparison, the concourses stamped by a particular airline's signature (and money) look sybaritic: waiting travelers linger in a variety of bars, restaurants, stores, and spruced-up lounges. American Airlines' Concourses H and K, started by one firm and finished by another, are pleasant but read as a weak echo of the stunning United Airlines Terminal. American's G Concourse is more original and better communicates the sense of imminent flight. Delta Airlines' expansive steel-framed Concourse L was the first of the 1980s generation. Its greater width allows more spacious passage as well as more efficient handling at the ground level. The glass-walled gate at the far end is popular with plane watchers.

6 Rotunda Building
1962, C. F. MURPHY ASSOCS.
When O'Hare opened, jet travel was a spectator sport as well as a means of transportation. The Rotunda, with its bars, restaurants, and expansive views, was the airport's social center. The circular building linking Terminals 2 and 3 and Concourse G not only relieves the rectilinearity but is also a practical connecting shape. To enhance circulation, the building is column-free, with a precast-concrete slab roof suspended by steel cables from a central steel ring—Chicago's only such structural tour de force. C. F. Murphy's young designer of the Rotunda was Gertrude Lempp Kerbis, one of a handful of women in the male-dominated profession at that time.

7 Former Control Tower
1970, I. M. PEI
O'Hare's original central nervous system was built from Pei's prototype designed for the Federal Aviation Administration. The glass bubble 200 feet in the air was the radome.

8 O'Hare Hilton Hotel
1972, C. F. MURPHY ASSOCS.
The slight curve relieves its immense (720-foot) length.

9 Heating Plant
1961, C. F. MURPHY ASSOCS.
Another Stanislav Gladych design, this is Chicago Modern at its best. Considered O'Hare's finest Miesian building, it undergoes a transformation at night, when the dark glass curtain wall vanishes and the mechanical equipment inside appears as if on a giant TV screen.

10 Parking Garage
1973, C. F. MURPHY ASSOCS.
The largest construction contract ever awarded by the city and the world's largest garage at the time of its completion, it offers a total of seventy-nine acres of parking on six levels.

O'Hare International Terminal

11 International Terminal

1993, PERKINS & WILL

Long underserved at O'Hare, the international airlines fill this gateway building. The gentle arc of the long curvilinear roof recalls old hangars while evoking an architecture of movement. The transparency, intended to enhance the traveler's orientation and conserve energy, makes the terminal dazzling at night.

WEST SIDE AND OAK PARK

see West Town map, p. 264

Kinzie

Carroll

Fulton

Walnut

Lake

Randolph

Maypole

19 Horner Homes

Maypole

Washington

Warren

United Center

Madison

22

CTA Ashland Station

15

Gilman House

17

Harrison Monument

13

16

First Baptist Congregational

Harvest Commons

Belt

Western

see Garfield Park map, p. 316

Metropolitan Missionary Baptist **18**

Manning Branch Library **20**

220-230 S Hoyne **21**

Monroe

Wilcox

Oakley

Belt

Leavitt

Hamilton

Seeley

Damen

Hoyne

Honore

Wood

Hermitage

Paulina

Pond House

Nye House

30

Church of the Epiphany **31**

Chalmers House **32**

Gladys

Malcolm X College

51

Ogden

Eisenhower Expwy I-290

700 Block S Claremont

59

Flournoy

Chicago Medical Center **60**

CORE Center **61**

Former Cook Co Hospital

65

67

Rush Univ Medical Center

62

64

66

Flournoy

Bowler St Row Houses

Stroger Hospital

Lexington

56

57

801-811 S Oakley

52-54

63

Vietnam Survivors Memorial

55

Bowler

Polk

Univ of Illinois College of Medicine

68

Wood

Paulina

Marshfield

Ashland

Belt

Claremont

Taylor

Fillmore

Ogden

Chicago Hope Academy

Hamilton

Hoyne

Seeley

UIC Outpatient Care Center **69**

Hermitage

58

Claremont Cottages

Grenshaw

Roosevelt

70

FBI **71**

13th

Washburne

72

Chicago Children's Advocacy Center

Wolcott

Illinois Center for Rehabilitation & Education

Hastings

14th

14th Pl

Western

see Lawndale map, p. 360

Damen

Wolcott

Wood

16th

17th

18th

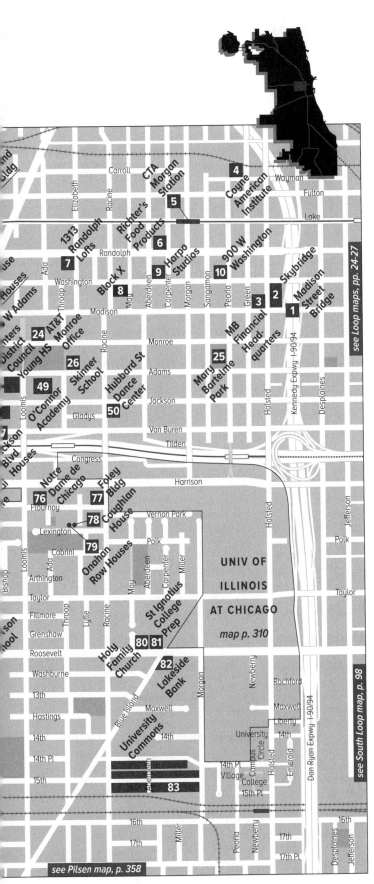

Carroll

Elizabeth

Racine

CTA Morgan Station

Wayman

4 Coyne American Institute

Fulton

5

Lake

1313 Randolph Lofts

Ada

Richter's Food Products

6

Randolph

900 W Washington

Skybridge

see Loop maps, pp. 24–27

7

Washington

9 Harpo Studios

10

Carpenter

Morgan

Sangamon

Peoria

Green

3

2

Madison Street Bridge

Block X

8

Aberdeen

May

Madison Street Bridge

Houses

Throop

W Adams

District

24 AT&T Monroe Office

Council

26

Young HS

Madison

1

MB Financial Head-quarters

Kennedy Expwy I-90/94

Desplaines

Monroe

25

49 O'Connor Academy

Skinner School

Hubbard St Dance Center

Adams

Mary Bartelme Park

Loomis

Jackson

50

Gladys

Jackson

Van Buren

Halsted

Blvd

Tilden

Houses

Congress

Notre Dame de Chicago

76

77 Foley Bldg

Harrison

Halsted

Jefferson

Flournoy

78 Coughlan House

Vernon Park

Lexington

Polk

Polk

Cabrini

79 Onahan Row Houses

Ada

Arthington

May

Aberdeen

Carpenter

Miller

UNIV OF ILLINOIS AT CHICAGO

map p. 310

Taylor

Bishop

Loomis

Taylor

Fillmore

Throop

Lytle

Racine

Grenshaw

St Ignatius College Prep

Roosevelt

80 **81**

Washburne

Holy Family Church

82 Lakeside Bank

Newberry

Rochford

see South Loop map, p. 98

13th

Morgan

Hastings

Maxwell

Maxwell

14th

Blue Island

Liberty

14th Pl

University Commons

14th

University

14th

Campus Circle

Dan Ryan Expwy I-90/94

15th

Aberdeen

14th Pl Village

College

Halsted

Emerald

83

15th Pl

16th

Mitter

Peoria

Newberry

17th

Desplaines

Jefferson

17th

17th Pl

see Pilsen map, p. 358

NEAR WEST SIDE

The Near West Side is a patchwork of past and present, with historic blocks separated by vast stretches of urban renewal and pockets of blight. From a Civil War–era residence and church to converted industrial lofts and modern institutional complexes, the area displays the cycles of growth, decline, and rebirth that characterize mature industrial cities. Exclusive Victorian residential districts that devolved into blight have been reborn, while immigrant ghettos have yielded to modern university buildings.

The area is split east–west by the Eisenhower Expressway (I-290), completed in 1960. To the south, the former immigrant area around Hull House continues to be replaced by the growing University of Illinois at Chicago, which demolished the historic Maxwell St. Market for redevelopment. A pocket of an Italian neighborhood survives between this campus and the massive Medical Center, which occupies the half mile from Ashland Blvd. west to Damen Ave. Modern residential construction fills the eastern flank of the Medical Center, while the gentrifying Tri-Taylor Historic District forms its western boundary.

North of the Eisenhower Expressway, the expanding central business district grows toward Greek Town on Halsted St. and the Randolph St. Market area, where most of the wholesale grocers have been replaced by trendy restaurants. Industrial loft buildings predominate: many of them have been converted to residences, offices, and art galleries. Historic districts near Union Park and along Jackson Blvd. recall some of Chicago's premier Gilded Age addresses. West of this narrow strip are vast stretches of vacant land, parking, and replacement housing built during the construction of the United Center. As in other areas, new town houses have replaced public housing high-rises with lower-scaled developments. Churches represent a wide variety of faiths and provide stability amid the whirling winds of the Near West real estate market.

The Near West Side has witnessed immigrant struggle at Hull House and immigrant success in Tri-Taylor, Yankee prosperity along Ashland Ave., and 1960s racial strife and frustration along Madison St. The area reflects the social engineering implicit in large-scale urban renewal at the University of Illinois campus and affirms Chicago's enduring commercial vitality in the Randolph St. Market. Eternally half-made and half-mad, the Near West Side is Chicago's private face, a thousand miles distant from its lakefront profile.

—VINCENT MICHAEL

1 Madison St. Bridge
Madison St. and the
Kennedy Expressway
1996, DESTEFANO & PARTNERS

This bridge was a prototype for the other bridges over the Kennedy. The red handrail sports motifs drawn from the Chicago flag, and a curbside barrier wall protects pedestrians. Unique to this bridge is the decorative fascia mounted with a strip of 300 bright blue pinpoint lamps. The bridge was rebuilt in this decorative style just in time for the 1996 Democratic National Convention, which was held farther west on Madison in the United Center. When the convention was coming and the Chicago Bulls were winning, local wags called this bridge the Road to Oz.

2 Skybridge
1 N. Halsted St.
2003, PERKINS & WILL

This residential high-rise is so far west of the bulk of downtown skyscrapers that it is a powerful sculptural presence from almost any direction. The building's two towers are connected by glass-enclosed walkways. The facades are rich compositions with opaque and transparent, solid and void elements coming to a balance. The giant roof trellis creates a distinct profile and shelter for outdoor recreation and entertainment.

3 MB Financial Headquarters
800 W. Madison St.
2005, BOOTH HANSEN

This cleanly detailed crystalline box makes the most of its corner location near the freeway with a logo-laden red cube that pops out of the roof. Looking like a scaled-down version of its skyscraper brethren on Wacker Dr., the building has large expanses of very clear glass at lobby level and tinted glass trimmed with stainless steel on the upper stories.

4 Coyne American Institute
330 N. Green St.
2005, BOOTH HANSEN

The concept of building as billboard is given a new twist in this low-budget educational facility tucked in an out-of-the-way location. Atop each of the five steel piers that support an overhanging roof is a giant letter, collectively spelling out *Coyne*.

5 CTA—Morgan Station
958 W. Lake St.
2012, ROSS BARNEY ARCHITECTS

Shimmering by day, glowing by night, this El station suits the glamorous but gritty character of the Fulton Market District. A more generous budget allowed for materials and design features that are value-engineered out of most transit projects. A glass-enclosed bridge links the two towers and offers million-dollar skyline views.

Richter's Food Products

6 Richter's Food Products
1040 W. Randolph St.
1933, H. PETER HENSCHIEN

This rare local example of an Art Deco factory produced sausages as well as smoked and boiled meats; Henschien's specialty was meatpacking facilities. The closely spaced piers frame striking geometric designs; the elegant entrances are framed in black terra-cotta flecked with gold.

7 1313 Randolph Street Lofts
(Chicago Florists' Center)
1313 W. Randolph St.
1928, FOX & FOX
2012, CONVERSION TO RESIDENTIAL, HARTSHORNE PLUNKARD ARCHITECTURE

Large Art Deco posies grace this concrete loft structure, which concentrated the wholesale floral trade in the Randolph St. Market area of meat and produce distributors.

8 Block X
1141–1151 W. Washington St., 15, 23 and 27 N. Racine St., 16, 24, and 26 N. May St., and the alley north of Madison St.
1999, PAPPAGEORGE/HAYMES

CTA—Morgan Station

Block X

By the late 1990s, developers ran short of the most suitable industrial loft buildings for residential conversions, so new construction resumed in this area after a hiatus of almost a century. While many of these structures are literal re-creations of converted factories, this project is clearly modern even as the materials and massing respond to its context. Parking is hidden beneath the buildings and grassy interior courtyard.

9 Harpo Studios
1058 W. Washington Blvd.
1989, REMODELING, NAGLE, HARTRAY & ASSOCS.

Pieces of this block-long Art Deco Revival office and studio complex have served as a stable, a bowling alley, and a film studio. The remodeled whole is owned by the palindromic Oprah (read it backward) Winfrey, who taped her popular talk show here until it went off the air in 2011.

10 900 W. Washington St.
2011, 4240 ARCHITECTURE

A metal screen—pierced, angled, or otherwise ornamented—has become a popular device for jazzing up tired facades, but in this new building it serves the functions of providing privacy for the law firm's clients (at least from the waist up) and filtering the southern sun while admitting ample daylight. The laser-cut pattern of per-forations is meant to evoke a strand of carbon fiber, a key component in the Ferraris beloved by the lawyer who commissioned the building.

Union Park
Lake St., Randolph St., Ogden Ave., Warren Blvd., Ashland Ave.
1853

The history of Union Park reflects the changing fortunes of its neighborhood. In 1853, local landowners seeking to increase the value of their property successfully lobbied the city to make this area a park. Named in honor of the Union cause, the park was the centerpiece of a wealthy residential area. Described in the 1870s as the "Bois de Boulogne of the West Side," it included a band shell, gazebos, and a bridged lagoon. By the 1920s, the surrounding streets were no longer fashionable, and many mansions on Ashland Ave. had become labor union headquarters, lending an interesting twist to the name Union Park.

11 Field House
(West Park Commission Headquarters)
1888, WILLIAM LE BARON JENNEY
1909, NORTH ADDITION, WILLIAM A. OTIS

Jenney's original Shingle Style building has been defaced by subsequent remodelings; only the stair tower suggests his original design. Since

1934, brick facades have concealed the original wood structure. The West Park System was headquartered here from 1888 until it moved to Garfield Park in 1928.

12 Locker and Gym Building
1917, JAMES B. DIBELKA

Most notable is the large pergola of concrete columns.

13 Carter Henry Harrison Monument
1907, FREDERICK C. HIBBARD

A relentless city booster, Harrison was the Richard J. Daley of his era, serving five terms as mayor (1879–87, 1893) and fathering Carter H. Harrison II, who was elected to the post in 1897. The quote on the monument's base, taken from Harrison's October 28, 1893, speech at the World's Columbian Exposition, captures the city's 1890s spirit: "Genius is but audacity, and the audacity of Chicago has chosen a star. It has looked upward to it and knows nothing that it fears to attempt and thus far has found nothing that it cannot accomplish." Later that day, Harrison was assassinated in his home at the southwest corner of Ashland and Jackson Blvds. The statue's pose is mayoral, but the rendition is naturalistic, especially the drape of the trousers and the soft felt hat clutched in the mayor's hand.

14 Harvest Commons Apartments
(Viceroy Hotel; originally Union Park Hotel)
1519 W. Warren Blvd.

1930, BENJAMIN ALBERT COMM
2013, REHABILITATION, LANDON BONE BAKER ARCHITECTS

This gem of an Art Deco apartment hotel had fallen on hard times along with its neighborhood. The gut rehab created transitional and affordable units with an emphasis on sustainability inside and out—a vegetable garden is a key landscape element. The ground floor houses support services that include a teaching kitchen.

15 CTA—Ashland Ave. Station
1601 W. Lake St.

1893, ARCHITECT UNKNOWN

Look north as you cross Ashland Ave. to see a relic of the Metropolitan West Side Elevated Railroad's early days. The station is sided with stamped metal panels and crowned with an ornate metal cupola.

16 First Baptist Congregational Church
(Union Park Congregational Church)
60 N. Ashland Ave.

1869–71, GURDON P. RANDALL

The attenuated spire and yellowed, rusticated Joliet limestone mark one of Chicago's oldest churches. But the prim and dignified Gothic facade won't prepare you for the warm and encircling interior, the oldest remaining amphitheatrical nave in Chicago. The speaker is surrounded by the congregation, in contrast to the celebrant-worshiper division apparent in Catholic and Episcopalian churches. The enormous Kimball organ still joyfully rocks the trussed ceiling during services.

First Baptist Congregational Church

17 William Gilman House

1635 W. Washington Blvd.

1887, LOUIS J. BOURGEOIS

This essay in Gothic is smoothly finished and lavished with crocketed arches, a corner oriel, and an elaborate third-floor dormer.

18 Metropolitan Missionary Baptist Church

(Third Church of Christ, Scientist)
2151 W. Washington Blvd.

1901, HUGH M. G. GARDEN

Garden combined the Greek Revival forms favored by Christian Scientists with his own Prairie Style details, especially the window surrounds on the west facade and the art glass. Gray granite columns have inverted capitals reminiscent of Secessionist architecture and of Wright's Heller House in Hyde Park.

Metropolitan Missionary Baptist Church

19 Henry Horner Homes

W. Washington Blvd., Leavitt St., Lake St., and Damen Ave.

1998, LEAVITT ST. TO HOYNE AVE., SOLOMON CORDWELL BUENZ & ASSOCS.

1999, HOYNE TO DAMEN AVES., JOHNSON & LEE, MASTER ARCH.; BROOK ARCHITECTURE AND HAMMOND BEEBY RUPERT AINGE, ASSOC. ARCHS.

Horner was one of the first Chicago Housing Authority properties to have its high-rises replaced by town houses. It is also an early example of the CHA encouraging a variety of architectural signatures rather than a single look. Architects for the later Westhaven Park development east of Damen Ave. include UrbanWorks; DeStefano & Partners; Cordogan, Clark & Assocs.; and Landon Bone Baker Architects.

20 Chicago Public Library— Mabel Manning Branch

6 S. Hoyne Ave.

1994, ROSS BARNEY & JANKOWSKI

The forty-foot tower glows at night, but even during the day, this small civic gem is a beacon in its busy neighborhood. Directed by the city to give the library a Prairie School appearance, the architects honored that intention while creating a modern composition that holds the street wall and plays off its contrasting horizontal and vertical, rectangular and circular ele-

Chicago Public Library—Mabel Manning Branch

ments. The diversity of spaces and uses within the small building is expressed with varied fenestration and massing.

21 220 through 230 S. Hoyne Ave.

1992, LANDON ARCHITECTS

Dubbed "the houses the Bulls built," this tidy row of capacious two-flats was erected for homeowners displaced by construction of the new United Center. Each is pleasingly neo-Victorian, complete with a low stoop and an embellishing tickle of decoratively laid brick in the gable.

22 United Center

1800 W. Madison St.

1994, HOK SPORTS FACILITIES GROUP

This buttoned-down sports facility is a weak echo of the "madhouse on Madison" that was the old Chicago Stadium. Surrounded by surface parking on three sides, the building extends all the way to the sidewalk on Madison St. and has large windows that provide views in and out of the spacious upper lobbies. Among the long list of staggering statistics about this building is the fact that the "megatruss" roof support system required 3,000 tons of steel.

23 Isaac N. Camp Row Houses

1526–1528 W. Monroe St.

EARLY 1870S, ARCHITECT UNKNOWN

The height of each story diminishes as these exaggeratedly vertical town houses rise; large blocks of Joliet limestone are striated to appear as many stacked, smaller blocks.

24 AT&T—Monroe Office

1340 W. Monroe St.

1932, HOLABIRD & ROOT

This cool, severe, but lovely Art Deco switching office is trimmed with black granite and cast aluminum. Abstract bas-relief panels above the entrance depict the transmission of sound.

25 Mary Bartelme Park

115 S. Sangamon St.

2010, SITE DESIGN GROUP

Named for the first female judge in Illinois, the one-square-block park provides much-needed green space for the many residents of a formerly industrial neighborhood. Low seating walls incorporate fragments of the infirmary that originally occupied the site. At the northwest corner, five stainless steel gates tilt at different angles and, in warm weather, spray a fine mist of water.

26 Mark T. Skinner West Elementary School

1260 W. Adams St.

2009, SCHROEDER MURCHIE NIEMIEC GAZDA-AUSKALNIS ARCHITECTS

In 2007, Mayor Richard M. Daley kicked off a construction boomlet

Mary Bartelme Park

Mark T. Skinner West Elementary School

christened Modern Schools Across Chicago. Schroeder Murchie Niemiec Gazda-Auskalnis was chosen as the elementary school design architect and was also the architect of record for several buildings, including Skinner. The firm designed an L-shaped prototype (the other two are linear and C-shaped) that groups amenities such as the gymnasium and library in a "Community Core" that can be separately accessed outside of school hours. Here, the core is a metal-wrapped tower that boosts the street presence of a building whose classroom wing is oriented toward the park. The library's top-floor location allows it to have large windows that overlook the green roof as well as a salvaged water tower that is now used as a rainwater cistern.

27 Painters District Council 14
1456 W. Adams St.
1956, VITZTHUM & BURNS
A pristine echo of the Art Deco style, this blocky little corner building is one of thirty union headquarters in the neighborhood. It provides an artful show of the beauties of limestone and polished granite—with not a painted surface in sight.

28 1529 W. Adams St.
1888, ARCHITECT UNKNOWN
In the early 1990s, this 520-ton house was purchased for one dollar on the condition that it be relocated from its original site at 1706 W. Jackson Blvd. The arduous move was chronicled by Home and Garden Television (HGTV).

29 Iram Nye House
1535 W. Adams St.
1874, ARCHITECT UNKNOWN
The flat, crisp wall of large unbroken blocks of Joliet limestone is treated like a canvas on which incised ornament is stiffly embroidered. The ornament is a miniaturized element adapted from more lavish, overtly "French"-style homes; incised ornament was also cheaper than carved hood molds and keystones.

30 Walter M. Pond House
1537 W. Adams St.
1879, ARCHITECT UNKNOWN
The profusion of pilasters and engaged columns, together with the mansard roof with its pedimented dormers, mark this as a rare surviving example of a full-blown Second Empire town house.

31 Church of the Epiphany
201 S. Ashland Blvd.
1885, BURLING & WHITEHOUSE
Here is one of Chicago's earliest and best examples of the Richardsonian Romanesque, a style known as Norman in the 1880s. The basic forms are simple and geometric—broad gables, a stocky tower, and roundheaded doors and windows—while the wall surfaces are complex. Rich, ruddy Lake Superior sandstone is carved into rectangles, squares, slivers, voussoirs, and colonnettes that fit together like an intricate jigsaw puzzle. Although the interior has taken some hard hits, including stained-glass theft and water infiltration, it remains a comfortable Victorian cave, punctuated by rows of deep-set windows.

Church of the Epiphany before completion of tower

The wall treatment is most unusual: unglazed terra-cotta tiles in alternating squares of fluid ribbons and pods that seem to have been squeezed from a pastry tube. Against the dark backdrop of wood and terra-cotta, the remaining windows and the Venetian glass mosaic murals in the sanctuary glow softly, visual feasts of Victorian polychromy.

32 William J. Chalmers House
315 S. Ashland Blvd.
1885, TREAT & FOLTZ

Uniform in material but richly varied in form, this house exhibits in stone many Queen Anne elements that are usually executed in wood: a turreted corner tower, windows (some mullioned) of many shapes and sizes, and a complex, irregular roof. Although only brownstone is used, it is carved, rusticated, planed smooth, and set in a checkerboard pattern for the stringcourse.

33 B. Dorr Colby House
1539 W. Jackson Blvd.
1894, RUSSELL B. POWELL

The robust Richardsonian Romanesque personality derives from the prominent turreted entry tower with second-floor loggia.

34 Richard Norman Foster House
1532 W. Jackson Blvd.
1892, PATTON & FISHER

The formula for this elegant limestone Romanesque town house includes a shallow facade, off-center entry, combination of smooth and rusticated stone, eaveless gable, and acanthus leaf carvings.

35 Mortimer and Tapper Houses
1533–1537 W. Jackson Blvd.
1881, ARCHITECT UNKNOWN

The flat fronts and emphasized roofline of these Italianate row houses set the stylistic tone for the developing block.

36 Flora M. Chisholm House
1531 W. Jackson Blvd.
1886, JOHN M. VAN OSDEL

Queen Anne breaks through the Italianate with a broadened bay and two-tone brickwork.

37 Norman Bridge House
1529 W. Jackson Blvd.
1883, ARCHITECT UNKNOWN

38 William Messenger House
1527 W. Jackson Blvd.
1884, ALFRED SMITH

39 Mary J. Dodge Houses
1526–1530 W. Jackson Blvd.
1885, WILLIAM STRIPPELMAN & CO.

These early Queen Anne designs retain the flat fronts and mansard roofs of slightly earlier styles.

40 William P. Henneberry House
1520 W. Jackson Blvd.
1883, FURST & RUDOLPH

The Second Empire facade is ironed almost flat, with shallow pilasters and incised ornament surrounding

William P. Henneberry House

the door and windows. An aggressively overscaled dormer interrupts the mansarded tower.

41 Henry C. Morey House
1519 W. Jackson Blvd.
1884, JOHN J. FLANDERS

Queen Anne exuberance bubbles up at the roofline, with a pink slate mansard and unusual semicircular metal pediments filled with symmetrical flowering plants.

42 John C. Nicol House
1515 W. Jackson Blvd.
1879, ARCHITECT UNKNOWN

The gargantuan blocks of Joliet limestone and the high level of the first floor are hallmarks of one of the block's oldest houses.

43 Andrew T. Merriman House
1516 W. Jackson Blvd.
1884, JOHN M. VAN OSDEL
44 George Ross House
1514 W. Jackson Blvd.
1884, JOHN M. VAN OSDEL

Not a match but balanced, the slopes of the mansard roofs are the perfect foil for the robustly pedimented dormers.

45 Matilda Hale House
1513 W. Jackson Blvd.
1883, L. GUSTAV HALLBERG

Even this three-story residence wears a shallow mansard lid.

46 1506 and 1508 W. Jackson Blvd.
1884, EDWARD BAUMANN

Designed by Baumann for himself,

these are late examples of "marble front" (Joliet stone) Italianates.

47 1501–1509 W. Jackson Blvd.
1882, ARCHITECT UNKNOWN

These Second Empire town houses are united by wide cornices and a broad stringcourse with grape leaf decoration. Lumber merchant Benjamin Franklin Ferguson lived at 1501. In 1905, when he died, he left almost $1 million to establish a fund for public sculpture to be administered by the Art Institute.

Apart from a brief spurt of public and semipublic construction in the late 1920s, there was very little development in the area north of Congress St. for decades. In the early 1970s, three large government-funded projects in the Miesian style (entries 48–49 and 51) put a stamp of brawny modernism on these rough-edged precincts.

48 Whitney M. Young Magnet High School
211 S. Laflin St.
1971, PERKINS & WILL PARTNERSHIP

This steel-framed trio has the cold efficiency of a factory for learning. The enclosed truss bridge spanning Jackson Blvd. links the fine arts building to the south with the academic and physical education buildings.

49 Timothy J. O'Connor Training Academy
(Chicago Police Training Center)
1300 W. Jackson Blvd.
1976, JEROME R. BUTLER JR., CHICAGO CITY ARCH.

When the building was constructed, the courtyard at its center sheltered the Haymarket Riot monument, which had attracted numerous attacks over the years. In 2007, the sculpture was moved to the Chicago Public Safety Headquarters at 3510 S. Michigan Ave.

50 Hubbard St. Dance Center
1147 W. Jackson Blvd.
2006, FACADE RENOVATION, KRUECK & SEXTON ARCHITECTS

A perforated metal veil shimmies and bends around a former automobile showroom, layering extra energy atop silkscreened depictions of dancers. The syncopated rhythm

2148–2158 W. Bowler St.

is created with just three different panel shapes.

51 Malcolm X College
1900 W. Van Buren St.
1971, C. F. MURPHY ASSOCS.
This state-operated junior college was designed to serve a student population of 10,000 as well as the local community. The steel frame has brick-and-glass infill; in contrast to Whitney Young and the Training Academy, the building's structural expression is limited to the first-floor columns. The third floor has two open-air courtyards.

South of the Eisenhower Expressway (I-290), the steady growth of the University of Illinois and the Medical Center has spurred residential redevelopment since the mid-1980s. Historic buildings have been renovated, and clusters of town houses have sprouted. Of special note is the pocket between Polk St., Ogden Ave., and Western Ave., part of the Tri-Taylor Historic District. A "second settlement" community, it received upwardly mobile immigrants graduating from the Maxwell St. area on the Near West Side. Tri-Taylor contains many examples of 1880s working- and middle-class housing (entries 52–59).

52 2125–2133 and
2135–2145 W. Bowler St.
1881, ARCHITECT UNKNOWN
53 2147–2159 and
2136–2146 W. Bowler St.
1882, ARCHITECT UNKNOWN
54 2148–2158 W. Bowler St.
1882, EDBROOKE & BURNHAM

This remarkable ensemble was developed by James L. Campbell. With the exception of the red-brick row houses with Gibbsian quoins framing the windows and doors at 2148–2158, all are Italianate with neoclassical details. The Joliet limestone facades are of massive ashlar blocks, and each row shares a pressed-metal cornice with brackets and dentils.

55 Chicago Hope Academy
(St. Callistus Church)
2189 W. Bowler St.
NORTH BUILDING, 1926,
JOHN G. STEINBACH
The northernmost portion was built as a combination church and school for St. Callistus Parish, with a ground-floor worship space and classrooms above. This pragmatic building type is scattered across Chicago neighborhoods and can be distinguished from regular parochial schools by a tall first floor, ornamental emphasis on the front door, and other ecclesiastical features. The tower here is an unusual embellishment

56 801–811 S. Oakley Blvd.
LATE 1870S, ARCHITECT UNKNOWN
The Italianate row houses at 801 and 811 were moved from a site two blocks north and now bookend similar neighbors.

57 Vietnam Survivors Memorial
815 S. Oakley Blvd.
1987, WILLIAM S. LAVICKA
One of the city's quirkiest pieces of folk art is this assemblage of ten cast-iron columns taken from the interior of the Page Bros. Building and

arranged around a granite marker. Lavicka, a structural engineer, Vietnam veteran, and preservationist, erected the memorial on his property with the help of other volunteer veterans.

58 Claremont Cottages
1000 block of S. Claremont Ave.
1884, ARCHITECT UNKNOWN

Turn west on Grenshaw St. and north on Claremont Ave. for an unexpected delight: a block of small Queen Anne brick cottages. A speculative development by Turner & Bond, they feature projecting gables, dormers, and overhanging eaves with slightly recessed entrances.

Claremont Cottages

59 700 Block of S. Claremont Ave.
1886–87, ARCHITECT UNKNOWN

This is an unusually cohesive streetscape of Queen Anne two-flats. Almost all of them were developed by George N. Hull and feature deep red face brick, stringcoursing, and pressed-metal cornices. Much rehabilitation took place on this block after 1983, when it was added to the National Register of Historic Places as part of the Tri-Taylor Historic District.

60 Chicago Medical Center
Ashland Ave. to Oakley Blvd.;
Congress Pkwy. to Roosevelt Rd.

In 1941, the state legislature created the Chicago Medical Center Commission and empowered it to acquire land on a 305-acre tract surrounding existing medical buildings. The com-

mission was charged with clearing blighted slum areas, allocating sites to medical institutions (five hospitals and ten professional schools), encouraging them to expand their facilities and create new housing for their employees, and apportioning land for small parks. The scheme's promoters envisioned a "Garden of Health," a very different image from what confronts the visitor to this gritty urban complex.

More than a century of health-care architecture is represented here. Most of it is fairly undistinguished, burdened by the strained budgets and ever-changing needs that beat the beauty out of most hospital architecture. But there are a few gems—and several curiosities. Almost every facility has been expanded and remodeled, some of them many times. Only the original architects of major visible sections are noted here.

61 CORE Center
2020 W. Harrison St.
1998, PERKINS & WILL; CAMPBELL
      TIU CAMPBELL, ASSOC. ARCHS.

This specialized outpatient clinic for the treatment of HIV/AIDS and related infectious diseases is organized vertically around a light-filled atrium that serves as a community room. As the floors go up, so does the level of patient treatment, from a first-floor screening clinic behind the curved brick wall to the infusion room at the top of the building, where the most seriously ill benefit from abundant space and daylight.

62 Former Cook County Hospital
1835 W. Harrison St.
1913, PAUL GERHARDT
1914, ADDITION, RICHARD E. SCHMIDT
1916, 1926 ADDITIONS, ERIC E. HALL

In response to lobbying by West Side real estate interests, the county located the area's first hospital here in 1874 as an anchor institution. A replacement hospital was completed in 2002 just to the south, and plans were announced to demolish this classical revival building. A furor ensued, and in 2010 the county agreed to pursue alternatives for adaptive reuse.

63 John H. Stroger Hospital of Cook County

1901 W. Ogden Ave.

2002, CCH DESIGN GROUP (LOEBL SCHLOSSMAN & HACKL, MCDONOUGH ASSOCS., GLOBETROTTERS ENGINEERING CORPORATION, HDR)

An assortment of modules in handsome materials form this replacement for an eighty-nine-year-old hospital. The interconnected modules were arranged to improve patient flow through the complex.

64 Rush–Presbyterian–St. Luke's Cohn Research Building

1753 W. Harrison St.

2000, PERKINS & WILL

65 Rush–Presbyterian–St. Luke's Medical Center Atrium Building

1653 W. Congress Pkwy.

1982, HANSEN LIND MEYER AND SOLOMON CORDWELL BUENZ & ASSOCS.

66 Rush–Presbyterian–St. Luke's Johnston R. Bowman Health Center

West side of S. Paulina St. between Harrison and Polk Sts.

1976, 1977, METZ, TRAIN, OLSON & YOUNGREN

Presbyterian Hospital was established here in 1883 and merged with St. Luke's in 1956. Rush Medical College, the first of its kind in Illinois, was founded in 1837, deactivated in 1942, and revived in 1969 as part of Presbyterian–St. Luke's. Still visible on Congress Pkwy. are the 1888 Presbyterian Hospital (a mangled Queen Anne structure by Stephen V. Shipman) and the 1956 Presbyterian–St. Luke's. The constricted site led to dramatic solutions for the 1970s and 1980s expansions. Paulina St. was closed; the block-long metal-paneled Rush Medical College and Bowman Health Center bestride Harrison St. and the elevated tracks. The El is further enclosed by the Atrium Building, which emulates a modern hotel, with many patient rooms facing pleasant atria.

67 Rush University Medical Center Tower

1620 W. Harrison St.

2011, PERKINS & WILL

The dramatic curves of the bed tower give Rush a powerful identity along the Eisenhower Expressway and bring patient rooms closer to nursing stations. Below is a three-story "interventional platform" that consolidates operating rooms with other treatment areas. The ground-level emergency department includes a bioterrorism preparedness center that can be sealed off from the rest of the hospital. In one of the great ironies of Chicago architecture, this hospital opened while preservationists were losing the battle to save Bertrand Goldberg's Prentice Women's Hospital, which pioneered the concept of a multi-lobed bed tower above a rectilinear base.

Rush University Medical Center Tower

68 University of Illinois College of Medicine Complex

(Research and Educational Hospitals of the State of Illinois)
Bounded by Polk St., Wolcott Ave., Taylor St. and Wood St.

College of Medicine West Addition

(Medical and Dental College and Laboratories)
1853 W. Polk St.
1931, GRANGER & BOLLENBACHER

College of Medicine West

(Research Laboratory & Library)
1819 W. Polk St.
1924, RICHARD E. SCHMIDT,
  GARDEN & MARTIN

Clinical Sciences North Building

(General Hospital and Clinical Institute)
1819 W. Polk St., inside courtyard
1925, RICHARD E. SCHMIDT,
  GARDEN & MARTIN

College of Medicine East

(Medical and Dental College Laboratories)
808 S. Wood St.
1937, GRANGER & BOLLENBACHER

Clinical Sciences Building

(Hospital Addition)
820–840 S. Wood St.
1954, HOLABIRD & ROOT & BURGEE

Neuropsychiatric Institute

912 S. Wood St.
1941, C. HERRICK HAMMOND

Biological Resources Laboratory

(Medical Research Laboratory)
1840 W. Taylor St.
1959, SKIDMORE, OWINGS & MERRILL

The original scheme for this two-square-block complex, developed in 1920 by Richard E. Schmidt, Garden & Martin, was followed closely for the northern half of the site, which was built out by later architects working in an Art Deco–influenced version of the 1920s English Gothic. The south half was to have contained one huge courtyard, but this plan was abandoned in 1930 with the construction of a nurses' residence; the 1954 Hospital Addition further injured the scheme. The hidden treasures among these red-brick buildings are the secluded courtyards. On Polk St. near Wood St., enter the picturesque north courtyard through an arched entryway lined with Works Progress Administration mosaics of astrological motifs. Sculptures of Aesculapius (the Greek god of medicine) and Hygeia (his daughter, the goddess of health) by Edouard Chassaing grace the west end of the court. In the Neuropsychiatric Institute courtyard above the entrance, a bas-relief of a brain is surrounded by names of famous brain researchers.

69 UIC Outpatient Care Center

1801 W. Taylor St.
1999, PERKINS & WILL

This building with fine proportions and muted colors fits gracefully into a neighborhood of buildings of many materials. A three-story, glassy pedestrian bridge over Taylor St. links several facilities and provides a focal point.

UIC College of Medicine Complex

70 Illinois Center for Rehabilitation and Education
1151 S. Wood St.
1965, HARRY WEESE & ASSOCS.

This small-scale village of linked brick buildings has a welcoming presence sorely lacking among its large institutional neighbors.

71 FBI Chicago Field Office
2111 W. Roosevelt Rd.
2006, LOHAN ANDERSON

An incongruous sight along Roosevelt Rd., this complex seems to have been airlifted from a suburban office park. The design achieves an open, welcoming appearance despite the necessary security features.

72 Chicago Children's Advocacy Center
1240 S. Damen Ave.
2001, TIGERMAN MCCURRY ARCHITECTS

To create a nonthreatening, non-institutional environment for the center's young clients, the exterior includes glazed brick in pastel tones, windows shaped as a child would draw them, and, facing the parking lot, a colorful mural by Christine Tarkowski with abstract images of stuffed animals.

73 St. Basil Greek Orthodox Church
(Temple Anshe Sholom)
733 S. Ashland Blvd.
1910, ALEXANDER L. LEVY

The Greek Revival temple front made the synagogue well suited for conversion to a Greek Orthodox church in 1927, after the original congregation had moved to what is now the Independence Blvd. Seventh-Day Adventist Church in Lawndale. The dome, originally ribbed but now asphalt-shingled, gives the building the height of a spired church while maintaining the classical language of the ensemble.

74 Garibaldi Square
1400–1600 W. Harrison St., south side
1984–88, NAGLE, HARTRAY & ASSOCS.

An unfussy low-rise development fits eighty-six town houses, forty-two condominiums, and a hotel onto an irregular 7.5-acre site. The red-brick-and-Indiana limestone buildings fit the neighborhood well.

75 Thomas Jefferson Public School
1522 W. Fillmore St.
1884, JOHN J. FLANDERS

As Board of Education architect, Flanders designed dozens of schools during the 1880s and early 1890s; only a handful from the era before his partnership with William Carbys Zimmerman (1886–98) remain in use. Tall and foreboding, most of them have even lost Flanders's signature Flemish gables, replaced with a flat parapet requiring lower maintenance.

Landon Bone Baker Architects has designed a new **National Museum for Public Housing** *to occupy the rehabilitated shell of the sole remaining building of the demolished Jane Addams Homes at 1322 W. Taylor St.*

76 Notre Dame de Chicago Church
1336 W. Flournoy St.
1887–92, GREGORY VIGEANT
1982, RENOVATION, HISTORIC BOULEVARD SERVICES

French Catholics built this nearly circular church, whose transept walls are almost entirely filled with stained glass. The bronze Virgin Mary atop the dome replaced a lead-coated wooden version struck by lightning.

77 James Foley Building
626 S. Racine Ave.
1889, PATRICK J. KILLEEN

This Queen Anne "flats above the store" sports pressed-metal bays, terra-cotta panels, a cast-iron storefront, and a foliate cornice.

78 John Coughlan House
1246 W. Lexington St.
1871, ARCHITECT UNKNOWN

79 William J. Onahan Row Houses
1254–1262 W. Lexington St.
MID-1870S, ARCHITECT UNKNOWN

The street was an Irish stronghold named Macalister Pl. when these Italianate houses were built. The row houses' huge blocks of yellow Joliet limestone are scored to resemble smaller blocks, a technique that enlivened the surface and saved on labor costs.

William J. Onahan Row Houses

80 Holy Family Church

1080 W. Roosevelt Rd.

1857–59, ATTRIB. TO
  DILLENBURG & ZUCHER
1860, INTERIOR AND FACADE,
  JOHN M. VAN OSDEL
1874, UPPER STEEPLE, JOHN PAUL HUBER
1886, SOUTH ADDITION,
  ARCHITECT UNKNOWN
1991–2002, RESTORATION, OFFICE
  OF JOHN VINCI AND WISS,
  JANNEY, ELSTNER ASSOCS.

A hardy survivor, the church is a tribute to the craftsmanship of neighborhood workers and to the leadership of Jesuits from the parish's founder, the Reverend Arnold J. Damen, to Father George Lane, the head of a 1990s restoration campaign. The phlegmatic German Gothic structure is bent with age; some of the tall Gothic pillars are as much as eighteen inches out of plumb, displaced by the weight of the slate roof. But generations of embellishments crowd the nave and sanctuary. The spired and crocketed wooden reredos (1865), painted white to imitate marble, was crafted by nearby resident Anthony Buscher, a carver of cigar store Indians. The altar front features a folksy Last Supper—down to carved knives and forks.

81 St. Ignatius College Prep

(St. Ignatius College)
1076 W. Roosevelt Rd.

1866–74, TOUSSAINT MENARD
1895, NORTHWEST ADDITION,
  ARCHITECT UNKNOWN

The upstanding and disciplined facade is decidedly French, from the mansard roof to the projecting pavilion, the stringcourses, and the quoining. The formal five-part facade features a columned entry atop a

St. Ignatius College Prep

double-axial staircase. A typical feature of late-nineteenth-century schools is the assembly room or library on the top floor, where a clear span space was structurally easier to include. The fourth floor here contains a fabulous example. Now known as the Brunswick Room, it was originally a natural history museum donated in 1873 by John M. Brunswick, a leading manufacturer of billiard tables and bowling equipment.

The grounds of St. Ignatius feature a trove of architectural fragments from demolished structures, including part of the cornice from Adler & Sullivan's 1894 Stock Exchange Building, bas-reliefs from the Chicago Stadium, and plaques from Art Deco bridge houses on the Ogden Ave. viaduct.

82 Lakeside Bank
(Illinois Regional Library for the Blind and Physically Handicapped)
1055 W. Roosevelt Rd.
1975–78, STANLEY TIGERMAN & ASSOCS., IN ASSOCIATION WITH JEROME R. BUTLER JR., CHICAGO CITY ARCH.
2005, RENOVATION, PAPPAGEORGE/HAYMES

The original design featured bold colors and shapes for the specialized library's patrons. The building fell into disuse before finding new life as a bank. The red walls are now white except for the Blue Island Ave. facade, where a vivid blue sets off the 165-foot-long window whose enigmatic curves represented the library's circulation plan. To provide sufficient daylight, the east wall is now glazed in a pattern that replicates that of the original metal panels. The design of the freestanding drive-up canopy was inspired by the curves and circles of Tigerman's building.

83 University Commons
(South Water Market)
1033–1151 W. 14th Pl. and
1000–1151 W. 15th St.
1925, FUGARD & KNAPP
2007, CONVERSION TO CONDOMINIUMS, PAPPAGEORGE/HAYMES

The property seemed like the ultimate white elephant when it was vacated in 2003 by the wholesale produce market that had moved here from South Water St. seven decades earlier. The six sprawling terra-cotta buildings now house 929 loft condominiums. Loading docks were converted to private outdoor terraces, and new triangular balconies were integrated into an open grid that evokes the original warehouse canopy. New top-floor units are set back far enough to disappear from most vantage points, and parking is mostly hidden in an underground garage.

NEAR WEST SIDE

University of Illinois at Chicago
(University of Illinois at Chicago Circle)
East Campus: Eisenhower Expressway to Roosevelt Rd.; Halsted to Racine Sts.
1965, 1967, SKIDMORE, OWINGS & MERRILL

Hailed as the college of the future when it opened in 1965, UIC is one of Chicago's strongest individual architectural statements—and one of the most violently disliked. The opening salvo was fired by architecture critic M. W. Newman, who shortly after its opening dubbed it "Fortress Illini." The succeeding decades saw no softening of opinion, and an extreme makeover began at the campus core in the mid-1990s and continues well into the twenty-first century.

Designed by Walter A. Netsch Jr., UIC is an unmistakable product of an era proud of grand schemes and social engineering; few college campuses have been so strongly shaped by their original architect. Although many of the social and aesthetic principles that guided the design are now considered outdated, the university itself prospered far beyond original expectations. Planned as an undergraduate branch of the well-established University of Illinois, it became a major research institution, with a third of its 25,000 students enrolled in graduate and professional programs.

The first and most lasting controversy surrounding the school was its location. In 1946, the university had opened a Chicago branch at Navy Pier to provide a two-year college course for returning servicemen. The predicted crush of Baby Boomers created a need for a permanent site for a four-year college;

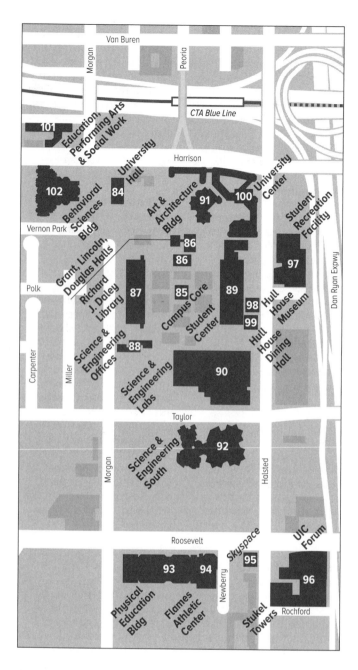

the search began a decade later. In 1959, Mayor Richard J. Daley proposed a fifty-five-acre site at Harrison and Halsted Sts. The densely populated neighborhood, already designated for urban renewal, was variously considered an expendable slum or a vibrant community—depending on the source. Community activists in the affected area tried to fight City Hall, but almost everyone else—including other West Siders—favored the site. The 1960 Democratic electoral landslide (President John F. Kennedy was a grateful Daley supporter) gave the mayor the backing he needed to acquire the site and finance the project.

In 1961, SOM presented a campus master plan, and construction began two years later. The university opened in February 1965, and five more buildings were added in Phase II by 1967. After this initial burst of construction, the pace slowed considerably until a second boom began in the 1990s.

Probably the only university named for a traffic interchange, the campus was originally known as the University of Illinois at Chicago Circle, the "spaghetti bowl" freeway tangle just to the east. In 1982, this campus was merged with the university's long-established medical center to the west, and the combined institution was renamed the University of Illinois at Chicago. The earlier name was not inappropriate, however, as Netsch had taken many cues from his own theories of transportation and movement.

The campus had two main organizing principles: a double-level system of walkways and a central hub consisting of a raised plaza surrounded by the most heavily used buildings. Netsch described the plan as "concentric rings with elements of most intense usage in the center; activity decreases and specialization increases with outward movement." This scheme was gradually abandoned as more specialized graduate divisions were added, but the core continues to function as planned, with a central area of lecture halls flanked by the library and student union. The walkway system and the raised plaza at the campus core were demolished in 1995. A few vocal fans of the original work cried foul, but most students and faculty welcomed the friendly ground-level plaza that forms the new center of campus.

The original campus building materials were exposed concrete, dark brick, and brown-tinted glass, which eliminated the need for window treatments. The reinforced-concrete structure is exposed on all the early buildings except Science and Engineering, and the decision to use concrete of uniform strength everywhere led to huge amounts of it in buildings with heavier structural loads. In an excessive refinement of the visible-structure principle, the concrete that carries heavier loads is sandblasted more than other concrete so that it has a coarser aggregate. The brutalist aesthetic is extended inside the buildings, where concrete ceilings support exposed mechanical and lighting elements.

A major expansion of the campus got under way in 2002 with the creation of University Village on a sixty-eight-acre site south of Roosevelt Rd. This expansion raised almost as great an uproar as the original campus proposal did in 1959, because it entailed demolition of the lively Maxwell St. Market. The new parking and retail structures that march down Halsted St. incorporate twenty-one of the street's historic facades. The major architects of University Village, which includes town houses, mid-rises, two dormitories, academic buildings, shops, restaurants, and parking facilities, are Roy H. Kruse & Assocs., Pappageorge/Haymes, FitzGerald Assoc. Architects, and Solomon Cordwell Buenz & Assocs.

In addition to new construction, emphasis in the twenty-first century is on renovating the 1960s buildings to improve function, appearance, and energy efficiency. Glass curtain walls are gradually replacing deteriorating concrete and dark windows to bring in natural light and provide a welcoming glow after dark. But as architects gradually sand off the roughest edges of the campus's brutalist character, what was once a cohesive, even overpowering environment is looking more and more like any other urban university.

Explore the campus on foot.

84 University Hall
601 S. Morgan St.
1965, SKIDMORE, OWINGS & MERRILL

Looming over the campus is its only skyscraper—the campanile, to use Netsch's metaphor—this twenty-eight-story office building for faculty and administration. In a paradoxical display of structuralism, the building becomes wider as it rises, with fewer columns creating bays of increasing width. The number of stories in each of the upper tiers—five, eight, and thirteen—was derived from another of Netsch's aesthetic principles: use of the golden section.

Continue south toward the center of campus. The blocky structure on the left is the Commonwealth Edison **Vernon Park substation,** *a vivid reminder of the logistical difficulties of planning a new campus over a century-old grid of city utilities.*

85 Campus Core
821 S. Morgan St.

1965, SKIDMORE, OWINGS & MERRILL
1995, REDESIGN, DANIEL P.
COFFEY & ASSOCS.

An amphitheater (Circle Forum) and rooftop-level plaza (the Great Court) originally covered the core of the campus, but both were removed in the 1990s renovation; the Great Court composed the common roof for several lecture halls. The new ground-level elliptical "piazza," designed to a human scale and furnished with benches, planters, and torcheres, has finally created the casual social environment originally envisioned.

86 Grant, Douglas, and Lincoln Halls
703, 705, and 707 S. Morgan St.

1965, SKIDMORE, OWINGS & MERRILL
2007–11, RENOVATION, SMITHGROUP;
DESIGN ORGANIZATION; ARCHITECTS
ENTERPRISE; HARLEY ELLIS DEVEREAUX,
ASSOC. ARCH. FOR DOUGLAS HALL

SmithGroup worked with the university on the pioneering renovation of Grant Hall, which became a model for how to green and improve the appearance of campus buildings. The design concept was modified by Design Organization for Lincoln Hall and then Architects Enterprise for Douglas. A geothermal well field serves all three LEED-certified buildings. A new glass curtain wall wraps around the concrete structure, increasing transparency and energy efficiency. The rhythm of the new facades relates to the adjacent buildings.

87 Richard J. Daley Library
801 S. Morgan St.

1965, SKIDMORE, OWINGS & MERRILL
The library was among the first buildings constructed. An interior renovation by David Woodhouse Architects in 2011 provides a good example of turning the old brutalism into the new cool.

88 Science and Engineering Offices
851 S. Morgan St.

1965, SKIDMORE, OWINGS & MERRILL
The exterior expression of the scissor stairs where the buildings are offset provides an unexpected point of interest.

89 Student Center
750 S. Halsted St.

1965, C. F. MURPHY ASSOCS.
This is the only one of the original buildings designed by a firm other than Skidmore, Owings & Merrill. Walk through it for a shortcut to Hull House.

90 Science and Engineering Laboratories
900 W. Taylor St. and 950 S. Halsted St.

1965, SKIDMORE, OWINGS & MERRILL
1990, ADDITION, HANSEN LIND MEYER
This hulk forms the south wall of the campus core. The giant structural bays are divided by concrete columns five feet square at the base. The bricks are twice as large as those on other campus buildings, and the concrete aggregate is coarser.

91 Art and Architecture Building
845 W. Harrison St.

1967, SKIDMORE, OWINGS & MERRILL
In this building, Netsch developed his "field theory," rotating squares into complex geometries that radiate out from a center core. In drawings, the plans look like lovely snowflakes, but in three dimensions, the building is dark and confounding, with no perceptible spatial logic. The raw walls on the exterior indicate where a planned expansion never happened.

At the entrance to the Art and Architecture Building is the only remaining section of the second-story walkway system. This section is atypical, constructed of steel rather than concrete and granite.

92 Science Engineering South
845 W. Taylor St.

1968, SKIDMORE, OWINGS & MERRILL
The last of Netsch's "field theory" trio of buildings was based on a complex geometry that the architect developed while collecting op-art paintings.

93 Physical Education Building
901 W. Roosevelt Rd.

1967, HARRY WEESE & ASSOCS.
Remarkable chiefly for its enormous bulk, the building was reoriented by Weese from its north–south axis on the plan to close the campus off on the south.

UIC Art and Architecture Building

94 Flames Athletic Center
839 W. Roosevelt Rd.

1999, MEKUS STUDIOS; SASAKI
ASSOCS., CONSULTING ARCH.

A new glass entrance and circulation space join the Physical Education Building to this converted ice rink, which houses administrative and support space and has a southern addition containing basketball courts.

95 UIC Skyspace and Earl Neal Plaza
Southwest corner of Halsted St. and Roosevelt Rd.

2006, JAMES TURRELL, ARTIST

Easily overlooked on this bustling corner is the only Turrell skyspace publicly accessible at all times. One must enter and gaze up at the oculus—preferably at dawn or dusk—to perceive the visual magic for which the artist is world-famous.

96 UIC Forum
725 W. Roosevelt Rd.
James Stukel Towers
718 W. Rochford St. and
1253 S. Halsted St.

2008, HELLMUTH, OBATA &
KASSABAUM; VASILKO, HAUSERMAN
& ASSOCS., ASSOC. ARCH.

The transition from commuter to residential campus took another giant leap with the four towers of this 750-bed complex. The adjacent Forum has an auditorium that seats 3,000 and a small theater as well as retail.

97 Student Recreation Facility
737 S. Halsted St.

2006, PSA DEWBERRY, DESIGN
ARCH.; MOODY NOLAN,
PROGRAMMING AND PLANNING

This recreational pleasure palace jogs in and out along Halsted St., seeming to taunt the lugubrious campus buildings to the west.

98 Jane Addams's Hull House Museum
(Charles J. Hull House)

1856, ARCHITECT UNKNOWN
99 Hull House Dining Hall
800 S. Halsted St.

1905, POND & POND
1967, RECONSTRUCTION OF MUSEUM AND DINING HALL,
FRAZIER, RAFTERY, ORR & FAIRBANK

Representative more of Hull than of Addams is this rebuilding of a first-generation Italianate "cube and cupola." The Italianate style reigned in Chicago from the 1850s to the 1880s. The symmetry, low foundations, arched windows, shallow sloped roof, and heavy bracketed eaves offer a rare view of a pleasing composition of the pre–Civil War era.

NEAR WEST SIDE

Jane Addams's Hull House Museum

By the 1880s, rapid expansion had overtaken the area, and the house was a furniture shop prior to its conversion to a settlement house by social reformers Jane Addams and Ellen Gates Starr in 1889. During the 1890s and early 1900s, thirteen buildings covering two city blocks were built around the house. The resulting complex, which offered social, cultural, and educational facilities for the urban poor and underprivileged, was inspired by the Progressive Reform movement and the Toynbee Hall settlement house in London. The Dining Hall, a simple Craftsman-style building, is the sole survivor of the complex; its architect, Allen Pond, was a social activist and supporter of the settlement. The house was substantially altered prior to Addams's death in 1935, gaining a third story and losing its wide veranda.

In 1963, the property was acquired by the University of Illinois and dedicated to a museum of Jane Addams's good works. As the other buildings in the Hull House complex were demolished, the house itself reemerged and was reconstructed. Furnishings from Addams's era were restored, and others were gleaned from antique stores, creating an interior that is a comfortable Victorian mélange. The fireplaces and moldings are original; the chandeliers were reproduced from photos. The Dining Hall, relocated from its nearby site, is now used for exhibits and presentations.

100 University Center Housing and Commons

700 S. Halsted St.

1988, SOLOMON CORDWELL
BUENZ & ASSOCS.

1993, WEST ADDITION, SOLOMON
CORDWELL BUENZ & ASSOCS.; LOEBL,
SCHLOSSMAN & HACKL, ASSOC. ARCHS.

A marked departure for the campus in form and function, these buildings are the first undergraduate housing here as well as the first complex to create a street wall and a grassy courtyard.

101 Education, Performing Arts, and Social Work

(Education, Communications, and Social Work)

1040 W. Harrison St.

1968, HARRY WEESE & ASSOCS.

This balconied bunker meets the standard of bleakness set by the first phase of campus construction.

102 Behavioral Sciences Building

1007 W. Harrison St.

1967, SKIDMORE, OWINGS & MERRILL

The torturous floor plan of this "field theory" building is the butt of many jokes about rats in a maze.

GARFIELD PARK/AUSTIN

To those traveling from Western Ave. to the city limits—past empty lots, crumbling six-flats, well-maintained graystones, battered retail areas, and sturdy churches—the suburban origins of these neighborhoods may seem remote and invisible. But the area from Western Ave. to Harlem Ave. in Oak Park and from North Ave. to Pershing Rd. was once Cicero Township, an independent political entity founded in 1857. Its villages, which grew up along the train lines, were coveted by Chicago politicians eager to add their public properties and tax assessments to the city's holdings.

In 1869, a seminal year for the West Side, Chicago annexed most of the easternmost two miles of Cicero Township, from Western Ave. to what is now Pulaski Rd. That year also saw the establishment of the West Park Commission, which immediately began acquiring property for what are now Humboldt, Garfield, and Douglas Parks. Selection of the Garfield Park site spurred speculation in surrounding properties, but construction accelerated only after transportation had improved. In the early 1870s, a station on the Chicago & North Western Railroad at Kedzie Ave. led to residential development there,

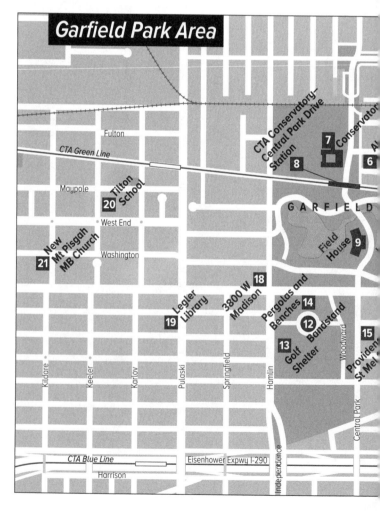

but not until the 1890s, with the advent of the Metropolitan West Side Elevated and better streetcar service, did the area begin to flourish.

In the huge 1889 annexation that quadrupled Chicago's size, the city bit off another chunk of Cicero Township: Central Park and Moreland, the two communities immediately west of Garfield Park. Pulaski Rd. (then 40th St.) was already a transportation center; at Kinzie were the carbarns for the Chicago & North Western Railroad, and at Madison was the transfer point from city streetcars to suburban lines such as the Cicero & Proviso St. Railway. The latter intersection grew into a vibrant urban center, a mini-downtown midway between the Loop and Oak Park shopping areas. In the 1920s, developers put up high-rise hotels, apartments, dance halls, and clubs. But the area was hard hit by the riots and fires that erupted after the 1968 assassination of Dr. Martin Luther King Jr. Despite massive disinvestment in the area, the intersection remains a retail hub, one of the few shopping centers between the West Loop and the city limits.

Annexation's pros and cons were long debated in Austin, which retained its autonomy as a village in Cicero Township until 1899. Austin and Oak Park,

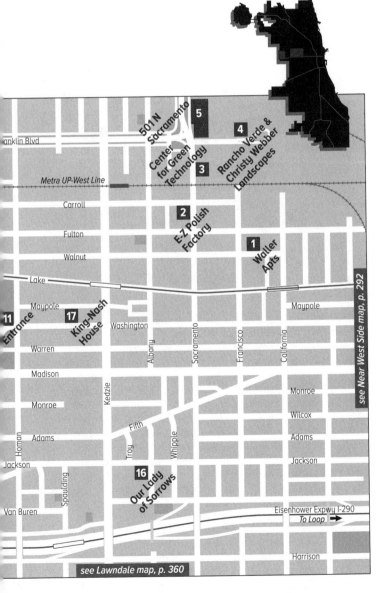

see Near West Side map, p. 292

see Lawndale map, p. 360

GARFIELD PARK/AUSTIN

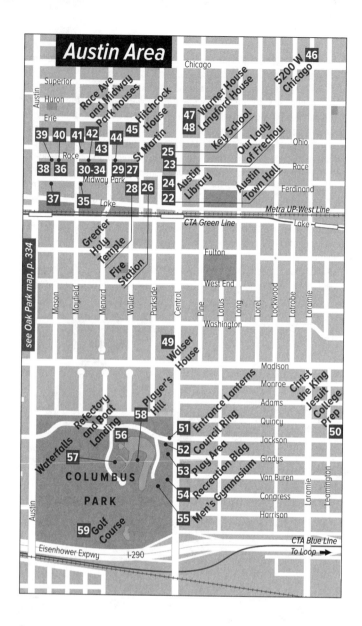

Austin Area

Chicago

5200 W Chicago

46

Warner House
Langford House

Superior

Race Ave and Midway Park houses

Austin

Huron

Erie

Hitchcock House

47

48

Key School

Our Lady of Frechou

Ohio

39 40 41 42

44

45

St Martin

25

23

Austin Library

Austin Town Hall

Race

Race

43

Ferdinand

38 36

30-34 29 27

Midway Park

24

22

Lake

37

35

28 26

Metra UP-West Line

CTA Green Line

Lake

Greater Holy Temple

Fire Station

Fulton

see Oak Park map, p. 334

West End

Mason

Mayfield

Menard

Waller

Parkside

Central

Pine

Lotus

Long

Lorel

Lockwood

Latrobe

Laramie

Washington

49

Walser House

Madison

Christ the King Jesuit College Prep

Monroe

Entrance Lanterns

Adams

Player's Hill

58

Quincy

51

Council Ring

Jackson

50

Refectory and Boat Landing

56

52

Play Area

Gladys

Waterfalls

57

53

Recreation Bldg

Van Buren

COLUMBUS PARK

54

Men's Gymnasium

Congress

Laramie

Leamington

55

Harrison

Austin

59

Golf Course

CTA Blue Line
To Loop ➜

Eisenhower Expwy

I-290

the township's two largest villages, battled for decades over funds in a rivalry that came to a head in the 1890s. Austin had some sentiment for annexation, largely among developers and investors in the Metropolitan West Side Elevated. Antiannexation fervor was much stronger in Oak Park, but seceding was difficult, with a majority of the entire township needed. In 1895, Austin thwarted Oak Park's efforts to secede, increasing bitterness and leading Oak Parkers to redouble their efforts to become independent. The *Oak Park Vindicator* editorialized, "The larger the municipality the greater are the opportunities for boodlers—vile men, who can no more appreciate the fine sentiments of patriotism than can Satan the sweet melodies of heaven. The Chicago boodler is the worst type in existence. The question before fair Cicero is, will she willfully put her head into his yoke?" The majority of Austin residents felt the same way. But in the decisive April 1899 election, Oak Park vanquished its rival, leading the township's villages in voting Austin into Chicago despite Austin's 972–516 vote to remain.

Austin retains preannexation features such as Merrick and Town Hall Parks, many churches and widely spaced homes, and the fire station on Waller Ave. During the 1920s, apartment and commercial buildings replaced single-family homes along major arteries such as Lake St., Central Ave., and Jackson and

Washington Blvds. The 1920s also saw the completion of Jens Jensen's masterpiece, Columbus Park.

The West Side shows typical inner-city scars of age and blight. There is little new construction, and empty lots outnumber buildings on some blocks; the building stock is aging faster than money becomes available to save it. But the positive effects of dedicated institutions and strong individuals are seen in every neighborhood, from the well-tended church and school complexes of Garfield Park to the rehabilitated homes of central Austin to the restored sections of Garfield and Columbus Parks.

—ALICE SINKEVITCH

Two lesser-known works of Frank Lloyd Wright are located in an area east of Garfield Park that is difficult to navigate because of railroad embankments and street conditions (entries 1–2).

1 Edward C. Waller Apartments
2840–2858 W. Walnut St.

1895, FRANK LLOYD WRIGHT

Real estate developer Waller was interested in low-income housing; these apartments were among the few of his schemes that were built. Four of the five units remain; all once backed up to Waller's more famous Wright-designed project, the Francisco Terrace Apartments, demolished in 1974 and partially re-created in Oak Park.

2 E-Z Polish Factory
3005 W. Carroll Ave.

1905, FRANK LLOYD WRIGHT
1913, ADDITION, HARRY H. MAHLER

This greatly altered factory is Wright's earliest essay in reinforced concrete. After commissioning him to design their homes, William E. Martin of Oak Park and his brother, Darwin E. Martin of Buffalo, hired Wright to design this stove- and shoe-polish factory. The windows have been bricked in and two floors have been added; the only exterior suggestion of Wright's involvement is the detailing around the entries and the ordered geometry of the facade.

3 Chicago Center for Green Technology
(Sacramento Stone Co.)
445 N. Sacramento Blvd.

2002, FARR ASSOCS.

A small abandoned factory on a former brownfields site was transformed into a showcase for energy efficiency. Photovoltaic panels are on the roof and in the place of awnings. The barrels on the front of the building catch the rain for reuse on the landscape. High-performance insulation, HVAC using ground source heat technology, and a rooftop planted with sun- and drought-tolerant greenery all help the building achieve its LEED platinum rating, the first building in the Midwest and the third in the world to earn this rating.

4 Rancho Verde and Christy Webber Landscapes
2900 W. Ferdinand St.

2007, FARR ASSOCS.

Following the success of the Center for Green Technology, the city decided to turn the remaining twelve acres of brownfield into an eco-industrial park. Christy Webber, a full-service landscape firm, agreed to become the anchor tenant and founded Chicago GreenWorks to develop the property, which was christened Rancho Verde. A sophisticated system harvests rainwater to irrigate plants in the greenhouses, one of which is atop the roof of this LEED platinum building. Power sources include a seventy-foot-tall vertical aeroturbine, solar panels, and a geothermal system.

5 501 N. Sacramento Blvd.
(Sprague, Warner & Co.)

1941, A. EPSTEIN

The Art Deco tower anchors this stretch of the boulevard system, developed as an industrial area because of nearby railroads. Food processors Sprague, Warner brought in raw materials and shipped out finished goods via a railway siding directly connected to the first floor. The tower housed offices and concealed the water tank.

6 Al Raby School for Community and Environment

(Lucy L. Flower Vocational High School)

3545 W. Fulton Blvd.

1927, JOHN C. CHRISTENSEN

The structurally expressive facade has light touches of Gothic detailing, a favorite design type of Board of Education architect Christensen. "Flower Tech" first opened in 1911 on the South Side as an open-enrollment high school for girls. Technical education included sewing, millinery, the "home arts," and later business classes.

Garfield Park

(Central Park)

Metra railroad tracks to W. Fifth Ave.; Hamlin Blvd. to S. Central Park Blvd.; central section extends east to N. Homan Ave.

1869–74, WILLIAM LE BARON JENNEY

1877–93, OSCAR F. DUBUIS

1905–20, JENS JENSEN

The middle of the West Park System's three great parks (Humboldt and Douglas Parks are the others) still clearly shows the work of William Le Baron Jenney and Jens Jensen, two of the commission's major talents. Starting with a 185-acre tabula rasa, Jenney began transforming the flat, treeless site into a picturesque landscape of winding lagoons and romantic vistas. Among the first improvements was the "pretty little inland sea," a fifteen-acre lagoon. Although he resigned as the West Park Commission's chief engineer in 1874, the year the first forty-acre portion was completed, Jenney was retained as a consultant until the 1890s.

From 1877 to 1893, Oscar F. DuBuis continued developing acreage, somewhat modifying Jenney's plans. When Jens Jensen became general superintendent and chief landscape architect in 1905, he redesigned the park to reflect his vision of a prairie landscape. Jensen also introduced Prairie School architecture into the park, hiring William Carbys Zimmerman and Schmidt, Garden & Martin for major improvements.

Only some of Garfield Park's structures remain, but several—such as the Bandstand, Conservatory, and West Park Commission Headquarters—are prime examples of their styles.

The park's most interesting historic landscape features are between Lake St. and Jackson Blvd. Jenney intended the area north of Lake St. as an open green meadow for "croquet parties, military parades, and baseball games." It became the site of several of the park's largest buildings, including the Conservatory and a cluster of much-altered service buildings that are difficult to see and in varying states of repair. The **Power Plant** (West Park Light Plant, 1896, JOSEPH L. SILSBEE) was designed to serve a large part of the West Park; it no longer has the top half of its chimney. West of the Conservatory are the *Bulls with Maidens* sculptures. The pair was originally created in plaster for the 1893 World's Columbian Exposition by Daniel Chester French and Edward C. Potter and was then cast in bronze in 1912. The sculptures depict a Native American goddess of corn to symbolize the New World and Ceres, the Roman goddess of grain, to represent the Old.

7 Conservatory

300 N. Central Park Blvd.

1906–7, JENS JENSEN AND SCHMIDT, GARDEN & MARTIN; HITCHINGS & CO., ENG.

1998, ENTRY PAVILION AND LANDSCAPING, BOOTH HANSEN ASSOCS.

1995–2000, AROID HOUSE RESTORATION, HORTICULTURE HALL AND
    CHILDREN'S GARDEN REHABILITATION, EIFLER & ASSOCS.

2007, CITY GARDEN, DOUG HOERR LANDSCAPE ARCHITECTURE

Considered revolutionary when it opened, the Conservatory was conceived by Jensen as a work of landscape art under glass and was designed in collaboration with a New York engineering firm that specialized in greenhouse design. Unlike Victorian hothouses, which had showy floral displays that often included potted plants, benches, and exposed pipes, the Conservatory was designed as a series of internal landscapes of tropical plantings, stonework, and water features.

Those who know Jensen as the dean of the Prairie landscape style might conclude that this work strayed from his usual efforts to convey symbolically the Midwest's indigenous landscape. Some of the gardens, however, were meant to emulate poetically the tropical appearance of the Chicago region during prehistoric times. In addition, according to Jensen, the structure's form was inspired by "the great haystacks which are so eloquent of the richness of prairie soil." Jensen, who served as the West Park System's chief landscape architect from 1905 to 1920, had recommended replacing small greenhouses in Humboldt, Douglas, and Garfield Parks with one economical, centrally lo-cated facility, which was touted as the world's largest conservatory under one glass structure.

The Conservatory plan consists of a large rectangular palm house and several small square rooms configured around the structure's premier space, the fern room. In the center of this compelling landscape is a small naturalistic lagoon framed by lush ferns on stratified stonework meant to emulate natural stone outcroppings. A path winds past the lagoon to the far end of the room, where stepping-stones cross a rocky brook fed by a "prairie waterfall." In a 1930 interview, Jensen explained that when the waterfall was being con-structed, he was consistently dissatisfied with the stonework and required the mason to dismantle and rebuild it several times. When the workman became frustrated, Jensen suggested that he listen to Mendelssohn's "Spring Song." After hearing the music, the mason constructed the waterfall perfectly, so that the "water tinkled gently from ledge to ledge, as it should in a prairie country."

The Conservatory's original vestibule and the decorative art-glass fea-tures in the palm house were designed by Schmidt, Garden & Martin. Unfor-tunately, they were lost in 1958, when the palm room's elegant, lacy truss system was demolished and replaced with a bolder structure of I-beam construction.

Although the Conservatory's annual attendance had reached half a million visitors in the 1920s, the facility began to deteriorate over the next few decades. Construction projects in the 1950s failed to take into account the structure's historic character. The neighborhood began declining and attendance dropped.

After winter storm damage in 1994, the Chicago Park District began to fully turn around that cycle. The Garfield Park Conservatory Alliance formed to upgrade programming and visitor services. The Aroid House was restored, the Horticultural Hall rehabilitated, and a new Children's Garden completed in 2000.

In 2001–2, the *Chihuly in the Park: A Garden of Glass* exhibit attracted more than half a million visitors. Several lily-like Dale Chihuly glass artworks

Garfield Park Conservatory

are now on permanent display in the Aroid House. Subsequent improvements include removing the 1950s fiberglass sheathing, reglazing the Palm House, and creating a new City Garden. A severe 2011 hailstorm caused millions of dollars of destruction, necessitating major restoration work on the Fern Room, Desert House, and Show House.

—JULIA S. BACHRACH

8 CTA—Conservatory and Central Park Dr. Station
3630 W. Lake St.

2001, CHICAGO TRANSIT AUTHORITY

Portions of the canopies and the station houses came from a former station at nearby Homan Ave. These preserved and restored pieces were fashioned into a new structure meant to look like the oldest stations on the line—those built for the Lake St. elevated railroad of the early 1890s. Modern technology was also incorporated into this increasingly busy facility, which serves several schools and the Garfield Park Conservatory.

9 Field House
(West Park Commission Administration Building)
100 N. Central Park Ave.

1928, MICHAELSEN & ROGNSTAD

Field House

Bertram Goodhue's Spanish Baroque Revival creations for the 1915 Panama-California Exposition in San Diego were cream-hued, grand, and bristling with sculpture. Their popularity changed the direction of architecture in Southern California and filtered east to inspire a new decorative vocabulary. Goodhue's California State Building from the exposition influenced this structure, which as the headquarters of the politically powerful West Park Commission housed its administrative offices, engineering department, and police force.

The facade is exuberantly if rather breathlessly punctuated with a Churrigueresque entry pavilion of spiral Corinthian columns, cartouches, and portrait sculptures. The gold terra-cotta dome shelters a rotunda with a geometric terrazzo floor. Four panels sculpted by Richard W. Bock pay homage to Art and Architecture (figures hold a model of this building), Chicago's parks and playgrounds, and the Illinois highway system. After the 1934 consolidation of the city's park districts, the building became a field house, with the commissioner's boardroom still used as a meeting room.

From the front of the Field House are excellent views of the eastern Lagoon and Suspension Bridge, the park's oldest elements.

10 Lagoons and Island
1870, WILLIAM LE BARON JENNEY
Suspension Bridge
1870, WILLIAM LE BARON JENNEY

The lagoons are the most notable remnants of Jenney's landscape design, and the area east of Central Park Blvd. is the oldest preserved landscaped space in a Chicago park. Done on an intimate, romantically miniaturized scale, the very irregular shoreline creates many inlets and changing vistas. Here one can imagine Chicagoans escaping to the city's edge to promenade, view the landscape, and partake of such amenities as the healthful water from the artesian well (which ran dry and was later removed by Jensen). Jenney's Suspension Bridge, the sole survivor of a group of ornamental bridges, is a miniature display of his engineering talents and an elegant adornment. Steel cables support a wooden deck hung from concrete piers, which have replaced the stone originals.

11 Washington Blvd. Entrance
Washington Blvd. at Homan Ave.

1907, WILLIAM CARBYS ZIMMERMAN

Originally laid out in a semicircle by Jenney, the entrance was reemphasized by Jensen, who hired Zimmerman to design the architectural enhancement, of which only fragments remain.

12 Bandstand
Music Ct. east of Hamlin Ave.

1896, JOSEPH LYMAN SILSBEE

A one-hundred-piece orchestra could fit on the broad platform of this white marble octagon, sheltered by the fantastic copper roof. Arabian patterns inspired the trefoil arches and the calligraphic mosaic panels.

13 Golf Shelter

1907, ATTRIB. TO HUGH M. G. GARDEN

While greatly altered, the area south of Madison St. shows Jensen's contribution to the landscape. He placed a semicircular earth berm south of the Bandstand to create a gently sloped amphitheater and a spot from which to view the golf course (now eradicated) that he created to the south. The Golf Shelter (now used for storage) had a full-width pergola across its southern facade.

14 Pergolas and Benches

1907, ATTRIB. TO HUGH M. G. GARDEN

Jensen linked the Bandstand to the western Lagoon by the siting of a large formal garden with reflecting pools running north. They were on axis with the Boathouse (burned in 1981; a fragment of the stair remains on Washington Blvd.), which stood on the southern edge of the western Lagoon. The pergolas are now fragmentary and merely suggest their original role as pleasant walkways and frames for pedestrians' views of the park.

15 Providence–St. Mel School
(Providence High School)
119 S. Central Park Blvd.

1929, MORRISON & WALLACE

The Tudor style, particularly that of Oxford and Cambridge Universities, was a popular model for Chicago public high schools from 1898 through the 1930s. The Central Park Blvd. entrance, derived from a fifteenth-century Gothic gatehouse, features carved reliefs of young scholars. One peers at a plant through a magnifying glass; the other, her hair in a fashionable 1920s bob, studies in a library.

16 Our Lady of Sorrows Basilica
3121 W. Jackson Blvd.

1890–1902, HENRY ENGELBERT, JOHN F. POPE, AND WILLIAM J. BRINKMAN

It's Bramante on the Boulevard—with a coffered, barrel-vaulted ceiling rising above the long nave. The stolid classical facade is enlivened by an English Baroque steeple. (Its mate was destroyed by lightning.)

17 King-Nash House
(Patrick J. King House)
3234 W. Washington Blvd.

1901, GEORGE W. MAHER

An interesting counterpoint to Maher's smooth, finely finished, Roman-brick–and–stucco houses is the occasional appearance of a megalithic work. Richardsonian influences are apparent in this husky limestone city house, with its exquisitely carved columns, capitals, and urns. The rhythmically recurring motif is the thistle, seen in the capitals and dormer and used extensively inside. The monochromatic palette originally offset jewellike glass mosaic panels, fragments of which remain beneath the second-floor window. Elongated Roman tray shapes, a favorite Maher motif, appear in the tall fence. Patrick Nash, a later owner, was a prominent politician.

King-Nash House

18 3800 W. Madison St.
(Midwest Athletic Club)
1926, MICHAELSEN & ROGNSTAD

The Spanish Baroque Revival palette and decorative vocabulary translated beautifully into terra-cotta. The fifth-floor shields commemorate the short-lived athletic club, which offered West Side businessmen all the amenities of a Loop club—including two ballrooms, an Olympic-size pool, a gym with a running track, plus a fabulous view across the park to the city skyline—before sinking into receivership in 1930.

19 Chicago Public Library— Henry E. Legler Regional Branch
115 S. Pulaski Rd.
1919, ALFRED S. ALSCHULER

This dignified Beaux-Arts building with its elegant raked brickwork was Chicago's first regional library. Seventeenth-century priest/ explorer Jacques Marquette is portrayed on the wall of the study room in a Works Progress Administration mural by R. Fayerweather Babcock.

20 George W. Tilton Public School
4152 W. West End Ave.
1908, DWIGHT H. PERKINS
1965, ADDITION, SAUL SAMUELS

In 1910, *Architectural Record* declared this school "the most successful of all Mr. Perkins's designs." The architect's bold hand sculpted a strong, geometric facade deriving drama from the articulate layering of planes—from windows to walls to towering piers. The virtuoso masonry is in

Tilton School

unusually rich tones of mustard and burnt-orange brick.

21 New Mount Pisgah M.B. Church
(St. Thomas Aquinas Church)
4301 W. Washington Blvd.
1923–25, KARL M. VITZTHUM

Austin resident Vitzthum's grandest local project is Gothic Moderne, a house of worship yearning to be a soaring skyscraper. The Celtic cross atop the tower provides the clue that this church was built for a predominantly Irish congregation. Inside, extensive gold mosaic work and opalescent grisaille glass make the nave worth a visit.

22 Austin Town Hall Park Field House
5610 W. Lake St.
1929, MICHAELSEN & ROGNSTAD
1992, RENOVATION, CHICAGO
PARK DISTRICT

From 1871 to 1928, the Cicero Town Hall stood on this site, which was donated by Henry W. Austin. When the West Park System took over the property in 1927, planning began for a "patriotic memorial hall for Austin organizations." This Georgian Revival recreational facility features a tower modeled on Independence Hall in Philadelphia.

Chicago Public Library—Henry E. Legler Regional Branch

23 Church of Our Lady of Frechou

(Austin Methodist Church)

502 N. Central Ave.

1900, SIDNEY R. BADGLEY

1909, BADGLEY & NICKLAS

A staid facade in plain-Jane Gothic hides an unusual rotated plan with the altar in the northwest corner. The west wall of the nave could be raised to increase the size of the worship space. When the church burned in 1909, the congregation again hired Cleveland architect Badgley and rebuilt to his original design.

24 Chicago Public Library— Henry W. Austin Branch

5615 W. Race Ave.

1928, ALFRED S. ALSCHULER

This Beaux-Arts library subtly integrates Egyptian forms in the papyriform capitals.

25 Francis Scott Key Public School

517 N. Parkside Ave.

1906, DWIGHT H. PERKINS

This solid, unfussy design is from Perkins's early years as Board of Education architect.

26 Fire Station

(Cicero Township Fire and Police Station)

439 N. Waller Ave.

1899, FREDERICK R. SCHOCK

The last municipal building erected before Austin's annexation to Chicago is now one of the West Side's oldest firehouses. The eclectic facade is dominated by the very flat, vaguely Gothic stone trim around doors and windows.

Begin a tour of Austin's finest residential area on the other side of the cul-de-sac of Midway Park at Waller Ave., where the Congregationalists and the Episcopalians had a stylistic face-off. The Episcopalians clung more tightly to tradition, while the Congregationalists threw caution to the winds (entries 27–28).

27 St. Martin's Episcopal Church

(St. Paul's Methodist Episcopal Church)

5700 W. Midway Park

1901, ALLAN M. BARROWS

The interior of this simplified Tudor Revival church is a small glory, with a beautiful timbered ceiling and rich stained glass. In the chapel are five stained-glass windows saved from the wooden church (1880) that originally occupied this site. The rectory, at 5710, echoes the Gothic church in the pointed-arch forms of the side entry, the dormer windows, and the porch piers.

28 Greater Holy Temple, Church of God in Christ

(First Congregational Church of Austin)

5701 W. Midway Park

1908, WILLIAM E. DRUMMOND

Drummond's first independent commission owes much in plan and massing to employer Frank

Fire Station

Greater Holy Temple

Lloyd Wright's design for Unity Temple in Oak Park. After you enter through a small, low-ceilinged vestibule, the worship space at the top of the stairs seems very spacious. A central nave with an ornamental colored-glass skylight is flanked by lower side aisles. Unlike Wright's design, the social hall and kitchen here are underneath the raised worship space, a variation on the typical "church basement" style.

29 5744 W. Midway Park
1988, JOHN KRAII

Donated materials and services made possible this unique home built by West Side Habitat for Humanity and the Home Builders Association of Greater Chicago. It was designed for a quadriplegic child and her family; ease of access was a prime consideration.

The simple gable and the veranda enable it to slip unobtrusively into the nineteenth-century streetscape.

30 Frederick R. Schock House
5804 W. Midway Park
1886, FREDERICK R. SCHOCK

The empress of Queen Annes, this richly inventive design was Schock's home for almost fifty years. Schock purchased the property just when central Austin was beginning to boom as a desirable residential location. The house was his architectural calling card, announcing his talents to new residents buying lots in the area, and it still stops traffic. The rusticated stone base supports a riot of materials and forms, among them slate shingles and arched window surrounds that look like wood but are actually pressed metal. The extremely varied roofline is topped by

Frederick R. Schock House

a large crest shaped like a handle—an invitation, perhaps, to carry this dollhouse away. Inside, the architect finished or remodeled rooms during different eras: there is a Queen Anne entry hall, a French parlor, and a Craftsman dining room.

31 Frederick Beeson House (2)
5810 W. Midway Park
1892, FREDERICK R. SCHOCK

Manneristic excesses abound in this Queen Anne house—the wooden "keystone" piercing the Palladian window form, the cartoonish broken pediments atop the second-floor bay windows, the stable's peculiar gable. The lavish budget was a step up from Beeson's modest Schock-designed first house in South Austin, and it paid for the stone and leaded colored glass as well as interior finishes such as African mahogany and walnut.

Frederick Beeson House (2)

32 Frederick Beeson House (4)
5830 W. Midway Park
1922, FREDERICK R. SCHOCK

With the construction of this amiable Georgian residence, the peripatetic Beeson ceased his restless architectural wandering of Midway Park.

33 Frederick Beeson House (3)
5840 W. Midway Park
1901, FREDERICK R. SCHOCK

The rounded second-floor bay and the Baroque gable whisper nineteenth-century eclecticism, while the hipped roof, deep eaves, urns, and Roman brick herald the emerging Prairie style.

34 Edward Funk House
5848 W. Midway Park
1886, HOLABIRD & ROCHE

Originally a shingled, turreted counterweight to Schock's extravaganza on the eastern end of the block, this house is now greatly altered.

35 Alvin F. Davis Flats
5849 W. Midway Park
1912, FREDERICK R. SCHOCK

Austinites favored the suburban look even after annexation to the city in 1899. Although the depth of the building bespeaks a multifamily residence, the facade—with the sort of geometric detailing popularized in nearby Oak Park—could pass for that of a single-family home.

36 William Ford House
5928 W. Midway Park
1893, JAMES BEVINS

Some embellishments on this Queen Anne are of recent vintage, but all are in the spirit of the original style.

37 Frank Barrett House
5945 W. Midway Park
MID-1890S, ARCHITECT UNKNOWN

This Queen Anne features almost every kind of window, most notably the circular series atop the turret.

38 Charles A. Carlson House
5964 W. Midway Park
1910, ROBERT M. HYDE

This Craftsman house has an arched corner entry and a battered dining room bay at the rear. The chimney's prominent placement bisecting the facade shows the importance of the fireplace, a key element in the Craftsman style.

39 Benjamin Wikoff House
5939 W. Race Ave.
1894, OLIVER C. SMITH

The picturesque tower and gambrel dormer pierce the gambrel roof of this large but snug Queen Anne.

40 Elwood Riggs House
5929 W. Race Ave.
1895, ARCHITECT UNKNOWN

Although neoclassical on the front, with a curiously dissected Palladian dormer, the sides are more stubbornly irregular and eclectic.

With its billowing wall plane, the third-floor dormer on the east side could have been plucked from a Shingle Style house.

41 5850 W. Race Ave.
1901, JOHN D. CHUBB
Builder Henry Hogan and owner Henry W. Austin Jr. developed the property with this very late Queen Anne–style house.

42 Francis Pray House
5837 W. Race Ave.
1904, ARCHITECT UNKNOWN
This fine example of a transitional style is still Queen Anne in plan and overall proportions but simpler and more rectilinear. Across the street at **5824** and **5830** are two more of the same era.

43 Catherine Schlecht House
5804 W. Race Ave.
1887, FREDERICK R. SCHOCK
This house could have been assembled from two different kits—it has two prominent entrances, both flat and rounded sides, and porches on several levels. The best element is on the west side: the high and hooded third-floor balcony flanked by shingled tourelles.

44 Marie Schock House
5749 W. Race Ave.
1888, FREDERICK R. SCHOCK
Schock designed this house for his mother, then had it published in

Building Budget as "A Cheap Suburban Residence." All wall surfaces and roofs were originally covered in stained shingles.

45 Charles Hitchcock House
5704 W. Ohio St.
1871, ARCHITECT UNKNOWN
This archetypal suburban Italianate house is strongly vertical

Charles Hitchcock House

and frosted with elaborate paired brackets and a porch balustrade made with a fretsaw. Most suburban Italianates were built of wood, and many mimic grander masonry homes. Here, the wooden window molding imitates incised keystones.

Before continuing south on Central Ave., a detour east to Laramie Ave. will take you to one of the city's finest terra-cotta neighborhood business blocks (entry 46).

Catherine Schlecht House

5200 W. Chicago Ave.

46 5200 W. Chicago Ave.
(Laramie State Bank)
1928, REMODELING, MEYER & COOK

What started out as a one-story addition and remodeling of a modest 1909 building grew into a major overhaul. The celery, mustard, and off-white facades are terrific examples of the craftsmanship of the Northwestern Terra Cotta Co. Decorative panels portray men at work, clouds of gigantic coins, and bees and squirrels—familiar symbols of industry and thrift.

47 Seth P. Warner House
631 N. Central Ave.
1869, ARCHITECT UNKNOWN

Compare this symmetrical Italianate with the Charles J. Hull House (1856) on S. Halsted St. to see how slowly architectural styles changed

Seth P. Warner House

Christ the King Jesuit College Prep

in the mid-nineteenth century. The projecting central pavilion, pediment, central stair-hall plan, and cupola typify this phase of the style.

48 Thomas J. Langford House
621 N. Central Ave.
1895, ARCHITECT UNKNOWN

On their property, the Langfords spanned the architectural generations. The roundheaded windows in the Queen Anne turret echo the cupola of the Seth P. Warner House to the north. To the south stands the Langford, an English Gothic six-flat developed by Langford in the 1920s.

49 Joseph J. Walser House
42 N. Central Ave.
1903, FRANK LLOYD WRIGHT

One of the last single-family houses built on Central Ave. during its

heyday as a fine residential street, it has been altered by the removal of leaded-glass windows and by the addition of side porches.

50 Christ the King Jesuit College Preparatory School
5088 W. Jackson Blvd.
2010, JOHN RONAN ARCHITECTS

Blue and gray fiber cement panels create a lively, tough-as-nails facade for a challenging neighborhood. Beautifully patterned glass block walls wrap the eastern end of the ground floor to fill the chapel with morning light. The L-shaped plan responds to the siting of an existing Jesuit middle school to the northeast and creates a semicourtyard that features images of Stations of the Cross printed on a series of exterior panels.

Columbus Park
W. Adams Blvd. to the Eisenhower Expressway; S. Central Ave. to S. Austin Blvd.
1920, JENS JENSEN
1992, RESTORATION, CHICAGO PARK DISTRICT

Jensen's prairie vision for Chicago's parks was most completely realized here, and the spirit lives on. The landscape, whether natural or shaped by humans, was filled with emotional content for Jensen, who wrote of this work, "Looking west from the river bluffs at sundown across a quiet bit of meadow, one sees the prairie melt away into the stratified clouds above. . . . [T]his gives a feeling of breadth and freedom that only the prairie landscape can give to the human soul."

Concerns that nearby Oak Parkers would use a park on their border mitigated against a city park at this location. The West Park Commission explored the expansion of its tax district to include the neighboring village but was defeated by the Oak Park lobby. Because it was the last large piece of land in the area, the property was acquired anyway; the Knights of Columbus suggested the name. Noting the lingering resentment toward Oak Park, sociologist W. R. Ireland commented, "Memorializing the great explorer and the patron saint of travelers, the park's name links to one another the Italian and Irish co-religionists of nearby populations and looks across the city limit to the Protestant 'Indians' of Oak Park who failed in their part of a projected bargain."

A shared public space that portrayed the beauties of the country was of great spiritual value to city dwellers, Jensen felt. Although largely human-created, the lines of the park feel natural and informal. When Jensen began work, the land was almost flat, rising only seven feet from east to west, an elevation he interpreted as an ancient glacial beach. Drawing inspiration from the landscape of northern Illinois, Jensen created a symbolic "prairie river": the lagoon that flows south and east from the Refectory and features two rock-ledge waterfalls. Dirt excavated to form the river was used to create a ridge shielding the body of the park from the city to the east and, originally, from the railroad to the south. Jackson Blvd. was rerouted slightly to flow through the park's north end. North of Jackson Blvd. is an area intended by Jensen for casual strolling and tennis courts.

The sheltering ridge and lagoon were truncated when the park's southern end was destroyed during construction of the Eisenhower Expressway in the 1950s. The extreme tip of the original lagoon still exists as a small pond just behind the athletic fields north of the expressway. A parking lot and bus turnaround have also been carved from the park's southeastern corner.

Though heavily used for swimming, golf, and other sports, the park also harbors less-healthful activities. Major buildings are heavily programmed and welcome visitors; the paths around the lagoon should be explored in groups.

51 Entrance Lanterns
Jackson Blvd. at Central Ave.
1918, SCHMIDT, GARDEN & MARTIN

Hipped-roof copper lanterns hover atop the concrete bases of the massive light fixtures, which are identical to those designed for Humboldt Park.

52 Council Ring
Central Ave. and Jackson Blvd.
1920, JENS JENSEN

The Council Ring, one of Jensen's trademarks, was a large circular bench intended to inspire fellowship and storytelling in the Native American tradition of gathering around a campfire. Most are circles of layered flagstone piers, originally topped by solid slabs of stone.

53 Children's Play Area
S. Central Ave. near Gladys Ave.
1920, JENS JENSEN; SHELTER ATTRIB. TO JOHN S. VAN BERGEN

The play lot shelter (with modern metal roof), wading pool edge, and Council Ring are all built from stratified limestone, one of Jensen's favorite materials. The shelter has been attributed to John S. Van Bergen, who did sketches for Jensen.

Columbus Park entrance lantern

54 Recreation Building
(Locker and Shower Building)
S. Central Ave. south of Van Buren St.
1918, JOHN C. CHRISTENSEN

An eclectic English brick building with a spreading U plan, it originally contained changing facilities for Jensen's rock-ledged swimming pool (since replaced by a modern pool).

55 Men's Gymnasium
(Stable)
West of Recreation Building
1917, JAMES B. DIBELKA
1936, CONVERSION TO GYMNASIUM

One of the handsomest remaining stable buildings in the Chicago Park

Columbus Park Refectory

District reveals its intended function on the west wall, where outlines of the original doors are still visible. Built on Central Ave. at Lexington St., the structure was moved here from the path of the expressway in 1953, when the former stable was connected to the Field House. Columbus Park's bridle paths were the only ones on the West Side; visitors rented horses at the stable.

56 Refectory and Boat Landing
South of Jackson Blvd. between Waller and Menard Aves.
1922, CHATTEN & HAMMOND
1992, RESTORATION, CHICAGO
   PARK DISTRICT

Jensen envisioned Prairie School architecture in his park and was dismayed at the commissioners' insistence on more traditional styles. He may have been disappointed by the revivalist design chosen for the

Refectory, but the rolling arches are romantic and rhythmic. The Refectory and the "prairie river" provide beautiful vistas for each other. The primary space is a light-filled dining room/meeting hall, where the Columbus theme is evoked by a mural on the west wall depicting his three ships. The painting is by Roy L. Terwilliger, who was an artist in the interior design department of Marshall Field's. On the Refectory's eastern end are a concrete boat landing and dining terrace. On the lower level, there were forty boats available for rental in the summer and a thousand pairs of ice skates in the winter.

57 Waterfalls
CA. 1920, JENS JENSEN

The sources of Jensen's "prairie river" are two waterfalls built of stratified limestone and designed

Columbus Park waterfalls

to resemble an Illinois river bluff in miniature.

58 Player's Hill
CA. 1920, JENS JENSEN

Jensen was committed to the idea of education through community theater, with open-air performances heightening communication with nature. The grassy slope between the two waterfalls was the stage, and the audience looked up to it from the meadow to the southeast. The hill originally was much more heavily planted; clearings provided natural dressing rooms shielded from the audience by greenery.

59 Golf Course
CA. 1920, JENS JENSEN

Under Jensen's hand, the nine-hole golf course occupying the park's western half became a miniaturized prairie—broad and expansive, dotted with clusters of vegetation. The starter shed, first tee, and concession stand were moved to their present locations in 1953.

OAK PARK

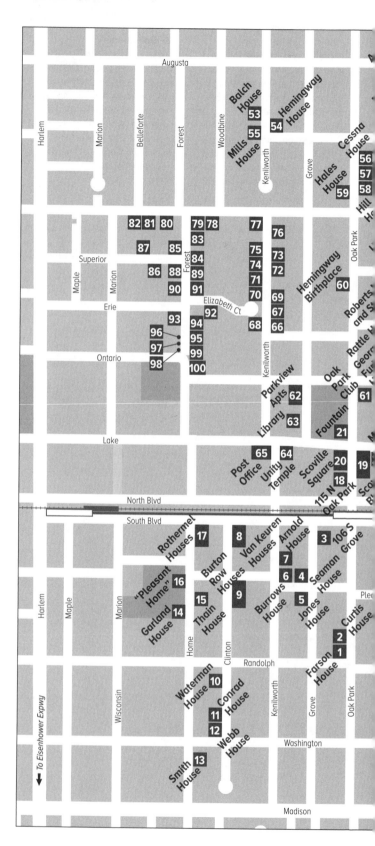

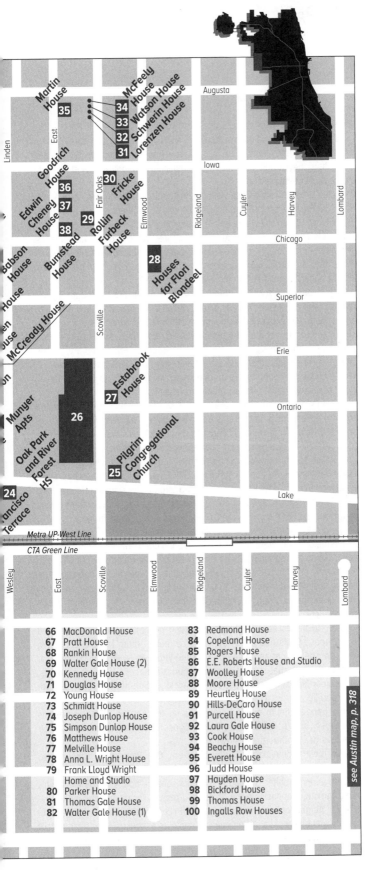

Augusta

Iowa

Chicago

Superior

Erie

Ontario

Lake

Martin House

35

East

Linden

McFeely House

34 Watson House

33 Schwerin House

32 Lorenzen House

31

Goodrich House

36

Edwin Cheney House

37

38

Fair Oaks

30 Fricke House

Elmwood

Ridgeland

Cuyler

Harvey

Lombard

29 Rollin Furbeck House

Babson House

Bumstead House

en House

use

 use

McCready House

28 Houses for Flori Blondeel

Scoville

Estabrook House

27

Munger Apts

26

Oak Park and River Forest HS

Pilgrim Congregational Church

25

24 ancisco Terrace

Metra UP-West Line

CTA Green Line

Wesley

East

Scoville

Elmwood

Ridgeland

Cuyler

Harvey

Lombard

66 MacDonald House
67 Pratt House
68 Rankin House
69 Walter Gale House (2)
70 Kennedy House
71 Douglas House
72 Young House
73 Schmidt House
74 Joseph Dunlop House
75 Simpson Dunlop House
76 Matthews House
77 Melville House
78 Anna L. Wright House
79 Frank Lloyd Wright Home and Studio
80 Parker House
81 Thomas Gale House
82 Walter Gale House (1)

83 Redmond House
84 Copeland House
85 Rogers House
86 E.E. Roberts House and Studio
87 Woolley House
88 Moore House
89 Heurtley House
90 Hills-DeCaro House
91 Purcell House
92 Laura Gale House
93 Cook House
94 Beachy House
95 Everett House
96 Judd House
97 Hayden House
98 Bickford House
99 Thomas House
100 Ingalls Row Houses

see Austin map, p. 318

OAK PARK

Arriving in waves after the Chicago Fire, settlers came to Oak Park by the thousands to build homes: freestanding, sun-filled, hygienic, secure. Fleeing the city's crowded, combustible flats and row houses, cholera epidemics, and corruption, they sought to create a community in harmony with God and with the help of like-minded souls.

Today, tens of thousands of visitors come to tour those houses, for it was in Oak Park that the modern American home was born. Twenty-seven designs by Frank Lloyd Wright still stand, among them fanciful experiments from his early years, his own home and studio, and mature Prairie School masterpieces. The geometric lines, the nature-inspired ornament, the hovering deep-eaved roofs, and the artful plans reflected a cohesive aesthetic vision and were Wright's heartfelt response to the need for shelter.

The twenty-two-year-old Wright moved here in 1889, brought by his mother, who distrusted "the raw winds of the lake." Oak Park was a border-land community, separated from similar settlements by stretches of prairie but connected to the city and to other suburbs by train lines. Real estate agents extolled the artesian wells, the many churches, and the public library, but the streets were largely unpaved, and houses were only just being numbered. Wright chose for his homesite an overgrown lot on the edge of an undeveloped prairie where he often went for nature walks.

During Wright's formative years in Oak Park, the community was dominated by hard-nosed British immigrants and transplanted Yankees. Disciplined, resourceful, and inventive, they sought to shape their environment and to have local control of taxes, school, transportation, and development. Threatened by annexation to Chicago, which had already swallowed up townships such as Lake View and Hyde Park, determined Oak Parkers stopped the city's westward movement. They created and pushed through the state legislature a law enabling towns to withdraw from townships and set up independent village governments. The new village of Oak Park was incorporated in 1902.

Up to 1880, settlers had built cottages and small villas with Greek Revival, Italianate, or Gothic detailing. As the population boomed, the prairie filled with subdivisions of wooden houses, from the structurally expressive Stick Style to the heavily ornamented Queen Anne and classical revival. No one style prevailed; unschooled architects and builders delighted in miniaturizing elements from grand houses and uninhibitedly combining them for maximum picturesque effect.

Later in his career, Wright blasted such designs: "These overdressed wood house walls had cut in them, or cut out of them to be precise, big holes for the big cat and little holes for the little cat. . . . The whole exterior was be-deviled, that is to say, mixed to puzzle-pieces with corner-boards, panel-boards, window-frames, corner-blocks, plinth-blocks, rosettes, fantails, and jiggerwork in general. . . . Simplicity was as far from this scrap-pile as the pandemonium of the barnyard is far from music." But the designs themselves stimulated him, and in the 1890s, he worked with some of their forms before synthesizing his own ideas.

Like most middle-class suburbs of its era, Oak Park was a conservative community, a temperance town nicknamed Saint's Rest for its many churches. But the young architect thrived in this atmosphere—nourished by the town's rapid growth, emphasis on the home, and respect for resourceful individualists. His neighbors became his friends and clients; their commissions constitute the nation's most amazing open-air museum of houses. Their freshness of concept and beauty of form, their modernity and originality, are strikingly set amid not only their Victorian predecessors but also their offspring designed by Wright's employees and contemporaries.

Wright entered a new phase of his life when he broke the bonds of Oak Park propriety with his 1909 trip to Germany. He had gone there to oversee the preparation of the Wasmuth edition of his work, taking with him his lover, Mamah Borthwick Cheney, wife of one of his Oak Park clients, Edwin H. Cheney. The voyage was a turning point in many respects. Now in midlife and with a new love, he was seeking fresh challenges and an international profile. In the two decades of his residence, Oak Park's population of 4,500 had quadrupled. No longer a suburban frontier, Oak Park had become an established center of its own, concerned less with innovation than with the status quo. Along the streets of his village, Wright could see his ideas interpreted and rehashed not only by younger architects who had worked in his studio but also by speculative builders cashing in on the look.

The frontier had disappeared; locally, his aesthetic was mainstream. Seeking new horizons, he moved on to Taliesin, his home in Wisconsin, leaving behind his family, his friends, and a dazzling body of built work.

—ALICE SINKEVITCH

1 John Farson House (1)
237 S. Oak Park Ave.
1888, ARCHITECT UNKNOWN
Farson's Queen Anne was a comfortable, commodious, and picturesque home for an up-and-coming young investment banker. After rapid financial success, he sought something more avant-garde, so in 1897, he commissioned the modern Pleasant Home a few blocks to the west.

2 Edward P. Curtis House
231 S. Oak Park Ave.
1889, FRANK ELLIS
Considered Oak Park's first architect, Ellis was actually a builder with a certain flair. This rectilinear Queen Anne house differs from his slightly earlier Stick Style houses only in the addition of a rounded corner bay with an exotic onion-shaped cap.

Edward P. Curtis House

3 106 S. Grove Ave.
1914, JOHN S. VAN BERGEN
A former Wright employee, Van

Bergen excelled at designing small houses with flowing plans and horizontal lines for deep but narrow lots. Tucked into the side, the entry brings the visitor directly into the heart of the house.

106 S. Grove Ave.

4 John A. Seaman House (1)
139 S. Grove Ave.
1894, FIDDELKE & ELLIS
The 1893 World's Columbian Exposition, a gleaming White City built to an awesome scale, created an enormous appetite for the classical revival style: this grand wedding cake was one of the first homes in

John A. Seaman House (1)

Oak Park to reflect the fair's influence. A profusion of garlands decorate porch and dormer pediments. A plainer sibling, also designed by Fiddelke, was built diagonally across the corner in 1899.

5 John I. Jones House
209 S. Grove Ave.

1887, CICERO HINE

From the second-floor row of miniature Moorish arches to the Tudor half-timbering to the multitude of window shapes and styles, this picturesque snapshot captures the uninhibited freedom of the Queen Anne style. The robust porch and well-broken skyline and wall surfaces still appear fresh, lively, and inventive. The exterior walls and the roof originally were covered with stained shingles, making them read like a uniformly fuzzy fabric.

6 Asa W. Burrows House
142 S. Kenilworth Ave.

1887, FRANK ELLIS

Devoid of historical references, geometrically paneled frame houses such as this one were in their era called modern and are now called Stick Style. The exterior cladding suggests the underlying balloon frame, with bands of wood dividing all wall planes into a series of clapboard and shingle rectangles. The wooden porch echoes the house's structure, framing the view of the world outside. The banded, rotated corner bay is a rectilinear version of the rounded Queen Anne tower.

7 Wesley A. Arnold House
130 S. Kenilworth Ave.

1888, WESLEY A. ARNOLD

Many homes of the 1880s that became Painted Ladies in the 1980s have been bedecked in colors that would have been chemically impossible and aesthetically undesirable at the time of construction. Here is a rare opportunity to study a true Victorian color palette. Built with unusually expensive materials, such as Darlington sandstone and slate, Arnold's own home promoted his talents. The pleasing but sober colors of nature favored in the late 1880s are displayed in the hard materials, which Arnold bent to his will, rounding off every corner. The rich-

Wesley A. Arnold House

est element is the doorway, framed by beveled-glass sidelights and a Moorish arch.

8 William J. Van Keuren Houses
100 and 102 S. Clinton Ave.

1896, WILLIAM J. VAN KEUREN

Oak Park architect Van Keuren built these late–Queen Anne houses himself as an investment.

9 Edmund F. Burton Row Houses
200–208 S. Clinton Ave.

1892, WILLETT & PASHLEY

Five Queen Anne dwellings with Romanesque details are shoehorned into a space that could have accommodated only two freestanding houses. The most elaborate occupies the eye-catching corner plot; its first tenant was Wright's future client, Arthur Heurtley. A disastrous 1979 fire destroyed 202 and damaged the others; sensitive rebuilding has brought them back.

10 Henry B. Waterman House
309 S. Clinton Ave.

1894, WILLIAM J. VAN KEUREN

Oak Parkers were fond of the no-nonsense Stick Style, with clapboards and rotated corner bay, which persisted here well into the era of Queen Anne and classical revival.

11 Isaac N. Conrad House
321 S. Clinton Ave.

1902, EBEN E. ROBERTS

Roberts created dozens of versions of this classic Oak Park house. Typical elements include the exaggerated breadth, the very low hipped roof and deep eaves, the manneristic brackets scrolling down the walls, and the disproportionately large abacus between the porch roof and columns.

12 George D. Webb House
329 S. Clinton Ave.

1896, ARCHITECT UNKNOWN

Showing the influence of the then-recent Columbian Exposition, this high-shouldered house features a New England curbed gambrel roof, dentils, and decorative columns.

13 George W. Smith House
404 S. Home Ave.

1898, FRANK LLOYD WRIGHT

Designed in 1895, this house of contrasts looks both forward and backward. The walls are subtly broken into rectangular planes like a Stick Style house but are covered in shingles rather than clapboard. Although as tall as its Queen Anne and classical revival neighbors, the house has proto–Prairie School elements: the entrance is hidden from view, and the house hugs the ground. Originally shingled like the walls, the steep double-pitched roof is now covered with pink asphalt, making the house look like a crazed pagoda.

14 Garland House
241 S. Home Ave.

EARLY 1850S, ARCHITECT UNKNOWN

Beneath the stucco, which dates

from around 1910, is one of Oak Park's oldest houses. According to local lore, it was moved from Lake St. in the mid-1880s. The symmetry, the rows of modillions, and the cornice return on the sides hint at the Greek Revival design.

Richard S. Thain House

15 Richard S. Thain House
210 S. Home Ave.

1892, PATTON & FISHER

The tall roof with the eaveless edge and the combination of robust forms with thin, crisp, clapboard siding are hallmarks of this firm's version of the Queen Anne style. Every room on the first two floors except the kitchen was designed with a bay, providing expansive views and a charmingly irregular form.

16 Pleasant Home

(John Farson House 2)
217 S. Home Ave.

1897–99, GEORGE W. MAHER

Designed in 1897 for investment banker John Farson, Pleasant Home was named for the streets that bound it. Maher considered it a "type for an American style," representative of the indigenous architecture that he and other Prairie School architects were creating. It became a prototype for many of Maher's houses.

Pleasant Home—exterior

Pleasant Home—dining room

Pleasant Home is approached through a formally landscaped, raised garden that emphasizes the facade's symmetry. The original ornamental fence and garden urns are preserved; the stable and greenhouse are not. Many aspects of the house relate to the William H. Winslow House in River Forest (1893) by Frank Lloyd Wright, with whom Maher had apprenticed in the office of Joseph Lyman Silsbee. The low-pitched roof, horizontality, buff-colored Roman brick, and simple stone window enframements respond to Wright's work. Maher introduced the emphasis on symmetry, the broad front porch, the elaborate centralized dormer, and the use of a floral motif in the decoration.

Pleasant Home's decoration introduced a personal design philosophy that Maher later called motif-rhythm theory. Selecting three decorative motifs—the American honeysuckle, the lion's head, and the shield—Maher unified the exterior details with art glass, mosaics, woodwork, light fixtures, and furniture. The art-glass door and windows at the entrance repeat the honeysuckle pattern and shield of the porch medallions; lion's heads appear on the porch and are carved into the hall's oak mantel. Maher designed the dining room table, chairs, and sideboard that are on view.

Maher developed a highly successful residential practice in the Chicago suburbs, especially in Kenilworth; his Chicago work is best represented on Hutchinson St. He developed his motif-rhythm theory to create visual unity in later commissions, exploiting the thistle in the James Patten House (Evanston, Illinois, 1901), the coral lily at Rockledge (Homer, Minnesota, 1911), both demolished, and the poppy in the Ernest Magerstadt House (Chicago, 1908). His subsequent furniture and interior decorations link his work to modern European design after 1900.

Herbert S. Mills, the house's second owner, sold the house to the Park District of Oak Park in 1939.

—KATHLEEN CUMMINGS

17 Samuel A. Rothermel Houses
100–110 S. Home Ave.
1891, WILLIAM J. VAN KEUREN
South and North Blvds. were originally the Boulevard, a broad street split by train tracks at grade and one of the village's earliest residential streets. With increasing traffic on the train lines, lots on the Boulevard became less desirable for fine homes and were developed as rental properties. Miniaturizing a variety of Queen Anne fronts, the design maximizes the number of units and features a style whose "stage set" quality is literally only skin-deep.

18 115 N. Oak Park Ave.
(Cicero Gas Co. Building)
1893, PATTON & FISHER
This narrow business block springs from a base of beautifully detailed

Roman brick. Local fraternal organizations could rent an upstairs hall.

19 Scoville Block (1)
116–132 N. Oak Park Ave.
1899, PATTON, FISHER & MILLER
1901, NORTH ADDITION, EBEN E. ROBERTS
1929, GROUND-FLOOR REMODELING,
   ROY J. HOTCHKISS

With this project, developer Charles B. Scoville accelerated the change of the Oak Park Ave./Lake St. district from single-family residential to commercial. Unusual for Oak Park are the Flemish stepped gables and the rich burnt-orange Roman brick and terra-cotta. Scoville is memorialized in medallions under the bays on the south wall. The original design was echoed beautifully in Roberts's Lake St. addition. The building remains a "flats above, stores below" complex.

20 Scoville Square
(Scoville Block 2)
137 N. Oak Park Ave.
1908, EBEN E. ROBERTS
1982, RESTORATION, OFFICE
   OF JOHN VINCI

This business block contained offices and a Masonic hall above shops. Bands of windows are divided by piers and topped by a row of roundheaded windows, a Sullivanesque organization of the wall popular with Oak Park architects Roberts and Normand S. Patton. The hipped roof and overhanging eaves are distinctly Prairie Style. Step inside to see a bright and breezy arcade.

21 Horse Show Association Fountain
Lake St. at Oak Park Ave.
1969 REPLICA OF 1909 ORIGINAL,
   RICHARD W. BOCK, SCULPTOR

The relationship between humans and their four-legged friends was a favorite sentimental theme of the period; this sculptured fountain symbolically and practically united them. People were to drink from the highest level, horses and dogs from the lower two. Bock showed a preliminary design to his friend and professional associate Frank Lloyd Wright, whose buildings frequently featured Bock's sculpture. Wright suggested the opening in the middle, leading to the apocryphal story that Wright had designed the fountain.

22 Medical Arts Building
715 W. Lake St.
1929, ROY J. HOTCHKISS

If Raymond Chandler's private eye, Philip Marlowe, had prowled the streets of Oak Park, his office would have been in this Art Deco mini-skyscraper. In contrast to the overgrown domesticity of much suburban commercial architecture of the 1920s, the unrestrained verticality and geometric decorative panels suggest that Oak Parker Hotchkiss looked to Loop high-rises for inspiration. The simple interior has been altered very little and is worth a look, especially for the light fixtures near the elevators and in the office corridors.

23 Archstone Apartments
675 W. Lake St.
1987, NAGLE, HARTRAY & ASSOCS.

This handsome, modern interpretation of the Prairie School idiom privatizes as much open space as possible, creating a tranquil spot that turns its back on the noise of Lake St. and the train tracks. Careful massing and choice of materials visually diminish the bulk. The lobby continues the look, featuring a fireplace with inglenook and Prairie School light fixtures and leaded glass.

Archstone Apartments

24 Francisco Terrace
W. Lake St. at N. Linden Ave.
1978, HARRY WEESE & ASSOCS.

This was among the first—and remains one of the best—Prairie School Revival projects in Oak Park. In 1973, as Frank Lloyd Wright's Francisco Terrace apartments in Chicago were about to be demolished, quick action on the part of real estate agent John Baird, attorney and historian

Devereux Bowly, and architect Ben Weese salvaged the terra-cotta arch, cornice, decorative panels, and other ornamentation. Adapting Wright's plan, Weese created a courtyard complex of seventeen town houses, replicating the original massing and details. The entry arch forms a beautiful terminus to Linden Ave.

25 Pilgrim Congregational Church
(Second Congregational Church)
460 W. Lake St.
1889, SOUTH HALF, PATTON & FISHER
1899, NORTH HALF, PATTON,
   FISHER & MILLER

The design bends a knee not to God but to H. H. Richardson, emulating his materials, polychromatic palette, bold forms, and confident vision. The rock-faced walls are trimmed in red brick, an inexpensive stand-in for Richardson's favored reddish Longmeadow stone. The Lake St. facade is unaltered; the remodeled office and chapel retain only the leaded-glass windows and fireplace. The addition to the north blends seamlessly, the stone base supporting a tall, rectilinear tower and an immense gable filled with a roundheaded window. More than 1,100 worshipers could be seated by raising the wall between the body of the church and the galleried Sunday school rooms to the east.

26 Oak Park and River Forest High School
201 N. Scoville Ave.
1906, NORMAND S. PATTON
   AND ROBERT C. SPENCER
1908, 1911, PATTON & MILLER
1913, ERIE ST. ADDITION,
   EBEN E. ROBERTS
1921, HOLMES & FLINN
1924, PERKINS, FELLOWS & HAMILTON
1928, FIELD HOUSE AND
   GYMNASIUM, CHILDS & SMITH
1968, ONTARIO ST. INFILL ADDITION,
   EVERETT I. BROWN & ASSOCS.

The clumsy late-1960s addition linking the field house and gym to the original school north of Ontario St. obscures the design, best seen from the Scoville and East Aves. sides. This project was a political marriage for Oak Parker Patton and River Forest resident Spencer: the school board split the design com-

Oak Park and River Forest High School—Erie St. Addition

mission between them. Sometimes described as Italian Renaissance, the school actually descends directly from Richardson's and Sullivan's organization of a large building block and strongly resembles Patton's best work as Chicago Board of Education architect in 1897–98. A school designer with twenty years' experience, Patton had favored roundheaded windows since the 1880s; combined with the deep eaves and hipped roofs, the whole has a Prairie spirit. The additions filling out the block from Ontario St. north to Erie St. emulate the original design.

27 Torrie S. Estabrook House
200 N. Scoville Ave.
1909, TALLMADGE & WATSON

The gabled roofs and projecting vertical piers are typical of this firm's work. Like many bungalows of the era, it has a large footprint; the cruciform plan included not only kitchen, living, and dining rooms on the first floor but also a den, a music room, and two bedrooms. This house was considered noteworthy in its time for the basement garage, entered from the rear of the property.

28 Houses for Flori Blondeel
426, 432, and 436 N. Elmwood Ave.
1913–14, JOHN S. VAN BERGEN

This pleasing trio of Prairie School houses is symmetrical and simply detailed. The center house is one of Van Bergen's many versions of Frank Lloyd Wright's "Fireproof House for $5,000," an economical design published in the *Ladies' Home Journal* in April 1907 and imitated by Van Bergen and others for years.

Houses for Flori Blondeel

29 Rollin Furbeck House

515 ～～～～ve.

1897, ～～～ WRIGHT

Wright's first emphatically forward-looking design in Oak Park excites with its remarkable experimentation. The variety and broken roofline of the Queen Anne style would have been comfortably familiar to any nineteenth-century viewer, while the dynamic composition and geometric detailing catapult boldly into the twentieth century. With its towering central pavilion, the design was an odd choice for this already elevated lot, which rolls over the remnants of an ancient glacial beach. Despite the placement of the first floor low on a water table and the horizontal banding of materials, the house reads as very tall, getting shyer as it rises. The very open picture window on the first floor contrasts sharply with the recessed diamond-paned windows above.

30 William G. Fricke House

540 N. Fair Oaks Ave.

1902, FRANK LLOYD WRIGHT

1907, GARAGE (FOR EMMA MARTIN),
FRANK LLOYD WRIGHT

This dazzling and dynamic arrangement of planes was originally anchored by a loggia and porch that ran to the south. Without them, the massive tower pulls the composition vertically. Even so, the interplay of wall and roof planes and the diamond-shaped entry bay on the north are the work of a rapidly maturing visionary.

31 Charles F. Lorenzen House

635 N. Fair Oaks Ave.

1906, EBEN E. ROBERTS

32 Charles Schwerin House

639 N. Fair Oaks Ave.

1908, EBEN E. ROBERTS

These typical Foursquare houses are refracted through the Oak Park prism, their exaggerated breadth

Charles F. Lorenzen House

William E. Martin House

and horizontality adorned with geometric Prairie School details from the front porch to the chimneys. Roberts frequently inflated the third-floor dormers on hip-roofed houses to give them maximum flair. The dormer at 639 owes a debt to George W. Maher, particularly his nearby house for Charles R. Erwin.

33 Vernon S. Watson House
643 N. Fair Oaks Ave.

1904, VERNON S. WATSON

Watson designed this modest house before he joined Thomas Tallmadge in practice. Built for $2,000, it is sided with horizontal board-and-batten and clapboard. Watson later added bays at the front and rear.

34 Otto H. McFeely House
645 N. Fair Oaks Ave.

1905, VERNON S. WATSON

Architects and owners valued concrete's fireproof qualities, especially after Chicago's disastrous Iroquois Theater fire of 1903. But the cost of constructing the forms was high, necessitating simple repetitive shapes and little or no ornament. This severe little experiment in concrete is softened somewhat by the porch and the Prairie-influenced stringcourse and wide eaves.

35 William E. Martin House
636 N. East Ave.

1903, FRANK LLOYD WRIGHT

Of this house, Wright wrote in his autobiography, "Here entered the important new element of Plasticity. . . . The windows would sometimes be wrapped around the building corners as inside emphasis of plasticity and to increase the sense of interior space. I fought for outswinging windows because the casement window associated house with the out-of-doors, gave free openings outward."

This mature Prairie School design offsets its great height by three layers of hipped roofs, which emphasize the horizontal and shield sparkling ribbons of leaded glass.

36 Harry C. Goodrich House
534 N. East Ave.

1896, FRANK LLOYD WRIGHT

The steeply pitched fedora roof with flared edges and the off-center porch are in the same vein as the George W. Smith House. The thin, crisp clapboard that covers so many Queen Anne houses in Oak Park reaches its true rectilinear potential here.

37 Edwin H. Cheney House
520 N. East Ave.

1904, FRANK LLOYD WRIGHT

Eye-catching in its dramatic horizontality yet guarding the path to penetration, this house protects as it entices. Even the location of the front door (in the middle of the south wall) is difficult to guess; the route to entry is circuitous and engaging. The lot slopes down to the east; the house snuggles into the same slight ridge that Wright's nearby Rollin Furbeck House (1897) surmounts. From the street, the terrace walls and the massive, low hipped roof hide most of the facade, with its dazzling art glass. No wonder Cheney's wife, Mamah Borthwick, fell in love with Wright! Their trip to Europe in 1909 was the beginning of the end for their marriages and for Wright's Oak Park life and Chicago practice; they moved together to Spring Green, Wisconsin, in 1911. She is buried there at Wright's home, Taliesin East, where she and her two children were among those murdered by a servant in 1914.

38 Dale Bumstead House
504 N. East Ave.
1909, TALLMADGE & WATSON

This successful design, with its signature narrow vertical piers and emphasized entry bay, became a formula for the firm.

39 Gustavus Babson House
415 N. Linden Ave.
1913, TALLMADGE & WATSON

By the time this split-level house was built, the Prairie School had become mainstream Oak Park, mingling with massive Georgians on Linden Ave.

40 Salem E. Munyer Apartments
175–181 N. Linden Ave./643–645 W. Ontario St.
1916, JOHN S. VAN BERGEN

Stripped and spare, this Prairie School building has a severity that looks ahead ten years to the International Style. It gracefully rounds the corner, balancing the horizontals of roof, raked mortar joints, and stone lintels with piers, chimneys, and stacks of sunporches.

41 Cheney Mansion
(C. A. Sharpe House)
208 N. Euclid Ave.
1913, CHARLES E. WHITE JR.

This mansion, now owned by the Park District of Oak Park, is notable chiefly for its size and craftsmanship.

42 George W. Furbeck House
223 N. Euclid Ave.
1897, FRANK LLOYD WRIGHT

This snug exercise in symmetry has a prominently placed door (in an enclosed porch, altered in the 1920s) but gives little indication of the interior layout. Wright loved to play with the viewer's sense of anticipation by giving false clues. A favorite subtly confusing device used here is the visual "stretching" of the first floor and shortening of the second by placing the stringcourse very high on the facade, directly under the second-floor windows. The textured surface, complex but well ordered, features Chicago common brick that interlocks and projects at the corners. Diagonal piers projecting from the sides of the bays resemble those on the front of the Rollin Furbeck House, done the same year for the owner's brother. The house was a wedding present from the resident's father, investor Warren Furbeck.

43 Edward W. McCready House
231 N. Euclid Ave.
1907, SPENCER & POWERS

This work—perhaps the firm's greatest—derives its grace from a subtle balancing of details: low urns, the high stringcourse, the deep-set door framed by glittering art-glass windows. The palette is simple but rich, the raked masonry joints of the orange brick emphasizing horizontality. It's a practical plan for a corner, often compared to H. H. Richardson's scheme for the John J. Glessner House on Prairie Ave. The north wall continues straight back to the garage, shielding the yard from the street.

Edward W. McCready House

44 Herman W. Mallen House
300 N. Euclid Ave.
1905, GEORGE W. MAHER

Damaged by fire and greatly altered, the house was originally stuccoed and sported open porches on the east and west. But beautiful art glass still adorns the second-floor bays of the Euclid Ave. facade.

45 Calvin H. Hill House
312 N. Euclid Ave.
1904, PATTON & MILLER

The style is colonial revival, but the massiveness is characteristic of the firm's Queen Anne work.

46 Thomas S. Rattle House
315 N. Euclid Ave.
1885, GEORGE O. GARNSEY

As editor of the monthly *National Builder*, a pattern-book magazine, Garnsey was one of Chicago's influential architects. This simple Queen Anne house has Stick Style details.

47 Charles E. Roberts House
321 N. Euclid Ave.
1883, BURNHAM & ROOT
1896, REMODELING, FRANK
LLOYD WRIGHT

Most of Wright's work was on the interior; some of his leaded glass can be glimpsed from the alley. Roberts was a great champion of the young architect and a prominent member of the Building Committee for Unity Temple.

48 Charles E. Roberts Stable
317 N. Euclid Ave.
1896, FRANK LLOYD WRIGHT
1929, CONVERSION TO HOUSE,
WHITE & WEBER

Perhaps Wright remodeled an exist-

ing stable; if so, it was a complete remodeling. From the front, it reads as stacked volumes; from the sides, as decorated planes.

49 Unity Church
(James Hall Taylor House)
405 N. Euclid Ave.
1912, GEORGE W. MAHER

This formal house resembles Maher's grand designs for Hutchinson St. in Chicago. The colossal flanged segmental arch over the door was one of his favorite details of this period. The deep, unusually detailed roofline features wide soffits and fasciae.

50 Charles R. Erwin House
530 N. Euclid Ave.
1905, GEORGE W. MAHER

Look at the tall narrow windows above the scalloped door arch to see the pattern in the art glass that once graced all the windows. It was echoed in a beautiful wrought-iron gate and fence.

51 George G. Page House
637 N. Euclid Ave.
1896, HARVEY L. PAGE

The grandeur and formality of this Federal Revival residence contrast sharply with other Oak Park houses of the era. Page had recently moved from Washington, D.C., and his academically correct cornice, pilasters, dentils, and Palladian windows have a measured and almost exotic beauty amid the efforts of Wright and Maher.

52 Harry S. Adams House
710 W. Augusta St.
1914, FRANK LLOYD WRIGHT

The unusual width of the lot allowed Wright to sprawl beyond his usual

George G. Page House

limits in this, his last Oak Park house. The breadth of the low chimney echoes the sweeping lines of the roof, stringcourse, and porte cochere. The sheltered entry features one of Wright's loveliest front doors.

53 Oscar B. Balch House
611 N. Kenilworth Ave.

1911, FRANK LLOYD WRIGHT

Wright had remodeled a store on Lake St. for decorator Balch and his partner, Frank Pebbles, in 1907. The music, living, and dining rooms flow straight across the front of the house, which is similar in first-floor plan to the Edwin H. Cheney House.

54 Clarence E. and Grace Hall Hemingway House
600 N. Kenilworth Ave.

1906, HENRY G. FIDDELKE

Grace Hemingway collaborated with the architect on the design, which included offices for Dr. Hemingway and a large music room. Ernest Hemingway lived here from the age of six until he left home at eighteen.

55 Walter Thomas Mills House
601 N. Kenilworth Ave.

1897, PATTON & FISHER

The simplicity and lack of fuss, the reliance on powerful forms already characteristic of the firm's work in the Queen Anne style, are edging here toward something more modern and rectilinear. The symmetrically placed corner windows on the second floor are noteworthy.

56 Charles E. Cessna House
524 N. Oak Park Ave.

1905, EBEN E. ROBERTS

Roberts indulged in rich materials: clay tile for the roof, a brick base, stone trim and brackets, and dazzling art glass. The emphasis on the horizontal is greatly exaggerated by the generous hipped roofs. The dormers are so deep that they subvert their function of admitting light into the attic space, much as the cavelike porch darkens the living room. The lack of light is a small price to pay for such a grand house.

57 William M. Luff House
520 N. Oak Park Ave.

1886, THEODORE V. WADSKIER

Even on this street of excessive architectural personality, this rare, well-preserved Swiss chalet version of the Stick Style holds its own. The wooden members that frame the rectangular panels of shingles and clapboard break through the plane of the wall, forming picturesque balconies. These, in turn, increase the complexity of the surface as the sun moves across the house, casting bars of shadow across its face.

58 Walter C. Hill House
516 N. Oak Park Ave.

1897, HARVEY L. PAGE

As strict an exercise in Federal Revival as can be seen in Oak Park, it is rigidly symmetrical and well proportioned.

William M. Luff House

59 Burton F. Hales House
509 N. Oak Park Ave.

1904, HENRY G. FIDDELKE

Oak Park's grandest mansion is this sober brick–and–Bedford limestone Gothic house.

60 Ernest Hemingway Birthplace
(Ernest Hall House)
339 N. Oak Park Ave.

1890, WESLEY A. ARNOLD

Ernest Hemingway was born in the second-floor turret bedroom in 1899. Hall was his maternal grandfather.

61 Oak Park Club Condominiums
721 W. Ontario St. (Oak Park Club)

1923, MILLER, HOLMES & FLINN

156 N. Oak Park Ave. (YMCA)

1904, POND & POND

1991, CONVERSION TO
  CONDOMINIUMS, BAUHS & DRING

The Georgian YMCA and the Renaissance/Prairie Oak Park Club served diverse social needs for decades. The club is the last major local descendant of the handsome building blocks seen in Oak Park and River Forest High School and Scoville

Square. Designed by Normand S. Patton's successor firm, it shifts to a more overtly revival style with Palladian detailing.

62 Parkview Apartments
173–181 N. Grove Ave.

1922, EBEN E. ROBERTS

As developer of this quality apartment house, Roberts billed it as "late English Gothic" and marketed it as "owner-occupied." Included were maids' rooms in the basement, a vacuum-cleaning system, "sound deafening" between floors, and a "radio-receiving apparatus" on the roof, with outlets in each unit. Faces loom at the parapet, styled on the north side as an iceman and a deliveryman to identify the service entrances.

63 Oak Park Public Library
834 W. Lake St.

2003, NAGLE HARTRAY
  DANKER KAGAN MCKAY

The third library to stand on this site still faces Lake St. but is oriented more toward Scoville Park.

64 Unity Temple
875 W. Lake St.

1905–8, FRANK LLOYD WRIGHT

Throughout his life, Wright was absorbed with pathways of discovery. At Unity Temple, the experience is both physical and spiritual. The route from the radical and uncompromising Lake St. facade to the warm and intimate temple is a sequence of spaces as compelling as any Wright ever created.

After their Gothic Revival church burned in June 1905, Oak Park's Universalists asked Wright to design a new building for four hundred members. The chosen site was prominent but small and close to noisy streetcar and train tracks. The budget was a modest $45,000.

These limitations and a deep understanding of the principles of the Universalist faith stimulated Wright's creativity. For reasons of economy, the architect selected reinforced concrete, usually used for important buildings only if covered with another material or molded to resemble stone. Construction technology and economics dictated broad, unornamented expanses and

Unity Temple—exterior

Unity Temple—interior

repetitive shapes. High walls and side entries set far back would shield worshipers from as much noise as possible.

Two similar but unequal blocks—"Unity Temple" for worship and "Unity House" for social-service functions—are joined by a low entry link. The deep overhang of the slab roof covers the walkway; the monumentally scaled planter cuts off the view of the street as one ascends the short flight of stairs. The visitor is sheltered and then encircled by the building before ever crossing the threshold. Facing the doors, the sheer walls of the two blocks and the entry parapet dramatically emphasize the sky, presaging the temple space. The inscription above each entry, "For the Worship of God and the Service of Man," reflects the Universalist belief that a house of worship must serve both sacred and secular needs.

Inside, the low-ceilinged entry area leads circuitously to even more confining cloisters from which one enters the dramatic temple space. Only thirty feet from the clamor of Lake St. is another world, flooded with light from amber-colored skylights that create the impression of what Wright called a "happy cloudless day." Three sets of galleries for the congregation and an alcove for the choir create a Greek cross within the square, with the corners occupied by square stair towers. No seat is more than forty-five feet from the pulpit, and most seats are just barely above or below the speaker's eye level. There are no religious symbols; the Universalists chose to focus all attention on the speaker. Wright placed doors to either side of the pulpit so the congregants would exit toward the minister.

Even before it gained worldwide renown, Unity Temple was widely praised both by the congregation and by local newspapers. Despite the unorthodox form and materials, they recognized that Wright had given form to a deeply rooted spirituality. It remains a transcendent work, bound to the earth and open to the heavens.

—ALICE SINKEVITCH

65 U.S. Post Office—Oak Park Station

901 W. Lake St.

1933, WHITE & WEBER

Here, sober Art Moderne is enlivened with amusing details, among them the sculptured panels over the entrances that document the world of mail delivery: birds carrying letters, a mailbag and cap, the Pony Express, a mail truck, a covered wagon, a train and plane. Studded with patriotic stars, Art Deco sconces and chandeliers light the pale interior.

66 William J. MacDonald House

300 N. Kenilworth Ave.

1890, WESLEY A. ARNOLD

Although added in 1911, the porch, with its foundation of boulders, complements the Queen Anne house.

67 George B. Pratt House

308 N. Kenilworth Ave.

1886, ARCHITECT UNKNOWN

This fine Stick Style house is modest in scale but boldly articulated on both front and sides.

68 John Rankin House

245 N. Kenilworth Ave.

1891, PATTON & FISHER

A grand parade of Kenilworth Ave. Queen Annes begins with this behemoth. The massive bays are tightly wrapped in thin clapboards. The octagonal corner turret appears to bulge from the effort of containing the great spaces within.

69 Walter H. Gale House (2)

312 N. Kenilworth Ave.

1905, HENRY G. FIDDELKE

This symmetrical Colonial Revival work has a detailed cornice and front door with sidelights.

70 David J. Kennedy House

309 N. Kenilworth Ave.

1888, PATTON & FISHER

Kennedy was a real estate investor and part owner of the Cicero & Proviso St. Railway. His barnlike Queen Anne features a layered gable front with flared edges.

71 William A. Douglas House

317 N. Kenilworth Ave.

1893, PATTON & FISHER

1908, ADDITION, PATTON & MILLER

Capacious, rambling, and generously scaled, the Douglas House has one of Oak Park's best porches. As in the John Rankin House, shingled, rolled edges frame the third-floor dormer.

72 Harrison P. Young House

(W. E. Coman House)

334 N. Kenilworth Ave.

1870S, ARCHITECT UNKNOWN

1895, REMODELING, FRANK LLOYD WRIGHT

The porch and the leaded diamond-paned windows are the most visible part of Wright's work.

73 John Schmidt House

400 N. Kenilworth Ave.

EARLY 1870S, ARCHITECT UNKNOWN

This early Oak Park cottage has Italianate detailing. The wood molding around the exaggeratedly vertical windows imitates masonry.

74 Joseph K. Dunlop House

407 N. Kenilworth Ave.

1897, EBEN E. ROBERTS

75 Simpson Dunlop House

417 N. Kenilworth Ave.

1896, EBEN E. ROBERTS

The Dunlop brothers were real estate developers and capitalists who established a bank in Oak Park in 1886. These magnificent houses are often labeled rectilinear Queen Anne, because although they are quite geometric on the outside, the plans still open out from the Queen Anne great hall.

76 Charles E. Matthews House

432 N. Kenilworth Ave.

1909, TALLMADGE & WATSON

The facade is sedate and formal, focusing on the entrance, which has art-glass windows that illuminate the stair hall.

77 Americus B. Melville House

437 N. Kenilworth Ave.

1904, EBEN E. ROBERTS

Americus B. Melville House

Roberts abandoned the box for this free-flowing stucco house, which is complex in elevation and sophisticated in plan. His characteristic brackets don't really support anything but have grown to gigantic proportions, dripping down the walls and porch piers.

78 Anna L. Wright House
(John Blair House)
931 W. Chicago Ave.

BEFORE 1873, ARCHITECT UNKNOWN
Wright bought the steeply gabled Gothic Revival house and large lot from Blair, a landscaper. On the Forest Ave. side of Blair's property, Wright built his own house; Wright's mother continued to live in Grandmother's Cottage.

79 Frank Lloyd Wright Home and Studio

951 W. Chicago Ave.
1889–1911, FRANK LLOYD WRIGHT
1976–86, RESTORATION, RESTORATION COMMITTEE OF THE FRANK
 LLOYD WRIGHT HOME AND STUDIO FOUNDATION

Wright's love was designing houses, and in seventy-two years of architectural life, he created more than 270 of them. This was his earliest as well as the first that he called home. Containing the seeds of all the rest, it was built on a corner lot acquired in 1889. The shingle-clad houses that Wright saw in architectural magazines gave aspect to the Forest Ave. facade, but the forms are sharply cut, crystal-clear products of the childhood training in geometric shapes that infused his entire career.

In keeping with the Shingle Style tradition, Wright's house is divided into three horizontal bands of base, walls, and roof. The base, of Chicago common brick, not only provides a protective wainscot but also roots the house in the suburban prairie. With what would be characteristic care for the setting, Wright retained most of the lot's tangle of native and exotic plants as a nest for his cottage. The wood-shingled middle zone almost disappears in the undulations of its wings and octagonal bays and in the transparency of its wide casement windows—a hint at the dissolution of the wall that characterized the Prairie School. The great gabled roof dominates the composition with proclamations of "shelter" and "home," as it always would for Wright. A dining room addition to the south and a kitchen/playroom addition to the rear completed the home about 1895.

Wright's studio addition (1898), facing Chicago Ave., shows a bold massing that came out of his love for pure geometric grammar. The exterior is a direct expression of the octagonal spaces within—a cubic two-story drafting room to the east of the entry and a library to the west. Commercial in scale, as befits an architectural office, the studio is nonetheless visually coupled to the house through the use of the same materials. Decorative elements by Wright and sculptor Richard W. Bock highlight the studio's elevations.

The organic, flowing, harmonious, and reposeful qualities that pervaded Wright's interiors can be found throughout, especially in the dining room,

Frank Lloyd Wright Home and Studio—exterior

Frank Lloyd Wright Home and Studio drafting room

playroom, drafting room, and library. The heating and lighting as well as the furnishings are everywhere integrated into the architectural environment.

After leaving Oak Park, Wright remodeled the studio as living quarters for his family, and the home was rented out; the complex was later remodeled into six apartments. The property was acquired by the National Trust for Historic Preservation in 1974. A National Historic Landmark, restored by the Frank Lloyd Wright Home and Studio Foundation to its 1905–9 appearance, it offers an intriguing look at the early home life and workplace of a master architect.

—DONALD G. KALEC

80 Robert P. Parker House
1019 W. Chicago Ave.
1892, FRANK LLOYD WRIGHT

81 Thomas H. Gale House
1027 W. Chicago Ave.
1892, FRANK LLOYD WRIGHT

These "bootlegged" houses were designed by the moonlighting Wright while he was still employed by Adler & Sullivan; local real estate agent Thomas Gale probably knew Wright through the Unitarian community. Both houses are a slight variation on a popular Queen Anne style, with a two-story corner bay topped by a turret. Wright's version is more geometric; the octagonal bay is a prominent element on both front and back, and the windows are massed in a band.

82 Walter H. Gale House (1)
1031 W. Chicago Ave.
1893–94, FRANK LLOYD WRIGHT

Construction of a cottage by architect L. D. Beman began in the spring of 1893 but apparently had not gotten far when Gale bought the lot later that year. This Queen Anne, with its sweeping roof, offers a rare example of Wright's skillful handling of spindles, an element frequently

Walter H. Gale House (1)

used to define interior spaces. Unusually tall and thin, they are so closely spaced that they appear as a solid wall as one approaches the house. Not until one is directly in front does the view of the wall behind suddenly emerge.

83 Andrew J. Redmond House
422 N. Forest Ave.
1900, EBEN E. ROBERTS
A giant step past the Victorianism of the Dunlop Houses, this is the first of a fifteen-year series of low, broad, beautifully detailed boxes. Maher's influence emerges in the urns, the emphasized third-floor dormer, the broad porch, and the formal symmetry.

84 William H. Copeland House
(William Harman House)
400 N. Forest Ave.
EARLY 1870S, ARCHITECT UNKNOWN
1908, GARAGE, FRANK LLOYD WRIGHT
1909, REMODELING, FRANK
  LLOYD WRIGHT
Known in Wright literature for later owner Copeland, this was originally an Italianate home in a yellowish

Milwaukee brick. An earlier renovation had already raised the roof when Wright remodeled the entry and interior, adding wood-mullioned windows and sidelights.

85 Sampson Rogers House
401 N. Forest Ave.
1890, FRANK ELLIS
This immense Queen Anne is made even larger by layers of porches, at least some of which were additions.

86 Eben E. Roberts House and Studio
1019 W. Superior St.
1911, REMODELING, EBEN E. ROBERTS
It has a cozy, hand-built look; most of the interest is in the interior, which is filled with detailed woodwork, art glass, and a built-in grandfather clock.

87 Francis J. Woolley House
1030 W. Superior St.
1893–94, FRANK LLOYD WRIGHT
A curiosity in Wright's development, this house bears a greater resemblance to Oak Park builders' houses of 1910 than to his later work.

88 Nathan G. Moore House
333 N. Forest Ave.
1895, FRANK LLOYD WRIGHT
1923, REMODELING, FRANK
  LLOYD WRIGHT
This generously scaled and lovingly detailed house is the product of two stages of Wright's career. Moore came to the architect in 1894 for a remodeling of the frame house on this site, then decided it would be too

Nathan G. Moore House

small and directed Wright to create something "Elizabethan." The bold and impressive Tudor Revival house was imitated by local architects for the next twenty years. Wright wrote in his autobiography, "Anyone could get a rise out of me by admiring that essay in English half-timber. 'They' all liked it and I could have gone on unnaturally building them for the rest of my natural life."

In December 1922, the house burned down to the top of the first floor. Wright, who happened to be in Chicago, contacted Moore and received the commission to rebuild. This opulent hybrid, with touches of Gothic, Sullivanesque, and Mayan design, was the result. Charles E. White Jr. was Wright's local coordinator for the project and is credited with the very traditional interior.

Arthur Heurtley House

89 Arthur Heurtley House
318 N. Forest Ave.

1902, FRANK LLOYD WRIGHT

Rich, challenging, and satisfying, open yet mysterious, firmly rooted to the ground yet removed from prying eyes, this is one of Wright's most magnificent homes. The raised living rooms enable occupants to look out through uncurtained art-glass windows without being seen. An overscaled brick half wall shields the roundheaded portal, rendering the front door invisible. The great hipped roof, utterly simplified, hovers over bands of richly leaded casement windows and a variegated battered-brick wall laid in a complex, textured pattern.

90 Edward R. Hills–Thomas DeCaro House
313 N. Forest Ave.

1883, CHARLES C. MILLER
1900–1906, REMODELING,
   FRANK LLOYD WRIGHT
1976, RECONSTRUCTION (FOR THOMAS
   DECARO), JOHN TILTON ASSOCS.

After several reincarnations, this gift from Nathan Moore to his daughter, Mary, is in excellent condition. The original Stick Style frame house stood just to the north with its narrow end facing Forest Ave. Wright and Moore moved it, turned it ninety degrees, and overhauled it so dramatically that they might as well have started from scratch. Although built in 1906, the house had apparently been designed in 1900, which partially accounts for the roofline with its flared eaves. The restored shingled roof is one of its most interesting features. Even here, Wright emphasizes the horizontal, with every fifth row of shingles a double layer. The small structure in the side yard is a ticket booth from the 1893 World's Columbian Exposition.

91 Charles A. Purcell House
300 N. Forest Ave.

1893, ARCHITECT UNKNOWN

This sober Queen Anne was built for architect William Gray Purcell's father, who once commented to his family, "If that Wright don't quit, he'll have our street ruined."

92 Laura Gale House
6 Elizabeth Ct.

1909, FRANK LLOYD WRIGHT

A stylistic step beyond even the boldest of Wright's Forest Ave. homes, this cantilevered composition looks forward twenty-five years to Fallingwater in Pennsylvania. Wright wrote, "In integral architecture the room-space itself must come through. The room must be seen as architecture or we have no architecture." Here, the porches are not applied appendages but "room-spaces" thrust through the wall, uniting exterior and interior. The leaded windows are screens, not barriers, protecting from the weather while enhancing the view.

93 Edgar Cook House
231 N. Forest Ave.

1870S, ARCHITECT UNKNOWN

One of the first generation of Forest Ave. houses, this simple cottage is vertically oriented, with jigsawed bargeboards under the eaves. Most of the other cottages from this era were either remodeled beyond recognition or moved after 1885 to other, less expensive sites.

94 Peter A. Beachy House
238 N. Forest Ave.
1906, FRANK LLOYD WRIGHT

The original commission was to re-model a modest cottage, which was ultimately obliterated by this grand Prairie School work. The thick lines of the eaves, lintels, and corner piers and the wood-mullioned windows have led to speculation that the talented hand of Wright employee Walter Burley Griffin contributed much to the design.

Joseph D. Everett House

95 Joseph D. Everett House
228 N. Forest Ave.
1888, WILSON, MARBLE & LAMSON

An overriding preference for the rectilinear once again harnesses the Queen Anne style.

96 Henderson Judd House
219 N. Forest Ave.
1881, ARCHITECT UNKNOWN

The Italianate was in its final years of popularity when this house

was built. In plan it resembles the emerging Stick Style, with an entry and stair hall pushed to the side. A very similar house was built at the same time at 223; remodeled after 1900, it is now unrecognizable as Italianate.

97 George T. Hayden House
209 N. Forest Ave.
1893, W. K. JOHNSTON

The riot of materials includes brick, stone, and shingles. The turret, porch, and shingled colonnettes dis-play more round forms than do most of Oak Park's other Queen Annes.

98 R. K. Bickford House
203 N. Forest Ave.
1885, ARCHITECT UNKNOWN

This Stick Style house retains a fea-ture long lost on most houses of the era: the scrolling open brackets that enhance the second-floor porch and corners and cast moving shadows on the clapboard.

99 Frank W. Thomas House
210 N. Forest Ave.
1901, FRANK LLOYD WRIGHT
1922, REAR ADDITION,
  TALLMADGE & WATSON
1975, RESTORATION

Turning a blind eye to the Victorian timidity on its flanks, the Thomas House is considered Wright's first constructed Prairie School house. "First thing in building the new house, get rid of the attic, there-fore the dormer," Wright wrote in *An Autobiography*. "Get rid of the useless false heights below it. Next, get rid of the unwholesome

Frank W. Thomas House

basement, yes absolutely—in any house built on the prairie. Instead of lean, brick chimneys bristling up everywhere to hint at Judgment, I could see necessity for one chimney only." This house meets the ground with a simple water table, above which the walls rise unbroken to the line of dazzling art glass. The entry sequence is complex and unpredictable. The roundheaded portal appears to shield a door but actually conceals a stair leading up and back to the real front door.

100 Emerson Ingalls Row Houses
200–208 N. Forest Ave.
1892, WILLIAM J. VAN KEUREN

Looking like an overgrown Queen Anne house, this symmetrical composition is interesting mainly for its sharp contrast with the Prairie style, which emerged on the lot next door in 1901.

PILSEN/HEART OF CHICAGO/ LITTLE VILLAGE/LAWNDALE

The communities of Pilsen, Heart of Chicago, Little Village, and Lawndale grew up with Chicago's industry, thriving in the 1870s when the city was becoming an industrial powerhouse and declining a century later as the manufacturing base withered away. The flats, cottages, and commercial buildings that met the needs of generations of factory workers suffer from decay and neglect, but lively areas persist in the immigrant neighborhoods, which continue to attract new arrivals.

Pilsen, the oldest community, is bounded on the south by the Illinois & Michigan Canal (1848) and was developed with lumberyards and breweries; on the north, Pilsen ends at railroad tracks laid in the 1860s. Its major development occurred after the Great Fire of 1871, when burned-out industries and workers moved west. Immigrants from Bohemia were the earliest settlers, and they named the community for their homeland's second-largest city. Polish and Yugoslavian immigrants arrived in the early twentieth century and were replaced beginning in the 1950s by Mexicans and Puerto Ricans. Pilsen's early role as a port of entry called for flats, apartments, and combination retail-residential buildings, built mostly by investors for rental. It remains a first-stop immigrant neighborhood but has also attracted artists priced out of the city's North Side. The area has a concentration of buildings from the 1870s and 1880s, many of which feature the mansard roof characteristic of those decades. In 1875, the city's ongoing sewer project reached the Pilsen area. This process of raising streets and sidewalks above new sewer and drainage systems left many buildings with their first floors eight to ten feet below street level.

Heart of Chicago, which is west of Ashland Ave., also boomed after the 1871 fire, when industries began to cluster along the river. Germans, Poles, and Northern Italians were the major ethnic groups. The leading industry was the McCormick Reaper (later International Harvester) works at Western and

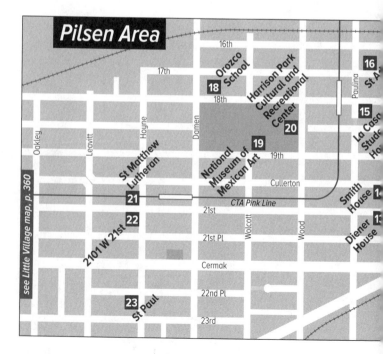

Blue Island Aves.; like other large employers, it is long gone. The southern stretches of both Pilsen and Heart of Chicago contain many barren former industrial sites, but the residential portions remain vital.

Little Village, or La Villita, was originally known as South Lawndale and was renamed in the mid-1970s by its Mexican American majority. Both Lawndales were primarily open swamplands west of the city limits at Western Ave. in 1863, when the Chicago, Burlington & Quincy Railroad was laid out on a southwesterly course that became the boundary between the two areas. Annexed by Chicago in 1869, South Lawndale witnessed residential development around 1885, with the general westward expansion of the built-up city, but it contained on the south and west by the accelerating development of industry. Immigrants from Bohemian Pilsen were among the first occupants of the area's small brick houses, followed in the 1930s by Poles and since 1960 by increasing numbers of Hispanics. By 1980, the community had the city's largest concentration of Mexicans.

Ogden Ave., built in the 1850s as a plank road along the portage trail linking Lake Michigan to the Des Plaines River, largely demarcates North Lawndale. Residential development progressed westward along Roosevelt Rd., the commercial street at Lawndale's northern edge, after 1895, when the Garfield Park elevated train inaugurated service to Cicero Ave. The bulk of the residential construction—primarily rental apartments and two-flats—took place between 1910 and 1925. The earliest occupants were Russian Jews moving from the Near West Side; in the 1920s, the area had seventy synagogues. After World War II, African Americans began following the same westward route and constituted 90 percent of the population by 1960. The West Side riots following the 1968 assassination of Dr. Martin Luther King Jr. closed some businesses, and the refusal of insurance companies to renew policies closed many more.

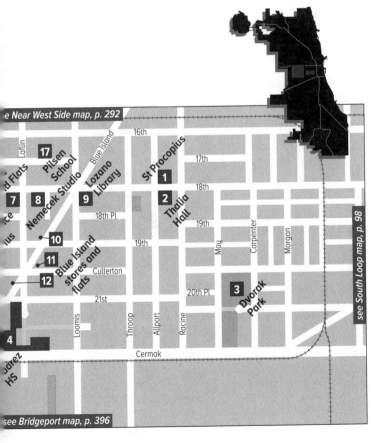

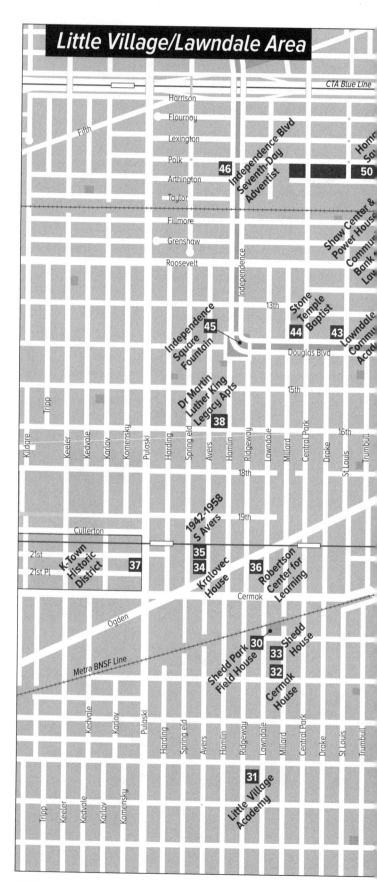

Little Village/Lawndale Area

CTA Blue Line

Harrison
Flournoy
Lexington
Polk
Arthington
Taylor

Fifth

46

Independence Blvd
Seventh-Day Adventist

Home Sav

50

Fillmore
Grenshaw
Roosevelt

Independence

Shaw Center & Power House

Commu Bank Law

13th

Stone Temple Baptist

44

43

Lawndale Commu Acad

Independence Square Fountain

45

Douglas Blvd

Dr Martin Luther King Legacy Apts

38

15th

Tripp
Kildare
Keeler
Kedvale
Karlov
Komensky
Pulaski
Harding
Spring eld
Avers
Hamlin
Ridgeway
Lawndale
Millard
Central Park
Drake
St Louis
Trumbull

16th

18th

1942-1958
S Avers

19th

Cullerton

21st
21st Pl

K-Town Historic District

37

35
34

Kralovec House

36

Robertson Center for Learning

Cermak

Ogden

Shedd Park Field House

30

33

Shedd House

32

Cermak House

Metra BNSF Line

Kedvale
Karlov
Pulaski
Harding
Spring eld
Avers
Hamlin
Ridgeway
Lawndale
Millard
Central Park
Drake
St Louis
Trumbull

31

Little Village Academy

Tripp
Keeler
Kedvale
Karlov
Komensky

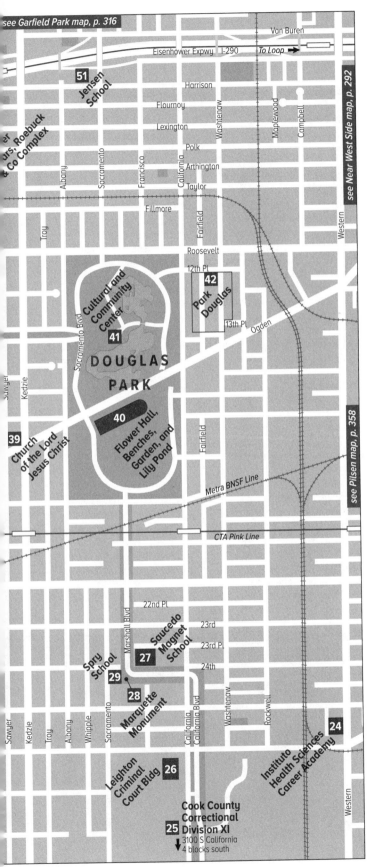

see Garfield Park map, p. 316

Van Buren

Eisenhower Expwy   I-290   *To Loop* →

51
Jensen
School

Harrison

Flournoy

Lexington

Polk

Arthington

Taylor

Fillmore

ers, Roebuck
& Co Complex

Albany

Sacramento

Francisco

California

Washtenaw

Maplewood

Campbell

Western

see Near West Side map, p. 292

Troy

Roosevelt

12th Pl

42

Park
Douglas

13th Pl

Ogden

Cultural and
Community
Center

41

Sacramento Blvd

DOUGLAS
PARK

40

Flower Hall,
Benches,
Garden, and
Lily Pond

Fairfield

Fairfield

Sawyer

Kedzie

39

Church
of the Lord
of Jesus Christ

Metra BNSF Line

see Pilsen map, p. 358

CTA Pink Line

22nd Pl

23rd

Saucedo
Magnet
School

23rd Pl

24th

Spry
School

27

Marshall Blvd

29

28

Marquette
Monument

Sawyer

Kedzie

Troy

Albany

Whipple

Sacramento

California

California Blvd

Washtenaw

Rockwell

24

Instituto
Health Sciences
Career Academy

Leighton
Criminal
Court Bldg   26

Cook County
Correctional
25 Division XI
↓ 3100 S California
4 blocks south

Western

Industrial properties have been vacated as the city shifted from a manufacturing to a service orientation. Lawndale's landscape is now characterized by aging housing stock, with blocks of neat graystones interspersed with vacant lots and crumbling buildings. Infill housing projects have appeared throughout the area but have not kept pace with the rate of decay.

—VINCENT MICHAEL

1 St. Procopius Church
18th St. at Allport St.
1883, JULIUS H. HUBER

The design of this "mother church" of Chicago's Bohemian parishes was inspired by the Romanesque Revival that occurred in the early to mid-nineteenth-century in Germany and Eastern Europe; it was then translated into inexpensive local materials. As in nearby flats and commercial buildings, walls of common brick are trimmed with Joliet limestone, sparely embellished with incised ornament. The leaded-glass windows are filled with plant forms and fleurs-de-lis, with religious imagery limited to small medallions.

2 Thalia Hall
1807 S. Allport St.
1893, FABER & PAGELS

This husky Romanesque mixed-use building served Pilsen's Bohemian community as a social and political center and hosted musical and theatrical productions. Apartments and stores helped support the hall, named for the Greek muse of comedy. Above the entry hovers a "green man," with hair, beard, and mustache of acanthus. A popular pagan figure co-opted by Christians, he can be traced to the head-hunting and -worshiping Celts.

He enjoyed a revival on turn-of-the-century buildings, particularly those faced with limestone, along with other elements borrowed from the Romanesque.

3 Dvorak Park
Cullerton to 21st Sts.;
Carpenter to May Sts.
1908, WILLIAM CARBYS ZIMMERMAN
    AND RICHARD E. SCHMIDT,
    GARDEN & MARTIN

Surviving features of this Progressive Reform movement park—used by 2,500 people a day during its first decade—include Zimmerman's original field house and fence posts; Schmidt, Garden & Martin's iron lamp standards; and 1920s fencing. Zimmerman's pool building has been heavily altered.

4 Benito Juárez High School
2150 S. Laflin St.
1977, BERNHEIM, KAHN & LOZANO
2011, ADDITION, ARCHITRAVE;
    OWP/P, ASSOC. ARCH.

Built for Pilsen's growing Mexican American community, this school was designed in consultation with Pedro Ramírez Vázquez, a Mexican architect. The geometry of the elevations was meant to evoke pre-Columbian temples but unfortunately has none of their drama or

Thalia Hall

rich narrative details. The addition is linked to the existing building by a glass-and-metal bridge.

5 St. Pius V Roman Catholic Church
1901 S. Ashland Ave.
1885–92, JAMES J. EGAN

Egan brought a light touch to the Romanesque Revival style, preferring smooth masonry to the rough ashlar favored by other Chicago church architects such as Burling & Whitehouse and Edbrooke & Burnham. The finely detailed arched entrances and windows are echoed on the interior, which, although modernized, retains a powerful trio of roundheaded arches, embellished with Norman carving and stencils, in the sanctuary. On the facade, the flowing geometric designs of the impost blocks and the band connecting the upper windows are in the vein of Frank Furness and Louis H. Sullivan.

6 U.S. Post Office—Pilsen Station
1859 S. Ashland Ave.
1935, JOHN C. BOLLENBACHER

The Pony Express goes Moderne in the reliefs above the windows of this blocky post office, one of the finest of its era.

Both sides of 18th St. from Loomis St. west to Damen Ave. are lined with well-worn but still heavily used retail, recreational, and residential buildings. Although many of them are remuddled and hung with modern signs, they remain vividly eclectic.

7 John Novak Store and Flats
1501 W. 18th St.
1887, ARCHITECT UNKNOWN

This deep tenement (with a fourth floor squeezed under the mansard roof) above a storefront grabs for glory with an effusively ornamented pressed-metal corner tower.

8 Francis D. Nemecek Studio
1439 W. 18th St.
1907, FRANK RANDAK

This tiny Baroque storefront for a photographer had a well-lit studio space above a metal–and–leaded-glass storefront, which has been well preserved.

9 Chicago Public Library— Rudy Lozano Branch
1805 S. Loomis St.
1990, JAY CAROW ARCHITECTS

Bands of red and blue terra-cotta ornament pierce the curved glass facade to run through the library's interior. The motif of the decorative tile is derived from pre-Columbian structures at Mitla, in Oaxaca.

On S. Blue Island Ave. from 19th to 20th Sts. is a cluster of three decades of typical Chicago "flats above the stores" buildings (entries 10–12).

10 Store and Flats
1870 S. Blue Island Ave.
1899, FROMMANN & JEBSEN

Working for Schlitz agent Edward G. Uihlein, the architects bent their Germanic Queen Anne taproom formula around this oblique corner to visually command the intersection.

11 Jan Kralovec Stores and Flats
1923–1929 S. Blue Island Ave.
1886, ARCHITECT UNKNOWN

Between the second and third floors are cast-iron columns with foliate capitals and ornate spandrels. The cornice, which is of pressed metal with paired brackets on Blue Island Ave., changes to a simpler brick corbel table around the corner on Cullerton St.

12 George Van Dolen Stores and Flats
2008–2010 S. Blue Island Ave.
1879, ARCHITECT UNKNOWN

This Italianate building has retained its cast-iron pillars carrying elaborate capitals and stone window hoods bearing prominent keystones.

13 Gustave Diener House
1529 W. Cullerton St.
1886, ARCHITECT UNKNOWN

14 Frank Smith House
1530 W. Cullerton St.
1887, ARCHITECT UNKNOWN

This street of late Italianate two- and three-flats is notable for the "boomtown" fronts (straight cornices disguising gable fronts) with straight or arched pediments projecting from the center. On each of these buildings, the cornice line leaps over an attic window to form a semicircle, a characteristic of Pilsen two-flats.

15 La Casa Student Housing
1805 S. Paulina St.
2012, URBANWORKS

The building represents a new paradigm in college housing, its location determined by the students' neighborhood rather than proximity to academic institutions. Students from the area live in shared suites, with living/dining rooms at the glassy corners. Building residents attend two- or four-year colleges in all parts of the city.

La Casa exterior

16 St. Adalbert Roman Catholic Church
1656 W. 17th St.
1914, HENRY J. SCHLACKS

On a street so narrow that the 185-foot towers reach almost out of sight stands Schlacks's basilica-plan masterpiece. Grand and formal, intended to inspire awe rather than familiarity, the facade and worship space are Renaissance Revival, typical of Chicago's Polish churches. The imposing colonnaded porch combines granite columns and door surrounds with terra-cotta capitals and pediment. Inside, the long nave is filled with golden light from tall clerestory windows. The sanctuary wall, painted with scenes from Polish history, frames a fabulous Baroque baldachin over the marble altar. Polish saints including Casimir and Stanislaus Kostka are commemorated in F. X. Zettler's rich stained-glass windows.

17 Pilsen Academy School
1420 W. 17th St.
1898, NORMAND S. PATTON

The arches and stone carvings give an unusual interest to this small school, which was designed during Patton's stint as Board of Education architect.

18 José Clemente Orozco Community Academy
1940 W. 18th St.
2000, ALPHONSE GUAJARDO ASSOCS.; URBANWORKS, ASSOC. ARCHS.

Art teacher Francisco Mendoza worked with students to create drawings of Mexican and Mexican American icons and scenes. The drawings were then digitized and turned into mosaic mural panels. The resulting band of images, which distinguishes this school, is a stunning display of talent and history.

19 National Museum of Mexican Art
(Harrison Park Natatorium)
1852 W. 19TH ST.
1914, WILLIAM CARBYS ZIMMERMAN
1978, RENOVATION, ADRIAN LOZANO
2001, ADDITION, ADRIAN LOZANO

Brick, concrete, and glass block transformed an aging natatorium into a museum.

20 Harrison Park Cultural and Recreational Center
S. Wood St. at W. 18th Pl.
1992, CHICAGO PARK DISTRICT

The facade is bent like an exedra to welcome visitors while respecting the park's original grid plan and maximizing the green space.

21 St. Matthew Lutheran Church
(Evangelische Lutherische St. Matthäus Kirche)
2100 W. 21st St.
1888, FREDERICK AHLSCHLAGER

The *Chicago Inter-Ocean* noted in 1888 that Ahlschlager "is getting the retainer for about everything Lutheran." His church is a rare surviving example of the off-the-shelf late-nineteenth-century Gothic Revival that so many congregations replaced with larger, more academically correct buildings. Common brick and Lemont limestone are joined by pressed metal that pinch-hits for stone in places such as the arcaded corbel table. The three entrances are topped by the original tympana of colored leaded glass, and the main door is surrounded by eight cast-iron columns.

22 2101 W. 21st St.
(Evangelische Lutherische Schule)
1882, ARCHITECT UNKNOWN
A very early private school is rendered in the Italianate style of the neighborhood's flats and storefronts. On the roof is a pressed-metal cupola with delicate cresting.

23 St. Paul Roman Catholic Church

(St. Paulus Kirche)
2234 S. Hoyne Ave.
1897–99, HENRY J. SCHLACKS

St. Paul Roman Catholic Church

The parish dreamed beyond reason, the architect designed beyond budget, and St. Paul's became Chicago's greatest Gothic leap of faith. In a working-class neighborhood of modest homes and flats, the 245-foot towers soared higher than the Loop's Reliance and Monadnock Buildings. Thrillingly out of scale in both size and expense, the construction left the parish deeply in debt and led Archbishop James Quigley to replace the pastor. The church was completed in just two years by an architect acting as contractor and by parishioners donating their skilled labor. Its strength lies in the boldness of scale, the integration of interior and exterior, and the selective embellishment that achieves maximum drama. Most of the building (and the surrounding parish complex) is modest common brick; the east facade and interior are a light-brown face brick. Molded brick is used where Schlacks would have used stone on a more expensive design, such as the colonnettes and rib vaulting; only where absolutely necessary did he resort to terra-cotta.

St. Paul's held Schlacks's interest for several decades. He designed the main altar (1910), communion railing (1912), and side altars and pulpit (1916) in a complementary Gothic style in white marble. The luminous Venetian mosaics that decorate the interior and facade were the final major element. Installed in 1930, they combine natural forms with symbolic and pictorial content. Completing the lush but harmonious decoration are stained-glass windows. The transept windows, which depict six scenes in the life of Christ, are particularly fine, with unusually well-detailed architectural backdrops and plant forms. Across the street to the north is St. Paul Parochial School (1892), also designed by Schlacks and connected by a second-story bridge to Casa Claret, once St. Paul's convent.

24 Instituto Health Sciences Career Academy

2520 S. Western Ave.
2011, JGMA, DESIGN ARCH.; GHAFARI ASSOCS., ARCH. OF RECORD
An old brick building is slipcovered in aluminum panels coated with an iridescent paint that changes color depending on the light and vantage point. The interior of this new high school is also saturated with vivid colors.

25 Cook County Maximum Security Facility Division XI

3105 S. California Blvd.
1995, ROULA ASSOCS. ARCHITECTS; KNIGHT ARCHITECTS ENGINEERS PLANNERS, ENGINEERING AND PROGRAM MANAGEMENT; PHILLIPS SWAGER ASSOCS., SECURITY CONSULTANTS
With a capacity of 1,600 inmates, this jail is one of the nation's largest. The X-shaped configuration provides

Leighton Criminal Court Building

a master control center for four self-sustaining "pods," each of which has a control area and outdoor yard for 200 two-person cells.

26 Leighton Criminal Court Building

(Cook County Criminal Court House and Jail)
2600 S. California Blvd.
1927, HALL, LAWRENCE & RATCLIFFE

Although far from the Loop's Cook County headquarters, this site was chosen because it adjoined the Bridewell House of Correction and offered room for expansion. This severe monument to criminal justice is realized in a brand of flat classicism most notable for its rich sculptural program, which is largely the work of Peter Toneman of Joseph Dux Studios in conjunction with the Indiana Limestone Co. Above each of the giant Doric columns rises an allegorical figure: Law, Justice, Liberty, Truth, Might, Love, Wisdom, and Peace. *S.P.Q.C.*, inscribed under the adjacent eagle panels, is Chicago's variant of the classical *S.P.Q.R.* (the Senate and People of Rome). The bison above the doors grow their pelts in a Greek meander pattern.

27 Maria Saucedo Magnet School

(Carter H. Harrison Technical High School)
2850 W. 24th Blvd.
1912, ARTHUR F. HUSSANDER

Ponderous classicist Hussander succeeded Prairie School designer Dwight H. Perkins as architect for the Chicago Board of Education in 1910. The roofline of this heavily ornamented structure bristles with acroteria, the shell-shaped protrusions generally found only at the apex and corners of a pediment.

28 Jacques Marquette Monument

S. Marshall Blvd. at W. 24th Blvd.
1925, BASE, HOLABIRD & ROCHE
1926, HERMON A. MACNEIL, SCULPTOR

Explorers Jacques Marquette and Louis Joliet are accompanied by an Algonquin Indian. Chicago's first known European inhabitant, Father Marquette spent the winter of 1674–75 near what is now the intersection of Damen Ave. and 26th St. Bronze tablets at the bridge's northeast corner commemorate his stay.

29 John Spry Community School

2400 S. Marshall Blvd.
1899, NORMAND S. PATTON
1919, ADDITION, ARTHUR F. HUSSANDER

Patton's gently Romanesque central section was the Board of Education's first fireproof school.

Subdivided in 1870 by Alden C. Millard & Edwin J. Decker, Millard Ave. south of the Chicago, Burlington & Quincy Railroad tracks was fashionable in the late nineteenth century. It retains a whisper of elegance in a sampling of Gothic Revival, Italianate, and Queen Anne houses, most of which have been greatly remodeled. The railroad had a station at what is now Shedd Park (entries 30 and 32–33).

Shedd Park Field House

30 Shedd Park Field House
(Recreation Building)
3660 W. 23rd St.
1917, WILLIAM DRUMMOND
1928, GYMNASIUM ADDITION,
MICHAELSEN & ROGNSTAD

By 1885, John G. Shedd had re-subdivided part of Millard & Decker's subdivision and set aside just over an acre for a private park. After unsuccessful efforts to assess local homeowners for improvements, the land was transferred to the city in 1888 and to the Chicago Board of Park Commissioners ten years later. Although nothing remains of Jens Jensen's landscape (1917), the field house is one of the best examples of Prairie School architecture in the Chicago Park District. Above the south entrance, a large but delicately detailed wood pediment contains a fine tympanum with thin glass windows between vertical wooden slats. The sensitively realized gymnasium is recessed forty feet behind the main entrance and repeats the horizontal massing and stringcoursing of Drummond's original.

31 Little Village Academy
2620 S. Lawndale Ave.
1996, ROSS BARNEY & JANKOWSKI
A tight site dictated an efficient,

Little Village Academy

compact building, but this public school building is no blank box. Sculptural elements seem to burst out of the facades, symbolizing an energy generated from within. These include the white trapezoidal library, horizontal sunscreens outside the computer room, and the angled fiberglass walls of the science room. The most dramatic punctuation is the entry and skylit stair tower, the functional and symbolic heart of the school. Its flat interior wall features a precisely oriented sundial. The sun motif, symbolic of the community's Mexican heritage, is carried through in the lobby flooring and extends outdoors to the plaza. Color and playful elements carried out in economical materials create a sense of fun throughout the building.

1952 S. Avers Ave.

32 Anton J. Cermak House
2348 S. Millard Ave.

1920, RANDAK & REZNY

This stolid essay in Bohemian Bourgeois was built by Cermak, a solid citizen, a state senator, chair of the Cook County Board, and Chicago's mayor from 1931 until 1933, when he was felled by an assassin's bullet intended for President-Elect Franklin D. Roosevelt.

33 John G. Shedd House
2316 S. Millard Ave.

1888, ARCHITECT UNKNOWN

1886, STABLE, CHARLES A. WEARY

Shedd rose from stock boy to partner to president of Marshall Field & Co. His robust Queen Anne house is remarkably intact, retaining its original porch with simple turned columns.

Just a few blocks northwest of Shedd Park, somewhat isolated by Ogden Ave. and one-way streets, is a cluster of unusually fine rusticated limestone homes (entries 34–35).

34 Jan Kralovec House
2102 S. Avers Ave.

1892, FREDERICK B. TOWNSEND

35 1942 through 1958 S. Avers Ave.

1893–94, ATTRIB. TO FREDERICK B. TOWNSEND

In anticipation of a new streetcar line on Cermak Rd., the Czech-born Kralovec began developing homes nearby. His own residence is an imposing example of the Richardsonian Romanesque style and has a matching coach house. The four adjacent houses he built are also of rusticated limestone, although only two of them continue the Romanesque style; those at 1942 and 1950 are classically inspired.

36 Carole Robertson Center for Learning
(Jubilee Family Center)
3701 W. Ogden Ave.

2002, ROSS BARNEY & JANKOWSKI

Creative use of durable, cost-effective materials makes this child-care center a source of neighborhood pride. Masonry on the north and south facades is patterned to resemble Kente cloth, an African fabric originally worn only by royalty. At the entrances to the building and to classrooms, colored floor tiles form "floor mats" that look like Zairian raffia cloths. A central courtyard provides protected play space and abundant daylight.

---

37 K-Town Historic District
W. Cullerton St. to W. Cermak Rd., S. Pulaski Rd. to S. Kostner Ave.

Listed on the National Register of Historic Places in 2010, K-Town is a well-preserved enclave of residential architecture in an area plagued by vacant lots and abandoned buildings. Its single-family homes and flats were constructed primarily between 1901 and 1918, though some are from the 1920s. It started as a Czech neighborhood convenient to industrial jobs. The most prominent remnant of the community's ethnic heritage is the former John Hus Memorial Building (1915, ANTON CHARVAT) at **4236 W. Cermak Rd.**, built as a community center for Bohemian freethinkers.

The most intact streetscapes are on 21st Pl., 21st St., and Cullerton St. As residential development proceeded west from Pulaski Rd., the Queen Anne and Romanesque Revival graystones were superseded by brick buildings with simple Prairie or classical revival details. The transition of style and materials is nicely illustrated by a trio of houses on W. 21st Place between Keeler and Kildare Aves.: **4224** is a typical two-story graystone built in 1911; **4228** is a simple brick three-flat built the following year; and **4230** is a Prairie School brick two-flat from 1914 (J. B. REZNY, ARCHITECT). Many of the buildings' architects are not documented; among the names that do appear frequently are Adolph Lonek and Joseph Houda.

The district has a higher concentration of single-family residences than many other ethnic working-class neighborhoods of the period. Most unusual are the single-story houses of brick or limestone that look like truncated multistory flat buildings. The greatest concentration of the "shoebox graystones" built between 1903 and 1908 (architects unknown) can be found at **4014 through 4052 W. Cullerton St.** There is a cluster of charming single-story brick residences at **4147 through 4155 W. Cullerton St.** (1911, ARCHITECTS UNKNOWN). Also of note are scattered brick two- and three-flats with simple pedimented entry porches and elaborately shaped gables: a good example is at **4122 W. 21st Pl.** (1906, JOSEPH B. DIBELKA).

---

38 Dr. Martin Luther King Legacy Apartments
1550 S. Hamlin Ave.
2011, JOHNSON & LEE

In 1966, Dr. Martin Luther King Jr. brought his crusade for social justice to the North and moved with his family into a three-flat at 1550 S. Hamlin Ave. Although that building and many others no longer stand, the Lawndale Christian Development Corporation has spearheaded plans to honor King's legacy with a four-acre historic district featuring new buildings and green spaces. This colorful mixed-use development is a strong start. It provides affordable rental housing and ground-level commercial space. Images of King and his family grace

Dr. Martin Luther King Legacy Apartments

the sidelights and transoms of the exterior residential entrances. Projecting window frames further enliven the facade, and the northernmost one on the third floor marks the approximate location of King's apartment in the demolished building.

39 Church of the Lord Jesus Christ of the Apostolic Faith
(Douglas Park Auditorium)
3202 W. Ogden Ave.
1910, RUSY & REZNY

Stores, offices, club rooms, and a dance hall filled this massive, *retardataire* Second Empire structure lavished with terra-cotta.

Douglas Park
W. Roosevelt Rd. to W. 19th St.; S. California Ave. to S. Albany Ave.
1871, WILLIAM LE BARON JENNEY
1885, OSCAR F. DUBUIS
1906, JENS JENSEN

Created along with Humboldt and Garfield Parks by the West Park Commission in 1869, Douglas Park was developed and redesigned over the next forty years. Jenney was starting from scratch; the park had to be raised to grade level by filling it in with manure and sand. The *Land Owner* reported on progress in 1874: "To enhance the beauties of the place, there have been 40,000 yards of Stock Yards' manure deposited there in an imposing mass, not to speak of the thousands of yards of the same romantic material scattered broadcast over the other parks. . . . The manure is magnificent soil medicine and its effects can be plainly traced in the improved vegetation and general fertility of a region that two years ago was not much removed from 'a howling wilderness.'"

The most important surviving element of Jenney's design is the northernmost portion of the lagoon, framed by the **Iron Bridge** (1892, ATTRIB. TO ADOLPH GOTTLIEB) to the south and by the **Stone Bridge** (1897, DESIGNER UNKNOWN) to the north. Later neighborhood residents put this lagoon to good use; the Federal Writers Project's *Illinois Guide* (1939) noted that annually "in early autumn, orthodox Jews gather at the lagoon for a ritualistic casting away of their sins."

Jensen's work is visible in the southern half of the park. At the Marshall Blvd. entrance at 19th St. are the wooden pergola and reflecting pools. The other surviving features of his design are the Prairie Meadow, with its berms and hawthorn trees (favored by Jensen for their horizontal branching pattern), and the formal flower garden ensemble that parallels Ogden Ave.

The most glaring of many subsequent alterations to the park was the intrusive siting of **George W. Collins High School** (1968, ANDREW HEARD & ASSOCS.), just north of the Douglas Blvd. entrance.

40 Flower Hall, Benches, Garden, and Lily Pond
CA. 1907, ATTRIB. TO SCHMIDT, GARDEN & MARTIN

The reinforced-concrete Flower Hall (covered walkway) is classical in form but Prairie Style in its integrated execution, with copper coping, extended cornice lines, and linear benches reinforcing the horizontality. The rectangular lily pond was designed to reflect the hall and enhance the structure by serving as an entrance to Jensen's long, linear formal garden. Benches and lantern standards mark the east end of the garden, which is now planted with species similar to but less invasive than Jensen's original choices. The Flower Hall, gardens, and major elements such as lights were restored in 2001.

41 Douglas Park Cultural and Community Center
(Field House)
1928, MICHAELSEN & ROGNSTAD

A virtual twin to the Humboldt Park field house in both Georgian style and siting, the building originally faced onto the lagoon and also served as the boathouse.

Douglas Park Flower Hall

42 Park Douglas Phase 1
S. Washtenaw and S. Fairfield
Aves. between 12th and 13th Pls.
2012, PAPPAGEORGE HAYMES
  PARTNERS AND KOO & ASSOCS.

Nineteen buildings on scattered sites represent an effort to provide stability and affordable housing by a partnership of city agencies, developer Brinshore-Michaels, and local employer Sinai Health System. Pappageorge Haymes was responsible for the master plan and the larger buildings, while Jackie Koo designed the three- and six-flats that incorporate limestone ornament from demolished structures.

Douglas Blvd. was once lined with former synagogues and other reminders of the area's Jewish heritage. Jews began moving here just before World War I, and between the wars, Lawndale and Garfield Park were known as Chicago's Jerusalem. Most of Chicago's synagogues built during the 1910s and 1920s were classically inspired, but Byzantine motifs surfaced with increasing frequency (entries 43–44).

43 Lawndale Community Academy
(Jewish People's Institute)
3500 W. Douglas Blvd.
1927, KLABER & GRUNSFELD

The Moorish capitals, religious symbols, glazed polychrome terra-cotta tile, abstract medallions, and ornamental brickwork evoke Judaism's Middle Eastern origins.

44 Stone Temple M.B. Church
(Congregation Anshe Roumania)
3622 W. Douglas Blvd.
1926, J. W. COHN & CO.

Classical facades lent themselves to discreet ornamental clues about a building's use and purpose. Here, the Star of David is included on the modified composite capitals, and a menorah and the Torah are depicted on stone medallions below the blind arcade.

45 Independence Square Fountain
(American Youth and Independence Day Fountain)
Independence Sq. at W. Douglas and Independence Blvds.
1902, CHARLES J. MULLIGAN

Bronze children joyously celebrate Independence Day with Roman candles (the fountain's original waterspouts), musical instruments, and a flag.

46 Independence Blvd. Seventh-Day Adventist Church
(Anshe Sholom Synagogue)
3803 W. Polk St.
1926, NEWHOUSE & BERNHAM

The congregation's history vividly illustrates the rapid westward migration of the neighborhood's Jewish community. This synagogue replaced one built only sixteen years earlier on Polk St. at Ashland Blvd. (now St. Basil Greek Orthodox Church). Here, the austere classical style of its predecessor continues, with a stone entablature bearing a Hebrew inscription.

47 Community Bank of Lawndale

1111 S. Homan Ave.

1982, WEESE HICKEY WEESE

Louis H. Sullivan's National Farm-

ers' Bank (1906–8) in Owatonna, Minnesota, inspired this crisp, blocky bank, which was one of the neighborhood's first new buildings in decades.

48 Former Sears, Roebuck & Co. Complex

900–930 S. Homan Ave.

1905–6, NIMMONS & FELLOWS

The lonely tower of the demolished Merchandise Building stands sentinel over remnants of the former Sears complex and the new housing that has sprung up in its shadow.

In 1906, the world's largest mail-order company moved into the world's largest commercial building. Founded in 1886, Sears sent out its first large general catalog ten years later and within another decade was mailing catalogs and orders to 35,000 customers a day. The business was then conducted exclusively with a rural clientele: according to *Architectural Record*, "No business is solicited with people living in large cities, and, in fact, this firm refuses to fill any order from a citizen of Chicago." Two hundred carloads of freight went out each day; all goods were shipped within twenty-four hours after the order was received.

The centerpiece of this monument to efficiency and speed was the Merchandise Building, with 1.7 million square feet of optimally planned space. The second floor of the nine-story (plus tower) building was the central shipping location. Pneumatic tubes carried orders from the Administration Building to the upper floors, where workers sent goods down to the second floor on spiral conveyors controlled by gravity and centrifugal force. Orders were loaded onto freight cars waiting in a train shed that spanned the space between the building's west wings. Completing the complex are the five-story (originally two-story) Administration Building, the four-story Printing Building to the east, and the Power Plant to the south. All are of brown brick trimmed in white terra-cotta with blue accents. The only elaboration is at the pedimented entrance to the Administration Building and at the entrance and top of the tower—the original "Sears Tower," with an observation room for visitors. The large arcades and red-tiled roof were inspired by the Tuscan style that the architects thought most appropriate for the simple materials.

In 1925, Sears expanded into retail operations and opened its first store in this complex. The company maintained its dominance as the nation's largest

Former Sears, Roebuck & Co. Complex

retailer and in 1974 moved to the world's tallest building, the Sears Tower (now Willis Tower). A 1992 move to suburban Hoffman Estates brought Sears full circle—back to a sprawling low-rise complex in a residential area.

49 Charles H. Shaw Technology and Learning Center and Henry Ford Academy: Power House High
(Sears Power Plant)
931 S. Homan Ave.
1905, NIMMONS & FELLOWS
2009, ADAPTIVE REUSE, FARR ASSOCS.

What seemed to be the campus's least likely candidate for reuse—the massive Power Plant—was imaginatively and sustainably converted into a charter high school with after-hours community service functions. The glazed brick interior of the north half was preserved as a voluminous gathering space, while the south half was gutted to insert three floors of classrooms. The gantry crane structure on the south facade originally served to unload coal from train cars on the rail spur; it now provides sun shading and emergency access for firefighters.

50 Homan Square
W. Lexington to W. Fillmore Sts., S. Kedzie Ave. to S. Independence Blvd. Phase 1, S. Homan to S. St. Louis Aves., W. Polk to W. Lexington Sts.
1995, NAGLE HARTRAY
DANKER KAGAN MCKAY

A joint venture of Sears and the Shaw Co., this residential development represents the first large-scale investment in North Lawndale since the 1960s. Targeted at low-income buyers and renters, the Phase 1 town houses and apartments have a clean, modern look that was not consistently maintained in subsequent residences. Later developments include the **Homan Square Community Center** at 3559 W. Arthington St. (1999, BOOTH HANSEN ASSOCS.) and **Holy Family Lutheran School** (2008, FGM ARCHITECTS) at 3415 W. Arthington St.

In 2012, the **Ulrich Children's Advantage Network** *hired Moody Nolan and Johnson & Lee to design a headquarters and seventy-bed youth home at Fillmore St. and Independence Blvd.*

51 Jens Jensen Public School
3030 W. Harrison St.
1961–63, HARRY WEESE & ASSOCS.

Built of warm, natural materials and on a human scale, the hexagonal classrooms establish the unusual geometry of this village-like school complex rendered in brick.

SOUTH AND SOUTHWEST

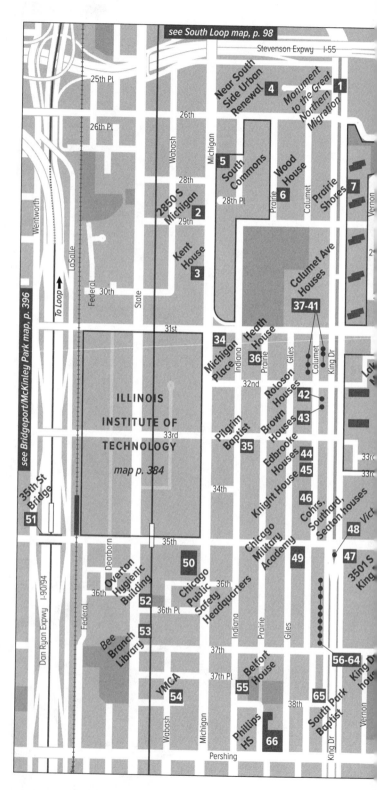

see South Loop map, p. 98

Stevenson Expwy I-55

25th Pl

26th

26th Pl

Near South Side Urban Renewal **4**

Monument to the Great Northern Migration **1**

Wabash

Michigan

5 South Commons

Wood House

Prairie **6**

Calumet

Prairie Shores **7**

Vernon

2850 S Michigan **2**

28th

28th Pl

29th

Kent House **3**

Federal

30th

State

LaSalle

Wentworth

To Loop

see Bridgeport/McKinley Park map, p. 396

31st

Calumet Ave Houses **37-41**

25

34 Michigan Place

Heath House

Indiana

Prairie **36**

Giles

Calumet

King Dr

Lak M

ILLINOIS INSTITUTE OF TECHNOLOGY

map p. 384

32nd

Roloson Houses **42**

Brown Houses **43**

Edbrooke Houses **44**

45

33rd

33rd

35th St Bridge **51**

33rd

Pilgrim Baptist **35**

Knight House **46**

34th

Cohrs, Southard, Seaton houses **48**

Vict

47 3501 S King

Dearborn

35th

Chicago Military Academy **49**

Overton Hygienic Building

50

Chicago Public Safety Headquarters **52**

36th

36th

I-90/94

Federal

Dan Ryan Expwy

36th Pl

53 Bee Branch Library

Indiana

Prairie

Giles

37th

37th Pl

Belfort House **55**

56-64

King Dr

hous

YMCA **54**

Wabash

Michigan

65 South Park Baptist

38th

Phillips HS **66**

King Dr

Vernon

Pershing

LAKE
MICHIGAN

Oakland/Kenwood map, p. 410

To Loop

Lake Shore Drive

E. Dearborn Dr

10
Pl

33rd
33rd Pl.

11-17

Douglas
Memorial
18

Cardinal
Meyer
Center
19

36th

ng

Cottage Grove

Lake Park

Ellis

Pershing

Oakwood

Groveland
Park

Lake Shore Drive

NEAR SOUTH SIDE

The Near South Side offers striking examples of urban renewal on a variety of scales, from multiacre developments to individual houses. It has some of the city's earliest residential neighborhoods, which were also among the first to be leveled and rebuilt as part of grand schemes in the 1940s. Sandwiched between the redeveloped areas is a neighborhood known as the Gap, which retains a nineteenth-century character that is especially notable on Calumet and Giles Aves. between 31st and 35th Sts. Renewed interest in Bronzeville recalls a time when this was a hub of African American business and culture second only to New York City's Harlem.

The area's history began with the arrival of the Illinois Central Railroad in the 1850s and remained closely tied to it for the next century. The railroad first spurred residential development near the commuter stations and later brought thousands of African Americans from the South. In 1863, the city limits were extended to 39th St., where they remained until the 1889 annexation of Hyde Park Township. Politician and real estate speculator Stephen A. Douglas created the area's first planned residential development. He bought sixty acres of lakefront property between 33rd and 35th Sts. in 1852 and three years later recorded his Oakenwald subdivision, with lots fronting on two private parks. Two short-lived institutions helped attract attention to the area: the first University of Chicago, whose Baptist founders accepted Douglas's donation of ten acres and had a small campus here from 1859 until 1886, when the enterprise went bankrupt; and Camp Douglas, which opened as an army training camp in 1861 and housed Civil War prisoners.

Residential development boomed in the 1870s and 1880s. German Jews moved to the area, establishing Michael Reese Hospital in 1881 and building a new structure for KAM Synagogue (the city's oldest Jewish congregation) in 1890. Working-class Irish lived in cottages along Federal St., close to the stock yards and other industrial jobs.

A black community was centered at 22nd and State Streets beginning in the 1870s, and the building frenzy that preceded the 1893 World's Columbian Exposition resulted in increased housing opportunities for middle- and upper-class African Americans. The time around World War I saw the large influx of African Americans that historians call the Great Northern Migration. Pullman porters on the Illinois Central trains to New Orleans brandished copies of the *Chicago Defender*, the city's premier black-owned newspaper, that painted Chicago as a desirable destination offering greater freedom and higher-paying industrial jobs.

By 1920, Black Metropolis or Bronzeville (commemorated in the title of a 1945 collection of poems by Gwendolyn Brooks) had developed into a city within a city. State St. between 26th and 39th Sts. was called the Stroll, and its jazz clubs and entertainment venues were famous throughout the country. But its glory days were fleeting. In 1927, the new Savoy Ballroom shifted the epicenter south to 47th St., and the Great Depression devastated many of the community's black-owned businesses. And as the newcomers from the South were barred from settling in other areas of the city, they were forced into increasingly overcrowded and run-down buildings, accelerating the transformation of once-fashionable houses into slum dwellings.

In the 1940s, two of the area's major institutions, Michael Reese Hospital and the Illinois Institute of Technology, joined forces to plan a program of urban renewal, eventually redeveloping seven square miles. Dilapidated housing was razed, and shiny new Modernist buildings near the lakefront were among the first in the city to welcome a racially integrated population. Around the same time, the city demolished the Federal St. slum and replaced it with enormous tracts of high-rise public housing. In the 1980s, restoration of historic properties began around Calumet Ave. and 32nd St., including the only extant row houses designed by Frank Lloyd Wright, and in 1998 the Black Metropolis–Bronzeville Historic District received landmark status. The turn of the twenty-first century brought more large-scale demolition—the Michael Reese campus on the east and public housing on the west—resulting in huge swaths of vacant land. The pace of renovation and construction was slowed by the Great Recession, but the Near South Side remains anchored by a thriving IIT and healthy residential areas in both historic and midcentury neighborhoods.

—JOSEPH D. LA RUE WITH LAURIE MCGOVERN PETERSEN

1 Monument to the Great Northern Migration
King Dr. at 26th St.
1994, ALISON SAAR

This fifteen-foot bronze statue of a man carrying a worn suitcase in his left hand and gesturing toward the north with his right symbolizes the migration of African Americans from the rural South to Chicago and other northern cities in the early twentieth century. The sculpture can also be viewed as a gateway to the Black Metropolis–Bronzeville Historic District, the city's oldest African American neighborhood. A close look at the figure's bronze suit reveals that it is made of the soles of shoes, suggesting the arduous journey to Chicago. This statue is part of the effort to repave and landscape King Dr. from 25th to 35th Sts. Other King Dr. Gateway Project elements that are worth seeing include the many artist-designed benches and sidewalk plaques that make up the Bronzeville Walk of Fame and the Historic Bronzeville Street Map (on the median at 35th St.).

2 2850 S. Michigan Ave.
(Vesta Accumulator Co.)
1919, PUCKEY & JENKINS

This was initially a deep, one-story sales and service building that housed a shock absorber business. A shallow second floor is now hidden behind a blind facade. The elaborate terra-cotta, which includes tympana of paired griffins, demonstrates the exuberance that enlivened auto-related architecture in the 1910s.

3 Sidney A. Kent House
2944 S. Michigan Ave.
1883, BURNHAM & ROOT
1982, CONVERSION TO APARTMENTS, SWANN & WEISKOPF

"Subdued richness" aptly describes this mansion. The ornamentation and styling, including the enhanced central pavilion carried above the cornice line, were consciously drawn from the châteaus of Francis I. But the essentially cubic massing, the unusual expanses of plate glass, the wide undecorated Philadelphia pressed-brick wall surfaces, and the uniform color all provide repose. Built when its neighbors were similar in size (60 × 100 feet), this house is now a rare example of the residential work of a major Chicago firm, surviving as five luxury apartments. The wrought-iron fence is truly French, having been purchased by Kent from a Columbian Exposition display.

4 Near South Side Urban Renewal
The character of the area between 26th and 35th Sts. is the result of decisions made in the 1940s, when the area's anchor institutions considered moving but instead stayed and exercised their influence on the neighborhood. The newly created Illinois Institute of Technology (formed in 1940 by a merger of two schools) was building a new campus, and Michael Reese Hospital needed room to expand. In 1945, the hospital created a planning staff with a mandate to devise a campus plan and to improve the character of its urban surroundings. Reginald

Near South Side Urban Renewal, including Lake Meadows, before demolition of Michael Reese Hospital

R. Isaacs served as director of the South Side Planning Board, while Walter Gropius held the post of architectural consultant. In what was perhaps the most comprehensive and ambitious essay in urban planning since Daniel H. Burnham's 1909 scheme for the entire city, the final report envisioned the complete redevelopment of seven square miles, from the lake west to the Pennsylvania Railroad tracks and from 12th St. south to 47th St. Taking a cue from Le Corbusier's model cities of the 1920s and 1930s, the planners advocated the abandonment of the urban grid in favor of towers set in open expanses of greenery. Also during this decade, the local, state, and federal governments resolved to address the lack of affordable urban housing. The housing shortage of the 1930s and 1940s, combined with a large influx of African Americans from the South whose areas of settlement were restricted by prejudice and covenant, had resulted in intolerable slum conditions on the South Side. In 1947, when Reese completed its two-year study, the city had just established a land-clearance program that made possible many of the study's recommendations. Lake Meadows became the city's first racially integrated middle-income housing, and Prairie Shores contin-

ued the success story. However, the "towers in a park" concept proved disastrous when governmental housing authorities applied it to low-income units. West of the lakefront, the State St. slum was demolished only to make way for a more vicious reincarnation, the high-rise projects of Stateway Gardens (State St. from 35th St. to Pershing Rd.) and the Robert Taylor Homes (State St. from Pershing Rd. to 54th St.), whose own demolition began in the late 1990s and was complete by 2007. Construction of new low-rise, mixed-income developments began on the cleared land in 2004 as the original street grid was restored to the superblocks that had been created for the public housing towers.

5 South Commons
26th to 31st St., Michigan to Prairie Aves.
1966–70, EZRA GORDON–JACK M. LEVIN & ASSOCS.; L. R. SOLOMON, J. D. CORDWELL & ASSOCS.

Planned as a small village with ambitious goals of racial and economic balance, this was one of the final building blocks in the grand plan of postwar urban renewal on the Near South Side. The town houses turn their backs on cars and streets, clustering around quiet, neighborly open courts, playgrounds, and stores.

Prairie Shores

6 George Ellery Wood House
2801 S. Prairie Ave.
1885, JOHN C. COCHRANE

The sole reminder of elegant "Lower Prairie Ave.," this Queen Anne house survives because its 1950s owners fought orders for the wholesale demolition of what was regarded as one of the city's worst slums.

7 Prairie Shores
2801–3001 S. Martin Luther King Jr. Dr.
1958–62, LOEBL, SCHLOSSMAN & BENNETT

This was Michael Reese Hospital's contribution to the plan it advocated. Comprising five apartment towers with a total of 1,677 units, the complex was intended primarily for hospital employees who wanted to live nearby. The narrow buildings are oriented north–south to maximize daylight, and each is massed as a pair of overlapping slabs. The curtain walls have ribbon windows and louvered spandrels of a different color on each building. Hideo Sasaki designed the landscaping here as well as at Lake Meadows and the Michael Reese campus.

8 Michael Reese Hospital Singer Pavilion (Psychosomatic and Psychiatric Institute)
S. Cottage Grove Ave. at 30th St.
1951, LOEBL, SCHLOSSMAN & BENNETT, ARCH. OF RECORD; WALTER GROPIUS, DESIGN CONSULTANT; JOHN T. BLACK AND REGINALD ISAACS, COORDINATING ARCHS. & MASTER PLANNERS

This is the lone survivor of the thirty-building Michael Reese Hospital campus, established here in 1881 and built largely in the 1950s.

Just as the city was clearing the land for a hoped-for 2016 Olympic Village, architect Grahm Balkany was uncovering evidence that the planning consultant, Walter Gropius, was more involved in the designs of the buildings themselves than had been assumed. A preservation furor ensued, and the Olympic bid fizzled, but Mayor Richard M. Daley's demolition edict held firm for all but this token building. Its boomerang-shaped plan and energy-conscious louvered sunshades hint at Gropius's influence.

9 Lake Meadows
S. Martin Luther King Jr. Dr. between 31st and 35th Sts.
1950–60, SKIDMORE, OWINGS & MERRILL

The overwhelming impression is of green, open space; the buildings cover only 9 percent of the land. The first housing constructed under the aegis of the Michael Reese plan, it was built on land assembled by the Chicago Land Clearance Commission and sold to New York Life Insurance Co. for about one-sixth of what the city paid for it. In 1946, *Architectural Forum* claimed that Lake Meadows would be "one of the first private housing projects to allow mixed Negro and white occupancy," an important advance in an area where as late as the 1930s properties carried covenants excluding sales to nonwhites. The seventy-acre, 2,033-unit complex includes ten apartment buildings, an office building, and a shopping center on 35th St.

10 Lake Meadows, 601 Building

601 E. 32nd St.

1960, SKIDMORE, OWINGS & MERRILL

The last and most luxurious building of the complex is the only one with floor-to-ceiling windows. Miesian influence is evident in the columns set behind the glass-and-steel curtain wall, the recessed brick or tile infill panels between the piers, and the inset wall on the ends.

11 Groveland Park

S. Cottage Grove Ave. at E. 33rd Pl.

In 1847, Senator Stephen A. Douglas moved to Chicago and began acquiring property, including a sixty-acre tract spreading from Lake Michigan west to King Dr. between 33rd and 35th Sts. His shrewd investment was made all the more valuable in the early 1850s when the Illinois Central Railroad—whose right-of-way Douglas had encouraged politically—built its tracks along the lakeshore. Douglas recorded the subdivision, Oakenwald, in 1855, setting aside the portion east of Cottage Grove Ave. for his own home and for two residential parks, Groveland and Woodland, with fifty-foot lots facing central open spaces. The depression of 1857 reduced the value of his holdings, which he mortgaged to finance his political campaigns. He was unable to redeem them before his death in 1861.

The property was developed only in 1873, after years of lawsuits had been settled in favor of Douglas's sons, when a Groveland Park homeowners' association was finally formed to oversee the maintenance of the common parklands. The first houses, clustered along the northern side of the park, have been destroyed. Many of the others are altered, but all enjoy frontage on this small, quiet park. The drives are a graveyard of demolished homes, lined with slabs and blocks of limestone, sandstone, and terra-cotta.

Groveland Park Gardener's Lodge

12 Groveland Park Gardener's Lodge

601 E. Groveland Park Ave.

EARLY 1870S, ARCHITECT UNKNOWN

This Gothic Revival dollhouse was originally trimmed with fancy bargeboards.

13 Charles W. and Edwin Pardridge Houses

607, 609, and 611 E. Groveland Park Ave.

LATE 1870S, ARCHITECT UNKNOWN

Three houses remain of the five built on lots subdivided in 1878. The "Athens marble" fronts, heavy pressed-metal cornices, and incised neo-Grec carving proved attractive to professors at the first University of Chicago, which was located on the west side of Cottage Grove Ave. from 1859 to 1886.

14 Hamilton Borden and William E. Selleck Houses

613 and 615 E. Groveland Park Ave.

1882, ARCHITECT UNKNOWN

Built by partners in a scales business, these rusticated sandstone houses have brownstone panels with robust leaf-and-tendril designs.

15 Frank N. Gage House

637 E. Groveland Park Ave.

1879, ARCHITECT UNKNOWN

Gothic details, such as the trefoil carved over the entrance and the pointed relieving arches in the windows, enliven an otherwise Italianate facade.

16 Edward S. Hunter and John B. Mallers Houses

639–641 E. Groveland Park Ave.

1886, FLANDERS & ZIMMERMAN

Mallers developed this double house with its brown sandstone facade; one half still has the original slate roof.

Soldiers' Home (now Cardinal Meyer Center)

17 John M. Gartside House
663 E. Groveland Park Ave.
1885, WILLETT L. CARROLL
This brick two-story and attic residence has a Euclid stone front.

18 Stephen A. Douglas Tomb and Memorial
636 E. 35th St.
1863–81, LEONARD W. VOLK
This is a monument as much to its era as to its subject, the Little Giant, Stephen A. Douglas. A larger-than-life bronze figure perches ninety-six feet in the air surveying Lake Michigan—or preparing to dive in, according to more than one critic. To offset the height, sculptor Volk placed four allegorical figures on freestanding plinths around the vault that contains Douglas's sarcophagus. The grounds were intended for Douglas's elegant home. Lack of funds delayed the statue's completion.

19 Cardinal Meyer Center
(St. Joseph Carondelet Child Care Center; originally Soldiers' Home)
739 E. 35th St.
1864, NORTH HALF OF EAST BUILDING, ATTRIB. TO WILLIAM W. BOYINGTON
1866, MAIN BUILDING (35TH ST.), WILLIAM W. BOYINGTON
1873, SOUTH HALF OF EAST BUILDING, ARCHITECT UNKNOWN
1878, NORTHWEST BUILDING, ARCHITECT UNKNOWN
2008, RENOVATION AND ADDITION, JAEGER, NICKOLA & ASSOCS.
A rare example of a surviving Civil War–era building in Chicago, this home was intended to serve soldiers who were sick, wounded, or merely in transit. Its intended function as a permanent home for disabled soldiers was made obsolete when Congress established national veterans' care in 1869, and this structure was used for a Catholic child-care facility from 1872 until 2005. The Catholic Archdiocese then renovated and expanded the building for offices. The simple Italianate style of Boyington's first buildings set the tone for all subsequent construction. The Northwest Building, which contains the entrance, has a second-floor chapel.

Illinois Institute of Technology (IIT)
S. Michigan Ave. to the Metra tracks, 31st–35th Sts.
IIT presents a remarkable example of a university campus that was shaped by a single architectural sensibility. Ludwig Mies van der Rohe's original plan as well as the buildings have continued to serve the campus well, especially in his choice of steel, brick, and glass materials; additions vanish seamlessly into the fabric of the original buildings. Designing the campus was his first American commission, and his buildings here develop ideas that he and his many students would apply throughout the world.

In the late 1930s, as the Nazis tightened their grip on Germany's cultural life, many talented artists fled to the United States. One of the most prominent of the Bauhaus architects, Ludwig Mies van der Rohe, was persuaded

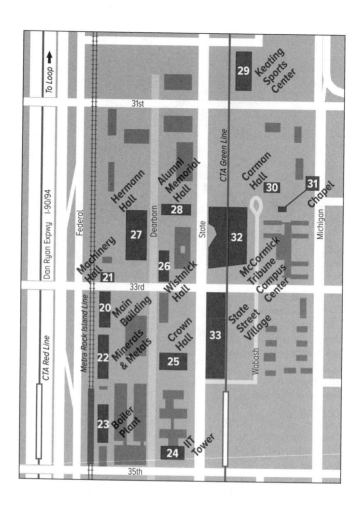

by Chicago architect John A. Holabird (son of William Holabird) to accept the directorship of the architecture department of the Armour Institute of Technology. Mies immigrated in 1938 and began his American career as a teacher and architect, a potent combination that exerted lasting influence. In 1940, Armour merged with Lewis Institute, a West Side technical school, to form the Illinois Institute of Technology.

Mies's campus plan for the new institution consisted of twenty buildings arranged symmetrically around 33rd St. between State St. and the railroad tracks to the west. Mies chose a module of 24 × 24 foot bays, 12 feet high, to determine both the bay size of individual buildings and the distances between them. The uniformity of the 24-foot length, a standard dimension for American classrooms at the time, allowed economies of construction and ensured a certain uniformity in campus design over time. The buildings are sited to form open spaces that are implied rather than defined. The buildings provided Mies with the opportunity to explore and elaborate on a new architectural vocabulary of skeletal steel construction. Welded steel frames are painted black and have infill panels of glass or tan brick. Guiding principles for all buildings are clarity of structure, appropriate use of materials, and sensitivity to proportions. Of his greatest achievement, Crown Hall, Mies said, "I think this is the clearest structure we have done, the best to express our philosophy."

Mies enlisted landscape architect Alfred Caldwell to design the landscape for the new campus and hired him to be a professor there. Caldwell favored native species such as the honey locust and a naturalistic placement of trees that complements the geometry of the campus and buildings.

After Mies retired as professor in 1958, he was replaced as campus architect by Skidmore, Owings & Merrill, one of the firms that had adopted his tenets most completely. Mies's twenty-two buildings were joined by others in the same vein, although many lacked the subtlety and refinement that had characterized his work. Results of a revitalization effort that began in the mid-1990s include the restoration of Crown Hall and two dramatic buildings that opened in 2003. Improvements to the landscape, including converting State St. into a green corridor and work done on the field north of Crown Hall (2000, 2001, HOERR SCHAUDT LANDSCAPE ARCHITECTS), which together added hundreds of trees, are consistent with Caldwell's vision and have reinforced connections between the two halves of the campus divided by State St.

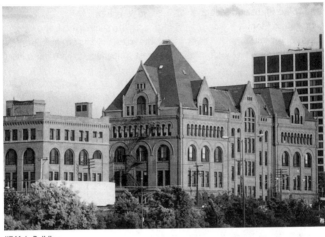

IIT Main Building

20 Main Building

(Armour Institute of Technology)

3300 S. Federal St.

1891–93, PATTON & FISHER

IIT's roots as a no-frills school for working people began here, when Philip D. Armour Sr. commissioned this manual training school. Designed as a companion piece to Burnham & Root's Armour Mission, a now-demolished settlement house across the street, it is rock solid and Romanesque. The rhythmic wall composition with its round-arched windows owes a great debt to Louis H. Sullivan, as do many of this firm's masonry buildings. The fourth floor, served by its own elevator, housed the "Girls' Department," with cooking and dressmaking workshops.

21 Machinery Hall

100 W. 33rd St.

1901, PATTON, FISHER & MILLER

This simplified version of the Main Building segregated noise-generating activities behind its Romanesque walls.

22 Minerals and Metals Research Building

3350 S. Federal St.

1943 (SOUTH), 1958 (NORTH), LUDWIG MIES VAN DER ROHE; HOLABIRD & ROOT, ASSOC. ARCHS.

This was the first campus building designed by Mies, and it established the basic concepts of subsequent classroom buildings. It was also his first constructed building in the United States and his first use of the rolled-steel I beam. Remarkably, it was completed during World War II despite the era's shortages of material, especially steel. Stripped down and startlingly severe, the glassy east side is now the only original piece easily seen. After many uses over the years, the building now houses the College of Architecture's model shop in the original three-story foundry space.

South of the Minerals and Metals building is a small plaza that provides access to the north end of the **35th Street / "Lou" Jones / Bronzeville Metra station** (2011, SKIDMORE, OWINGS

& MERRILL). *The angled steel roofs of the warming shelters at the south end of the station reference the 35th St. Bridge canopies. Wide ramps and stairs were designed to accommodate large crowds going to and from U.S. Cellular Field across the expressway. All the improvements to the bridge, CTA entrance, and Metra station have strengthened the IIT campus's connection to the city.*

23 Boiler Plant and Steam Generating Plant
3430 S. Federal St.
1945–50, LUDWIG MIES VAN DER ROHE; ALSCHULER & SINCERE, ASSOC. ARCHS.; FRANK J. KORNACKER, STRUCTURAL ENG.; SARGENT & LUNDY, MECHANICAL ENG.
1964, NORTH ADDITION, SARGENT & LUNDY

The six north bays follow Mies's original specifications. Steam is generated in the 1990 Co-Generation Building, a smaller version of the original.

24 IIT Tower
10 W. 35th St.
1963–64, SCHMIDT, GARDEN & ERIKSON
The tallest building on campus is the least sympathetic to earlier buildings.

When Crown Hall (entry 25) was constructed, 34th St. still ran through this part of campus, so the building's formal entrance was on the south facade.

25 S. R. Crown Hall

(College of Architecture, Illinois Institute of Technology)
3360 S. State St.
1956, LUDWIG MIES VAN DER ROHE; PACE ASSOCS. AND
C. F. MURPHY ASSOCS., ASSOC. ARCHS.
2003, SOUTH PORCH RESTORATION, FUJIKAWA JOHNSON & ASSOCS. AND MCCLIER
2005, RESTORATION, KRUECK & SEXTON ARCHITECTS AND MCCLIER;
LANDSCAPE RESTORATION, CHANDRA GOLDSMITH

During his American career, Mies came to believe that structure and space were the essential elements of architecture; as a result, his American reputation has centered on the expression of those concepts. In Crown Hall he exposed the structure and enclosed the space with a powerful balance of steel, glass, and light.

Mies's building for the College of Architecture was in design as early as 1950 and was completed in 1956. It is dominated by the steel-frame-and-glass pavilion of its upper level. Effectively a one-room school, the space is 120 × 220 feet and 18 feet high.

S. R. Crown Hall South Facade

Crown Hall's greatness derives from both its clarity and its comprehensive solution of all the problems it set out to solve. The building reads as a largely transparent glass box floating between its translucent podium and its roof, which is suspended from the four plate girders that punctuate its silhouette. The podium is actually a concrete frame on a 20 × 30 foot module, set with 8 feet below grade and with 4 feet above grade glazed with translucent glass.

During the day, Crown Hall seems a precisely defined, translucent, and transparent volume in perfect repose. At night, it becomes a reliquary of light, as its interior illumination appears to make the building almost seem to float on a cushion of light. The travertine main entrance stairs, centered on a long side of the building, also seem to float, inviting the visitor inside through entrances marked by floor-to-ceiling glass. Upon entering, one faces a central space defined by 8-foot-high oak partitions; the cross axis that divides this core into two parts helps orient visitors to the richly developed spaces of a building that seems initially to be without a plan. One could easily locate the physical center of the building only to discover that much of the greatness of the space comes from its development whereby no single place is seen to have priority.

Crown Hall departs from the module that Mies established for the campus in his master plan. As a result, it—rather than a more traditional campus structure, such as a library, administration building, or student union—becomes what Mies called representational. Such a building, Mies maintained, must declare the highest purposes and ideals of the institution. At the dedication of Crown Hall he said, "Let this building be the home of ideas and adventure" that would be "in the end a real contribution to our civilization."

—KEVIN HARRINGTON

The **circular fountain** *at the north-west corner of 33rd and State Sts. was designed by architect Myron Goldsmith, a partner at Skidmore, Owings & Merrill who was an IIT alumnus and professor.*

26 Wishnick Hall
(Chemistry Building)
3255 S. Dearborn St.
1946, LUDWIG MIES VAN DER ROHE;
ALFRED S. ALSCHULER AND R. N.
FRIEDMAN, ASSOC. ARCHS.
2008, RENOVATION, HOLABIRD & ROOT
Using the same materials and structure as Alumni Memorial Hall but with smaller windows (four per bay), this building became the standard for subsequent classroom buildings.

27 Grover M. Hermann Hall
3241 S. Federal St.
1962, SKIDMORE, OWINGS & MERRILL
This was originally the student union building; together with the library to the south, it follows Mies's plan for two large buildings on this site. But both are done with a heavier hand. Beams lie across the roof like logs instead of being gracefully integrated with the wall

as at Crown Hall. The original pre-cast concrete porch, similar to that of Crown Hall, has been replaced with granite. Unlike that building, the structure here is hidden behind the glassy skin. To the north is Morton Park, landscaped by faculty member Alfred Caldwell.

East of Hermann Hall sits **Man on a Bench** (1986, GEORGE SEGAL, SCULPTOR), *commissioned for the centennial of Mies van der Rohe's birth. The 6 × 9 foot area for the sculpture is Chicago's smallest official park.*

28 Alumni Memorial Hall
(Navy Building)
3201 S. Dearborn St.
1946, LUDWIG MIES VAN DER ROHE;
HOLABIRD & ROOT, ASSOC. ARCHS.
1972, ADDITION, MITTELBUSHER
& TOURTELOT
The first academic building completed after the war, this is also the first in which the glass panes fill the width of an entire twenty-four-foot bay. It was an archetype, with a primary structural frame of steel beams and a secondary structure of I beams attached to the exterior to support brick infill and window

frames. The hidden structural system is expressed in the reentrant corners, showing the secondary I beam welded to the primary column.

29 Arthur S. Keating Sports Center
3040 S. Wabash Ave.

1966, SKIDMORE, OWINGS & MERRILL

Here is another SOM building that hides the structure behind the walls, although nighttime illumination reveals the steel columns. The first floor is raised, and windows below it provide clerestory lights for the lower level.

30 Carman Hall Apartments
60 E. 32nd St.

1951–53, LUDWIG MIES VAN DER ROHE; PACE ASSOCS., ASSOC. ARCHS.

IIT built these apartments for faculty and married students. Rare for this campus, the concrete-frame buildings show Mies's signature receding columns, which carry less weight as they rise.

31 Robert F. Carr Memorial Chapel of St. Savior
65 E. 32nd St.

1952, LUDWIG MIES VAN DER ROHE

2009, EXTERIOR RESTORATION,

2011, PHASE 1 OF INTERIOR RESTORATION, HARBOE ARCHITECTS

Known on campus as the God Box, this is the only church that Mies ever designed. A nondenominational meditation chapel, its walls are clear glass on the east, translucent glass on the west, and brick on the north and south. This building is also Mies's only masonry bearing-wall construction outside of Europe.

Robert F. Carr Memorial Chapel of St. Savior

32 McCormick Tribune Campus Center
3201 S. State St.

2003, OFFICE OF METROPOLITAN ARCHITECTURE; HOLABIRD & ROOT, ASSOC. ARCHS.

Rem Koolhaas presented his design proposal for the IIT Campus Center as a critique of the planning philosophy that led to clearing the land for Mies's academic campus. The design intent was to restore within the building the density of the historic housing that had been demolished during the urban renewal era.

The center passes under the Green Line elevated tracks to unite the academic and residential zones of the IIT campus. Its primary visual element is the acoustic tube that encloses the trains as they pass overhead. Diagonal paths within the center connect the academic and residential destinations beyond. The spaces that remain between these paths house student and community activities.

IIT McCormick Tribune Campus Center

The Koolhaas design incorporates Mies's 1953 Commons Building, which retains its original function as a student cafeteria. Portions of two of the Commons's exterior walls complete the enclosure of a small courtyard within the Campus Center.

The exterior of the building is an expression of its interior spaces. Koolhaas incorporated a variety of levels into what is essentially a one-story building. The tube above seems to press the building into the ground, creating angles in the roof and multilevel spaces connected by ramps and stairs. Materials and color are used in unconventional ways, from the orange glow of the west wall to translucent honeycomb .restroom walls and printed graphics that depict Mies's face on the north entrance doors and donor portraits on the Founders Wall just inside.

33 State St. Village
3303, 3333, and 3353 S. State St.
2003, MURPHY/JAHN;
   HOERR SCHAUDT LANDSCAPE
   ARCHITECTS

Completed several months before the McCormick Center, this was the first major new building on campus in more than thirty years. Jahn, who studied under Mies in the 1960s, designed the 550-foot-long dormitory as three separate U-shaped buildings with passageways between, connected by corrugated stainless steel that curves to form both roof and facade. The dorm simultaneously encloses the open space north of Crown Hall, buffers the noise from the CTA tracks, and forms gateways for pedestrians crossing to the residential side of campus.

34 Michigan Place
3115 S. Michigan Ave.
2002, OPTIMA

Two midrise towers are sited to the north to provide maximum sun exposure for these town homes and their courtyard. Parking for the houses is concealed beneath landscaped berms that create a rolling courtyard.

35 Pilgrim Baptist Church
(Kehilath Anshe Ma'ariv Synagogue)
3301 S. Indiana Ave.
1890–91, ADLER & SULLIVAN

A devastating fire that broke out during a 2006 renovation reduced the once-glorious building to a masonry shell. Johnson & Lee drew up phased restoration plans that await funding. KAM (Congregation of the Men of the West) was Chicago's oldest Jewish congregation, founded in 1847; Adler's father had served as the synagogue's rabbi from 1861 to 1883. The architects

responded to programmatic needs by designing an auditorium (their specialty) expressed as two stacked rectangles—one for the worship space, the other for the clerestory necessary for good acoustics. For budgetary reasons, the top cube was clad in pressed metal rather than the originally specified stone, and it was destroyed in the fire.

36 Ira A. Heath House
3132 S. Prairie Ave.
1889, ARCHITECT UNKNOWN

Despite the long-standing attribution of this house to Adler & Sullivan, the residence that they designed for Heath was not the one built.

37 Samuel B. Steele House
3123 S. Calumet Ave.
1890, CHARLES S. FROST

Isaac Wedeles House
3127 S. Calumet Ave.
1890, CHARLES S. FROST

Carefully controlled Romanesque houses for partners in a wholesale grocery business, these stone-front dwellings feature two-story, gently projecting bays and strong stringcourses above their battered bases.

38 Thomas D. Stimson House
3132 S. Calumet Ave.
1886, GEORGE H. EDBROOKE

A scalloped roofline distinguishes this Romanesque house, a virtual duplicate of the one the architect had designed for himself up the block at **3314–3316**.

39 Carl D. Bradley House
3140 S. Calumet Ave.
1884, CHARLES M. PALMER

On the cusp of stylistic change, here is an Italianate house breaking out in a Queen Anne pox. This hybrid has the flat front, tall narrow windows, and bracketed cornice of the older style but the rounded elements, decorative roof peak, and varied materials of the new fashion.

40 Joseph Deimel House
3141 S. Calumet Ave.
1887, ADLER & SULLIVAN
This is the lone survivor of the more than twenty residential commissions that Adler & Sullivan undertook for Jewish clients in this part of town.

41 3144–3148 S. Calumet Ave.
1881, ARCHITECT UNKNOWN
Investors John J. Curran and Maximillian and Isaac Wolff were partners in a lumber-drying business and invested in several row house developments along Calumet Ave. This set, in which three of the eight units survive, was home to the Wolffs. It features angular neo-Grec styling, incised ornament of Joliet limestone facing, and strong metal cornices.

42 Robert W. Roloson Houses
3213–3219 S. Calumet Ave.
1894, FRANK LLOYD WRIGHT
1980, RENOVATION, FITCH/
 LAROCCA ASSOCS.
The only Wright row houses ever built date from the early years of his independent practice. Here, he reduced the Jacobean gable to a simple geometric form. The Roman brick wall is a severe but lovely backdrop for Sullivanesque terracotta panels.

43 Thomas Brown Houses
3221–3223 S. Calumet Ave.
1885, JULIUS H. HUBER
Terra-cotta spandrel panels featuring putti, masks, and foliage enliven this mansarded brick double house.

44 George H. Edbrooke Houses
3314–3316 S. Calumet Ave.
1884, GEORGE H. EDBROOKE
A Romanesque facade with a Flemish roofline marks Edbrooke's own home at 3316. The attached house is smaller, simpler, and set back in deference to its showier neighbor.

45 Clarence A. Knight House
3322 S. Calumet Ave.
1891, FLANDERS & ZIMMERMAN
The unusual palette and materials—pink-veined, rusticated orange Kasota stone and orange rock-faced

Clarence A. Knight House

Robert W. Roloson Houses

Roman brick—contribute to a very lively design by architects known for their picturesque work. The combination of burly Romanesque corner towers and fine Gothic detailing in the ogee arches is skillfully handled.

Chauncey E. Seaton House

46 John B. Cohrs, Albert R. Southard, and Chauncey E. Seaton Houses
3356–3360 S. Calumet Ave.
CA. 1890, ARCHITECT UNKNOWN

A trio of Richardsonian Romanesque town houses strike a harmonic chord in sandstone, greenstone, and limestone. The elaborate carving on 3360 portrays dragons and enigmatic men.

Dr. Martin Luther King Jr. Dr.
(Grand Blvd.)

In 1869, Frederick Law Olmsted and Calvert Vaux were commissioned to survey and plan two boulevards, eventually named Drexel and Grand. They were intended to link a park to be created in the township of Hyde Park with the city of Chicago, whose southern boundary was then at 39th St. As built, only Grand Blvd. was a continuation of an actual Chicago street. It ran from 35th St. to 51st St., curving gently into Washington Park for an impressive view of the huge meadow. Extensions to the north and south of the boulevard segment were named South Pkwy., and in 1968, the entire eleven-mile thoroughfare was renamed Dr. Martin Luther King Jr. Dr. Unlike the other boulevards that converge on Washington Park, King Dr. has no central planted median. Its six wide central lanes are flanked by slim grassy strips, which are in turn bordered by local drives.

47 3501 S. King Dr.
(Supreme Life Building; originally Liberty Life)
1921, ALBERT ANIS
2006, RESTORATION, PIEKARZ ASSOCS.

One of the major landmarks of Black Metropolis–Bronzeville regained its former glory with the removal of its 1950 metal skin. (The four Italianate town houses to the south on King Dr. were renovated at the same time.) Liberty Life Insurance was founded in 1919, bought this building five years later, and changed its name to Supreme Life Insurance in a 1929 merger. It was the first insurance company in the northern United States to be owned and operated by African Americans. The Chicago-born Anis later became one of the top designers of Art Deco buildings in Miami Beach.

48 *Victory*
S. King Dr. at 35th St.
1928, 1936, LEONARD CRUNELLE, SCULPTOR; JOHN A. NYDEN, ARCH.

Three larger-than-life figures—a soldier, a mother, and Columbia—are carved in high relief around a shaft to honor members of the African American Eighth Infantry, Illinois National Guard, who died in France during World War I. Their unit was incorporated into the U.S. Army 370th Infantry, 93rd Division, during the war. The statue was unveiled in 1928 and topped by the three-dimensional doughboy in 1936.

49 Chicago Military Academy—Bronzeville
(Eighth Regiment Armory)
3519 S. Giles Ave.
1915, JAMES B. DIBELKA
1999, EXTERIOR RESTORATION, INTERIOR REMODELING, WENDELL CAMPBELL ASSOCS.
2002, NORTH ADDITION, MAUREEN REAGAN ARCHITECTS

The long-abandoned armory has been reborn as the home for an innovative Chicago Public School program with a strong military emphasis. The original building, now the southern part, has a long, three-story facade of brown brick with limestone trim. It was the first armory in the country built for an African American regiment—the unit whose sacrifices in World War I are honored by the *Victory* statue. The link between the addition and existing building commemorates the history of Bronzeville and the armory by incorporating a clock tower with an informational plaque and military insignia plaques representing the five branches of the armed forces.

50 Chicago Public Safety Headquarters

3510 S. Michigan Ave.

2000, LOHAN ASSOCS.

A modern brick-and-curtain-wall building with a cantilevered canopy houses a technologically advanced police facility with an emphasis on community involvement and ease of use for the staff. At the west entrance, facing the parking lot, is one of Chicago's most infamous statues.

Haymarket Riot Monument

1889, JOHN GELERT

The figure of a police officer, his arm upraised, restrains an invisible mob, commanding peace "In the name of the people of Illinois." The controversy that surrounded the 1886 Haymarket Riot continued to plague this statue, which was originally erected near the site of the riot. Moved to Union Park in 1928 after a series of incidents that included being rammed by a streetcar, the monument was defaced with black paint and twice blown up by bombs during the 1960s. Placed under twenty-four-hour guard and moved to Central Police Headquarters, it was transferred to the courtyard of the newly built Chicago Police Training Center in 1976 before moving to this site in 2007.

51 35th St. Bridge

35th St. at the Dan Ryan Expressway

2003, GENSLER; ROSS BARNEY & JANKOWSKI, ASSOC. ARCHS.

Designed and built on a accelerated timetable to greet the crowds for the 2003 Major League Baseball All-Star Game, this bridge addition celebrates the destinations at either end in stainless steel letters over the expressway: *Chicago White Sox* and *Illinois Institute of Technology*. Canted galvanized steel canopies that tie into the existing CTA sta-

tion and cover the sidewalks on either side of the bridge create the impression of a single enclosed space. Chicago was the first U.S. city to include rail rapid transit in the middle of a major expressway. Stations designed by Skidmore, Owings and Merrill opened along the Dan Ryan and Kennedy I-90 in 1969–70, a decade after such service was inaugurated on the Congress (now Eisenhower) Expressway.

The demolished Stateway Gardens public housing high rises once occupied thirty-three acres west of State St. between 35th and Pershing (39th) Streets. A master plan by Skidmore, Owings & Merrill and Johnson & Lee envisioned a mixed-income low-rise community that began to take shape in 2004. The first development of what is now called **Park Boulevard** *is a trio of mixed-use buildings on the southwest corner of 35th and State Sts., all completed in 2007. The building at* **17 W. 35th St.** *was designed by Kathryn Quinn Architects; the one at* **3506 S. State St.** *was designed by Landon Bone Baker Architects; and* **3522 S. State** *was designed by UrbanWorks. The Park Boulevard Rental Residences at* **3622 S. State St.** *were designed by VOA Assocs. Other houses and flats in the development were designed by various firms, including Landon Bone Baker Architects and Brook Architecture.*

52 Overton Hygienic Building

(Overton Hygienic/Douglass National Bank Building)

3619 S. State St.

1923, Z. EROL SMITH

2000, 2008, RESTORATION, BAUER LATOZA STUDIO

Located close to the intersection of 35th and State, which was the heart of Bronzeville in the 1920s, the Overton Hygienic Building became the community's prime business address. The four-story structure was built by Bronzeville's leading entrepreneur, Anthony Overton, to house his successful cosmetics enterprise (the Overton Hygienic Co.), his Douglass Bank, and a variety of other shops and professional offices. It was promoted during construction as "a monument to Negro thrift and industry." Supported by a reinforced concrete frame, the Overton has street facades of dark-red brick with extensive trim in white-glazed terra-cotta. An impressive terra-cotta plaque in the center of the fourth-floor facade proudly carries the name *Overton Hygienic Company*.

53 Chicago Public Library—Chicago Bee Branch
(Chicago Bee Building)
3647 S. State St.
1931, Z. EROL SMITH
1995, RESTORATION OF EXTERIOR AND REMODELING OF INTERIOR, MCCLIER

Overshadowed for years by the massive public housing towers to the west, by the general bleakness of the streetscape, and by its own dilapidated condition, this colorful three-story building was easy to overlook. An award-winning restoration of the exterior has brought the green, black, and tan terra-cotta panels as well as the intricately incised ornamentation back to their original look and revealed the Chicago Bee Building to have one of the city's niftiest Art Deco facades. Built as the headquarters of a newspaper started in 1926 by Bronzeville entrepreneur Anthony Overton and then later used by his cosmetics firm, the building subsequently sat vacant until it became a branch of the Chicago Public Library.

54 Wabash Ave. YMCA
3763 S. Wabash Ave.
1913, ROBERT BERLIN
2000, RESTORATION AND REMODELING, WEESE LANGLEY WEESE ARCHITECTS

The great philanthropist Julius Rosenwald led the effort to build this

Wabash Ave. YMCA—interior

and many other YMCAs in African American communities in Chicago and elsewhere; architect Berlin designed several of them. This handsome building with bold piers and recessed spandrels features a subdued Arts and Crafts style on the interior, with a brick fireplace, oak trim, cast-metal balusters, ceramic tile, wood floors, and a 1936 mural by African American artist William Edouard Scott.

55 Belfort House, Teen Living Programs
3745 S. Indiana Ave.
2010, HARTSHORNE PLUNKARD ARCHITECTURE

The architects worked pro bono to design this haven for homeless teens. Concrete panels are tinted to harmonize with the neighborhood's brick facades, and the U-shaped plan allows for expanses of glass on the protected north side that includes the building's entrance. A historic marker notes that author Richard Wright lived in an apartment on this site in 1935.

56 Double House for Albert Mendel and James S. Toppan
3558–3560 S. King Dr.
1889, WILSON, MARBLE & LAMSON
57 Double House for John F. Finerty and Edward J. Mendel
3562–3564 S. King Dr.
1888, WILSON, MARBLE & LAMSON

Four rusticated limestone facades combine Gothic and Romanesque motifs.

58 John F. Whiting House
3568 S. King Dr.
1888, THOMAS W. WING

The great Queen Anne bay is robust and highly detailed, studded and pointed, serving as a signpost for this narrow house.

59 John J. Hill House
3608 S. King Dr.
1889, E. CLARKE JOHNSON

This dignified Romanesque house has a beautiful entry, with a curving wall of small beveled windows whose squares are echoed in the paneled wooden door.

60 John Tait House
3614 S. King Dr.

1888, HOLABIRD & ROCHE

The simple facade is made interesting by the lively use of a single material, a variegated brownstone. This house was an excellent advertisement for its owner, a stone collector, as well as for its architect, Tait's brother-in-law, Martin Roche. Both men lived here. Roche documented the construction in his diary.

61 John McCormick House
3616 S. King Dr.

1886, CHARLES E. KAUFFMANN

An idiosyncratic stone house, it has the tall, narrow proportions of the much earlier Gothic Revival.

62 Ida B. Wells House
(Martin Meyer House)
3624 S. King Dr.

1889, JOSEPH A. THAIN

This house is noteworthy for its 1920s owners. Wells was a black-rights activist and a crusading journalist who exposed the ugly reality of lynching. Her husband, Ferdinand Lee Barnett, was a lawyer and journalist. This was the earliest and largest of a succession of somewhat fussy Romanesque houses on this stretch of the boulevard that were designed by a prolific but little-known architect.

63 Charles H. Nichols House
3630 S. King Dr.

1886, RAE & WHEELOCK

Queen Anne exuberance is manifested in rich detailing in pressed metal, an elaborate iron porch rail, carved brownstone animal masks and terra-cotta panels, a foundation of novel Hummelstown striated brownstone, two very different oriels, and a high picturesque roof.

64 D. Harry Hammer House
3656 S. King Dr.

1885, WILLIAM W. CLAY

This is the king of King Dr., a rare surviving example of the large houses that anchored many corners of the South Side boulevards by the 1890s. Striking color—orange brick, brownstone, and copper trim—enhances the more usual corner features of two impressively gabled sides and an angled tower element. Terra-cotta detailing, wrought-iron grilles, and art glass abound on this design by one of the era's most flamboyant architects.

65 South Park Baptist Church
3722 S. King Dr.

1953, HOMER G. SAILOR

Here is a lingering postwar blast of Art Moderne styling. A broad expanse of narrow bright-orange brick, broken only by the vertical thrust of

D. Harry Hammer House

a limestone tower, dips inward at the street-level portal and outward as ribbon windows are introduced to light the office wing.

66 Wendell Phillips High School
244 E. Pershing Rd.
1902, WILLIAM B. MUNDIE
FOR JENNEY & MUNDIE

Hailed as one of Chicago's first modern high schools, Wendell Phillips was intended to grace an affluent neighborhood with a "stately presence" of red brick and a colossal Ionic order and to provide "everything that can vitalize and energize the school work." The building initially had forty-eight classrooms fully equipped for the manual and academic training of 1,700 students, a gymnasium, a lunchroom, spaces for extracurricular activities, and—recognizing the new notion that schoolhouses should be civic centers open day- and year-round—a large auditorium.

BRIDGEPORT/CANARYVILLE/
MCKINLEY PARK/BACK OF THE YARDS

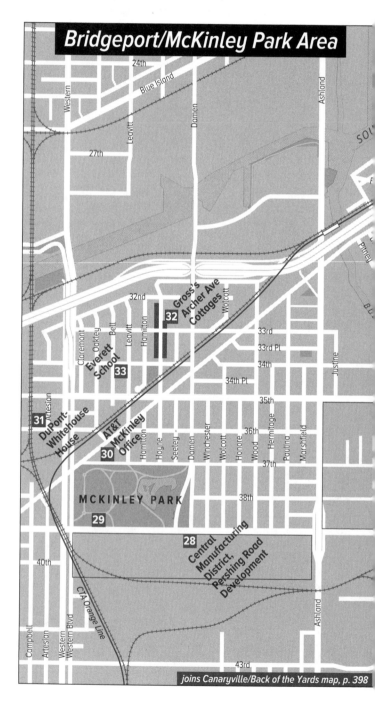

Bridgeport/McKinley Park Area

joins Canaryville/Back of the Yards map, p. 398

Pilsen map, p. 358

THE CHICAGO RIVER

Metra Heritage Line

CTA Orange Line

To Loop

see Near South Side map, p. 376

To Loop

Archer

23rd Pl
24th
24th Pl
25th Pl
25th Pl

Wentworth

27th

Palmisano Park **1**

Ling Shen Ching Tze Temple **2**

Morgan St Live Work **5**

3

4

31st Pl

32nd

32nd Pl

Monastery of the Holy Cross

Expwy I-55

Poplar
Throop
Quinn
Farrell
Keeler
Bonfield

31st Pl
32nd
32nd Pl
33rd St
33rd Pl

May
Aberdeen
Carpenter
Morgan

Lituanica
Halsted

May

acturing
rict,
st District

Lituanica
Sangamon
Lituanica

35th Pl
36th
37th
37th Pl
38th
38th Pl

Pershing

40th

Stock Yard District

Exchange

Union Stock Yards Gate **15**

12

Peoria

14

Stock Yards Bank

13

Post Office

41st

Root

43rd

26th
27th
28th
28th Pl

Emerald
Union
Lowe
Wallace
Parnell
Normal
Canal

Stewart
Shields
Princeton
Wells
Wentworth

29th
30th

31st

32nd

33rd

34th
34th Pl

Boys' & Girls' Club **10**

McClellan School

Armour Square Park **6**

35th

8

9

Richard J. Daley House

U.S. Cellular Field **7**

Dan Ryan Expwy I-90/94

CTA Red Line

Emerald
Union
Lowe
Wallace
Parnell
Normal

Halsted

Metra Southwest Service

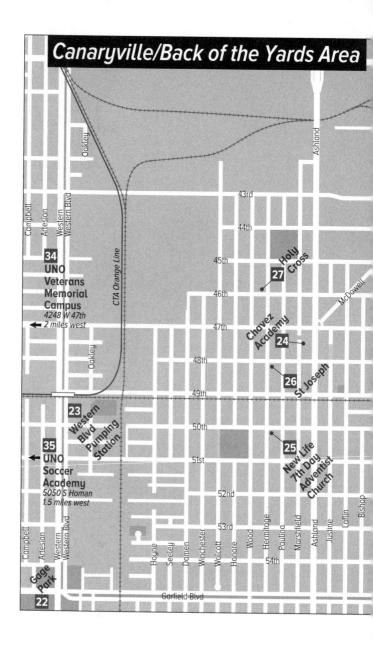

Canaryville/Back of the Yards Area

34
UNO Veterans Memorial Campus
4248 W 47th
← 2 miles west

35
← **UNO Soccer Academy**
5050 S Homan
1.5 miles west

23
Western Blvd Pumping Station

22
Gage Park

27
Holy Cross

24
Chavez Academy

26
St Joseph

25
New Life 7th Day Adventist Church

"They were left standing upon the corner, staring; down a side street there were two rows of brick houses, and between them a vista: half a dozen chimneys, tall as the tallest of buildings, touching the very sky—and leaping from them half a dozen columns of smoke, thick, oily, and black as night . . . stretching a black pall as far as the eye could reach." The great smoking chimneys that so awed and ultimately overwhelmed the young Lithuanian immigrants in Upton Sinclair's *The Jungle* (1906) no longer blacken the sky over this industrial neighborhood. But church spires still rise above modest homes and apartments, commemorating the waves of immigrants that poured into the South Side beginning in the 1830s to pursue the American Dream. The Lithuanians were only the most recent group in Sinclair's time. Canal construction and railroads, stock yards and slaughterhouses, steel mills and breweries had already brought the Irish, then the Germans, and then the Slavs and Balts in the 1880s and 1890s; after World War II, Hispanics and African Americans followed. These newcomers flowed into an area rigidly divided by the physical barriers of the river branches, the canal, the railroad tracks and embankments, and

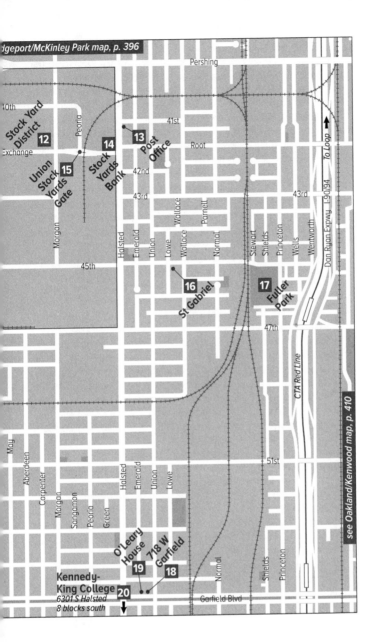

idgeport/McKinley Park map, p. 396

Pershing

10th

Stock Yard District

Peoria

41st

Exchange

12

14

13 Post Office

Root

Union Stock Yards Gate

15

Stock Yards Bank

42nd

43rd

43rd

Morgan

Halsted

Emerald

Union

Lowe

Wallace

Parnell

Normal

Stewart

Shields

Princeton

Wells

Wentworth

Dan Ryan Expwy. I-90/94

To Loop

45th

16 St Gabriel

Wallace

17 Fuller Park

47th

CTA Red Line

May

Aberdeen

Carpenter

Morgan

Sangamon

Peoria

Green

Halsted

Emerald

Union

Lowe

51st

Shields

Princeton

see Oakland/Kenwood map, p. 410

O'Leary House

718 W Garfield

19

18

Normal

Shields

Princeton

Kennedy-King College
6301 S Halsted
8 blocks south

20

Garfield Blvd

later the highways, creating a series of neighborhoods whose boundaries are more visibly defined than is the case in many other parts of Chicago.

Bridgeport, the first community to be settled, is one of the city's oldest. The Illinois & Michigan Canal, begun in 1836 to connect the Chicago and Illinois Rivers, offered construction jobs to Irish and later German immigrants, who settled along the Chicago River's south branch at the northern terminus of the canal. Originally referred to as Hardscrabble, Bridgeport was named for the port area created by a bridge near Ashland Ave. built so low that it obstructed river traffic and required the unloading and reloading of cargo. The narrow diagonal streets perpendicular to Archer Ave. still retain the atmosphere of this workers' community; though not the original shanties and frame houses, many homes are quite old and little changed. After the canal opened in 1848, Bridgeport attracted many new industries, primarily slaughterhouses and supporting businesses. The area east of Halsted St. and north of 31st St. was incorporated into the City of Chicago in 1853; the area from 31st to 39th Sts. was annexed in 1863.

The opening of the Union Stock Yards in 1865 consolidated Chicago's livestock trade between 39th and 47th Sts., Halsted St., and Racine Ave. The Union Stock Yard & Transit Co. (backed largely by the railroads' investors) purchased 345 acres and laid the Chicago Junction Railway to link the yards with all major lines entering the city: "As far as the eye can reach," Sinclair wrote, "there stretches a sea of pens. And they were all filled—so many cattle no one had ever dreamed existed in the world. . . . The sound of them here was as of all the barnyards of the universe." The stock yards and train lines that served them created physical barriers that still mark the divisions between ethnic and racial groups.

To the east of the yards' entrance at Halsted St. and Exchange Ave., Canaryville was originally a middle-class neighborhood. The Swifts, Libbys, and Hutchinsons settled on Emerald Ave., and the Irish community gradually expanded south from Bridgeport to be closer to the stock yards. St. Gabriel's Parish was established in 1880 to serve the Irish residents. In the 1890s, the upwardly mobile began to move south, with many of them building large houses on Garfield Blvd., still within easy distance of the stock yards.

West of Bridgeport lies McKinley Park, also settled by Irish canal workers. Originating as a farming community in the 1840s, it grew into an industrial center incorporated as the Town of Brighton in 1851. Samuel E. Gross created several developments of small-scale workers' cottages that still exist.

By the 1870s, after the introduction of the refrigerated railroad car, packing plants had moved to the area immediately west of the yards, creating Packingtown, isolated by industrial sites, garbage dumps, and railroads. Living conditions in Back of the Yards epitomized the worst of industrialization. The noxious stench of Bubbly Creek, a stagnant fork of the river's south branch, permeated the area. Essentially an open sewer, it carried offal from the slaughterhouses and packinghouses. These congested neighborhoods featured few or no municipal services.

Progressive reformers subsequently turned their attention to these inhumane working and living conditions. The Progressive emphasis on open areas, or "breathing spaces," led to the development of a significant type of public space, the neighborhood park, which combined recreational and social facilities. Not surprisingly, the severity of local conditions meant that the South Park Commission led the way. After its first success with McKinley Park, the commission hired D. H. Burnham & Co. and the Olmsted brothers to design a series of small parks, of which Sherman and Fuller are perhaps the finest examples.

By 1900, another industry was contributing to the area's development. Ten years earlier, a group of investors headed by Frederick H. Prince had purchased the Union Stock Yard & Transit Co. and the Chicago Junction Railway, and in 1902, they began to acquire land north of the yards. In 1905, they announced the creation of the Central Manufacturing District (CMD), a planned industrial site that housed manufacturing and warehousing operations and employed thousands of local residents.

Since the 1950s, little new construction has occurred in the area. The Union Stock Yards closed in August 1971 after years of declining trade. The eclipse of related industries and the replacement of most of the International Amphitheater's uses by McCormick Place effectively curbed the area's growth. The stock yards' land was turned over to the CMD for development into the Donovan Industrial Park. Low warehouses and light industrial buildings now sprawl behind the old Stock Yards Gate, a sanitized relic of a pungent past. The neighborhood retains the varied ethnic character established throughout its development.

—KATHLEEN NAGLE

Archer Ave. began as a path along the Illinois & Michigan Canal, named for canal commission member Colonel William B. Archer. Bridgeport's oldest neighborhoods are nearby and still contain early cottages and flats. Through Bridgeport, the Adlai E. Stevenson Expressway (I-55) runs along the site of the canal.

Palmisano Park

1 Henry G. Palmisano Park
2700 S. Halsted St.
2009, SITE DESIGN GROUP

A timeline of this park would begin 400 million years ago with the formation of dolomite limestone from a coral reef. It would fast-forward to the 1830s, when the stone was excavated to help build the new city of Chicago. Stearns Quarry operated until 1970 and then became a landfill for construction debris. Dynamic design brings the park into the twenty-first century. A quick drive around the perimeter does not reveal its treasures. Only after ascending the trail can visitors see the terraced water feature leading to a fishing pond in the preserved quarry or look north for a spectacular skyline view.

2 Ling Shen Ching Tze Temple
(Immanuel Presbyterian Church)
1035 W. 31st St.
1892, BURNHAM & ROOT

Looking past the recent additions reveals the severe simplicity of one of John Wellborn Root's last designs.

3 Monastery of the Holy Cross
(Immaculate Conception Roman Catholic Church and Rectory)
3111 S. Aberdeen St.
1909, CHURCH, HERMANN J. GAUL AND ALBERT J. FISCHER
1901, RECTORY, ALBERT J. FISCHER

The charming rectory creates a pleasing Gothic ensemble with the slightly later church, founded to serve a German parish.

4 St. Mary of Perpetual Help Roman Catholic Church
1035 W. 32nd St.
1889–92, HENRY ENGELBERT

The dull brick Romanesque exterior gives no hint of the lavishly shaped and decorated nave enriched with Stations of the Cross and stained-glass windows with Polish inscriptions. Three domes sail high above, the central one lit by a ring of lantern windows and sheathed in a copper roof. The nave is further decorated with fine scagliola work, three elaborate marble altars, and a suspended pulpit topped by a wedding-cake cupola.

5 Morgan St. Live + Work
3209 S. Morgan St.
2007, URBANLAB

Husband-and-wife architects Martin Felsen and Sarah Dunn give a uniquely modern twist to the idea of living above the store. The shallow office building clad in Cor-Ten steel with perforations at window level hugs the street. A similarly long, narrow volume is turned ninety degrees and its front end set atop the office. The other end of the residential structure, which is made from a prefabricated bridge, is perched atop a small hill in the backyard. The landscaped mound was created from the construction debris of the building previously on the site.

6 Armour Square Park
33rd to 34th Sts., from S.
Wells St. to S. Shields Ave.
1904–5, OLMSTED BROS.
1905, FIELD HOUSE, D. H.
   BURNHAM & CO.

Of the parks proposed by the South Park Commission in 1903, eight were to be "small parks" and six were to be "squares" of ten acres or less. The field house is one of the world's first. It was designed by Edward H. Bennett, who was the chief architect for all of the Burnham & Co. field houses. The central building faces the park on a diagonal, sheltered from the street by the two wings of the gymnasium.

7 U.S. Cellular Field
(Comiskey Park)
333 W. 35th St.
1991, HELLMUTH, OBATA & KASSABAUM

The new stadium for the Chicago White Sox was one of the last "modern" ballparks of the twentieth century. When HOK proposed a similar design for Oriole Park at Camden Yards, the client rejected it in favor of a "retro" version that was so well received it launched a new trend in ballpark design. So a series of renovations to the Chicago ballpark began in 2001, when it was just a decade old. Most significantly, in 2004, more than 6,000 seats at the top of the upper deck were removed and replaced with a steel truss-supported canopy. While the change did not alter the distance from the field or steep upper-deck pitch of thirty-four degrees, the roof enclosure helps those in the upper seats feel more a part of the action. Fences were adjusted to make the outfield less symmetrical, and seats were changed back to the classic green of the old ballpark.

8 George B. McClellan Public School
3505 S. Wallace St.
1881, ARCHITECT UNKNOWN
1896, SOUTH ADDITION, AUGUST FIEDLER

One of Chicago's oldest remaining public schools is in the popular, all-purpose, pedimented Italianate style.

9 Richard J. Daley House
3536 S. Lowe Ave.
1939, ERIC E. HALL

Although built after the 1920s vogue for bungalows had peaked in Chicago, this is a modest continuation of the formula. Daley was born at 3602 and was a lifelong resident of S. Lowe Ave.

10 Boys' and Girls' Clubs of Chicago—Louis L. Valentine Club
(Valentine Chicago Boys' Club)
3400 S. Emerald Ave.
1938, CHILDS & SMITH

The entrance to this Art Moderne temple to boyhood adventure is flanked by replicas of Alaskan Coastal Indian totem poles and is topped by a terra-cotta overhang suggesting a cliff cave entrance. The apparently romantic name is actually that of the donor, a retired furniture manufacturer.

Boys' & Girls' Clubs of Chicago—Louis L. Valentine Club

11 Central Manufacturing District, East District

35th St. to Pershing Rd., Morgan St. to Ashland Ave.

1905–15

The first American industrial park was established here in 1905 by a group of investors headed by Frederick H. Prince. They began acquiring land, mostly vacant except for three established industries, in 1902. By 1908, the 265 acres were serviced by individual switch tracks from the Chicago Junction Railways, and utilities, services, and street improvements were in place. The CMD built manufacturing buildings and warehouses designed by staff architects and engineers (until 1921 by S. Scott Joy, then A. Epstein) and financed the structures' lease or purchase by tenant companies. The CMD's architectural standards dictated design basics, whether companies used Joy's services or those of another architect. Among the companies that located here were the William Wrigley Jr. Co., American Luxfer Prism Co., Westinghouse Electric & Manufacturing Co., and Spiegel, May, Stern & Co. (later Spiegel). Many of the buildings have been demolished or are vacant, but some have found new life as art centers.

12 Stock Yard District

Clustered around the intersection of Halsted St. and Exchange Ave. are only a few structures recalling the days when Chicago was "hog butcher to the world." The city's location made it a natural trading hub and, after the invention of the refrigerated car, a processing center for many forms of livestock—a position further consolidated by the opening in 1865 of the Union Stock Yards. The stock yards attracted not only workers and livestock traders but also tourists, who marveled at the scale and efficiency of the operation. But by the mid-twentieth century, business was declining as trucking supplanted rail for transporting livestock products, and modern, decentralized packinghouses sprang up farther west. When the stock yards closed in 1971, the CMD began development of Donovan Industrial Park, a series of single-story, light-industrial buildings.

13 U.S. Post Office—Stock Yards Station

4101 S. Halsted St.

1936, HOWARD L. CHENEY

The U.S. eagle meets the stock yards cow on reliefs ornamenting this small Art Moderne post office.

14 Stock Yards Bank Building

W. Exchange Ave. and S. Halsted St.

1924, A. EPSTEIN

Philadelphia's Independence Hall inspired this anchor of the business district.

15 Union Stock Yards Gate

850 W. Exchange Ave.

1879, ATTRIB. TO BURNHAM & ROOT

A lonely symbol of the vanished stock yards, the stone gate is almost certainly the work of Burnham & Root, who did other projects for the stock yards' owners (including a house for its organizer, John B. Sherman, Burnham's father-in-law). This tripartite gate marked the entrance to the animal pens, providing a large central arch for livestock and wagons flanked by pedestrian arches. The great copper roof concealed an iron grille that was lowered each night over the main arch; the southern arch has its original, hinged iron gate. Above the central arch is a relief head of another Sherman, the steer that won the American Fat Stock Show in 1878.

16 St. Gabriel Roman Catholic Church

4501 S. Lowe Ave.

1887, BURNHAM & ROOT

St. Gabriel's Parish was organized by the Reverend Maurice J. Dorney in 1880 to serve Irish immigrant stock yard workers. According to Harriet Monroe, Root's biographer and sister-in-law, Root felt that "people too often attempted to build 'little cathedrals,' instead of being content with parish churches. . . . [T]he Romanesque was more suitable [than the Gothic style] to a simple home of the people." Monroe considered the church one of Root's most characteristic works, "as personal as the clasp of his hand."

The preliminary design called for a centrally planned stone church with a low, massive tower over the crossing. For cost reasons, the material was changed to brick and the tower was moved to the side but made much

St. Gabriel Roman Catholic Church

higher. The north facade was altered in 1914 by the addition of a portico and vestibule; it originally had a taller arch in the middle, as seen in the window arrangement on the west transept. In 1944, the 160-foot tower was shortened by 14 feet and lost its high pyramidal roof. The interior of the church, too, has been substantially altered.

East of the railway viaduct is the economically challenged Fuller Park neighborhood (entry 17).

17 Fuller Park
45th St. to 46th Pl., S. Princeton Ave. to S. Stewart Ave.

1905, SOUTH PARK COMMISSION
1910, BUILDINGS, D. H. BURNHAM & CO.
The creative plan fits many recreational amenities onto a tight site, even using the railway embankment for spectators' seating. The buildings are of poured-in-place concrete with integrally cast ornament, an economical alternative to cut stone known as "marble-crete" or "popcorn concrete" as a consequence of the roughness of the aggregate. The park has more original features than others of its size on the South Side, including an ornamented concrete bench that curves around the wading pool.

Fuller Park Field House

18 718 W. Garfield Blvd.
(Chicago Bicycle Club)
1898, ANDERS G. LUND

Club members departed from this late Queen Anne house on velocipede tours and other jaunts.

James J. O'Leary House

19 James J. O'Leary House
726 W. Garfield Blvd.
1901, ZACHARY T. DAVIS

O'Leary, whose mother owned Chicago's most famous cow, was a gambling king who operated from his saloon across from the Stock Yards. His busy, château-style house has Renaissance details such as the dormers and balustrades.

South of Garfield Blvd. is the Englewood neighborhood (entry 20).

20 Kennedy-King College
6301 S. Halsted St.
2008, JOHNSON & LEE AND VOA ASSOCS.

Though today they look like a lunar landscape, the blocks around the intersection of 63rd and Halsted once rivaled the Loop as a retail hub. The red-brick Kennedy-King buildings, simply but crisply detailed, strongly define the two east corners and create a modern quadrangle on Halsted. They also signal an attempt at revitalization of the beleaguered Englewood community.

The post office at **611 W. 63rd St.** *is on the site of H. H. Holmes' infamous "murder palace," described in Erik Larson's* Devil in the White City.

21 Sherman Park
W. 52nd St. to Garfield Blvd.,
S. Racine Ave. to S. Loomis St.
1904, OLMSTED BROS.
1904–5, BUILDINGS, D. H.
  BURNHAM & CO.
1996, FIELD HOUSE RESTORATION,
  BAUER LATOZA STUDIO
1998, POOL BUILDING REHABILITATION,
  GRAHAM, ANDERSON, PROBST & WHITE

This sixty-acre oasis achieves the pastoral qualities of much larger parks through the gentle berm around its perimeter, which creates a tranquil spot focusing on a large lagoon. The extensive use of water is unusual in the South Side parks but was suitable for this poorly drained site. The island encircled by the lagoon accommodates playing fields, which are reached by four bridges at the corners of the park. The field house contains an auditorium, meeting rooms, and a refectory. The restored murals in the auditorium were

Sherman Park

César Chávez Academy

created by students from the School of the Art Institute in 1912.

22 Gage Park
  W. 54th to W. 56th Sts., Claremont
  Ave. to Artesian and Maplewood Aves.
  1905, SOUTH PARK COMMISSION
  1928, FIELD HOUSE AND POOL HOUSE,
    SOUTH PARK COMMISSION

At the southwest corner of the original plan for the South Park System, Gage Park anchors the corner of Garfield and Western Blvds. The field house follows the earlier pattern established by D. H. Burnham & Co. Tom Lea's interior mural (1931) depicts a pioneer scene.

**23 Western Blvd.
Pumping Station**
  4919–4943 S. Western Blvd.
  1927, CHARLES KALLAL, CHICAGO CITY
    ARCH.; G. DWIGHT TOMPKINS, ASST.
    ENG., DEPT. OF PUBLIC WORKS

This dignified little box, encrusted with shells and crabs, is a decorative cap on a large node of Chicago's vast water system. At an intake crib three miles out into the lake, fresh water enters a tunnel running to the South District Filtration Plant. The purified water flows west through tunnels to this station (and others), where steam engines pump it to the area bounded by Pershing Rd., Indiana Ave., 79th St., and the city limits as well as to some southwestern suburbs. This station is one of the city's largest, with a capacity of 320 million gallons a day.

24 César Chávez Academy
  4747 S. Marshfield Ave.
  1993, ROSS BARNEY & JANKOWSKI

Joyful and playful, this building creates wonder and a heightened sense of anticipation to see what is inside. To meet the challenges of a long, narrow lot, the architects sited the building to shelter classrooms and outdoor play spaces from the alley to the east. A cube-shaped library pavilion topped with a translucent fiberglass skylight and a gymnasium/lunchroom building are broken out from the single-loaded classroom wing, saving on structural costs while enlivening the design. Bright colors and differing shapes suggest that school can be fun.

**25 New Life Seventh
Day Adventist Church**
  (Sts. Cyril and Methodius Church)
  5001 S. Hermitage Ave.
  1913, JOSEPH MOLITOR

**26 St. Joseph Roman
Catholic Church**
  1729 W. 48th St.
  1914, JOSEPH MOLITOR

**27 Holy Cross Roman
Catholic Church**
  1736 W. 46th St.
  1913–15, JOSEPH MOLITOR

Molitor, an immigrant from Bohemia, shaped the Back of the Yards skyline with this trio of towered churches. The Renaissance-style New Life Seventh Day Adventist, formerly a Bohemian Catholic church, is anchored by an Italian bell tower. The Romanesque St. Joseph, which still houses a Polish congregation, has twin Baroque towers and an exquisitely lit interior with rings of brass sconces and a leaded-glass chandelier. The Renaissance Revival Holy Cross features Lithuanian religious iconography, including facade sculptures of favorite saints George and Isidore, and rises to twin Baroque towers.

28 Central Manufacturing District, Pershing Rd. Development
Pershing Rd. between Ashland and Western Aves.

The brick–and–terra-cotta water tower at Damen Ave., flanked by massive warehouses, stands as a powerful signpost for this early industrial park. By 1915, the original East District was full, and the CMD purchased the entire south frontage of 39th St. from Ashland Ave. to Western Ave., extending 700 feet south to the Chicago Junction Railways' classification yards. The site included the infamous Bubbly Creek, which the CMD and the Sanitary District filled in and replaced with a sewer in the early 1920s.

Central Manufacturing District—Pershing Rd. Development

The Pershing Rd. Development extended the industrial-park concept to include such comprehensive services as a central power plant and sprinkler plant, central union freight stations, comprehensive railroad track arrangements, concrete traffic and utility tunnels connecting all buildings, brick-paved streets with water and sewer systems, sidewalks and grass parkways, and street lighting. The standardized buildings were constructed of concrete or heavy timber, with exteriors of pressed brick and terra-cotta. Most of the buildings had six stories and basement, with uniform floor areas of about 30,000 square feet. They epitomize the multistory "gravity" system of manufacturing, which lost favor to the "straight line production" system and its single-story buildings.

The first four units of the Union Freight Station and Loft Buildings (A, B, C, D) were built between March and October 1917, faster than any other buildings of their kind. The CMD architect for almost all of the work up to 1921 was S. Scott Joy, who was replaced by engineer A. Epstein in July 1921.

The view down Pershing Rd. is impressive, with the water tower dominating the mile of cohesive development. The terra-cotta logos such as Goodyear Tire & Rubber Co., Albert Pick & Co., and L. Fish Furniture Co. identify the original tenants.

29 McKinley Park
Damen Ave. to Western Ave., 37th St. to Pershing Rd.
1902–6, SOUTH PARK COMMISSION
1916, FIELD HOUSE, SOUTH
PARK COMMISSION

The lovely foreground to the Pershing Rd. Development is idyllic McKinley Park, the first of the South Park Commission's neighborhood parks and a model for the Progressive park movement. Designed by the commissioners and staff, the park was a laboratory for testing new ideas, with a swimming lagoon and changing rooms equipped with showers—an important amenity for occupants of cold-water buildings. When the commission retained the Olmsted brothers and D. H. Burnham & Co. to design the next series of parks and park buildings, their designs partially resulted from experiments here.

Planning began in 1900 under South Park Commission general superintendent J. Frank Foster. The park was enlarged in 1906 to include a fishing lagoon, bathhouse, wading pool, and music pavilion (demolished). The swimming lagoon no longer exists, and the changing room building is now a service facility. The field house was designed by staff architects, who adapted models originated by D. H. Burnham & Co. The Damen Ave. Viaduct truncated the park's eastern end. President William McKinley, assassinated in 1901, is commemorated with a statue by Charles J. Mulligan.

Samuel E. Gross's Archer Ave. Cottages

30 AT&T—McKinley Office
(Chicago Telephone Co.)
2240 W. 37th St.
1917, HOLABIRD & ROCHE
1938, ADDITION, HOLABIRD & ROOT

Eschewing their "Phone Company Georgian" formula, the architects delivered a Renaissance Revival building with rusticated base and Venetian windows. When it was first built, the building was only three stories tall and three bays (the easternmost) wide.

31 Du Pont–Whitehouse House
3558 S. Artesian Ave.
1876, OSCAR COBB & CO.

This unusually well documented house is a relic of the era when manufacturers stored explosives and gunpowder in what was then a sparsely populated area. E. I. du Pont de Nemours & Co.'s local agent, Junot J. Whitehouse, commissioned Cobb to design this residence, which was moved from 3616 S. Western Ave. in 1920. Gray cement parging partially conceals the original brick, but the incised stone hood moldings and the pedimented pavilion mark the house as a rare example of the Italianate country-house style that reigned from the 1850s through the 1870s.

32 Samuel E. Gross's Archer Ave. Cottages
3200–3300 S. Hoyne Ave.
1887, ARCHITECT UNKNOWN

The P. T. Barnum of working-class housing, developer Gross boasted that these houses, "for the price, are the handsomest, best built brick cottages in the city, with stone and brick trimmings, seven-foot basement, lake water and large lot." But, he admonished, "you must be quick if you want one at these prices and terms. They go fast. Go and see them and take your wife with you." He was

right: they sold out. But fortunately there was almost always another one under construction; his annual catalog for 1889 cites five developments in the Bridgeport/Back of the Yards area alone.

The uniformity of the long rows of rooflines hints at the development's original cohesiveness. The plain facades have served as blank canvases for widely varied remodelings. In this modest subdivision, Gross not only provided the lot and infrastructure but built the house as well, selling it for $1,050–$1,200, payable on "easy terms" of $50–$100 down and $8 a month (equivalent to the cost of renting). To save excavation and drainage costs, houses had basements aboveground; exterior stairs led to the main level, comprising a parlor, kitchen, two bedrooms, and a small pantry. The street level was later raised, placing the first floor virtually at grade. Many are now reached by a small footbridge between the sidewalk and the front door.

33 Edward Everett Public School
3419 S. Bell Ave.
1891, JOHN J. FLANDERS
1914, ARTHUR F. HUSSANDER

The corner towers of this archetypal Queen Anne school are visible from many nearby bridges and viaducts.

A detour to the Archer Heights and Gage Park neighborhoods takes in two very different schools built for the same organization (entries 34–35).

34 UNO Veterans Memorial Campus
4248 W. 47th St.
2010, URBANWORKS

An obsolete industrial bakery now houses a high school and two elementary schools, each on a separate floor. A glassy addition on 47th St.

UNO Soccer Academy

trumpets the new use while containing a shared gymnasium, cafeteria, and library that also collectively serve as a community center. The entrance on Kildare leads to a three-story atrium that connects public and school spaces. The success of this project inspired the CEO of the United Neighborhood Organization (UNO) to put a premium on architectural creativity in future projects rather than simply occupying decommissioned schools.

35 UNO Soccer Academy

5050 S. Homan St.

2011, JGMA, DESIGN ARCH.; GHAFARI ASSOCS., DESIGN-BUILDER

While Chicago Public Schools was restricting architects to tweak-ing prototypes, the UNO charter school network held a competition that emphasized inspiring, forward-looking design. Swooping ribbons of glass and stainless steel import the glamour of Chicago's Loop, which can be seen from many of the spaces. Hallways line the exterior, sharing light and views with glass-walled internal classrooms. The openness to the community is a deliberate rebuke to the fortress-like appearance of other public buildings in struggling neighborhoods. The elementary school is the first stage of a campus plan that includes a high school (2013, JGMA AND GHAFARI) and soccer stadium.

UNO Veterans Memorial Campus

see Near South Side map, p. 376

see Canaryville/Back of the Yards map, p. 398

38th

Pershing

Vincennes

**NEIU
Center**

Sherman
House

11

13

1

12

Oakwood

14

Holy
Angels

40th

Monur
Bapt

41st

41st

Bowen

10

Metropolitan
Community
Church

42nd

42nd Pl

Urban
Green
House I

First
Church of
Deliverance

43rd

Vernon

6

Champlain

Langley

43rd

9

44th

44th

45th

King Dr

44th Pl

Ebenezer
Church

5

45th Pl

46th

Michigan Blvd
Garden Apts

7

46th

4

Mount
Pisgah
Church

46th Pl

St. Lawrence

Champlain

Langley

Evans

47th

48th

Vincennes

Forestville

Corpus
Christi
Church

Calumet

Washington
Park Court

Ryerso
Hou

49th

3

1

McGill P
Cond

50th

2

Houses for
Hart & Frank

50th Pl

Nol
H

Educare
Center

8

51st

70

Washington
Memorial

51st Pl

52nd

69

Dyett
School

Jones
Armor

52nd Pl

State

Wabash

Michigan

Indiana

Prairie

52nd Pl

7

53rd

53rd

Payne

Chicago
Baking
Company

54th

Ellsworth

WASHINGTON

71

54th Pl

54th Pl

PARK

Garfield Blvd

55th Pl

Morgan

Rainey

Princeton

Yale

Wentworth

56th

72

Du Sable
Museum

74

Dearborn

57th

Pool and
Locker
Bldg

Russell

58th

LaSalle

Perry

Lafayette

DuSable
Museum
Roundhouse

7

59th

Payne

60th

Bess

To Loop

Federal

Dearborn

Princeton

Wells

Wentworth

Dan Ryan Expwy

CTA Green Line

CTA Red Line

Federal

Dearborn

Federal

Dan Ryan Expwy

51st Pl

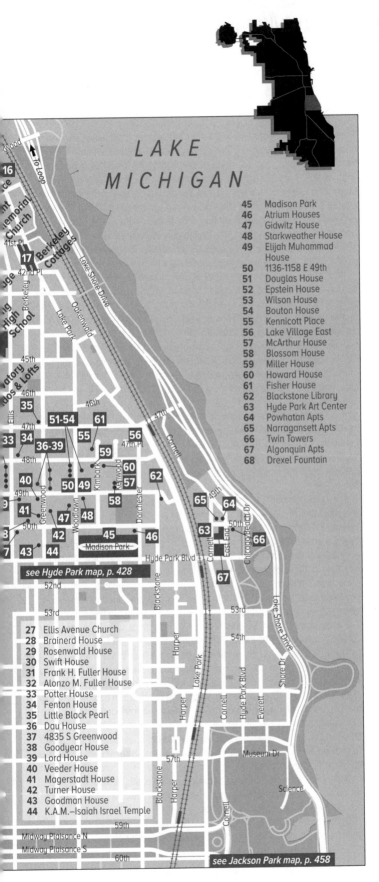

LAKE
MICHIGAN

45 Madison Park
46 Atrium Houses
47 Gidwitz House
48 Starkweather House
49 Elijah Muhammad
   House
50 1136-1158 E 49th
51 Douglas House
52 Epstein House
53 Wilson House
54 Bouton House
55 Kennicott Place
56 Lake Village East
57 McArthur House
58 Blossom House
59 Miller House
60 Howard House
61 Fisher House
62 Blackstone Library
63 Hyde Park Art Center
64 Powhatan Apts
65 Narragansett Apts
66 Twin Towers
67 Algonquin Apts
68 Drexel Fountain

see Hyde Park map, p. 428

27 Ellis Avenue Church
28 Brainerd House
29 Rosenwald House
30 Swift House
31 Frank H. Fuller House
32 Alonzo M. Fuller House
33 Potter House
34 Fenton House
35 Little Black Pearl
36 Dau House
37 4835 S Greenwood
38 Goodyear House
39 Lord House
40 Veeder House
41 Magerstadt House
42 Turner House
43 Goodman House
44 K.A.M.–Isaiah Israel Temple

see Jackson Park map, p. 458

SOUTH AND SOUTHWEST **411**

OAKLAND/KENWOOD

The residential development of this area reflects two contrasting ideals: the urban boulevard house and the country retreat. Chicago's earliest boulevards were established just north of Washington Park, and their popularity with wealthy homeowners set the pattern for other areas. Along the lake, Kenwood's large wooded lots created a secluded suburban setting that contrasted with the see-and-be-seen urbanity of the broad streets to the north and west. The fate of these neighborhoods began to diverge sharply as early as 1900, and today they have little in common. While the boulevards offer examples of past grandeur in decayed circumstances, the enclave of Kenwood south of 47th St. has retained its affluent character to a remarkable degree.

West of the lakefront communities of Oakland and Kenwood are the neighborhoods of Grand Blvd., which lies north of 51st St., and Washington Park, which includes the park itself and the streets to its west. Kenwood was the first to develop and closely followed Paul Cornell's establishment in 1853 of the village of Hyde Park. In 1856, Jonathan A. Kennicott, a dentist and horticulture enthusiast, bought eight acres of countryside near the Illinois Central Railroad tracks south of 43rd St. and named his estate *Kenwood*, after his mother's ancestral home in Scotland. A few wealthy families joined him in the area, and when the railroad added a station at 47th St. in 1859, it was named Kenwood.

In 1861, the area east of State St. from 39th to 63rd Sts. was incorporated as the township of Hyde Park. Separated by 43rd St. and sharing a western boundary at Cottage Grove Ave., Oakland and Kenwood grew as desirable lakefront suburbs over the next three decades. Kenwood outshone all its competitors, however, and was already known by 1874 as the Lake Forest of the South Side.

The neighborhoods west of Cottage Grove Ave. developed slightly later, receiving their impetus from the establishment of the boulevard-and-park system. Frederick Law Olmsted's 1870 plan for the South Park Commission, established in 1869, included a grand circuit of boulevards. Garfield Blvd. was planned as a link to the West Side parks; to the north, Grand (now Martin Luther King Jr. Dr.) and Drexel Blvds. were connected by Oakwood Blvd. to form a four-mile circuit popular for fashionable carriage promenades. In 1874, improvements began on Grand Blvd., which soon became lined with mansions whose styles were emulated by the more modest houses on the side streets. The area north of 51st St. was built up by the 1890s, when development spread south to the Washington Park neighborhood.

The 1890s witnessed the decline in fashionableness of the mature neighborhoods. The City of Chicago had swallowed the township of Hyde Park in 1889, and the elevated train line was extended to Jackson Park in time for the 1893 World's Columbian Exposition. Apartment construction began to exceed that of single-family houses, and the original Protestant residents moved on to other neighborhoods. By 1900, Grand Blvd. had become a second settlement area for German Jews, and large houses in Oakland were being subdivided to provide apartments for Irish stock yard workers. The establishment of a streetcar line on 47th St. created a commercial strip that forms the present boundary between Oakland and Kenwood. To the south, Kenwood remained an exclusive neighborhood of single-family houses, and its status became more closely tied to that of Hyde Park.

During and after World War I, the Great Northern Migration of African Americans from southern states greatly increased population densities in the traditional African American neighborhoods west and south of downtown. In the 1920s, middle-class African Americans began to move into the Grand Blvd. and Washington Park neighborhoods, and by the end of the decade, the thriving community of Bronzeville had shifted south from 35th to 47th St., where the old Regal Theatre hosted nationally famous entertainers. In the wake of another African American influx during World War II, overcrowding spilled into this neighborhood from the north, and middle-class residents fled. Decay overtook the area in the 1950s, and the absence of large institutions left a vacuum filled by the Chicago Housing Authority, which constructed the Federal St. corridor, a narrow but long strip of high-rises west of State St. In the late 1990s, the CHA's Plan for Transformation led to destruction of the notorious high-rises and their replacement (though in insufficient numbers) by hundreds of market-rate and subsidized units.

Oakland has shared the fate of its impoverished neighbors to the north and west. Success stories include the upgrading of a pair of CHA lakefront properties and the appearance of several mixed-income developments.

South of 47th St., Kenwood has benefited from its proximity to Hyde Park and the stabilizing influence of the University of Chicago, which spurred extensive redevelopment in the 1950s and 1960s. Home to the nation's first African American president, Kenwood remains one of the city's most racially integrated and economically stable neighborhoods.

—JOSEPH D. LA RUE WITH LAURIE MCGOVERN PETERSEN

1 Washington Park Court

S. Washington Park Ct.
from 49th to 50th Sts.
1895–1905, HENRY L. NEWHOUSE,
ANDREW SANDEGREN, AND OTHERS

The T. G. Dickinson real estate company created this one-block subdivision in 1892, specifying a ten-foot setback and selling the lots in clusters of two or three. Andrew and John M. Dubach developed at least twenty-five of the fifty-one lots, and Henry L. Newhouse was their architect for at least twelve designs. They set the tone of the street as an enclave of brick and limestone houses with common porch and cornice lines (third stories are often mansarded or recessed) and almost invariably with bay fronts.

2 Houses for the Hart & Frank Co.

4941–4959 S. Martin
Luther King Jr. Dr.
1901, PEABODY & BEAULEY

The subdivision that created Washington Park Court allowed Robert and Emil Hart and their partner in a mortgage-loan business, David L. Frank, to create an unusually harmonious streetscape. Details are drawn from Gothic and Châteauesque idioms in three cases and from classical and Renaissance Revival in the other four.

3 Corpus Christi Roman Catholic Church

4920 S. Martin Luther King Jr. Dr.
1916, JOSEPH W. MCCARTHY
1976, RESTORATION, PAUL J. STRAKA

Built by affluent Irish Catholics just before racial change swept the South Side boulevards, this twin-spired Renaissance Revival church has support buildings grouped around an adjacent cloister. The church features a magnificent coffered ceiling, a main altar that is a mosaic replica of that in Leonardo da Vinci's *The Last Supper*, and windows by F. X. Zettler depicting the church's members in procession with Pope Pius X. This was McCarthy's first major commission; as Cardinal Mundelein's favorite architect, he went on to build twenty-eight churches, most of them during the 1930s.

4 Mount Pisgah Missionary Baptist Church

(Sinai Temple)
4622 S. Martin Luther King Jr. Dr.
1909–12, ALFRED S. ALSCHULER

Alschuler capitalized on lessons learned as a tyro on Adler's Isaiah Temple to establish a widely copied formula for Reform synagogues: separate but linked community and worship buildings isolated daily activities from formal weekly ones. The freely adapted classical styling was regarded as expressing the broad views of the congregation. The temple proper is a wide, shallow space, cross-axial to a broad lobby and entrances. Alschuler conceded that they were modeled on those of the Auditorium Theater, emulating the ease of ingress and egress.

5 Ebenezer Missionary Baptist Church
(Isaiah Temple)
4501 S. Vincennes Ave.
1899, DANKMAR ADLER

Adler's last commission was an auditorium-style synagogue featuring a vaulted ceiling to create the "very nearly perfect" acoustics for which he was famous. Although the building sold out stylistically to the Georgian Revival, it was innovative in elevating school and community services from the basement to a separate but connected annex.

6 Urban Green House I
448 E. 44th St.
2007, DB STUDIO, IIT

Professors Eva Kultermann and Thomas Gentry and their students at IIT designed and constructed this prototype single-family house that is both sustainable and affordable. The south-facing atrium serves as a solar chimney, with a rock bed thermal storage system under the concrete floor that retains heat and releases it at night. Awnings and reflective roofs mitigate summer heat gain. On

the lot to the east is **Hybrid House** (2007, RAY/DAWSON), which has sustainable features and neotraditional architecture.

7 Michigan Blvd. Garden Apartments
4610–4646 S. Michigan Ave. and 40–78 E. 47th St.
1929, ERNEST A. GRUNSFELD JR.

Sears, Roebuck & Co. president Julius Rosenwald, one of Chicago's greatest philanthropists, planned the project to provide sound housing within the black community and a small return on investment. His inspiration was post–World War I municipal housing in Vienna (for example, the Metzleinstaler-Hof [1921–23]; the more famous Karl-Marx-Hof [1927–30] was contemporaneous with Rosenwald's effort). The architect was Rosenwald's nephew, who shared the design of numerous subsequent housing developments; his son-in-law, Alfred K. Stern, was in charge of the plan. For decades, the apartments were extremely attractive to working-class renters, but the profit was only 2.4 percent over seven years on a $2.7 million investment. After Rosenwald's death in 1932, Stern conceded that low-income housing required government support.

Five-story walls of cream brick are relieved with red-brick banding. Storefronts line the base along 47th St., and eight Art Moderne terracotta doorways lead into a spacious inner court of gardens and play-

Michigan Blvd. Garden Apartments before being vacated

grounds that provides access to the 421 walk-up apartments.

The complex was vacated and left to an uncertain fate in 2000.

8 Educare Center
5044 S. Wabash Ave.
2000, TIGERMAN MCCURRY ARCHITECTS

This village-like complex is designed to provide a sense of security in an impoverished neighborhood formerly dominated by towers of public housing. Intended as a national model for day care centers, it has a large interior courtyard surrounded by colorful classroom pavilions with sheltering gable roofs.

9 First Church of Deliverance
4315 S. Wabash Ave.
1939, WALTER T. BAILEY
1946, TOWERS, KOCHER BUSS & DEKLERK

The first African American architect in Illinois converted a former hat factory into this unusual Art Moderne church. It was one of the first houses of worship to have a Hammond electric organ, which gave its gospel music a unique sound. The church was also known for radio broadcasts of its services, which continue to this day.

The large swaths of vacant land west of State St. from Pershing Rd. to 54th St. were occupied by the twenty-eight high rises of the Robert Taylor Homes until 2007. The new development slowly rising in its place, **Legends South**, *consists of two- and three-story residential buildings whose designers include Landon Bone Baker Architects, Johnson & Lee, and Brook Architecture.*

10 Metropolitan Apostolic Community Church
(41st St. Presbyterian Church)
4100 S. Martin Luther King Jr. Dr.
1891, JOHN T. LONG
1913, SOUTH GABLE REMODELING, CHARLES S. FROST

A Romanesque church with a Greek-cross plan to accommodate semi-circular seating presents gable end walls with round arched openings that get smaller as they move up the variegated red sandstone faces.

Oakwood Blvd. provides a short, spacious link between Grand Blvd.

(now King Dr.) and Drexel Blvd. that allowed carriages and riders to make a four-mile grand circuit to Washington Park without backtracking. As a major thoroughfare, it was a natural location for neighborhood churches.

11 Isaac N. W. Sherman House
442 E. Oakwood Blvd.
1889, BURNHAM & ROOT

The severity of John Wellborn Root's Monadnock Building imbues this large house, which is dominated by a huge front gable.

12 Holy Angels Roman Catholic Church
607 E. Oakwood Blvd.
1991, SKIDMORE, OWINGS & MERRILL

When fire destroyed his 1896 church, Father George Clements recruited SOM to donate this design for the nation's first church heated and cooled by solar energy. Simplicity, flexibility, and energy efficiency characterize this concrete basilica with a pitched roof supported by exposed steel trusses. Stucco covers virtually all of the street elevations, while the south side has a glass-filled wall and a roof of solar collectors. The architects, the artists (Englebert Nveng, Richard Hunt, and Roy Lichtenstein), and most of the contractors worked pro bono.

13 Northeastern Illinois University—Center for Inner City Studies
(Abraham Lincoln Center)
700 E. Oakwood Blvd.
1898–1903, FRANK LLOYD WRIGHT AND DWIGHT H. PERKINS
1903–5, DWIGHT H. PERKINS
1971–76, RENOVATION, HEARD & ASSOCS.

A crusty client with a broad social reform agenda had a major hand in shaping this high-rise settlement house. Jenkin Lloyd Jones, Wright's uncle, was pastor of nearby All Souls Unitarian Church (demolished) and conceived the idea for this religious social center. Wright lived nearby when he first arrived in Chicago in 1887 and met his first wife, Catherine Tobin, at his uncle's church.

Pastor Jones's interests ranged far beyond Unitarianism. His desire for a nonsectarian facility led him to shun historic styles for his church

Northeastern Illinois University—Center for Inner City Studies

center. The brick base housed activity rooms and a library. The second and third floors, the site of the galleried auditorium-church, were identified by groups of windows united vertically. The three upper floors—devoted to meeting rooms, the pastor's quarters, and a top-floor gymnasium and domestic science rooms—were marked by decreasing window heights. Strong corner piers strengthen the elevations; the dark floor-line bandings cross the piers only four times. The 1970s renovation made extensive changes to suit the university's needs.

14 Monumental Baptist Church
(Memorial Baptist Church)
729 E. Oakwood Blvd.
1899, PATTON, FISHER & MILLER
This is one of Chicago's finest surviving examples of the central lantern church, a type popularized by H. H. Richardson's Trinity Church in Boston.

15 Mandrake Park Comfort Station
900 E. Pershing Rd.
2001, JOHNSON & LEE
The heavy timber structure is embellished with African-inspired motifs, including semicircular porches at each end and geometric patterns in the masonry, metal grilles, and roof shingles. A high pitched roof makes the small building more prominent from the street.

16 Lake Parc Place
(Victor A. Olander Homes and Olander Homes Extension)
3939 and 3989 S. Lake Park Ave.
1953, 1956, SHAW, METZ & DOLIO
1991, RENOVATION, DAVID A. SAUER

In a remarkable demonstration of how the Chicago Housing Authority can redevelop its dreary 1950s properties, two fifteen-story Y-shaped public housing blocks, distinguished only by their views of Lake Michigan, were meticulously rehabbed, imaginatively landscaped, and secured with attractive fencing that emblazons their trendy new name. The project's success in attracting a mixture of market-rate and public housing tenants led the CHA to adopt ambitious plans for creating mixed-income communities out of all of its holdings. One of these, **Lake Park Crescent** (BEGUN 2003, CAMPBELL TIU CAMPBELL, MASTER ARCH.), is immediately to the south, from 40th St. to 42nd Pl.

17 Berkeley Cottages
4119–4169 S. Berkeley Ave. and
4130–4162 S. Lake Park Ave.
1886–87, CICERO HINE
Sited back-to-back are twenty-six freestanding cottages with wood "simple work" and detailed with Queen Anne elements. They are the survivors of a development that was entirely the work of the English-born Hine, who had a brief solo practice before becoming staff architect for the Brunswick, Balke, Collender Co., where he designed pool halls and bowling alleys.

18 Drexel Blvd.
The most elegant of the South boulevards, Drexel was planned by Olmsted & Vaux in 1871 as a drive with traffic lanes on either side of a 100-foot-wide median, landscaped by H. W. S. Cleveland in 1873–74 with winding walks and formal plantings. The land was donated by the Drexel banking family of Philadelphia, which reaped the benefits of greatly increased value for family members' South Side holdings.

19 Grant Memorial African Methodist Episcopal Church
(First Church of Christ, Scientist)
4017 S. Drexel Blvd.
1897, SOLON S. BEMAN
The first of Beman's Christian Scientist churches, this one set the classical Greek pattern that was followed for decades. The architect of Pullman was invited to submit plans

for a 1,500-seat church with a "large vestibule hall" on a long, narrow site. He modeled his main elevation on the Ionic facade of the Erechtheion, on the Acropolis in Athens. A foyer is wrapped around three sides of the building, providing stairways to a column-free auditorium fitted with theater seats under a low Tiffany "fish scale" dome. The plan and styling were hailed for creating a distinctive architecture for the young religion.

20 Grant Village
4161 S. Drexel Blvd.
1991, JOHNSON & LEE

Grant Church developed this housing for senior citizens. To downplay the vertical block formula dictated by government guidelines while suiting the boulevard context, this eighty-unit, six-story development has two-tone brick banding and a third color on the windows, doors, grilles, and entrance canopy.

21 Martin Luther King Jr. High School
4445 S. Drexel Blvd.
1971, CAUDILL, ROWLETT & SCOTT

The concrete-framed school has its main entrance at the rear of an inner courtyard that flows toward the street, around the slab columns and beneath the second floor at the school's southwest corner. Glazing in metal frames is placed behind the deep columns as well as flush with their front planes. It was rehabbed and given a fresh color scheme in 2002.

22 The Observatory Condos and Lofts
(William E. Hale House)
4545 S. Drexel Blvd.
1885–86, BURNHAM & ROOT
1925, SCHOOL ADDITION, E. NORMAN BRYDGES

This vigorous house gets bigger as it rises, with ledges and corbels thrusting successive floors beyond the planes of lower ones.

23 Moses Born House
4801 S. Drexel Blvd.
1901, FROST & GRANGER

This smooth-faced limestone house demonstrates Charles S. Frost's masterly adaptation of historic styles.

24 Martin A. Ryerson House
4851 S. Drexel Blvd.
1887, TREAT & FOLTZ

This Richardsonian mansion was built shortly after the marriage of the lumber-fortune heir. The building's stern massiveness was at odds with the qualities of the French Impressionist masterworks that once hung here.

25 McGill Parc Condominiums
(John A. McGill House)
4938 S. Drexel Blvd.
1890, HENRY IVES COBB
1928, ANNEX FOR CARRIE MCGILL MEMORIAL YWCA, BERLIN & SWERN
1982, CONVERSION TO APARTMENTS, CARL R. KLIMEK & ASSOCS.

Cobb's penchant for picturesque styles led him to a medieval French model for this limestone-clad mansion. McGill left the land, house,

McGill Parc Condominiums

and funding to the YWCA, which added the annex of concrete and stucco with limestone details. After decades of use as a nursing home and cultist hangout, its derelict hulk was adapted to hold thirty-four units, some duplexed.

26 John H. Nolan House
4941 S. Drexel Blvd.
1887, BURNHAM & ROOT

This simply massed house of variegated brick dates from the last phase of Root's career, when strong gable facades characterized much of his work. The satisfied client wrote, "You not only can make a good picture of a house, but . . . when it comes to delivering up the keys make a man happier . . . than he expected he would be."

27 Ellis Ave. Church
(William M. Crilly House)
5001 S. Ellis Ave.
1908, WILLIAM CARBYS ZIMMERMAN

In partnership with John J. Flanders or on his own, Zimmerman designed houses in various styles for the Crilly family of developers and contractors. This one, in the mode of Richard E. Schmidt's Madlener House, might best be called Chicago School residential.

28 Ezra S. Brainerd House
1030 E. 50th St.
1867, ARCHITECT UNKNOWN

Built by a Civil War soldier with his mustering-out money, this back-lot frame house with an extensive veranda evokes Kenwood's era as a community of lakefront cottages.

29 Julius Rosenwald House
4901 S. Ellis Ave.
1903, NIMMONS & FELLOWS

The head of Sears, Roebuck gave the commission for his house to the pair of masterful designers who became Sears's virtual house architects. Perhaps they had some trouble ratcheting down to the domestic scale; apart from such Prairie School elements as the hipped roof and Roman brick, it's otherwise a grand, styleless galoot.

30 Gustavus F. Swift House
4848 S. Ellis Ave.
1898, FLANDERS & ZIMMERMAN

This meatpacker's palazzo features sweeping verandas, Palladian windows, and at each corner of the

Gustavus F. Swift House

third floor a terra-cotta lion bearing a shield emblazoned with a huge *S*.

31 Frank H. Fuller House
4840 S. Ellis Ave.
1891, FREDERICK W. PERKINS

32 Alonzo M. Fuller House
4832 S. Ellis Ave.
1890, FREDERICK W. PERKINS

A society architect who had been trained in Paris at the École des Beaux-Arts, Perkins combined rock-faced stone and steep roofs here for different effects. Alonzo's imposing house works tan stone into towers, gabled pavilions, and verandas wrapped around a hip-roofed core. Frank's uses a version of the gambrel roof, a battered rubblestone tower, and varied window shapes in a most pleasing, relaxed manner.

33 Edward C. Potter House
4800 S. Ellis Ave.
1892, CHARLES S. FROST

This brick house has the double-tower facade popularized by Charles F. McKim at East Coast resorts.

34 William T. Fenton House
1000 E. 48th St.
1899, WILSON & MARSHALL

All of the exuberance and care that characterized Benjamin H. Marshall's flamboyant career appear in this Georgian Revival study.

35 Little Black Pearl
1060 E. 47th St.
2004, REMODELING AND ADDITION, K2 ARCHITECTS

Two very different buildings zip together to house this nonprofit, which provides afterschool arts education to neighborhood students. The 1920s terra-cotta corner building was remodeled to contain an exhibit

4835 S. Greenwood Ave.

space, café, and gift shop on the first floor with offices above. The new structure to the north, assertively modern with an asymmetrical facade and angular roof, encloses a large multipurpose space and a variety of art studios and classrooms.

36 J. J. Dau House
4807 S. Greenwood Ave.
1897, GEORGE W. MAHER
Designed while Maher was working on his innovative Pleasant Home in Oak Park, this house demonstrates that the style, drawn from colonial American themes, was better served by a full-width veranda than by this hulking extended porch. The reddest of Roman brick is offset by limestone details, some of which introduce Maher's signature "motif-rhythm"—in this case, a round shield and berry-laden leaves.

37 4835 S. Greenwood Ave.
2001, VINCI/HAMP ARCHITECTS
A modern, volumetric composition is executed in rich Roman brick.

38 Charles A. Goodyear House
4840 S. Greenwood Ave.
1902, WILLIAM CARBYS ZIMMERMAN
An elaborate stone facade that invokes such Tudor details as a broad arched entryway and a sort of strapwork on the second-story balustrade also pairs lions within the tympanum and angels beside the arch.

39 John B. Lord House
4857 S. Greenwood Ave.
1896, CHARLES S. FROST
Frost again proves his deftness at

picking up on McKim, Mead & White's free handling of historical styles.

40 Henry Veeder House
4900 S. Greenwood Ave.
1907, HOWARD VAN DOREN SHAW
The site allowed Shaw to place the entrance on the long 49th St. facade. The house is organized symmetrically, with full-height bays at each end, but the door is off-center, occupying a space between four engaged columns. Shaw's free use of the classical vocabulary comes through in the Lego-like metope blocks on the cornices.

41 Ernest J. Magerstadt House
4930 S. Greenwood Ave.
1908, GEORGE W. MAHER
This is one of Maher's finest designs, sympathetic to the demands of a house whose narrow lot requires a side entrance. The carved poppies on the porch columns introduce the selected "motif-rhythm," repeated inside in moldings, mosaics, and leaded glass.

Ernest J. Magerstadt House

42 Edward H. Turner House

4935 S. Greenwood Ave.

1888, SOLON S. BEMAN

This Queen Anne house built entirely of masonry has the style's characteristic solidity but little of its picturesque variety.

43 William O. Goodman House

5026 S. Greenwood Ave.

1892, TREAT & FOLTZ

2007, RESTORATION, HASBROUCK, PETERSON, ZIMOCH, SIRIRATTUMRONG

The heavy hand of Fritz Foltz robs all possible grace from the Italian palazzo form.

44 Kehilath Anshe Ma'ariv– Isaiah Israel Temple

(Temple Isaiah Israel)

1100 E. Hyde Park Blvd.

1924, ALFRED S. ALSCHULER

1973, ADDITION, JOHN H. ALSCHULER

To be "distinctive in style, majestic in appearance, and Jewish by suggestion," the architect chose "Byzantine lines" for this synagogue. The walls are polychromatic brick in various shapes laid up randomly to suggest old, sunbaked walls, while the smokestack is disguised as a minaret. The acoustically perfect auditorium has a spherical Guastavino dome and a stone treatment also intended to suggest age. The addition, designed by the architect's son, adds a chapel and social facilities around a courtyard, one wall of which is the old building. Brick is again the main material, but it is used in a single shape.

45 Madison Park

Entrances on S. Woodlawn and Dorchester Aves. between 50th and 51st Sts.

In December 1883, John H. Dunham, a sugar merchant and banker who had acquired considerable property in Kenwood shortly after the Civil War, filed a subdivision of his holdings. Mostly he provided spacious lots for suburban homes but—apparently emulating Stephen A. Douglas's Woodland and Groveland Parks—he also set out very small city-size lots around an open common ground in Madison Park and along 50th St., which backs up against the park's lots. In no hurry to develop the tracts, he built a few rental houses along 50th St. but specified in his will that his holdings could not be sold until his last surviving heir had died. His heirs supplied a number of single and duplex rental houses, but major development was not possible until the 1920s, after the death of Dunham's daughters. Lots were then combined for the apartment construction that had become the norm in Hyde Park–Kenwood.

46 Atrium Houses

1366–1380 E. Madison Park

1961, Y. C. WONG

The windowless street facades give no clue to the light-filled interiors of these modernist town houses. Each is oriented to a glass-walled atrium deep within. With their severe tan-brick walls, beams for

Kehilath Anshe Ma'ariv–Isaiah Israel Temple

Atrium Houses

cornices, and simple doors, they have been praised as "the ultimate in reticence." Wong lived here with his family, including his son, Ernest, who became a landscape architect and founded Site Design Group. Y. C. Wong also designed the town house complex at **1239–1243 E. Madison Park** (1966).

47 Willard Gidwitz House
4912 S. Woodlawn Ave.
1947, RALPH RAPSON AND
JOHN VAN DER MEULEN

In the immediate postwar years, young architects wishing to build in the modernist manner of Walter Gropius and Marcel Breuer sometimes chose traditional materials to ensure acceptance. Here, the architects used the stone and wood of the existing house on the site but completely transformed them. The rubblestone of the recessed base came from the porch; stones from its huge piers were reused in the chimney. Other materials on the new elevations are wood panels, steel supports, and a glass-enclosed cantilevered steel stair.

48 Charles H. Starkweather House
4901 S. Woodlawn Ave.
1902, HOWARD VAN DOREN SHAW

As with Shaw's Veeder House one block to the west, this house faces 49th St. and offsets the symmetrical composition of the main block with an off-center entrance. The entrance contrasts with the

house's Georgian vocabulary with a pier-and-slab frame topped by a half-round window, creating a forced perspective that dramatizes the entrance.

49 Elijah Muhammad House
4855 S. Woodlawn Ave.
50 **1136–1158 E. 49th St.**
1971, MEESI

The leader of the Nation of Islam, his children, and his chief aides occupied this complex, a mix of Mediterranean and modernist elements. The stained-glass windows incorporate Muslim emblems.

51 James Douglas House
4830 S. Woodlawn Ave.
1907, HOWARD VAN DOREN SHAW

This is an archetype of the formal, symmetrical Georgian Revival house that set the pattern for countless thousands of center-entry colonials. A balustrade originally ran the length of the roof ridge from chimney to chimney.

James Douglas House

52 Richard Epstein House
4824 S. Woodlawn Ave.

1980, NAGLE, HARTRAY & ASSOCS.

The street side is a good neighbor, recalling the red brick and the fanlight door of the colonial revival home it replaced. The private side is a sculptural facade of stucco and large window openings.

53 Thomas E. Wilson House
4815 S. Woodlawn Ave.

1910, HOWARD VAN DOREN SHAW

By 1910, Shaw was better known for palatial suburban estates than for city houses in Kenwood and Hyde Park. Despite its urban location, this house has much in common with those rambling, artfully asymmetrical Tudor-inspired country houses.

54 Christopher B. Bouton House
4812 S. Woodlawn Ave.

1873, ARCHITECT UNKNOWN

2001, RESTORATION AND
    ADDITION, FARR ASSOCS.

Built as a substantial country villa on a large tract, this is regarded as the least-altered 1870s house in Kenwood–Hyde Park. While the window shapes suit the Italianate roofline, their framing suggests another, indeterminate, era.

55 Kennicott Place
4701 and 4721 S. Woodlawn Ave.

1991, DAVID SWAN

These eighteen single-family and duplex "cottage style" town houses have either high stoops or English basement entries (slightly below grade). The Queen Anne houses on Kimbark Ave. near 48th St. were their prototypes.

56 Lake Village East
4700 S. Lake Park Ave.

1971, HARRY WEESE & ASSOCS.;
    EZRA GORDON–JACK M. LEVIN
    ASSOCS., ASSOC. ARCHS.

The slim silhouette changes constantly as one moves around its thirty-eight brick-and-glass facets. The twenty-five-story tower with eight units per floor is one of several Ben Weese designs from the early 1970s that used "minimum perimeter" floor planning in response to demands for short corridors, interesting layouts, and structural

Lake Village East

economy. The multifaceted shape tends toward the circular—the most economical ratio of perimeter to floor area—but it also permits rectangular rooms. Window tiers were placed to capture the best lake and Loop views. The brick sections provide interior walls that welcome the large furniture that modernist apartment design generally found anathema and did not accommodate. The additional cost of the irregular (rather than rectangular) concrete structural system was offset by the lower cost of enclosing a reduced perimeter.

57 Warren McArthur House
4852 S. Kenwood Ave.

1892, FRANK LLOYD WRIGHT

58 George W. Blossom House
4858 S. Kenwood Ave.

1892, FRANK LLOYD WRIGHT

The most important of the "bootlegged" commissions done while he was working for Adler & Sullivan prove that the highly inventive Wright could create successful traditional designs. On the McArthur House, the gambrel roof and the porch with arched corner sections are colonial motifs; the bay windows nestle under the eaves and gable as they do on Wright's own Oak Park home; and the molding dividing the brick base from the stucco wall becomes part of the entrance arch.

The Blossom House appears coldly symmetrical on the front, with three Palladian openings on each street facade, but its plan is not the traditional central hall. A

George W. Blossom House

living room and hall combination spans the midsection from north to south; the first floor ends in a glassy, sunlit, half-circular dining area in the southwest corner. Note the coach houses: McArthur's is a miniature of the main house set at an angle, while Blossom's is a 1907 design exhibiting Wright's Prairie School themes.

59 George L. Miller House
4800 S. Kimbark Ave.
1888, GEORGE O. GARNSEY

Garnsey unabashedly appropriated and miniaturized H. H. Richardson's William Watts Sherman House (1874–76) in Newport, Rhode Island, almost detail for detail. Garnsey also advertised the plans for a double-

house version of the structure in his magazine, *National Builder*.

60 Joseph H. Howard House
4801 S. Kimbark Ave.
1891, PATTON & FISHER

Every peak, plane, dormer, and turret above the stone base is sheathed in the pink slate tiles found on numerous Queen Anne houses in Hyde Park and Kenwood but in few other places locally.

61 Reynolds Fisher House
4734 S. Kimbark Ave.
1890, PATTON & FISHER

The thin, tight clapboarding, high gables, and eaveless roof edges of the architect's own house are all typical Patton & Fisher elements.

George L. Miller House

62 Chicago Public Library— Blackstone Branch

(T. B. Blackstone Memorial Library)
4904 S. Lake Park Ave.
1902, SOLON S. BEMAN

Executed in Concord granite, this Beaux-Arts cupcake was modeled after Beman's Merchant Tailors Building. That miniature domed temple, facing the lagoon at the 1893 World's Columbian Exposition, had pleased both Blackstone and a critic, who described it as "one of the beauty spots of that grand architectural display."

63 Hyde Park Art Center

5020 S. Cornell Ave.
2006, GAROFALO ARCHITECTS

This is the only Chicago building by Doug Garofalo, one of the city's most respected and lauded architects. When he died in 2011, he was in his early fifties, a time when architects are generally embarking on their best work. He had come to national prominence as a pioneer in exploiting digital design for both collaborating online (Korean Presbyterian Church of New York) and creating fluid, biomorphic forms. But this small project is the opposite of a "starchitect" museum. The low-budget renovation of an old army warehouse creates a self-effacing yet extremely effective and innovative showcase for all types of art. The centerpiece is an "inhabitable digital facade," an eighty-foot-long glassy catwalk overhanging the sidewalk that allows interactive video or other artworks to be seen from both inside and out. The first floor's main gallery continues the theme of neighborhood engagement with overhead doors that open the room to the street. Inside, long bands of interior windows do double duty as vitrines to display smaller artworks.

64 Powhatan Apartments

1648 E. 50th St.
1928, ROBERT DEGOLYER AND CHARLES L. MORGAN

65 Narragansett Apartments

1640 E. 50th St.

Powhatan Apartments

1929, LEICHENKO & ESSER WITH
CHARLES L. MORGAN

In the late 1920s, developers attempted a South Side version of the North Side's fashionable Streeterville on landfill holdings of the Chicago Beach Hotel (demolished), a longtime resort at the foot of Hyde Park Blvd. (51st St.). Five apartment buildings were begun before the stock market crash: the jewels are the Powhatan and the Narragansett, both of which were developed by the Garard Trust, with Morgan in charge of aesthetics. Native American names and themes were chosen, primarily because they were untapped sources for the Art Deco designs that embellish the black bas-relief spandrels in the limestone bases and the earth-toned tile panels inserted in the upper elevations. The Narragansett also features goofy, flat-faced pachyderms solemnly gazing down on visitors and residents. The Powhatan is a reinforced-concrete structure with outer walls that could have been flat surfaces but are instead composed of a rhythmic pattern of projecting piers and mullions. It is the only large-scale Chicago apartment building that fully exhibits the "stripped architecture" of recessed spandrels and continuous piers introduced by Eliel Saarinen's entry for the Chicago Tribune Tower Competition of 1922.

66 Twin Towers

1645 and 1649 E. 50th St.

1951, A. EPSTEIN

The recessed spandrels, finished in horizontally striated metal, stretch the entire distance between strongly expressed corner piers, contrasting with their earlier neighbors' vertical orientation.

67 Algonquin Apartments

Hyde Park Blvd., E. 50th St.,
Cornell Ave., and East End Ave.

1950–52, PACE ASSOCS. AND HOLSMAN,
HOLSMAN, KLEKAMP & TAYLOR

These spartan, fourteen-story concrete-frame units perpetuate the Native American theme of the 1920s Chicago Beach development properties in name only. Ludwig Mies van der Rohe was associated with this complex but removed his name when plans were altered to include first-floor residences.

68 Francis M. Drexel Fountain

Drexel Sq. (Drexel Blvd.
and E. 51st St.)

1881, HENRY MANGER, SCULPTOR

Drexel Sq. serves as a transition space between Drexel Blvd. and Washington Park, a truncated version of the sweeping approach envisioned by Frederick Law Olmsted. The family of the Philadelphia financier commissioned the fountain, which depicts Drexel perched atop a pedestal with bas-relief imagery that includes Neptune and a harvest goddess.

69 Walter H. Dyett High School

555 E. 51st St.

1972, DAVID N. HAID

Between 1968 and 1973, the Public Buildings Commission, headed by architect Jacques C. Brownson, hired private architects to build twenty-six inner-city schools with universal modules and flexible plans. Park sites were sought to give underprivileged children the advantages of landscaped suburban schools, provoking protests from open-land advocates. The courts upheld the controversial invasion, but only three schools were eventually built on Chicago Park District property (including Collins High School in Douglas Park). Sensitive to arguments against the site, Haid designed two large-span steel structures with dark, fully glazed skins; the front building is below grade.

70 George Washington Memorial

S. Martin Luther King Jr.
Dr. at E. 51st St.

1904, DANIEL CHESTER FRENCH
AND EDWARD CLARK POTTER

French's rather stolid figure, in contrast to Potter's spirited horse, is meant to indicate Washington's rocklike support of freedom. The work is a second casting of a Paris monument.

71 Chicago Baking Co., International Brands Corporation

(Schulze Baking Co.)
40 E. Garfield Blvd.

1914, JOHN AHLSCHLAGER & SON

Paul Schulze planned his bakery

as part of an aggressive campaign to sell his "better than home-made" bread to tradition-bound, cleanliness-conscious housewives. Five-story walls of glazed cream terra-cotta suggest hygienic conditions. Blue lettering, stringcourses of rosettes, and foliated cornice ornament all carry associations of sunlight, fresh air, and purity, as do the 700 windows grouped in unified ranges. The ornamentation is abstract, Sullivanesque, and modern, not overtly classical and old, because Schulze's product relied on modern technology.

Washington Park
(South Park)
E. 51st St., S. Martin Luther King Jr. Dr., E. 60th St., and S. Cottage Grove Ave.
1871, PLAN, OLMSTED & VAUX, LANDSCAPE ARCHS.; EXECUTED BY H. W. S. CLEVELAND

Washington Park was designed in 1871 by Olmsted & Vaux as the Upper Division of a great "South Park" that also included a Lower Division (now Jackson Park) and a connecting strip, the Midway Plaisance. In contrast to Jackson Park's swampy lakefront site, Washington Park was flat prairie, which would not "elsewhere be recognized as well adapted to the purpose." It was also to be the terminus of three boulevards—Garfield from the west, and Drexel and Grand (now Martin Luther King Jr. Dr.) from the north.

Making an advantage of what they had, Olmsted & Vaux established in the park's northern half a "large meadowy ground," 100 acres of open space perceptible without break from all three approaches. The southern end was to be more verdant, with a pond that would connect—via a canal down the Midway—with the lagoon in Jackson Park. In 1872, park commissioners entrusted the plan's execution to an Olmsted associate, H. W. S. Cleveland, stipulating that he avoid "extensive alterations of the natural surface," thereby putting an end to the Midway's waterway linkage.

Around 1904, the members of the South Park Commission altered the original crescent-shaped lagoon, known as the Mere, to provide a full loop for boaters. A major improvement project in 2003 included restoration of the rocky brook created on the east side of the Mere a century earlier. Washington Park today retains its naturalistic character, with buildings restricted to the perimeter and with the main traffic lanes raised slightly so that visitors must descend into the park proper.

Washington Park and Midway Plaisance

72 Pool and Locker Building
(Refectory)
Pool and Russell Drs.
1891, D. H. BURNHAM & CO.
1992, EXTERIOR RESTORATION, A.
EPSTEIN & SONS WITH DUBIN,
DUBIN & MOUTOUSSAMY AND
HASBROUCK PETERSON ASSOCS.

This elegant, classically derived refectory was built near the site chosen by Olmsted for a pavilion to overlook his "Southopen Ground." It features a deep ground-level colonnade and four open rooftop corner towers. The much-needed restoration was done in conjunction with the creation of adjacent pool facilities.

73 General Richard L. Jones Armory
5206–5310 S. Cottage Grove Ave.
1928, PERKINS, CHATTEN & HAMMOND

The cubic, hard-edged profile of one of the nation's largest urban armories is softened by a crisply detailed bas-relief frieze of soldiers, vertical fluting, giant pilasters every fourth bay, and towers marking the entrances on the north and east sides. Ancient and modern (World War I) sentries emerge from the stone to guard the vehicular entrance.

74 DuSable Museum of African American History
(South Park Commission— Administration Building)
740 E. 56th Pl.
1910, D. H. BURNHAM & CO.
1992, ADDITION, WENDELL CAMPBELL ASSOCS.
2009, EXTERIOR RESTORATION, BAUER LATOZA STUDIO

The most elaborate of the firm's concrete buildings designed for the South Parks shows how a poured material can be manipulated to imitate a carved one; only the terra-cotta Ionic capitals at the main entrance are added on. The lightly sanded precast-concrete addition duplicates the original's color and fenestration, adding galleries, a theater, and exhibit space.

75 DuSable Museum Roundhouse
(Stable)
Payne Dr. south of 57th St.
1880, BURNHAM & ROOT
2012, EXTERIOR RESTORATION, BAUER LATOZA STUDIO

This rare roundhouse stable and its attendant buildings, all built of random ashlar Joliet limestone, were acquired by the DuSable Museum in 2004 to provide expansion space. Fund-raising challenges have delayed completion of the project.

HYDE PARK/SOUTH SHORE

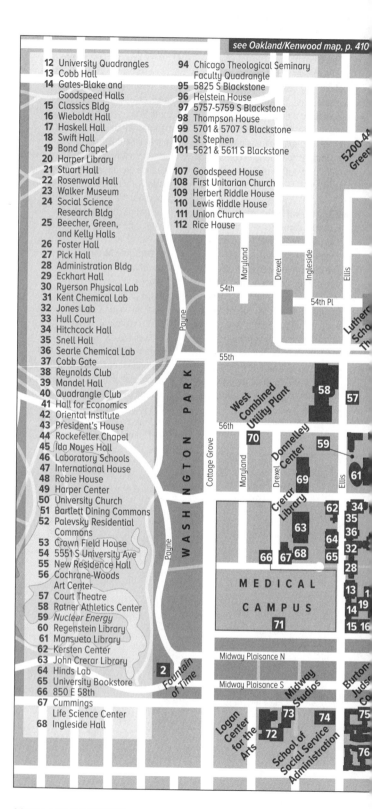

see Oakland/Kenwood map, p. 410

12 University Quadrangles
13 Cobb Hall
14 Gates-Blake and
   Goodspeed Halls
15 Classics Bldg
16 Wieboldt Hall
17 Haskell Hall
18 Swift Hall
19 Bond Chapel
20 Harper Library
21 Stuart Hall
22 Rosenwald Hall
23 Walker Museum
24 Social Science
   Research Bldg
25 Beecher, Green,
   and Kelly Halls
26 Foster Hall
27 Pick Hall
28 Administration Bldg
29 Eckhart Hall
30 Ryerson Physical Lab
31 Kent Chemical Lab
32 Jones Lab
33 Hull Court
34 Hitchcock Hall
35 Snell Hall
36 Searle Chemical Lab
37 Cobb Gate
38 Reynolds Club
39 Mandel Hall
40 Quadrangle Club
41 Hall for Economics
42 Oriental Institute
43 President's House
44 Rockefeller Chapel
45 Ida Noyes Hall
46 Laboratory Schools
47 International House
48 Robie House
49 Harper Center
50 University Church
51 Bartlett Dining Commons
52 Palevsky Residential
   Commons
53 Crown Field House
54 5551 S University Ave
55 New Residence Hall
56 Cochrane-Woods
   Art Center
57 Court Theatre
58 Ratner Athletics Center
59 *Nuclear Energy*
60 Regenstein Library
61 Mansueto Library
62 Kersten Center
63 John Crerar Library
64 Hinds Lab
65 University Bookstore
66 850 E 58th
67 Cummings
   Life Science Center
68 Ingleside Hall

94 Chicago Theological Seminary
   Faculty Quadrangle
95 5825 S Blackstone
96 Helstein House
97 5757-5759 S Blackstone
98 Thompson House
99 5701 & 5707 S Blackstone
100 St Stephen
101 5621 & 5611 S Blackstone

107 Goodspeed House
108 First Unitarian Church
109 Herbert Riddle House
110 Lewis Riddle House
111 Union Church
112 Rice House

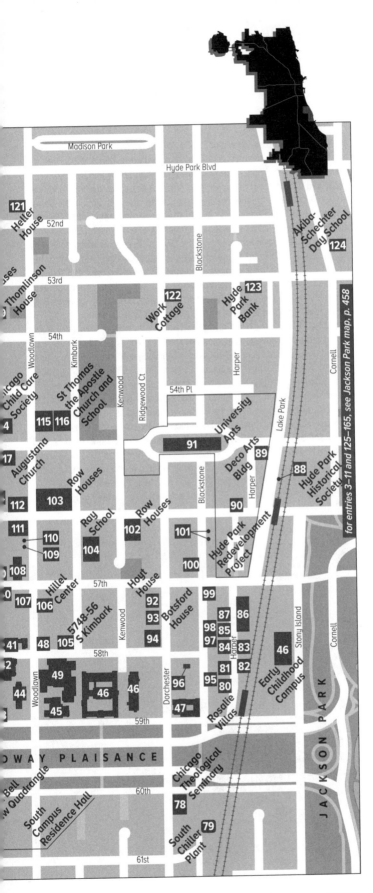

Madison Park

Hyde Park Blvd

121 Heller House

52nd

Blackstone

Akiba-Schechter Day School

124

Thomlinson House

53rd

122 Work Cottage

Hyde Park Bank 123

Woodlawn

Kimbark

54th

Chicago Child Care Society

St Thomas the Apostle Church and School

Kenwood

Ridgewood Ct

54th Pl

University Apts

Harper

Cornell

for entries 3–11 and 125–165, see Jackson Park map, p. 458

4

115 116

91

Deco Arts Bldg

89

88

Hyde Park Historical Society

17 Augustana Church

Row Houses

Row Houses

Blackstone

Lake Park

Harper

112

103

Ray School

102

90

111

110 109

104

101

100

Hyde Park Redevelopment Project

108

Hillel Center

57th

Hoyt House

92

93

94

Botsford House

99

87 86

Stony Island

107 106

5748-56 S Kimbark

Kenwood

98 85

97

84 83

82

46

Early Childhood Campus

Cornell

41 48 105

58th

96

95 81

80

49

46

46

Dorchester

47

Rosalie Villas

Harper

JACKSON PARK

44

45

Woodlawn

59th

WAY PLAISANCE

Bell

Quadrangle

South Campus Residence Hall

Chicago Theological Seminary

60th

78

South Chiller Plant

79

61st

HYDE PARK/SOUTH SHORE

The World's Columbian Exposition of 1893 had a powerful and lasting impact on Chicago's urban development, and nowhere were these effects felt as strongly as in Hyde Park. The enormous annexation of 1889, in which the city swallowed up huge townships like Lake View, Jefferson, and Hyde Park, was prompted in part by the theory that the larger the city's population, the better its chances of being named the site of the fair. In April 1890, after Chicago had won this prize, civic pride demanded the creation of institutions befitting the nation's second-most-populous city. One of these new institutions was the University of Chicago, founded the same year. Other preparations for the exposition included the long-postponed landscaping of Jackson Park (chosen as the site of the fair), the extension and expansion of public transportation from the Loop, and massive construction of hotels and apartments. Hyde Park would never again be the quiet suburb envisioned by its founder.

In 1853, Paul Cornell, a Chicago lawyer newly arrived from New York, bought three hundred acres of lakefront land between 51st and 55th Sts. and deeded sixty of those acres to the Illinois Central Railroad in return for a train station located in his new community of Hyde Park. He knew that his hopes for a prosperous residential development depended in equal measure on perceived seclusion from urban woes and easy access to the city's commercial and cultural institutions. Hyde Park was incorporated as a township in 1861 (with boundaries that vastly exceeded those of the small settlement by that name) and as a village in 1872. Originally concentrated around 53rd St. and Hyde Park Blvd. (near the train station at 53rd St. and Lake Park Ave.), commercial development continued to follow the train's southward path, with districts emerging along Stony Island Ave. and East 71st, 75th, and 79th Sts.

Local businesses were the only nonresidential users of land in Hyde Park;

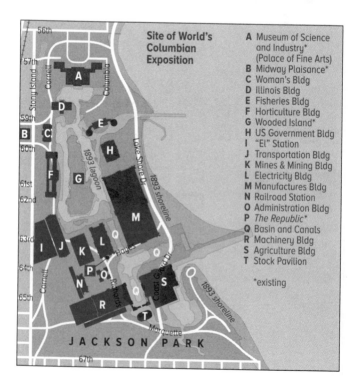

Site of World's Columbian Exposition

A Museum of Science and Industry* (Palace of Fine Arts)
B Midway Plaisance*
C Woman's Bldg
D Illinois Bldg
E Fisheries Bldg
F Horticulture Bldg
G Wooded Island*
H US Government Bldg
I "El" Station
J Transportation Bldg
K Mines & Mining Bldg
L Electricity Bldg
M Manufactures Bldg
N Railroad Station
O Administration Bldg
P *The Republic**
Q Basin and Canals
R Machinery Bldg
S Agriculture Bldg
T Stock Pavilion

*existing

industry was deliberately excluded. Cornell hoped that a large institution would become an anchor for the area, but this did not come to pass until after his death, when the University of Chicago was founded. The lakefront location, although swampy and not very attractive in its unimproved state, gave the area great potential as both a resort location and a year-round suburban community. Hotels were among the earliest large buildings, and housing ranged from villas and cottages to row houses and apartment buildings.

The area's most ambitious landscape improvements resulted from the 1869 creation of the South Park Commission, of which Cornell was a member. The commission established an extensive system of connected parks and landscaped boulevards and hired Frederick Law Olmsted and Calvert Vaux to design the enormous South Park (now Washington and Jackson Parks and the connecting Midway Plaisance). Although several features of the original plan were altered or omitted, the overall character of these parks comes remarkably close to Olmsted's pastoral vision.

The slow pace of land acquisition and a lack of money delayed the landscaping of Jackson Park. Not until 1890, when it was chosen as the site for the World's Columbian Exposition, did work progress, but it then proceeded at a breakneck pace that made up for two decades of neglect. The White City created here was intended to show how parks, boulevards, and buildings could be planned in a unified manner that would bring harmony and order to the chaos of the industrial city. The fair sowed the seeds of the City Beautiful movement, which culminated in Daniel H. Burnham's 1909 *Plan of Chicago*. Two of the plan's features that had the greatest impact on this area were the dedication of all lakefront land to public use and the creation of wide thoroughfares to facilitate access to and from the central city.

The increasing ease of transportation to the Loop—frequent train service was supplemented in the twentieth century by automobile and bus access—brought greater density to Hyde Park and spurred development to the south. The South Shore became a fashionable middle-class area, with an elegant country club and a planned subdivision, Jackson Park Highlands.

The diverse architecture of Hyde Park comprises excellent examples of almost every urban building type and style, from modest frame cottages to luxurious lakefront high-rises. The area is particularly rich in houses from the 1890s, the era of its most feverish development. Many of them were designed by architects later grouped as the Chicago School, a term that includes both the Prairie School and less radical colleagues such as Pond & Pond and Howard Van Doren Shaw. All were experimenting with new forms and rethinking what the house should be. Frank Lloyd Wright's Robie House is the most outstanding example.

Some of Hyde Park's finest houses were designed for faculty members of the university, which has continued to play a pivotal role in the community and was instrumental in the large-scale redevelopment of the 1950s. Its reassuring presence has helped to maintain the desirability of the Hyde Park neighborhood for the last century and will no doubt continue to do so for at least the next hundred years.

—R. STEPHEN SENNOTT

1 Midway Plaisance
Between E. 59th and 60th
Sts. from Washington Park
east to Jackson Park

Although its name is a contradictory mix of the tawdry and the elegant, the Midway Plaisance is actually a broad boulevard with a vast sunken grassy median. The first half of its name resulted simply from its location midway between the two large parks that it connected. Its use as a grounds for the Ferris wheel and other amusements during the 1893 World's Columbian Exposition—in contrast to the high-minded, educational quality of the exhibits farther east—made *Midway* synonymous with carnival grounds everywhere. A *plaisance* was one of Frederick Law Olmsted's landscape types and referred to a pleasure grounds with winding, shrub-lined paths for strolling and picnicking. Ironically, the Midway was never developed with such a landscape. Nor did it ever become the great water link between parks that Olmsted had envisioned, with its median canal planned to unite Jackson Park's lagoons to a lake in Washington Park. In 1894, the members of the South Park Commission hired Olmsted, Olmsted & Eliot to create a plan that would fulfill the vision of a canal. Some excavation occurred, lowering the level of the land, but the plan was never completed. Today it serves as a broad greensward that sets off the neo-Gothic grandeur of the University of Chicago campus.

Twenty-first-century work on the Midway includes an **ice rink and warming house** (2002, NAGLE HARTRAY DANKER KAGAN MCKAY PENNEY ARCHITECTS) that occupies the exact site of the Ferris wheel, a discovery made during construction. The **Midway Crossings** (2010–13, JAMES CARPENTER DESIGN ASSOCS., BAUER LATOZA STUDIO, AND SCHULER SHOOK) at Ellis, Woodlawn, and Dorchester Aves. are forty-foot-tall light masts that help to visually unite the north and south parts of the campus.

2 *Fountain of Time*
Midway Plaisance at entrance to Washington Park
1922, LORADO TAFT
BASE DESIGN, HOWARD
  VAN DOREN SHAW
2002, 2007, RESTORATION,
  CHICAGO PARK DISTRICT AND
  BAUER LATOZA STUDIO

One of Chicago's most impressive monuments anchors the west end of the Midway, which Taft wanted balanced by a Fountain of Creation at the east end. Inspired by lines from an Austin Dobson poem,

> Time goes, you say? Ah no!
> Alas, Time stays, we go. . . .

Taft depicts a hooded figure leaning on a staff and observing a panorama of humanity that rises and falls in a great wave. The statue's ambitious theme, size, and scope overshadow its original purpose, which was to commemorate a century of peace between England and the United States in the wake of an 1814 treaty resolving Canadian border conflicts. Taft envisioned the group sculpted from marble, but the material's high cost and vulnerability to Chicago's weather made it impractical. Bronze, his second choice, was also prohibitively expensive, leading to the selection of a pebbly concrete aggregate. The hollow-cast concrete form reinforced with steel was cast in an enormous 4,500-piece mold. Taft himself appears among the figures that line the west side of the monument; he is wearing a smock, head bowed and hands clasped behind him.

Jackson Park
(South Park)
E. 56th–67th Sts., S. Stony Island Ave. to Lake Michigan
1871, OLMSTED & VAUX
1895, OLMSTED, OLMSTED & ELIOT

Although Olmsted & Vaux had prepared a comprehensive plan for the South Parks in 1871, Jackson Park did not receive major improvements for two decades. The primary features of the plan were aquatic:

Fountain of Time

a channel cut through the beach would link a 200-foot pier with a series of lagoons that would lead to canals along the Midway and eventually to a small lake in Washington Park. During the 1870s, dredging of the swampy land began, and in the 1880s a permanent beach was completed from 56th to 59th Sts.; it was later paved with granite blocks down to 63rd St. When planning began in 1890 for the World's Columbian Exposition, it finally created an impetus to complete work on Jackson Park, the main site of the fair. Frederick Law Olmsted designed the fairgrounds, and his vision of a watery paradise was fulfilled with a ceremonial basin called the Court of Honor, canals, a lagoon with a wooded island, and a pond. The only tangible reminders of the fair's glory are the Museum of Science and Industry, the Lagoon and Wooded Island with its Japanese garden, and Daniel Chester French's statue, *The Republic*.

The third and most influential plan for the park was drawn up by Olmsted, Olmsted & Eliot in 1895. The theme of water was central to the plan and can still be seen despite the loss of several links between ponds and lagoons. Improvements were made on a grand scale, so that by 1904, Jackson Park contained beautifully scenic greens, shrubbery, trees, walks, bridges, and driveways. The encroachment of the automobile has destroyed much parkland, but the essential character remains.

3 Museum of Science and Industry

(Palace of Fine Arts)
S. Lake Shore Dr. at E. 57th St.
1893, D. H. BURNHAM & CO.
1929–40, RECONSTRUCTION, GRAHAM,
    ANDERSON, PROBST & WHITE
1998, GARAGE AND UNDERGROUND
    ADDITION, E. VERNER JOHNSON
    & ASSOCS., A. EPSTEIN AND SONS
    INTERNATIONAL, JACOBS/RYAN ASSOCS.
2005, U-505 SUBMARINE CONSERVATION
    AND RELOCATION, GOETTSCH PARTNERS

Built as the Palace of Fine Arts of the World's Columbian Exposition, this is the sole remnant of the great 1893 fair and its only fireproof structure. Designed by Charles B. Atwood (1849–95) to display paintings and

Museum of Science and Industry—detail

sculpture assembled from all over the world, the Palace of Fine Arts was the greatest of Atwood's structures at the exposition.

Following the fair, the building housed the Field Museum of Natural History until 1920. It then stood empty and deteriorating while architect George W. Maher, who called its neoclassical architecture "unequaled since the Age of Pericles," spearheaded an effort by the AIA to save it. In 1930, Julius Rosenwald, philanthropist and president of Sears, Roebuck & Co., contributed $5 million to rehabilitate the structure and to establish a world-class museum. The rebuilding, completed in 1940, produced a stylistic anomaly. The original exterior of staff, a hemp-and-plaster compound, was replaced exactly in marble and limestone, while the interior received Art Moderne streamlining.

Handsome changes at the museum's imposing grand entrance facade occurred in 1998. An unsightly 1,300-car surface lot was transformed by Jacobs/Ryan into six acres of green space. The garage was transferred below; exhibition space was expanded, and a dashing new underground entry was designed by Epstein to complement the museum's 1930s Moderne interior.

With its Ionic colonnades, caryatid porches, and domed roofs, the Palace of Fine Arts represented the acme of the classicism that made the fair a White City of marble temples. After Chicago won out over New York in a fierce rivalry to host the fair, Frederick Law Olmsted was hired to plan the grounds on a 700-acre site in Jackson Park. John Wellborn Root was selected the architect in charge of design; and his partner, Daniel H. Burnham,

Museum of Science and Industry

was to be chief of construction. Buildings of "high architectural importance" were to be designed by East Coast establishment architects, some of whom had been educated at the École des Beaux-Arts in Paris. These men included Richard Morris Hunt, third president and a founder of the AIA; Atwood; and the firm of McKim, Mead & White.

However, Root's sudden death in January 1891 and his replacement by Charles Atwood left the architects free to agree among themselves that classical motifs would be stressed throughout. This choice not only secured the reputation of academically trained architects for decades to come but also ensured that classicism would become the standard dress for practically every city's major cultural, commercial, and municipal institutions virtually until the Great Depression. Burnham's role as coordinator with total charge over the exposition launched him as the nation's top city planner.

—SUSAN S. BENJAMIN

4 Columbian Basin

This reflective pool, designed as part of the 1895 plan, replaced an informal pond but conveys the character of the fair's Court of Honor, which had been farther south in the park. At the south end of the basin is the Clarence S. Darrow Bridge, named for the lawyer who lived nearby and had his ashes scattered over the bridge into the lagoon.

5 Music Court

The radiating layout of the paths and some of the original trees date to the 1895 plan.

6 Wooded Island and Lagoon, Osaka Garden

A survivor of the 1893 Exposition, the island was the site of the Ho-o-den, a group of three Japanese pavilions that strongly impressed Frank Lloyd Wright with their inventive organization of space. The gardens were installed near the Ho-o-den in 1935 using lanterns and plant materials from the Japanese Garden at the recently closed Century of Progress world's fair (the building itself burned down in the 1940s). In 1981, a new Japanese teahouse was built and the first of many garden restorations was undertaken. The island is now a nature sanctuary, and its planting of native midwestern foliage framed by

the lagoon strongly evokes Olmsted's turn-of-the-century vision for the park.

7 *The Republic*

1893, DANIEL CHESTER
FRENCH (CAST 1918)
1992, RESTORATION, CHICAGO
PARK DISTRICT

The "Golden Lady" is, surprisingly, Jackson Park's only sculpture. It was cast from a plaster model of the original, which was almost three times as big and graced the eastern end of the fair's Court of Honor. Now located on the site of the fair's Administration Building, which terminated the western end of the Court of Honor, the statue symbolized the advanced

The Republic

state of civilization on the 400th anniversary of Columbus's landing.

8 Jackson Park Beach House
(64th St. Beach Pavilion)
1919, SOUTH PARK COMMISSION
1999, RESTORATION, MANN, GIN, DUBIN
   & FRAZIER AND DLK ARCHITECTURE

This enormous classically inspired concrete bathhouse was modeled on the many buildings of this type designed by D. H. Burnham & Co. It included a covered promenade and an infirmary in addition to the lockers and showers. As restored, it is again a grand lakeside amenity.

9 Former U.S. Coast Guard Station
1906, ARCHITECT UNKNOWN
1992, RESTORATION, CHICAGO
   PARK DISTRICT

This building was commissioned by the federal government to serve the crowds of bathers and boaters flocking to the park. The shingled surfaces and roof terrace are like those of more remote Great Lakes Coast Guard stations.

10 Hayes Dr. and Coast Guard Dr. Bridges
These are two of the four rusticated stone bridges erected in Jackson Park around 1904, when walkways, boulevards, meadows, and other landscape features were being completed. Part of the 1895 plan, the bridges are decorated with figures and reptiles meant to evoke the theme of wind and water. The southern bridge, designed by Peter Weber, was rehabilitated in 2004 by Johnson Lasky Architects.

11 La Rabida Children's Hospital and Research Center
65th St. and Lake Michigan
1931, GRAHAM, ANDERSON,
   PROBST & WHITE
1952–59, ADDITIONS, FRIEDMAN,
   ALSCHULER & SINCERE
   AND PACE ASSOCS.
1992, ADDITION, VOA ASSOCS.

The name comes from the Spanish pavilion at the 1893 Exposition, which replicated the convent where Columbus awaited Queen Isabella's decision about his voyage to the New World. Converted to a children's hospital, it was later replaced by the present structure.

University of Chicago Campus
Because campus buildings are organized around landscaped quadrangles with little or no automobile access, the campus is best seen on foot. This walking tour begins at the southwest quadrangle of the central campus, where the earliest buildings are located.

12 University of Chicago Quadrangles
Bounded by Ellis and University Aves. and E. 57th and E. 59th (Midway Plaisance) Sts.
1891–30
PLAN AND BUILDINGS TO 1900: HENRY IVES COBB
LANDSCAPE DESIGN: OLMSTED BROS., BEATRIX FARRAND, AND OTHERS

The Gothic quadrangles of the University of Chicago were built on land donated by or purchased from Marshall Field in 1890, the year of the university's charter. With three exceptions, the site's thirty-four buildings employ various interpretations of the Gothic that are faithful to the spirit of the initial plan and to the trustees' dream of a unified, organic, self-contained campus that would nurture and sustain the ideal of a great research university.

Henry Ives Cobb, creator of the Fisheries Building at the 1893 World's Columbian Exposition as well as structures for the Chicago Historical Society and the Newberry Library, designed the original scheme and its early modifications. It consists today of six broken quadrangles, three on the north side, three on the south, paralleling a larger, less defined central rectangle that runs between University and Ellis Aves. (Other academic buildings and complexes, many also wearing Gothic dress, are on adjacent streets.) Most of the structures built during the university's first ten years were designed by Cobb, including complexes running along the west and east sides of the southern half of the quadrangles and in the center on the northern half. Cobb also designed the university's Yerkes Observatory in Wisconsin and its President's House on University Ave. He was succeeded as master designer in 1901 by

University of Chicago Quadrangles

Shepley, Rutan & Coolidge, whose more elegant and elaborate structures include the Hutchinson Court complex in the northeast corner and Harper Memorial Library to the south. Other contributors of variations of campus Gothic included Dwight H. Perkins, Charles Z. Klauder, and Coolidge & Hodgdon.

Adorned with carved references to ancient and modern history, to classical mythology, and to Christianity and folklore while featuring lancet windows, hammer-beam ceilings, loggias, corbels, gargoyles, and all the other elements of the Gothic, the picturesquely assertive buildings define a symmetrical plan whose scale and clarity recall the Beaux-Arts vision of the Columbian Exposition. The beauty of these structures has also been enhanced by the work of an important series of landscape designers.

Derided by modernists for their archaic conceits, the quadrangles survive as one of the country's most remarkable expressions of commitment to a scholarly or priestly dream, one containing great stylistic variety within the larger Gothic vocabulary. The forty years of construction now seem all of one piece, the only jarring elements projected by three structures put up after World War II. By then, fortunately, this central campus was almost complete, and modern designers could build only in surrounding areas.

—NEIL HARRIS

13 Cobb Lecture Hall
5811–5827 S. Ellis Ave.
1892, HENRY IVES COBB

This was the university's first building, one of eighteen designed by Cobb during his tenure (1891–1901) as campus architect. Named for donor Silas B. Cobb (no relation to the architect), it established the Gothic style that would be followed for the next four decades—but with a chunky, robust character that hints at the architect's attraction to the Romanesque (as do the red tile roofs). Cobb, in fact, had to be persuaded to adopt the Gothic instead of the Romanesque style of his Newberry Library. The trustees felt strongly that the ecclesiastical and educational associations of the Gothic made it more appropriate to a university than was the Romanesque, which was then popular for commercial structures. Despite his initial hesitancy, Cobb executed a masterful rendition of the Gothic style, with gables and dormers piercing steeply pitched roofs and crowned with vigorous crockets. Oriels, bays, and pavilion-like projections break the wall planes and give a suitably medieval impression of picturesque irregularity despite the buildings' essential symmetry.

The fourth floor contains the Bergman Gallery, where for many decades the Renaissance Society has exhibited important modern art.

14 Gates-Blake and Goodspeed Halls
(Middle Divinity, Graduate, and South Divinity Halls)
5845 S. Ellis Ave.
1892, HENRY IVES COBB

Originally dormitories for fifty men each, they contained suites of two bedrooms on either side of a study. They continue the style of Cobb Hall, with an extra story added to Gates Hall to break up the roofline. A former reading room is now a recital hall and features its original windows and wood-trussed ceiling.

15 Classics Building
1010 E. 59th St.
1915, SHEPLEY, RUTAN & COOLIDGE

After the initial flurry of the 1890s, campus construction was heavily concentrated within three periods: 1901–4 (see the Tower Group), 1912–16, and 1926–32. The second of these building booms, heralded by the long-awaited completion of Harper Memorial Library, was a period of increasing attention to architectural symbolism. No longer content with crockets and gargoyles, the university requested carved ornament indicative of activities inside the buildings, an obsession that would persist for a decade. The Classics Building is ornamented on the south with the heads of Homer, Cicero, Socrates, and Plato; characters from Aesop's fables; and depictions of the labors of Hercules.

16 Wieboldt Hall
1050 E. 59th St.
1928, COOLIDGE & HODGDON

Dating from the last efflorescence of campus Gothic, Wieboldt resembles its earlier neighbor, the Classics Building. The west wall of the archway linking them had embedded in it a stone from the old University of Chicago, which went bankrupt in 1886. Represented on this building for the study of modern languages are authors Lessing, Goethe, Schiller, Ibsen, Dante, Molière, Hugo, Cervantes, Chaucer, Shakespeare, Milton, and Emerson.

17 Haskell Hall
(Haskell Oriental Museum)
5836 S. Greenwood Ave.
1896, HENRY IVES COBB

The building's original purpose as a museum is signaled by the unusual roof, which had skylights to illuminate the galleries. The university's collection of ancient Near Eastern art and artifacts was displayed here until the completion of the Oriental Institute in 1931. The cornerstone bears inscriptions in Hebrew, Latin, and Greek.

18 Swift Hall
1025 E. 58th St.
1926, COOLIDGE & HODGDON

The Divinity School's central campus location, planned long before construction or even design of the buildings began, was meant to symbolize the centrality of religious belief to all fields of study at the university. The richly decorated interior includes a carved, hammer-beam ceiling in a third-floor lecture hall, which was a reading room for the school's library.

19 Bond Chapel
1926, COOLIDGE & HODGDON

The intimate interior is a jewel; if it is dark, look for light switches to the left of the front door. Appropriately connected to Swift Hall by a cloister, this small and beautifully ornamented chapel narrates a wide range of Christian doctrine on the exterior as well as interior. Adam and Eve flank a window on the west, while angelic and devilish figures play tag across the roofline and cornices. An orchestra of angels plays above a pierced inscription of the Beatitudes that scrolls across the walls. The designers (including Charles J. Connick, whose Boston firm executed the windows) had expert iconographical guidance from the Divinity School faculty, especially Edgar J. Goodspeed, chair of the Dept. of New Testament and Early Christian Literature.

20 William Rainey Harper Memorial Library
1116 E. 59th St.
1912, SHEPLEY, RUTAN & COOLIDGE
1972, RENOVATION, METZ, TRAIN, OLSON & YOUNGREN

Punctuating the skyline with two massive towers, this library formed the first important component in the southern wall of buildings oriented toward the Midway. Its location resulted from a comprehensive campus plan formulated in 1902 that called for concentrating the humanities and social sciences buildings in the southern part of the quadrangles, which would henceforth be academic and not residential. As other buildings in the plan were completed

William Rainey Harper Memorial Library

Rosenwald Hall—exterior detail

(the last one in 1929), second-story bridges linked the library to reading rooms and department libraries in Haskell and Stuart Halls. Visit the third-floor reading room, a grand space marked on the exterior by the long row of arched, double-height windows. Look for the university's coat of arms, devised during this time so that it could be included in the room's iconography along with those of other distinguished institutions. Cross the bridge into another reading room, modernized but retaining an elaborate ceiling, that is actually part of Stuart Hall.

21 Harold Leonard Stuart Hall
(Law School)
5835 S. Greenwood Ave.
1904, SHEPLEY, RUTAN & COOLIDGE
The building is carved with figures of kings and magistrates (predemocratic dispensers of justice) and features Moses and the Ten Commandments atop the roof.

22 Rosenwald Hall
1101 E. 58th St.
1915, HOLABIRD & ROCHE
1972, RENOVATION, SAMUEL A. LICHTMANN
The shield next to the door proclaims Dig and Discover. Better yet, look up and discover: use binoculars and a telephoto lens to capture all the beasts on this building. This was the home of the geology and geography departments, and the carvings reflect the interests of these disciplines and honor the donor, Sears, Roebuck magnate Julius Rosenwald, with a frieze of roses around the entrance. The octagonal tower originally held meteorological instru-

ments, and its gargoyles represent the four winds and four birds of the air. The square tower has four symbols of continents, with the buffalo, bull, elephant, and lion representing North America, Europe, Asia, and Africa, respectively.

23 Walker Museum
1115 E. 58th St.
1893, HENRY IVES COBB
1980, RENOVATION, NAGLE, HARTRAY & ASSOCS.
Cobb designed this to be a natural history museum, pushing the stair tower out the south wall to allow space in the exhibition hall for prehistoric skeletons. It was used instead for desperately needed classrooms, laboratories, and offices; the prehistoric collection was eventually given to the Field Museum of Natural History. When the Graduate School of Business moved into the building, architects took advantage of the generous ceiling heights to squeeze five floors of space into the three-story structure.

24 Social Science Research Building
1126 E. 59th St.
1929, COOLIDGE & HODGDON
When this structure completed the south wall of buildings in 1929, it represented the fulfillment of the 1902 plan for the original campus quadrangles. It was designed to bring together the departments of history, sociology, economics, and political science to foster the interdisciplinary study of society. The elaborate program of ornament, which by this era of campus design was less concerned with historicism than with representational imagery, includes measuring devices such as calculators and calipers.

25 Beecher, Green, and Kelly Halls
5848 S. University Ave.
1893, 1899 (GREEN HALL),
HENRY IVES COBB

26 Foster Hall
1130 E. 59th St.
1893, HENRY IVES COBB
1902, WESTERN ADDITION,
WILLIAM A. OTIS

Coeducational since its founding, the university provided women's dormitories on the southeastern edge of the main quadrangle, mirroring the original four buildings to the west. Green Hall, which was completed later for financial reasons, is a story higher than its neighbors, just as Gates Hall stands out on the opposite side. Cobb emphasized the prominent Midway corner of Foster Hall with a profusion of crockets and gargoyles on the corner turret. Marion Talbot, dean of women from 1892 to 1925, influenced Cobb's plans for the Women's Quadrangle. She recommended four smaller buildings rather than a single large one, and single rooms rather than the two-bedroom-and-study arrangement used for the men. She also made sure that the women's dorms would have parlors and dining rooms for socializing; the men's facilities had woefully inadequate public spaces.

27 Albert Pick Hall for International Studies
5828 S. University Ave.
1971, RALPH RAPSON & ASSOCS.,
BURNHAM & HAMMOND,
AND J. LEE JONES

A modern attempt to evoke the Gothic tradition, this limestone building shares the materials, vertical proportions, and irregular profile of its earlier neighbors. Unfortunately, the prominent caulk lines make it look like a suit with the tailor's chalk marks still showing.

28 Administration Building
5801 S. Ellis Ave.
1948, HOLABIRD & ROOT & BURGEE
Cobb originally envisioned a library and "university hall" for this prominent site, and later plans called for a Gothic administration building. When final planning for this building began in earnest in 1945, the Gothic style was not considered aesthetically or economically appropriate, so this utilitarian structure was erected instead. Truly a wallflower, it modestly directs attention to its more elaborate neighbors.

29 Eckhart Hall
1118 E. 58th St.
1930, CHARLES Z. KLAUDER
A late Gothic addition to the main quad, Eckhart Hall offers further proof of the style's power to unify the work of different architects. Klauder was nationally known for his Collegiate Gothic buildings at Princeton, the University of Pennsylvania, and the University of Pittsburgh. During the 1926–32 campus construction boom at the University of Chicago, each building design was assisted by a faculty committee on symbolism. The ornament of this building related to the physics, astronomy, and mathematics departments housed within.

30 Ryerson Physical Laboratory
1100 E. 58th St.
1894, HENRY IVES COBB
1913, NORTH ANNEX, SHEPLEY,
RUTAN & COOLIDGE

31 Kent Chemical Laboratory
1020 E. 58th St.
1894, HENRY IVES COBB
This pair of ornate science buildings had complex interior requirements that combined with the lavishness of architectural ornament to drive the cost way over budget. Inside is a bronze relief of the donor, Sidney A. Kent, designed by Lorado Taft. The octagonal Kent Theater to the north was the university's assembly hall until the 1903 completion of Mandel Hall.

32 George Herbert Jones Laboratory
5747 S. Ellis Ave.
1929, COOLIDGE & HODGDON
Room 405 is a National Historic Landmark, because it was where plutonium was first isolated and weighed.

33 Hull Court and Biological Laboratories
1025–1103 E. 57th St.
1897, HENRY IVES COBB
Entered from the south through the wrought-iron Hull Gate, this

courtyard contains four laboratory buildings (anatomy, botany, physiology, and zoology) designed as a group in a simpler and less costly style than Kent and Ryerson Laboratories. Joined by loggias and arcades, the buildings surround but do not actually face Hull Court and Botany Pond, both planned by landscape architect John C. Olmsted, as was the nearby Hutchinson Court.

34 Hitchcock Hall
1009 E. 57th St.

1902, DWIGHT H. PERKINS

Here is the university's most original interpretation of the Gothic style prior to World War II. Perkins's application of Prairie School principles can be seen in the low pitched roof, low dormers, and generally horizontal character of the building. The ornament was also a departure, with geometric stained-glass windows and corncobs and other prairie vegetation substituting for abstracted English flora. Perkins was a family friend of the donor, Mrs. Charles Hitchcock, and was one of the few outside architects brought in to design a campus building.

35 Snell Hall
5709 S. Ellis Ave.

1893, HENRY IVES COBB

Snell was the only one of the original men's residence halls that was designed for undergraduates.

36 Searle Chemical Laboratory
5735 S. Ellis Ave.

1967, SMITH, SMITH, HAINES, LUNDBERG & WAEHLER

2009, REHABILITATION AND NEW ENTRANCE, WILSON ARCHITECTS

Elements that relate to the existing campus include limestone, window and spandrel size, and building height.

37 Cobb Gate
South side of E. 57th St. between Ellis and University Aves.

1900, HENRY IVES COBB

After budgetary constraints had curbed his use of ornament on campus buildings, Cobb let his decorative impulses run wild on this fanciful ornamental gate, which he donated to the university. It ended up being his swan song, as he was replaced as campus architect the following year. The trustees felt that his attention was being diverted by efforts to build a national practice out of his newly opened office in Washington, D.C. Ironically, the firm that replaced him, Shepley, Rutan & Coolidge, was based in Boston.

Cobb Gate

Hutchinson Court and the Tower Group
38 Mitchell Tower, Hutchinson Commons, Reynolds Club
39 Mandel Hall
Southwest corner of E. 57th St. and University Ave.

1903, SHEPLEY, RUTAN & COOLIDGE

1981, MANDEL HALL RENOVATION, SKIDMORE, OWINGS & MERRILL WITH THE OFFICE OF JOHN VINCI

Shepley, Rutan & Coolidge made a significant campus debut with this monumental group of buildings, which anchors the northeast corner of the main quadrangle. It marks an increasing emphasis on historicism, including an effort to make the interiors correspond with the style of the facades. Shepley, Rutan & Coolidge's buildings generally have more elaborate wall planes than Cobb's, with arched and traceried windows. The rooflines, however, are simpler, with rows of crenellations replacing the profusion of gables and dormers.

Seeking early on to associate their fledgling institution with significant historic European (especially English) universities, donor Charles L. Hutchinson

Hutchinson Commons

and architect Charles A. Coolidge traveled to Oxford to study its collegiate architectural tradition. The design of Mitchell Tower, the first purely ornamental building on campus, was derived from the bell tower of Magdalen College. The ten Palmer chimes, named for the first dean of women, Alice Freeman Palmer (see the Daniel Chester French plaque in the lobby), are still used for change ringing, a traditional English style of play that some find cacophonous. Originally a men's dining hall, Hutchinson Commons was modeled after Oxford's Christ Church Hall. Enjoy a modestly priced meal in the grand dining room, remarkable for the hammer-beam ceiling and the many portraits of trustees and benefactors, including John D. Rockefeller and Martin Ryerson.

Reynolds Club was derived from St. John's College at Oxford, and its domestic feeling is enhanced by a stair hall that could have come straight out of an English manor house.

40 Quadrangle Club
1155 E. 57th St.
1922, HOWARD VAN DOREN SHAW
Shaw deliberately designed this faculty club in red brick with a multi-colored slate roof to contrast with the surrounding gray limestone buildings.

41 Hall for Economics
(Chicago Theological Seminary)
5757 S. University Ave.
1926, RIDDLE & RIDDLE
2014, RENOVATION, ANN
   BEHA ARCHITECTS
The two wings of the former seminary are connected by a second-story arched corridor that spans the alley. The east wing contained residential quarters; the west wing housed two chapels, a library, and classrooms. Chicago Theological moved to a new home south of the Midway in 2011 so that this complex could be transformed into a home for the university's economics department.

42 Oriental Institute
1155 E. 58th St.
1931, MAYERS, MURRAY & PHILLIP
1997, ADDITION, HAMMOND,
   BEEBY & BABKA
This building was designed by the successor firm to Bertram Grosvenor Goodhue Assocs. (architects of Rockefeller Memorial Chapel) with an Art Deco simplicity that tempers the Gothic gables, bays, and buttresses. Egyptologist James H. Breasted, director of the institute from 1919 to 1935, designed the symbolic bas-relief over the north entrance. It illustrates elements of civilization from the ancient Near East and the Western world, including the Sphinx and architect Goodhue's Nebraska State Capitol.

43 University President's House
5855 S. University Ave.
1895, HENRY IVES COBB
The pale Roman brick, less expensive

than limestone, blends with the surrounding buildings, as does the peaked tile roof with dormers. Many alterations have been made over the years.

44 Rockefeller Memorial Chapel
(University Chapel)
5850 S. Woodlawn Ave.
1925–28, BERTRAM GROSVENOR
  GOODHUE ASSOCS.
2010, RESTORATION, INSPEC

Towering over the Midway, this massive limestone church of load-bearing masonry employs traditional Gothic structural devices of arches and buttresses. Goodhue was a nationally famous proponent of the Gothic Revival and the Arts and Crafts movements, and this design is his interpretation of Modern Gothic. The university administration was heavily involved in the design process, and its president, Ernest DeWitt Burton, toured famous English cathedrals to satisfy himself that the design was appropriate. The greatest departure from medieval Gothic is in the proportions, with un-

usually wide bays and tall clerestory windows over low side aisles, and in the abundance of smooth, flat surfaces. Lee Lawrie designed the facade sculpture up to thirty feet from the ground; Ulric H. Ellerhusen was responsible for the higher designs. The interior has a cool, restful palette (except for some unfortunate brightly colored modern windows) and an unusual example of Guastavino tile vaulting, a technique in which the tile is structural rather than merely ornamental. The sculpture includes religious as well as allegorical and historical figures along with coats of arms and inscriptions. A statue of Goodhue on the east transept wall personifies architecture, with Rockefeller Chapel in his hands and West Point Chapel behind him. Opposite him is Bach, representing music.

45 Ida Noyes Hall
1212 E. 59th St.
1916, SHEPLEY, RUTAN & COOLIDGE
1986, MAX PALEVSKY CINEMA, VICKREY,
  OVRESAT, AWSUMB ASSOCS.

Lavishly decorated in a domestic Tudor Revival style, it was designed to offer women the kind of social and recreational facilities provided to men in the Tower Group buildings. It became a general student center in 1955, when women were no longer excluded from the men's premises. The lounge, library, and Cloister Club contain rich ornament and fixtures. Climb the elaborately carved staircase to see a third-floor student theater with *The Masque of Youth*, an early mural by Jessie Arms Botke that depicts a performance given at the building's dedication.

Rockefeller Memorial Chapel—interior detail   Ida Noyes Hall

46 The University of Chicago Laboratory Schools

1362 E. 59th St. and 5823 S. Kenwood Ave.

1903, EMMONS BLAINE HALL, JAMES GAMBLE ROGERS

1992, MIDDLE SCHOOL, NAGLE, HARTRAY & ASSOCS.

2000, KOVLER GYMNASIUM, NAGLE HARTRAY DANKER KAGAN MCKAY

Amid the older Lab School buildings, which are University of Chicago Gothic, stand two newer projects that fit in beautifully. The middle school was built to the east of a 1960s green-glass high school addition by Perkins & Will with Eero Saarinen, which is no longer visible from the street. Kenwood Ave. was closed off to create play space for the lower grades. Across the space is Kovler Gym, which is connected to the 1929 Sunny Gym with an arcade. Both the middle school and gym are "streamlined Gothic," designed to complement the existing buildings.

In the fall of 2013, the youngest students moved to **Earl Shapiro Hall** (VALERIO DEWALT TRAIN ASSOCS.; FGM ARCHITECTS, ARCH. OF RECORD) on the newly created **Early Childhood Campus** at 5800 S. Stony Island Ave. The **University of Chicago Child Development Center—Stony Island** (2013, WHEELER KEARNS ARCHITECTS) occupies the south end of the small campus.

47 International House

1414 E. 59th St.

1932, HOLABIRD & ROOT

With the completion of this building and the Henry Crown Field House, Holabird & Root ended the first era of Collegiate Gothic with a stripped-down, Art Deco interpretation. Campus building did not resume for more than fifteen years—and then in a strictly utilitarian style. "I-House" rises elegantly on its long, shallow site and has an attractively landscaped interior courtyard.

48 Frederick C. Robie House

5757 S. Woodlawn Ave.

1908–9, FRANK LLOYD WRIGHT

RESTORATION BEGUN 1997 BY THE FRANK LLOYD WRIGHT PRESERVATION TRUST

This house, which Frank Lloyd Wright designed in 1908 for a bicycle and motorcycle manufacturer, is one of the world's most famous buildings. Magnificently poised, like a great steamship at anchor, it is the distilled essence of Wright's Prairie style and the culmination of his search for a new architecture. It is also among the last of his Prairie houses; during construction, Wright abandoned both his Oak Park practice and his family to embark on a new phase of his long career.

The Robie House faces west and south on a lot measuring 60 × 180 feet. Its basic form consists of two parallel, rectangular two-story masses at the meeting of which rises a smaller, square third story. The massive chimney effectively anchors these separate parts. The main living quarters occupy the second floor, with three bedrooms above. There is no basement. The exterior formulation of base, wall, and cornice, common to all of Wright's Prairie houses, is repeated in every part of the elevations. Here it is expressed by thin, long Roman bricks and limestone trim. Floors and balconies are reinforced concrete, while the great overhangs are made possible by numerous concealed steel girders, some as long as 60 feet.

Frederick C. Robie House

Frederick C. Robie House—interior

Space is defined not by walls, in the conventional sense, but by a series of horizontal planes intercepted by vertical wall fragments and rectangular piers. These horizontals extend far beyond the enclosures, defining exterior space as well and echoing the flat midwestern landscape that so inspired the architect. The chief embellishments are the exquisite leaded- and stained-glass doors and windows, which not only provide accents of color and ornament but also screen interior from exterior space while preserving the unity between outside and inside.

The Robie House's calculated asymmetry, irregular form, and striking silhouette excite curiosity and invite exploration of its carefully arranged sequences of spaces. This picturesque manner of composition can ultimately be traced to the freely experimental buildings of the Shingle Style that Wright had learned in the 1880s from his first significant employer, Joseph Lyman Silsbee. The beautiful abstraction of the building's surfaces, clean geometry of form, and personal manner of decoration—its emphatic style—as well as the strong central axis that orders its raised living and dining rooms are the legacy of Wright's "Lieber Meister," Louis H. Sullivan. Only by uniting these seemingly opposing traditions was Wright able to create a personal modern style in 1900 and give it its perfect expression eight years later in the Robie House.

—PAUL KRUTY

49 Charles M. Harper Center/ Chicago Booth School of Business
5807 S. Woodlawn Ave.

2004, RAFAEL VINOLY ARCHITECTS

The cantilevers, the horizontal massing and detailing of the stone, and most important, the siting well back from Woodlawn are a collective tip of the hat to neighboring Robie House. But inside is a soaring twenty-first-century-Gothic winter garden that rivals the interior of Rockefeller Chapel. Four colossal white steel columns branch up and out to create a vaulted glass roof. They also serve as internal downspouts, funneling rainwater into a hidden reservoir, and bear the brunt of the snow load. Clustered around this luminous space are a variety of classrooms, offices, and other functions that formerly occupied six different buildings.

50 University Church
(University Church of the Disciples of Christ)
5655 S. University Ave.

1921, HOWARD VAN DOREN SHAW
AND HENRY K. HOLSMAN

This austere Gothic church is almost primitive. An unusual feature of its spare but lovely interior is the fireplace at the back of the west aisle.

Charles M. Harper Center/Chicago Booth School of Business

51 Bartlett Dining Commons
(Frank Dickinson Bartlett Gymnasium)
5640 S. University Ave.
1904, SHEPLEY, RUTAN & COOLIDGE
2002, CONVERSION, BRUNER/
   COTT & ASSOCS.

Go up a few steps to see the romantic medieval-style mural and a stained-glass window that features a scene from *Ivanhoe*. The gym was donated by university trustee and hardware merchant Adolphus C. Bartlett in memory of his son. The mural was painted by another son, Frederic Clay Bartlett, who also executed designs in the Tower Group. The former gymnasium on the second floor is now a dining hall, with the old running track providing a seating mezzanine.

52 Max Palevsky Residential Commons
5630 S. University Ave., 1101 E. 56th St., and 5625 S. Ellis Ave.
2002, RICARDO LEGORRETA

The most colorful building on campus is of orange brick with a bright blue roof and has purple, yellow, and pink elements, one for each of its three sections. It runs for two blocks along 56th St., creating courtyards that soak up the southern sun.

53 Henry Crown Field House
(Field House)
5550 S. University Ave.
1932, HOLABIRD & ROOT
1977, 1979, RENOVATIONS,
   HOLABIRD & ROOT

Designed and redesigned over a five-year period, the building reflects the lines of its Gothic predecessors only in the vestigial buttresses and tall, arched windows. Earlier, more elaborate designs had proved too costly, and the winds of modernism had penetrated even the ivy walls of this august institution.

54 5551 S. University Ave.
1937, GEORGE FRED KECK
   & WILLIAM KECK

Here is timeless, first-generation modernism from the firm that had gained fame (but few commissions) for its futuristic House of Tomorrow at Chicago's 1933 Century of Progress Exposition. A three-flat, it is unrelated to any of its predecessors. The innovative louvers make curtains unnecessary and help conserve energy. Even the garage doors are building blocks for the facade's simple geometry.

5551 S. University Ave.

55 New Residence Hall

E. 55th St. and S. University Ave.

In 2013, the university demolished Pierce Hall (1960, HARRY WEESE & ASSOCS.) and unveiled designs for a new residential complex by Studio Gang Architects.

56 Cochrane-Woods Art Center

5540 S. Greenwood Ave.

1974, EDWARD LARRABEE BARNES

57 Court Theatre

5535 S. Ellis Ave.

1981, HARRY WEESE & ASSOCS.

Planned as the nucleus of a never-completed Arts Quadrangle, Barnes's simple limestone buildings house the art department and the Smart Museum of Art. The Court Theatre is one of many Weese-designed performing arts facilities, of which the most famous is Arena Stage in Washington, D.C.

58 Gerald Ratner Athletics Center

5530 S. Ellis Ave.

2003, CESAR PELLI & ASSOCS., DESIGN ARCH.; OWP/P, ARCH. OF RECORD

The volumes are broken up and one wing set back to create a plaza that leads to a welcoming rotunda. On display in the lobby is the first Heisman Trophy, awarded in 1935 to University of Chicago halfback Jay Berwanger. The mast-and-cable roof supports of the natatorium and gymnasium buildings are meant to evoke the flying buttresses of the university's Gothic architecture.

59 *Nuclear Energy*

East side of Ellis Ave. between E. 56th and 57th Sts.

1967, HENRY MOORE

Intended to suggest a human skull and a mushroom cloud, this abstract bronze form commemorates the moment on December 2, 1942, when Enrico Fermi and his colleagues created the first self-sustaining, controlled nuclear chain reaction. This initiation into the atomic age took place in a squash court under the bleachers of the now-demolished Stagg Field, site of the Regenstein Library.

60 Joseph Regenstein Library

1100 E. 57th St.

1970, SKIDMORE, OWINGS & MERRILL

Walter A. Netsch Jr. brought the concrete brutalism of his University of Illinois at Chicago to this traditional campus, where it landed with a thud on the site of Stagg Field. The irregular massing and profile, slit windows, and vertically grooved facade are meant to allude to the surrounding Gothic buildings but are more a product of Netsch's own idiosyncratic design concepts. Fortunately, two of the seven floors are underground.

61 Joe and Rika Mansueto Library

1100 E. 57th St. (entrance through Regenstein Library)

2011, MURPHY/JAHN

Like Regenstein, some of Mansueto's floors are underground, but otherwise the buildings could not be more different. Here, a transparent, self-supporting dome, made up of 691 rhombus-shaped glass panels, seems to hover above a light-filled reading room. Beneath are five floors of storage space for some 3.5 million volumes, all quickly accessible by a mind-boggling robotic retrieval system. While Jahn likes to describe his work as "archineering" because of the often-innovative engineering that undergirds the projects, the overall goal is "elegant minimalism," which Mansueto delivers marvelously.

Joe and Rika Mansueto Library

*HOK, working with light designer James Carpenter, designed the **William Eckhardt Research Center**, scheduled to open in 2015 on the west side of the 5600 block of S. Ellis Ave.*

62 Samuel Kersten Jr. Physics Teaching Center

5720 S. Ellis Ave.

1985, HOLABIRD & ROOT; HAROLD H. HELLMAN, UNIVERSITY ARCH.

The Ellis Ave. facade presents a subtle modern contribution to the

Collegiate Gothic tradition, while the Science Quadrangle facade reflects the brash modernity of its neighbors with a glass curtain wall that steps back to form a series of terraces.

63 John Crerar Library
5730 S. Ellis Ave.
1984, HUGH STUBBINS ASSOCS.; LOEBL,
SCHLOSSMAN & HACKL, ASSOC. ARCH.

The use of limestone, the window proportions, and the emphasis on the entry attempt to relate to the Gothic, while the projecting third floor provides cover, as in Gothic arcades and loggias.

64 Henry Hinds Laboratory for the Geophysical Sciences
5734 S. Ellis Ave.
1969, I. W. COLBURN & ASSOCS.
AND J. LEE JONES

Colburn was a consulting architect to the university from 1964 to 1973, and his quirky, expressionistic Esperanto Gothic style dominates the Science Quadrangle. Bay windows and an irregular, sculptural facade loom above surrounding buildings. Step inside the small foyer to be immersed in Ruth Duckworth's 1969 ceramic artwork, *Earth, Water & Sky*.

65 University Bookstore
(University Press Building)
5750 S. Ellis Ave.
1902, SHEPLEY, RUTAN & COOLIDGE

Another red-brick building in a sea of gray, this one sports a variety of gabled forms. The unusually open first-floor facade has rows of tall arched windows.

66 850 E. 58th St.
(American School of Correspondence)
1907, POND & POND

This is one of the city's finest examples of the architects' unique version of the Arts and Crafts style. The banded piers and tower may have been inspired by Secessionist architecture that the Ponds had seen at the 1904 St. Louis World's Fair; Irving Pond wrote an early and influential essay on the movement in 1905. The American School of Correspondence offered courses in a variety of subjects, including architecture and engineering, and after its 1902 move to Chicago,

many of its texts featured work by local designers such as Frank Lloyd Wright and Pond & Pond.

67 Cummings Life Science Center
920 E. 58th St.
1973, I. W. COLBURN & ASSOCS.;
SCHMIDT, GARDEN & ERIKSON

The tallest building on campus has forty red-brick towers—exhaust ducts aspiring to be medieval chimney stacks.

68 Ingleside Hall
(Quadrangle Club)
956–960 E. 58th St.
1896, CHARLES B. ATWOOD

Moved here in 1929 from its original location on the site of the Oriental Institute, the vaguely neoclassical building is the only one designed for the campus in the 1890s by an architect other than Cobb.

69 Donnelley Biological Sciences Learning Center and Knapp Research Center
924 E. 57th St.
1994, STUBBINS ASSOCS.; LOEBL,
SCHLOSSMAN & HACKL, ASSOC. ARCHS.

The window shapes and limestone cladding help this huge modern science center blend with its surroundings.

70 West Campus Combined Utility Plant
5615 S. Maryland Ave.
2010, MURPHY/JAHN

The building's stark, prismatic form—like a glass ice cube—gets jazzed up by the display of its innards, as at Helmut Jahn's earlier South Plant.

71 Medical Campus
E. 57th to E. 59th Sts., S. Ellis
to S. Cottage Grove Aves.

The medical campus alone has more square footage than many small colleges. Twenty-first-century additions include the **Knapp Center for Biomedical Discovery** (2009, ZIMMER GUNSUL FRASCA WITH PROGRAMMING BY PERKINS & WILL) and the **Center for Care and Discovery** (2012, RAFAEL VINOLY ARCHITECTS WITH PLANNING BY CANNON DESIGN).

Reva and David Logan Center for the Arts

72 Reva and David Logan Center for the Arts

915 E. 60TH ST.

2012, TOD WILLIAMS BILLIE TSIEN ARCHITECTS, DESIGN ARCH.; HOLABIRD & ROOT, ARCH. OF RECORD

The Logan created a stir from day one for its size, cost, and ten-story tower as well as for the dramatic signal it sends about the university's increased commitment to the visual and performing arts. A warm and light-colored Missouri limestone (remarkably like Jerusalem, that most beautiful of limestones) is cut into the shapes of oversized Roman bricks, softening the severe geometry of the tower and the lower studio block. The interior program presented major challenges, above all the need to accommodate many different functions—practice rooms, painting studios, three theaters of various sizes, classrooms. Colors and materials, including a pressed-felt wall covering developed for the building, are understated but winning. Logan is an instant landmark.

73 Midway Studios

6016 S. Ingleside Ave.

1906, POND & POND

1929, OTIS F. JOHNSON

Sculptor Lorado Taft and a group of fellow artists lived and worked in this cluster of studios and living quarters, which expanded gradually from the original converted carriage house. This is where Taft created the *Fountain of Time*, located at the west end of the Midway, and the *Fountain of the Great Lakes*, outside the Art Institute. The setting now provides studio and gallery space for the university's studio art program.

74 School of Social Service Administration

969 E. 60th St.

1965, LUDWIG MIES VAN DER ROHE

School of Social Service Administration

The purest example of modernism on campus was designed by the master himself. Inside the black steel-and-glass box is a large lobby that is an exercise in Miesian "universal space," rather like his U.S. Post Office in the Loop.

75 Burton-Judson Courts
1005 E. 60th St.
1931, ZANTZINGER, BORIE & MEDARY

The university jumped the Midway in constructing this pair of dormitories. Plans formulated in the 1920s called for the creation of a self-contained undergraduate campus south of the Midway, but they were scrapped in favor of continued northward expansion. This remains the plan's only built component. The small landscaped quadrangles are worth a peek.

76 South Campus Residence Hall and Dining Commons
6031 S. Ellis Ave.
2009, GOODY CLANCY & ASSOCS.

Through an inventive combination of design elements—setbacks, glass-and-limestone cladding, a handsome courtyard—what could have been a bulky addition to the south campus instead fits into it nicely. The glass-walled lower levels of this large (811-student) building fill the community spaces with a cheery light.

77 Laird Bell Law Quadrangle
1111 E. 60th St.
1959, EERO SAARINEN & ASSOCS.
1998, ADDITION, OWP/P
2008, LAW LIBRARY RENOVATION, OWP/P

This complex is Saarinen's most significant contribution to the campus that resulted from his 1950s master plan. Following the tradition of clustering buildings of similar disciplines around a central court, Saarinen designed a group of four buildings (Constitution Hall, a classroom building, the law library, and the administration building) around a reflecting pool and fountain. In November 1960, *Architectural Record* quoted Saarinen as saying that "by stressing a small, broken scale, a lively silhouette, and especially verticality in the library design, we intended to make it a good neighbor with the Gothic dormitories." The bronze sculpture, *Construction in Space in the 3rd*

and 4th Dimension, was designed for this space by Antoine Pevsner, a Russian-born sculptor who worked in the cubist and constructivist styles. Highlights of the multiyear renovation include a sensitive updating of the library, which is the star of the complex, and the replacement of the original water feature with a new reflecting pool.

78 Chicago Theological Seminary
1407 E. 60th St.
2011, NAGLE HARTRAY DANKER
KAGAN MCKAY PENNEY

The seminary moved here after selling its 1920s Gothic complex to the university. Several pieces of stained glass made the move south of the Midway and have been incorporated throughout the new building.

South Campus Chiller Plant

79 South Campus Chiller Plant
6035 S. Dorchester Ave.
2009, MURPHY/JAHN

Helmut Jahn's trio of campus buildings began with this elegant stainless-steel–and–glass utility plant. The see-through walls reveal stairwells and machinery in various colors and patterns, while the stainless steel curves at the top echo the arched windows of the **heating plant** to the south (1929, PHILIP MAHER). This head-on contrast—glassy modernism meets brick–and–terracotta Gothic Revival—is terrific.

Rosalie Villas
The 5700 and 5800 blocks of S. Harper Ave. (originally called Rosalie Ct.) contain many of the houses built as part of Rosalie Villas, the area's first planned community. Rosalie Buckingham bought this land in 1883 and subdivided it into lots for forty-two freestanding houses. She hired Solon S. Beman, fresh from his planning of Pullman,

to supervise the design and construction of the houses and of the commercial buildings planned for the corner of 57th St. At that time, the Illinois Central Railroad's tracks ran at grade, giving the houses on the east side of the street views of open land and the lake beyond. By the end of the decade, several of the lots had been subdivided for smaller frontages, and an apartment building anchored 57th St., giving the development a less rural character than originally planned. The houses are currently in various states of repair, ranging from pristine to tumbledown (entries 80–87).

80 5832–5834 S. Harper Ave.
1884, SOLON S. BEMAN
Beman was one of the first to create an exception to the detached-residence rule when he designed this double house for John A. Jackman Jr. It is composed as a unified facade, however, with a shared chimney creating a focal point at ground level with a large terra-cotta panel. A manager at the Pullman Co., Jackman also commissioned Beman to design the house at **5824**.

81 William Waterman House
5810 S. Harper Ave.
1884, HENRY F. STARBUCK
One of the few brick houses in this clapboard-and-shingle enclave, it has an especially fine terra-cotta cornice and the rotated bay frequently seen in Stick Style homes.

82 5809 S. Harper Ave.
1888, E. CLARKE JOHNSON
This Queen Anne town house was turned on its side to fit an unusual site: broad and shallow rather than long and narrow.

83 5759 S. Harper Ave.
1884, SOLON S. BEMAN
The details of this frame Queen Anne, especially on the well-preserved porch, are typically robust, showing an emphasis on cutouts and screens.

84 Charles Bonner House
5752 S. Harper Ave.
1889, WILLIAM W. BOYINGTON
This greatly altered frame house offers tantalizing glimpses of original details such as the inset second-floor balcony.

85 Ernest W. Heath House
5744 S. Harper Ave.
1886, W. IRVING BEMAN
This greatly altered house is difficult to piece together. W. Irving Beman was Solon's brother and worked in the Pullman architectural offices.

86 5719 through 5745 S. Harper Ave.
1888, ROBERT RAE JR.
The similarity between these houses is obscured by their varying states of integrity and upkeep. The three southernmost houses (5739 through 5745) are from 1888, which seems a likely date for the others as well. They all offer noteworthy examples of the vigorous punched ornament popular on late-nineteenth-century frame houses. Unfortunately, it is often removed or replaced by spidery mass-produced spindle work.

87 M. Cochran Armour House
5736 S. Harper Ave.
PRE-1888, ARCHITECT UNKNOWN
Then as now, this is one of the most lavish houses on the block. The exuberant forms include a two-story elliptical bay, curved corner windows, and inset balconies. Fish-scale shingles, carved plaques, and half-timbering provide a potpourri of textures.

88 Hyde Park Historical Society
(Chicago St. Railway Co. Station)
5529 S. Lake Park Ave.
1893, ARCHITECT UNKNOWN
1981, RENOVATION, OFFICE OF JOHN VINCI
This small station once served passengers at the southern terminus of a cable car line, completed in anticipation of the 1893 World's Columbian Exposition. When the Illinois Central trains were elevated in the late 1920s, this building was tucked into their embankment.

89 Deco Arts Building
(Ritz 55th Garage)
E. 55th St. at Lake Park Ave.
1929, M. LOUIS KROMAN
This is an Art Deco paean to the glamour of the roadster. The terra-

M. Cochran Armour House

Deco Arts Building

cotta facade cruises from one automotive image to the next: engines,
stoplights, tires, gearshifts—and of
course a flivver itself, with jauntily
clad driver. The first floor, now altered, once included a chauffeurs'
lounge.

90 Hyde Park Redevelopment Project

53rd to 57th Sts., west of the Illinois Central Railroad
1957–59, I. M. PEI AND HARRY WEESE & ASSOCS.; BARTON
ASCHMAN, CIVIL AND LANDSCAPING CONSULTANT

91 University Apartments

1400 and 1450 E. 55th St.
1961, I. M. PEI AND LOEWENBERG & LOEWENBERG

The lush gardens and well-kept public spaces that mark the Hyde Park
Redevelopment Project testify to the continuing success of a pioneering
effort to combat middle-class flight from this distinguished Chicago neighborhood. They belie, however, the controversy that surrounded the project
in the mid-1950s. Flight to the newly burgeoning suburbs was in full force,
and the University of Chicago was threatened by the increasing decay of
the once substantial neighborhood that surrounded it. In 1957, a large area
of blighted buildings was torn down; they were replaced by some 150 two-
and three-story town houses and two ten-story apartment buildings. The
project was financed by a combination of federal, city, and private monies
and was strongly backed by the university.

This effort differed from other 1950s urban renewal schemes, which cut
great swaths in the existing city fabric that seldom were artfully replaced.
Such projects were often like ocean liners moored in the middle of the city—
separate, apart, and a world unto themselves, with little direct relationship to
surrounding street patterns or building types. Here in Hyde Park, however,
great care was taken to relate the new construction to the existing neighborhood, which comprised a mixture of single-family homes from the 1880s and
small pre–World War I apartment buildings.

The project was guided by an overriding concern to preserve the urban
neighborhood spirit. The master plan emphasized low buildings to provide

Hyde Park Redevelopment Project

University Apartments

the strong relationship to the street characteristic of healthy and safe neighborhoods. Parklike public spaces were created, and town houses were built around inner squares. These shared spaces are now filled with greenery and animated by playgrounds and basketball courts. The inclusion of a shopping center (since replaced) recognized that traditional neighborhoods have necessary goods and services close at hand.

Probably the most radical urban planning move was placing the mid-rise University Apartments in the middle of 55th St. and splitting traffic lanes on either side, thereby creating an island to discourage high-speed traffic. This placement was directly inspired by planning principles of the modern movement as espoused by Le Corbusier in *La Ville Radieuse* (1935). The island has not had its intended effect; traffic speeds up on the split street, and pedestrians are discouraged from crossing.

Within the strong traditional forms of the overall plan, the architecture asserts a modernist design ethic. University Apartments saw the early use of fiberglass forms for poured-in-place concrete as well as a convenience unique at the time, a closed-circuit television entry system.

The two- and three-story town houses scattered throughout the area were the work of the New York office of I. M. Pei and the Chicago firm of Harry Weese & Assocs. Town houses had not been constructed in Chicago since the early 1900s and were a new element in this neighborhood. Pale brick sets them apart from their predominantly red-brick antecedents. Inspired by eighteenth-century English town house rows, or "terraces," Pei and Weese reinterpreted Georgian regularity and harmony. The strong horizontals of ground-floor recesses and third-floor clerestories unify the rows, while evenly placed door and window elements maintain symmetry throughout the project.

This project not only succeeded in combating middle-class flight but also spurred private renovation in the surrounding area. In addition, the town house form reintroduced here has been used in smaller infill sites throughout the city. The Hyde Park Redevelopment Project is notable as an outstanding example in Chicago of rebuilding a large urban area without creating a "project."

—CYNTHIA AND CATHARINE WEESE

92 William H. Hoyt House
5704 S. Dorchester Ave.
1869, ARCHITECT UNKNOWN

93 Charles H. Botsford House
5714 S. Dorchester Ave.
1860, ARCHITECT UNKNOWN

These Italianates are the granddaddies of the block, dating from the settlement of this area. Their form is typical of the suburban or country villa of the period, with symmetrical facades, tall, narrow windows, and bracketed cornices. The cupola (originally larger) of the Botsford House once provided a view of the lake and aided in ventilation by drawing hot air up the central stairwell.

94 Chicago Theological Seminary Faculty Quadrangle
E. 58th St. and S. Dorchester Ave.

1963, LOEBL, SCHLOSSMAN, BENNETT & DART

Edward D. Dart designed this cluster of three- and four-bedroom units as rental faculty housing for the seminary. Set on diagonals at the perimeter of the lot, with heights varied to increase privacy, they surround a central common intended as a children's play area. The village-like enclave recalls the work of Finnish architect Alvar Aalto.

95 5825 S. Blackstone Ave.
1909, MARSHALL & FOX

A building inspired by nineteenth-century Paris stands out among its Anglophile neighbors. This elegant four-flat has tall, narrow proportions (note the triple-sash windows) that had not been a prominent feature in this neighborhood since the Italianate boom of the 1860s and 1870s.

96 Helstein House
5806 S. Blackstone Ave.

1951, BERTRAND GOLDBERG

Goldberg used his favorite materials, concrete and glass, to create an uncompromisingly modern house. The placement well back on the lot provides privacy despite the expanses of glass and avoids shocking its traditional neighbors.

97 5757–5759 S. Blackstone Ave.
1899, NIMMONS & FELLOWS

This double house presents a handsome Chicago interpretation of the Louis XIII style, with a flattened front and slightly bowed bays.

98 James Westfall Thompson House
5747 S. Blackstone Ave.

1899, POND & POND

The diaper pattern of bricks on the top floor was a popular motif in the 1890s among architects inspired by the Arts and Crafts movement, because the design was derived from the materials themselves rather than from applied color or ornament. Pond & Pond, which designed many settlement houses, probably used the motif more than anyone else.

99 5701–5703 and 5705–5707 S. Blackstone Ave.
1905, CARL M. ALMQUIST

This pair of typical six-flats has fluted columns supporting porches on all levels. Leaded-glass windows and brick quoins increase the grandeur.

100 St. Stephen's Church of God in Christ
(Tenth Church of Christ, Scientist)
5640 S. Blackstone Ave.

1919, COOLIDGE & HODGDON

University of Chicago architects Coolidge & Hodgdon gave this church a classical facade, a break from their campus Gothic. The shallow inward curve of the street wall draws people in and then cuts off views of the neighboring buildings, maximizing the potential of the midblock site.

Chicago Theological Seminary Faculty Quadrangle

101 **5621 and 5611 S. Blackstone Ave.**

1886, FLANDERS & ZIMMERMAN

These sharply contrasting buildings were built for the same client, architect William Carbys Zimmerman himself. At 5621 is a classic example of the Shingle Style, while 5611 is almost proto-Prairie, with its deep-set door and its porch hollowed out of the building's mass and inset with square columns.

102 **5603–5615 S. Kenwood Ave. and 1357–1361 E. 56th St.**

1903, MANN, MACNEILLE & LINDEBERG

103 **5558 S. Kimbark Ave. and 1220–1234 E. 56th St.**

1904, MANN, MACNEILLE & LINDEBERG

Several groups of cooperative row houses were designed for university faculty by this New York firm. Charles Riborg Mann was a professor of physics at the university and probably referred colleagues to his brother's firm. The group is noteworthy for its intact tile roof and for the variety of window and door treatments.

104 **William H. Ray Public School**
(Hyde Park High School)
5631 S. Kimbark Ave.

1893, JOHN J. FLANDERS
1915, ASSEMBLY HALL, ARTHUR
   F. HUSSANDER
1996, SOUTH ADDITION, FOX & FOX

This highly decorated Queen Anne school is distinguished by Flanders's signature bands of ornament and full-height octagonal bays rising to an unusually lively roofline.

105 **5748, 5752, and 5756 S. Kimbark Ave.**

1985, DAVID SWAN

These stucco-and-brick houses are starkly modern and geometric, with sweeping curves and metal railings that recall Art Deco forms.

106 **Hillel Center**
(Arthur J. Mason House)
5715 S. Woodlawn Ave.

1904, HOWARD VAN DOREN SHAW

107 **Edgar Johnson Goodspeed House**
5706 S. Woodlawn Ave.

1906, HOWARD VAN DOREN SHAW

Shaw's Hyde Park and Kenwood houses demonstrate his admiration for the English Arts and Crafts move-

Hillel Center

ment, which flourished in Chicago beginning in the 1890s. Shaw had great respect for materials and craftsmanship and a deep appreciation of English vernacular residential architecture as well as classical and historical forms. At 5715, the treatment of the elaborate door surround and the inventive ornamentation on the pilaster capitals exemplify his freedom with the classical vocabulary.

108 **First Unitarian Church of Chicago**
5650 S. Woodlawn Ave.

1931, DENISON B. HULL

This textbook example of English Perpendicular Gothic design fits in easily with the limestone facades and Gothic ornament of many Hyde Park residences and campus buildings. It was built around the Hull Memorial Chapel (1897, WILLIAM A. OTIS), which is now the south transept.

109 **Herbert Hugh Riddle House**
5626 S. Woodlawn Ave.

1912, RIDDLE & RIDDLE

110 **Lewis W. Riddle House**
5622 S. Woodlawn Ave.

1912, RIDDLE & RIDDLE

Built for brothers who practiced architecture together, these houses share the same massing and push the entrance to one side, so that the street facade has only windows. Lewis's house is a sober Georgian composition, while Herbert's has a distinctly French flair. Don't miss the metal-and-glass entrance canopy, reminiscent of Hector Guimard's Art Nouveau design for a Paris Métro entrance.

111 **Hyde Park Union Church**
(Hyde Park Baptist Church)
5600 S. Woodlawn Ave.

1906, JAMES GAMBLE ROGERS

The congregation of this church was closely associated with founders of the University of Chicago, and the building's construction was financed largely by John D. Rockefeller. The massive orange sandstone facade on Woodlawn Ave. is anchored by square entry towers marked by round arches. The round-arch motif is repeated on the interior, which also has beautiful stained-glass windows by Louis C. Tiffany of New York and Charles J. Connick Studios of Boston.

112 Theodore F. Rice House
5554 S. Woodlawn Ave.

1892, MIFFLIN E. BELL

One of the neighborhood's best-preserved Queen Anne houses is distinguished by a wonderful color palette: the brownstone base harmonizes with the dark pink and gray tiles above.

113 Lutheran School of Theology
1100 E. 55th St.

1966, PERKINS & WILL

A far cry from Collegiate Gothic, this triple-winged complex is a structural tour de force, with six concrete Vierendeel trusses (normally used for bridges) poured in pairs, 175 feet long and 2 feet thick. Three-piece steel rockers transfer the load to concrete pedestals carried on cruciform piers. The quadrangle is enclosed on the north side by the **McCormick Theological Seminary** (2003, M & W ZANDER).

114 Chicago Child Care Society
5467 S. University Ave.

1963, KECK & KECK

The concrete floors extend beyond the glass walls and are perforated to provide a sunscreen.

115 St. Thomas the Apostle Roman Catholic Church
5472 S. Kimbark Ave.

1924, BARRY BYRNE

116 School
5467 S. Woodlawn Ave.

1929, SHATTUCK & LAYER

This remarkable break from traditional Catholic church design was executed by Barry Byrne, who had previously worked for Frank Lloyd Wright. This affiliation with the Prairie School may account for the naturalistic hues of the bricks, the innovative massing, and the

unique design of the sculpture and ornament, especially the terra-cotta surrounding the entry and windows. Alfonso Iannelli, an important sculptor who often collaborated with Prairie School architects, worked closely with Byrne on the design of the facades and interior spaces.

Verticality has always been a meaningful metaphor in church design, and here the narrow lancet windows, doorway sculpture, and sculpted brick surfaces ascend dramatically to a richly ornamented roofline. The worship space is free of columns and has pews set close to and almost encircling the altar, which is pushed forward into the nave. The resulting proximity of celebrant and congregation anticipated Roman Catholic liturgical reforms of the early 1960s. Sculptor Alfeo Faggi designed the bronze Stations of the Cross with an expressive simplicity appropriate to the interior.

117 Augustana Evangelical Lutheran Church of Hyde Park
1151 E. 55th St.

1968, LOEBL, SCHLOSSMAN, BENNETT & DART

Edward D. Dart's solid design of interconnecting masses has a low and inviting entry to provide shelter from the rush of traffic on 55th St. The sculpture of Christ (*Ecce Homo*, 1939) was Egon Weiner's first important work after emigrating from Europe in 1938. He also designed the St. Paul sculpture in the 1985 Memorial Garden.

St. Thomas the Apostle School

118 5200–5244 S. Greenwood Ave.

1903, JOSEPH C. BROMPTON

Charmingly deceptive, the entire block is lined with twenty row houses with set-back common walls mimicking detached houses. It was created by Charles Counselman, a local meatpacker, and Samuel E. Gross, an active real estate developer. Like Gross's contemporaneous Alta Vista Terrace on the North Side, the row features a variety of styles, materials, and colors, but with a remarkable unity deriving from the common scale and setbacks.

119 Joseph A. Thomlinson House

5317 S. University Ave.

1904, SOLON S. BEMAN

One of the neighborhood's most eccentric designs bears a great gambrel roof ornamented with stone brackets above a rock-faced stone facade.

120 53rd and University Town Houses

1119–1125 E. 53rd St.

1985, DAVID SWAN

The severe northern facade gives no clue to the personable southern side, where tiers of terraces overlook back gardens.

121 Isidore Heller House

5132 S. Woodlawn Ave.

1897, FRANK LLOYD WRIGHT

This important early Wright design has many of the radical features that characterize his slightly later Prairie School houses. The bands of windows tucked under the low horizontal eaves and the potential for cross-axial spatial relationships suggest what was to follow in the Robie House. The frieze by Richard W. Bock (an important collaborator of many Prairie architects) and the two-tone brick banding of the top story emphasize the horizontal divisions of the wall plane. Despite the narrow and deep I-shaped plan, the interior space is open and expansive because Wright pulled the dining room out to the south and created a long east–west hallway axis perpendicular to the entry. Unlike the frontal entrances of most 1890s houses, the all-important entrances to Wright's houses—here marked by relief

Isidore Heller House

sculpture—are frequently set into the side for privacy and to dramatize the entry process.

122 Henry C. Work Cottage

5317 S. Dorchester Ave.

1859, ARCHITECT UNKNOWN

Look south from 53rd St. to see what is thought to be Hyde Park's oldest house, a tiny cottage that has long been part of the larger house facing Dorchester Ave. The original board-and-batten siding has been re-created; it and the steep pitch of the roof and of the lone dormer identify the style as Gothic Revival. Work was a renowned composer of Civil War and temperance songs.

123 Hyde Park Bank

1525 E. 53rd St.

1929, KARL M. VITZTHUM & CO.

2004, RENOVATION, FLORIAN ARCHITECTS

The grandeur of the second-floor banking hall was restored and rejuvenated, with subtle modern materials such as metal mesh and translucent glass used to create new workspaces. A combination of new and restored lighting shows it all off.

124 Akiba-Schechter Jewish Day School

5235 S. Cornell Ave.

2005, JOHN RONAN ARCHITECTS

Hebrew letters were cast into rough-textured structural concrete wall panels, economically evoking stone tablets and reinforcing the school's identity. The facade that forms an entry courtyard with the existing preschool building is clad in oxidized copper. Inside is a multipurpose room with retractable stage that makes the most of limited space and budget—also a key strategy in Ronan's subsequent Gary Comer Youth Center.

In 2012, Studio Gang Architects unveiled revised plans for a development called **City Hyde Park** *for the site at 1501 E. Hyde Park Blvd.*

125 5312–5318 S. Hyde Park Blvd.
1908, ANDREW SANDEGREN

The bulging glassy bays are an early form of the boxy sunroom additions that became so popular on flat buildings in the following two decades.

126 5451–5455 S. Hyde Park Blvd.
1907, FROMMANN & JEBSEN

The carved Art Nouveau ornament is more reminiscent of Barcelona than Chicago on this fanciful example of a luxurious six-flat, built when the street was dominated by large single-family residences.

127 5487–5499 S. Hyde Park Blvd.
1908, DOERR & DOERR

This prototypical Hyde Park luxury six-flat has giant classical columns supporting large open porches on the upper floors. This type of multi-balconied six-flat is more common in Hyde Park than in any other area of the city.

128 5501–5503 S. Hyde Park Blvd.
1909, HENRY W. TOMLINSON

Tomlinson's residential and commercial buildings in Hyde Park frequently exhibit flared cornices and a robust modern interpretation of classical ornament. This particular building retains the most integrity, with its basement retail shops, iron railings, intact cornice, and other original features.

129 William B. Conkey House
5518 S. Hyde Park Blvd.
1888, ATTRIB. TO GEORGE W. MAHER

This house presents several features typical of an idiosyncratic, highly decorative style. The window lintels are massive blocks of rough stone, so large that they seem structurally impossible. The second-floor window is pushed behind the wall plane, with a fat splayed column placed in front of it. The third-floor window is a variation on a Palladian theme, with the central section squeezed almost into oblivion. The rough stone and rock-faced brick are of a similar color and texture.

130 N. Anderson House
5522 S. Hyde Park Blvd.
1888, ATTRIB. TO GEORGE W. MAHER

The facade has an unusual combination of pale yellow and green sandstone.

131 Windemere House
(Windemere East Hotel)
1642 E. 56th St.
1924, C. W. AND GEORGE L. RAPP

The 1920s were the golden age of residential hotels, and this lakefront area is particularly rich in fine

5451–5455 S. Hyde Park Blvd.

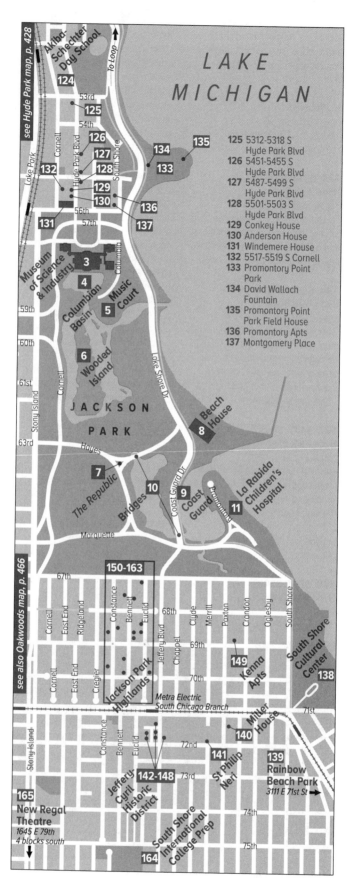

see Hyde Park map, p. 428

Akiba-Schechter Day School

124

To Loop

LAKE
MICHIGAN

53rd
125

54th
126
127
128
132
129
130
131
56th
57th

Lake Park

Cornell

Hyde Park Blvd

South Shore

134
135
133
136
137

125 5312-5318 S
    Hyde Park Blvd
126 5451-5455 S
    Hyde Park Blvd
127 5487-5499 S
    Hyde Park Blvd
128 5501-5503 S
    Hyde Park Blvd
129 Conkey House
130 Anderson House
131 Windemere House
132 5517-5519 S Cornell
133 Promontory Point
    Park
134 David Wallach
    Fountain
135 Promontory Point
    Park Field House
136 Promontory Apts
137 Montgomery Place

Museum of Science & Industry

3
4
5
6

Columbian Basin

Music Court

Columbia

Cornell

59th
60th
61st
63rd

Stony Island

Wooded Island

J A C K S O N

P A R K

Lake Shore Dr.

Hayes

7

The Republic

Bridges

10

9

Coast Guard Dr.

Coast Guard

Beach House

8

Promontory

11

La Rabida Children's Hospital

Marquette

see also Oakwoods map, p. 466

150-163

67th

Cornell
East End
Ridgeland
Constance
Bennett
Euclid

68th

Jeffery Blvd
Chappel
Clyde
Merrill
Paxton
Crandon
Oglesby
South Shore

69th

149

Kenna Apts

South Shore Cultural Center

138

70th

Cornell
East End
Cregier
Jackson Park Highlands

Metra Electric
South Chicago Branch

71st

Miller House

Stony Island

Constance
Bennett
Euclid

72nd

140

142-148

Jeffery-Cyril Historic District

73rd

141

St Philip Neri

139

Rainbow
Beach Park
3111 E 71st St →

165

New Regal
Theatre
*1645 E 79th
4 blocks south*
↓

74th

South Shore International College Prep

75th

164

examples. Designed to house both transient and permanent guests, the Windemere offered single rooms (many with kitchenettes), as well as suites that could be combined to create apartments of up to five rooms. Typically for this building type, all the architectural exuberance is concentrated on an elaborate entry pavilion.

132 5517–5519 S. Cornell Ave.
1891, ATTRIB. TO GEORGE W. MAHER

Built by real estate broker Alex F. Shuman, presumably to Maher's designs, these houses have wildly original ornament, with almost no repetition of forms or detail.

133 Promontory Point Park
(55th St. Promontory)
55th St. at S. South Shore Dr.
1937, ALFRED CALDWELL

This point of land is the highlight of Burnham Park, which stretches north all the way to Grant Park, serving as a lakefront link to Jackson Park. The area of this park had been filled in by 1926 but was not landscaped until after Works Progress Administration funding became available in 1935. Alfred Caldwell, a follower of the Prairie School landscape tradition of Jens Jensen, envisioned a prairie and meadow landscape planted with native flowering trees. Following the point's fiftieth anniversary in 1987, Caldwell was hired to restore the landscape. The improvements included previously unexecuted circular limestone benches, modeled after Jensen's larger council rings, and the planting of hundreds of trees that had been on his original plan.

134 David Wallach Fountain
1939, ELIZABETH & FRANK HIBBARD

Wallach donated money to design a fountain for "man and beast." The husband-and-wife sculptors (who designed the marble base and the bronze doe, respectively) were students of Lorado Taft at the School of the Art Institute. Elizabeth Hibbard was also an assistant at his Midway Studios.

135 Promontory Point Park Field House
1937, EMANUEL V. BUCHSBAUM
1991, RENOVATION, CHICAGO
PARK DISTRICT

This Lannon stone field house, with its circular lookout tower, was modeled after a lighthouse.

136 Promontory Apartments
5530 S. South Shore Dr.
1949, LUDWIG MIES VAN DER ROHE,
PACE ASSOCS., AND HOLSMAN,
HOLSMAN, KLEKAMP & TAYLOR

This was Mies's first constructed high-rise and his first collaboration with developer Herbert S. Greenwald, who became one of Mies's most important clients. The original design had a curtain wall of steel and glass that was the forerunner of 860–880 N. Lake Shore Dr. The columns taper as they rise, giving visual expression to their decreasing structural load.

137 Montgomery Place
5550 S. South Shore Dr.
1991, NAGLE, HARTRAY & ASSOCS.

Crisp red-brick walls are punctuated by angled bay windows that maximize light and views in a design influenced by Richard M. Bennett's 1350–1360 N. Lake Shore Dr. This luxurious high-rise for seniors was built over an existing underground garage and was sited to minimize blockage of its neighbors' light and views.

138 South Shore Cultural Center
(South Shore Country Club)
7059 S. South Shore Dr.
1916, MARSHALL & FOX
1983, RENOVATION, NORMAN
DEHAAN ASSOCS.

Established in 1906, South Shore prospered along with the neighborhood to become one of the city's renowned country clubs, and Marshall & Fox's modest clubhouse (1906) was replaced with this palatial Mediterranean-style structure that incorporated the original (now south) ballroom. Spacious and elaborately decorated corridors connect two grand ballrooms with a glazed solarium on the east as well as with dining and meeting rooms overlooking the lake. Inside, the north ballroom is like an enormous glass box with a Wedgwood lid. The wall-to-wall windows could be raised to open the room to the surrounding terrace. The splendid colonnaded driveway, on axis with the entrance

South Shore Cultural Center

gatehouse (unrestored), provides a grand approach. The sixty-five-acre property, purchased by the Chicago Park District in 1974, includes a beach, a golf course, tennis courts, an outdoor stage, and a riding arena as well as traces of the original bowling green and shooting area. The stables are now used by the Chicago Mounted Police. The abandoned shooting lodge to the north was built at the same time as the main clubhouse.

139 Rainbow Beach Park Buildings
3111 E. 71st St.
2000, DAVID WOODHOUSE ARCHITECTS

The previously neglected park received a jolt of creative architecture with the addition of these small but imaginative structures. The translucent oval canopies were meant to evoke clouds.

140 Allan Miller House
7121 S. Paxton Ave.
1915, JOHN S. VAN BERGEN

This extremely well preserved house is the only surviving building in Chicago by this Prairie School architect, most of whose work is found in the North Shore suburbs. Its open plan is derived from Wright's "Fireproof House for $5,000," but the generous seventy-five-foot lot width allowed Van Bergen to expand the cube with a large porch, giving the composition some of the expansiveness associated with suburban Prairie houses.

141 St. Philip Neri Roman Catholic Church
2126 E. 72nd St.
1928, JOSEPH W. MCCARTHY

The golden hues of Plymouth granite set off this Tudor Revival design. Bedford limestone is used for the carving around the entrance and the

Beach House at Rainbow Beach Park

tracery in the large rose windows. The copper spire adds height to this large church, which is set on a landscaped base raised above the street.

142 Jeffery-Cyril Historic District
7100 block of S. Jeffery and S. Cyril Blvds.

The rejuvenation of this enclave provides an excellent example of the benefits available under mid-1980s tax incentives for historic preservation. The busy intersection of E. 71st St. and Jeffery Blvd. was developed in the late 1920s with six apartment buildings in widely varied styles. All but one had small to medium units (one to four rooms) marketed to middle-class tenants. Varying in height from five to thirteen stories, the buildings form a group that dominates the low-rise residential and commercial landscape. In 1987–88, four of them were restored and modernized by a development subsidiary of South Shore Bank.

143 E. 71st Pl. Building
1966–1974 E. 71st Pl.
1928, PAUL FREDERICK OLSEN
1987, RENOVATION, LISEC & BIEDERMAN

A Spanish colonial revival building of brick and terra-cotta, it has a two-story lobby on 71st Pl. and storefronts (altered) along Jeffery Blvd.

144 Bedford Villa Apartments
7130 S. Cyril Ave.
1929, PAUL FREDERICK OLSEN

This Gothic Revival apartment building has a distinctive entrance with gargoyles and fleurs-de-lis.

145 Shore Manor/ Eleanor Manor
7150 S. Cyril Ave.
1928, DANIEL J. SCHAFFNER

This pair of Georgian Revival apartment buildings rises over an English basement that contains the lobbies.

146 The Highland
7147 S. Jeffery Blvd.
1927, MCNALLY & QUINN
1987, RENOVATION, LISEC & BIEDERMAN

Gabled parapets and a traceried entrance give this brick-and-limestone structure a Tudor flavor.

147 Jeffery-Cyril Apartments
7144 S. Jeffery Blvd.
1927, JULIUS J. SCHWARZ
1988, RENOVATION, LISEC & BIEDERMAN

The two-story entryway of this Tudor building is decorated with crockets. Unlike its neighbors, it was originally a cooperative, with larger apartments of five or six rooms.

148 The Regency
(Jeffery Terrace Apartments)
7130 S. Jeffery Blvd.
1929, PAUL FREDERICK OLSEN
1987, RENOVATION, LISEC & BIEDERMAN

Although designed by the same architect as two other buildings in this group, this one represents a complete break with their historically

The Regency (Jeffery Terrace Apartments)

inspired styles. It is a jazzy essay in Art Deco, with ornament created only by geometric shapes. Arcades along Jeffery Blvd. provide sheltered entries for the commercial spaces. The apartment entrance is surrounded by gold glazed tile.

149 Kenna Apartments
2214 E. 69th St.
1916, BARRY BYRNE & RYAN CO.
The unusually severe composition, perhaps influenced by Byrne's contact with California protomodernist Irving J. Gill in 1913, is enlivened by Alfonso Iannelli's wonderful ornament around the entrance and windows.

Kenna Apartments

150 Jackson Park Highlands
Euclid, Bennett, and Constance Aves. between 67th and 71st Sts.
Named for its location atop a ridge, this middle-class residential neighborhood was established as an eighty-acre subdivision in 1905. It was developed by Frank I. Bennett, a Chicago alderman, lawyer, and real estate agent, and Charles J. Bour, an "advertising agent." Most of the houses were built between 1905 and 1940, and they present an impressive array of the styles—mostly revivalist—of the period. The design standards included minimum lot widths of fifty feet, a thirty-foot setback from the street, no alleys, and buried utilities. Facade

materials were restricted to brick or stone, while roof materials were limited to tile or slate. As a group, the houses retain an unusually high degree of architectural integrity, rewarding visitors with superbly handled materials, ornamental details, and early landscape and gardening features. This subdivision grew as automobile ownership was increasing: a look down the original narrow, two-track concrete driveways reveals auto sheds that match the houses.

151 6700 S. Euclid Ave.
1952, SPITZ & SPITZ
One of the few postwar houses in this subdivision, this 1950s classic has a big front-entry fin.

152 6826 S. Euclid Ave.
1905, ARCHITECT UNKNOWN
The two-story temple front proclaims its Greek Revival style, but in an unusual twist, the triangular pediment is half-timbered. There is a similar house at **6931**.

153 6840 S. Euclid Ave.
1905, ARCHITECT UNKNOWN
This is a good example of the simplification of Queen Anne forms after the turn of the century. The large bays are still present, but the massing is simpler and the facade is symmetrical.

154 6955 S. Euclid Ave.
1909, FRANK D. CHASE
This Tudor Revival house and matching two-story auto shed show the influence of the English Arts and Crafts movement.

155 6956 S. Bennett Ave.
1936, PAUL SCHWEIKHER
This International Style house in brick has metal-framed corner windows, a low roof with a central chimney, and glass blocks in windows on the north and south sides. Schweikher practiced in Chicago from 1933, when his work was exhibited at the Museum of Modern Art, to 1953, when he left to teach at Yale University.

156 6926 S. Bennett Ave.
1908, WILLIAM L. PAGELS
Maher's influence is strong in this house, with its octagonal columns

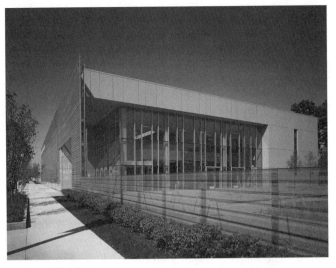
Gary Comer College Prep

Glassy and colored a youthful lime green, Comer Prep looks very different from the earlier building. A perforated stainless steel protective screen that was used to wrap the youth center's parking lot became an exterior design element of the school, visually unifying the campus. The screen makes it difficult to see into the building in the daytime but very easy to see out. It responds to the design challenge of creating a safe environment that does not feel like a bunker. The hallway walls of the classrooms are glass, increasing light and transparency throughout. During the school day, students use the youth center's gym and lunchroom. The school even loans umbrellas and outerwear to allow the pupils to pass between the two buildings in inclement weather.

The youth center was championed and funded by Gary Comer, who was born and raised in Greater Grand Crossing in the 1930s and 1940s before finding immense wealth as the founder of mail-order retailer Lands' End. Comer died in October 2006, five months after the youth center was dedicated. The charter school he had envisioned was named in his honor, and the family-run Comer Science and Education Foundation continues its involvement with the community.

—LEE BEY

167 Oak Woods Cemetery

1035 E. 67th St.

The Oak Woods Cemetery Association was formed in 1853. Like Chicago's other historic cemeteries, Graceland and Rosehill, it was located beyond the growing city but close to a railroad line. In 1866, the Illinois Central began operating a spur line to the cemetery. The association hired Adolph Strauch, superintendent of Spring Grove Cemetery in Cincinnati, to assist in the planning, thus ensuring that Oak Woods would reflect the most up-to-date thinking. Beyond establishing a parklike environment, Strauch promoted the idea known as the lawn plan, in which no walls, fences, curbing, or coping mark the edges of the plots. His plan for Oak Woods included three lakes surrounded by curving roadways and gently rising mounds.

Oak Woods has one of Chicago's most significant concentrations of Civil War commemorations. The **A | Confederate Mound Monument,** erected in 1893 and officially dedicated on Memorial Day 1895, marks the North's largest burial site for Confederate soldiers and sailors. The two-acre site, acquired by the federal government in 1867, marks the graves of 6,000 prisoners of war who died in Chicago's Camp Douglas of disease and deprivation. General John C. R. Underwood, a civil engineer and Confederate veteran, led the movement to build this memorial and designed it himself. The graves are arranged in concentric trenches around the sloping base of the forty-foot-tall monument. In 1911, bronze tablets bearing the names and ranks of the 4,275

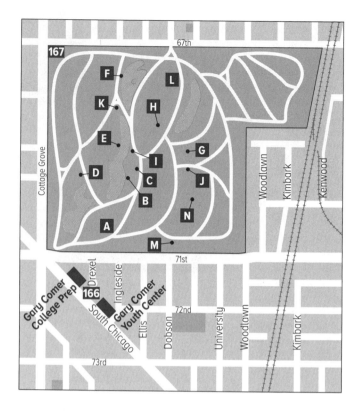

men identified in official records were added to the mound. Atop a twelve-foot column, its capital carved to resemble a battlement, is a bronze sculpture of a Confederate infantryman, based on a figure in Appomattox, a painting by Confederate veteran John A. Elder.

The 1890s saw the erection of numerous monuments to the Civil War in both the North and the South. Sufficient time had passed for the national rift to have begun to heal, and those with firsthand memories of the war wanted to commemorate their experiences before it was too late. In the northwest corner of the cemetery are plots held by the Soldiers' Home, Abraham Lincoln Post No. 91, Dept. of Illinois, the Grand Army of the Republic, and the Chicago Veterans Association. A statue of a Union soldier with a rifle (partially missing) and a cannon and shot marks the plot of the Soldiers' Home (now Cardinal Meyer Center), which still stands on E. 35th St. A 1905 replica of Charles J. Mulligan's *Lincoln the Orator* (*The Gettysburg Lincoln*) (1903) marks off the plot for members of a local post of the GAR, the major Union veterans' organization.

The tallest monument is the limestone obelisk marking the burial site of **B | William Hale "Big Bill" Thompson,** Chicago's mayor from 1915 to 1923 and from 1927 to 1931. A boorish lout with a theatrical manner, he opposed U.S. involvement in World War I and Prohibition at home, threatening to fire any policeman who interfered with a citizen's "personal liberty"—the selling or consumption of alcohol. Thompson's was one of the loudest roars in the Roaring Twenties.

A gray granite mausoleum is the final resting place of **C | Harold Washington**, state legislator, member of the U.S. Congress, and the first African American mayor of Chicago.

A simple granite column with four sloping sides marks the grave of architect **D | Solon S. Beman**.

E | George A. Fuller was trained as an architect but achieved fame as originator of the modern contracting system in building construction. His firm, based in Chicago with a branch in New York City, built the Monadnock Building and the Rookery in Chicago and the Flatiron (originally Fuller) Building in New York. Bruce Price designed the monument, the only work in Chicago by this New York architect. It is a limestone pergola of fluted columns on

George A. Fuller Monument

which rest three layers of supporting beams representing steel, stone, and wood construction. Curiously, on the underside of the topmost, or "wooden," beams, are carved stone rivets—characteristics of modern steel-frame construction. The classical details convey an impression of a traditional, albeit somewhat peculiar, design.

The red granite monument to **F | Jesse Owens** features the Olympic rings that recall his achievements at the 1936 Games in Berlin, at which he won the broad jump and the 100- and 200-meter dashes.

Crossed baseball bats and a ball mark the grave of **G | Adrian C. "Cap" Anson,** a baseball player and manager of the Chicago White Stockings (forerunner of the Cubs) in the newly formed National League.

Eastman Monument

The monument to **H | Gale Cramer,** a young train engineer who sacrificed himself to save his passengers, features a model of the train in which he died.

I | The Firmenich Family Monument is a very tall statuary group that stands out dramatically at Symphony Lake. Atop a large, heavy base are three female figures representing Faith, Hope, and Charity.

J | The Eastman Monument features a life-size bronze figure of a woman wearing classical dress and bearing a wreath in her right hand while she leans mournfully against a pink granite slab.

K | Paul Cornell's plot features a very large monument made of a material known as white bronze. In 1853, he founded the town of Hyde Park and cofounded Oak Woods Cemetery.

Paul Cornell Monument

Oak Woods Cemetery Chapel

L | The Chapel and Crematory (1903, WILLIAM CARBYS ZIMMERMAN) is reminiscent of a rural English Gothic church but exhibits some Prairie School elements in its steeple and entrance porch. The **Tower of Memories** (1960) is a communal mausoleum and columbarium. Prairie School architect **M | George C. Nimmons**, who specialized in industrial buildings, is buried here.

Along the south edge of Oak Woods are a group of Jewish cemeteries, each demarcated by a fence. These plots, held by congregations or fraternal organizations, resemble traditional European graveyards with close-set headstones and no open space apart from walkways. In the cemetery proper, among another area of Jewish graves, is a monument known as the **N | Eternal Light**. In every synagogue burns an eternal light; this one is a memorial to victims of the Holocaust. Its base shaped like a Star of David, the red granite tower contains in its top a radioactive material that absorbs sunlight by day and glows at night.

—JOAN POMARANC

In 2011, Brinshore Development and the Rebuild Foundation, created by artist and planner Theaster Gates, commissioned Landon Bone Baker Architects to design the **Dorchester Artist Housing Collaborative**. The two-story town houses comprising the abandoned Dante Harper housing project (1980, CHICAGO HOUSING AUTHORITY) on E. 70th St. at Dante and Harper would be redeveloped into thirty-two mixed-income rental units, with an arts center created from four units at the heart of the complex.

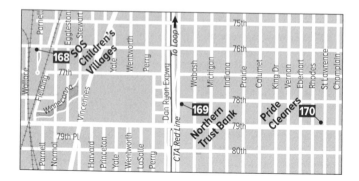

SOS Children's Villages Lavezzorio Community Center

168 SOS Children's Villages Lavezzorio Community Center
7600 S. Parnell Ave.
2007, STUDIO GANG ARCHITECTS

Like a Gee's Bend quilt that creates beauty from fabric remnants, this building celebrates and transforms its disparate donated materials. A fluid pattern was coaxed from different types of concrete to form a "strata wall" that evokes the layers below the earth. The wall folds around three sides of the building and makes a dramatic frame for the entrance, which faces the cul-de-sac of the foster-family Children's Village. Large areas of glass in the brick-and-concrete walls at 76th and Parnell encourage public use of the second-floor community room.

169 Northern Trust Bank South Financial Center
7801 S. State St.
1996, JOHNSON & LEE

The Prairie School style is a nod to the neighborhood's residential character, while the clock tower gives the building high visibility from the Dan Ryan Expressway. Loggias and overhanging roofs mitigate solar heat gain on the south and west exposures.

170 Pride Cleaners
558 E. 79th St.
1959, GERALD SIEGWART

This is the wildest roof in Chicago, a concrete slab that swoops from ground to sky. Pride's freestanding sign, with its colorful pointed oval shapes, completes this ensemble of eye-catching roadside architecture. The style is sometimes referred to as Googie, named for a chain of California coffee shops that exemplified the exuberantly non-traditional architecture of the 1950s and 1960s. Architect Siegwart also designed houses, including a 1953 commission for *Better Homes and Gardens* that appeared in a thirteen-page article, "This Is the House You Asked For."

BEVERLY/ MORGAN PARK

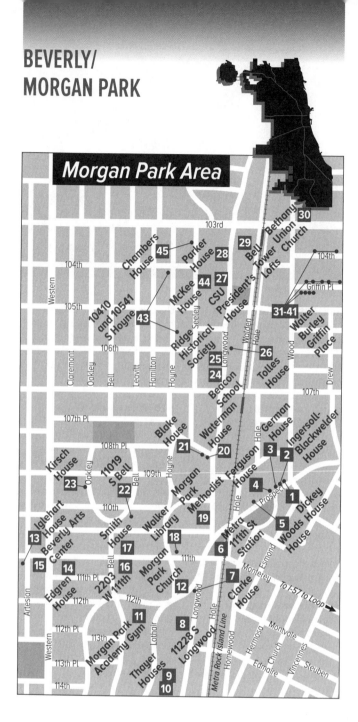

Morgan Park Area

If communities still adopted Latin mottos, Beverly–Morgan Park might bill it-self as *Suburbia in Urbe*. With its towering trees, broad lawns, and sprawling old houses, it looks more like an affluent North Shore suburb than a Chicago neighborhood. The hilly topography and winding streets also set it apart from the flat urban grid to the east. The small rail stations, which retain much of their charm despite heavy-handed remodelings, recall the area's origins as a commuter suburb.

Morgan Park is the older community. In 1844, an Englishman named Thomas Morgan bought a large tract of land along the Blue Island Ridge (the hill that rises west of Longwood Dr.) from 91st to 119th Sts., which remain the north and south boundaries of the combined neighborhoods. It remained a sleepy farm community until 1869, when the Blue Island Land & Building Co. bought the land and hired another Englishman, Thomas F. Nichols, to lay

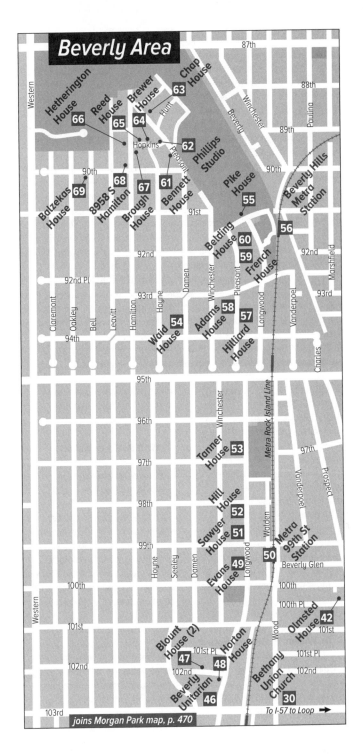

Beverly Area

joins Morgan Park map, p. 470

To I-57 to Loop →

out the subdivision of Morgan Park south of 107th St. The curving streets and generous greenswards of this area result from Nichols's picturesque planning principles.

Although not incorporated as a village until 1882, Morgan Park developed significantly in the 1870s. In the first year of the decade, the Chicago, Rock Island & Pacific Railroad established a branch line that provided the area with convenient service to the Loop. Three institutions were established here in quick succession: the Morgan Park Military Academy, founded in 1873, which continues—minus the military aspect—to be a prominent preparatory school;

the Chicago Female College, established in 1875; and the Baptist Union Theological Seminary, which moved here from Chicago's Douglas neighborhood in 1877. The presence of the seminary, led by Thomas W. Goodspeed and William Rainey Harper, raised hopes that the proposed University of Chicago might establish its new campus here. When the more centrally located Hyde Park was chosen instead, the seminary left to become the university's Divinity School. Morgan Park remained a quiet residential village whose community life centered on a handful of Protestant churches. Even a fiercely fought annexation to the city in 1914 did little to alter its subdued character.

The community of Beverly, also called Beverly Hills, developed slightly later but followed a similar pattern. It was part of the village of Washington Heights to the east, which was annexed to Chicago in 1890 but retained its own small-town identity. Like Morgan Park, it developed from east to west. In 1889 the Chicago, Rock Island & Pacific Railroad opened a station at 91st St. and named it Beverly Hills, which came to be the name for the whole community north of 107th St. along the ridge. Residential development proceeded swiftly, with the biggest boom taking place in the 1920s.

North of 95th St., an important commercial artery, the enclave of North Beverly is the area's most exclusive community. The deep wooded lots on rolling hills shelter large Revival-style houses from the 1920s and 1930s. As geographically distant from the Loop as are the suburbs of Evanston and Riverside, North Beverly shares their sylvan sense of shelter.

—LAURIE MCGOVERN PETERSEN

1 Luther S. Dickey Jr. House
10990 S. Prospect Ave.
1912, CHATTEN & HAMMOND
Set far back on a four-acre lot is a stellar example of the Arts and Crafts–influenced eclectic house often found in the North Shore suburbs. Picturesque elements—a half-timbered double gable, sloping brick buttresses and piers, and a flanged segmental entry arch—are freely combined into a masterfully integrated composition.

2 Ingersoll-Blackwelder House
10910 S. Prospect Ave.
1874; 1887, FRONT ADDITION,
ARCHITECTS UNKNOWN

3 Dr. William H. German House
10924 S. Prospect Ave.
1884, FREDERICK G. GERMAN
Ingersoll-Blackwelder is a catalog of the decorative possibilities of wood sheathing: clapboards laid horizontally, vertically, and even diagonally; applied fretwork; and shingles in three patterns. The German House is comparatively restrained but adds a touch of half-timbering to the mix.

4 William G. Ferguson House
10934 S. Prospect Ave.
1873, ARCHITECT UNKNOWN

5 Dr. Arthur W. Woods House
10970 S. Prospect Ave.
1872, ARCHITECT UNKNOWN

Deep, ornately bracketed fascia characterize these altered but charming Italianates.

6 111th St. Metra Station
(Chicago, Rock Island & Pacific Railroad—Morgan Park Station)
111th St. and Hale Ave.
1891, JOHN T. LONG
Set on a large greensward, this station has a deliberately domestic scale and was meant to advertise the comfortable suburban character of early Morgan Park. The first floor was designed to be faced in brick but was constructed entirely of wood.

Like Prospect Ave., Longwood Dr. developed early as a fashionable street. At the top of the hill are many of the oldest houses, which have long front yards stretching down to Longwood, frequently with newer houses at the base of the hill. Some now have addresses on Lothair Ave., one block to the west (entries 7–10).

7 Sarah D. Clarke House
(W. S. Kiskaddon House)
11156 S. Longwood Dr.
1892, JOHN GAVIN
This prim Queen Anne dollhouse miniaturizes diverse stylistic elements with bracketed charm. The Italianate corner tower shrinks as it rises.

8 **11228 S. Longwood Dr./
11213 S. Lothair Ave.**
1935, REMODELING, CHARLES
D. FAULKNER

Probably dating from the late nineteenth century, this house was completely transformed with a Jacobean brick-and-stone veneer and addition.

9 Dr. Henry E. Thayer House (2)
11347 S. Lothair Ave.
1874, ARCHITECT UNKNOWN

10 Dr. Gilbert Thayer House (1)
**11359 S. Lothair Ave./11410
S. Longwood Dr.**
1873, ARCHITECT UNKNOWN

Almost lost to view in leafy summer are these grand hilltop Italianates with their breathtaking eastward views.

**11 Morgan Park
Academy Gymnasium**
2147–2155 W. 112th St.
1900, DWIGHT H. PERKINS

The geometric end gables and some of the windows hint at Perkins's Prairie School affinities. This is the oldest extant Morgan Park Academy building.

**12 Morgan Park Church
of God in Christ**
(Morgan Park Congregational Church)
11153 S. Hoyne Ave.
1916, PATTON, HOLMES & FLYNN

Domestically scaled and comfortable, it is Chicago's best-preserved Craftsman church, here blended with Mission touches. The interior retains the original lanterns and woodwork.

13 Charles D. Iglehart House
11118 S. Artesian Ave.
1857; 1870S, FRONT ADDITION,
ARCHITECTS UNKNOWN

Tucked away on a mundane street of mid-twentieth-century brick houses is one of Chicago's earliest dwellings. The rear half of this Italianate house was a small cottage where Iglehart's daughter, Mary, was born in 1857—the first birth in Morgan Park. The house is in remarkably good condition for an 1870s frame building.

14 Johan Alexis Edgren House
2314 W. 111th Pl.
1882, PALLISER, PALLISER & CO.

The design for this unusually well preserved house was purchased from Palliser, Palliser & Co., producers of some of America's most influential pattern books for homeowners and builders. This style is now called Stick Style, for the wood laid atop the building's clapboard walls. It articulates the structure below and was considered modern during the 1870s and 1880s.

15 Beverly Arts Center
2407 W. 111th St.
2002, WHEELER KEARNS ARCHITECTS

One of this firm's greatest talents is to develop a noble project on a small budget. Crisp planes of brick and glass create an imposing street presence on the busy corner and a welcoming courtyard facing the parking lot. The modest budget was stretched to include a 420-seat theater, art gallery, and studio space.

Morgan Park Church of God in Christ

Harry Hale Waterman House

16 2203 W. 111th St.
1873, ARCHITECT UNKNOWN

17 Justin A. Smith House
2204 W. 111th St.
1872, ARCHITECT UNKNOWN

These early, altered houses share
a cross-gabled massing, triangular
second-floor window hoods, and the
bracketed front gables so popular in
early 1870s cottages. The structure
at 2203 was formerly the Morgan
Park Academy Headmaster's House.

**18 Chicago Public Library—
George C. Walker Branch**
11071 S. Hoyne Ave.
1890, CHARLES S. FROST
1933, ADDITIONS, DOERR & DOERR
1995, RENOVATION AND NORTHERN
   ADDITION, VOA ASSOCS.

This library is reminiscent of H. H.
Richardson's suburban train stations,
but the twin towers with inward-
facing windows have a slightly
pigeon-toed charm all their own.
The end and rear rooms came later,
and the interior has been completely
remodeled.

**19 Morgan Park United
Methodist Church**
*(Morgan Park Methodist
Episcopal Church)*
11000 S. Longwood Dr.
1913, HARRY HALE WATERMAN
1926, ADDITION, PERKINS,
   FELLOWS & HAMILTON

Simple, powerful elements dominate
this Craftsman church: the exagger-

atedly broad gable, the anchoring
tower, and the entry cut like a cave
from the body of the church.

Along Longwood Dr., architects dealt
with a problem rare in Chicago: the
rolling lot. The houses nestle into,
perch on, strut across, or lord it
over their hilltop sites with varying
degrees of success (entries 20 and
24–28).

20 Harry Hale Waterman House
10838 S. Longwood Dr.
1892, HARRY HALE WATERMAN

With its terraced entry, it snuggles
more cozily into the ridge than any
other house on Longwood Dr. Punctuated by an exaggerated gable at
the entry porch, the high hipped roof
gives a whimsical sense of dispro-
portion to this overgrown cottage,
the architect's own home.

21 J. T. Blake House
2023 W. 108th Pl.
1894, HARRY HALE WATERMAN

Typical of many of Waterman's
charmingly irregular designs, the
asymmetrical, steeply pitched gable
roof and jutting stairway bay form an
entrance facade combining stone,
stucco, and wood.

22 11019 S. Bell Ave.
EARLY 1880S, ARCHITECT UNKNOWN

Two narrow wings meet stiffly at
an angled wall that grows into a

tower—a massing with French precedents that is little seen in Chicago.

23 Kirsch House
10920 S. Oakley Ave.
1888, ARCHITECT UNKNOWN
Queen Anne meets the Kremlin in this exuberant house with a gilded turret.

24 Beacon Therapeutic School
(E. J. Barker House)
10650 S. Longwood Dr.
1910, HARRY HALE WATERMAN
1992, ADDITION, PHILLIP
   PEECHER & ASSOCS.
The horizontal massing and simple lines show a Prairie School spirit worlds apart from the picturesque irregularity of Waterman's houses from the 1890s.

25 Ridge Historical Society
(James P. Driscoll House, originally Herbert S. Graver House)
10616 S. Longwood Dr.
1922, JOHN TODD HETHERINGTON
The terraces take better advantage of the dramatic hilltop site than any house on the street.

26 Harry N. Tolles House
10561 S. Longwood Dr.
1911, WALTER BURLEY GRIFFIN
Though related to the houses on Griffin Pl., this house has an altered porch, a relocated main entrance, glass block, and replaced window muntins that detract from its appearance.

27 Chicago State University—President's House
(Frank Anderson House)
10400 S. Longwood Dr.
1924, OSCAR L. MCMURRY
This very formal, elegant rendition of 1920s Italian Renaissance Revival has simple classical pediments above the first-floor openings.

28 Hiland A. Parker House
10340 S. Longwood Dr.
1894, HARRY HALE WATERMAN
Site and style combine here for high drama. The base of huge rusticated brownstone blocks rises from the hill to form arches on the big semicircular porch. The tall roof, pierced with steeply pitched gabled dormers, exaggerates the height.

29 Bell Tower Lofts
(Thirteenth Church of Christ, Scientist)
10317 S. Longwood Dr.
1916, HOWARD L. CHENEY
1992, CONVERSION TO APARTMENTS,
   STOWELL COOK FROLICHSTEIN
A ponderous Greek Revival box, this typical Christian Scientist church has taken on a new mission with its conversion to apartments.

30 Bethany Union Church
1750 W. 103rd St.
1927, RAYMOND M. HOOD
The narrow facade of this lovely and severely simple church has been overwhelmed by the mundane support building to the west.

31 W. 104th Pl./Walter Burley Griffin Pl.
A 1973 article in the *Prairie School Review* revealed that detective work by architect Wilbert R. Hasbrouck and architectural historian Paul E. Sprague had uncovered a significant concentration of houses by Walter Burley Griffin in Beverly. All of the houses were commissioned by Russell L. Blount, an aspiring developer whose early successes in selling houses designed by Griffin led to a string of projects. Griffin was at the height of his American career at the time; he had worked in Frank Lloyd Wright's studio from 1901 to 1905 and had a substantial solo practice until he left for Australia in 1913 to design the capital city, Canberra.

Blount's association with Griffin began in 1909, when Blount commissioned a house for himself and his fiancée to be built on her father's property on 104th Pl. Before the house was complete, he received an attractive offer for it from Edmund C. Garrity, leading him to commission a new one for himself next door (Blount House 1) and a speculative one down the block that was later sold to Harry G. Van Nostrand. In 1912–13, Blount commissioned three more houses from Griffin: the Blount House (2), which became his by default when the intended purchaser reneged, and the Salmon and Jenkinson Houses. Griffin was listed as providing "plans only" for the Jenkinson House, and it differs in several respects from the previous five, which are considered purer examples of his work.

Shortly after Griffin left for Australia, Blount built four other houses in the area, three based on the Van Nostrand House design (Williams, Hornbaker, Clarke) and one on the Salmon House (Furneaux). Sales of the later houses never lived up to the expectations generated by the quick offers received for the first few, and by 1915 Blount was building undistinguished rows of cracker-box houses.

This remarkable street, renamed Walter Burley Griffin Pl., reflects an innovative approach to the design of small, inexpensive houses. All of Griffin's houses are 1.5 or 2 stories, are built of wood and stucco on a concrete basement, and have very compact square plans, similar to Wright's 1907 design of "A Fireproof House for $5,000." The living and dining rooms are defined rather than separated by a large fireplace; the kitchen is tucked into the remaining corner; and open porches extend the spaces outdoors. Griffin invariably covers the foundation with clapboards, often continuing them to the sill line of the first-floor windows. The porch's location is determined by the desire to give it at least one southern exposure. The windows are casements with robust wooden mullions in geometric patterns, sometimes quite elaborate. The roof is occasionally hipped but most often has a large open gable with extended ends that enhance its sheltering quality. Gables over the screened porches echo the main gable and add variety to the basic cube. This group is part of Griffin's rustic work, with rough brown siding, pale stucco, and naturally weathering shingles making the houses seem suited to their bucolic location.

32 Harry G. Van Nostrand House
1666 W. Griffin Pl.

1911, WALTER BURLEY GRIFFIN

The plan is a smaller version of the Garrity House and was reused in others. Except for an added front dormer, the house is in close to original condition. It is especially rewarding to see the porch still screened—as so many of them were—rather than enclosed.

33 Edmund C. Garrity House
1712 W. Griffin Pl.

1909, WALTER BURLEY GRIFFIN

The quick and profitable sale of this newlyweds' house launched Blount

on his career. The second-floor dormers were added later, although the mullion pattern was thoughtfully reproduced.

34 Russell L. Blount House (1)
1724 W. Griffin Pl.

1911, WALTER BURLEY GRIFFIN

When Garrity bought Blount's first house, he commissioned this replacement. The clapboard "hoop skirt" covering the foundation exaggerates the horizontal with inexpensive flair. Griffin grouped first-floor windows to break through the wall at all four corners.

Edmund C. Garrity House

Russell L. Blount House (1)

35 Walter O. Salmon House

1736 W. Griffin Pl.

1912, WALTER BURLEY GRIFFIN

The unusual two-story screened porch has been enclosed on the first floor.

36 Arthur G. Jenkinson House

1727 W. Griffin Pl.

1912, WALTER BURLEY GRIFFIN

The partial extension of the clapboard siding above the first-floor level may be Blount's alteration to Griffin's design. It is similar to the facade treatment of the Newland House, whose architect of record was Spencer & Powers.

37 William N. Clarke House

1731 W. Griffin Pl.

1913, WALTER BURLEY GRIFFIN

Blount shifted the Van Nostrand House plan ninety degrees here and moved the porch. The windows have lost their distinctive muntins.

38 Harry C. Furneaux House

1741 W. Griffin Pl.

1913, WALTER BURLEY GRIFFIN

This plan is a reversed version of the Salmon House but with a single-story porch and different details. The triangular roof brackets may have been inspired by those on the Newland House.

39 Harry F. Newland House

1737 W. Griffin Pl.

1912, SPENCER & POWERS

This house may have been begun by Griffin. The roof brackets and the extension of the clapboarding above the first floor are not found in his work.

40 William R. Hornbaker House

1710 W. 104th St.

1914, WALTER BURLEY GRIFFIN

This heavily altered variation of the Clarke House has had all the windows replaced and large dormers added.

41 Ida E. Williams House

1632 W. 104th St.

1913, WALTER BURLEY GRIFFIN

Despite the addition of a small dormer, this house retains much of its original appearance and still has a screened porch with the wood muntins. It is of the same plan and tiny dimensions as the Van Nostrand House.

42 Frank N. Olmsted House

1624 W. 100th Pl.

1910, WALTER BURLEY GRIFFIN

A reversal of the Blount House (1) plan, it has lost the "hoop skirt" clapboarding at the base.

43 10410 and 10541 S. Hoyne Ave.

1917, FRANK LLOYD WRIGHT

These are products of American System-Built, a short-lived collaboration of Wright and Richards Bros. of Milwaukee that sold Wright designs prepackaged and ready to build. Novelist Sherwood Anderson was the company copywriter and touted the modestly priced houses as examples of an American architecture "as brave and direct as the country." These designs were derived from Wright's "Fireproof House for $5,000" but are far less successful schemes and were

10541 S. Hoyne Ave.

unsupervised by Wright. Other, more popular models included duplexes and bungalows.

44 James R. McKee House
10415 S. Seeley Ave.
1908, JOHN M. SCHROEDER
This house packs all its punch into one element, the projecting sunroom capped by a graceful broken arch. The simple entrance is hidden away on the side, behind the battered front wall.

James R. McKee House

45 Chambers House
10330 S. Seeley Ave.
1874, ARCHITECT UNKNOWN
This remarkably well preserved house is a classic suburban villa, complete with "French" tower. The garden veranda on the south side

Chambers House

was meant to frame the view and provide a suitable vantage point for the beauties of nature.

46 Beverly Unitarian Church
(Robert C. Givins House)
10244 S. Longwood Dr.
1886, ARCHITECT UNKNOWN
Modeled after an Irish castle and built of Joliet limestone, this imposing edifice was the work of an early developer who wanted to give the area a fashionable image.

Beverly Unitarian Church

47 Russell L. Blount House (2)
1950 W. 102nd St.
1912, WALTER BURLEY GRIFFIN
The plan is the same as for the earlier Blount House (1), but the bedrooms have cathedral ceilings that are echoed in the exterior trim. The family lived here from 1914 to 1916, when Harry Furneaux bought this house and the Blounts purchased his Griffin-designed house on Griffin Pl.

48 Horace Horton House
10200 S. Longwood Dr.
1890, JOHN T. LONG
This house is an imposing example of the severely academic colonial revival style and appears to be based on McKim, Mead & White's H. A. C. Taylor House (1886) in Newport, Rhode Island.

49 Robert W. Evans House
9914 S. Longwood Dr.
1908, FRANK LLOYD WRIGHT
Here Wright builds onto the hill, not into it. The pinwheeling of forms around a central chimney resembles that of his Ward W. Willitts House (1901) in Highland Park, Illinois, but

the stucco has been defaced with a layer of stone.

50 99th St. Metra Station
(Chicago, Rock Island & Pacific Railroad—Walden Station)
99th St. and Wood St.
1889, ARCHITECT UNKNOWN
2008, RESTORATION AND NEW PLATFORM SHELTER, EDWARDS & KELCEY

This uniquely charming Queen Anne–style station is one of the smallest on the rail line. An oversized hipped roof with flared eaves is further embellished with ornamental Craftsman-style brackets and topped with metal finials. The east side, which faces the tracks, is dominated by an enormous octagonal dormer.

51 Frederick C. Sawyer House
9822 S. Longwood Dr.
1908, HORATIO R. WILSON
52 Bryson B. Hill House
9800 S. Longwood Dr.
1909, ALBERT G. FERREE

These classically inspired mansions coexisted with the Prairie School and will never go entirely out of style.

53 Louis A. Tanner House
9640 S. Longwood Dr.
1909, TALLMADGE & WATSON

The simple but pleasing facade retains an element typical of this firm's smaller projects: the trellised porch with cutout balusters.

54 Dan Everett Waid House
9332 S. Damen Ave.
1894, ARCHITECT UNKNOWN
1906, ALTERATION, HENRY K. HOLSMAN

This lively Queen Anne house has an unusual triple-gable composition that is symmetrical yet highly picturesque.

55 E. S. Pike House
1826 W. 91st St.
1894, HARRY HALE WATERMAN

Expect Hansel and Gretel to come tripping past this house set on the edge of the woods. Huge blocks of red sandstone anchor the first floor and contrast with the light stucco above.

E. S. Pike House

56 Beverly Hills Metra Station
(Chicago, Rock Island & Pacific Railroad—Beverly Station)
91st St. and Prospect Sq.
1889, CHARNLEY & EVANS

Only the picturesque towered and gabled massing hint at the Queen

Beverly Hills Metra Station

Anne character. Modernizations have removed the original small-paned windows and the elaborate cladding of shingles.

57 Edwin P. Hilliard House
9351 S. Pleasant Ave.

1894, HARRY HALE WATERMAN

Like the Pike House, this small variation on Waterman's picturesque theme features a tower breaking through the curbed gambrel roof and half-timbered stucco over a heavy stone base. The half-timbering frames the edges of the windows, organizing rather than fragmenting the wall plane.

58 William and Jessie M. Adams House
9326 S. Pleasant Ave.

1900, FRANK LLOYD WRIGHT

1913, REAR ADDITION, ROBERT HYDE

This house is quiet by Wright standards but has a typically intriguing entry sequence.

59 William M. R. French House
9203 S. Pleasant Ave.

1894, WILLIAM A. OTIS

This classical revival house is sophisticated and straightforward among its picturesque Waterman-designed and oblique Wright-designed neighbors. The second-floor central doorway treatment is as elaborate as that on the first floor.

60 Hiram H. Belding House
9167 S. Pleasant Ave.

1894, HARRY HALE WATERMAN

Described in *Inland Architect* as "Norman-French style," it has an L-shaped plan with a prominent stair tower and colossal stone base, favorite Waterman elements.

61 Arthur J. T. Bennett Jr. House
8944 S. Pleasant Ave.

1937, MURRAY D. HETHERINGTON

Hallmarks of Hetherington's talents are the artfully integrated garage and the emphasis on site and landscape; the garden entrance is framed by a stone gate extending from the wall of the house. The conical corner-entrance tower and hipped roof pierced by arched dormers identify the style as French Provincial.

62 Madge Phillips Studio
8910 S. Pleasant Ave.

1954, WILLIAM CARNEGIE

This is a latter-day version of the Walter Burley Griffin idiom as seen on 104th Pl. Although a sprawling single-story house rather than a compact cottage, it has the deep eaves and patterned wooden muntins of Griffin's distinctive style.

63 Ignatius Chap House
8831 S. Pleasant Ave.

1928, HOMER G. SAILOR

A dollhouse masquerading as a hacienda, it has a miniature entrance tower with blind arches. Painted tiles are inset into the rough stucco.

64 Everett Robert Brewer House
2078 W. Hopkins Pl.

1924, MURRAY D. HETHERINGTON

The irregular roofline, with its variegated slate hewn into random-sized slabs, evokes the craftsmanship of a preindustrial era. But the twentieth century asserts itself in the orderly arrangement of large windows in the projecting central section.

65 George W. Reed House
2122 W. Hopkins Pl.

1929, JAMES ROY ALLEN

The irregular massing of this sprawling house, with four wings spinning off the central block, was probably intended to suggest an English country house enlarged over the centuries. The style is early Renaissance, with classical details grafted onto medieval forms.

66 Murray D. Hetherington House
8918 S. Hamilton Ave.

1924, MURRAY D. HETHERINGTON

Second-generation Beverly architect Hetherington's home is endear-

Murray D. Hetherington House

S. P. Balzekas House

ingly and un-self-consciously pretty. It's the perfect Cotswold cottage, from the irregular massing and roofline to the rough-hewn materials to the flagstone-lined miniature streambed. The front bears a shield with the construction date in a stucco panel.

67 James Alex Brough House
8929 S. Hamilton Ave.
1927, MURRAY D. HETHERINGTON

This folksy stucco Spanish Revival home could be a stage set for *The Barber of Seville*, even down to the balcony.

68 8958 S. Hamilton Ave.
1951, JOSEPH EMIL HOSEK

If North Beverly is a symphony of architectural styles, here's the tuba. Everything is overblown: the five-foot eaves, the picture windows, and the first-floor coat of many colors that could have been the inspiration for PermaStone. The finishing touch is the highly manicured yard, complete with marshmallow and corkscrew topiary.

69 S. P. Balzekas House
9000 S. Bell Ave.
1935, WILLIAM SEVIC

In this multilevel Prairie and Moderne mishmash, the flat roofs projecting at many levels shelter metal-framed corner casement windows.

PULLMAN

In 1878, the swampy land now locked between the Dan Ryan and Calumet Expressways contained a few Dutch farms in the community of Roseland, high ground along what is now Michigan Ave., and fewer than twenty houses in the village of Kensington, centering on the railroad junction at 115th St. and Cottage Grove Ave. Five years later, the population had soared to seven thousand, most of them laborers drawn by new industry. The leading attraction was the company town of Pullman, begun by railroad car manufacturer George M. Pullman in April 1880 on five hundred acres between the western edge of Lake Calumet and the Illinois Central Railroad right-of-way. Pullman's plans called for a model town set on the north and south sides of the Pullman Palace Car Co.'s works. Superior living quarters in a healthful setting far from urban problems, he believed, would attract good workers and enhance productivity. Pullman insisted that his venture was not philanthropy but good business, and he expected everything in the town—houses, stores, the stable, and even the church—to bring in a return of 6 percent on investment.

Pullman's architect was Solon S. Beman, newly launched from the office of East Coast architect Richard M. Upjohn. The landscape designer was New Yorker Nathan F. Barrett, an avowed formalist whose work contrasted with the popular naturalism of Frederick Law Olmsted. Barrett's aesthetic gave the Pullman layouts their strongly French tone, with housing units arranged in carefully balanced sets, adorned with undulating walls like French pavilions, and oriented toward garden spaces. Beman's facades, constructed of bricks made from Lake Calumet clay, reveal the French predilection for indicating the underlying construction, even if only with a course of black brick at a floor line. Slate-covered mansard stories equaling one-third the building's height are grace notes throughout the town.

Other developers capitalized on the popularity of this famous experiment. In particular, the West Pullman Land Association was formed in 1890 to exploit the area west of State St. and south of 119th St. One portion, Stewart Ridge, was reserved for large houses on spacious lots. But Pullman's paternalism as well as other ambitions for the area were thwarted by the depression of 1893 and by the notorious Pullman Strike the following year. Workers' protests that rents remained high while wages were cut escalated into a national confrontation between railroad owners and the nascent railroad union led by Eugene V. Debs. The coup de grâce came in 1898, when the Illinois Supreme Court found the company in violation of a state law forbidding businesses to own land in excess of their industrial needs. By 1907, the court-ordered sale of Pullman had been completed.

The communities of Pullman, Roseland, Kensington, and West Pullman grew during the industrial buildups of the world wars and stagnated as industries departed in the 1980s. The Pullman works closed in 1981, leaving behind an area that had seen rapid racial change in the 1960s. Residents strive to maintain their town, wrested from developers by the Historic Pullman Foundation, which gained national landmark status for Pullman. Restoration of the state-owned Florence Hotel and former Pullman Administration Building, which was almost destroyed in a 1998 conflagration, continues into the twenty-first century.

—MARY ALICE MOLLOY

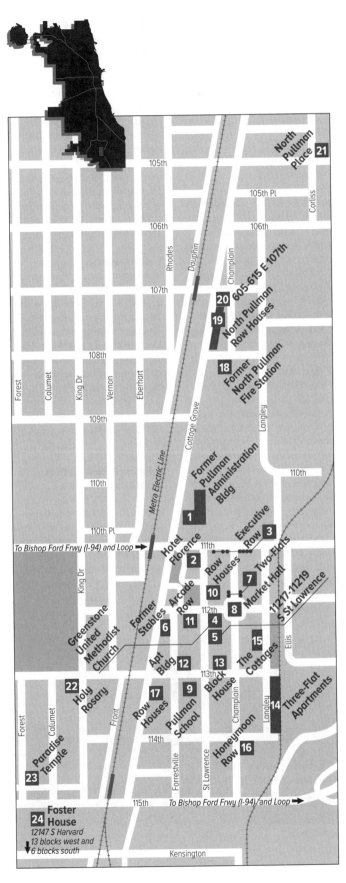

North Pullman Place **21**

Corliss

105th

105th Pl

106th

106th

Rhodes

Dauphin

Champlain

605-615 E 107th

107th

20
19 North Pullman Row Houses

18 Former North Pullman Fire Station

Forest

Calumet

King Dr

Vernon

Eberhart

108th

Langley

109th

Cottage Grove

Metra Electric Line

110th

Former Pullman Administration Bldg

110th

1

110th Pl

110th Pl

To Bishop Ford Frwy (I-94) and Loop →

Hotel Florence

Executive Row **3**

111th

Row Houses

Two-Flats

King Dr

2

7 Market Hall

Arcade Row

10

1217-1219 S St Lawrence

Former Stables

6

11

8

112th

4

Ellis

Greenstone United Methodist Church

5

15 The Cottages

Apt Bldg **12**

13 Block House

Forest

22 Holy Rosary

17 Row Houses

9 Pullman School

113th

Champlain

14 Three-Flat Apartments

Front

Calumet

Paradise Temple

114th

Honeymoon Row **16**

Langley

23

Forrestville

St Lawrence

115th

To Bishop Ford Frwy (I-94) and Loop →

24 Foster House
12147 S Harvard
13 blocks west and
↓ 6 blocks south

Kensington

PULLMAN

SOUTH AND SOUTHWEST **483**

1 Former Pullman Administration Building and Clock Tower

S. Cottage Grove Ave.
north of E. 111th St.
1880, SOLON S. BEMAN

The original focal point of the Pullman complex was gutted by a fire in 1998.

2 Hotel Florence

11111 S. Forrestville Ave.
1881, SOLON S. BEMAN

Named for Pullman's favorite daughter, this "large gingerbread country villa" with fifty guest rooms introduces the robust wooden embellishments on porches, gables, and stairs that characterize Beman's Queen Anne work. The trim is painted in "official" Pullman colors, two greens and a deep red, researched and reformulated by Pullman neighbor Sherwin-Williams.

3 Executive Row

619–623 through 641–645 E. 111th
CA. 1881, SOLON S. BEMAN

Employees' status within the Pullman company dictated the type of houses in which they could live and the homes' location relative to the factory. These double houses directly across 111th St. from the factory complex were reserved for management, hence the street's unofficial name, Executive Row. These were the largest and most elaborate houses in Pullman, commanding rents between twenty-eight and fifty dollars per month.

4 Greenstone United Methodist Church

(Greenstone Church)
11211 S. St. Lawrence Ave.
1882, SOLON S. BEMAN

The only significant importation of materials for Pullman was the serpentine rock quarried in New England for the town's only company-owned church. It was intended as a union church, with all denominations sharing the use and cost. This showpiece combines the peaked roofs of the Gothic with the round-arched openings and rock-faced masonry popularized by H. H. Richardson.

5 11217–11219 S. St. Lawrence Ave.

CA. 1881, SOLON S. BEMAN

Originally built as a rooming house, this building was converted to a hospital in the early 1900s with the construction of a rear addition. The building was restored to residential use after the construction of Roseland Community Hospital in 1924. The original two-story porch wrapped around the corner of the rectilinear turret to the north side of the house.

6 Former Pullman Stables

11201 S. Cottage Grove Ave.
CA. 1881, SOLON S. BEMAN

Time and unsympathetic readaptation have dimmed but not erased the charm of the wooden horses' heads, the wide entrance, and the shingle facing of this communal barn. The building was erected to reduce town

Hotel Florence

maintenance by keeping horses off most Pullman streets.

7 Two-Flats
11146–11148 and 11147–11149 S. Champlain Ave.
CA. 1881, SOLON S. BEMAN

These two-story buildings are four- or five-room two-flats constructed to resemble row houses. Variations in this type appear in the placement of the front doors as well as in roof details.

8 Market Hall and Colonnade Apartments and Town Houses
E. 112th St. and S. Champlain Ave.
1892, SOLON S. BEMAN

Four excruciatingly narrow curved units with bachelor apartments above arcades are bookended by matching town houses in this touch of Italy. They were inserted into the town fabric after a market hall on this site burned down. In the center is the remaining single story of the second Pullman Market Hall.

Market Hall and Colonnade Apartments and Town Houses

9 George M. Pullman Public School
11311 S. Forrestville Ave.
1910, DWIGHT H. PERKINS

Beman's school was replaced by a distinctively Perkinsian stylized Gothic block that features thick terra-cotta copings and angle buttressing against rust-brick walls.

10 Five-Room Row Houses
11145–11151 S. St. Lawrence Ave.
1880, SOLON S. BEMAN

A significant contribution to 1880s residential design was Beman's plan for a five-room worker's cottage, introduced in this block of row houses,

the first to be completed in Pullman. The houses, which range from fourteen to twenty-two feet wide, feature front parlors and rear kitchens/dining rooms on the main floor. Upstairs, each house has a front bedroom and two small rear ones split by a skylit stair hall that leads to a water closet. Beman picturesquely grouped his row houses. Here, a pair that shares a dormered, mansarded second story is linked with another pair in which an enhanced central element is topped with a purlin gable. No Pullman five-room house is unaltered; additions here include porches with details drawn from the Hotel Florence.

11 Arcade Row Houses
533–535 E. 112th St.
1881, SOLON S. BEMAN

In Pullman, the best buildings were placed in the most conspicuous locations. These two are among the best-preserved examples in a row of gambrel-dormered, three-story row houses that face the town's park. These units, large by Pullman standards, were not restricted to middle-class tenants. They were available to anyone who could afford the rents, a group that included the Pullman school principal, who lived at 533 in 1889, and a collection of carpenters and foremen for whom 535 was a boardinghouse.

12 Corner Apartment Building
11261 S. Forrestville Ave.
CA. 1884–86, SOLON S. BEMAN

This nearly square corner building houses its third story under an unusually high, curbed mansard roof. Similar structures are found along 113th St. at **11260 S. St. Lawrence Ave.** and **11270 S. Champlain Ave.**

13 Block House
614 E 113th St.
CA. 1881, SOLON S. BEMAN

Tenements anywhere else, they were called block houses in Pullman and offered individual rooms for rent. In a long row along the town's eastern edge, their low status and backbench location called for simple common brick facades, yet on each block house, the third story featured an extended central section set off from the mansard roof. This building now houses two-bedroom apartments. Other surviving block houses are at **11127 S. Langley Ave., 644–646 and 645–647 E. 113th St.**, and **704–706 E. 112th St.**

14 Three-Flat Apartment Buildings
S. Langley Ave. between 113th and 114th Sts.
1880–82, SOLON S. BEMAN

An entire block of identical three-story, three-flat units stands with the backs of the units against the railroad tracks. Although built of the most modest materials, they have some of Pullman's most formal layouts. In three places, units are pulled out to the sidewalk, creating two forecourts.

15 The Cottages
11218–11250 S. Langley Ave.
1880–82, SOLON S. BEMAN

Seventeen five-room row houses a mere fourteen feet wide demonstrate the great variety of facades that Beman and his associates, among them Irving K. Pond, designed in Pullman's early years for even the least expensive houses.

16 Flats on Honeymoon Row
11401–11403 S. Champlain Ave.
1888, SOLON S. BEMAN

These four-flat units employ common brick picked out with red brick in the manner of industrial housing worldwide in the late nineteenth century. The highly unusual plan features a trapezoidal bay with three doors. The two on the sides opened into the main-floor flats, and the central one led to stairs to two upper units. There were originally four water closets at the rear of the main floor, one for each unit.

17 Five-Room Row Houses
11307–11309 S. Cottage Grove Ave.
1888, SOLON S. BEMAN

Houses seen by the public from passing trains received special treatment, even when they were modest dwellings. These row houses have triangular bays, wide pedimented porches, and carefully balanced contrasts between light and dark brick that are unknown elsewhere in Pullman. The units to the south have the town's only roundheaded windows.

18 Former North Pullman Fire Station
623 E. 108th St.
1895, SOLON S. BEMAN

With a limestone pedimented truck door, ranks of arched windows, and an attenuated hose-drying tower, this Renaissance fire station was the last gasp in Pullman construction. It reflects the prevailing mode of the 1890s as surely as the initial Pullman buildings document the previous decade.

Former North Pullman Fire Station

The Cottages

19 North Pullman Row Houses

10701–10739 S. Cottage Grove Ave.

CA. 1884–85, SOLON S. BEMAN

The first sight of Pullman from trains leaving Chicago was this picturesque row, which steps forward to follow the angle of the street. Anchored by a large corner rooming house and distinguished by particularly high false rooflines, the buildings share simple, flat, red-orange brick facades.

20 605–615 E. 107th St.

1880S, SOLON S. BEMAN

The workers' houses in this row are noteworthy for their small size as well as for the way they seem to be wedged in between only slightly larger houses at each end of the block. Recent careful restorations of the houses at 605 and 609 show the potential of the rest of the houses on the block.

21 North Pullman Place

10461 S. Corliss Ave.

1880S, ARCHITECT UNKNOWN

2008, REHABILITATION, LANDON
  BONE BAKER ARCHITECTS

Similar to the block houses by Beman (and thus probably designed by him), this former rooming house was restored to its original appearance on the outside and converted to six residential units within. The new front porch and the wood trim display the official Pullman colors.

The former three-flat building at 10406 S. Maryland Ave. houses the **A. Philip Randolph Pullman Porter Museum** *(open seasonally), with exhibits focusing on African American contributions to the American labor movement.*

22 Holy Rosary Roman Catholic Church

11300 S. Martin Luther King Jr. Dr.

1890, SOLON S. BEMAN

Built on Pullman-held land for company employees, this church replays in brick the Greenstone Church's round arched windows under peaked roofs and steep tower cap. But details such as the self-corbeling, the arched detailing on the tower, and the small rose window appear to reflect the communicants' Germanic background rather than the donor's preferences.

23 Paradise Temple Church of God in Christ

(Shomre Hadath Synagogue)

11437–11445 S. Forest Ave.

1928, HARRY L. MORSE

This is a late example of the curved gable synagogue; the design was popularized by the Grande Synagogue of Paris, in the rue de la Victoire (1874, A. P. ALDROPHE). But Morse used twentieth-century Chicago materials: wire-cut brick, exposed concrete as trim, and an inset band of multicolored tiles.

Several blocks to the southwest, in the community of West Pullman, is an unusual house by Frank Lloyd Wright (entry 24).

24 Stephen A. Foster Residence and Stable

12147 S. Harvard Ave.

1900, FRANK LLOYD WRIGHT

The house with the hat marks Wright's brief flirtation with Japanese variations on the Shingle Style theme. The tall, brimmed roof is echoed in the dormers and all but swamps the shingle-clad base.

PHOTO CREDITS

*The position of photographs on a page has been abbreviated in the following manner: **T**, top; **B**, bottom; **L**, left; **R**, right; **M**, middle.*

The Shaping of Chicago: page 2T From Lewis University's Canal and Regional History Collection; **2B** Courtesy Chicago History Museum; **3** Courtesy The Art Institute of Chicago; **4** Courtesy Chicago History Museum; **6** Courtesy Chicago History Museum; **8** Courtesy Chicago History Museum (cropped); **9** Courtesy of the Commission on Chicago Landmarks; **11** Courtesy Chicago History Museum; **12** Courtesy Chicago History Museum (cropped); **15** Courtesy Chicago History Museum; **16** Hedrich Blessing photograph, courtesy Chicago History Museum (cropped); **18** Courtesy Chicago History Museum (cropped); **19** Courtesy Chicago History Museum (cropped); **20** Photo by Ron Gordon.

The Loop: page 29 Jon Miller photograph © Hedrich Blessing; **30** Hedrich Blessing photograph, courtesy Chicago History Museum (cropped); **32** Steve Hall © Hedrich Blessing; **33** James Steinkamp © Steinkamp Photography; **34** Hedrich Blessing photograph, courtesy Chicago History Museum (cropped); **35** Barbara Crane for the Commission on Chicago Landmarks; **38** Lawrence Okrent; **39** Peter J. Schulz; **41** Courtesy Chicago History Museum (cropped); **42T** Hedrich Blessing photograph, courtesy Chicago History Museum (cropped); **42B** Bob Thall, courtesy The Art Institute of Chicago; **44** Courtesy Chicago History Museum (cropped); **45T** Chicago Park District Special Collections; **45B** Barbara Karant, Karant & Associates, Inc.; **46** Photo by Alice Sinkevitch; **47T** Barbara Crane for the Commission on Chicago Landmarks; **47B** Courtesy of the Commission on Chicago Landmarks; **49** © 2002, Steinkamp/Ballogg Photography; **50** Tom Rossiter; **51** Courtesy of the Commission on Chicago Landmarks; **54T** Hedrich Blessing, courtesy Chicago History Museum (cropped); **54L** Hedrich Blessing photograph, courtesy Chicago History Museum (cropped); **54R** SOM/© Tom Rossiter; **56** Courtesy of the Commission on Chicago Landmarks; **57** Craig Dugan © Hedrich Blessing; **59** Courtesy of the Commission on Chicago Landmarks; **60** Courtesy of the Commission on Chicago Landmarks; **61** Hedrich Blessing photograph, courtesy Chicago History Museum (cropped); **63T** Courtesy of Chicago History Museum (cropped); **63B** Photo by Howard N. Kaplan, © HNK Architectural Photography, Inc.; **64L** Hedrich Blessing photograph, courtesy Chicago History Museum (cropped); **64R** Courtesy The Art Institute of Chicago; **65** Courtesy Chicago History Museum (cropped); **66** Photo by David Clifton; **67** Photo by Howard N. Kaplan, © HNK Architectural Photography, Inc.; **69T** Hedrich Blessing photograph, courtesy Chicago History Museum (cropped); **69B** © Hedrich Blessing; **71** Hedrich Blessing photograph, courtesy Chicago History Museum (cropped); **72** Hedrich Blessing photograph, courtesy Chicago History Museum (cropped); **73** Hedrich Blessing photograph, courtesy Chicago History Museum (cropped); **74** James R. Steinkamp, courtesy of Murphy/Jahn—Lester B. Knight & Associates, A Joint Venture; **75** © Hedrich Blessing; **77T** Hedrich Blessing photograph, courtesy Chicago History Museum (cropped); **77B** James R. Steinkamp, Steinkamp/Ballogg, Chicago; **78T** Courtesy Chicago History Museum (cropped); **78B** Nick Merrick, Hedrich Blessing, courtesy of McClier; **79** Nick Merrick, Hedrich Blessing, courtesy of McClier; **80** Photo by John Gronkowski; **81** James R. Steinkamp, courtesy of Murphy/Jahn; **83T** Chicago Architectural Photographing Co. for the Commission on Chicago Landmarks; **83B** Hedrich Blessing photograph, courtesy Chicago History Museum (cropped); **84** Jon Miller, © Hedrich Blessing; **85** Harold A. Nelson, architect/photographer; **86** James Steinkamp © Steinkamp Photography; **87L** Scott McDonald, © Hedrich Blessing; **87R** Nick Merrick, © Hedrich Blessing; **88** Photo by Greg Murphey; **89** Robert Shimer, Hedrich Blessing, courtesy of Merchandise Mart Properties, Inc.; **91T** Jon Miller © Hedrich Blessing; **91B** James Steinkamp © Steinkamp Photography; **92** Photo by Timothy Hursley; **93** © Anthony May; **94L** © Judith Bromley; **94R** Hedrich Blessing photograph, courtesy Chicago History Museum (cropped); **95** Nick Merrick, © Hedrich Blessing; **96** William Kildow Photography; **97** Nick Merrick, © Hedrich Blessing.

South Loop: page 101 © William Zbaren; **102** Leslie Schwartz Photography; **103** Leslie Schwartz Photography; **104T** © Judith Bromley; **104B** James Caulfield, courtesy of Glessner House Museum; **105** Hedrich Blessing photograph, courtesy Chicago History Museum (cropped); **106** Courtesy Chicago Architecture Foundation; **107** © Fred Leavitt Photography; **108** Nick Merrick, © Hedrich Blessing; **110T** Kate Roth Photography; **110B** Photo by Ron Gordon; **111** © Judith Bromley; **112T** Photo by David Pilarczyk, courtesy of Schroeder Murchie Laya

489

218, Barbara Karant, Karant & Associates; **219** William Kildow Photography.

Lakeview / Ravenswood / Uptown: page 223T Hedrich Blessing photograph, courtesy Chicago History Museum; **223B** Photo by Howard N. Kaplan, © HNK Architectural Photography, Inc.; **224L** Bob Thall for the Commission on Chicago Landmarks; **224R** *Architectural Record*, v. 21, Feb. 1907, courtesy of The Art Institute of Chicago; **225T** Bob Thall for the Commission on Chicago Landmarks; **225B** Bob Thall for the Commission on Chicago Landmarks; **226L** Kate Roth Photography; **226R** Kate Roth Photography; **228T** Photostat line drawing by Schroeder Murchie Laya Associates Ltd.; **228B** Scott McDonald, © Hedrich Blessing; **229L** Russell B. Phillips Photography; **229R** Photo by David Clifton; **230T** Richard Nickel for the Commission on Chicago Landmarks; **230B** Courtesy Chicago Public Schools; **232** Barbara Crane for the Commission on Chicago Landmarks; **233** Bob Thall for the Commission on Chicago Landmarks; **234** Photo by Barry Bebart; **235T** Courtesy The Art Institute of Chicago; **235B** Bob Thall for the Commission on Chicago Landmarks; **236** Barbara Crane for the Commission on Chicago Landmarks; **237T** Photo by Howard N. Kaplan, © HNK Architectural Photography, Inc.; **237B** Leslie Schwartz Photography; **238T** William Kildow Photography; **238B** Leslie Schwartz Photography; **239** Courtesy of the Commission on Chicago Landmarks; **240T** Christopher Barrett Photography; **240B** Mark Ballogg, © Steinkamp/Ballogg Chicago; **241** Leslie Schwartz Photography; **242L** Photo by David Clifton; **242R** © Hedrich Blessing; **243L** Courtesy Chicago Public Schools; **243R** Photo by David Clifton.

Edgewater / Rogers Park: page 247 Photo by Ron Gordon; **248T** © Fred Leavitt Photography; **248B** Photo by David Vincent Forte, AIA; **249** Leslie Schwartz Photography; **250T** William Kildow Photography; **250B** Leslie Schwartz Photography; **251** Photo by Mati Maldre; **252T** Photo © Lawrence Okrent; **252B** Photo © by Lawrence Okrent; **254** © George Lambros/Lambros Photography Inc.; **255T** Photo by Ron Gordon; **255B** Photo by Mati Maldre; **256T** Courtesy Chicago Public Schools; **256B** Jon Miller, © Hedrich Blessing; **257T** Leslie Schwartz Photography; **257B** Alice Sinkevitch; **258** Alice Sinkevitch; **259** © George Lambros/Lambros Photography; **260** Photo by Barry Bebart; **261T** Photo by Barry Bebart; **261M** Bob Thall for the Commission on Chicago Landmarks; **261B** Photo by Barry Bebart; **263** Steve Hall, © Hedrich Blessing.

West Town: page 268T Steve Hall, © Hedrich Blessing; **268B** Barbara Karant, Karant & Associates; **269** Historic American Buildings Survey (Library of Congress) Repository, HABS ILL,16-CHIG,71—1, Harold Allen, Photographer; **270** Photo © Lawrence Okrent; **271** Photograph by Felicity Rich; **272T** Andreas Simon, *Chicago, die Gartenstadt*, 1893, courtesy of The Art Institute of Chicago; **272B** Photo by Felicity Rich; **273T** Neal A. Vogel,

Restoric, LLC; **273BL** James R. Steinkamp, Steinkamp/Ballogg, Chicago; **273BR** Doug Fogelson; **274** Marty Peters, Marty Peters Photography; **276** Alice Sinkevitch; **277T** Charlie Mayer Photography; **277B** Barry Rustin Photography; **278** Sean J. Reidy; **279TL** Courtesy Chicago History Museum (cropped); **279TR** Sean J. Reidy; **279B** Photo by Felicity Rich; **280** Barbara Crane for the Commission on Chicago Landmarks; **281** Steve Beal for the Commission on Chicago Landmarks; **282** © Fred Leavitt Photography; **283** Timothy Hursley, courtesy of Murphy/Jahn.

Chicago–O'Hare International Airport: page 286 James R. Steinkamp, courtesy of Murphy/Jahn; **287** Timothy Hursley, courtesy of Murphy/Jahn; **288** Hedrich Blessing photograph, courtesy of Chicago History Museum (cropped); **289** James Steinkamp, Steinkamp/Ballogg Chicago.

Near West Side: page 295T Leslie Schwartz Photography; **295B** Kate Joyce Studios; **296** George Pappageorge; **297** Neal A. Vogel, Restoric, LLC; **298T** Elaine S. Baxton for the Commission on Chicago Landmarks; **298B** Steve Hall, © Hedrich Blessing; **299** Site Design Group; **300** John Faier; **301** Courtesy The Art Institute of Chicago; **302** Barbara Crane for the Commission on Chicago Landmarks; **303** Neal A. Vogel, Restoric, LLC; **304** Photo by Felicity Rich; **305** James Steinkamp © Steinkamp Photography; **306** Courtesy the University of Illinois at Chicago, The University Library, University Archives; **308T** Neal A. Vogel, Restoric, LLC; **308B** Bob Thall for the Commission on Chicago Landmarks; **313** Lawrence Okrent; **314** © Judith Bromley; **315** Nathan Kirkman.

Garfield Park / Austin: page 321 Courtesy of Chicago Park District Special Collections; **322** Courtesy of Chicago Park District Special Collections; **323** Bob Thall for the Commission on Chicago Landmarks; **324T** Photo © Lawrence Okrent; **324B** Chicago Historic Resources Survey of the Commission on Chicago Landmarks; **325** Photo by Josh Goldman; **326T** *Western Architect*, v. 21, Feb. 1915, Courtesy of The Art Institute of Chicago; **326B** Photo by Alice Sinkevitch; **327** Photo by Josh Goldman; **328T** Neal A. Vogel, Restoric, LLC; **328B** Photo by Josh Goldman; **329T** Photo by David Clifton; **329B** Copyright © Thom Clark; **330** Nathan Kirkman; **331** Neal A. Vogel, Restoric, LLC; **332T** Courtesy The Art Institute of Chicago; **332B** Courtesy of Chicago Park District Special Collections.

Oak Park: page 337L © Suzette Bross; **337TR** © Suzette Bross; **337BR** Photo by Josh Goldman; **338** Photo by Josh Goldman; **339T** Photo by Josh Goldman; **339B** Leslie Schwartz Photography; **340** Courtesy of the Historical Society of Oak Park and River Forest; **341** Marco Lorenzetti, © Hedrich Blessing; **342** Photo by Josh Goldman; **343T** Alice Sinkevitch; **343B** © Suzette Bross; **344** Alice Sinkevitch; **345** Photo by Josh Goldman; **346** Photo by Alice Sinkevitch; **347** Photo by Josh Goldman; **348** © Judith Bromley; **349** © Judith Bromley; **350** Photo by Alice Sinkevitch; **351** Donald G. Kalec, courtesy of the Frank Lloyd Wright Preservation Trust; **352** Jon Miller, © Hedrich Blessing, courtesy of the Frank Lloyd Wright Preservation Trust; **353T** Photography by Thomas A. Heinz © 2003, Copyright Thomas A. Heinz; **353B** Photo by Josh Goldman; **354** Alice Sinkevitch; **355T** Alice Sinkevitch; **355B** Alice Sinkevitch; **357** Anthony May Photography.

Pilsen / Little Village / Lawndale: page 362 Photo © by Lawrence Okrent; **364** Anthony May Photography; **365** Courtesy Chicago History Museum; **366** Courtesy Chicago History Museum; **367T** Photo by Felicity Rich; **367B** Steve Hall, © Hedrich Blessing; **368** Chicago Historic Resources Survey of the Commission on Chicago Landmarks; **369** Walter Street, Johnson & Lee; **371** Photo by Felicity Rich; **372** Lawrence Okrent.

Near South Side: page 380 © by Lawrence Okrent; **381** Hedrich Blessing photograph, courtesy Chicago History Museum (cropped); **382** Neal A. Vogel, Restoric, LLC; **383** Courtesy Chicago History Museum; **385** By permission of University Archives, Paul V. Galvin Library, Illinois Institute of Technology, Chicago; **386** Bill Engdahl, Hedrich Blessing photograph, courtesy Chicago History Museum; **388T** By permission of University Archives, Paul V. Galvin Library, Illinois Institute of Technology, Chicago; **388B** Ali Razfar / flickr, CC BY 2.0; **390T** Courtesy The Art Institute of Chicago; **390B** Neal A. Vogel, Restoric, LLC; **391** Neal A. Vogel, Restoric, LLC; **393** Bruce Van Inwegen; **394** Photo by Ron Gordon.

Bridgeport / Canaryville / McKinley Park / Back of the Yards: page 401 Site Design Group; **402** Neal A. Vogel, Restoric, LLC; **404T** Photo by Lawrence Okrent; **404B** Neal A. Vogel; Restoric, LLC; **405T** Neal A. Vogel, Restoric, LLC; **405B** Courtesy of the Chicago Park District Special Collections; **406** Steve Hall, © Hedrich Blessing; **407** Lawrence Okrent; **408** Chicago History Museum; **409T** Tom Rossiter; **409B** Christopher Barrett Photography.

Oakland / Kenwood: page 414 Hedrich Blessing photograph, courtesy of Chicago History Museum (cropped); **416** Robert Shimer, © Hedrich Blessing; **417** © Judith Bromley; **418** © Judith Bromley; **419T** Christopher Barrett, © Hedrich Blessing; **419B**

© Judith Bromley; **420** Barbara Crane for the Commission on Chicago Landmarks; **421T** Site Design Group; **421B** Helena Chapellín Wilson, copyright © 1993; **422** Photo by Philip Turner, courtesy of Benjamin Weese; **423T** © Judith Bromley; **423B** Barbara Crane for the Commission on Chicago Landmarks; **424** Hedrich Blessing photograph, courtesy Chicago History Museum (cropped); **426** Courtesy of Chicago Park District Special Collections.

Hyde Park / South Shore: page 432 Bauer Latoza Studio; **433** Courtesy of the Museum of Science and Industry, Chicago; **434T** Courtesy of the Museum of Science and Industry, Chicago; **434B** Courtesy of Chicago Park District Special Collections; **436** The University of Chicago Archives; **438L** © Judith Bromley; **438R** Kate Roth Photography; **440** Kate Roth Photography; **441** The University of Chicago Archives; **442L** © Judith Bromley; **442R** Steve Hall, © Hedrich Blessing; **443** Richard Nickel for the Commission on Chicago Landmarks; **444** © Judith Bromley; **445T** Tom Rossiter; **445B** © Judith Bromley; **446** Rainer Viertlboeck; **448T** Tom Rossiter; **448B** Hedrich Blessing photograph, courtesy of Chicago History Museum (cropped); **449** Rainer Viertlboeck; **451TL** © Judith Bromley; **451TR** © Judith Bromley; **451B** Hedrich Blessing photograph, courtesy Chicago History Museum (cropped); **452** Hedrich Blessing photograph, courtesy Chicago History Museum (cropped); **453** Kate Roth Photography; **454** © Judith Bromley; **455** © Judith Bromley; **456** © Judith Bromley; **457** Photo by David Clifton; **460T** Courtesy of Chicago Park District Special Collections; **460B** Barbara Karant, Karant & Associates; **461** Helena Chapellín Wilson, copyright © 1993; **462** Dennis M. Ryan; **463T** Courtesy of Helena Chapellín Wilson, copyright © 1993; **463B** Steve Hall, © Hedrich Blessing; **464** Steve Hall, © Hedrich Blessing; **465** Steve Hall, © Hedrich Blessing; **467T** William Kildow Photography; **467M** Courtesy of the Commission on Chicago Landmarks; **467B** Courtesy of Helena Chapellín Wilson, copyright © 1993; **468** Helena Chapellín Wilson, copyright © 1993; **469** Steve Hall, © Hedrich Blessing.

Beverly / Morgan Park: All photos in this section by Mati Maldre.

Pullman: All photos in this section by Harold A. Nelson, architect/photographer.

INDEX

Every building described in the Guide is listed as a primary entry in the index by the building's previous and current names.

Main entries for street names beginning with "North," "South," "East," or "West" are alphabetized under those words, but subentries are alphabetized by N., S., E., or W. Building and street names beginning with numbers are alphabetized as if spelled out.

The names of persons, firms, organizations, and government offices involved in creating the works listed in the Guide appear in SMALL CAPS. Unless otherwise indicated, they are architects or associated artists.

Names of towns, historic districts, and communities within Greater Chicago appear in **boldface**. Major divisions and tours appear in **BOLD UPPER CASE**. A page reference in **boldface** indicates that an illustration of the building, area, or other work appears on that page.

The following abbreviations appear in the index:

adapt.	adaptation	Corp.	Corporation	P.S.	Public School
add.	addition	Ct.	Court	R.C.	Roman
alt.	alteration	Dept.	Department		Catholic
Apts.	Apartments	Dr.	Drive	Rd.	Road
Assn.	Association	Expy.	Expressway	rebldg.	rebuilding
Assocs.	Associates	Hosp.	Hospital	recon.	reconstruction
attr.	attributed to	H.S.	High School	rehab.	rehabilitation
Ave.	Avenue	Intl.	International	rem.	remodeling
Bldg.	Building	M.B.	Missionary	renov.	renovation
Blvd.	Boulevard		Baptist	rest.	restoration
Bros.	Brothers	M.S.	Middle School	RR	Railroad
Cem.	Cemetery	Natl.	National	St.	Street
Co.	Company	Pkwy.	Parkway	Univ.	University
Condos.	Condominiums	Pl.	Place		
conv.	conversion	pres.	preservation		

ABAKANOWICZ, MAGDALENA
  Agora, 48
Abbott (Wallace C.) House, 241
ABBOTT, FRANK B.
  Fulton House (North American Cold Storage Co.), 170
  Heisen (Carl C.) House, 176
Abbott Hall, 144
ABC-WLS Bldg., 55
ABN / AMRO Plaza, 96
Abraham Lincoln (Standing Lincoln) (Court of the Presidents), 44
Abraham Lincoln: The Head of State (The Seated Lincoln) (Lincoln Park), 215
Access Living, 163
Adams (Henry S.) House, 345–346
Adams (William and Jessie M.) House, 480
Adams Express Co. Bldg., 9
Addams (Jane) Homes, 15, 307
Addams (Jane) Hull House Museum, 313, **314**
Addams, Jane, 14, 106, 281, 313–314
ADDISON, JOHN
  Second Presbyterian Church Bell Tower, 111
ADLER, DANKMAR, 8
  Auditorium Bldg., 47–48
  Ebenezer M.B. Church (Isaiah Temple), 414
ADLER, DAVID
  Abram House, 211
  grave, 234

N. Astor St. No. 1500 (Elinor Patterson–Cyrus H. McCormick Mansion) add., 178
  Ryerson (Joseph T., Jr.) House, 179
  Ryerson (Mrs. Arthur) House, 211
ADLER & SULLIVAN, 8, 19, 64, 352, 422
  Auditorium Bldg., 7, 8, 9, **47** 48, 101, 414
  Barker-Haskell-Atwater Bldgs., 51
  Charnley-Persky House, 180,
  Chicago Stock Exchange, 6, 8, **18**, 19, **42**, 43, 76, 232, 309
  Chicago Stock Exchange Arch, 43
  Clinton St. Lofts, 95
  Deimel (Joseph) House, 390
  Halsted (Ann), houses for, **191**
  Halsted (Ann) House, 206
  Heath (Ira A.) House, 389
  Jewelers Bldg., **51**, 52
  Kaufmann (Ferdinand) Store and Flat Bldg., **204**
  Mannheimer (Leon) House, 205
  Pilgrim Baptist Church (Kehilath Anshe Ma'ariv Synagogue), 389
  Schiller Bldg., 8, 19, 161, 189
  Standard Club, 109–110
  Victoria Hotel, 210
Adler Planetarium and Astronomy Museum, 49–50, **49**
African Methodist Episcopal Chapel, 110

Scoville Block (1), 340
Scoville Block (2), 340
Scoville Square, **337**, 340
Seaman (John A.) House (1), 337–338
SEARL, LINDA
  Ohio House, **268**
SEARL & ASSOCS.
  N. Rush St. No. 660 (Double House for
    Leander McCormick and son, Robert
    Hall McCormick) conv., 155
Sears, Roebuck & Co., 282
Sears on State, 58
Sears Power Plant, 373
Sears Roebuck & Co. Complex (former),
  372–373, **372**
Sears Tower, 16, 19, 54, 92–93, **92**, 141, 143,
  145, 205, 232, 373
Seaton (Chauncey E.) House, 391, **391**
Second Congregational Church, 341
Second Franklin Bldg., 115, **115**
Second Leiter Bldg., 7, 62–63, **63**
Second Presbyterian Church, 111, **111**
Second Studebaker Bldg., 113
Seigle Residence, 200
Self Park (60 E. Lake St.), 52
Selwyn Theater, 71
Senn (Nicholas) H.S., 251
Seventeenth Church of Christ, Scientist, 52
SEVIC, WILLIAM
  Balzekas (S.P.) House, 481, **481**
Seward Park Field House, 168
Seward Park Field House Clock Tower, 168
The Sexton, 166, **166**
Sexton (James A.) P.S., 165
Sexton (John) & Co., 166, **166**
SEYFARTH, ROBERT E.
  N. Ridge Ave. No. 7114, 258
Seymour (Claude) House, 236, **236**
Shakespeare Theater, 145
SHANKLAND, EDWARD E., 58
SHANKLAND & PINGREY
  River West Lofts (J. P. Smith Shoe Co.)
    add., 169
Sharp Bldg., 51
Sharpe (C. A.) House, 345
SHATTUCK & LAYER
  St. Thomas the Apostle School, 455, **455**
Shaw (Alfred) grave, 234
Shaw (Charles H.) Technology and Learning
    Center and Henry Ford Academy: Power
    House High (Sears Power Plant adaptive
    reuse), 373
SHAW, ALFRED, & ASSOCS.
  E. Monroe St. No. 55 (Mid-Continental
    Plaza) and Park Monroe, 51
SHAW, HOWARD VAN DOREN, 431, 454
  Armour (Lester) House, 225
  Astor Court (William O. Goodman House), 180
  Douglas (James) House, 421, **421**
  E. Cermak Rd. No. 350 (R. R. Donnelly &
    Sons Co. Calumet Plant), 107–108, **107**
  Fortune (Peter) Houses, 178–179
  Fountain of Time base design, 432
  Fourth Presbyterian Church, **140**
  Goodspeed (Edgar Johnson) House, 454
  Graceland Cem.: Goodman family tomb,
    233; Shaw family plot, 231
  Hillel Center (Arthur J. Mason House),
    454, **454**
  Intl. Museum of Surgical Science (Eleanor
    Robinson Countiss House), 177

Mentor Bldg., 61
N. Lake Shore Dr. No. 1130 (90 E. Elm St.), 176
N. Lakeview Ave. No. 2450, 211
S. Plymouth Ct. No. 731 (Lakeside Press
    Bldg.) four north bays, 114
Second Presbyterian Church rebldg.,
    111, **111**
The Spirit of Music Sculpture and Park, 48
Starkweather (Charles H.) House, 421
Symphony Center (Orchestra Hall) top floor
    add., 43
Univ. of Chicago: Quadrangle Club, 441;
    University Church (of the Disciples of
    Christ), 444–445
Veeder (Henry) House, 419
Wilson (Thomas E.) House, 422
SHAW, METZ & ASSOCS.
  Art Institute of Chicago Morton Wing, 42
  One East Wacker, 55
SHAW, METZ & DOLIO
  Lake Parc Place (Victor A. Olander Homes
    and Olander Homes Extension), 416
  S. State St. Nos. 211–227, 61
SHAW, NAESS & MURPHY
  DePaul Univ., O'Connell (Michael J.) Center,
    202
SHAW & ASSOCS.
  Burnett (Leo) Bldg., 72
  Chicago Board of Trade 1980 add., 77
  N. State St. No. 515, 153–154
  S. La Salle St. No. 190, 80
SHAW ENVIRONMENTAL AND INFRASTRUCTURE
  Lincoln Park, Peoples Gas Education
    Pavilion and South Pond Nature
    Boardwalk, 215–216
Shaw family plot, 231
SHAW SUSTAINABLE SOLUTIONS OF ILLINOIS
  Lincoln Park, Peoples Gas Education
    Pavilion and South Pond Nature
    Boardwalk, 215–216
SHAYMAN & SALK
  Ohio House Motel, 164
Shedd (John G.) Aquarium, 50
Shedd (John G.) House, 368
Shedd, John G., 367
Shedd Park Field House (Recreation Bldg.),
    367, **367**
Sheldon (Edwin B.) Row Houses, 190
SHEPLEY, GEORGE F., 104
SHEPLEY, RUTAN & COOLIDGE, 435
  Art Institute of Chicago, 42–43
  Art Institute of Chicago Ryerson and
    Burnham Libraries, 42
  BMO Harris Bank, 75
  Chicago Cultural Center (Chicago Public
    Library), 34–35
  Fountain of the Great Lakes Basin, 43
  Univ. of Chicago: Bartlett Dining Commons
    (Frank Dickinson Bartlett Gymnasium),
    445; Classics Bldg., 437; Harper
    (William Rainey) Memorial Library,
    437–438; Hutchinson Commons,
    440–441, 441; Mandel Hall, 440–441;
    Mitchell Tower, 440–441; Noyes (Ida)
    Hall, 442; Reynolds Club, 440–441;
    Ryerson Physical Laboratory north
    annex, 439; Stuart (Harold Leonard)
    Hall (Law School), 438; University
    Bookstore (University Press Bldg.), 447
Sheraton Chicago Hotel & Towers, 148
Sheridan (Nicholas J.) House, 227

Alice Sinkevitch is former executive director of AIA Chicago. **Laurie McGovern Petersen** is a writer for *Chicago Architect* magazine. **Geoffrey Baer** is the host of WTTW-TV's popular television specials about Chicago architecture and history. **Perry Duis** is professor emeritus of history at the University of Illinois at Chicago and the author of *Challenging Chicago*.

The University of Illinois Press
is a founding member of the
Association of American University Presses.

Designed by Kaelin Chappell Broaddus
Composed in 9/10.5 Proxima Nova Condensed
by Lisa Connery
at the University of Illinois Press
Manufactured by Sheridan Books, Inc.

University of Illinois Press
1325 South Oak Street
Champaign, IL 61820-6903
www.press.uillinois.edu